The Journals and Miscellaneous Notebooks of RALPH WALDO EMERSON

VOLUME I

1819–1822

Emerson's journals and miscellaneous notebooks

The Journals and Miscellaneous Notebooks of RALPH WALDO EMERSON

EDITED BY

WILLIAM H. GILMAN ALFRED R. FERGUSON
GEORGE P. CLARK MERRELL R. DAVIS

THE BELKNAP PRESS
OF HARVARD UNIVERSITY PRESS
Cambridge, Massachusetts
1960

Distributed in Great Britain by Oxford University Press, London

Typography by Burton J Jones

Printed in the U.S.A. by the Harvard University Printing Office

Bound by Stanhope Bindery, Inc., Boston, Massachusetts

Library of Congress Catalog Card Number: 60–11554

This edition
of his grandfather's journals
is dedicated to
EDWARD WALDO FORBES

Preface

This new edition of Emerson's journals is planned in approximately sixteen volumes, with a final index which will combine the entries in the individual indexes. Like all large undertakings it could not have come into existence without the aid of numerous individuals and agencies, and the editors take pleasure in acknowledging their separate and collective debts:

to Edward Waldo Forbes and to the Ralph Waldo Emerson Memorial Association, for permission to publish the manuscript journals, now in the Houghton Library of Harvard University, and for grants which have provided for one half-year leave-of-absence, for microfilming of the manuscripts, and for other materials;

to Professor William A. Jackson, Director of the Houghton Library and member of the Ralph Waldo Emerson Memorial Association, for direct and indirect aid of many kinds;

to Miss Carolyn Jakeman of the Houghton Library for innumerable acts of professional and personal assistance;

to Mrs. Linda Gallasch, who among many other important tasks made rigorously accurate transcriptions of the text of volume I from the microfilms and did research for the notes; to Ralph H. Orth and to Mrs. Seymour Scher, who assisted with both text and notes; and to James C. Ballowe and Mrs. A. Dwight Culler, who proofread a part of the typescript;

to the University of Rochester, Ohio Wesleyan University, the University of Washington, and the Research Board of the University of Illinois, for providing funds for research assistance, travel, and freedom from summer teaching;

to the American Council of Learned Societies for a grant for a research assistant;

to the John Simon Guggenheim Memorial Foundation for a research fellowship;

to the staffs of the libraries of the University of Rochester, Ohio

Wesleyan University, the University of Illinois, the University of Washington, and Harvard University;

to Professors Kenneth B. Murdock, Perry Miller, Mark DeWolfe Howe, Glyndon G. Van Deusen, Harrison Hayford, and Elmer G. Suhr, and to William H. Bond and Herbert Cahoon for help of various kinds;

to scholars of the past and the present whose studies of Emerson have been indispensable — James Elliot Cabot, Edward W. Emerson and Waldo Emerson Forbes, Ralph L. Rusk, and Kenneth W. Cameron;

and to Professor Howard Mumford Jones, who labored with faith and wisdom to prepare the way.

Quotations from the "Records of the Immediate Government of Harvard College" are by permission of Harvard University. Unless otherwise noted, translations from Greek and Latin are from the Loeb Classical Library and are reprinted by permission of the Harvard University Press and the Loeb Classical Library. "Universe No. 7" is printed by permission of the Pierpont Morgan Library.

W.H.G. A.R.F.
G.P.C. M.R.D.

Contents

INTRODUCTION

Emerson in His Journals xiii
The Manuscripts xxxiv
The Publication Plan xxxvi
The Editorial Method xxxvii
The Source of the Text xlii

FOREWORD TO VOLUME I

The Early Journals xlv
Chronology xlvii
Symbols and Abbreviations xlix

PART ONE

THE TEXTS OF THE JOURNALS

Wide World 1 3
Wide World 2 33
Wide World 3 59
Wide World 4 91
Wide World 6 114

PART TWO

THE TEXTS OF THE MISCELLANEOUS NOTEBOOKS

[*College Theme Book*] 161
No. XVII 206
No. XVIII 249
The Universe 358
Catalogue of Books Read, 1819–1824 395

Editorial Title List 403

Alphabetical Title List 413

Textual Notes 416

Index 419

Illustrations

Frontispiece

Emerson's journals and miscellaneous notebooks in Houghton Library

Following page 158

Plate I	*Wide World 1, page 1*
Plate II	*Wide World 2, page 34*
Plate III	*Wide World 2, page 38*
Plate IV	*College Theme Book, front cover verso*
Plate V	*No. XVII, page 3*
Plate VI	*No. XVII, pages 12 and 13*
Plate VII	*No. XVII, page 18*
Plate VIII	*No. XVII, page 34*
Plate IX	*No. XVII, page 51*
Plate X	*No. XVII, page 58*
Plate XI	*No. XVIII, page 62*
Plate XII	*No. XVIII, page 79*

The reproductions have been chosen to illustrate Emerson's idiosyncrasies in keeping his journals and notebooks, a substantial number of typical textual problems, and some of the more difficult passages.

Introduction

EMERSON IN HIS JOURNALS

When the first volume of the Emerson-Forbes edition of Emerson's Journals appeared half a century ago the conditions were exactly right for the kind of work the editors published. Interest in nineteenth-century American Olympians amounting to idolatry had been patent in the steady printings, ever since the 1880's, of "collected" or "complete" editions of Hawthorne, Holmes, Whittier, Bryant, Longfellow, Lowell, and Thoreau. Emerson himself had been collected in sixteen volumes in 1883–1887 and in the twelve-volume Centenary Edition of 1903–1904, edited by Edward W. Emerson. Devotees of the great had been slower about getting what journals and notebooks there were into print, but Sophia Hawthorne had led the way in the late sixties with bowdlerized volumes of her husband's private records, and room had been made for Thoreau's Journals in the twenty-volume edition of his *Writings* in 1906. A formidable wave of biography accompanied this flood of original work. For a whole generation after 1880, it seems, the public provided a good market for the works and histories of America's great Victorians. If the level and taste of this audience apparently helped to determine the policies of the editors and biographers, these literary gentlemen (as often as not members of the writer's family or close friends) seem also to have had tacit agreements about what should be said in print, and what scruples should be observed. Essential privacy was not to be invaded, no one was to be embarrassed, texts were to be made grammatical and "correct," "trivia" were to be eliminated. The general aim, perhaps, was to do for their subjects what James Elliot Cabot had tried to do for Emerson in his *Memoir*—to "fill out and define more closely" for the friends and readers of the great man "the image of him they already have."

The Emerson-Forbes edition of the journals is very much in

this tradition. Completed in 1914, it was largely the work of Emerson's son Edward Waldo, with some help from Waldo Emerson Forbes, his nephew. Throughout the ten volumes there floats the image of a nineteenth-century gentleman, consistently referred to, and virtually titled "Mr. Emerson." Mr. Emerson was permitted to be quoted as writing "You must on no account say 'stink' or 'Damn'," and "I will not obey it, by God," but even a nineteenth-century gentleman was allowed a touch of earthiness, and on a moral issue like the Fugitive Slave Law of 1850, a little profanity would never hurt his reputation. Undoubtedly the first edition of the journals deepened and widened the understanding of Emerson. Cabot's early statement that the journals "do not often bring us closer to him than we are brought by his published writings" was rather wide of the mark. He was more accurate when he told Edward Emerson that readers of "Emerson's first record of his thoughts [would] come nearer to the man than in the essays carefully purged of personality." Edward Emerson revealed much of the introspective young collegian, the sickly theological student, the anguished widower, the lonesome champion of heterodoxy and individualism, the aroused moralist, and the puzzled observer of irreconcilable principles like freedom and fate. For all this, the portrait of Emerson is a work of subtle and elusive artistry, created through thousands of selected passages and hundreds of stippled footnotes in a kind of editorial *pointillisme*. The ectoplastic philosopher of the essays took on human shape and color in the journals, but he was still what his chief editor felt impelled to make him, still more the mystic than the Yankee, and always, from beginning to end of the five thousand well-printed pages, "Mr." Emerson.

If this title tends to invest Emerson with a halo which alienates modern readers, editorial principles, overt or tacit, have had their share in creating difficulty and misunderstanding. Readers have long known that they were getting selections only, and most of them, even scholars, have been content to take what they were given without further inquiry. They have gone along with the knowledge that the editor left out most of the matter Emerson used in his essays, that he deleted some personal references, corrected quotations, and printed incomplete lists of the books Emerson read. Some of these techniques were thoroughly defensible. An edition designed to be published commercially for a much larger segment of the reading public than it would appeal to today could hardly have been definitive. Not all the 182 "journals" could be published, and the 94 chosen for excerpting were in general the best. Even so, the manuscripts were pruned without real cause, some omissions were indicated and others were not, omissions were shown where there were none, some editorial insertions were bracketed and others were not, dates and sources were omitted and silent alterations made, sentences were grouped into paragraphs, the order of passages was needlessly changed, and of course the entire text "cleaned up," so that the real spontaneity and informality of the manuscripts completely disappeared. Misreadings, though bothersome, are relatively few, but the omission of cancellations and other material is often a serious defect. What all these practices combined to produce was a sublimated picture of the Emerson the chief editor knew best and a model of the nineteenth-century American gentleman.

There can be no doubt that Emerson was the nineteenth-century gentleman, but the image we have had is a created image, not the true one. The true image is richer, deeper, earthier, more persuasively that of a live man, rather than an idealized type. The preference for the ideal over the real in late nineteenth-century thought, which produced what Willard Thorp has called the "defenders of ideality," seems clear if one studies the pattern of editing in the first edition of these journals. The subject is one for extended scholarly study. But major clues to the recovery of the true image of Emerson may at least be suggested here by a brief examination of specific editorial practices and samples of suppressed passages taken almost at random from journals kept at various periods of Emerson's life. Some passages, to be sure, may be printed elsewhere in Emerson, but their original significance lies in their original context. What appears as a personal revelation in the journals, for example, consistently becomes a generalized or dramatized statement in the essays.

One such cluster of passages seems to have been dropped to protect Emerson's privacy. A few entries, like the recollection of a mastiff who blocked the entrance to a house, record those most private of man's experiences, his dreams. Others are self-estimates, or accounts of physical or social activities the reason for whose exclusion is often puzzling. Once Emerson brooded, Byronically, over his college days, retrospectively picturing himself

> . . . in the crude blood of sixteen
> When the red tides run swift & being chafed
> Do hastily mount into the mantling cheek,

a "poor proud, & solitary," young man who walked alone in the moonlight to ease his suffering. He went to the morgue in Paris and gazed in horror at three corpses exposed for identification. In 1848 he innocently "went to see the dwarf of dwarfs, Tom Thumb." Assailing the respect for professional pugilists held by Englishmen, he mentioned with embarrassing familiarity some American boxers, whose names, he wrote, defaced the very page he was writing on. He admitted to himself that he had no ear for music, and that he had "no joy so deep as the stings of remorse." In the midst of the crisis over the Communion Service he became sick and observed that "a stomach ache will make a man as contemptible as a palsy. Under the diarrhoea have I suffered now one fortnight & weak am as a reed. Still the truth is not injured, not touched. . . ." That the printed text begins with "The truth is not injured" suppresses not only a distasteful physical fact but also the dogged sense of glory in the triumph of the taut spirit over the helplessly limp flesh. In one of many other sentences scissored from its context he wrote: "Without horror I contemplate the envy, hatred & lust that occupy the hearts of smiling, well dressed men & women but the simplest most natural expressions of the same thoughts in action astonish & dishearten me." He confessed to an embarrassment at the animal spirits of a host who tickled his wife and daughter after dinner. He spent many hours with an unidentified "child" whom others thought "romantic & insane & exaggerating," though she seemed "the most real" of all persons to him. It can hardly be meaningless that this deleted passage immediately follows the record of a visit to Charles K. Newcomb with Caroline Sturgis, that her name, with others, is dropped from a list of people to whom Emerson sent copies of his second *Essays,* that a record of his purchase of prints, together with a note that "The Daniel of M. Angelo was taken by C. S.," is cut out, and that hers is the only name of five excised from a passage about society as "a curiosity shop full of odd excellences. . . ." Then, too, when he pays merely conventional respects to the intellectual beauty of his wife but describes a house guest as "the lofty maiden who represents the Hope of these modern days . . . and whose beautiful impatience of these *dregs of Romulus* predict to us a fairer future," "Caroline Sturgis" in the manuscript is reduced to "C. S.," presumably to hinder identification of the "lofty maiden." It will be one of the tasks of responsible scholarship to determine, when the entire record is available, the significance of these and other passages relating to Caroline Sturgis.

Three other passages will delight or inform the student of Emerson the man. During the return from England in 1833 he wrote, in a mood of almost reckless intellectual and physical indulgence, "I have been nihilizing as usual & just now posting my Italian journal. . . . Never was a regular dinner with all scientific accompaniments so philosophic a thing as at sea. I tipple with all my heart here. May I not?" In a long analysis, from the perspective of a year or so, of his abortive college friendship with Martin Gay—whose name he habitually disguised or cancelled—he justified, at least in the printed text, his own aloofness: "From the first, I preferred to preserve the terms which kept alive so much sentiment rather than a more familiar intercourse which I feared would end in indifference." But the printed text omits the dynamic, one-word commentary Emerson added later—"Pish." It seems to speak with most miraculous organ his honest acknowledgment that he had pompously rationalized a failure to achieve a warm, human relationship. That warmth is terribly apparent, however, in the omitted sections of his journal recording the death of his first wife. Not only did he describe it in detail but he uttered an anguished lament on his own sinfulness and loneliness, the deletion of which, even more than of the other passages, foreshortens the picture of the truly private man.

The first editor of Emerson's journals wrote that "Most of the personal references, unless too private, are given. Mr. Emerson's notes are free from offense in this particular." Like his comments on himself, his notes on others, direct or quoted, are certainly free from offense; but they are not free from candor, wry humor, and other qualities the full evidence of which deserves restoration. However honorable the motive of the earlier editor—was it to protect living people or their immediate descendants from possible embarrassment? —it is no longer a sanction for changing "A. and M." to "X and Y" because Emerson said they were venal; or for omitting the identification of Judge Wilbur because Emerson said he was not a great man; or George Ripley's[?] remark about Margaret Fuller's husband, the Marchese Ossoli—"I suppose that title is about equivalent to Selectman here"; or the usually genteel William Ellery Channing's quip that "a cockney was a horse-louse curried from a horse"; or the gossip that John Adams' son John Quincy could "at any time excite him in a moment to great indignation"; or the devastating statement, snipped from a comment of the senior Henry James, that Thackeray was "immoral in his practice, but with limits, & would not commit adultery." It is now fair to restore, too, Emerson's comments on friends or neighbors—his shrewd observation, for instance, of the pains Mr. Lyman took to be thought happy as against his private admission of misery; or the blunt contempt for artifice in the note that "In Mr. Levi Bartlett's farm every slope & duct was so arranged that you could not so much as spit without its being carried off to the muck-heap." We can now know, too, that he finally lost patience with Sampson Reed, who "entrenched . . . in another man's mind," made you "feel as if you conversed with a spy . . . ," and whose church was guilty of "immense arrogancy & subtle bigotry." No one should now complain even at the restoration of his disillusion with Charles K. Newcomb (whose name is reduced in the printed version to a single unidentifiable capital), a friend whose conversation had once been Emerson's highest privilege, but which was now "sloth & weariness . . . and a consumption of my time," in whose company there was now "no frankness, no pleasure; . . . nothing but unmixed pain." Besides supplementing the life of Emerson, these and many other reactions should be useful in the biographies of Emerson's contemporaries.

As for omissions dealing with Emerson's family they are innocent indeed—like the memorandum, curiously enough in French, about expenses for his feeble-minded brother Robert, or the abortive verses written shortly after his engagement to Ellen Tucker:

I've found the dainty malice out
Of Ellen's hypocritic eye
She's wound her gipsy nets about

I thought it was no harm to watch
The features of an artless maid

Considering the intensity of his love for Ellen, the lines could hardly have grown from serious qualms; they were probably the good-humored lament of a bachelor over the willing loss of his freedom, a cheerful acquiescence in the face of feminine wiles. If they qualify the image of Emerson as the unrestrained idealizer of his first love, they contribute something more to the paradox of his personality. He could, to be sure, be disturbed by the conventional forms of entertainment he found even in his own home, and while the printed text gives some clue to this it omits the final response to Lidian's soirées — "There is no refuge but in oblivion of such misdemeanors." More amusing is his equanimity and tacit approval when "Queenie," as he often called her, exceeded his own impatience with do-gooders: "Queenie (who has a gift to curse & swear) will every now & then in spite of all manners & christianity rip out on Saints, reformers & Divine Providence with the most edifying zeal." The reference was too private in 1911, but it was then and is now without offense and deserves its role in the re-assessment of its author.

Another representative group of excisions has the effect of sharply restricting Emerson in what he took to be the right of freedom and frankness in commenting upon or alluding to women, love, and sex. He observed that a man who "approaches a woman unlawfully [and] thinks he has overcome her . . . will shortly discover that he has put himself wholly in the power of that worthless slut." In disgust at Fourier's views on women he described him as "one of those salacious old men . . . in [whose] head it is the universal rutting season." He observed that Swedenborgism had been misrepresented as "a red rag of whoredom," and that knowledge of "the doctrine of sexual relations of [Fourier]" would induce "rowdies . . . [to] flock in troops & gangs to so fair a game." He quoted Behmen's judgment on woman, that "the temptation might take hold of her most readily[,] being herself a kind of temptation."

He wrote down what some bitterly frank woman may have said to him: "Nature does with us as N. Y. villains." The late nineteenth-century image of the gentleman apparently made no provision for such thought or language. The instances are easily multiplied. Once Emerson declared that "Every woman has a design on you — all — all — if it is only just a little message." Commenting upon the wrong done to women who are unconsciously desired for their sex alone he wrote: "Love rights all this deep wrong." This is printed, but as so often it is the unprinted remark that makes for the real meaning — on this occasion, "but who ever knew in real life a genuine instance of seasonable love?" The process of deletion of his comments on women catches many other aberrations in its nets — even the innocent observation on the trip to Egypt in 1873 that "the women too are as straight as arrows from their habit of carrying everything on their heads" — and of course the laconic note, "I told A. [Alcott?] the current story about the dancing girl at New Orelans & he replied that he should like to have been one of the party."

But it is not just on this topic that justification was found for drawing Emerson's teeth. No matter what the subject, the editor seems to have blue-penciled Emerson's language or thought whenever it struck him as too intemperate. That much of the acidity is gone is thoroughly clear from a variety of examples which prove that Emerson, even more than other young men of the time, was born with a knife in his brain. He either copied or wrote (as acidly as Mark Twain on medieval nobles), "The proof of his humanity amounts to this, that driving out on one occasion he did not run over a child, when he had a good opportunity." Impatient with what he called "goodies," he wrote that "we will almost sin to spite them," but he was not permitted the frankly contemptuous sequel, "Better indulge yourself, feed fat, drink liquors, than go straight laced for such cattle as these." He wrote that in people of thievish manners suicide would "be a high act of virtue." Revulsion at seeing the individual personality submerged at evening parties, where everybody said the same thing no matter what the question, provoked the angry "a soirée [is] a heap of lies. . . ." He was disgusted with "great cities, enormous populations, if they be Paddy populations" — but the last clause was deleted. It all came at one point to the misanthropic conclusion, rising to a most "ungentlemanly" feeling that profanity was the only way you could tell the mob how barbarous they were:

> I see not how we can live except alone. Trenchant manners, a sharp decided way will prove a lasting convenience. Society will ⟨paw & paddle⟩ coo & claw & caress. You must curse & swear a little: they will remember it, & it will do them good. What if they are wise & fine people[?] I do not want ⟨their⟩ your silliness, though you be Socrates, and if you indulge them, all people are babyish. Curse them.

So vexed was Emerson at substitution of communal for individual activity that he labeled the Puseyite Church a "clubhouse"—deleted, of course, so that the printed description—"a balance and overpoise to the conscience" is mild, to say the least. The most influential religion in New England came off little better in his note, "The Unitarian the milk & water era, the day of triviality and verbiage," but the first phrase was blue-pencilled. With all this deletion one is far from surprised to find perhaps the roundest of all condemnations of the age's "superstitions" dropped quietly from sight: "Public opinion is a hobgoblin, Christianity a hobgoblin, the God of popular worship a hobgoblin."

The limitation imposed on Emerson's frankness in these matters extends to others too. A rather large number of deletions can be explained by assuming an archaic standard of delicacy. But what the defenders of ideality seemed to consider coarse will scarcely seem more than a refreshing frankness in the twentieth century. We are not a bit bothered by Emerson's note that thoughts sometimes pour into the mind like bile into the mouth during retching, or his description of "that hand-breadth of greener grass where the cattle have dropped dung . . ." as "the first lecturer on Agriculture." We are amused by the omitted anecdote of the reformed sailor at Father Taylor's prayer meeting who said, "Jesus Christ is my grog shop," and we are educated in the flexibility of Emerson's mind by the restoration of the suppressed phrase (editors' italics) in the query, "What is there of the divine in a load of bricks? What is there of the divine in a barber's shop *or a privy*? Much. All." That this is no slip of the blue pencil seems clear from a similar deletion when Emerson subjected Spinoza's theory that there is "but one substance" to the skepticism of a boy who told him "he thought the pinelog was God, & that God was in the jakes. What can Spinoza tell the boy?" The image of the gentleman allowed for no such imaginative neighborliness between scatology and ontology—or anything else, it appears, for having momentarily glimpsed the figurative possibilities of the jakes, Emerson did not leave it alone. The very next entry, omitted of course, is "Even Dickens is doubtless of much use to this country, though in so humble a way as to circulate into all towns & into the lowest classes the lesson which is pasted in the water-closets of public houses,—*Do not spit, & please close the covers.*" That a nineteenth-century gentleman had been not only in a public house but also in its water-closet was apparently a damning fact. The gentleman could be frank to a point, but to live up to the later image was to avoid the slightest taint of indelicacy. Presumably it was the indelicate simile which got this fusion of heaven and earth banished: "The sublime enters into everything even into a baker's score or a schoolboy's multiplication table, as the light beams into privies & garrets." One indelicate word probably lost us "Malthus revolts us by looking at a man as an animal. So do those views of genius semi-medical which I spit at." And delicacy ruled out other kinds of coarseness besides the scatological; perhaps this was why Emerson was not allowed to recount the anecdote heard in a stagecoach of a "lady who took an egg in her hand & the warmth of her body hatching it the little serpents came out & ran all over her hand." That extended passages of this genre are missing from the early journals may be accounted for on the grounds that the writing is juvenile, but one can't avoid the suspicion that the gentleman was not expected to enjoy the grotesque.

This picture of the lost Emerson might easily be expanded, but it is not the purpose of this introduction to exhaust the recovered materials. Hopefully, enough has been said to show that if left to himself, left to follow the full bent of his feeling and to say exactly what he wanted to say, Emerson is a significantly different man from the person who emerged from the printed journals half a century ago. What was left out, of course, no more constitutes the whole Emerson than does the result of a subtly weighted editing. The fair and reasonable reader will not take the parts for the whole, but will conscientiously fit them in and observe the product in the right perspective. He will come to know Emerson's personality not from any restorations of detail, however revealing, but from a comprehensive view of the entire picture.

If we now turn our attention away from Emerson the man to Emerson the thinker and compare the original journals with the abridgment, we shall find that though less, perhaps, is to be recovered, what there is has its own fascination and value. It should be clear from some of the passages to be cited that the praiseworthy effort to reduce bulk by cutting out juvenilia, repetition, and trivia by no means explains the editing in full. Certain ideas and attitudes seem to have been expunged either because they were not considered worthy of a "gentleman" or because they did not fit the editor's picture of what Emerson, at various times, believed or stood for.

The variety, the many-sidedness, even the polarity of Emerson's ideas are extensively represented in the published journals. It may well seem temerarious to suggest that these ideas had even wider range than we have known. Yet this is the clear implication if we look at selected omissions of certain literary and social views, religious ideas, and moral or philosophical concepts. For example, here is a journal entry of February 1850 in which unusual editorial bias is apparent in the ruthlessness of the abridgment. What we have read and what we now can read are distinguished by italics (except for the Italian word); the reader may find a certain pleasure in reading the roman print first and then the roman and italic together:

> Carlyle is wonderful for his rhetorical skill. This trick of rhyme, burden, or refrain, which he uses so well, he not only employs in each new paragraph, suddenly treating you with the last *ritornello*, but in each new essay or book quoting the Burden or Chorus of the last book — You know me, and I know you; or, Here we are again; come take me up again on your shoulders, — is the import of this. *'Tis curious, the magnificence of his genius, & the poverty of his aims.* He *draws his weapons from the skies, to fight the cause of some wretched English property or monopoly or prejudice or whim. A transcendental John Bull delighting in the music of Bowbells, who cannot see across the channel, but* has the skill to make divine oratorios in praise of the Strand, Kensington and Kew. *I was to have said just now that* he contrives in each piece to make, out of his theme or lucky expression, a proverb before he has done; and this conclusion of the last is the exordium of the next chapter.

Admittedly, the exact reversal of meaning here which results from the excision is rare in the published journals, but it dramatizes the loss readers have suffered in the full understanding of Emerson. Such a loss is again exhibited in the editorial treatment of slavery and the Negro. Thus from an early treatise on compensation is missing a one-sentence illustration of the effects of revolution, which might give property and freedom to twenty million slaves but brings loss of property and death to innocent and deserving men. More telling is the absolute deletion of four passages which express grave doubt that the Negro is human. The first occurs in 1822, when the nineteen-year-old Emerson is speculating philosophically upon slavery and the Negro, and giving full rein to his instinct for exploring the arguments on both sides of a question, no matter how "revolting" a subject might seem to him. Thus in examining the biological status of the Negro he is forced to admit that though generally speaking the possession of Reason separates man from beast, the line gets lost as individuals of one species are compared with individuals of another. This is printed, but it leaves the question of the Negro's status conveniently generalized. Emerson, in his honesty, did nothing of the kind. He went on:

> It can hardly be true[,] I think[,] that the difference lies in the attribute of Reason; I saw ten, twenty, a hundred large lipped, lowbrowed black men in the streets who, except in the mere matter of language, did not exceed the sagacity of the elephant. Now is it true that these were created superior to this wise animal, and designed to controul it? And in comparison with the highest orders of men, the Africans will stand so low as to make the difference which subsists between themselves & the sagacious beasts inconsiderable. It follows from this, that this is a distinction which cannot be much insisted on.

Emerson continued in the same unprinted section to query a distinction based on "the upright form, and countenance raised to heaven,—fitted for command." "The Monkey resembles Man, and the African degenerates to a likeness of the beast." Thus if "the distinction between the beasts and the Africans is found neither in Reason nor in figure . . . ," he asks, "where then is the ground of that distinction? is it not rather a mere name & prejudice and are not they an upper order of inferior animals?"

His conclusion that slavery is "the worst institution on earth" would have gained more force than it has in the printed text if the reader had known that Emerson could arrive at it even though Negroes seemed to him like animals. Two passages written as late as July 1853 show that this attitude continued. In one he sees the Negro as "standing . . . in nature below the series of thought, & in the plane of vegetable & animal existence"; in the other, headed "The Sad Side of the Negro Question," he repeats that the Negro is "created on a lower plane than the white, & eats men & kidnaps & tortures, if he can," and insists that "the brute instinct rallies & centres in the black man."[1] Later, he would observe sardonically, "Nature every little while drops a link. How long before the Indians will be extinct? Then the negro? Then we shall say, what a gracious interval of dignity between man & beast!" That Emerson could hold these views and at the same time take an active part in the anti-slavery movement is only more testimony to his astonishing ability to achieve his own goal—to "look farther than to the simple fact and perhaps aid our faith by freer speculation."

On other topics also, Emerson's views, philosophical, religious, or moral, have suffered some loss in the original excavations. The gentlemanly archaeologists of 1909–1914 left many a stone untouched and brought back many a cropped photograph from their prodigious dig. Only extensive scholarship can adequately restore the full remains—and this scholarship should have implements unavailable even now, such as a full index-concordance, to make absolutely certain that passages were not omitted from one context because they were printed elsewhere, whether in the journals, the essays, the extended notes to the essays, the lectures, or the letters. At the moment it is only possible to mention what seem to be significant passages and to speculate on the significance of their omission. Thus one wonders why the following passages dealing with the idea of God are cut:

1. Emerson's argument that God established his system by miraculous agency.

[1] It is true that Cabot prints both passages entire in his *Memoir* (II, 429), but here they are undated and are placed between a speech given in 1837 and a journal passage of 1844. At least one scholar of Emerson's views on abolition has been misled by Cabot's failure to give the original location.

2. A sentence which means that the reward of heroism is largely in God's approval, not in the individual's sense of merit (where the printed text puts it).
3. A passage on the death of Clay which shows unequivocally Emerson's belief that God inspires all human effort.
4. From an essay on God's benevolence, which ends (in the printed text) "If God is good, why are any of his creatures unhappy?" the following sentence: "It seems to me that a liberal view of the subject should reconcile the mourner to his transient affliction, and his affliction to the benevolence of God." Emerson's thought is scarcely done justice in a prior footnote: "The young man confesses his inability to satisfactorily account for all misery. . . ."
5. Some four pages of reflection on mutability, "the unsubstantial pageant" of life, decay, loss of youth and beauty, the vanity of opposing "this tremendous fate," and the certainty of the grave — all culminating in the assertion that the only antidote is trust in the Lord.
6. A rebuke to the man who gets sick, prays, gets well, then wonders whether his recovery is due to the efficacy of prayer or of medicine. "Man of little faith," Emerson admonished, "it is God that always gives efficacy to wretched human means."
7. The flat statement, so much the reverse of the creed ordinarily associated with Emerson, that "To believe too much is dangerous because it is the near neighbour of unbelief. Pantheism leads to Atheism."
8. The retrospective rejection of his own training: "It is a great happiness to escape a religious education. ⟨It⟩ ↑Calvinism↓ destroys religion of character."

Such an accumulation, small as it is, raises the suspicion that something of Emerson's youthful orthodoxy has been tempered out of the text, especially since all the passages but the last occur before 1831.

The suspicion gains some strength from the deletion of a number of passages from about the same period on the subject of sin. In one of these the doctrine of original sin supports anti-Primitivism and a traditional conservatism. The young Emerson was not surprised that travelers found savages lacking in virtue, for depravity was not, he thought, the product of civilization but something common to all men. In fact the growth of virtue coincided with the growth of civilization or the security of property. Another group of passages stresses the continuing sinfulness of man and his disposition to sin in secret. Emerson develops at length a paragraph beginning: "It is not enough considered by us how much it is the fault of each of us that there is so much sin & evil in the world." Another full paragraph asserts that "sin is in our cities, at our doors, in our chambers, in our bosoms," that "it is the nature of man to sin in secret," that "he falls from innocence & like Adam in Eden is ashamed & seeks to hide himself." Here the doctrine of original sin has been surgically removed, as though it were some cancer in the mind of the young radical. That some policy was being carried out is the implication of removing another tumorous passage, "My friends[,] we are sinful men. We can copy from our own memories the fatal history of the progress of sin." The excision turns a hard-headed, particularized statement into an earnest but gentle admonition that slights the sympathetic involvement of all men in the sins of the wicked. If the concern with sin is not obsessive either here or elsewhere, the young Emerson's intense conviction of sin still suggests more kinship between him and Nathaniel Hawthorne than we have hitherto realized.

Such editorial treatment pretty clearly rejects a body of evidence which conflicts with the image of Emerson as cosmic optimist. Not that the editor disposed of all such evidence. Emerson's frustration, bad health, and loneliness, his anguish of spirit in the early years, and other experiences in a minor key all have their voice in the published journals. But some of the extremes of the anguish and certainly some of the darker shades of doubt and pessimism have been lost to two generations of readers. Thus, during the cure for incipient tuberculosis at St. Augustine, Emerson gloomily reflected that "the sun will shine on your funeral as bright as he did at your bridal day," and that "when two or three weeks of decent grief are gone those of your own household will quote the day of your death as a convenient date. . . ." The dedication to an early Wide World journal begins with a long section on the corruption of the body, and the murderous passions, vices, injustice, and ignorance of men in the past, against which it weighs the familiar vision of the Party of the Future in America, with its prospect of realizing the splendid dreams of men "as the consummation of Time." But that Emerson had not yet completely joined the party is clear from the next sentence: "But if this also be an illusion, and Time hoards no halcyon scene as a retribution for his sorrows — mine eye passeth over his bound, for a glimpse of the shoreless abyss — Eternity! There are beings and events involving felicity *there,* — if such there be in the Universe." The last qualifying doubt, worthy of Melville in 1851, only sharpens the refusal of the young skeptic to be blinded by conventional hopes either of time or of eternity. Yet the printed version begins with none of this; it begins only with the single sentence, "To the Genius of the Future, I dedicate my page." That Emerson was not quite so sure of the future as this and its sequel make him seem is clear in another omitted passage a page or two further on in which he vents dark, even morbid thoughts on the "transitory Universe" and the grave. Much in tune with all this are two pages from an earlier journal whose omission veils Emerson's direct recognition of evil and of the blindness and distortions of Hope, and his certainty of evil days to come. Whatever his position later on — a position which included the pregnant and deleted statement in 1848, "The past with me turns to snakes" — it should be clear that he arrived there after more struggle than the first printing of the journals reveals.

Three other flaws contribute to ignorance or misunderstanding of Emerson — misreadings of the text, rejection of canceled passages, and erratic representation of Emerson's reading. We have had ". . . the beauty of God makes me feel my own sinfulness the more," where Emerson wrote "the bounty of God"; ". . . the Union is only perfect when all the Unities are absolutely isolated," but Emerson's word is "Uniters"; and ". . . the fire of the robust, united, burning, radiant fuel," where the error "fuel" for "soul" makes the thought ridiculous. One of his basic metaphors gets lost when the text reads "Morals as the foundation of nobility" instead of "fountain," and both thought and parallelism suffer when "satisfy" is misread "justify" in "Always too young or old, I do not justify myself: how can I satisfy others?" We have had, too, "I do not wish to hold, nor to help you to hold them," where Emerson wrote "wish to hold slaves." His thought is lost entirely in paragraph two of the following passage:

Correcting manuscripts and proofs for printing makes apparent the value of perspective as essential to good writing. Once we said genius was health; but now we say genius is Time.

This doctrine of results, too, from which flows genius, also [appears?] to be geometrical and mechanical, or, that gravitation reaches up into the sacred soul.

Emerson's actual comment was: "This doctrine results too from that which shows genius also to be geometrical & mechanical, or, that gravitation reaches up into the sacred soul." There is similar loss or distortion of his thought in all the following (the error is bracketed): "The artificial is [read] rent from the eternal"; "[Humility] Humanity characterises the highest class of genius, Homer, Milton, Shakespear"; "[He reserves] Here serves however the Spartan in us . . ."; "The wise [may] man, that is the healthy mind learns . . ."; "Indeed it was the common opinion of the [day] boys that Mr. Thoreau made Concord"; "Hell is better than Heaven, if the man in Hell [knows] honors his place, and the man in Heaven does not." Many more misreadings have been found. If they are not likely to revolutionize our reading of Emerson, they will at least make it more accurate.

The elimination of most cancelled passages in the first edition does, of course, have the advantage of excluding what Emerson supposedly thought inferior or irrelevant. Yet if much trivial matter has been suppressed, much of interest to the scholar studying composition and style as well as thought and personality is lost. Instances abound on page after page of the present edition, especially in the earlier volumes; the reader may make his own comparison with the old edition. A few examples will indicate the kinds of observation or thought which Emerson himself deleted: "What is good in itself ⟨no circumstances can make bad⟩ can be bad to nobody"; "⟨The fly & the musquito are as untameable as the hyena & jaguar⟩ The fly strikes against the window pane until at last he learns that though invisible there is an obstacle there"; "Get the soul out of bed, . . . out into God's universe, . . . and your pros⟨ing⟩y ↑selfish↓ sensualist

⟨selfish Capitalist⟩ awakes, a God, . . ."; "⟨I have a nasty appetite which I will not gratify⟩". To make his expression more accurate, to curb extravagance, to suppress too candid a self-revelation—these and other motives may be discerned in the numerous instances of cancellation. Restored deletions and corrected readings should provide in themselves a solid basis for various studies of Emerson.

The record of Emerson's reading, as it appears in book lists and quotations, has added to the difficulties of scholars, especially those who have tried to study Emerson's sources. Edward Emerson did what he could to provide clues by printing some quotations and by listing for each year the books or authors referred to in the journals of that year. But besides the innumerable unpublished quotations in the regular journals a half dozen volumes given over almost entirely to quotations had to be left out. With the correction of what quotations were printed went the evidence as to Emerson's accuracy or inaccuracy—and the student of Emerson and the classics particularly will find much to interest him on this score. As for book lists and author lists, they sometimes conceal as much as they reveal. That a book is mentioned does not mean that Emerson read all of it; that an author is quoted means frequently that Emerson merely copied a passage out of one of the many reviews or other secondary sources which he read. Access to the available facts about Emerson's reading should correct many a false impression and open the road to important exploration of his use of sources.

The last group of omissions to be dealt with here, and certainly the most extensive and valuable, consists of those journal entries which had appeared in the same or mostly the same form in the Centenary Edition of Emerson's works, edited by Edward W. Emerson in 1903–1904. "Such paragraphs," we learn in the Introduction to the *Journals*, "are for the most part left out, but sometimes, if important, are referred to. In some instances it seems well to give the original form, which may show the conditions." The motive for this policy was doubtless to give the greatest amount of Emerson's thought that was financially possible, and its implementation deserves the highest praise. Something like total recall was required, since Emerson's compositional habits might lead him to derive a paragraph for any given essay from three or four notebooks, or to distribute the thoughts in a journal paragraph into three or four essays. The cross references to the printed matter entered by Edward Waldo Emerson in pencil in the manuscript journals as a guide to what to omit constitute an amazing feat of memory. They are incorporated into the present edition, and those who use them will be aware of the profound debt they owe to Edward Emerson for his painstaking labor. Together with the full text they will supply the basis for precise studies of Emerson's creative habits, the provenience of his essays, the relation between the times of composition and the times of publication, and the role played by James Elliot Cabot in the organization of *Letters and Social Aims* and the posthumous essays, and numerous other subjects. Such studies ought to find, among other things, that though some journal passages are inferior to their formal counterpart, others are plainly better. By and large the omitted matter is more concrete, more detailed, or more personal than the essay version. Students of Emerson's habits of mind will be able to see even further how he characteristically generalized the cluster of illustrations which accompanied his first thoughts. Conversely, what seems remote, abstract, or impersonal in the essays will often turn out to be rooted in immediate experience and an active sense of life and persons, and to have what Henry James called "solidity of specification."

Here is a typical example of reduction in Emerson's thought. In his journal he wrote: "We have no prizes offered to the ambition of generous young men. There is with us no Theban Band. . . ." In print, the entry is cut off with the note, "The rest is printed in 'Aristocracy.'" There we read, as the "rest" of the passage, "We have a rich man's aristocracy, plenty of bribes for those who like them. . . ." But what Emerson actually wrote is: "We have a Brummagem aristocracy, O plenty of cambrichandkerchief [sic] nobles, & grocer gentlemen, cake, cigars, & champagne, musty parlours & irritable women." Similarly, when Emerson writes of our fondness for "a good superlative"—and here the omission is not indicated—he lavished instances in his journal: "Everybody climbs Mont Blanc, if he can; nor will travellers rest until they have looked off Himalaya. We go under the flood of Niagara at Table Rock. The Flying Childers who ran a mile a minute, must be seen, if to see; and General Thumb, the smallest man that ever grew,—or grew not." The dehydrated essay version reads only "Our travelling is a sort of search for the superlatives or summits of art,—much more the real wonders of power in the human form" (and these are exemplified by Newton, Caesar, and others). In at least one instance, the restoration of the journal source combined with the essay passage provides some fascinating clues to history. Take the following, for example:

I wrote formerly what seemed the experience of some of our rural socialists, that the purity of the sexes depended on plain speaking, and that to redress the wronged pudency, it needed—to come nearer. A good lamp is the best police.

In Brook Farm was this peculiarity, that there was no head . . . ; each was master or mistress of his or her actions; happy, hapless anarchists. They expressed, after much perilous experience, the conviction that plain dealing was the best defence of manners and moral[s] between the sexes. People cannot live together in any but necessary ways.

Put together, the two passages seem pretty clearly to imply that the Brook Farmers of the essay were the "rural socialists" of the journal, and that their experience with sexual behavior must have been somewhat more critical than the essay indicates to call forth the mordant "A good lamp is the best police." In many another instance the excised journal passages clarify the meaning of the essays—especially where the thought in the essays is itself blurred.

The raw journals also illustrate something else—the way Emerson himself sometimes toned down or altered his original thought when he presented it for public consumption. In the essay on "Politics" he writes about Americans: "Born democrats, we are nowise qualified to judge of monarchy, which, to our fathers living in the monarchical idea, was also relatively right." This represents something of a retreat from the first version: "We are . . . democrats, & are nowise qualified to judge of monarchy, which to our fathers living & thinking in the monarchical idea was just as exclusively right." Again—and this helps to confirm what was said before about Emerson and the racial status of the negro—he wrote in "Worship," published in 1860, "Christianity, in the romantic ages, signified European culture,—the grafted or meliorated tree in a crab forest. And to marry a pagan wife or husband was to marry Beast, and voluntarily to take a step backwards towards the baboon. . . ." The first version, written in 1848, is identical — except that the last clause reads " a step backwards towards the negro & baboon." Finally, consider a passage in "The Preacher" and then fit into it the significant cancelled phrases in the original, deleted journal passage: "What sort of respect can these ⟨ ⟩ preachers or newspapers inspire by their weekly praises of texts and saints, when we know that they would say just the same things if ⟨ ⟩ Beelzebub had written the chapter, provided it stood where it does in public opinion ⟨ ⟩." Into the first space insert "unitarian or presbyterian"; into the second "the Devil"; into the third "which they flatter & serve." Distressing as the practices of his first editors may have been, they had some sanction in Emerson himself. Whether he merely wished to modulate his thought, whether he actually changed his mind between the study and the lecture platform, or whether, despite his own courage, he dared not utter his frankest reflections — these are problems for systematic investigation. Let us hope the investigators will recognize the complex difficulties of determining motives.

"Emerson's revised reputation," writes a scholar who has patiently saturated himself in Emerson, "will be founded upon a thoroughgoing critical revaluation of the Journals." The prediction deserves fulfillment. The thoroughgoing critical revaluation, so far beyond the scope of a mere introduction, will one day be made. The introduction is but the preview, like the dumb show to a play. Its deductions about editorial motives in the first edition are open to inspection; perhaps even its sketch of the lost Emerson, most certainly due to be expanded, will also be revised. But until the record is complete, until all the lost mosaic fragments are back in their proper places, the conclusions must stand. In the first printing of the journals we lost much of Emerson. The Montaigne in him was unduly overshadowed by the Plotinus, the brooding doubter by the cosmic optimist, the private man in his freedom and infinitude by the public man in the confining garments of "the gentleman." We also lost the full means of knowing his habits of writing, the extent of his sources and his use of them, his knowledge of the classics, and particularly the slow, intricate ways in which his thought grew, fascinating as a banyan tree in all its apparent lawlessness. Without this knowledge we are something less than the transparent eyeball we should be to take in the great universe of Emerson's mind. Thoreau once wrote that "the real facts of a poet's life would be of more value to us than any work of his art." He might have added, "and the full facts." At any rate, it is the premise of this edition that Emerson's first thoughts, the hardheaded things written for himself only, the personalia, sometimes even the false starts and unfinished sallies of thought, as well as the things which did go into the essays—all these are real facts to be valued along with the finished works in the study of Emerson, and all are needed for the revision of Emerson's reputation.

THE MANUSCRIPTS

For more than half a century Emerson fulfilled his own admonition that one primary duty of the American scholar should be to sit "in his private observatory, cataloguing obscure and nebulous stars of the human mind . . . watching days and months sometimes for a few facts; correcting still his old records." Emerson's observations, catalogues, records, and corrections of his old records now fill several crowded shelves with manuscript volumes even more diverse in content than in size, shape, and appearance. Their physical life began when as a Harvard sophomore Emerson started jotting down his ideas in composition books or on mere gatherings of paper later sewed together, probably by his mother. In time he habitually used hard-covered, octavo notebooks, though on his travels he carried pocket-size leathered-covered notebooks, and occasionally he recorded a fleeting thought in small, leather-bound diaries with calendars and printed dates.

Carefully treasured, they must have bulked large in the Concord study by the time of the fire in 1872. Unlike so many of Melville's manuscripts, which have disappeared in various conflagrations, Emerson's seem to have survived this one virtually intact, thanks to the care of friends. After the fire the manuscripts probably went to the temporary study set up in the Concord Court House for Emerson, and finally back to the restored house and study. James Elliot Cabot, Emerson's literary executor, used them for his *Memoir* in 1887 and made some attempt to arrange the early ones chronologically, supplying paper covers where needed and pasting on little lettered squares of the same paper for identification. After Emerson's death in 1882 the journals came into the possession of his heirs, Ellen Tucker Emerson, Edith Emerson Forbes, and Edward Waldo Emerson. The latter had selected passages transcribed for the edition of 1909–1914. In 1903, at the urging of Edward W. Forbes, a safe was built in the Concord house and the journals were deposited in it. About 1930 they were moved to a safe in the Fogg Art Museum at Harvard, and finally, in 1941, to the Houghton Library. Nearly all of them have the marks of time and heavy wear. Emerson went over and over them, adding comments and afterthoughts, culling out and lining through passages used in lectures or essays, making cross references, copying from one into another, indexing, or just reading. Yet none is seriously damaged, and the sturdy and handsome hand-lettered boxes in which they now rest will preserve them pretty much in the condition in which Emerson left them.

Including only holograph items, the collection contains 234 manuscripts that can be called Emerson's journals and notebooks; but the number is misleading, for of these 31 are pocket diaries and memoranda of engagements, 13 are account books including the covers of 1 account book, 9 are notebooks containing Emerson's copies of the personalia of family members or friends, and one is a late notebook, scarcely used. If the manuscript journal at the Pierpont Morgan Library and the transcript of a notebook at the Houghton Library are added, the total of Emerson's regular journals and notebooks is 182. At least two and perhaps three or more journals have disappeared. But Bliss Perry's statement that the first sixteen journals have also been lost is probably untrue. The "lost" numbers can be accounted for by a reconstruction of Emerson's probable numbering system. Loose pages of putative journal material exist in the general Emerson collection at Harvard. Some of these may have been torn out from journals listed here, but many of them, as Professor Rusk has said, are probably isolated scraps of paper which Emerson inserted in letters to Mary Moody Emerson. The present edition takes as its starting point all the journals of Emerson which are known to exist.[1]

[1] Nothing is known of Emerson's journal in the country mentioned in *L*, I. 115. For explanations of the manuscript total, of the missing journals, and of Professor Perry's statement, see pp. 403–412.

THE PUBLICATION PLAN

If journals are daily accounts of transactions and events, of experiences and observations, the title customarily used to describe this body of Emerson's manuscripts is only partially accurate. What he called his "savings Bank" contains many different forms of money, from coined gold to shin plasters of merely historical value. Some volumes are composed almost exclusively of materials which fit the standard definition of journals. Other volumes are exclusively or almost exclusively books of compositions, accounts, addresses, poetry, indexes, quotations, jokes, records of trees planted, and special topics. Other "non-journal" materials in the collection include clippings, letters, book-lists, property records, memoranda, and statistical data. A more nearly accurate title for the collection is "journals and miscellaneous notebooks." Journals are taken to mean those volumes which consist predominantly of Emerson's prose records of his experiences and thoughts, set down more or less in day-to-day order. Miscellaneous notebooks include composition books, quotation books, volumes on special topics, and records of various kinds. Such a division is the intended design in this edition. In publication the principle of first things first will prevail. The printing of volumes entirely or largely given over to accounts, addresses, indexes, and such factual information must be postponed in favor of the personal, literary, and intellectual records. Whether it is feasible to publish these factual volumes will be decided later. Volumes composed entirely or mostly of poetry do not seem to warrant immediate printing, in view of Professor Carl Strauch's forthcoming edition of the poems. Also postponed are topical volumes in which Emerson gathered together his thoughts on individuals like Thoreau, Margaret Fuller, or Alcott, or on special subjects, like "War," "Art," and "Fate." These and other volumes, though sometimes recording new thought, are typically composed of passages drawn from previous journals. The focus in the edition is on Emerson's thought at the time he first wrote it down. Even with this as a guide the problem of recognizing and dealing with repetition arises. But where duplicated material is easily perceived, as in the topical volumes, it is easily assigned a low publication order.

It would be fortunate indeed if the contents of each volume fitted the division into regular journals and miscellaneous notebooks, but unhappily they do not. Kinds of material which do not merit immediate publication when concentrated in a single volume appear in various quantities scattered through other volumes. Not only poetry, but accounts, addresses, index material, and other records of fact intrude into pages essentially concerned with thought or observation. Sometimes systematic, sometimes haphazard, Emerson frequently turned his journals into nightmares of miscellanea, creating bewildering editorial problems. But on the theory that some factual details, though tedious in quantity and isolation, have a certain contrasting interest or usefulness when scattered about among the real products of Emerson's mind, the editors have included many of them. Poetry which appears in regular journal volumes is printed because it and its context illuminate each other. Quotation books, invaluable indices to Emerson's reading and intellectual tastes, are also printed.

THE EDITORIAL METHOD

The first, the basic premise, of the editorial plan, was that Emerson's journals should be made available as rapidly as was consistent with the most elementary requirements for a scholarly text—accuracy and completeness. All other considerations have been subordinated to this. Extensive documentation, location of all sources and quotations, the designation of passages already printed, the arrangement of every entry in precise chronological order, these desiderata of the ideal edition had to be sacrificed whenever they became obstacles to prompt publication. The second premise, which followed from the first, was that each journal would be presented intact. With some few and necessary exceptions the individual volumes were to be printed as units rather than broken up and distributed by the date or supposed date of each entry. The value of keeping Emerson's journals pretty much in the form in which he wrote them was assumed to balance the unattainable advantages of a rigorously chronological arrangement. The other major premises were that minimum interference with the text, maximum intelligibility, and maximum feasible honesty with the reader were the proper attributes of a modern scholarly edition.

The Text. The text, while partially emended, comes as close to a *literatim* transcription into print as is feasible. It represents what Emerson wrote, in the way he wrote it, including cancellations, revision, and variants. Omitted silently are Emerson's miscellaneous markings, practice penmanship, false starts at words, isolated words or letters, and other trivia, if in each instance there is maximum certainty that the element omitted has neither meaning nor significance. Omitted, but with symbol or descriptive annotation, are pen or pencil sketches, Emerson's letters, and certain index material and repetitions. The manuscripts bear extensive markings in pencil or crayon, mostly parentheses or brackets, but occasionally verbal clarifications. These are assumed to be by Edward Emerson or Cabot and hence are ignored, but wherever they may be Emerson's they are noted.

Emendation of Prose. The aims of the emendation have been the maximum of intelligibility consonant with minimum interference, and a text which can be quoted with the fewest possible brackets and *sics*. Thus, though Emerson's punctuation is often casual, hurried, or non-existent, it is stylized only when some addition is indispensable for clarity or will simplify meaning without serious disturbance to the original. Stylization is indicated by square brackets except in a few recurring situations. A period is silently added to any declarative sentence lacking terminal punctuation but followed in the same paragraph by a sentence beginning with a capital letter. If a declarative sentence lacking a period is followed by a sentence beginning with a small letter, either a bracketed semicolon is supplied, or a bracketed period is supplied and the small letter is silently capitalized. In the second instance the reader will automatically know that the capital was originally a small letter. If a direct question lacking a question mark is followed by a sentence in the same paragraph beginning with a capital the question mark is silently added.

Some other punctuation and capitalization is normalized, in

accordance either with Emerson's prevailing practice or with requirements for quotation today. Punctuation of items in a series, since Emerson habitually set them off, is silently inserted. Small letters at the beginning of unquestionable paragraphs or of sentences which follow a sentence ending with a period are silently capitalized. Where indispensable for clarity a silent period is added to an abbreviation. Quotation marks, dashes, and parentheses missing from intended pairs have been silently supplied. Apostrophes have been silently inserted or normalized in possessives and contractions. Superscripts have been lowered and double or triple underscorings have been interpreted by italics. Emerson's underscoring to indicate intended revision is not reproduced. His single carets under insertions are assimilated into the editors' insertion marks. Indisputable cancellations are shown, but lines Emerson drew to show he had used a passage in an essay or copied it somewhere are deleted, with annotation where necessary. Where Emerson cancelled by writing over a word, in whole or in part, the cancelled matter is shown in the conventional angle brackets and the substitute matter is printed immediately after it, with no intervening space (e.g., "the⟨m⟩ir," or "⟨seven⟩eight").

Emendation of Poetry. On the whole, Emerson's poetry has been left as it stands in the manuscripts. Apostrophes and some commas, periods, and question marks have been supplied, in accordance with the rules for emending prose, but only where Emerson's intention was unmistakable. The verse is characteristically unrevised, or fragmentary. The difficulties of deciding in every instance exactly what rhythm or stress Emerson would have chosen had he put in punctuation have proved entirely too formidable.

Emerson's spelling, reflecting both interesting American practice and his own individuality, is retained, except for metatheses (the original is printed in the textual notes), demonstrably meaningless slips of the pen, and common Emersonian contractions like *yt* for *that*, *ye* for *the*, *wh* for *which*, *wd* and *shd* for *would* and *should*, and *bo't* for *bought*.

Emerson's syntax and grammar are retained with these exceptions: careless repetitions of a single word are omitted, and careless grammatical errors and syntax unintelligible because of imperfect revision are corrected in the text, if possible, with the originals in textual notes or footnotes. The text follows Emerson's specified changes in order, with the original order shown in textual notes or footnotes. Thus in Wide World 1, p. [2], Emerson's "*does not*$_2$ or *cannot*$_1$" becomes "cannot or does not." Here and elsewhere textual notes are indicated by a superior "n" (^{n}). Matter the intended order of which is not clear is inserted in the text if some logical place can be found for it; otherwise it is put in the notes; in either case descriptive annotation or explanatory symbol is provided.

Annotation. Annotation is intended to fulfill only the minimum obligations. As a rule, those authors and other persons not included in *Webster's Biographical Dictionary* are identified, titles of unfamiliar works are supplied, and some biographical information is provided. Information given in the first reference to such matters, since it may be found through the index, is not usually repeated. Some cross references are provided, using either the page numbers of this edition or those of the manuscript journals. Except in the headnotes the latter are bracketed to avoid confusion. In the location of sources and quotations, reference is made either to the edition Emerson used, to a standard edition, or to a readily available one. In some instances, an intermediate source is cited, for Emerson frequently copied passages from periodicals or secondary works, rather than from the original author. Minor misquotations are not ordinarily noted.

Quotations. Translations of classical quotations are from the Loeb Classical Library, unless otherwise noted. Except for apostrophes, quotations are unaltered. Emerson's quotation marks at the beginning of each line of a quoted passage have been dropped. Phrases, lines, or passages which Emerson is known to have quoted from other authors are set down in smaller type, unless they are syntactically or structurally a part of what he wrote.[1] This system of identification has been confounded by Emerson's occasional trick of putting his own words in quotation marks, as though he were an established author. Where he has marked the passages with his symbol of personal authorship, there is no problem. But there are also passages in quotation marks (and some without), which the editors have not been able to identify with certainty as either Emerson's or

[1] Because of the limitations of printing, both Emerson's and the editors' identifications of such passages are also set in smaller type.

another writer's. Questions about the authorship of such passages are ordinarily indicated by the query "By Emerson?" Exhaustive research will doubtless be able to establish the proper authorship where it is dubious. Meanwhile caution signs have been erected.

Order. When the journals fit into a logical time sequence, this is adhered to; when they overlap in time they are generally presented in order of prior beginning; when a journal falls in one period but contains a substantial sequence of entries for another, those entries are printed with the journals to which they are nearest in time. Double-enders (journals kept at different times and written from back to front as well as from front to back) are treated as two separate volumes and placed in their respective periods. For the most obvious reasons quotation books and topical journals are not broken up by supposed date of the entries but printed as units.

Dating. The dates of innumerable journal entries are uncertain and unascertainable. The fact that a passage falls between two dates does not necessarily mean that it was written on the first date or even before the second. It may be earlier or later than both, since in some journals and especially in the miscellaneous notebooks Emerson skipped about from one page to another, used back or middle pages before front pages, and returned, sometimes much later, to add entries or use up the empty pages for economy's sake. Besides reversing journals and making two out of one Emerson sometimes reversed a journal several times, so that some matter appears upside down on the page. The precise chronological relation of these entries to each other and to those appearing right-side up is frequently baffling. For these, as for other dating problems, Emerson's handwriting offers some assurance, especially after it settles down in the twenties to a regular form, but in the early volumes he uses confusingly different styles. The determination of dates by means of ink studies has not been undertaken. A task likely to take at least as long as the preparation of the edition itself, it is still open to someone with the necessary time and money. All the ready means of dating have been used, such as Emerson's dates, historical events and personal experiences, book withdrawals, and Emerson's marginal arithmetic (e.g., when he subtracts from the year 1821 the year 1617, 1821 is taken as the date of the matter on the page). Where an entry or passage seems to have been written significantly later or earlier than its context, this is indicated in a note. The year date of material on each two pages, as far as it is ascertainable, is printed as a running head in the gutter margin of the right-hand page, with queries where appropriate. Despite all these difficulties in dating, the reader can be sure of the year date of the vast majority of passages and reasonably certain of the period within the year; and Emerson himself supplies a reassuring number of day and month dates. When he does this at the end of a passage his date is printed in its original position and form, but is also bracketed at the beginning in normalized form. When the date is to be supplied for an undated passage and it differs from that in the running head, a bracketed and italicized date is inserted at the head of the passage.

Page Numbers. Ordinarily, where Emerson fails to supply page numbers, they are silently supplied. A subscript letter to a page number means that the page is an insert. A subscript number to a page number means either that the page number is repeated in the manuscript or that the editors have repeated it in order to clarify the use or the sequence of the manuscript pages, as when Emerson directs material from one page to be inserted on another; when he writes both from front to back and from back to front; when editorial pagination of unnumbered pages necessitates the repetition of a manuscript page number, or whenever other such unusual situations occur. When a page number is repeated, its first occurence bears a subscript "1" ($_1$). These and other occurrences of unusual pagination are annotated.

THE SOURCE OF THE TEXT

Between 1929 and 1938 the Ralph Waldo Emerson Memorial Association undertook the expense of *literatim* transcripts for about two thirds of the journals in order to save wear and tear on the journals themselves. These are surely among the most faithful possible attempts to execute copies of manuscripts. Within the limits of a typist's resources the manuscript pages are duplicated — cancellations are struck through, letters are struck over where Emerson wrote over them, interlineations are inserted as such, the position and arrangement of marginalia are imitated. Where the typewriter was inadequate, india ink was used, and sketches, practice penmanship, or idle markings were not only copied but sometimes painstakingly traced. These transcripts have been most useful in the physical preparation of the present edition, but since they have not proved absolutely accurate, the working text has been derived from microfilm. This text has been fully collated with the manuscripts to provide the final text for volume I; in future volumes any necessary deviation from this practice will be noted. Cruxes have been studied by magnifying devices, and where necessary, high-contrast photography has been used. Every feasible step has been taken to present exactly what Emerson wrote.

Foreword to Volume I

THE EARLY JOURNALS

Emerson apparently began keeping regular journals in January, 1820, when he dedicated his first "Wide World" to the recording of "new thoughts (when they occur)" and "old ideas," and to "all the various purposes & utility real or imaginary which are usually comprehended under that comprehensive title *Common Place book.*" His primary aim was the capture of inspired thought. This is clear from the dedications with which so many journals begin. Variously he invoked the "Spirits of Earth, Air, Fire, Water," "the Muse, the fairies, the witches, and Wisdom," as well as Imagination, Nature, and Time, "to preside over [his] creations." Imagination in particular he chose to appoint "the generallissimo & chief marshal of all the luckless ragamuffin Ideas which may be collected & imprisoned hereafter in these pages. . . ." Perhaps of even more moment was the dedication of his seventh Wide World to "the Spirit of America . . . to that living soul, which *doth* exist somewhere beyond the Fancy. . . ." Despite an obvious addiction to accepted models of thought and form, and to conservative preachers, thinkers, books, and periodicals, despite the air of reason and orthodoxy and sense which dominate such matters as the arguments for the existence of God or for the depravity of the stage, Emerson deep down was an enthusiast. Almost instinctively, it seems, he joined the other romantics in the pursuit of the unattainable and sought spiritual and imaginative freedom through inspiration from some powerful but hidden and undefined source. Much later, he was to discover that the source was simultaneously and equally "within" and "above." The early journals still retain all the faint tracks and footsteps of the hunt for direct inspiration, for what is "a little beyond," as Emerson once agreed to define Transcendentalism.

It is conventional to acquiesce in Edward W. Emerson's verdict that these manuscripts are "journals, not of incidents and persons, but of thoughts." There is more intellectual history here than autobiography. Yet a fair image of Emerson as a young man emerges, especially from previously unpublished passages. A sparkle of a passion or a conflict, perhaps imperfectly revealed or suppressed outright, will gleam here and there from the pages. A few cancellations designed to conceal private thoughts from public gaze will carry their own mute message. "Mr Somebody, will it please your impertinence to be conscience-struck," wrote Emerson in a journal he seriously expected to burn. What he hoped would escape prying eyes is not sensational; even so, his is the fate of all public figures whose stature justifies every effort to recapture their most intimate thoughts and feelings. One would prefer a great deal more but what there is recovers something at least of the private Emerson.

The first volume contains those journals and miscellaneous notebooks which Emerson kept from the spring of his second year at Harvard to the summer of 1822. The cut-off point, though partially determined by the need for some uniformity in the printed volumes, is not as arbitrary as it may appear. The regular journals, Wide Worlds 1–4 and 6, which came to be "peculiarly devoted to original ideas," consist mostly of dated entries from January 25, 1820 to July 10, 1822. The miscellaneous notebooks have various materials set down with little regard to logical or chronological order, but ranging from 1819 to the latter half of 1822. Thus the volume contains the various expressions of Emerson's mind and interests in the period, whether daily meditation, compositions and essays, or favorite passages. In the Wide Worlds Emerson notes his critical responses to college friends, especially the mysterious Martin Gay, to the eloquent lectures and sermons of George Ticknor and Edward Everett, and to college exhibitions and commencements. Here, too, are estimates, sometimes hopeful, more often pessimistic, of his progress towards the distinction he sought; here is something like the self-analysis and examination of conscience familiar in the tradition of Puritan diarists like Cotton Mather, Samuel Sewall, and Jonathan Edwards. The personal focus largely changes in the journals of the post-graduate year as Emerson, rather quickly maturing, develops more extended views on religion, the nature of God, greatness, the passions, or whatever engages his roving mind. Here the materials begin to merge with those he first tended, on the whole, to enter in the miscellanies, set apart chiefly for original compositions to be presented in public. Ultimately, as everyone knows, the regular journals became as much a source of published work as the original miscellaneous notebooks.

The miscellaneous notebooks are in some respects more interesting than the journals. Aside from quotation books, they are composed mostly of notes for or rough drafts of college themes, Bowdoin prize essays, poems or essays for literary clubs, wild romances, and other formal compositions, and they provide a new basis for study of his early intellectual and creative processes. Thus the "Dissertation on Ethical Philosophy" may now be traced from its inception in "detached phrasula," quotations, and experimental sentences and paragraphs through a more orderly state into the final version which Edward Everett Hale printed, with some errors, many years later. Much of the original version of Emerson's first published work, "Thoughts on the Religion of the Middle Ages," is here. These and other "essays" make it clear that Emerson early thought of himself as a speaker and a writer. The college themes and essays for literary clubs are the earliest evidence of what shortly emerges as a major ambition — to write for publication, to make his thought known and felt in the world around him. Contrary to what Edward Emerson wrote, Emerson wanted to and did publish shortly after finishing Harvard. As early as January, 1822, he confided to his journal some thoughts on contrast only because he felt unable "to shine upon this topic in *theme, poem,* or *review.* . . ." The miscellaneous notebooks are in part the inchoate chronicle of Emerson's attempts to be somebody. For all their trivia they form, for the regular journals, an indispensable supplement.

CHRONOLOGY 1803–1822

1803: May 25, Emerson is born in his father's house on Summer Street, Boston.

1811: William Emerson, the father, dies.

1812–1817: Emerson attends Boston Public Latin School.

1817–1818: August, Emerson is admitted to Harvard; lives in Wadsworth House as President Kirkland's freshman; during winter and spring vacations, teaches in Uncle Samuel Ripley's school in Waltham.

1818–1819: Emerson rooms at 5 Hollis Hall with William B. Dorr; joins a college book club; November, votes against tyrannical treatment of the sophomore class by the Government of Harvard and joins the Conventicle Club; during the winter, serves as waiter in the Junior class dining hall; on April 24, becomes charter member of a nameless literary society; before June 14, is elected to the Pythologian Society; on July 5, reads essay on "Sentimental Feeling" to the literary society; teaches during vacations at Uncle Samuel Ripley's school in Waltham.

1819–1820: Emerson lives at 15 Hollis Hall with John G. K. Gourdin; November 27, is appointed secretary of the nameless literary society; in January, begins "Dissertation on the Character of Socrates"; in the spring, attends lectures by Professor Edward Everett on Greek literature; April 20, delivers his poem "Improvement" before the Pythologian Society; April 26, reads poem at first anniversary meeting of the literary society; May 15, ends term as secretary of the literary society; in July, wins second place in the Bowdoin prize competition with "Dissertation on the Character of Socrates"; in August, wins one of three second prizes in the Boylston oratorical contest; in August? first sees Martin Gay.

1820–1821: Emerson rooms in Hollis 9 with his brother Edward; November–May, attends lecture course by Professor George Ticknor on French and Spanish literature; January 3, begins "Dissertation on the Present State of Ethical Philosophy"; February 26, reads an essay before the literary society. In April, his mother moves to 26 Federal Street, Boston. Before April 17, Emerson drops "Ralph" and calls himself "Waldo"; April 24, reads poem, "Indian Superstition," at College Exhibition; July 16, ties for second-place Bowdoin prize with "Dissertation on the Present State of Ethical Philosophy"; July 17, reads class poem; August 29, at Harvard Commencement, takes part in conference "On the Character of John

Knox, William Penn, and John Wesley," admires Sampson Reed's essay on genius, and graduates; in the fall, begins teaching in his brother William's school for young ladies in Boston; October 21, begins series of essays on the drama, perhaps for publication.

1822: May–early June, goes on walking trip with brother William to Northboro, Mass.; in July, begins essay on "The Religion of the Middle Ages" (published in *The Christian Disciple* for November and December).

SYMBOLS AND ABBREVIATIONS

⟨ ⟩	Cancellation
↑ ↓	Insertion
/ /	Variant
‖ . . . ‖	Unrecoverable matter, normally unannotated. Three dots, one to five words; four dots, six to fifteen words; five dots, sixteen to thirty words. Matter lost by accidental mutilation but recovered conjecturally is inserted between the parallels.
⟨‖ . . . ‖⟩	Unrecoverable cancelled matter
‖msm‖	Manuscript accidentally mutilated
[ ]	Editorial insertion
[. . .]	Editorial omission
[ ]	Emerson's square brackets
⌊ ⌉	Marginal matter inserted in text
⌈ ⌋	Page numbers of original manuscript
n	See Textual Notes
☞ ☜ ☟	Hands pointing

^	Emerson's symbol for intended insertion
[R.W.E.]	Editorial substitution for Emerson's symbol of original authorship. See plate VII.
*	Emerson's footnote

ABBREVIATIONS AND SHORT TITLES IN FOOTNOTES

W	*The Complete Works of Ralph Waldo Emerson.* With a Biographical Introduction and Notes, by Edward Waldo Emerson. Centenary Edition. Boston and New York: Houghton Mifflin Co., 1903–1904. 12 vols.
J	*Journals of Ralph Waldo Emerson.* Edited by Edward Waldo Emerson and Waldo Emerson Forbes. Boston and New York: Houghton Mifflin Co., 1909–1914. 10 vols.
L	*The Letters of Ralph Waldo Emerson.* Edited by Ralph L. Rusk. New York: Columbia University Press, 1939. 6 vols.
E t E	Kenneth W. Cameron. *Emerson the Essayist.* Raleigh, N.C.: The Thistle Press, 1945. 2 vols.

"Books Borrowed." Kenneth W. Cameron, "Books Borrowed from the Boston Library Society by Ralph Waldo Emerson and His Mother (1815–1845)," in *Emerson the Essayist*, II, 149–186.

"Early Reading List." Kenneth W. Cameron, "Emerson's Early Reading List (1819–1824)," *Bulletin of the New York Public Library*, LV, 315–324 (July 1951), reprinted with additions in *Transcendentalists and Minerva* (Hartford, 1958), pp. 415–424.

"Emerson's Reading." Kenneth W. Cameron, *Ralph Waldo Emerson's Reading*. Raleigh, N.C.: The Thistle Press, 1941.

PART ONE

The Journals

Wide World 1

1820

Emerson used the title Wide World with an accompanying number for what seems to have been originally a series of thirteen regular journals. At present only twelve such journals are known to exist, since Wide World 5 is missing. In the middle of his junior year at Harvard, on January 25, 1820, Emerson began the first of these journals, Wide World 1, and made periodic entries in the homemade booklet through August 24.

Like the rest of this series of journals, Wide World 1 is made out of sheets of unlined foolscap, folded folio and hand-stitched into gatherings which are then re-stitched at the fold to form a simple uncovered booklet. Forty-six of the original forty-eight pages exist; the leaves vary slightly in size according to the condition of their edges but measure approximately 16.8 x 21.4 cm each. There are six gatherings in the manuscript, each containing four leaves. In gathering 5, however, leaf 20 (for pages that were numbered 39 and 40) is torn away, leaving only faintly decipherable letters on the stub of the recto and lines for an index on the verso. Tipped to the top of the page numbered 32 is an unnumbered insert leaf, verso blank, of different paper, measuring 11.1 x 16.4 cm, affixed so that the writing on it is perpendicular to that of the numbered page.

[1] —The Wide World.[1]— No. 1.

[Jan. 25, 1820] Mixing with the thousand pursuits & passions & objects of the world as personified by Imagination is profitable & entertaining. These pages are intended at this their commencement to contain a record of new thoughts (when they occur); for a receptacle of all the old ideas that partial but peculiar peepings at antiquity can furnish or furbish; for tablet to save the wear & tear of

[1] To enclose the title Emerson drew a flat hexagonal frame and painted it light blue in water color. The first page of this journal is reproduced as plate 1.

weak Memory & in short for all the various purposes & utility real or imaginary which are usually comprehended under that comprehensive title *Common Place book.* O ye witches assist me! enliven or horrify some midnight lucubration or dream (whichever may be found most convenient) to supply this reservoir when other resources fail. Pardon me Fairy Land! rich region of fancy & gnomery, elvery, sylphery, & Queen Mab! pardon me for presenting my first petition to your enemies but there is probably one in the chamber who maliciously influenced me to what is irrevocable; pardon & favour me! — & finally Spirits of Earth, Air, Fire, Water, wherever ye glow, whatsoever you patronize, whoever you inspire, hallow, hallow, this devoted paper. — Dedicated & Signed Jan 25, 1820, Junio.[2] —

[2] [Jan. 26] After such a dedication what so proper to begin with as reflections on or from Edward Search?[3] It is a fine idea which he either intends to convey or else the form of expression unintentionally did (pray let us believe the latter for the credit of Originality) that those parts of the world which man cannot or does not[n] inhabit are the abodes of other orders of sentient being invisible or unpercieved by him. To amplify — Perhaps the /cent⟨er⟩re/interiour/ of the earth, the bottomless depths & the upper paths of Ocean, the lands circumjacent to the poles, the high rock & clefts of the rock are peopled by higher beings than ourselves; — animals cast in more refined mould; ↑not↓ subject to the inconveniencies, woes &c of our species to whom as to us this world appears made only for them & ⟨to⟩ ↑among↓ whom our very honest & honourable species are classed ↑only↓ as the highest order of brutes — perhaps called of the *bee* kind. — When Imagination has formed this class of beings & given them the name of Supromines it will be perfectly convenient

[2] Emerson discontinued the use of this pen name after August 24, 1820, the last day of his junior year.

[3] Pen name of the English philosopher Abraham Tucker (1705–1774), author of numerous volumes of metaphysical speculation. On Oct. 21, 1815, and Sept. 19, 1816, either Emerson or his mother had borrowed from the Boston Library Society Tucker's *Abridgement of the Light of Nature* (London, 1807). For this and other information about Emerson's reading, the editors have consulted the studies by Kenneth W. Cameron, making corrections and additions where necessary: *EtE*; "Books Borrowed"; "Early Reading List"; and "Emerson's Reading." See the table of abbreviations for the full bibliographical facts.

to rise again to an order higher than these last, holding our self complacent friends the Supromines in as utter contempt as they, us, or as we the beasts, & then she may rise to another & another till for aught I know she may make this [3] world one of the Mansions of heaven & in parts of it though in & around yet thoroughly unknown to us the⟨y⟩ ↑seraphim & cherubim↓ may live & enjoy. I have now already fallen into an errour which may be a very common one[,] to hunt an idea down when obtained[,] in such a remorseless manner as to render dull & flat an idea originally plump, round, & shining. —But before I proceed further, I do hereby nominate & appoint "Imagination" the generallissimo & chief marshal of all the luckless raggamuffin Ideas which may be collected & imprisoned hereafter in these pages[n] (signed) Junio.—Jan 26th ⟨It⟩

It enlarges the mind & certainly gratif⟨ys⟩ies it to hold large contemplations regarding the material Universe. Perhaps our system and all the planets [&] stars we can discover, nay, the whole interminable Universe is moving on as has been supposed in ⟨a⟩one grand circle round the centre of light & since the world began it has never completed a single revolution. It is an improvement on the grandeur of this supposition to suppose there is a source of light before [4][4] us & the whole vast machinery has been forever & is ↑now↓ sweeping ⟨on⟩ forward in a direct line through the interminable fields—extensions of space.—It is a singular fact that we cannot ⟨imagine⟩ ↑present to the imagination↓ a longer space than just so much of the world as is bounded by the visible horizon; so that even in this stretching of thought to comprehend the broad path lengthening itself & widening to recieve the rolling Universe stern necessity bounds us to a little extent of a few miles only. But what matters it[?] We can talk & write & think it out. We can imagine the shadow of the incomprehensibly large[,] glorious mass blackening the infinity behind it[;] we can send Conjecture forth to ride on the wings ⟨of⟩that are bearing the worlds forward & sit & explore & discover what is to ⟨be its er⟩ occur when the wheels shall stop & the wings fall ⟨before⟩ in the im-

[4] "Astronomical reveries" is written vertically in the left margin upward from "what is" (below) to "miles" (above). Such marginalia in this and other journals are index headings for the matter to which they apply.

mediate presence of the source of light ↑to which for ages past & ages to come they have been & will be advancing↓. Conjecture weary & overwhelmed only exclaims Time shall be no more.—Everett's[5] "⟨|| . . . ||⟩Man standing on the confines of that other world where Goodness & Happiness those stranger sisters shall meet together & know each other, & ⟨she[?]⟩ seeing creation on creation sweeping [5][6] by to their doom, then he shall learn to pity little Man piling up his monuments of marble & calling it fame"—is very very fine. Chateaubriand's "the universe is the imagination of the deity made manifest" is worthy him.—Personification of moral attributes or things is a fine employment. Grandeur would make a fine personage in poem. Represent him sitting in pomp of silence on the high places of the world holding a creative wand & the unborn glories & minds & powers of monarchs & men strewed round him in embryo. Let[n] him bestow on the bold Genius of ancient Rome all ⟨the⟩ splendour & majesty↑;↓ ⟨of the⟩ but Destiny is abro[ad] & his magnificent chariot must roll on. It set forth in its career before the systems of existence were compacted, it has long been upon the earth & its heavy wheels are ↑now↓ hastening from the north. Hark the lumbering of its wheels is already sounding in the ears of Rome! it came,—it passed over her⟨;⟩—Grandeur flung away his withered wand & his crown fell, the wide world was ⟨hastening to Decay⟩ ↑yielding↓ before the coming [of] Destiny but Nature & the powers of the universe interpose[d], averted the course of his steeds & smoothed away his frown. New nations arose from beneath the ruins of Rom[e] [6][7] like Milton's ⟨bad⟩ angels from the superincumbent mountains & Grandeur resumed his crown & wand.—

"Mount on thy own path to Fame nor swerve for man or more

[5] Edward Everett (1794–1865) was at this time Eliot Professor of Greek Literature at Harvard, editor of *The North American Review*, and a Unitarian minister. Emerson is quoting from a sermon preached in the Brattle Street Church in Boston in late Dec. 1819, or early Jan. 1820. His recollection of the passage was somewhat different when he quoted it in a letter to his brother Edward Bliss Emerson, Jan. 31, 1820 (*L*, I, 89).

[6] The phrase "grandeur & destiny personified" is written vertically in the text upward from "Hark" (below) to "piling" (above).

[7] "Independence" is written vertically in the left margin upward from "great" (below) to "all" (above).

than man" says Caswallon (in Samor)[8] & it will be a fine motto by striking out the last four words. It were a sublime spirit that implicitly followed the rule. I may admire[,] I fear I cannot obey[,] & there is an apology which every man makes for himself when his independence is put to the test that by nature we are social beings & it is utterly against the order of things for a single man to presume to encounter all the prejudices & violence & power & war of the world[,] ⟨so⟩ invidious & alone. With this plausible answer he stands his ground, worms himself into good opinion & patronage of men & secures himself present peace by the sacrifice of his high honour. But there are on earth great men who disdainful alike of the multitude's scorn & the multitude's applause elevate themselves by their own exertion to heights of human exaltation where the storm of varying opinion cannot hurt them & the levin-bolts of furious envy & disappointed passion will not reach or harm them. Every man of talents & application [7][9] has it in his power to be one of these.—

In "Samor" the judgement scene in the close of the book is well described. Indeed the eloquence of the senate, bar, or pulpit, or indeed ↑of↓ any occasion where one is addressing a multitude on an affair of any importance as it is in itself able to produce in the orator an agony of excitement[,] is a noble subject for description. Gather together an august conv⟨a⟩ocation of a nation's *wise* on a subject where the passions are awake & knowledge is full & power is strong —then give place to one that is eminent; let him come forth with dignity and all eyes will see him & him alone[;] they will hang with speechless & intense observance on every look, word, motion.—When he gives animation to high sentiments the thrill of soul will *valde* tremefacere ⟨ullos⟩ *eos*;[10] the mind of all & every hearer will dilate & contract, will triumph & droop, as he shall desire. But no prosing— let us suppose ⟨that⟩ a pulpit Orator to whom the path of his profession is yet untried but whose talents are good & feelings strong & his independence as a man in opinion and action is established[;] let

[8] Henry Hart Milman, *Samor, Lord of the Bright City* (New York, 1818), lines 257–258, misquoted.

[9] "Samor" is written diagonally left to right in the text upward from "convocation" (below) to "judgement" (above). "Pulpit eloquence" is written vertically upward in the left margin from "please" (below) to "But no" (above).

[10] "Really make them tremble" (Ed.).

him ascend the pulpit for the first time not to please or displease the multitude but to expound to them the words of the book & to waft their minds & devotions to heaven. Let him come [8][11] to them in solemnity & strength & when he speaks he will chain attention with an interesting figure & an interested face. To expand their views of the sublime doctrines of the religion he may embrace the universe & bring down the stars from their courses to do homage to their Creator. Here is a fountain which cannot fail them. Wise Christian orators have often & profitably ⟨elaborated⟩ ↑magnified↓ the inconcievable power of the creator as ⟨evinced⟩ ↑manifested↓ in his works & thus elevated & sobered the mind of the people & gradually drawn them off from the world they have left by the animating ideas of Majesty, Beauty, Wonder, which these considerations bestow. Then when life & its frivolities is fastly flowing away from before them & the spirit is absorbed in the play of its mightiest energies & their eyes are on him & their hearts are in heaven then let him ⟨unfold⟩ discharge his fearful duty, then let him unfold the stupendous designs of celestial wi↑s↓dom, & whilst admiration is speechless let him minister to their unearthly wants and let the ambassador of the most high prove himself worthy of his tremendous vocation. Let him gain the ↑tremendous↓ eloquence which stirs men's souls, which turns the [9] world upside down, but which loses all its filth & retains all its grandeur when consecrated to God. When a congregation are assembled together to hear such an apostle you may look round & you will see the faces of men, bent forward in the earnestness of expectation & in this desirable frame of mind the preacher may lead them whithersoever he will; they have yielded up their prejudices ⟨& [?]⟩ to the eloquence of the lips which the archangel ha⟨ve⟩th purified & hallowed with fire & this first sacrifice is the sin offering which cleanseth them. One of the most grand subjects which the Christian religion contains is the judgement & ⟨one of⟩ the noblest theme for eloquence. To picture the world destroyed & all the peoples thereof & whole human race assembled. All the ⟨rejoicing⟩ nations that the world ever saw & all their generations from ⟨a⟩Adam to ⟨n⟩Noah & from Noah to the last child that shall be born. Yes they shall come & their righteous-

[11] "Pulpit eloquence" is written vertically in the left margin upward from "gradually" (below) to "which cannot" (above).

ness & unrighteousness, their glory & degradation, their sin & their sacrifice, yea all that they have done shall come with the[m] to judgement. And the archangels shall marshal them to the stupendous tribunal of inexorable Justice.

[10] Then shall the blinding influence of prejudice pass away from all eyes; and things shall be seen as they are when human passions & folly & ambition & interest & hope are removed. & behold the loud clamour of rejoicing nations is hushed—astonishment hath made them dumb. The heavens & all their host are rolled together as a scroll—they are folded up & changed[;] the world is bla⟨s⟩zing beneath them [n] & its flame is ascending forever & ever[;] the pillars of the universe are falling to decay & creation's fabrick is mouldering away hitherto deemed eternal in vain. All all is vanishing but the throne of the ⟨eternal⟩ ↑everlasting.↓—

Feb. 6th The immediate presence of God is a fine topic of sublimity. In charging a minister for instance "above all remember the omniscience of God—His allseeing eye is upon you now, it will always be upon you—& in his immediate presence we now charge you fear him[,] obey him." His throne is founded far above the stars.—Descend ye Nine—

[Feb. 7] Mr K. a lawyer of Boston gave a fine character of a distinguished individual in private conversation [n] [11][12] which in part I shall set down. "Webster is (Feb 7th) a rather large man, about 5 feet, 7, or 9, in height & 39 or 40 years old—he has a long head, very large black eyes, bushy eyebrows, a commanding expression,—& his hair is coal black & coarse as a crow's nest. His voice is sepulchral.—There is not the least variety or the least harmony of tone—it commands, it fills, it echoes, but is harsh & discordant.—He possesses an ↑admirable readiness, a↓ fine memory and a faculty of perfect abstraction, an unparallelled impudence & a tremendous power of concentration—he brings all that he has ever heard, read, or seen to bear on the case in question. He growls along the bar to see who will run & if nobody runs he *will* fight. He knows his ⟨own⟩ strength,

[12] "(Webster)" is centered beneath "shrewd & sarcastic" at the bottom of the page.

has a perfect confidence in his own powers & is distinguished by a Spirit of fixed determination[;] he marks his path out & will cut off fifty heads rather than turn out of it; but is generous & free from malice & will never move a step to make a severe remark. His genius is such that if he descends to be pathetic he becomes ridiculous. ⟨h⟩He has no wit & never laughs though he is very shrewd & sarcastic & sometimes [12] sets the whole court in a roar by the singularity or pointedness of a remark. His imagination is what the light of a furnace is to ⟨his⟩ ↑its↓ heat[,] a necessary attendant — nothing sparkling or agreeable but dreadful & gloomy." This is the finest character I have ever heard pourtrayd & very truly drawn with little or no exaggeration. With respect to the cause of a town's condition of bad society he said well "there is stuff to make good society but they are discordant atoms" & regarding the contrasting & comparing the worthy and great dead — "you may not tell a man 'your neighbour's house is higher than yours' but you may measure gravestones & see which is the tallest." —

Cambridge March 11th 1820

Thus long I have been in Cambridge this term (three or four weeks) & have not before this moment paid my devoirs to the Gnomes to whom I dedicated this quaint & heterogeneous manuscript. Is it because matter has been wanting — no — I have written much elsewhere in prose, poetry, & miscellany — let me put the most favourable construction on the case & say that I [13][13] have been better employed. Beside considerable attention however unsuccessful to college studies I have finished Bisset's Life of Burke as well as Burke's regicide Peace together with considerable variety of desultory reading generally speaking highly entertaining & instructive. The Pythologian Poem[14] does not proceed very rapidly though I have experienced some poetic moments. Could I seat myself in the alcove of one of those public libraries which human pride & literary rivalship have made costly, splendid, & magnificent it would indeed be an enviable situation. I would plunge into the classic lore of chivalrous story &

[13] "Fairy land" is circled and centered beneath "magnificent" at the bottom of the page.

[14] See p. 25 and pp. 235–242.

of the fairy-land bards & unclosing the ponderous volumes of the firmest believers in magic & in the potency of consecrated crosier or elfin ring I would let my soul sail away delighted in to their wildest phantasies. Pendragon is rising before my fancy & has given me permission to wander in his walks of Fairy-land & to present myself at the bower of Gloriana. I stand in the fair assembly of the chosen; the brave & the beautiful; honour & virtue, courage & delicacy are mingling in magnificent joy. Unstained knighthood is [14][15] sheathing the successful blade in the presence of unstained chastity. And the festal jubilee of Fairy land is announced by the tinkling of its silver bells. The halls are full of gorgeous splendour & the groves are joyous with light & beauty. The birds partake & magnify the happiness of the green-wood shades. & the music of the ↑harp↓ comes swelling on the gay breezes. Or other views more real[,] scarcely less beautiful should attract, enchain me. All the stores of Grecian & Roman literature may be unlocked & fully displayed—or with the Indian enchanters send my soul up to wander among the stars till "the twilight of the gods[.]"

April 2d. Spring has returned & has begun to unfold her beautiful array, to throw herself on wild flower couches, to walk abroad on the hills & summon her songsters to do her sweet homage. The Muses have issued from the library & costly winter dwelling of their votaries & are gone up to build their bowers on Parnassus, & to melt their ice-bound fountains. Castalia is flowing rapturously & lifting her foam [15] on high. The hunter & the shepherd are abroad on the rock & the vallies echoe to the merry merry horn. The Poet of course is wandering while ⟨the &⟩ Nature's thousand melodies are warbling to him. This soft bewitching luxury of vernal gales & accompanying beauty overwhelms.—It produces a lassitude which is full of mental enjoyment & which we would not exchange for more vigorous pleasure. Although so long as the spell endures little or nothing is accomplished, nevertheless,[n] I believe it operates to divest the mind of old & worn-out contemplations & bestows new freshness upon life & leaves behind it imaginations of enchantment for the

[15] "Spring" is written vertically in the lower left margin upward from "are" (below) to "homage" (above).

mind to mould into splendid forms & gorgeous fancies which shall long continue to fascinate, after the ⟨natural⟩ physical phenomena which woke them have ceased to create delight. Perhaps we have dwelt too long on the beautiful & fanciful [16][16] of thought & forgot or perhaps avoided too sedulously what is darksome & grand. But we hope in time to devote pages to this department of the moral world. At all events we will now prosecute the chase for the lovely & beautifying. The Nai⟨d⟩ads are bathing in their streams[,] the Dryads & Fauns are threading the wild-wood — the eagle is mounting aloft — "mewing his mighty youth & kindling his undazzled eyes at the full mid-day beam"[17] — the cattle are lowing on a thousand hills & the far voice of joy resounds in the solitary place. Who can wonder that at such an hour we forsake the abodes of solemn sorrow or reject the discordant voice that summons us to mourn & plunge deeply into pure & boundless happiness[?] The unimproved hour may refuse to return.

[17][18] April 4th 1820. Judging from opportunity enjoyed I ought to have this evening a flow of thought rich, abundant, & deep; after having heard Mr Everett deliver his Introductory Lecture, in length 1 & ½ hour, having read much & profitably in the Quarterly Review and lastly having heard Dr Warren's introductory lecture to Anatomy,[19] — all in the compass of a day — & the mind possessing a temperament well adapted to recieve with calm attention what was offered. Shall endeavour to record promiscuously rec.[eive]d ideas. Though the literature of Greece give us sufficient information with regard to later periods of their commonwealth[,] as we go back before the light of tradition comes in the veil drops. "All tends to the mysterious east." From the time of the first dispersion of the human family to the time of Grecian rise every thing in the history of man is obscure & we think ourselves sufficiently fortunate "if we can write in broad lines the fate of a dynasty" tho we know nothing

[16] "(Spring)" is centered beneath "may" at the bottom of the page.

[17] Misquoted from Milton, *Areopagitica.*

[18] "Greece" is written diagonally left to right across the text downward from "mind possessing" (above) to "of Greece" (below). "Greece" is circled and written beneath "invention" and "Everett" beneath "much" in the bottom margin.

[19] John C. Warren, M.D. (1778–1856), was Hersey Professor of Anatomy and Surgery.

of the individuals who composed it. The cause is the ↑inefficiency &↓ uncertainty of tradition in those early & ignorant times when the whole history of a tribe was lodged in the head of its patriarch & in his death their history was lost. But ↑even↓ after the invention of letters much[,] very much[,] has ⟨escaped⟩ never [18] reached us. This we need not regret. What was worth knowing was transmitted to posterity[,] the rest buried in deserved forgetfulness. Every thing was handed down which ought to be handed down. The Phenicians gave the Greeks their *Alphabet* yet not a line of all which they wrote has come down while their pupils have built themselves an imperishable ⟨name[?]⟩monument of fame. The Greeks have left us a literature the most complete in all its parts which the world has ever shown. The long controversy which has made so much stir in the world with regard to the comparative merit of ancient & modern literature is senseless. We do not judge of the literature of Greece considering its age but considering its merit. The moderns' best efforts have only imitated them, & the mod[erns]. ⟨had⟩ composed theirs with them for models but they theirs without. Some history of the controversy will be useful. It commenced long ago for Quinctilian speaks of it & holds up the Grecian models to admiration—Horace also recommends them, & Cicero, but mention the dispute then commenced regarding superiour merit of ancient or mod[ern]. It was inherited through a succession of lines by France in 15 & 1600[,] the subject then warmly agitated. Boileau, Fontenelle, Racine on the side of the ancients.

For Everett See P. 21 (Everett—lecture on Greece)

Fontenelle having in [19] youth espoused the cause applied four times for a place in French Academy & "4 times Demosthenes, Plato, Theocritus pleaded against him." Undoubtedly many sensible people thought correctly of the dispute & engaged on neither side but it is immaterial to know. From France the quarrel passed over to England & Sir William Temple wrote for the moderns & was answered by Wattle [Wotton] whose work is superiour, for he seconds his arguments with the illustrious "names of Bacon, Bentl⟨y⟩ey, Boyle, Locke, Milton, Shakspeare, & weak must be the cause or powerful the advocate which is not assisted by these auxiliaries." [20]

[20] Emerson (and perhaps Everett) misstates the story. Temple, of course, dis-

Swift joined the controversy by writing The battle of the books, a work which has not even the uncertain merit of originality as a French work had previously been published in France[,] Le combat des livres. Swift's wit is wholly that which Locke has defined wit[,] unexpected association of ideas. Addison's posthumous works contained some reflections on this questio||n.|| Since then it has slumbered.

(The above is a very concise abstract of Prof. E's lecture as far as the Eulogy — not more —)

Greece is the land of contrast. A principle of contrast runs through all that we know of it. Drama, Manners, Climate, [20] Houses, Women — every thing — *Destiny* presided in their Tragedy very sublimely. — They passed the temples of the Furies without daring to behold them.

[Apr. 10] I here make a resolution to make myself acquainted with the Greek language & antiquities & history with long & serious attention & study⟨,⟩ (always with the assistance of circumstances.) To which end I hereby dedicate & devote to the *down-putting* of sentences quoted or original which regard Greece [—] historical, poetical, & c[rit].ical[,] page 47 of this time honoured register. By the way[,] I devote page 44[43] to the notation of Inquirenda & of books to be sought signed Apr. 10th Junio. There is a fascination which the elegance & genius of the ancients has thrown over their productions ↑here stenography begins↓ & wh rndrs mdrn lbrs cntmptbll .n cmprsn. I mst rd Hrdts & Arstphns & ll Grk trgdns snr or ltr. Wld tht sm rlcks of Egptn ltrtr rmnd I wld prse thm ||w||th .rdr & strnge .ntrst! Bt nthng .s lft .s bt . fw prd smbls .f dprtd grndr. It ws rmrkd in th Qrtrl Rvw tht .s you g. wst sprsttn grws mr fntckl & inhmn; i.e. Hndstn .s mr crl .n hr crmns & [...][21] thn Egpt, & Egpt thn Erp. But .t .ll .vnts ths stngrphy .s msrble. —[22]

---

paraged the moderns, and Wotton, though defending modern learning, thought the ancients superior in literature.

[21] "pnhts[?] [or] pnhcs[?]" or some other combination of letters. Emerson seems to have intended a stenographic abbreviation for *punishments.*

[22] Emerson's unsuccessful experiment with shorthand may be expanded as fol-

[21] Apr 30th. Have malignant demons possessed themselves of my mind & my pen & my tongue & my book? It is rarely that I s⟨ea⟩it myself down to this common place book which was intended to restore the sinking soul, to keep alive the fire of enthusiasm in literature, & literary things, to be the register of desultory but valuable contemplations. Etherial beings to whom I dedicated the pages of my "Wide World" do not I entreat you neglect it; when I sleep waken me; when I weary animate! Wander after moon-beams, fairies! but bring them home here. Indeed you cannot imagine how it would gratify me to wake up from an accursed Enfield lesson [23] & find a page written in characters of light by a moon-beam of Queen Mab! I will give you a subject — a thousand if you wish; — for instance 'Pendragon,' your own Pendragon[;] record his life & his glories. — 'Prince Arthur' if it is not too trite; or 'the Universe' or a 'broom stick'; either or all of these or 50 thousand more. "In the Capuchin Church at Vienna sixty six emperours are sleeping; — none of your mock emperours; none of your mushroom kings but &c" *Mr Everett* —

[May] Sabbath Evening. Would not Pestilence be a good personage in poetry for description? [n] Wrapt in the long white robes of sickness, entering the town in her awful chariot & her slow approach heard afar off [22] by the anxious fearful listeners — it comes — it rolls over the distant pavement — it draws near — the haggard ter-

---

lows: "and which renders modern libraries contemptible in comparison. I must read Herodotus and Aristophanes and all Greek tragedians sooner or later. Would that some relicks of Egyptian literature remained. I would peruse them with ardor and strange interest! But nothing is left us but a few proud symbols of departed grandeur. It was remarked in the Quarterly Review that as you go west superstition grows more fanatickal and inhuman; i.e. Hindustan is more cruel in her ceremonies[?] and punishments[?] than Egypt, and Egypt than Europe. But at all events this stenography is miserable." Emerson is paraphrasing from Robert Southey's review of Thomas D. Fosbrooke's "British Monachism," *Quarterly Review,* XXII (July 1819), 66, but he has reversed the sense of the opening statement: "Superstition has always lost something of its grossness as it proceeded from east to west." A system of shorthand based upon the omission of vowels was used regularly by Thomas Jefferson. See George F. Sensabaugh, "Jefferson's Use of Milton in the Ecclesiastical Controversies of 1776," *American Literature,* XXVI (Jan. 1955), 558–559.

[23] William Enfield, *Institutes of Natural Philosophy,* was a required text in the junior year at Harvard.

rifick form is presented to their view & in vain they fly; she stretches forth her hand & withereth & polluteth & destroyeth — in vain they strive & struggle to avoid her grasp: her arm stre⟨ct⟩tches out, her form enlarges to a supernatural size, ↑like the magnified limb in a distorted mirrour↓[,] as they retreat; & she goes on unchecked, unrelenting, diffusing mad desolation & dismay. — Every where the roaring voices of Joy are still, & the mourners go about the streets. But ⟨h⟩Health dwelleth in his tabernacle on the mountain & is waking the woods at dawn with the shout & noise of industry & the joyous peal of the hunter's merry merry horn — he is climbing the cliff & swimming the flood & labouring in the field. — The mountains & the grove are his dominions & Pestilence may not come near them. May 27 Thou changest his countenance & sendest him away! — May 28th I am now sitting before the *Pedagogue's* Map of Europe & startled almost to behold the immense region which Alexander governs. The ample domains [23][24] of the emperour of Russia are nearly equal to the rest of Europe. One man is insignificant in the extremest degree set down in this mighty land[;] yet all the millions of population planted in this stretching territory ↑& seemingly bound by no ties but the eternal bands of their common earth↓ bow to the despotism of an individua[l] like themselves. One would think his mind would dilate, "expand with strong conception" to meet the grandeur of circumstances with which God has surrounded him & accomodate himself to his vast commission. The bell rings[.]

In unison with the idea is that of Byron; after describing the magnificent dome of St Peter's at Rome he proceeds —

Enter. its Grandeur overwhelms thee not
And why? it is not lessened; but thy mind,
Expanded by the genius of the spot
Has grown colossal, &c ⟨can only find⟩
(and afterwards —) "and thou shall one day" (says he)
See thy *God*, face to face, as thou dost now
His Holy of Holies, nor be blasted by his brow.

([*Childe Harold's Pilgrimage*] CLV Stanza —
4th canto — [lines 1–4, 6–9])

[24] "Byron" is written diagonally left to right in the left margin upward at the bottom of the page from "one day" (below) to "And why?" (above).

June 4th ("The fiery soul sits murmuring in her shattered clay")[25]

[24][26] June 7th — A very singular chance led me to derive very sensible answers to the two questions I proposed to Virgil. For the first I opened to the line

O crudelis Alexi, nihil mea carmina curas.[27]

for the other I opened to a line, Dryden's translation of which is

Go let the gods & temples claim thy care.

— Have been of late reading patches of Barrow & Ben Jonson;[28] & what the object — not curiosity? no — nor expectation of edification intellectual or moral — but merely because they are authors where vigorous phrases & quaint, peculiar words & expressions may be sought & found, the better "to rattle out the battles of my thoughts." I shall now set myself to give a good sentence of Barrow's (the whole beauty of which he has impaired by a blundering collocation) in purer & more fashionable English. Obvious manifestations may be sometimes seen of the ruling government of ⟨g⟩God: Sometimes in the career of triumphant guilt when things have come to such a pass that iniquity & outrage do exceedingly prevail so that the life of the offender becomes intolerably grievous a change comes upon the state of things however stable & enduring in appearance, a revolution in a manner sudden & strange & flowing from causes mean & unworthy which overturneth the towering fabric of fortune & reduces its gigantic dimensions, [25][29] and no strugglings of might, no fetches of policy, no circumspection or industry of man availing to uphold it; there is outstretched an invisible hand checking all such force & cross-

[25] Paraphrased from Dryden, *Absalom and Achitophel*, I, 156–158.

[26] "Lottery" is written diagonally left to right across top left page from "translation" (below) to "opened" (above). "(Barrow)" is centered beneath "reduces its" at the bottom of the page.

[27] "O cruel Alexis, care you naught for my songs?" *Eclogues*, II, 6. Emerson is consulting the *Sortes Virgilianae*, that is, opening Virgil at random and taking the first passage sighted as an oracle.

[28] See p. 27, n. 55.

[29] "Barrowistical" is written vertically across middle six lines of text upward from "over" (below) to "originally" (above).

ing all such devices—a stone cut out of the mountain without hands & breaking in peices the iron & the brass & the clay & silver & the gold.—In looking over the sentence however though the grand outline of the whole was originally Rev Isaac Barrow's yet we very self complacently confess that great alterations have rendered it editorially Mr Ralph Emerson's & I intend to make use of it hereafter after another new modelling for it is still very susceptible of improvement. People prate of the dignity of human nature. Look over ⟨its⟩ the whole history of its degradation & find what odious vice, what sottish & debasing enormity the degenerate naughtiness of man has never crouched unto & adored? to things animate & things inanimate, to the ghosts of dead men whose li⟨f⟩ves were bloody & cruel,[n] lewd & fo⟨w⟩ul.—to beasts & grovelling reptiles, dogs, serpents & crocodiles—they have bowed down & adored—nay with a brutal folly more revolting than this they have prostituted their obedience & worship, they have sacrificed their dearest pledges of life & fortune, fawning in abominable adulation they have abandoned their interests & welfare to the cursed fiends of hell. Ingenuity has been exercised [26][30] to drag forth new unimagined objects such as these ⟨to⟩on whose ⟨idols⟩ ↑altars↓ mankind might offer their devotion, pay their respect, & repose their confidence. But it is a joyful change to see human nature unshackling herself & asserting her divine origin;—employed in encountering prejudices & detecting frauds; checking & chastising profane abuse; subjecting to legitimate controul those fiery passions which corrode & fret the soul; & woe to those whose malignity would fright her from her pursuit. Let these men vilif⟨ie⟩y ⟨&⟩their own nature, & disparage themselves as they please, we will acknowledge & avow that "Mentem e coelesti demissam traximus arce,"[31] that the soul hath appetites & capacities by which when well guided ⟨it⟩ ↑she↓ soars & climbs continually towards perfection & is backed by omnipotence in her magnificent career. The whole complication of good affections & actions pushing forward this object should spur on conscientious endeavour despite the torment of unprosperous envy & baffled mal-

[30] "Barrowistical" is written vertically across middle twelve lines of text upward from "spur on" (below) to "fiery" (above).

[31] Misquoted from Juvenal, *Satires*, XV, 146: "We have drawn from on high that gift of feeling. . . ."

ice,[n] in whose destruction providence seems to exceed or contravene the ordinary course of nature; their estates without visible means do moulder & [27][32] decay[,] a secret moth devouring them.—

June 19th When those magnificent masses of vapour[n] which load our horizon are breaking away disclosing fields of blue atmospher there is an exhilaration awakened in the system of a susceptible man which so invigorates the ⟨facu⟩ energies of mind & displays to himself such manifold power & joy superiour to other existences that he will triumph & exult that he is a man. I love the picturesque glitter of a summer morning's landscape; it kindles this burning admiration of nature & enthusiasm of mind.

We fecl at these times that eternal analogy which subsists between the external changes of nature & scenes of good & ill that chequer human life. Joy cometh but is speedily supplanted by grief & we look at the approach of transient adversities like the mists of the morning fearful & many but the fairies are in them & *White Ladies* beckoning. —— For better recollection of the meridian of papal power—mark this. In A.D. 1077 Henry ⟨f⟩IV emperour of Germany waited barefooted & bareheaded for three days at the outer gate of the fortress of Canosa in the depth of winter—expecting the pardon & forgiveness of Gregory VII.——

[28][33] July 23d. And then we journeyed to Logyle. After travelling long upon plain ground we were relieved by the appearance of a hill in our front. As we ascended gradually our ears were attracted by the sound of a waterfall—we continued to ascend till arriving at the summit, the hill was abruptly terminated by a precipice; but a noble prospect rewarded our toils. On the right from a

[32] "Exhilaration" is written vertically across middle eight lines of page upward from "look at" (below) to "will" (above). "Henry IV" is written beneath "forgiveness" and the notations "WX" and "PQ" beneath "Gregory" at the bottom of the page.

[33] "PICTURE" is printed in large letters diagonally left to right across the center of the page upward from "heaths" (below) to "were relieved" (above). Tipped on the page at the bottom is a small water-color sketch illustrating the landscape and buildings described in the text. It is not certain that either the description or the sketch is by Emerson.

bank beneath our precipice rose a similar steep cliff serving for the foundation of a square castle which retained the characteristics of feudal grandeur in architecture notwithstanding its modern improvements. Immediately in front was the waterfall & upward along the country a sheet of silver daz⟨l⟩zled the eye for a tract of many miles. The fall was but a few feet perpendicular & about 20 feet wide which has given a ↑beautiful↓ green border to the barren heaths of this unfruitful land. On the left a higher hill rose opposite the one I before mentioned but covered on its top with 3 singular edifices giving a picturesque tone to the view. One was a ⟨r⟩Round Tower, the second a sort of watch-keep or observatory, the third was a state-office of some kind under the old government & larger than the others. The soil here presents every variety of colour but nowhere more than about this hill. — Far before us there were mountains, clouds, trees, & castles all black[,] very little bright colouring [29][34] on any scenery. I enclose a sketch of the scene —

THE[35] phantasies of imagination & bad dreams. —

July 25 If power could make man happy the ancient great Roman citizens ought to have been the happiest of subjects. It was a strange state of Society. Pompey or C⟨ea⟩aesar or Milo though private citizens ⟨builded⟩ from their own revenues builded edifices & exhibited shows which would ruin a king of modern Europe. This immense flowing in of national treasuries to the coffers of private citizens throws a splendour & magnificence around eminent Romans which we feel for no other human beings. But we are told that their lives were an unceasing struggle with embarassments, enmities, & terrors; that they were harassed by petulant Tribunes or awed by rival nobles — oh it was worth their factions & their fears to live in that agony of high excitement, those tremendous strivings for power, enjoying the more than mortal grandeur of Roman glory!

[34] "Roman" is circled and written above "Phantasies of imagination" at the top of the page.

[35] "THE" is elaborately illuminated with a water-color sketch of the heads and shoulders of two men in medieval dress, a tower, an orb, a unicorn's head, a scepter, and other objects.

Since those mighty times there has been no man of whom it might be said that he stood forth like a Consul of Rome as proud as all earth's crowded honours could render a man! —

[30][36] Aug 8th Have been reading the Novum Organum. Lord Bacon is indeed a wonderful writer; he condenses an unrivalled degree of matter in one paragraph. He never suffers himself "to ⟨wander⟩ ↑swerve↓ from the direct forthright" or to babble or speak unguardedly on his proper topic, & withal writes with more melody & rich cadence than any writer (I had almost said, of England.) on a similar subject. Although I have quoted in my "Universe" of composition,[37] (by which presumptuous term I beg leave to remind myself that nothing was meant but to express — wideness & variety of range) yet I will add here a fine little sentence from the 30th section of the 2d Vol of the Novum Organum. Speaking of bodies composed of two different species of things he says; "but these instances may be reckoned of the singular ⟨or extraordinary⟩ heteroclite kind as being rare & extraordinary in the universe; yet for their dignity they ought to be separately placed & treated. For they excellently indicate the composition & structure of things; & suggest [31][38] the causes of the number of the ordinary species in the universe; & lead the understanding from that which is, to that which may be."

There is nothing in this sentence which should cause it to be quoted more than another. It does not stand out from the rest; but it struck me accidentally as a very different sentence from those similarly constructed in ordinary writers. For instance in the last three clauses (beginning "For they excellently") it is common to see an author construct a fine sentence in this way with idle repetitions of the same idea, embellished a little for the sake of shrouding the deception. In this, they all convey ideas determinate but widely different

[36] "Bacon" is written diagonally left to right across the page at top and bottom, upward from "Universe" (below) to "babble" (above) and again from "excellently" (below) to "different" (above).

[37] See p. 375.

[38] "Bacon" is written diagonally left to right across the middle of the page upward from "embellished" (below) to "ordinary" (above). "GAY" is written across the three lines — "There is a strange face . . . & should" — at the bottom of the page.

& all beautiful & intelligent. — But says Sterne, "the Cant of Criticism is the most prov⟨ing⟩oking."[39]

— There is a strange face in the Freshman class whom I should like to know very much. He has a great[n] deal of character in his features & should [be] [32][40] a fast friend or a bitter ⟨||. . . ||⟩enemy. His name ⟨is[?] Gay[41]⟩ I shall endeavour to be↑come↓ acquainted with him & wish if possible that I might be able to recall at a future period the singular sensations which his presenc[e] produced at this. —

[39] *Tristram Shandy*, III, ch. 12, slightly misquoted.

[40] "Comets" is written diagonally left to right in the left margin upward from "commemorates" (below) to "this." (above). Tipped to the top of the page is an unnumbered half sheet, verso blank, with this note: "If it be an adage of ethics that there is no law ||th||at does not bend to Circumstances what is virtue today being vice tomorrow, much more is it sure that the⟨re are not common⟩ ↑feelings↓ of men must accomodate themselves to their condition. I cannot concieve that the poor Ethiopian feeding swine in the shadow of the Pyramids in Lower Egypt while a Turkish Pasha insults the sublime observatories & sepulchres of his primeval ancestry should burn with poetic or ||a||mbition like him , who on our towering ||m||ountains or foaming cataracts[.]" Though the linen tipping material was available in Emerson's day, the insertion seems to have been made later, perhaps by Edward Waldo Emerson. The tipped page might have been from a college exercise or from another journal. There is no way of being sure that it belongs chronologically with its context.

[41] When Emerson set down his feelings about Gay, he usually went back later and carefully deleted or disguised them. A young man of the same age, who had entered Harvard from Hingham in 1819, Martin Gay was to haunt Emerson for over two years. A few months after this occasion he took part in a class "rebellion," and in his senior year he and thirty-four classmates were dismissed for engaging in "a combination to resist the Authority of the College. . . ." Nevertheless he took an M.D. degree at Harvard in 1826 and went on to become a prominent Boston physician and chemist, and a member of the Boston Society of Natural History and Fellow of the American Academy of Arts and Sciences. He was eulogistically described as even-tempered, amiable, modest, a noble and virtuous man with a "delicate regard for the feelings of others," a lover of "the beautiful in nature and art" who was interested in music, painting, and sculpture both at home and on travels in Europe. He sometimes gave lecture courses on chemistry and mineralogy, and lawyers liked his clarity and accuracy when he testified in cases of suspected poisoning. "No one could know him," we are told, "without feeling that no temptation could move him from his purpose to be a perfectly upright and honorable man." Despite his public career in Boston there is no evidence that Emerson met him in later life. His death in January 1850 was recorded with great regret and sorrow ("Records of the Immediate Government of Harvard College," X, 1822–1829, 1828; Boston *Post*, Jan. 14, 1850; Boston *Daily Advertiser*, Jan. 28, 1850).

Enfield on the subject of the Comets.

commemorates Dr Halley's successful predictions. Apian mentioned a comet appearing in 1531 & Kepler made observations on one appearing in 1607. Dr Halley found reason to believe that ⟨it was⟩ ↑both saw↓ the same comet which he himself saw in 1682. After mentioning these reasons he adds—"Hence I think I may venture to foretel that it will return again in the year 1758." The comet did appear December 14th 1758. "Dr Halley therefore, had the glory first to foretel the return of a comet & the event answered, in a remarkable manner, to his prediction."[42] This was a most splendid triumph for human science. And could the philosophic prophet have seen the fulfilment of his word what a big moment must it have been to *him.* I should think, if he had been an enthusi[33]astic man it must have overwhelmed him with tumultuous feeling.—If it is not retarded or accelerated by the action of the planets it must of course look upon the ⟨world⟩ ↑Earth↓ again in 1833. As I am upon Astronomy let me recollect that Orion the most beautiful constellation will be over head in this latitude on the 6th of Aquarius—25th of January at 9 or 10 o'clock P.M.—

Aug 10th Today we read our Forensics on Virtue as measured by Utility. Mr Frisbie[43] gave his opinion on the negative of the question, that is, that Utility is not essential to Virtue. He expressed a singular opinion with regard to the subject which opinion may be thus stated—Whereas for works in the material world which display intellectual & designed utility we do not feel the sentiment of moral approbation with which we applaud virtue; & whereas it appears from other considerations, that there are no general rules in morals,[n] i.e. none which do not bend to [34][44] circumstances, it is reasonable to suppose that the pleasure we recieve from the observation of virtue is a distinct power of the soul & may be illustrated by analogous instance in the intellect. For, when we see an exquisite specimen of painting—whence does the pleasure we experience arise? from the *resem-*

[42] Enfield, *Institutes of Natural Philosophy* (Boston, 1802), p. 308.

[43] Levi Frisbie (1783–1822), at this time Alford Professor of Natural Religion, Moral Philosophy, and Civil Polity at Harvard.

[44] "Virtue" is circled and centered beneath "for" at the bottom of the page.

blance, it is immediately answered, to the works of nature.[n] It is granted that this is in part the cause but it can't explain the whole pleasure we enjoy; for we see more perfect resemblances (as a stone apple or fruit) without this pleasure.—No it arises from the *power* which we immediately recollect to be necessary to the creation of the painting.—So [when] in Morals We see Virtue what is it pleases us? not the Utility; but the idea of moral power & beauty which strike us as necessary to give birth to the action.—This idea is strongly confirmed by our experience of the different sentiments with which we regard different virtues, bestowing slight regard on the homely every-day virtues which are the most useful but reserving our strong moral approbation for the more rare & lofty [35][45] displays of virtue which require a mightier effort—

The above is a pretty faithful transcript of the substance of Mr. Frisbie's observations on the subject.—

A strange idea or two may find place here to relieve this metaphysical prolixity. Imprim⟨s⟩is. In Lapland the intense cold freezes the words of men as they come out in breath & they are heard not until the sun thaws them! Item[.] When Astrology was much in vogue, a mighty man of gramarye repaired to Gregory VII to give the science a patron saint. The pontiff—well pleased directed him to make his choice from the ⟨p⟩Pantheon. Accordingly the conjurer was hood-winked & marched into the building and ⟨found his way⟩ took hold first of the statue of the *Devil* as combating with the Archangel Michael! Item. Lord Bacon notices a singular fact that the opposite shores of S. America & Africa correspond—bay to cape—gulf to coast &c "which could not be without a cause." Vide Map.

[36][46] Aug 21st. In the H[arvard]. C[ollege]. Athenaeum I enjoyed a very pleasant hour reading the life of Marlborough[n] in

[45] "Notes to Hudibras" is written between long rules vertically along the left margin upward from "building" (below) to "the sun" (above). "LAPLAND" is circled and written beneath "cause.' Vide Map." and "Lord Bacon" is circled and written beneath "could not be" at the bottom of the page.

[46] "Futurity" is circled and centered beneath "interea, fugit" at the bottom of the page.

the Quarterly Review.[47] I was a little troubled there by vexatious trains of thought; but once found myself stopping entirely from my reading & occupied in throwing guesses into futurity while I was asking myself if, when ten or a dozen years hence, I am gone far on the bitter perplexing roads of life, when I shall then recollect these moments ⟨shall⟩now thought so miserable shall I not fervently wish the possibility of their return & to find myself again thrown awkwardly on the tilted chair in the Atheneum study with my book in my hand; the snuffers & lamps & shelves around ⟨me[?]⟩; & Motte[48] coughing over his newspaper near me & ready myself to saunter out into gaiety & Commons when that variously-meaning *bell* shall lift up his *tongue.*

"Sed fugit interea, fugit irreparabile tempus." [49]

[37] Aug 23d 1820. Tomorrow finishes the Junior year. As it is time to close our accounts we will conclude likewise this book which has been formed from the meditations & fancies which have sprinkled the miscellany-corner of my mind for two terms past. (It was begun in the winter vacation.) I think it has been an improving employment decidedly. It has not encroached upon other occupations & has afforded seasonable aid at various times to enlarge or enliven scanty themes &c. Nor has it monopolized the energies of composition for literary exercises. Whilst I have written in it I have begun & completed my Pythologian Poem of 260 lines—& my Dissertation on the character of Socrates.[50] It has prevented the ennui of many an idle moment & has perhaps enriched my stock of language for future exertions. Much of it has been written with a view to their preservation as hints ⟨of⟩for a peculiar pursuit at the distance of years. Little or none of it was elaborate—its office was to be a hasty sketchy composition containing at times elements of graver order.

[47] The reference is apparently to the review of William Coxe, *Memoirs of John Duke of Marlborough,* XXIII (May 1820), 1–73.

[48] Emerson's classmate, Mellish Irving Motte, from Charleston, S.C. He was minister of the South Congregational Church in Boston from 1828 to 1842 (from *J*, I, 30, n. 1).

[49] "But time meanwhile is flying, flying beyond recall." Virgil, *Georgics,* III, 284.

[50] See p. 10, pp. 235–242, and No. XVII, *passim.*

[38][51] [Aug. 24, 1820] So fare ye well gay Powers & Princedoms! To you the sheets were inscribed. Light thanks for your tutelary smiles. Grim witches from Valhalla, & courteous dames from Faerylond, whose protection was implored, & whose dreams were invoked to furnish forth the scroll — adieu to you all; — you have the laughing poet's benison & malison, his wish & his forgetfulness. Abandoning your allegiance he throws you to the winds, recklessly defying your malice & fun. Pinch the red nose; lead him astray after will-o'-the-wisp over wilderness & fen; fright him with ghastly [n] hobgoblins — wreak your vengeance as you will — He gives you free leave on this sole condition, — if you can. ——

Junio. August 24. 1820.

||[39]–[40]||[52]

[41] A Common Place Book[53]

[51] A small water color of Emerson's room (Hollis 15) is painted at the bottom left of the page. It is reproduced in *J*, I, 4.

[52] Nearly all of the leaf containing these pages is torn out. A few unintelligible letters remain on p. [39], and on p. [40] are the vestiges of the first page for the alphabetical index to the journal.

[53] This title is for a page ruled off in ten rectangles equally spaced in two columns and lettered "M, N, O, P, R, S, T, U, X, Z," with each rectangle subdivided by lines bearing the vowels of the alphabet in order. The "u" subheading under the rectangle "R" is omitted. The letter "Q" is added below "Z" in the final rectangle before the "u" subheading and is separated by a double line. The whole page is a continuation of the index begun on p. [40], now mutilated. Thirteen numerals citing page numbers in Wide World 1 appear on the index lines, nine of which can be positively identified as referring to the subjects of "Pestilence" (22), "Picture" (28), "Roman" (29), "Samor" (7), "Spring" (14, 16), "Virgil" (24), "Virtue" (34), "Webster" (11), and four as referring to subjects less certainly identified as "Mind"? (for "Mentem"? 26), "rolling Universe"? (4), "Rome"? (or "Russia"? 23), and "*White Ladies*"? (27), all subjects appearing on pages bearing the specified number. Emerson's index is based generally on John Locke's system of indexing, as illustrated in *A Common Place Book, Upon the Plan Recommended and Practised by John Locke, Esq.* (Boston, 1821), a copy of which was owned by Edward Bliss Emerson (Houghton 156a). The system listed each letter of the alphabet separately, with the exception of "I" and "J" and "U" and "V," which were combined as single entries, and it identified subjects by the first letter and the first succeeding vowel. Emerson either knew an earlier edition than the 1821 edition his brother owned or added the index in 1821 on blank pages of this journal. He was later to make variations on the system in the index pages of his journal XVIII[A].

[42] ⟨(Mr Locke's Common place Book)⟩

[43] [54] Books to be sought — [55] *Inquirenda*

Wordsworth's Recluse

Quarterly Rev. Sept. 1819.

⟨l⟩Liv. VIII of Buchanan's Scotland-Wallace.

Spenser's view of the state of Ireland

Extent — history of the *Troubadours*?

Pendragon x Sir W Raleigh's conceipt of the Faery Queen

x Valhalla x Archipelago x Paestum

x Taillefer at the battle of Hastings x Illumination (graphic.)

[54] Three pen and ink profiles of men are sketched at the bottom right of the page, in a vertical row under column of "Inquirenda," from "Bayle's Dictionnaire" (above) to "Sir Charles Grandison" (below).

[55] Emerson began this list on or after April 10 (see p. 14). His ascertainable knowledge and use of the listed books in the approximate period of this volume are here outlined. For some works, only a conjectural identification is supplied. The appearance of a work in the list below does not necessarily mean that Emerson is known to have read it. Items are listed alphabetically, by author or title, whichever Emerson gives. Where known, editions or probable editions are supplied. A number of works were almost certainly suggested to Emerson by the periodicals which he was reading regularly at this time (see especially "Catalogue of Books Read," *passim*). Because his impressions of the works may owe much if not all to the reviews where he probably encountered them first, they are also cited. For further evidence of Emerson's reading in the works on his list, see Index. See also "Books Borrowed" and "Early Reading List."

Isaac Barrow, *Sermons Preached upon Several Occasions* (London, 1678). See pp. 17–18 and the quotation at p. 368.

Pierre Bayle, *The Dictionary Historical and Critical of M. Peter Bayle* (*with Life of the Author by M. Des Maizeaux*), 5 vols. (London, 1734–1738). Volumes 4 and 5 withdrawn from Harvard College Library, 1824(?).

Richard Bentley, *A Dissertation upon the Epistles of Phalaris . . .* (edition unknown).

Boccaccio, *The Decameron*, 2 vols. (London, 1804). Volume 1 withdrawn from the Boston Library Society May 13, 1820.

George Buchanan, *The History of Scotland*, the eighth book of which is concerned with William Wallace (edition unknown).

Richard Burton, *The Anatomy of Melancholy* (London, 1660). Withdrawn from the Boston Library Society, Feb. 1, 1821.

William Camden, *Annales rerum Anglicarum et Hibernicarum regnante Elizabetha* (edition unknown). Quoted pp. 32 and 361.

Geoffrey Chaucer, *Works* (edition unknown). See p. 158 for a quotation from Chaucer — which may, of course, have come from a secondary source. See also p. 362.

Camden's annals of ⟨Ph.⟩ Queen Eliz.
Kennet's life & characters of Greek poets
Hody de illustribus Graecis.
Middleton's Cicero. Burton's Melancholy
Barrow's Sermons Hobbes' Leviathan
Joinville's life of St. Louis
Froissart's history of England
Chaucer's Works: Bayle's Dictionnaire
"Corinne." Massinger's Plays.
Fletcher's do. Bentley's Phalaris
Peter's Letters. Letters from Eastern states
Waverley. Cogan on the passions
Sir Charles Grandison
x Griselda of Boccace x
x Walter Raleigh's account of Theories of Paradise
x Water spouts. x

Thomas Cogan, *A Philosophical Treatise on the Passions* (edition unknown).

Corinne, ou L'Italie, by Madame de Staël, 3 vols. (Paris, 1812). Volume 1 withdrawn from the Boston Library Society March 18, 1820, March 14 and Oct. 19, 1822; volumes 2–3, Nov. 23, 1822.

John Fletcher, Francis Beaumont and, *The Works* (edition unknown). Listed in "Catalogue of Books Read," and probably read between Feb. and July 1821. A review of Stephen Jones's *Biographica Dramatica*, *The Quarterly Review*, VII (June 1812), 282–292, discusses the work of Fletcher without Beaumont. *Beggar's Bush* is quoted, p. 330 and *The Nice Valour*, p. 353.

Jean Froissart, *Sir John Froissart's Chronicles of England, France, Spain, and the Adjoining Countries*, transl. Thomas Johnes, 3d ed., 12 vols. in 6 (London, 1808). Volume 1 withdrawn from the Boston Library Society Sept. 21, 1820; volume 4, Oct. 27, 1821. An earlier edition was reviewed in *The Edinburgh Review*, V (Jan. 1805), 347–362. See pp. 181–183.

Thomas Hobbes, *Leviathan* (edition unknown).

Humphrey Hody, *De Graecis Illustribus* . . . (London, 1742). Quoted, p. 366.

Jean de Joinville, *Memoirs of John Lord de Joinville, Grand Seneschal of Champagne, Written by Himself; Containing a History of Part of the Life of Louis IX, King of France* . . . , transl. Thomas Johnes (Hafod, 1807). Reviewed in *The Edinburgh Review*, XIII (Jan. 1809), 469–477. Joinville is cited, p. 264.

Basil Kennett, *The Lives and Characters of the Ancient Grecian Poets* (London, 1697). Listed in "Catalogue of Books Read." Quoted pp. 209(bis) and 360.

[44] Pillory. Ladies of the pillory.[56]

[45][57] There was a little city of the world
Where former times saw Grecian banners furl'd
Free as the winds that swept its mountain rock
Stern time in vain renewed his frequent shock

⟨Honour & virtue⟩
Nature in strength had built its little walls

Letters on the Eastern States, by William Tudor, New York, 1820. Listed in "Catalogue of Books Read." Reviewed in *The North American Review,* XI (July 1820), 68.

The Plays of Philip Massinger, 2d ed., 4 vols. (London, 1843). Volumes 1–2 withdrawn from the Boston Library Society Sept. 2; volumes 3–4 Sept. 14, 1820. Listed in "Catalogue of Books Read." Quoted, p. 371.

Conyers Middleton, *The Life of Marcus Tullius Cicero,* 3 vols. (London, 1801 or 1810, or Boston, 1818). Listed in "Catalogue of Books Read," and probably read between April and Aug. 1820. Quoted, p. 362.

Peter's Letters to His Kinsfolk, by John Gibson Lockhart, 3 vols. (Edinburgh, 1819), or 1 vol. (New York, 1820). Listed in "Catalogue of Books Read," and read in Aug. 1820. Quoted, pp. 217, 225.

The Quarterly Review, Sept. 1819. There was no such issue. Emerson probably meant the July issue. See p. 15, n. 22.

Sir Walter Raleigh, *The History of the World* (edition unknown). In the London edition, 1614, Book I, ch. 3, is entitled "Of the Place of Paradise."

———, "A Vision upon This Conceipt of the Faery Queene." This is prefixed to Spenser's *The Faery Queene* (edition unknown).

The History of Sir Charles Grandison, by Samuel Richardson, 7 vols. (London, 1754 or 1781). Volumes 1–2 withdrawn from and returned to the Boston Library Society May 23, 1818; volume 3 withdrawn Nov. 21, 1822; volumes 3–7, April–May 1829; volumes 1–7, Sept. 1832.

Waverley, by Sir Walter Scott, 2 vols. (Boston, 1815). Volume 1 withdrawn from the Boston Library Society Dec. 23, 1820; volume 2, April 13, 1822. *Waverley* was reviewed in *The Edinburgh Review,* XXIV (Nov. 1814), 208–243, and *The Quarterly Review,* XI (July 1814), 354–377.

William Wordsworth, *The Excursion, Being a Portion of The Recluse, a Poem* (edition unknown). Quoted and discussed pp. 270–272. Reviewed in *The Edinburgh Review,* XXIV (Nov. 1814), 1–30, and *The Quarterly Review,* XII (Oct. 1814), 100–111.

[56] The rest of the page is filled with rough pen and ink sketches of human heads, torsos, and full figures, a tower, and a furled banner.

[57] At the top of the page are two rough pen and ink sketches, one on either side of the verse, each sketch representing the head and shoulders of a man. A similar sketch appears in the bottom left margin below an elaborate design.

And Freedom built his altar in the halls
Fast by Albani⟨s⟩as ⟨ancie⟩giant mountains stood
The fortress breasting the Ionian flood.

A pleasant ↑fount↓ has gushed in Araby
From yellow sands the waves are leaping high
Where tropick suns have ⟨bent their⟩ ↑darted↓
fervid rays
Where the ⟨mute⟩ ↑strong↓ camel trembles as
he strays
Where caravans have found their horrid ⟨tomb⟩
grave
O'erwhelmed & choked with that unnatural wave
There the green turf is freshly blooming now
And the fair palm exalts her towering bough.

When the round moon surmounts the eastern clouds
In graceful pride emerging from ⟨her⟩ the shrouds
Which envious mantle o'er her lovely beam
In glorious beauty — Is it not a dream? — Boo!

(the sun bursting from the clouds his swaddling garments.)

[46][58] [Letter omitted]

[47] [59] Composition in prose began with the use of alphabetick writing about 6 centuries before Christ. Gillies' Greece.[60] The first prose writers or more properly the first writers were Pherecydes of Syros, Acusilaus of Argos, Hellanicus of Lesbos, Hecataeus & Dionysius, both of Miletus the last of whom flourished in the 65th Olymp.

[58] The several very rough pen and ink profile sketches and pencilled heads drawn through the writing on this page were already there when on March 21, 1824, Emerson entered a copy of a letter to his Aunt Mary, filling this page and most of [48]. The letter is printed in *J*, I, 356–359.

[59] Emerson had saved this page for notes on Greece. See p. 14.

[60] John Gillies (1747–1836), *The History of Ancient Greece . . .*, 4 vols. (London, 1787).

520 years B.C. & immediately preceded Herodotus. G.'s Greece. Here are the twelve Gods — viz.

> "Juno, Vesta, Minerva, Ceres, Diana, Venus, Mars, Mercurius,
> Jovi, Neptunus, Vulcanus, Apollo." [61]
>
> Ennius [*Annals*, I, 60–61]

Melampus & Linus are both mentioned by Homer, & Herodotus ignorant of this thought they lived after the great poet!

> "Movet Amphion lapides canendo" [62] Hor[ace].
>
> [*Odes*, III, XI, 2]

θεοισι και ανθρωποισι αειδειν [63] Hom[er]. [*Odyssey*, XXII, 346] Acc. to Herodotus the Delphian oracle predicted to Archilochus that his fame should descend to the latest ages of the world. Give us a song of Alcaeus or Anacreon was a common saying in the age of Socrates. (Athenaeus L. X. c. VIII) as quoted by Gillies. A period of 20 years was required among the Druids to complete the poetical studies of a candidate for the priesthood. Caesar de bello Gallico. L. VI. "Νυν δ'επι κιμμεριων στρατος ερχεται ομβιμοεργων." [64] Callinus. [*Odes*, 2, 1]

> Nullum numen habes si sit prudentia; sed *te*
> *Nos facimus fortuna deam,* caeloque locamus.[65]
>
> Juv[enal]. [*Satires*, X, 365–366]

Vid. Spenser [*The Faerie Queene*] B. vi. C. ix. S. XXIX.[66]

[61] "Jovi" is misquoted for *Jovis* (Jupiter).

[62] "Amphion with his measures moved the rocks." "Movet" is a misquotation for "movit."

[63] "[I] who sing to gods and men."

[64] "And now the fearful army of the Cimmerians draws near" (Ed.). Emerson misquotes the last word.

[65] "Thou wouldst have no divinity, O Fortune, if we had but wisdom; it is we that make a goddess of thee, and place thee in the skies."

[66] " 'In vaine,' said then old Meliboe, 'doe men
The heavens of their fortunes fault accuse,
Sith they know best what is the best for them:
For they to each such fortune doe diffuse,
As they doe know each can most aptly use.
For not that which men covet most is best,
Nor that thing worst which men do most refuse;
But fittest is, that all contented rest
With that they hold: each hath his fortune in his brest.' "

Poetis funus ducentibus.[67] [William] Camden[,] de Spenser [in *Annales rerum Anglicarum et Hibernicarum*]. Τιδε (said Aeschines to the Rhodians) τιδε ει αυτον τον θηριον ακηκοειτε; [68] [Pliny, *Letters*, II, iii, 10]. χαιρωμεν χαιρετε! [69] exclaimed the messenger from Marathon in the Athenian senate & expire||d|| immediately.

[48][70] [continuation of letter omitted]

[67] "His hearse being carried by poets" (Ed.). See p. 364.

[68] "But how would you have been affected, had you heard the wild beast's own roar!" Emerson misquotes the last word.

[69] Usually given as χαίρετε, νικῶμεν ("Rejoice, we conquer"). See Lucian, *Works*, ed. W. Tooke (London, 1820), II, 402.

[70] See p. 30, n. 58.

Wide World 2

1820–1821

The dated entries in this journal cover most of Emerson's senior year at Harvard, running from October 3, 1820, to June 10, 1821.

The manuscript is composed of foolscap paper like that in Wide World 1; the sheets are folded folio into five gatherings of four leaves each, each gathering hand-stitched and combined by hand-stitching along the fold. The only irregularity in the forty pages is that the end page numbered 40 is blank. The leaves vary slightly in size, measuring approximately 16.5 x 20 cm.

[1] The Wide World[1] No 2.

October 1820.

↑I have determined to grant a new charter to my pen,↓ ⟨H⟩having finished my common-place book which I commenced in January & with as much success as I was ambitious of — whose whole aim was the small utility of being the exchequer to the accumulating store of organized verbs, nouns, & substantives, to wit, sentences. It has been a source of entertainment & accomplished its end & on this account has induced me to repeat or rather continue the experiment. Wherefore On!

[Oct. 3, 1820] To forget for a season the world & its concerns, & to separate the soul for sublime contemplation till it has lost the sense of circumstances & is decking itself in plumage drawn out from the gay wardrobe of Fancy is a recreation & a rapture of which few men can avail themselves. But this privilege in common with other

[1] The title is framed in a rectangle.

great gifts of nature is attainable if not inborn. It is denied altogether to three classes at least of mankind[,] viz[.] the *queer*, the downright, & the ungainly. This is by no means a careless or fanciful classification although rather a restricted sense belongs to [2] these epithets. By "the queer" I understand those animals of oddity whose disgusting eccentricity flows from a conceited [n] character & the lack of commonsense. I characterize "the downright" only as people who do *jobs*. And "the ungainly" points exclusively at some gaunt lantern countenances who have at one time and another shocked my nerves & nauseated my taste by their hideous aspects. With cautious explanation we advance from these degraded stages of intellect, this doleful frontispeice of creation to prouder orders of mind. Ordinary men claim the intermittent exercise of this power of beautiful abstraction; but to the souls only of the mightiest is it given to command the disappearance of land & sea, & mankind & things, & they vanish. — Then comes the Enchanter illuminating the glorious visions with hues from heaven, granting thoughts of other worlds gilded with lustre of ravishment & delight, till the Hours teeming with loveliness & Joy roll by uncounted. Exulting in the exercise of this prerogative the poet, truly called so, has entreated the reluctant permission

> "And forever shalt thou dwell
> In the spirit of this spell."

[Byron, *Manfred*, I, i, 210–211]

Oct. 3, 1820

Instruction by *Dictation* is a mode of teaching older than the art of printing. Owing to the scarcity of books, the [3] professor possessed himself of a classic, perhaps the only copy in the community & dictated a sentence from it to the students. This they immediately copied off — each for himself — & the Professor proceeded to make ⟨re⟩his remarks on the sentence which also it was the duty of the scholars to note down. Slavish as was this custom it survived the Invention of printing & is practised to this day in the Dutch Universities. It is done with exact minuteness; when the professor comes to a stop he exclaims "Comma," when to a period "punctum," & when he begins a paragraph — "nova linea." The lectures are universally Latin. (The above was related to the class by Prof. Everett.) A good illustration of Dr. Blair's[2] observation that in imperfect languages the most important word in the sentence comes first — is the Indian beggary in ⟨New Orleans⟩ Alibama as related by ⟨JA⟩JUA. "Sugar — ⟨a⟩ little bit — give me some."

Oct 6th 1820

I thought I percieved the fit coming — the humour of inspiration & straightway seized the pen. I fear it was a false alarm. I have listened this evening to an eloquent lecture of the elegant Professor of French & Spanish Literature.[3]

[4][4] On the subject of the extent of the language, a subject which bears on the face of it dulness & dread — every soul present warmly acknowledged the force of delineation when the great deluge of the French language sweeping down all the feeble barriers of ephemeral dialects carried captive the languages & literature of all Europe while in the commotions of politics the German thrones were dashed to peices against each other on this great & wide sea.

When bounding Fancy leaves the clods of earth
To riot in the regions of her birth
Where robed in light the Genii of the Stars
Launch in refulgent space their diamond cars
Or ⟨dwell⟩ in pavilions of celestial [n] pride
Serene above all influence beside
Vent the bold joy which swells the glorious soul
Rich with the rapture of secure controul
Onward, around their golden visions stray
Till only Glory can their range delay[.]

Well I began with prose & have mustered up 10 lines of poetry which will answer rarely to lighten the labour of the next theme. It is half past 10 — & time to put away the Wide World [n] & its concerns

[2] Emerson found the observation in Hugh Blair's *Lectures on Rhetoric*, one of the texts required in the curriculum. See the Philadelphia, 1853, edition, Lecture VII, p. 68.

[3] George Ticknor (1791–1871) was Smith Professor of French and Spanish Languages and Literature, and Professor of Belles Lettres (1819–1835).

[4] At the end of the first paragraph below, "sea" is followed by a small pen and ink sketch of a man's head.

& consign my indolent limbs to comfortable repose. Ergo cease, my pen,

"To witch the world with noble *pen*-manship."[5]

[5] October 9th 1820

The eloquence of the bar belongs to the *useful* departments of life. Although to the details of the barrister belongs little of the charm which fancy or elegance casts over other ranges of intellect, though destiny denies ⟨him⟩ ↑to his name↓ that light which is traced far down the long line of human generations, emanating from the crystal fountains of Genius when its course is free. poor

Evening.

Hugo de Tabarin[n] an old French Poet of the XII century wrote the history of his adventures in the Crusades. In a skirmish he was taken & thus becoming the captive of the Turkish Sultan, after some rough conversation had passed between them, the Sultan offered him his liberty if he would make him a knight. This for a time he sternly refused but afterwards consented telling him however at the same time that to bestow the holy gift of knighthood on him a heathen was like covering a dunghill with silk to prevent its being offensive & that he did it only because he was now his slave.—

Prof. Ticknor[.]

October 12th.

I should write a theme this evening but cruel Destiny forbids the thoughts of rainbow colours to rise—I want to write poetry to add to "When bounding" &c.

[6] Continued.—

They read the silent mysteries of fate
The slow revealings of the ⟨coming⟩ ↑future↓ state
Trace the colossal shades of coming time
Pregnant with unknown prodigies of crime
While passing on to find their direful birth

[5] Cf. "To witch the world with noble horsemanship" (Shakespeare, 1 *Henry IV*, IV, i, 110).

Low in the hapless atmosphere of earth
    Life's motley revelry had scarce begun
With Ariel youngest offspring of the Sun
In gay Peru where genial climes ⟨unfold⟩ ↑behold↓
The heavens reflected in earth's treasured gold
When holy love enchained his youthful mind
Before the thrones where Incas sat enshrined.
Th⟨e⟩at ancient priesthood claimed the princely boy
Whilst mighty visions swelled his heart with joy.
And hoary seers unrolled the tales of time
The proud religion in its honoured prime
Pointed the Source whence their fair faith began
Till Ariel wept to think himself a man,
Till bounding Fancy left the clods of earth
&c (Vide Page 4)
Enthroned they sit & vigilantly gaze
Far in the dusky wilderness of space
Lest their ⟨bright orbs far⟩ ↑swift star↓ from the
    ↑far↓ centre hurled
Cross the bright orbit of another world
Or travelling its long pilgrimage be lost
In the wild myriads of the shining host.
[7] But thoughts which human tongue may not ↑impart↓
Fell on the tranced stillness of his heart
Lightening its human load of sin & pain
That when Young Ariel weked to Earth again

Oct. 15th 1820

Different mortals improve resources of happiness which are entirely different. This I find more apparent in the familiar instances obvious at college recitations. My more fortunate neighbours exult in the display of mathematical study, while I after feeling the humiliating sense of dependance & inferiority which like the goading soul-sickening sense of extreme poverty, palsies effort, esteem myself abundantly compensated, if with my pen, I ↑can↓ marshal whole catalogues of nouns & verbs, to express to the life the imbecility I felt.

Mr Everett says — The shout of admiration is lost ere it reaches the arches of heaven but there is an allseeing eye which looks deep down into the recesses of the obscurest heart. It is a small matter to abstain from vice to which there is no temptation or to perform a Virtue which is standing by you with crowns for your head; but it is the obscure struggling & unsuccessful virtue which meets with reward.——

[8] Oct 20.

The supreme Pontiff sent a confessor to Rabelais on his deathbed charging him to recieve absolution. Rabelais dismissed the messenger & bid him tell the Pontiff He was now going to visit the great *Perhaps.*

⟨Gay hit[?] g||...||⟩[6]

Oct [24]

Exhibition night.[7] This tumultuous day is done. The character of its thought-weather is always extremely singular. Fuller than any other day of great thoughts — & poets' dreams, of hope & joy & pride & then closed with merriment & wine evincing or eliciting gay fraternal feeling enough, but brutalized & defiled with excess of physical enjoyment; leaving the mind distracted & unfit for pursuits of soberness. ⟨Barnwell's⟩ Oration contained sublime images. — One was of great power — a terrible description of the fire tempest which ⟨||ruined||⟩[n] ↑overshadowed↓ Sodom & Gomorrha. — Another description of the waterspout of the Pacifick was noble. A great struggle of ambition is going on between ⟨Barnwell⟩ & ⟨Upham⟩.[8] [9][9] Thundering & lightning are faint & tame descriptions of the course of astonish-

[6] To the left is a small sketch of a bird and what might be a dish with eggs in it, or a lamp, with the word "DULL" printed on it.

[7] Since 1756, Harvard had conducted exhibitions in both spring and fall in which "Selected students of the two upper classes" presented "debates, dialogues, and orations, mostly in the English language . . ." (S. E. Morison, *Three Centuries of Harvard*, 1936, pp. 89–90).

[8] Robert Woodward Barnwell, of South Carolina, and Charles Wentworth Upham, of Salem, were classmates of Emerson. See *J*, I, 68, n. 1.

[9] Centered beneath the last line of the first paragraph is a pen and ink sketch of the head and shoulders of a man. To the left of the figure is written "Boah" and to the right "Friar Boan" (repeated).

ing eloquence. You double the force of painting if you describe it as it is. The flashing eye, that fills up the chasms of language; the living brow, throwing meaning & intellect into every furrow & every frown; the stamping foot, the labouring limbs, the desperate gesture, these must all be seen in their strong exercise, before the vivid conception of their effect can be adequately felt. — And then a man must separate & discipline & intoxicate his mind before he can enjoy the glory of the orator, when mighty thoughts come crowding on the soul; he must learn to harrow up unwelcome recollections & concentrate woe & horror & disgust till his own heart sickens; he must stretch forth his arm & array the bright ideas which have settled around him till they gather to forceful & appalling sublimity.

Oct. 24th

I begin to believe in the Indian doctrine of eye-fascination. The cold blue eye of   has so intimately connected him with my thoughts & visions that a dozen times a day & as often ⟨in the⟩ ↑by↓ night I find myself wholly wrapped up in conjectures of his character & inclinations. ⟨The t⟩ We have had already two or three long profound stares at each other. Be it wise or weak or superstitious I must know him.[10]

[10] Oct. 25

I find myself often idle, vagrant, stupid, & hollow. This is somewhat appalling & if I do not discipline myself with diligent care I shall suffer severely from remorse & the sense of inferiority hereafter. All around me are industrious & will be great, I am indolent & shall be insignificant. Avert it heaven! avert it virtue! I need excitement.

"Delivery from Sun-burning & Moonblasting." [11]

Nov. 1.

My opinion of ☟ was strangely lowered by hearing that he was "proverbially idle." This was redeemed by learning that he was a

[10] Presumably Martin Gay.

[11] Milton, *An Apology Against a Pamphlet Called a Modest Confutation . . . The Works of John Milton*, Columbia ed. (N. Y., 1931), III, pt. I, 352.

"superior man." This week, a little eventful in college, has brought a share of its accidents to him.[12]

October

Perhaps thy lot in life is higher
    Than the fates assign to me
While they fulfil thy large desire
    And bid my hopes as visions flee
But grant me still in joy or sorrow
    In grief or hope to claim thy heart
And I will then defy the morrow
    Whilst I fulfil a loyal part.

[11] [Nov. 1] Wednesday Night

A new epoch was brought about in French Literature by a trivial circumstance, says Fontenelle. A gentleman introduced his friend to a lady with whom he ↑(the first)↓ was in love; his friend won the affections of the lady & made his own triumph on the ruin of the introducer's hopes. Elated with his success, he wrote a comedy on the incident.—That comedy was Mélite, & that false friend, *Corneille.* (Prof Ticknor.) —— Here follows a sentence from the author of Paradise Lost—& such a sentence!

"A bishop's foot that has all its toes (maugre the gout) & a linnen sock over it, is the aptest emblem of the Prelate himself; who being a Pluralist, may under one Surplice hide four benefices besides the great metropolitan *Toe* which sends a foul stench to Heaven." [13]

I wish I might be so witched with study, so enamoured of glory for a little time, that it were possible to forget self & professions & tasks & the dismal crowd of ordinary circumstances in a still [n] & rapid & comprehensive course of improvement. How immensely would a scholar enlarge his power could he abstract himself wholly, body &

[12] The reference here and in the following lines of verse must be to Martin Gay. The hand sign points to a sketch of Gay[?] which Emerson did on a scrap of paper and tipped onto the lower part of the page over the verse. The sketch is reproduced in *J*, I, opposite p. 70. For the "eventful" week and the "accidents" see p. 244, n. 95.

[13] Misquoted from *An Apology* . . . (See p. 39, n. 11 and Milton, *The Works*, III, pt. I, 308).

[12] mind from the dinning throng of casual recollections that summon him away, from his useful toil to endless, thankless, reveries; informing him for instance, for a whole rueful half hour of what he has done, is doing, & will do today, all which he knew at six o'clock in the morning & is condemned to learn anew twenty times in the course of the day. Perhaps this ugly disorder is peculiar to myself & I must envy that man's uninterrupted progress, who is not obliged ↑by his oath to nature↓ to answer this idle call. If this is to continue it will weaken the grasp with which I would cling,—with which every young man would cling, to "visions [n] of glory." My talents, (according to the judgement of friends or to the whispered suggestions of ⟨fancy⟩ vanity,) are popular, are fitted to enable me to claim a place in the inclinations & sympathy of men. But if I would excel & outshine the circle of my peers those talents must be put to the utmost stretch of exertion, must be taught the confidence of their own power; and lassitude & these desultory habits of thinking with their melancholy pleasure must be grappled with & conquered. These soliloquies are certainly sweeter than Chemistry!

[13] Nov. 2.

What a grand man was Milton! so marked by nature for the great Epic Poet that was to bear up the name of these latter times. In "Reason of church government urged against Prelaty" written while young his ⟨|| . . . ||⟩spirit [n] is already communing with itself & stretching out into its colossal proportions & yearning for the destiny he was appointed to fulfil. He says, "It hath been imputed to me that some self-pleasing humor of vain[-]glory hath incited me to contest with men of high estimation now, while green years are upon my head."—But I must quote a great deal now that I have begun. —"For me, I have determined to lay up as the best treasure & solace of a good old age, if God voutsafe it me, the honest liberty of free speech from my youth, where I shall think it available in so dear a concernment as the Churche's good. For if I be either by disposition, or what other cause too inquisitive or suspicious of myself or mine own doings who can help it? But this I foresee that should the church be brought under heavy oppression & God have given me ability the while to reason against that man that should be the author of so foul a deed; or should she by blessing from above on the industry & courage of faithful men, change this her distracted estate into better days, without the least furderance or contribution of *those few talents which God hath lent me* I foresee what stories I should hear within myself, all my life after, of discourage & reproach. Timorous & ingrateful the church of God is now again at the foot of her insulting enemies & thou bewailst; what matters it for thee or thy bewailing? When time was, thou couldst not find a syllable of all thou hadst read or studied to utter in her behalf. Yet ease & leasure was given thee for thy retired thoughts, out of the sweat of other men. [14][14] Thou hadst the diligence, the parts, the language of a man when a vain subject were to be adorn'd or beautifi'd; but when the cause of God & his church was to be pleaded, for which purpose that tongue was given thee which thou hast, God listened if he could hear thy voice among his zealous servants, but thou wert dumb as a beast."— He then supposes the contrary side [—] the triumph of the church — & concludes with — "These & such lessons as these would have been my matins daily & my even-song."

Nov. 10.

"*The Abbot*" must be to its author "a source of unmixed delight & unchastened pride."

Nov 10

A Recipe!!!

Young Waldo, when in your thick-coming whims, you feel an itching to *engrave*, take a piece of glass & cover it with a thin film of wax or isinglass & trace the proposed figure with a steel point. Place this over a vessel containing a mixture of powdered fluor spar & sulphuric acid gently heated. The acid gas coming into contact with the uncovered parts of the glass combines with & removes the silex, as well probably as the alkali with which it is united & lines more or less deep are thus formed — according to Gorham's Chemistry[15] — (Article — Silicon —) page 265 — Vol. I.

[14] A pen and ink profile of a man's head is sketched above "author" and below "Matins" in the center of the page.

[15] John Gorham's *Elements of Chemical Science*, 2 vols., 1819, a required text in the Harvard curriculum.

Item. On a Grave Stone in Framingham is a poetical Epitaph concluding with these words.—
[15][16]—"Killed by lightning sent from heaven
In——— 1777."——

Nov 15th

De La Fontaine was an easy lazy sort of a gentleman from whom also Scott derived some of his notions of Dominie Sampson particularly the manner of furnishing him with new clothes. He was a child of genius whom every body protected & when one of his patronesses died, who had said that she had dismissed everything except her three domestic animals[—] her dog, her parrot, & De La Fontaine—the old man then at the age of 70 was taken up as one who had not yet arrived at years of discretion merely from the delight which was awakened by his simple, childlike & original genius. Madame de   said to him, that he should ⟨direct⟩ ↑dedicate↓ his tale to the king; — So I think said De la Fontaine & did it, but with an ignorant simplicity, which loved to defeat its own purposes, informed the king in the dedication that he did [so] by the orders of Madame de   . He informs us that he spent half his time in sleeping & the other half in doing nothing: & that he holds money to be a thing not necessary. So much for Jean de la Fontaine & Mr Ticknor.

Observe this. Mr Everett notices that a temperate climate has always been found necessary to a high national character. Also Mr. Waldo if you would like to find the sublimest attainable sayings on the destruction of Nations.—Vide 4th book of the Sybilline Collections[.][17]

[16] A pen and ink sketch of skull and cross-bones is written at the top left of the page beneath "1777." The profile of a man labelled "Mr. Gray" is sketched beneath "heaven" at the top right. The writing in the upper center of the page flows around a profile of the head and shoulders of a man. It is dated "Nov. 12th" and identified as "FATHER AMBROSE" in block printing. There is a faint pencil sketch of a man's face following "De la Fontaine" at the center of the page.

[17] The *Oracula Sibyllina,* a collection of pseudoepigraphical literature of the era 150 B.C.–300 A.D., and supposedly the utterances of the ancient Sibylls. Book

[16] Nov 18th

I shall subjoin some recipes for the cure of the horrible void which ruins ever & anon the mind's peace, & is otherwise called Unhappiness.

1. Take Scott's Novels & read carefully the mottoes of the chapters; or if you prefer reading a novel itself take the Bride of Lammermoor.

2. Sometimes (seldom) the finest parts of Cowper's Task will answer the purpose. I refer to the home-scenes.

3. For the same reason ↑that↓ I would take Scott's Mottoes I would also take an old tragedy such as Ben Jonson's, Otway's, Congreve's[,] in short, any thing of that kind which leads as far as possible from the usual trains of thought.

4. Make recipes to add to this list.

[17] December 4th 1820

Here at Cambridge in my cheerless schoolroom. Sunday Evening I heard Mr Everett preach at the Old South [18] a charity sermon — one of his most (perhaps the most) eloquent efforts.

Abstract. The most recommended virtue in the New Testament is *charity*. Witness the ⟨par⟩ 25 Matt. where the Judgement day is described & everlasting happiness promised to him who giveth one cup of cold water &c. But it cannot be the ⟨apparent⟩ ↑real↓ intention as it is the apparent one to describe ⟨it as th⟩[n] almsgiving as the first virtue &c for it is easier to give to a famishing brother than to withhold it — it is a very easy thing to dispense of the store with which heaven has lavishly supplied us. It is harder a thousand yea a thousand times harder to pull one plume from the mountain pinion of Ambition — or to drive from the heart one of the accursed vanities of this world. This cannot be the *tribulation* with which we must be saved — this cannot be the toil & agony which must be endured to the end — if it is[,] vainly have all the strugglings & penances of christians been endured ⟨f⟩— foolishly aye madly has the ↑holy↓

IV traces the destruction of proud and impious people from the early Assyrians to the later Romans through war, earthquake, flood, and fire, and ends with a prophecy of the last judgment.

[18] The Old South Church, in Boston.

blood of martyrs been poured out. No this cannot be. Charity in its scripture use means something more than almsgiving—it means the great virtue of general benevolence & a sister spirit[,] an upholding principle of the christian religion. And in this I am persuaded I shall be supported by the general Judgement of the World. It is common [18] to rail at the world as hollow & vain, as fond[n] to flatter an idol & forgetting to notice merit. But if this be said absolutely we deny it as absurd. By the generall judgement of the world I do not mean the generation of which we are a part—the folly & fashion of the day—but if the world is the unbroken line of the wise & pious—the glorious company of the ⟨wise⟩ ↑great↓ & ⟨pious⟩ ↑good↓ which has not failed, God be praised, since the world began—the great uncorrupted Church—then the assertion is *idle*. This great principle divides itself into 1. Love to God & 2. Love to men. ⟨As⟩ 1. *We* must be charitable as the dispensers of his bounty. Our wealth & our wisdom is not our own.—Shall not I do what I will with mine own?—these are not the words of man they are the words of the most high God—not a son ⟨or daughter⟩ of Adam shall dare to take a syllable of them to himself[,] not a man shall dare lay his hand on a cup of cold water & call it his own. Your science cannot add a sparkle of a star[,] you cannot prevent the fall of a leaf in the lonely woods. If therefore there be wisdom & prudence it belongs to the weak & foolish—if there be power[,] to the timid—2.

[19] Lastly. The sense of our accountableness hereafter will teach us the duty of charity. We are not going alone[;] the highways of eternity are crowded[;] crowds of pilgrims are thronging with us & the widow & the orphan whom our kindness has relieved or our hardness famished are going there to bless or to curse us. We are not going to whisper a secret tale in the ear of the Judge but every word shall be rung out by angel trumpets from the borders to the borders of the universe. Thank ⟨g⟩God then that your silver & your gold will b⟨y⟩uy you imperishable crowns,[n] & recollect that every widow's sigh & every orphan's prayer unattended shall rise up in testimony against us!

They shall all arise at the same trumpet with their imperfections on their head whether a pyramid or a cypress cover them now[.]

⟨No[v]⟩Dec 5th

It appears to me that it is a secret of the art of eloquence to know that a powerful aid would be derived from the use of forms of language which were generally known to Men in their infancy & which now under another and unknown [20][19] garb but forcibly reminding them of early impressions are likely to be mistaken for opinions whose beginning they cannot recollect & therefore suppose them innate. At least if by such operation they cannot convince the mind they may serve to win attention by this awakening but ambiguous charm. By these forms of language I mean a paraphrase of some sentence in a *Primer* or other Child's book common to the country.—The spell would be more perfect perhaps if instead of such a paraphrase the words of a sentence should be modulated to the cadence of the aforesai⟨n⟩d infant literature. I dare not subjoin an example.

[21] Dec

The human soul, the world, the universe are labouring on to their magnificent consummation. We are not fashioned thus marvellously for nought. The straining conceptions of man, the monuments of his reason & the whole furniture of his faculties is adapted to ⟨grand⟩mightier views of things than the mightiest he has yet beheld. Roll on then thou stupendous ⟨||...||⟩ Universe in sublime incomprehensible solitude, in an unbeheld but sure path. The finger of God is pointing out your way. And when ages shall have elapsed & time is no more[,] while the stars shall fall from heaven & the Sun become darkness & the Moon blood, human intellect purified & sublimed shall mount from perfection to perfection of unmeasured & ineffable enjoyment of knowledge & glory↑.↓—⟨to⟩ ↑Man shall come to↓ the presence of Jehovah. (In the manner of Chateaubriand.)

Dec 15th

I claim & clasp a moment's respite from this irksome school to saunter in the feilds of my own wayward thought. The afternoon was gloomy & preparing to snow,—dull, ugly weather. But when I came out from the hot, steaming, stove-ed, stinking, dirty, a "b"-spell-

[19] Pasted to the page at the close of the text is a small water color sketch of three men at sea in a bowl with an inscription "Three Wise Men of Goshen" beneath it.

ing school room I almost soared & mounted the atmosphere at breathing the free magnificent air, the noble [22] breath of life. It was a delightful exhilaration; but it soon passed off. — It is impossible that the distribution of rewards ⟨& punishments⟩ hereafter should not be in gradation. ⟨h⟩How inconsistent with justice would it be that all the boundless varieties of desert & condition should be levelled to a single lot — all from the agonized martyr who was sawn asunder for the faith to the deathbed of a modern christian where a soul which was never tempted & a sinless innocence which was never tried has ⟨been⟩ sighed out a harmless life on beds of down & accompanied & piloted to heaven by the prayerful sympathy of the saints on earth. In the manner of Everett.

The other day read Edin. Review of Drummond's Acad. Questions.[20] The review & the reviewed are both beautiful specimens of an elegant metaphysical style. For an idea of Drummond see Universe No 5.[21]

Attended Mr Ticknor's Lecture on Voltaire. — Wonderful homage accorded to him on his appearance at Paris after 27 years absence. The greatest triumph which literary history can boast. — Various fortune of Voltaire's Adelaide de Guesclin — first representation was hissed throughout. Voltaire only said "Saturday I witnessed the burial of Adelaide & I was glad to see so respectable a procession." The next time a little altered it was decently recei[23]ved. The third time it was tumultuously applauded & those parts most clamorously praised which before were the most hissed. Voltaire says, "I ⟨am⟩can only say with the Venetian advocate to his judges 'Last week your ⟨e⟩Excellencies judged thus — today your ⟨e⟩Excellencies have judged exactly the reverse — and in both cases your ⟨e⟩Excellencies have judged admirably well.'"

Dec 19. I am going to set apart a page or two of this variety-shop for unconnected reflections or allusions to the day of retribution to the human race. Teeming with such importance so universal & so intense, ⟨that⟩ it cannot be named too often or pressed with too much force. Expressions of worth may sometimes occur which it

[20] Vol. VII (Oct. 1805), 163–185. The review was by Francis Jeffrey.

[21] See p. 376.

will be well to record—if not I shall but have to regret the loss of paper to my miscellany. (Turn to page 26)

The Day of Judgement.

They shall all arise at the same summoning call whether they sleep now under a pyramid or a primrose. When the solemn day of decision shall come & the world—and its crowded fulness shall appear at the throne of him who judgeth righteously the thoughts of the heart & its lofty pride—the little triumphs of human intellect & its low degradations—the boasts & blemishes of moral purity & last the history of the soul's religion [—] of its holiness or apostacy—of its vigorous overflowing piety or its devilish unbelief [n] shall all be developed by the hand of truth.

[24][22] As for the wicked[,] God shall laugh at them in heaven & the laugh of demons ↑shall scare them↓ from below. We were sent into the world on the same great errand on which thousands have been sent & which some ↑have↓ accomplished & others not. We are hastening to bear the tidings of fulfilment or neglect to the throne of the Omniscient.

[25] X Most of the prevailing opinions concerning Ancient philosophy are probably travesties of the true systems by the comic poets e.g. Pythagoras taught the old doctrine of Anima mundi into which the Soul of the individual was absorbed and afterwards emanated again. From this it is probable the poets took occasion to specify the individual men and animals, through which one or another portion passed, and attributed the conceit to Pythagoras.[n]

A tenet of philosophy is with difficulty transmitted unaltered through a succession of men; hence the Schools denominated Ionic, Academic, &c did not always defend the same opinion[.] X Prof Everett Lecture

[26] Jan 9th 1821. How frequently I am led to consider the distinguished advantages which this generation enjoy above our fathers. Have heard today another consecrated display of genius—of the insinuating & overwhelming effect of eloquent manners & style

[22] "Mr James" is interlineated in the first sentence.

when made sacred & ⟨powerful⟩ impregnable by the subject which they are to enforce. Mr Everett's sermon before the Howard Benevolent Society. He told a very affecting anecdote. "I have known a woman in this town go out to work with her own hands to pay for the wooden coffin ⟨in⟩ which ⟨her only child was enclosed⟩ ↑was to enclose the dust of her only child↓ I prayed with her when there was none to stand by her but he who was to bear that ⟨child⟩ ↑dust↓ to the tomb."

There was a vast congregation, but while he spoke, as silent as death. Unluckily, in the pauses, however they shook the house with their hideous convulsions; for when he raised his handkerchief to his face after a pause in the sermon it seemed almost a concerted signal for the Old South to cough[.]

Let those now cough who never coughed before
And those who always cough cough now the more.[23]

[27] Feb 7th

The religion of my Aunt is the purest & most sublime of any I can conceive. It appears to be based on broad & deep & remote principles of expediency & adequateness to an end—principles which few can comprehend & fewer feel. It labours to reconcile the apparent insignificancy of the field to the surpassing grandeur of the Operator & founds the benignity & Mercy of the Scheme on adventurous but probable comparisons of the Condition of other orders of being. Although it is an intellectual offspring of beauty & splendour, if that were all, it breathes a practical spirit of rigid & austere devotion. It is independent of forms & ceremonies & its ethereal nature gives a glow of soul to her whole life. She is the Weird-woman of her religion & conceives herself always bound to walk in narrow but exalted paths which lead onward to interminable regions of rapturous & sublime glory.

[28] Feb 1821—Martial ⟨saith⟩ in one of his Epigrams complains that Livy takes up his whole library & he has room for no

[23] Emerson paraphrases the refrain from *Pervigilium Veneris*: "Cras amet qui nunquam amavit, quique amavit cras amet." "Tomorrow let him love who has never loved before, and who has loved, let him love the more" (Ed.).

more.[24] Such was the clumsy length of a great work in the miserable copying system which prevailed in those days.[n] I must give Mr Channing[25] a theme on the influence of weather & skies on mind; I have tried poetry but do not succeed as well as might be wished. Plan — The poor inhabitants of Indostan are distressed & degraded by the horrors of a flimsy & cruel Superstition. The iron hath entered into their souls, & their situation is in all respects abominable. Why is it their misery is thus darkened & deepened far different from the lot of the rejoicing nations of Europe & America[?] It is because a flaming sky boils their blood & blackens their skin & maddens their nature enervating the mind while it renders it fiercer & more brutal. It is just so in other climes an Indian day fires the spirits, a dull day depresses them, & a glorious one exhilarates, & Man vainly endeavours to oppose the order of nature & contend with superiour ordinations.[26] [29][27] Discurse a little & done with the same.

Feb 18th.

The honours which it remains for the living to pay the dead are but fleeting & thankless. But it is well to discharge the debt to those that are silent for the sake of the monitory lesson which it is intended to impart. And it is also some poor consolation to bereavement to listen to the praises which would rescue the memory of the dead from premature & offensive oblivion. A friend shoul[d] show his friendship by noticing the loss of which the world is unmindful. The deceased hath merit[ed] uncommon honours & his death has spread an unusual gloom upon the aspect⟨s⟩ of Society. His name & memory do not share the low lot of the unbefriended & inconsiderable mem-

[24] "Narrowed into scanty skins is bulky Livy, the whole of whom my library does not contain." *Epigrams*, Book XIV, cxc.

[25] Edward Tyrrell Channing (1790–1856), Boylston Professor of Oratory and Rhetoric.

[26] The "theme" seems to have been a part of the process of reflection which culminated in the poem "Indian Superstition," delivered by Emerson at the exhibition April 24, 1821. (See Kenneth N. Cameron, ed., *Indian Superstition*, 1954, pp. 17 and 24.)

[27] A pen and ink sketch of the head and shoulders of a man appears between "little" (above) and "honours" (below) at the top of the page.

bers of the community but his fellow men have accorded him the sincere praise of comely sorrow & de[30]cent approbation. His estate was not ⟨outward⟩ large among men but the extraordinary grasp of his mental powers made ample amends. He was possessed of an ardent & passionate imagination, wh⟨i⟩ose burning zeal outran the boundaries of creation[,] whose career was unchecked by the ordinary limits of human thought but whose lofty dignity disdained every thing which was licentious or profane. But the flights of such an imagination did not interfere with the sobriety of his judgement or the sedateness of his life. In the walks of life he was seen without pomp or pride to bear a soul as pure & exalted as ever panted for a higher nature. Heaven hath granted his wish & set aside ours. He was elevated in public notice by the dignity & urbanity of manners which never failed to ensure his welcome in the private circle or at the crowded assembly. He was esteemed as he deserved to be as the upright man, the elegant scholar, the accomplished gentleman, the fast friend. A model of social life he concentrated the affections ↑of all↓ upon himself—& established his praise in the heart which acknowledges him.

[31] March 14th 1821

I am reading Price on Morals[28] & intend to read it with care & commentary. I shall set down here what remarks occur to me upon the matter or manner of his argument. On the 56 Page Dr Price says that right & wrong are not determined by any reasoning or deduction but by an ultimate perception of the human mind. It is to be desired that this were capable of satisfactory proof but ↑as it↓ is in direct opposition to the sceptical philosophy it cannot stand unsupported by strong & sufficient evidence. I will however read more & see if it is proved or no.—He saith that the Understanding is this ultimate determiner[.]

[28] Richard Price (1723–1791), *A Review of the Principal Questions and Difficulties in Morals.* . . . Emerson was almost certainly using the second edition (London, 1769). But in Price the phrase Emerson renders as "an ultimate perception of the human mind" is really "some *immediate* power of perception in the human mind" (p. 57).

[32][29] Cambridge, March 25 1821
— Sabbath —

I am sick — if I should die what would become of me[?] We forget ourselves & our destinies in health, & the chief use of temporary sickness is to remind us of these concerns. I must improve my time better. I must prepare myself for the great profession I have purposed to undertake. I am to give my soul to God & withdraw from sin & the world the idle or vicious time & thoughts I have sacrificed to them; & let me consider this as a resolution by which I pledge myself to act in all variety of circumstances & to which I must recur often in times of carelessness and temptation [—] to measure my conduct by the rule of conscience.

[33] Cambridge April 1

It is Sabbath again & I am for the most part recovered. Is it a wise dispensation that we can never know what influence our own prayers have in restoring the health we have prayed God to restore? It has been thought by Some that in these immediate effects they have [n] no influence in general, that their good is prospective, & that the world is governed by Providence through the instrumentality of general laws which are only broken on the great occasions of the world or other portions of the Creator's works. But what have I wandered from[?] I think that it infinitely removes heavenly dispensations from earthly ones — this manner of giving gifts without ⟨assigning⟩ expressing the reason for which they are bestowed & leaving it to the heart to make the application & to discover the Giver is worthy of a supreme, ineffable Intelligence.

[34] Well, I am sorry to have learned that my friend[30] is dissolute; or rather the anecdote which I accidentally heard of him shews ⟨me⟩him more like his neighbours than I should wish him to be. ⟨Bef⟩ I shall have to throw him up, after all, as a cheat of fancy. Before I ever saw him, I wished my *friend* to be different from any individual I had seen. I invested him with a solemn cast of mind, full

[29] A pen and ink sketch of the profile of a bearded man is at the top of the page, above the date.

[30] Presumably Martin Gay. See p. 39, n. 10, and p. 40, n. 12.

of poetic feeling, & an idolater of friendship, & possessing a vein of rich sober thought.ⁿ When I saw ⟨ 's[31] pale but expressive face & large eye, I instantly invested him with the complete character which fancy had formed and⟩ though ⟨entirely unacquainted with him was pleased to observe the notice which he appeared to take of me[?]. For a year I have ent⟩ertained towards him the same ⟨feelings & should be⟩ sorry to lose him altogether ⟨before we have e⟩ver exchanged above a dozen words.

NB By the way this book is of an inferiour character & contains so much doubtful matter that I believe I shall have to burn the second number of the Wide World immediately upon its completion.

---

[35] Apr 10th

It is a wonderful attestation of the art of man that all the books of antiquity are preserved from age to age despite the turbulent little windy stormy life which is allotted him. Not a month passes without some physical occurrence to signalise & mark it as hostile to the comfort of man — either a deluging rain; or a whirlwind instead of a day; or a day of sevenfold heat like the flame of the furnace — exceeding hot; or mild January day in which the mercury amuses itself & the learned by freezing in the Sun.ⁿ In fact it is an excessively paltry humbug of a world, — and every circumstance of human comfort is a triumph of human ingenuity.

— "The fame of England" — pray what is that? The petty talk of the idle gossips in the ⟨|| . . . ||⟩ other dozen nations of the world, despised for their prating among the industrious of the nations. And what else? Nothing; for to two or three even of the existing nations as the Birman empire & the Hottentots her name has hardly penetrated. Here then is her glory circumscribed; for after she has gone to these few nations on her own globe, she must stop. Impermeable space separates the concerns of this world forever from mingling with those of any other.

[31] Emerson omitted Martin Gay's name but later filled the blank space with meaningless letters and pseudo-letters intended to mislead prying eyes. Gay's name should presumably fill the two blank spaces on p. [36]. See plate II.

[36] May 2d 1821

Mr Ticknor has finished his course of lectures.[32] French literature is a confined literature of elegant society, therein distinguished from all others which have appeared, for all others are national; the results of the feelings, situation, circumstances, & character of the whole people which produced it. But in France, from the Court of Louis XIV went out the rules & spirit to which all its classics conform, & must continue so to do.

Professor Ticknor named six characteristics of the Body of French Literature.

1. Such a conventional regularity
2. So little religious enthusiasm & feeling
3. Such a false character in the expression of love
4. So little deep sensibility
5. Such an ambition of producing a brilliant effect
6. So remarkable a restriction of success to those departments which will give some kind of entertainment.

⟨I am more puzzled than ever with ’s conduct. He came out to meet me yesterday and I observing him, just before we met turned another corner and most strangely avoided him. This morning I went out to meet him in a different direction and stopped to speak with a lounger in order to be directly in ’s way, ⟨and[?]⟩but ||...|| turned into the first gate and went towards Stoughton.⟩ [37][33] ⟨All this baby play pe||rsists|| without any apparent design, and as soberly as if both were intent on some tremendous⟩ affair.[34] With a most serious expectation of burning this book I am committing to it more of what I may by and by think childish sentiment than I should care to venture on vagabond sheets which Some-

[32] One of the courses in the history and criticism of French and Spanish literature which Ticknor had introduced at Harvard in 1819. He sometimes provided students with printed syllabi. (See S. E. Morison, *Three Centuries of Harvard*, p. 230, and George S. Hillard, *Life, Letters, and Journals of George Ticknor*, 1876, I, 325*n*.)

[33] A pen and ink sketch of a man’s head and shoulders in profile is at the right center of the page, with the text flowing around it from “my Magician!” (above) to “voice and” (below).

[34] The whole passage is heavily cancelled, some words or phrases being overwritten two or three times. “first gate” and “pe||rsists||” are blotted, but the dark letters of “first gate” show up legibly against the blot.

body else may light upon. (Mr Somebody, will it please your impertinence to be conscience-struck!)

May 10th Huzza for my Magician! he engages me finely. I am as interested in the tale and as anxious to know the end as any other reader could be. By the by this tale of mine might be told, with powerful effect by a man of good voice and natural eloquence.[35]

June 10 Mr Everett in his Artillery election Sermon,[36] to preface his own prophecy that the century now begun (i.e. third century since the Plymouth landing) will be the most important in determining the future fates of America[,] told this Story. In 1417 when Huss was bound to the stake at Prague, he declared amid his tortures that after a hundred years a retribution should be made on papacy. The inhabitants of Prague wrote his words "Post centum annos" upon their standard and in their records; and in 1517 the Reformation by Luther began.

[38] Books — Inquirenda[37]	Subjects for themes
Mather's Magnalia	Destruction of a city. poetry
Dunlop's history of Fiction.	(Forensic) Whether Civil Government be founded on a compact expressed or implied.
Mattaire.	
Swift. Froissart.	

[35] Emerson is probably referring to a story about the witch Uilsa and her son Vahn, the Magician, the surviving parts of which appear in No. XVIII, beginning on p. [26]. See p. 266.

[36] The sermon preached at the annual election of officers of the Ancient and Honorable Artillery Company of Massachusetts.

[37] Emerson's ascertainable knowledge and use of the works on pp. [38] and [39] for the approximate period of this volume are here outlined. For some works, only a conjectural identification is furnished. The appearance of a work in the list below does not necessarily mean that Emerson is known to have read it. Items are listed alphabetically by author. Where known, editions or probable editions are supplied. A number of works were almost certainly suggested to Emerson by the periodicals which he was reading regularly at this time (see especially "Catalogue of Books Read," *passim*). Because his impressions of the works may owe much to the reviews where he probably encountered them first, they are also cited. For further evidence of Emerson's readings in the works on his lists, see Index. See also, "Books Borrowed" and "Early Reading List." Page [38] is reproduced as plate III.

Alexander Adam, *Roman Antiquities* (edition unknown). A required freshman text in 1817.

Davy's Chemistry
Teignmouth's life of Jones.
Simmon's life of Milton —
— 3 Vol of [Wrangham's] Brit. Plutarch
Chaucer

The domestic relations as restraints on an adventurous ↑spirit↓

Influence of weather on intellectual temperament.

Hugh Blair, *An Abridgement of Lectures on Rhetoric* (edition unknown). A required sophomore text in 1818.

Sir Humphrey Davy, *Elements of Chemical Philosophy* (?) (London, 1812); *Elements of Agricultural Chemistry*(?) (London, 1813). The latter work was reviewed in *The Edinburgh Review*, XXII (Jan. 1814), 251–281.

Sir William Drummond, *Academical Questions* (London, 1805). Listed in "Catalogue of Books Read." Quoted p. 376, undoubtedly from *The Edinburgh Review*, VII (Oct. 1805), 179–180.

John Colin Dunlop, *The History of Fiction* . . . , 3 vols. (London, 1814). Volume 1 withdrawn from the Boston Library Society Sept. 22, 1821. Reviewed in *The Edinburgh Review*, XXIV (Nov. 1814), 38–58.

François de Salignac de la Mothe-Fénelon, *Les Aventures de Télémaque* (edition unknown). Emerson had begun reading this as early as Nov. 1816 (see *L*, I, 25).

Alexander Humboldt, *Personal Narrative of Travels to the Equinoctial Regions of the New Continent (1799–1804)*, transl. Helen Williams, 3 vols. (London, 1814). Reviewed in *The Edinburgh Review*, XXV (June 1815), 86–111. *Researches Concerning the Institutions and Monuments of the Ancient Inhabitants of America* . . . , transl. Helen Williams (London, 1814), was reviewed in *The Edinburgh Review*, XXIV (Nov. 1814), 133–157.

Henry Kett, *Elements of General Knowledge* . . . (edition unknown).

Silvestre Francois Lacroix, *Elements of Algebra*, transl. John Farrar (Cambridge, 1818). According to *The North American Review*, XIII (Oct. 1821), 363–380, this was one of the books especially translated and printed for the new course in mathematics at Harvard. A required freshman text in 1820.

John Locke, *Essay on the Human Understanding* (edition unknown). A required sophomore text in 1818.

Cotton Mather, *Magnalia Christi Americana*, 2 vols. (London, 1702, or Hartford, 1820). Quoted pp. 380–381. Reviewed in *The North American Review*, IV (Jan. 1817), 255.

Michael Maittaire, ed., Homer, *Ilias*, 2 vols. (London, 1816). A required junior text in 1820.

Michel Eyquem de Montaigne, *Essais*, 4 vols. (Paris, 1802). Volume 1 withdrawn from the Boston Library Society Sept. 7, 1820. (See also Charles L. Young, *Emerson's Montaigne*, pp. 1, 83ff.)

Richard Price, *A Review of the Principal Questions and Difficulties in Morals* . . . , 2d ed. (London, 1769). Quoted p. 347. See p. 51, n. 28.

William Robertson, *The History of America* (edition unknown).

Montaigne's Essays
Germany (Stael)
Drummond's Academical Questions
Price on Morals
Humboldt's Work on America
Smith's Virginia
Robertson's S. America
Hist of Philip 2 [Watson's]
Life of Shakspeare

[39] Books lent[39]
Kett's Elements, both Vols. to Angier

Character of any fancy portrait as for instance ☞[38]
My feet are gone. I am a fish. Yes I am a fish!

John Smith, *The Generall Historie of Virginia and the Summer Isles* (edition unknown). The London edition of 1626 was reviewed in *The North American Review*, IV (Jan. 1817), 145–155.

Anne Louise Germaine (Necker) baronne de Staël-Holstein, *De l'Allemagne*, 2d ed., 3 vols. (Paris, 1814). Volumes 1–2 withdrawn from the Boston Library Society May 21, 1822, and May 1(?), 1823. In College Theme Book, p. 202 below, Emerson cites the review of *De l'Allemagne* in *The Edinburgh Review*, XXII (Oct. 1813), 198–238.

Jonathan Swift, *The Works* (edition unknown). See "Catalogue of Books Read."

Charles Symmons, *John Milton: The Prose Works, with Life . . .*, 7 vols. (London, 1806). Volume 1 withdrawn from the Boston Library Society August 14, 1823.

Sir John Shore, Lord Teignmouth, *Life of Sir William Jones* (London, 1804). Reviewed in *The Edinburgh Review*, V (Jan. 1805), 329, which volume was withdrawn from the Boston Library Society Dec. 21, 1820.

John Walker, *Rhyming Dictionary*, probably the 3d ed., 2 vols. (London, 1819).

Robert Watson, *The History of the Reign of Philip the Second, King of Spain* (edition unknown).

Francis Wrangham, *British Plutarch*, 6 vols. (London, 1816). See "Catalogue of Books Read."

[38] The hand sign points to the figure of a grim-faced man with feet like a trifid fish tail. Beside the man are the amputated feet in the mouth of a great fish, and the words, "My feet . . . a fish!" Below the fish is some arithmetic in pencil.

[39] The identifiable friends to whom Emerson lent the books were: John Angier (1797–1863), Joseph Bancroft Hill (1796–1864), or his twin brother John Boynton Hill (1796–1886), and Jonas Henry Lane (?–1861), all seniors, and all but Lane

Telemaque [Fénelon] to Stackpole 1.
Lacroix to Gutterson
Locke 2. Vol. to Hill
III. & IV Cantoes of Childe Harolde — both lost
Guy Mannering to Lane
Rhyming Dictionary [Walker's] to Williams AB
Blair's Rhetoric (abridgement) to Hooper
Lay of the last Minstrel. Lothrop
Lady of the Lake to Idem
Adams' Antiquities

---

members of the nameless literary club to which Emerson belonged; and Joseph Lewis Stackpole (?–1847), Harvard '24, Nathaniel Leech Hooper (?–1831), Harvard '19, and Samuel Kirkland Lothrop (1804–1886), Harvard '25, nephew of President Kirkland of Harvard, and one-time tutorial student of Emerson's in 1817. Of Williams and Gutterson no records have been found.

Wide World 3

1822

There is no Wide World for the second half of 1821, but it is not exactly true that "Emerson seems to have kept no journal" for this period (*J*, I, 95). A considerable number of entries in No. XVIII are of the same kind as those in the Wide World manuscripts. The dated entries in Wide World 3 run from January 12 to February 20, 1822.

The manuscript of thirty-six pages is made up of three gatherings, of four, three, and two folded sheets respectively, all hand-stitched together. Most of the leaves measure approximately 17.2 x 23 cm, but some have been trimmed slightly. Tipped on to the page numbered 30 and attached by red sealing wax to the upper right hand corner is a large insert sheet, folded folio so that each leaf is 20 x 24.8 cm and then refolded at the bottom and at the right to fit this booklet. The four pages created by this insert leaf are numbered 1, 2, 3, and 4, but are indicated in the present text pagination by subscript letters (a, b, c, d) added to page 30, the number of the tip-on sheet.

[1] Wide World No 3[1]

Boston Jan 12, 1822.

After a considerable interval I am still willing to think that these commonplace books are very useful and harmless things,—at least sufficiently so, to warrant another trial. Besides every one writes differently when he composes for the eyes of others, and when his pen scampers away over mote and rut for the solitary edification of ⟨his⟩ ↑its↓ lord and master. The peculiar cause why this moment should be distinguished above others by the commencement of my third creation is that I am ambitious to say some fine things about

[1] The number and title of the journal are enclosed in the outline of a fish. A hand is pencilled in the middle of the first page and two pencilled outlines are shaded in.

Contrast, while, at the same time, the scattered undefined connection of my ideas leads me to mistrust my ability to shine upon this topic in theme, *poem*, or *review*.— What therefore is left, but for me to confide in the silent sheets of my book which cannot insult and will not betray?

Contrast is a law which seems to exist not only in the human mind with regard to the objects of imagination as an associating principle but also to obtain in the course of providence & the laws which regulate the World. When the day grows very bright and the atmosphere burns with unusual splendour, the mind reverts to the storm which will cloud, or the night which will speedily blacken it. Before the time of Mahomet and the comparative civilization of the deserts the merciless ⟨a⟩Arab celebrated a ⟨day⟩ feast of peace annually of seven days in which the deadliest enemy & the longest feud were forgotten & reconciled in ↑a religious↓ harmony & joy until the Close of the period.—And were the Arab tenfold more keen & terrible in his vengeance and his selfishness more sordid & savage than it is now, we feel sure, that [2] the feast should be longer & the friendship closer. ⟨than before⟩. The principle of Contrast which we find engraven within proves that such a state of things would follow. For how came it there, whence did we derive it? Either the Deity has written it as one of his laws upon the human mind or we have derived it from an observation of the invariable course of human affairs—and either of these suppositions proves the truth of the inference. For we could not have learned ourselves to range from one present object over all the immense circuit of intermediate objects to that one, most remote of all, from our present contemplation.

In this principle is lodged the safety of human institutions and human life. For suppose ambition excite against the peace of the World one of those incarnate fiends which have at different periods arisen to destroy the peace & good order of one community after another & of nation after nation. Gradually the lust of ⟨su⟩↑ex↓cess [n] engendered by sudden prosperity debauches every virtue and steals away the Moral sense. The insolence of power tramples upon the laws of God and the rights of man. The thirst of ⟨power⟩ ↑fame↓ arrays millions in the field ⟨and⟩ which the sword reaps down crying blood, blood! Which no vengeance can satisfy, no agony avert. Justice pleads in vain to the destroyer; Patriotism plots wisely, but her stern efforts are frustrated and [she] ↑dies by↓ the knife which was whetted for the tyrant. But the victor rides onward in his car of conquest exterminating the race which are made in the image of God until "Men said openly that Jesus and ⟨the⟩ ↑his↓ [2] Saints were asleep." Policy watches all night to contrive their destruction. The Statesman's aching brow,[n] the winning hand of the Merchant, the art [n] of the Engineer are joined for their persecution. Here, when the day of triumph burns with consuming splendour — here, the mind of itself pauses to anticipate change near at hand. The victor⟨y⟩[3] must cease. Else would the very stones cry out — Day and Night contend against [3] him; the Elements which he wielded rebel and crush him; the clouds nurse their thunders to blast him; he [n] is lifted up on rebellious spears between heaven and earth unworthy and abhorred of both, to perish.

Tnamurya.[4] "When that spell which can only be felt is thrown over the soul by the magic of genius, — 'now lettest thou thy servant depart where all is boundless genius,' — or 'let us tarry forever in this grave, if thus illuminated' — is the adoring language of the heart. — Is it not a well known principle of human nature that moments of enthusiasm can produce sacrifices which demand no proportionate virtue to those which never pretend to fame? Is not the real and perspective nature of moral grandeur thus proud? And of its ultimate and final cause — from which Utility cannot be excluded in the nature of things?"

The invisible connection between heaven and earth [,] the solitary principle which unites intellectual beings to an Account and makes of Men, Moral beings — Religion — is ⟨alike⟩ distinct and peculiar ↑alike↓ in its origin and in its end from all other relations. It is essential to the Universe. You seek in vain to contemplate the order of things apart from its existence: you can no more banish this than you can separate from yourself the notions of Space and Duration. Through all the perverse mazes and shadows of infidelity the Light still makes itself visible until the reluctant mind shudders to acknowledge the eternal encompassing presence of Deity. If you can abstract it from the Uni-

[2] The cancellation and insertion are both done in pencil.

[3] The "y" is cancelled in pencil, possibly not by Emerson.

[4] Mary Moody Emerson (1774–1863) was Emerson's paternal aunt. This and similar anagrams of her name mark frequent passages of her letters to him which he copied into his journals.

verse the soul is bewildered by a system of things of which no account can be given; instances[n] of tremendous power — and no hand found to form them; a thousand creations in a thousand spheres all pointing upward to a single point — and no object there to see and receive — it is all a vast anomaly. Restore Religion and you give to those energies a sublime [4] object. Every being and every world while it occupies its sphere exists to a purpose, — and far far above all is the throne of a Supreme Intelligence who fills up all the measure of perfection, and whose Wisdom animates the whole. In its view the wide Universe becomes one great Church encircling myriads of worlds and every world is an altar with its sacrifice of praise.[5]

The History of Religion involves circumstances of remarkable interest and it is almost all that we are able to trace in the passage of the remote ages of the world. It is a beautiful picture and just as it should be that in the character of Noah, of Abraham, and the early denizens of the world we trace no feature which does not belong peculiarly to their religion; — it was their life. It was natural that when the Mountains were just swelling upward under the hand of the Creator, when his bow was just built and painted in the sky, when the stone-tables were ⟨still[?]⟩ yet unbroken by Moses which now lie mouldering in fragments upon Sinai — that Men should walk with God. As we come downward and ⟨wander away from⟩ ↑leave↓ the immediate precincts of the tabernacle although we become sensible of the progressive departure from the truth yet each superstition ⟨possesses⟩ ↑retains↓ the inherent beauty of the first form, disguised and defaced in some degree, by ill adjusted and needless apparel. Indeed the only records by which the early ages of any nation are remembered is their religion. We know nothing of the first empires which grasped the sceptre of the earth in Egypt, Assyria, or Persia, but their modes [5] of worship. And this fact forcibly suggests the idea that the only true and legitimate vehicle of immortality, the only bond of connection which can traverse the long duration which separates the ends of the world and unite the first people to the knowledge and sympathy of the last people, is religion.

☞ Continued on page 10.

[5] The isolated name "Robert" appears between this and the following paragraph.

Every being is judged by his own law. Besides[,] these laws may never jar[,] may never come into comparison. They are as entirely unlike as the ideas of *reason* and a *daisy* and have no analogous points except perhaps the common analogies prevailing throughout the universe of a common creation by one ⟨m⟩Mind. They may severally be productions of several thoughts of the divine Mind. One system may be the representation, the Shadowing out of the *divine Imagination*; a second — of the *reason*; a third — of some other faculty incomprehensible to us. All this may take place just as the human sciences and arts are severally the embodyings of a faculty; — poetry, of the *imagination*; Mathematics of the reason; painting of sight; Music of the hearing &c &c. Each may be as different from the rest as one sense from another and yet when all are learned (as may take place when we are freed from the restraint of this one world) all may form a beautiful harmony, which shall be the perfection of knowledge. [R.W.E.] [6]

Will the disputes upon the Nature of God, upon Trinitarianism & Unitarianism, never yield to a [6] purer pursuit and to practical inquiry? It is possible, for all we know to the ⟨C⟩contrary that God may exist in a threefold ⟨form⟩ Unity; but if it were so, ↑since↓ it is inconceivable to us, ⟨and⟩ he would never have revealed to us such an existence which we cannot describe or comprehend. Infinite Wisdom established the foundations of knowledge in the Mind so that twice two cou⟨d⟩ld never make any thing else than four. As soon as this can be otherwise, our faith is loosened and science abolished. — Three may be one, and one — three.

Of Poetry [7]

⟨It is the language of the passions which do not ordinarily find their full expression in the sober strain⟨s⟩ of prose. We should rest our argument on this; that there seems to be a tendency in the passions to clothe fanciful views of objects in beautiful language. It seems to consist in the pleasure of finding ↑out↓ a connection between

[6] Here and elsewhere "[R. W. E.]" is substituted for Emerson's symbol of original authorship, which he first used July 26, 1819. See pp. 169, 215, and plate VII.

[7] The next two paragraphs are crossed out in pencil.

a material image and a moral sentiment. Few men are safe when they begin to describe poetry; they talk at random or hardly prevent the ends of the lines from rhyming and /are like/resemble/ the mimic of a madman ⟨run⟩ ↑who went↓ mad ⟨themselves⟩ ↑himself↓. Poetry never offers a distinct set of sensations. Science penetrates the sky, Philosophy explains its adaptation to our wants, and Poetry grasps at its striking phenomena and combines them with the moral sentiment which they ⟨occasion⟩ naturally suggest. Its images are nothing but the striking occurrences selected from Nature and Art and clothed in an artful combination of sounds. With regard to *poetical expression,* that is, a form of language which dignifies a common idea it depends a great deal upon the assistance of words to give definiteness and very much resembles [7][8] algebra in the principle whereon it is founded.⟩

⟨We say commonly that poetical expression gives a tinsel lustre to common thoughts and an ordinary reader is decieved into a respect beyond the merits of the peice. But poetical expression constitutes to half the world the beauty of poetry and in this it seems ⟨to us⟩ to resemble Algebra, for both make language an instrument and depend solely upon it without having any abstracted use..⟩

The Arts are mostly the production of some tendency in the human mind[.]

There are few things which the wellwishers of American literature have ⟨ne⟩ more at heart than our national poetry. For every thing else, for science, and morals, and art they are willing to wait the gradual /progress/developement/ but they are in haste to pluck the ⟨bright⟩ blossoms from the fair tree which grows fast by the hill of Parnassus. For when a nation has found time for the luxury and refinement of poetry it takes off the reproach of a sluggish genius and of ignorant indifference. Moreover, although the learned nations of the east and west acquired by their arts and learning a claim to re-

[8] Pencilled writing begins after "instrument" and continues to "There are few" (below). "The Arts" apparently served first as the heading for the second paragraph following. Roughly pencilled sketches of men's heads fill the spaces around the sentence "The Arts . . . mind[.]"

nown yet it was the Muse which inscribed that title upon the temple of fame and it would be a kind of fraud perhaps not unparalleled should we forestal our merit by writing the name before we deserved the record.

[8] Poetical expression serves to embellish dull thoughts but we love better to follow the poet when the muse is so ethereal and the thought so sublime that language sinks beneath it.

When the heart is satisfied and the pulse beats high with health man is apt to exclaim "Soul, thou hast much goods laid up for many years, eat drink and be merry; Life is long and time is pleasant,—I rejoice that my maker has clothed me with strength and poured this buoyant blood into the vessels of life; I will go to the banquet and the dance, I will go to the fields to play."—I would remind him that far off stand the ruins of Palmyra and Persepolis; the hands that builded them are unknown,—the gods that were worshipped there have perished also and for ages they have served as a memento of death and ruin—I would remind him of the vast cemetery of the dead which is peopled with countless nations and outnumbers a thousand fold the population of the earth.

Saturday Evg Jan 19th.

When a species of composition has been written with success in a brilliant period, and in another and remote land has been likewise known, and after having been discontinued and forgotten is revived ⟨again⟩ in another age and another country—we have every right to say that such an art is agreeable to the dictates of nature. This is the history of the Drama, and it has every reasonable indication that ↑it↓ will every where flourish under favourable circumstances. It is easy also to distinguish between those parts of it which are unnatural and the forced production of a state of society [9] and those which are the genuine offspring of the human spirit. In the Mysteries—the French ⟨d⟩Drama of the Middle ages,—such personages were introduced upon the stage as "Such," "Each one," and "Both," and performed their parts as gravely and as much to the satisfaction of a perverted public taste as ↑did ever↓ the most accomplished Iphigenia, Electra, or Caesar. Such a folly as this is evidently the appropriate spawn of the age of the Schools and the pleasantry of confirmed pedantry. It does not follow that if any thing be out of the common course of human experience, it is not natural to the drama and may not talk with ordinary agents. The representation of the dead consorts perfectly with the feelings of the most refined taste, and in every age has formed a part of dramatic entertainment. For the belief in unseen agents is so universal and indeed is a consequence of a belief in God that no mind ever revolts at the idea.

A constituent part of the Drama from its very invention was the ornament of scenery. This suggested itself unavoidably as an important element of the plan which ⟨is[?]⟩acts altogether by decieving the audience into the conviction that the actors ↑really↓ *are* the persons whom they represent. The illusion could be promoted best by removing all extraneous circumstances and affording the imagination the help of all the senses. Independently of this, it is a high gratification to be suddenly removed from all the common objects of daily occurrence and admitted to a spectacle of shining cities, of im[10][9]posing mountain scenery, of thrones, and of magnificent apparel.—I shall resume this subject when I have more to say.

The Dark ages comprehend six centuries 5,6,7,8,9,10, and the four following were the dawn of restoration of human honour. It is a fearful phemonenon that the Mind should thus sleep for six hundred years and under the influence of such tremendous dreams. But the causes which are assigned are adequate. In the annals of the mind they are counted out of the estimate and are only parallel⟨l⟩ed by the dark ages which marked the infancy of the world. It may be through such another ⟨V⟩valley of the ⟨S⟩shadow of death the World shall approach its extinction.

The Genius of the Universe assigned
To each long age a Guardian Spirit's care.
Lo! in Time's Temple where they stand sublime
And each bears written on his awful brow
The record of the World. Wo wo to him

[9] The series of numbers near the top of this page is linked to an inserted "Centuries" above by a brace which also encloses "DARK AGES" printed below the numbers. A pen and ink sketch of a hand and "(Continued from page 5)" are in the lower left margin.

Admitted to that mighty company
Who reads the frowning characters

☞ (Continued from page 5) Sat. Morning—

A nation which exists when the means ↑are few↓ of transmitting their memory, ⟨are few,⟩ is remembered, not by any partial or local institutions, ⟨but by⟩which their neighbours can neither copy nor understand; but they derive their best chance for immortality from their modes of embodying the principles which all feel—from their obedience to the common ne[11]cessities of human nature. Thus, the burial of the dead is a custom so natural and necessary, that we have easily traced its forms in every different nation; while, if we reason from our own experience of the vagaries of folly, fashion, and caprice, we can have no doubt that a thousand forms of society and a thousand temporary customs sprung up in the primitive ages, of which not the faintest trace remains in the world. The idea of eternity took strong hold of the mind, and being corroborated by their own natural feelings, and, when they looked to the condition of man, by the principle of contrast, it was soon exhibited in their prevailing national establishments. Such a gift to thought, as this notion, (if it were not intuitive) would be caught from soul to soul, from community to community so rapidly, that in ignorant times when the mind is readily kindled to fanaticism, no power, no deep rooted prejudices could withstand the enthusiasm. No man can doubt that if in such a state of newly acquired principles there had been a nation whose faith rested on absolute annihilation and refused the inspired doctrine, millions would have been ready to risk their life in a holy Crusade for the propagation of such a belief. Indeed I have such a confidence in human fortitude that I have no doubt in declaring that ⟨all men⟩ ↑two thirds of mankind↓ would consent to die for the belief of another existence. (Continued on page 17)

[12] Monday Evg Jan 21

To one who⟨m⟩ from this remote quarter of the globe, looks over the history of mankind, obviously the most remarkable event is the darkness of the Middle Ages. When seemingly the world had disengaged itself in all its great members from the swaddling bands of its infancy and all its powers ↑had been↓ unfolded and exposed to the genial influence of the elements; when time and moral causes had had their expected effects and all that improvement was realised of which it was known to be susceptible — a sudden revolution takes place in its ⟨condition⟩ character springing from itself through the cross operation of its internal energies. The wonder has forcibly suggested itself to the minds of all men as an emphatic night preceded and followed by Days of extraordinary glory. We understand the nature of the darkness and in many respects, how it was produced. We feel that from it has proceeded a mightier energy than has before operated upon the nations, that the Mind has laid her strong grasp upon hidden truths, that men are travelling the ways of human life in Continents which the Ocean hitherto concealed, and have adorned that life with unborrowed arts and inventions and revived all that was worthy in Ancient Science. Philosophy is extending her influence in a thousand branches, and in none does it more become her to walk than upon this dark portion of time.

[13][10] Whether the sudden developement of the mind in Arabia and the ⟨un⟩irresistible force with which the religion of Mahomet was carried from the banks of Euphrates to the banks of the Guadalquiver had any other connection with the deep sleep under which Europe was laid than the unknown laws ⟨of Contrast⟩ which take place to keep the level in human affairs, there is no reason to suppose. There was no union of commerce or interest, ↑no alliance,↓ no emigration which could serve to point out any relations between the fall of Rome, and the empire of the Saracens. Indeed the known causes of that prosperity are adequate to the end and entirely independent of any other power.

There are some portions of history which it is tedious to read because the mind is oppressed with a weary succession of disappointments and bad fortune and which are not compensated but summed up in ⟨a⟩the miserable event. Such is the disastrous tale of the overthrow of the Greek empire in which the humiliation of the emperors

[10] At the top of the page in the indented space before the first sentence Emerson subtracted 1453 from 182[2] (369 years since the fall of Constantinople). A large "G" appears in the space between the first paragraph and the paragraph beginning "There are" (below).

only equals the ↑ill-timed↓ treachery and avarice of their subjects and the selfish policy of their natural allies. In the fall of the first Greece our regret is always tempered by our sympathy with her high-minded conquerors but the indignation which kindles at the loss of Constantinople is aggravated by our abhorrence of the barbarous ⟨conquerors⟩ ↑invaders↓. The only sovereign remedy is acquiescence in the decrees of an equal fate which we see does prevail. The decrepitude of overgrown empire is as natural an ⟨‖...‖⟩event as the rise and progress. Rome wrested the Bosphorus from the barbarian and founded the Eastern [14] capital. The Turk built his throne there upon the ruins of Rome and the Russian at this day holds suspended over the Ottoman Capitol the same terrors ↑with↓ which ⟨t⟩he formerly menaced the sons of Constantine.

The ⟨fortun⟩ fall of empires does not depend so much upon individuals and their casual passions as the fortunes of small states. The government which gathers under its large circle a population of many millions stands more upon the feelings and interests of society than upon the attachments, resentments, and judgement[n] of its nominal head. The luxury which loosened the throne of Rome did not proceed directly from the conquered countr⟨y⟩ies to the court but was imparted and conveyed through the ranks of society by her merchants and rich inquisitive travellers. The character of the people will generally find a competent representative in the purple and it is impossible that a dissolute court should ⟨be maintained by⟩ ↑run the last lengths of extravagance amidst↓ a free, temperate, and powerful nation. Hence we do not deplore the fall of Rome; it was as desirable as it was inevitable that a mass so rotten should dissolve and cease to infect the air; but we deplore the succession of causes which led to that necessity; ⟨we deplore that the prosperity of nations is⟩ we[n] deplore that the elements of national prosperity are sown in the same soil with the seeds of decline and that the lofty philosophy which explores the secrets of history, the rise and fate of empires, should find no single exception to that fatality which ↑makes good-fortune ominous by↓ assign⟨s⟩ing decay as ⟨the⟩its immediate ⟨result⟩ ↑attendant↓.[11]

[11] A stray phrase — "under the damning influence which feeds his sensuality" — is written in pencil as the last line on the page.

[15] The President Montesquieu has written a masterly exposition of the causes which led to the Grandeur of the Roman Empire. ⟨We shall add a few considerations upon the means which should have ↑been↓ used to withstand the progress of decline in that nation.⟩ ↑The solitary student is apt to censure the error and deficiency↓. While the vigour of the ⟨empire⟩ ↑imperial resources↓ yet remained in the hands of the Caesars and the symptoms began to manifest themselves of approaching corruption it was in the power of the successors of Julius and Augustus and the scholars of a golden age to have a wise recourse to the ↑political↓ remedies. To have reestablished the responsibility and powers of the senate as far as an old and free aristocracy was compatible with their own sovereignty; to have at least restored the factious tribunes to an useful sense of importance; to have resolutely excluded from the privileges of citizenship the profane hands whose wealth was proffered to bribe it; these are obvious methods which suggest themselves to all as direct means of retarding the footsteps of fate. But it is easy at the distance of a thousand years for common minds to direct the sovereigns of Rome. These would have been cures if the evil had resided in the court or ⟨i⟩on the frontier; but while desperate private vice and abuse of public trust spread everywhere from the publican to the prince throughout the empire, some fiercer restorative should be sought, some new secret of art explored. We shall hardly venture to advise in such important crises; but it appears to us that if the modern ⟨dis⟩ inventions of perfect representation had ⟨occurred⟩ ↑been tried in↓ Rome it would have gone far to save the fortunes of the World. If we consider for a [16] moment what would have been the probable operation[,] we presume [n] not to say it would have been practicable in the deeply founded establishment of ranks to have created an independent representation, or that from such a wide mixture of nations and tongues it would have been possible to collect an adequate body of men ⟨and⟩ ↑who should be↓ intelligible to each other; we only affirm that the wise and fortunate principle of that system embodies such political power as was indispensable to the salvation of Rome. A body of men to whom is committed the correction of political mistakes may completely and safely revolutionize the government for it is to be recollected that it is in fact ⟨a device of⟩

⟨only a mode of carrying the people into the senate house⟩ a refinement upon democracy whereby the wisdom of the people is brought to the senate house purged of their ignorance and local bigotr⟨y⟩ies. And the nation which opposes or annuls what a few rulers have done cannot thus frustrate their own unanimous decrees. It is upon this science that our last hope rests that the union is not essential of ↑national↓ glory and decay. It is the indulgence of this rational [national?] hope of our own institutions which is ignorantly stigmatized abroad as the dreams of boyish imagination.

After the extinction of the ⟨ea⟩western Empire and the settling down of the northern emigrants in the South of Europe a long period of ten centuries ⟨comprises⟩ is embraced under the name of the Middle Ages.

Sir Knight of Corfu, the Republic of St Mark greets you thus. You have sunk our vessels, defrauded our mariners, and slain our captains, and have afforded us every just cause of war. Ninety-nine islands are subject to Venice, and all the prowess of your knights shall not withold the hundredth. [R.W.E.]

[17] (Continued from page 11)

We have said that the first nations were remembered by their religion; — and in tracing down their history a little farther until the time of written languages we find that the first efforts which the human genius made to commit its ideas to permanent signs were exercised upon the great topic which stood uppermost in an unperverted mind. Poetry attempted to fashion a probable picture of the Creation, to explore the character of Providence, to impress upon mankind the enlightened views of a moral government in the world which had been disclosed to her own eye. History alarmed the mind by reciting the vengeance which waited and fell on ⟨the⟩ impiety; and the dark imaginations which concieved the destruction of the Giants, the fire and vulture of Prometheus, the abode of the Furies and of the dead, sufficiently attest the nature of the principles which excited their hearts and founded their traditions. Philosophy set out from rude speculations upon the Being of God and borrowed from another age or gathered from its own observation the notion of Destiny. But the date of *writing* marks the second age in the history of Religion and we have parted from the more attractive memory of the first. The naked savage who ascends the ⟨dusky⟩ mountain,—because the ⟨grandeur of its⟩ dusky summit inclines him to believe that the Great Spirit /abides/inhabits/ there—and erects a stone as his simple and sincere tribute to the Majesty of that being, is an ⟨in⟩ object infinitely more agreeable to ⟨th⟩our imagination and feelings than the loftier and more excellent offering of lettered Science. And although reason teaches us that the deliberate devotion of a philosophic mind is more worth than the vague fears of a superstitious one, yet we are apt to inquire if the [18][12] pride of learning has not been known to harden the mind even to the plain proofs of Divine Providence. (Such a profane desire of knowledge which tempts arrogance to question the laws of truth is a damning moral Gluttony which by abusing the ⟨faculties⟩ ↑appetites and means of gratification↓ we possess debases the character.) Continued on page 20.

I was the pampered child of the East. I was born where the soft western gale breathed upon me the fragrance of cinnamon groves and through the seventy windows of my hall the eye fell on the Arabian harvest. An hundred elephants apparelled in cloth of gold carried my train to war and the smile of the Great King beamed upon Omar. But now—the broad Indian moon looks through the broken arches of my tower, and the wing of Desolation fans me with poisonous airs; the spider's threads are the tapestry which adorns my walls and the rain of the night is heard in my halls for the music of the daughters of Cashmere. Wail, wail for me, ye who put on honour as gay drapery!

The Grave.

Can thy gates shut, Oh City of the Dead!
And cease to add the eternal increment
Which crowds thy caverns from the worlds of life?
God spreads beneath us the enveloping gulf
And feeds its fell and gnashing gluttony
With our poor shrinking tenements of clay.
Who hath gone down inquisitive to see

[12] In the left margin, beside lines six to eight of the poetry, is profiled in pen and ink the head of a hawk-like bird.

Thy ribbed vaults, thy drear magnificence
The thrones of Death and Darkness, or to make
Acquaintance with thy countless colonies
Heirs to thy strength, dark subjects of thy sway?
Ask not, frail man, it boots thee not to know,
Myriads have sought, thyself shall speedily seek
In thy own turn the abysses of the pit
Whose silent horror tempts thee to be bold.
[19] Still I would pry unbidden and undone
Upon the Monitory secrets laid
Embosomed in the marble sepulchres.
⟨Is it not trifling⟩ Man trifles with thine arm
    omnipotent
To hang with blooming flowers the dismal Urn
And mocks Destruction with /the/love's/ roses gay.
Dark cheerless King! I venerate thy power.
What if the gaudy world, the vine-clad Muse,
The loud rejoicing nations, the bright Sun,
Nature and Art, Health, Happiness, and Love
Join to detest, defy, and curse the ⟨g⟩Grave; —
What are they all but writhing worms of pride
Rebelling 'gainst the /foot/giant/ which crushes them.
Thy pride is soothed by the fierce haste which heaps
Thy hecatombs and the red stream which sends
Its steaming incense to thy nostril, puffed
31 With Earth's perpetual pile of sacrifice.
Continued on the next page.

⟨Sunday Evg Jan 27⟩

The Feudal Institutions changing the state of society in every respect are to be examined in four respects; their *ecclesiastical, civil, judicial,* and *social* innovations; and these are all so connected that the ↑full↓ discussion of one of these involves all the rest. Energy and unscrupulous power was at the bottom of the system which growing from the muscular power of the barbarians who founded it distinguished it chiefly from the superannuated governments ⟨of⟩ which it displaced. Italy was the field in which all met, — the degenerate posterity of Rome, the tribes of barbarians, the merchants of Greece composed the miscellaneous population on which the feudal thrones were first erected; but they were loosely fixed and were soon shattered [20][13] in the cities where this mixture of population and the intelligence of commerce agreed better with the un⟨quench⟩↑govern↓able factions of Florence or of Pisa than with the quiet oppression of a baron. Nothing is so surprising as the contrasts which that state of society exhibits of untameable pride and of ⟨avarice⟩ rapacity, with the most prostrate superstition; of uncommonly barbarous features, with a delicate respect for the female sex.

Continued from page 19

Lord of the dead, not with a golden crown
Is thy brow girdled; ⟨at [?]⟩ thy dissolving touch
Crumbles the diamond diadem of Power
And scatters ashes on the victor's wreath.
Wide underneath our feet thy courts are spread
In unknown horror; gaily overhead
Thy palace-roof — the nations trample loud
Kings of the earth and high plumed conquerors
Young dancing Beauty and exulting Youth
⟨March o'er the false ground where
rose-leaves hide the chasm⟩
Haste o'er the chasm which blushing roseleaves hide.
— Far, far beneath where ⟨th[?]⟩Man hath never been
The ghastly giant bars the Gates divine
Which separate Eternity from Time.

Continued from page 18.

The difference between the primitive forms of religion and the second dispensation (and likewise the first) consisted in this, that the

[13] In the left center margin of the page, beside lines of verse four through eight, there is a pen and ink sketch of a mountainous landscape, with a castle and a bridge. Beneath it is a profile of a man's head and a crossed-out sketch of a winged dragon whose tail appears as a large numeral "6" and whose talons grasp a man holding aloft an unfurled pennant with the word "Body" printed across it. The title "Great Dragon" appears below the sketch.

first were the voluntary offerings of the imagination and the understanding to a sublime but unseen Spirit, while the last were the implicit [21] submissions of duty, of custom, of fear. For this reason we sympathise more with the savage. (in the last paragraph) It is somewhat remarkable that in the simple institutions of the barbarous nations God was worshipped through sublime and awful images, and nothing ⟨that was⟩ mean and disgusting was attributed to his character. It were needless to repeat that Caesar found the German nations without idols, ⟨and⟩ deeming it unworthy to build a house for him that made the Universe; — or to transcribe the Indian creed of the Great Spirit, so scrupulously pure that it rejected what it could not reconcile of an evil world[n] to a Benevolent Cause, and created an opposite, ↑active, evil↓ ⟨p⟩Principle on which to pile the sin and the storm, pain, and death which beset human life. Such also was the Persian faith which thought the Fire no unfit emblem of Divinity; and if the Druid sacrificed men on the altar, an oak forest was the temple and it was not offered to an ox or an ass — but to an adequate notion of the Supreme Being. In all these the ways of Providence were traced in the hurricane, the sea, the cloud, or the earth-quake and therefore the mind must needs be elevated that would converse with them. But as civilized life advanced and civil and social institutions were erected and life became more intellectual, devotion was degraded by a profane and vulgar idolatry; corrupt thoughts began to be imputed to the divine character; the vices found their way each to a temple and worshippers; the gods and demigods went fast below the standard of human respectability until the worship of Superior beings ↑the holiest feeling of which the h[uman]. soul is capable and that perhaps for which it was made↓ seems to have almost passed out of repute and name among honest patriots, and Olympus needed to be cleaned of its impurities and the throne of Heaven to be subverted for the peace of Society —

[22] This fact that the seeds of corruption are buried in the causes of improvement strikes us everywhere in the political, moral, & natural history of the world. It seems to indicate the intentions of Providence to limit human perfectibility and to bind together good and evil like life and death by indissoluble connection[.]

We have loosely[14] traced the leading features of the early History of Religion before the covenants were given and (which is the same thing) in the nations where they were not known. The idea of *power* seems to have been every where at the bottom of the Theology; the human mind has a propensity to refer all its higher feelings, all its veneration for virtue and greatness, to something wherein this attribute is supposed to reside. Cause and Effect is another name for the direction of this sentiment. It is felt by all. The terms of common speech, the names we give to immaterial things, all consent to this, and are qualifications of it. What is Honour, Mercy, Pride, Humility, Revenge — but sensations which have reference to in⟨trinsic⟩ ↑dwelling↓ *power?* Honour is the worthiness which it gives; — Mercy, the temperate forbearance of its exercise; Pride, the selfrespect which attends its possession; Humility, the acknowledgement of its existence; Revenge, a barbarous use to which it is put. — It is shared among all beings, but in all has a limit and a beginning, on which the mind's eye eagerly fastens with an immediate attempt to trace the sources whence the subtle principle was derived. It is a great flood which encircles the universe and is poured out in unnumbered channels to feed the fountains of life and the wants of Creation, but every where runs back again and is swallowed up in its Eternal Source. That Source is God.

[23] It was when the mind had thus embodied in systems its ideas of Deity that a necessity was found in the divine counsels for a new revelation. We now revert to the covenants made with Abraham & his posterity. It must be recollected that confused traditions of the Creation and of the Deluge were current among mankind and were almost the only vestiges of the early dealings of Providence with man. Continued on p. 25[.]

Battle of Lignano 1176[n]

War of Como

In the year 1118 the Milanese began the war with ⟨|| . . . ||⟩Como

[14] This is the passage which Emerson referred to at the end of a long discussion on omnipotence in Wide World 7, p. [47], when he wrote, Nov. 2–3, 1822: "For the conclusion of this paragraph see p. 22 Wideworld No 3 — beginning — 'We have loosely &c.' "

a little independent city in the neighbourhood of ⟨Milan⟩ ↑Switzerland↓, with some just pretexts for hostilit⟨y⟩ies. Some differences subsisted between the Emperour (Henry V) and the pope Honorius. Milan with the other Lombard cities adhered, as was common, to the Emperor whilst Como took part with the pope who had gratified them with a popular Bishop. Meantime Londolphe a ⟨bishop of⟩ noble Milanese was appointed to the same see by the antipope Burdino; and he coming with an armed retinue was surprised and taken prisoner by Guido his rival. Milan took up arms to avenge the affront and obtained the aid of several cities among which were Parma, Modena, Laguna, Vicenza, Cremona, Bologna, Mantua, Ferrara, Pavia, Plaisance, Novare, Alba, ↑Verona,↓ & others amounting to ⟨sixteen⟩ seventeen or 18.) With these powerful preparations the war was waged against the city for 10 years. The Comasques were the bravest people of Italy and in the first year repeatedly defeated and disgraced different members of the confederation. ⟨B⟩For eight years the contest was but weakly managed on the part of the Milanese; but in the year 1125 the Comasques lost their bishop Guido; and [24] in him expired the soul of their power and policy. The long war had weakened their resources and reduced their numbers[,] and their resistance to the annual incursion was feebler than before. In 1127 Milan redoubled its efforts, assembled a larger army, and advanced machines of assault to the walls of the beleaguered town. The intrepid Comasques performed prodigies of valour; but the engines of the beseigers which had effected a considerable breach in the wall made all their plans hopeless of saving the city. They promptly came to the determination to forsake their country and having constructed light boats for the purpose of conveying their families and property they embarked at night while a strong party of the garrison made a ↑sudden↓ sally to engross the attention of the enemy. The Milanese were afraid to enter the open gates of the city supposing a plot of ambuscade, and the Comasques reached unmolested, the fortified castle of Vico.

This history bears a striking analogy to the Trojan War, both in its duration and event. "All the states of Lombardy were convened against the unfortunate Comasques.[n] This was the first great exertion which the cities made of their strength; the[y] combated against the

Alpine mountaineers, the mariners of the lakes, the people of the valley of [n] St Martin; they thus became warlike and able to resist Frederic Barbarossa the formidable Xerxes of the Middle Age." Sismondi [*L'Histoire des Républiques Italiennes au Moyen Âge*] Chap VII Tome II.

↑"In the desart a fountain is springing,
In the wild waste there still is a tree,
And a bird in the solitude singing,
Which speaks to my spirit of thee." Byron.↓
["Stanzas to Augusta," lines 45–48]

[25] (Continued from page 23)

A vague notion of something miraculous, a stupid consciousness of going wrong, and a reminiscence of the right — attend the perversion of the mind in idolatrous countries. He does not believe — the most ignorant devotee — that his brass idol made the world; that a calf or an ox — a miserable animal which the slave despises [—] is the personification of that omnipotent Spirit which created the Universe and bound it together with a golden chain of attraction; which planted in the birth of Nature the seeds of perpetual succession; which formed the Reason of man, and curiously contrived the passions, & the Imagination, and adjusted their gratifications; which made the Soul and its sense of immortality. He does not believe that a Being whom his own human fancy has conceived to have built pavilions for the sons and daughters of light in remote gardens of the universe, will rob himself of his perfections to choose for his own habitation, the contemptible frame and faculties of a beast. There is a failure in imagination to reconcile such desperate absurdities, nor will the lying pandects of his faith nor the doctors of the law satisfy the abused reason. Meantime, while he kneels before the false altar, in obedience to a greater idol, Custom, the moral sense rebels within him, and warns him of another world and whispers to him of judgement. Of old, there was among the Chaldeans one who obeyed this secret voice and dared to proclaim his belief and abandon the wretched fortunes of a nation whose reason and human honour had been long wrecked in vice.

Continued on next page [n]

[26] Of the nature and causes of the Covenant with Abraham, we cannot safely speak, further ↑than↓ the Scripture account extends. We do not sufficiently understand the relations which fallen man sustains towards the Deity, before the Christian dispensation. We see that there are "cycles in the moral world," without knowing what differences, what walls of partition they erect between those who live under the one & the other. Perhaps it is one of those momentous privileges which enhance our danger while they add to our hope, and which, by their awful importance, make just the ordination, that the moments of life are to colour the ages of eternity. Probably, the influence and intention of that covenant reaches down to us through some moral channel, and may deeply affect our future condition. Certainly, it takes away from us the choice of religious feelings, which a Greek or Roman claimed, and compels their direction to an individual, immaculate, omnipotent principle. Apart from its unknown character in the counsels of Providence, we must reason upon its effects on mankind, according to the known laws of operation in the human mind. We know that a primitive nation never makes any considerable progress until it has first been acted upon by some foreign impulse. Now if we recur to our sacred books, we shall find that the first family upon earth rec⟨ie⟩eived their impulse to improvement directly from the Deity and the rapid progress which is recorded of the arts evinces the effect of a communication with such an Agent. After the Deluge some other exciting principle [27] was demanded to trouble the waters and prevent a stagnation. We shall be deeply sensible of such a necessity if we compare the history of the human mind then, with its other epocha. We know that every man is indebted for all the foundations of his attainments to the knowledge which he finds already accumulated in society;* that now when Newton has lived, an inquiring man has no need of going over for himself all which Newton has learned; but this is all done,—he begins from the point where Newton left off, and consequently his acquisitions must far outstrip his Master. Now if we carry back this idea to the family of Noah we immediately perceive that the tremendous judgement which had drowned the earth had likewise buried the accumulations of knowledge, & that while the forlorn

* Vide "Stewart's Philosophy of the Mind" Vol. I.

remnant began to lay again the foundations of society, the human spirit rose ⟨again⟩ ↑also↓ from its weary oblivion, to hoard anew its acquisitions. There were no general principles established; no discoveries of science recorded; the fie⟨e⟩lds of moral sentiment, of philosophy, of imagination were void; not a monument, not a name, not a book was left to afford example and stimulus to zeal. Under this view it might be expected that intellect would become a blank page, and that a retrograde ⟨motion⟩ progress would reduce the mind to a wretched level with the brutes. Some most extraordinary action was wanted to cause vibrations of life and harmony in the deadly moral stillness which was felt in the world. This want [28] was supplied by opening to the mind a communication the most elevating in its nature of any which thought can conceive, by awakening every capacity, every slumbering energy of the soul to a most lively exercise in direct intercourse with the Divine Mind. We know not how widely this influence was propagated; it may have entered deeply th⟨r⟩ough indirectly into the subsequent advancement of ⟨the world⟩ ↑mankind↓ in other countries. Continued on the 31 page.

Η γαρ φυσις βεβαιος, ου τα χρηματα [15]

Soph. [Euripides] Electra, 937 [941] l.

The Greek long ago reasoned thus upon the folly of the rich man's hope. "Is it well, he said, to ⟨please⟩ ↑value↓ thy self ⟨with⟩ ↑on↓ a pile of gold? for what is it, but to have ⟨b⟩seen ↑riches↓ familiar↑ly↓ for a little time; nature is stable, but not wealth; for Nature ⟨always⟩ remaining ↑forever,↓ corrects her own faults, but wealth, when it is unjustly acquired, or partaken with fools, having *displayed* * [n] *its plumage* a little while, flies out of the house." [16] He described it well when he said that *wealth* was only "*to see riches familiarly*," not to feel and enjoy them. To acquire riches, and to be rich, is to hope and to be disappointed, for Care & Pain keep so close to the chariot of Wealth, that they are not seen by those panting after it, until they have reached the wheel, and then the appetite of

*The word is ανθησας (q. v.), and therefore the figure inconsistent[.]

[15] " 'Tis character abideth, not possessions."

[16] Emerson is freely translating the passage from Euripides from which he quoted line 941 above.

pursuit is ⟨more than⟩ overpaid ↑by↓ the chagrin of success.—⟨Wealth⟩ Fortune is fleeting, and riches take to themselves wings, but is ↑the second part of his proposition true, is↓ Nature eternal? Is the rose on the cheek of youth perennial? Will the locks remain on the brow of manhood? All flesh is grass &c. Nothing ↑of nature↓ is firm but the eternal mountains and the naked rocks. But are these unchanged? The Winter has /stripped/shorn/ them, the earthquake has rent their foundations. ⟨a⟩And can the whole earth and the centres of nature show a fairer claim to permanence? I fear not. There are the Fire, the Wind, the Waters, Earth[29]quakes and lightning buried within it to tear it asunder. Without, there is an Order of the Universe—broken, if the Arm which sustains it be withdrawn; and the forerunner of this dissolution, the Angel of Prophecy has already published the day.—Watch[,] for the Time is at hand—when the heavens shall be rolled together as a scroll and the elements shall melt with fervent heat. What then is Nature?—it is the transitory pleasure of the Divine Mind.

Idealism.

Deep in the soul a strong delusion dwells,
A curious round of fairly fashioned dreams;
Yet quietly, the pleasant vision swells
Its gay proportions far around; the streams
Of the wide universe their wealth supply,
Their everlasting sources furnish forth
The fabled splendours, whose immortal dye
Colours the scene with hues which mock the summer sky

And oh how sweetly, in youth's seraph soul,
That vision, like the light of heaven, doth rest
Its name is Life; its Hours their circle roll
Like angels in the robes of morning drest;
And every phantom of the train is blest
Who shakes his plumes upon the odorous air,
Or lights a star upon his azure crest
And while the lovely beam reposes there
Joy in the guileless heart his welcome will prepare

[30][17] [Feb. 12, 1822]

I stand amid the wilderness. Disdain
Hath marked her victim; Hunger, Cold,
Misfortune shake their shrivelled hands at me
And gird me in their hideous company.
I have conversed too long with life, and fed
The appetites of dull mortality
With nectar from the paradise of God.
Unchastened, I have put my hand upon
The wheels of the revolving Universe
To pluck another nature thence than mine.
Amid the deafening battle of the clouds
The thunder of the ocean and the cry
Of [alarmed] Nature I have lifted up
No woman voice to hush the awful roar.
— Anguish hath visited my bower of strength,
A deluge hath come over my delights.
Wo! the bright gem which graced my crown of pride
Now burns my forehead with consuming fire.
Come! scatter ashes on my fragrant couch
I will shake hands with Death and hug Despair
So I may rid me of the iron fiends
Who haunt & hiss me.

[Feb 12 1822]

I see a rich country far over the sea
Where gold God [n] and freedom are hid from the ee
Who findeth the first shall be tortured and slain
⟨Who⟩ But merry live they who discover the twain.[18]

[30_a] *Of Italy.*

We judge ↑of the value↓ of every portion of history by its use-

[17] The date "Feb 12 1822" is written vertically in the bottom left margin upward from "where" (below) to "So" (above). Affixed to the top right edge of the page by sealing wax is a four-page essay, "Of Italy." written on a single folded sheet of paper and printed below as pp. [30_a], [30_b], [30_c], and [30_d]. Although it is incomplete, the formality of the composition and the careful hand in which it is written suggest that Emerson may have planned it for publication.

[18] Emerson quotes the lines in a letter to John Boynton Hill, March 12, 1822,

fulness in application to our own and other times. Can we learn from the greatness, or the disasters it recounts, how to mould our own governments, in order to ensure the benefits and avoid the faults of the nation we see?—then the history is valuable. But the annals of the Chinese monarchy could be of little comparative advantage to the European Statesman; certainly of much less, than those of the ancient European dynasties. Exactly the opposite of the great Asiatic anomaly, is Italy. I cannot accurately judge of the Chronicles of China since they are little accessible to many, and less so, to me; but from the vague knowledge we possess of that empire, and from our minute acquaintance with Italian history, we may learn this; that both are insupportably tedious from different causes. In the grave and never-ending series of sandaled Emperors whose lives were all alike, and whose deaths were all alike, and who ruled over myriads of animals hardly more distinguishable from each other, in the eye of an European, than so many sheeps' faces,—there is not one interesting event, no bold revolutions, no changeful variety of manners & character. Rulers & ruled, age and age, present the same doleful monotony, and are as flat and uninteresting as their own porcelain-pictures. On the contrary, in Italy, after the fall of the Empire, the scholar is shewn a line of twenty cities whose fluctuating policies perpetually vary through every form of government, and every variety of political connection. Numberless coalitions are formed & broken; ⟨C⟩confederate districts, cities, and families whom true interest should bind inseparably, work themselves up to acts of madness against each other by the fury of faction; the government, which was yesterday a cautious aristocracy, is today a fierce democracy, & will be tomorrow, a despotism. Each year is a disastrous repetition of tyranny, revolution, & bloodshed, [30_b] until the eye is lost in the hopeless confusion wherein nothing predominates but the names of War, Faction, Misery.

Such is the contrast of two distinct histories; the obvious lesson to be drawn from both, is to avoid the desperate defects which disgrace the poor construction of these governments. In one, since the days of its foundation[,] intelligence, improvement, and enlightened

and says they are "said to have circulated in England some centuries since" (*L*, I, 108).

happiness have never visited mankind; and peace has been purchased by a blind subjection of human interest, honour, & will to an ignorant & oppressive despot. By reason of the want of experiments we cannot say with confidence, that another government would have made another character in Canton and the Yellow Sea, but the analogies of other nations are in favour of such a supposition. In the other, all the faculties of the mind were perhaps diligently exercised, but owing to a clumsy ill-digested system in which private ambition was improperly nursed and directed, and no ⟨solid⟩ ↑permanent↓ balance formed among the parts, men passed a turbulent & perilous life in walled towns which might protect them from enemies without, but offered no defence against the formidable warfare within. That the miseries of the Middle ⟨a⟩Ages belonged to the ↑bad↓ governments under which society laboured is abundantly manifest from the different condition of the same country under the well organized domination of the first Rome.

I am inclined to consider the history of Italy as the most instructive ⟨which⟩ page which can be read in the registers of time. Because it demonstrates better than any other the remarkable & vast effects upon national prosperity of free Commerce & agriculture; which exalted individual character, and filled the public treasury with a boundless wealth which all the extravagance & spoliation of their wars could never exhaust, & seemed never to diminish. At the same time, it admonishes posterity to beware how it shall frustrate these eminent advantages by neglecting to lay deeply the foundations of civil order upon the sound principles of the interests and inclinations of men. It may be so studied, that the sufferings of Florence, of Pisa, of Genoa, [30_e] and of Rome may prevent the necessity of the after repetition of similar suffering, and the bloody sacrifice once made, may be made for the world.

To use this history aright, we ought, in looking over its events, to regard the distinguishing political features which were the cause of their calamities. I shall attempt therefore to set in order such of the remarkable faults of government as are most obvious, and most easily explained.

Most of the Italian cities were for a long period under the government of *Seigneurs,* who for the most part, were men of property or influence ⟨in the city⟩ who took advantage of some accidental panic or perplexity in the public circumstances, to ask or command their own election, to a municipal & military supremacy. This power was nearly allied to a *military despotism.* A jealous multitude were able to make some exceptions to its absolute controul, & perhaps to keep the *judiciary*, safe from encroachment. But the tendency of this dominion is to grow continually, untill it embraces, within its ample circle, every description of authority, and in ordinary cases it forces a reluctant repose throughout the state; this peace, the only merit of this kind of government, is not the tranquillity of satisfaction, but of fear. But in the cities of Italy even this poor merit was denied to the government of the *seigneuries.* For although a tyrant who is seated amid a band of armed & disciplined troops may scare into obedience all the members of a peaceful state, yet this power is abridged or neutralized in a nation of soldiers; and such, from the necessity of their situation in a warlike neighbourhood, were the Tuscan & Lombard commonwealths. Here then rests the evil. Under a warm and seductive sky, the government of the Seigneuries allowed all the licence and indulgence common to a camp in peace, without being able to allay or crush the fierce irritation which such manners provoked in the community. They were consequently short-lived, and the natural reaction in society from an abhorred servitude, led directly from this oppression to an intemperate democracy, whose opposite but equally pernicious troubles inclined men again to seek relief in the [30_d] dominion of one. Thus in small states which have been once ill governed and where sound politics are not understood, the public difficulties tend constantly to multiply & not to correct themselves.

The next great fault in the social order of the Italian Republics was the peculiarity of their military establishment. While the weak tie which connected them to the Germanic empire still subsisted, it became a necessary custom regularly following the election of an Emperor, that he should cross the Alps with eight or ten thousand Germans to recieve the iron crown at Monza and the homage of his Roman subjects. Upon the return of the monarch to his native states, a considerable portion of his soldiers generally preferred the rich soil & abundant wealth of Italy to ↑the↓ semi barbarous condition they had left at home, and chose to remain embodied troops for the chance of war or the hope of plunder. These instantly became formidable to the territories in their neighbourhood, who were compelled to purchase their departure at ⟨a⟩ consid↑e↓rable sums. They were ready also to enlist without distinction of party under any leader who should pay the highest wages. With this character, it is evident of what signal advantage their service must sometimes be to belligerent states. ⟨For⟩ ↑Venice or Florence↓ without the time & difficulty necessary to levy & discipline raw soldiers, ⟨they⟩ could command at once the force of a veteran army & skilful leaders, with this additional convenience that they could prosecute the war ↑abroad↓, without the smallest interruption to their commerce at home. As soon as this lucrative prospect filled Italy with "Condottieri" (as the mercenaries were called,) the military character of the states declined apace, as its necessity seemed to be superseded, until the country was left at the mercy of the armies which it supported. John Hawkwood's Company from England, was followed by another from France, until at last, native Condottieri took the place of foreigners, but not to lessen the calamities of Italy. Here the military schools of B↑r↓accia & of Sforza were instituted, and for a long time signalised against each other their destructive accomplishments. By his arms alone, the head of the latter school and the descendant of a soldier of fortune, acquired the duchy of Milan and left it to his family.

(?)

[31] From p. 28 Saturday Evg Feb 16

We leave the Abrahamic covenant to make a few reflections on what should perhaps have had the first place in any sketch of the history of Religion — human views of *providence*. By this term we understand — not the special exhibitions of the Deity to Abraham or to Israel, in the desart or on Sinai, but the general silent course of the Divine Government, manifested in the tendencies of human institutions and the human mind, — in the perfectness & imperfection, and their results, of brute or vegetable nature, in the daily events which take place and change the Universe. A child may ask — what are these tendencies? but none who is much travelled in the ways of the world, and who has pushed through the common experience of forty, thirty or twenty years can hesitate to identify them. There is a tendency in all things human to decay, a tendency in vice to hasten its own destruction, and in that fall, a tendency in the ruins of society towards new life. Now these proofs of the action of some single intelligent Principle are not offered to the Atheist from the Bible or from the priest but they are taken out from the *proverbs* and familiar sayings of all nations, which ⟨have⟩ are the first generalizations of the mind and have been repeated by the mouth of the million.

[32] As the peculiar language of experience, altogether independent of other purposes than as tried guides of life, *proverbs* demand notice. It was early found that there were a few principles which controuled society; that the mother of all the arts, the nurse of social feelings, the impeller of individual energies—was Necessity; (Geometry was invented and taught in Egypt, because the inundations of the Nile, sweeping away ⟨o⟩the⟨r⟩ landmarks, rendered other means of securing property indispensably requisite. V. Mitford Greece.[19]) and this was embodied in a maxim which has circulated through the world. ⟨—⟩ ↑It was also seen↓ that in the distribution of the advantages of life great inequality and variety took place,—that some did not partake and others were deprived—of these blessings; but it was found that in the place of lost and unknown[n] goods, a system of equivalents was substituted,—that if Age ⟨which⟩ palsied the Arm, and broke up the bodily enjoyments, yet Folly and Fancy and Appetite were dead, while the Understanding was matured and Experience filled up;—that where barrenness had cursed the land with poverty,—strength and intellect made good the loss, &c. &c. These truths, ascertained by the progress of society, and corroborated by the observation of each succeeding generation, were incorporated into these short maxims as rules for youth which maturity ↑would↓ establish. Every man /becomes/grows/ acquainted with the moral laws which govern his condition, as he does with the decencies of society—only by a growing familiarity with the order of the scene wherein he plays a part.

[33] Often, in the whirl of affairs, the Providence becomes very noticeable. Suppose a nation who have ascended the ordinary scale

[19] William Mitford, *History of Greece,* 6 vols. (London, 1795). Volumes 1–3 withdrawn from the Boston Library Society Feb. 16, 1822.

of progress with triumphant rapidity, and have touched the point of criminal ambition, have commenced that profligate tyranny over other communities which has been so often repeated, have emptied the coffers of the world into their own, and ↑finally↓ have plunged into that boundless luxury, which, in the order of things, is the consequence of empire, and the cause of decline — and at this time, when the nations looked for judgement, judgement did not ⟨ar⟩come, but the state went on from greatness to greatness, and sin to sin, on a tide which knows no ebb; — but suddenly, a check comes without adequate cause; — providence reaches out through the channels of success and the ↑fair↓ prospects of prosperity & the pillars of ↑social↓ strength to pluck down its life & honours root & branch — forcibly conveying to the mind the idea of Power, which we have said was at the bottom of the notion of Deity. This is but a transcript from many of the pages of Time, and this constant operation of a code of moral laws is a sufficient evidence of the government of Providence. We want no other testimony — we ask no higher miracle to attest the omnipresence of a wise & good Being, than the observation which a judicious mind makes upon the course of human affairs. And it is a fine view of science, to reflect that it is merely our own recorded observation of the ⟨d⟩Divine administration of the world.

[34][20] The circle of the sciences is no more firmly bound together than the circle of the virtues; but in the first a man cannot hope to be thoroughly acquainted with all, for they are in some degree incompatible; whereas in the last, his character will be defective if it do not combine the whole & form that harmony which results from all.

Proud of the rich variety of things
Thought never lacks her food. Her ardent search
Taxes the outmost orbit's ample road
To chase the star upon the wings of light.
Tired of her toil, now settles on the life

[20] In the left margin, opposite line one of the poetry, is a small pen and ink profile, and opposite lines two to six of the poetry, a pen and ink sketch of the head and shoulders of a man. In the right margin, from lines four to seven of the poetry, is a partially obliterated profile.

Of Man and finds its moral miracles
A miniature of the Universe[.]

[Tuesday Eve. — Feb. 20, 1822]

I shall close my book with some remarks upon a few of its pages from the kindness of one who was persuaded to read them.[21]

"The author of history of religion turned aside very happily ⟨itself⟩ for himself and for the episode (which ranges through some of the most extensive views of the moral & social world — brings ↑into the↓ delighted [35] vision of the theist, those universal laws or agency of God which he terms *providence*) from the Abrahamic covenant. To retrace that singular selection of an Idolater to found a nation, which was to become a mark of reproach to all the world and doomed to bear oppression & misery — is a task which might puzzle the pen which moves from the barm of excitement. The best theist sees a mystery in those arbitra⟨t⟩ry rites & in that unsuccessful ↑experiment of↓ theocracy itself, which can never be explained, but by the faith of a christian. In this view had the whole Jewish economy existed but to give the voice of Isaiah to ages before Jesus[,] it had been an evidence of inspiration worthy of God, who has eternity to use. The history of the Jews, as it respects their fortune and sufferings however singular, can be accounted for by the general laws which prevail over society as well perhaps as any nation who are persecuted (say Poland) but viewed by the light of their Scriptures & their fortunes became a strong proof of their miraculous history, and of their existence as a chosen nation, being wholly perspective & for the salvation of the world."

Tuesday Evg — Feb 20th 1822 Tnamurya

[36] "It's hame and it's hame and it's hame we fain would be
Though the cloud is in the lift & the wind is on the lea
For the Sun thro the mirk blinked blithe on mine ee
Says I'll shine on you yet in your own countree." Scott.
[*The Fortunes of Nigel*, ch. XXXI]

"Nec totam servitutem, nec totam libertatem pati possunt" Tac[itus].
[*Histories*, I, XVI, 38][22]

"Thou that art our queen again
And may in the Sun be seen again
Come Cares come

[21] Mary Moody Emerson.

[22] "[men who] can endure neither complete slavery nor complete liberty."

For the War's gone home
And the fields are quiet & green again." L[eigh]. Hunt.
[*Descent of Liberty*, III, 529–533]

"Incipe. Vivendi recte qui prorogat horam,
Rusticus expectat dum defluat amnis; at ille
Labitur ac labetur in omne volubilis aevum." [23]
Hor[ace]. [*Epistles*, I, II, 41–43.]

"His mother from the window looked
With all the longing of a mother
His little Sister weeping; walked
The greenwood paths to meet her brother."
[John] Logan ["The Braes of Yarrow," lines 25–28]

[23] "Begin! He who puts off the hour of right living is like the bumpkin waiting for the river to run out: yet on it glides, and on it will glide, rolling its flood forever."

Wide World 4

1822

The dated entries run from February 22 to March 10, 1822, covering a part of the second winter in which Emerson taught at his brother William's "school for young ladies."

The thirty-two numbered pages of the manuscript are made from four gatherings of two folded sheets each, hand-stitched with green yarn to each other and to a paper cover. The leaves measure approximately 16.3 x 20 cm.

[1] R Waldo Emerson

Wide World. No 4 [1]

Boston Feb 22 1822

DEDICATION.

I have invoked successively the Muse, the fairies, the witches, and Wisdom, to preside over my creations; I have summoned Imagination from within, and Nature from without; I have called on Time, and assembled about the slight work the Hours of his train. — But the Powers were unpropitious[,] fate was averse. Some other spell must be chaunted, some other melody sung. I will devote it to the dead. The mind shall anticipate a few fleeting hours, and borrow its tone fro[m] what all ↑that↓ have been ↑are,↓ and all that are, will shortly be. All that adorns this world are the gifts which they left in their passage through it. To these monuments which they bequeathed, and to their shades which watch in the universe, I apply for excitement, and I dedicate my short-lived flowers.

[1] The title and the number of the journal are enclosed in an irregularly traced rectangle. Below the framed title is a death's head lightly sketched in pencil. Sketches of towers are centered beneath "dedicate" at the bottom of the page.

[2][2] Saturday Eve. Feb 23

Continuation of some remarks upon Providence.[3]

No elaborate argument can remove the fact which strikes the senses, and which is the first & chief difficulty in the way of the belief of an omnipotent good Principle, namely, the ⟨great proportion of⟩ existence of evil in the world, and next, the great share it has in the texture of human life, and its successful opposition to virtue and happiness. If we suppose the character of the ⟨a⟩Author to be unmixed goodness, the work must be likewise pure [,] and an ultimate failure of success subtracts Wisdom and Omnipotence (if indeed the one be not involved in the other) from the qualities of the forming Being — that is — demonstrates him not to be God. Human wisdom sees the imperfection ↑of the part,↓ and labours to make out the perfection of the whole from the analogies of the universe which fall under its eye, from its judgements upon the language which testimony attributes to this Creator and from the intuitive and acquired conclusions which it forms upon — Nature.

But another great testimony to which the mind will naturally turn to confirm or efface its convictions of a superintending hand — is History; — to see if Time will fulfil any larger part of that Justice which should take place — than falls under the life of one man. — And this is an [3][4] evidence which grows with every year of time, which could not be open to the primitive races of mankind, and which, if its weight be found favourable, will develope ↑to the last ages↓ the connecting bonds which unite the fate of many generations, — the plan, of ample outline and intricate parts, which will reveal the obscure relations between one and another remote scene, whereby a succession ⟨of misery⟩ ⟨and⟩of misfortune & suffering is counterbalanced by an equal sum of happiness, and the unnatural success of vice and its undue preponderance over ages and nations of the world, is set right again by the triumphs of virtue over other ages and nations.

Moralists have regarded the adjustment of this great & perplex-

[2] "(Providence)" is centered under "one man." at the bottom of the page.

[3] The last previous discourse on Providence ends in Wide World 3, p. [33]. See p. 88.

[4] "(Providence)" is centered under "Christian dispensations;" at the bottom of the page.

ing variety in human condition as the exhibition to the Universe of a great Picture, in which, for the harmony of the whole, much is encompassed with deep shade; and the painted figures may not complain to the Artist because they have been arranged & coloured in such or such a manner. But is this a fair view? are free agents nothing more than painted emblems? are — (but I have left my proper course of thought and must return to it again)

I was about to say that it is History alone which can determine whether the means answer the end, and whether the design be fully accomplished in those schemes whose fulfilment involves many ages. e.g. to discover the typical and direct relations between the Jewish & Christian dispensations; and to watch the [4][5] fulfilment of prophecy. But whether these schemes be answered or not, the question still recurs — why did a good providence permit at all the existence of evil, or why does any one individual suffer from the vice of others or the sickness & unhappiness which he did not bring on himself but which is incident to his nature? The reply which each individual finds himself able to make to this question will go far to doubt or to justify his idea of Providence.

It may be well by way of solving this question to propose and answer two more — What is evil? and What is its origin?

What is evil? There is an answer from every corner of this globe — from every mountain and valley and sea. The enslaved, the sick, the disappointed, the poor, the unfortunate, the dying, the surviving, cry out It is here. Every man points to his dwelling or strikes his breast to say it is here. An enumeration of some of the most prominent evils in society will illustrate the variety & malignity of this disease[.]

[5][6] What is its origin? The sin which Adam brought into the world and entailed upon his children.

One of the finest chapters in the old Testament is the Song of Deborah & Barak, Judges V. Q. V.!!

The novelist must fasten the skirts of his tale to scenes or traditions so well known as to make it impossible to disbelieve and so ob-

[5] "(Providence)" is centered at the bottom of the page.

[6] A pen and ink sketch of the shoulders and profiled head of a man is in the right margin beside the date. "(Trash)" is centered beneath "Mater well," at the bottom of the page.

scure as not to obtrude repugnant facts upon the finished deception he weaves.

Tuesday, Evg. Feb. [26]

A ghost may not appear because *no* one answers the question—why should he appear. As soon as the cause is adequate, there is every reason in nature to expect such an appearance.

Somebody says that it makes no difference how many believe in a recieved opinion, but that it does weaken the presumption in its favour—how many dissent from it. If this be true, the vast number of voices who consent to be orthodox, and which seems at first the chief argument in its favour fall away at once from the purpose and the minority of cool-judging, prudent men who secede do greatly prejudice the cause.

I have not much cause, I sometimes think, to wish my Alma Mater well, personally; I was not often [6][7] highly flattered by success, and was ⟨often mortified by⟩ every day mortified by my own ill fate or ill conduct. Still, when I went today to the ground where I had had the brightest thoughts of my little life and filled up the little measure of my knowledge and ↑had↓ felt sentimental for a time, and poetical for a time, and ↑had↓ seen many fine faces, and traversed many fine walks, and enjoyed much pleasant, learned, or friendly society,[n]—I felt a crowd of pleasant thoughts—as I went posting about ↑from↓ place to place, and room to chapel. I met [.][8]

[Feb. 28, 1822] Few of my pages have been filled so little to my own satisfaction as these—and why?—because the air has been so fine, and my visits so pleasant, and myself so full of pleasant social feelings—for a day or two past that the mind has not possessed sufficiently the cold frigid tone which is indispensable to become so *oracular* as it hath been of late. Etsi mearum cogitationum laus et honor non tam magna quam antea fuit, tamen gaudium voluptatemque majorem accipit, quoniam sentire principia amoris me credebam. Vidi amicum, etsi veterem, ignotum; alteram vidi notam et

[7] "(Hark rascal)" is centered at the bottom of the page beneath the date.

[8] The omitted name may be that of the "ignotum amicum" or the "alteram notam" mentioned in the following paragraph.

noscendam; ambo, forsitan, si placet Deo, partem vitae, partem mei facient. Poenitet mei res magnas narrare cum verbis qualibus tyro uti solet.[9] —*Feb 28 1822*

[7][10] Such is the contrary condition of things that pride subjects a man oftenest to humiliation; for its nature being to render the possessor ever mindful of himself, that very mindfulness is exhibited in the features of the face, and serves only to provoke the frown, anger, and contempt of others. Every slight, while it irritates the pride, darkens the brow, and repels the more, the more fretful it becomes. Be content then to jostle with the multitude, to bow your head and let the world wag.

"Hark ⟨hated⟩ rascal!"
At mid day, in the crowd of care,
⟨The thought will start⟩
The unbidden thought will come,
And force the obedient blush prepare
Reluctant welcome home;
And in the corners of the heart,
And in the Passions' cell,
It bids my thoughts to battle start,
Which fain would peaceful dwell.
Peace, Pleasure, Pride, and Joy, and Grief
Awake the chaos wild,—
But worse and cursed the relief
Which sense & strife beguiled. (to wit Indifference.)

[9] Several words in this passage were altered in ink, apparently by Emerson, in order to make the text less readable. For example, *laus* was written over to read "teas," the letter "c" was prefixed to *amoris*, and "t" was appended to *sentire* and to both occurrences of *vidi*. The lines may be translated as follows: "Although the praise and honor of my thoughts has not been as great as before, yet it acquires a greater joy and pleasure, since I believed I felt the beginnings of love. I saw a [male] friend, though an old one, unknown; I saw another [female] known and to be known; both, perhaps, if it pleases God, will make a part of life, a part of me. I regret telling important matters with the words that a beginner is accustomed to use" (Ed.). The "[male] friend" may have been Martin Gay.

[10] In the right margin from "wag" (above) to "care" (below) is sketched the face of a man. From "heart" (above) to the end of the poem is a rough sketch of a soldier holding a shield. "(Pride)" is centered below "remembering" at the bottom of the page.

So much poetry for peculiar sources of pride old and inveterate and perhaps ⟨f⟩hereafter unintelligible. Still one's feelings are well worth speculation and I am desirous of remembering a date. (as that of the last page)

[8][11] —scripsi nomen, supra.

A beautiful thought struck me suddenly, without any connection, which I could trace, ⟨of⟩ with my previous trains of thought and feeling. It had no analogy to any notion I ever remembered to have formed; it surpassed all others in the energy and purity in which it clothed itself; it put by all others by the novelty it bore, and the grasp it laid upon every fibre; for the time, it absorbed all other thoughts;—all the faculties—each in his cell, bowed down and worshipped before this new Star.—Ye who roam among the living and the dead, over flowers or among the cherubims, in real or ideal universes, do not whisper my thought!

March 2 Saturday Eve ⟨Feb. 30⟩

There is no one fact in the economy of Providence more remarkable ⟨as⟩than the disproportionate influence which the social feelings exercise upon the mind. Other events and minds, which, on the scale of the universe, carry vast weight & consequence, sink, on the scale of individual life, below comparison in ↑their↓ importance. Many millions of men lived, toiled, and died, ages since, to help on the grandeur of the Assyrian empire; the intellectual energies of the choice minds of a hundred generations (?) were tasked to this end; the riches, refinement and pride which each generation, improving on the last, could accumulate in a rich soil and amid poet[9][12]ical scenery,—were poured in to build up and adorn the nation;—at the same time, all the round of moral events, the education and exercise of the affections, the balance of right and wrong, and finally, the *religion* wherein Nature instructed the soul—all wrote their record on the page of time, and completed a national history. And *now*, to what

[11] The Latin reads: "I have written the name above." "(Social Feelings)" is centered beneath "accumulate in a" at the bottom of the page.

[12] "(Social Feelings)" is centered at the bottom of the page beneath "rightly considered."

purpose, as far as regards our welfare, did all this laborious and eventful age exist? In the mind of one individual, in the history of one man's life the being of the Assyrian empire comes and passes like a shadow, while six or ten or twenty persons of ordinary or mean powers, and of no account in the whirl of affairs, occupy, almost exclusively, his mind through the greater part of his life. To more extraordinary intellects, it serves but a little higher purpose, — ⟨to⟩ as, to shew thereby the analogies of human condition, "to point a moral, or adorn a tale,"[13] while, to the rest, it is but a transitory vision, or perhaps a reluctant lesson. It is probable that these great concerns will some time bear an⟨d⟩ adequate esteem, and that their proper value and connection will be made out, when our knowledge is enlarged in another state; meantime we must be content to discover, that, wise ends are answered by the excessive interest with which we behold the persons and occurrences of the passing moment; and this we cannot fail to do, if they be rightly considered.

[10][14] It is manifest from a little reflection how little improvement is made in a separate *unsocial* state even supposing for a moment that the race could be reared and educated in solitudes. Indeed, every thing upon this topic is so plain and obvious, that it is hardly pardonable to state our views. Man was as evidently intended for society, as the eye for vision, or the ear to hear; and the yearning affection which the mother bestows upon her child, while it bears upon its front the marks of design and utility, leads us to imagine the effect, if our sympathies and affections went back to waste themselves on the remote & forgotten fortunes of departed empires. ⟨Youth⟩ Childhood — should lack needful nourishment while our tenderness journeyed back to the childhood of the world. Age — should languish and die alone, while the mind reverted to the decline of lettered Egypt, Persia and Greece; Sickness and sorrow pine unknown, because our philanthropy mourned over the broken arches of the ancient capitals. No education is correct and adequate which is not derived in part from the society of our equals in age and attainments. No developement of the human energies is complete which has been prevented from ex-

[13] Johnson, *The Vanity of Human Wishes*, line 222.

[14] "(Social Feelings)" is centered at the bottom of the page beneath "limited to themselves."

tending the affections, each to its appropriate object. Both mind and heart are sufferers and enjoy but half their ⟨life.⟩ ↑capacit⟨y⟩ies,↓ when the bursting buds of life are checked and limited to themselves. It is a part [11][15] of a plan ⟨I⟩ that we should be helpless here; it is a part of our education for another sphere, that we should *here* put forth all the energies which lie dormant within. It were alike unnatural and weak to avoid them, for, in their gratification is made to consist, the larger part of earthly happiness.

It will satisfy us how imperfect will be the education of a moral being, *out of social* life, if we but ⟨name⟩ consider for a moment the nature of the virtues. What is Charity⟨?⟩—Patriotism—Benevolence, Prudence, but the exercises of Duty towards fellow-beings? We do not deal with angels; we do not *compassionate*, *arouse*, *assist*, or *guide*—disembodied spirits. If we feel these emotions, which are the best part, next to God's love, of our nature, we must feel them for man. And what are the springs of action, which incite any one man to do noble and praiseworthy deeds?—Patriotism, Love, Emulation. And where were these begotten?—in Heaven? in unreal and fictitious scenes? in the silent groves, and the solitary hut of the ascetic? No; these form the atmosphere and the bond of union to *social*, cultivated, and active Man. Solitude has but few sacrifices to make, and may be innocent, but can hardly be greatly virtuous like Abraham, like Job, like the Roman Regulus or the apostle Paul. Great actions, from their nature, are not done in a closet; they are performed in the face of the sun, and in behalf of the world.

[12][16] To find if Man can dwell in Solitude, I must lead you back, gentle Reader, to the beginning of the world. We must quit the city, the house, the cleared road, the simplest improvement of civilization, and stand up on the banks of the river which no dams have confined, amid woods which no axe hath felled, in a solitude which none partakes but the invisible Being who hath just now made it. I think that person who stands there alone among the trees with his eye on the waters and his hand upon his lips—is an object of interest. His name is Adam. He is the venerable head of long & far following generations, the germ of whose distant destinies is lodged in him. In

[15] "(Social Feelings)" is centered beneath "of the sun," at the bottom of the page.

[16] "(Social Feelings)" is centered beneath "March" at the bottom of the page.

him are now kindling the passions, which, in his sons and his sons' generations, shall create more strange and awful scenes than gifted imagination can describe, which shall build up this wilderness into lofty cities, in their benign operation, and then desolate them in their wrath. He is the only one in the world in whom resides that miraculous combination of corruptible matter with incorruptible mysterious mind. He dwells in Paradise and is unacquainted with sickness, evil, and affliction. But he finds that it is not good to be alone, and lo! a companion is given to his prayers. Is solitude purer than Society? Eve yielded in solitude to the tempter, and the sin was done in retired shades, which "brought death into the world, and all our woe." [Milton, *Paradise Lost*, I, 3]

Sabbath March 3. Weather remarkably fine.

[13][17] Animi ardor de quo supra dixi non extinctus est, sed mihi videtur non esse tam potens tam clarus tam magnus quam antea. Timeo ne caderet. Spero ut viveret.[18]

March 4. A breathless solitude in a cottage in the woods beneath the magnificent splendour of this moonlight and with this autumnal coolness might drive one mad with excitement. Precipit⟨i⟩ous and shadowy mountains, thick forests and far-winding rivers should sleep under the light, and add their charm to the fascination. The silence broken only by the far cry of the night bird; or disturbed by the distant shout of the peasant, or, at intervals, by those melancholy moanings of the wind, which speak so expressively to the ear, — who would not admire? Let the Hours roll by uncounted, let the universe sleep on in this grand repose, but be the spell unbroken by aught of this world, by vulgar and disquieting cares; by a regret or a thought which might remind us of aught but Nature. Here is her Paradise, here is her throne. The stars in their courses roll silently; the oaks rock in their forests to the voice of the sighing breeze; the wall-flower [n] on the top of the cliff nods over its giddy edge, and the worshipping

[17] "(Vision)" is centered at the bottom of the page beneath "desolation!"

[18] "The ardor of spirit of which I spoke above is not extinguished, but seems to me not to be as powerful, as brilliant, as great, as before. I am afraid it may fade. I hope it will live" (Ed.).

enthusiast stands at the door of his tent mute and happy, while the leaves rustle down from the topmost boughs and cover his feet. A cry in the wilderness! the shriek and sudden sound of desolation! howl for him that [1⟨3⟩4][19] comes riding on darkness through the midnight; that puts his hand forth to darken the moon, and quenches all the stars. Lo! where the awful pageantry rolleth now to the corners of the heaven; the[n] fiery form shrouds his terrible brow behind the fragment of a stormy cloud, and the eyes of Creation gaze after the rushing chariot. Lo! he stands up in the Universe and with his hands he parts the firmament asunder from side to side. And as he trode upon the dragons I saw[20] the name which burned underneath — Wake, oh wake, ye who keep watch in the Universe! Time, Space, Eternity, ye ⟨e⟩Energies that live, for his name is DESTRUCTION! — who keep the *Sceptre* of its eternal order, for ⟨h⟩He hath reached unto your treasuries, & he feeleth after your Sceptre to break it in pieces. Another cry went up like the crash of broken spheres, the voice of dying worlds. It is night. — An exceeding noisy vision! —

Greatness

[March 6] Never mistake yourself to be great, or designed for greatness, because you have been visited by an indistinct and shadowy hope that something is reserved for you beyond the common lot. It is easier to aspire than to do the deeds. The very idleness which leaves you leisure to dream of honour is the insurmountable obstacle between you and it. Those who are fitly furnished for the weary passage from mediocrity ⟨and⟩ to greatness seldom find time or appetite to indulge [15][21] that hungry and boisterous importunity for excitement which weaker intellects are prone to display. That which helps them on to eminence is in itself sufficient to engross the attention of all their powers, and to occupy the aching void. Greatness

[19] "(Vision)" is centered beneath "find time" at the bottom of the page. "(Greatness)" appears to have been added later in pencil as a paragraph heading.

[20] The pencilled number "2" is written underneath "firmament" and over "the" in the phrase "upon the dragons" and the pencilled number "1" is written under "asunder" and over the space between "dragons" and "I". It is not clear which words or phrases the numbers are intended to reverse. Therefore the order has not been altered.

[21] "(Greatness)" is centered beneath "power which" at the bottom of the page.

never comes upon a man by surprise, and without his exertions or consent; No; it is another sort of Genii who traverse your path suddenly; — it is *Poverty* which travels like an armed man; it is *Contempt* which meets you in the corners and highways with a hiss, and *Anger* which treads you down as with the lightning. Greatness is a property for which ⟨a⟩no man gets credit too soon; it must be possessed long before it is acknowledged. Nor do I think this to be ↑so↓ absolutely rare and unattainable as it is commonly esteemed. This very *hope*, and panting after it, which was alluded to, is, in some sort, an earnest of the possibility of success. God doubtless designed to form minds of different mould, and to create distinctions in intellect; still the extraordinary effects of education attest ⟨the⟩ ↑a↓ capacity of improvement to an indefinite degree. And this is certain that every man may be higher and better than he is. It is ↑then↓ not only safe but salutary to make sacrifices and efforts for greatness, while it were madness and perdition to become stationary or retrograde. — It is very evident that there are two sorts of people in society; one which is capable of making those generalizations, and signal master-pieces of power which flow from and ascertain [16][22] greatness, and the other, which, sometimes with more pride and jealous self-respect, confines itself to the task of watching and analyzing those efforts. It is very observable that the second class is Argus-eyed, and that they are distinguished by an acuteness, which should seem destined for the first but fallen upon the second, to measure and compare, with lilliputian accuracy, the progress, conduct or defects of first minds. It may be cited as an example of what I affirm, that Newton was often at a loss when the conversation turned upon his own discoveries; ∧ that Shakspeare was indifferent or opposed to the publication of his works, and idly left his books, careless himself, for others, for Britain, or the world to boast of. It is impossible to make arithmetical computation of *mind*.[n] Still this indifference to trifles, and the sensibility to them, trace a very broad line of distinction between the first & second orders.

There is another remarkable trait about great moral or intellectual distinction which arises from the last; — I mean the obscurity in which it sometimes condemns itself to dwell, chiefly from its own self-willed unconcern to the rewards and prosperity which their fellow

[22] "(Greatness)" is centered beneath "that the highest" at the bottom of the page.

men have it in their power to bestow. And I am not sure but that the highest order of greatness, [17][23] that which abandons earthly consanguinity, and allies itself to immortal minds, is that which exists in obscurity and is least known among mankind. For, superiour intellects are only drawn out into society by the action of those inducements which society holds up to them. If, therefore, there are any who are above the solicitation of wealth, honour, and influence, and who can laugh even at the love of Fame, ↑that last infirmity of noble minds[,]↓ there will be nothing left worth offering them, to attract them from their solitudes; they must pass on through their discipline and education of life, unsympathised with, unknown, or perhaps, ignorantly despised. Thus the archangels pass among us unseen, for, if known, they could not be appreciated, and having faculties and energies which our organs can never measure, it is better that we never meet.

But this is speculating rather too boldly upon the distinctive features of a *social race*, and the nature of things will hardly sanction an opinion that those most able to direct the destinies of the mass, should, from their nature, depart from all intercourse among them. Moreover there are some men, whose talents, ill adapted to the multiplied details of business, do yet embrace grand and liberal views of politics and law, and are therefore exactly fitted for the offices of government, into which they naturally fall. It is so in every sphere from the lowest to the highest, and all are filled; which fact sufficiently [18] justifies the wisdom and *design* of the provision for *social* life, and still leaves room for the conjecture, that for unknown purposes, the *supreme* order of minds may suffer, think, and slumber, without acquaintance or respect in the world. ¶These last notions may serve to connect these remarks upon greatness with those upon *the social feelings* which were concluded on the 12 page.[24] March 6 —

[March 7] Be it recollected, that, in all adventurous speculations upon political society, this fact be borne in mind, that they are positively and obviously modified, throughout history, by some circum-

[23] The page number has been corrected from "19" to "17." "(Greatness)" is centered beneath "all are" at the bottom of the page.

[24] See Emerson's discussion of "Greatness" in Wide World 8, p. [39], which he prefaces: "Continued from W. [W.] No 4."

stances of climate or soil, which serve as stamina to keep a sameness and resemblance through all possible changes. e.g. Let Italy be assailed or prospered as she may, the government has always ⟨been⟩ tended to an indefinite division into small independent principalities, and has always from Alba Longa down to modern Naples displayed a marked inherent love of change.

⟨I am full sick of life⟩[25]
The Knight rode up to the castle-gate
But a grisly hag was there
She chattered in spite with muttered threat
And twisted her thin gray hair

2 Her half-bald pate was a sorry sight
But her eyes went wide askew
Two long dog-teeth like dim twilight
Shone over her lips so blue.

[19] 3 "Fair ladye of love!" the knight exclaimed,
And bent his body low
"Thou flower of beauty widely famed,
"Roses feed thee, I trow.

4 "The boy Cupide attendeth thee
"The Graces thy sisters be
"Oh give me a lock of thy golden hair
"And make a faithful knight of me"

5 The maiden clenched her shrivelled fist
And her eyes grew red with rage—
"You may mock, sir Simple, as loud as you list,
"But you shall be my chosen page.

6 "I'll give ye a lock of the hair that's left,
"Three hairs I'll give to thee;
"Beelzebub knows when I'm bereft
"I will the stronger be."

[25] In the left margin Emerson sketched the opening scene of the ballad, with the castle, the witch, and the knight on horseback. "(History. Ballad.)" appears in the bottom margin. Besides the changes shown in the text, Emerson underlined "shall be" and circled "chosen" (line 20), as though planning revision.

7 She plucked three hairs from her pye-bald head,
And shrieked like a fishhorn loud,
— Straight of those hairs three snakes were made,
That leaped on the champion good;

8 And one twined round his armed neck,
And one twined round each hand,
And the tails of the three in ⟨one⟩ ↑a black↓ braid met
In the grisly haggis hand,

9 And the hag she turned to a dragon green,
With these she flew away,
And never ⟨more⟩ ↑again↓ those two were seen,
Until the Judgement day.

[20][26] This book in ordinary is peculiarly devoted to original ideas but I cannot resist the pleasure of setting down, in black & white, verses which I have repeated so often. It is a charm in one of Ben Jonson's Masques.

"The faery beam upon you,
The stars to glister on you,
A moon of light,
In the noon of night,
⟨When⟩Till the fire-drake hath o'er-gone you.
The wheel of fortune guide you,
The boy with the bow beside you,

Run aye in the way,
Till the bird of day,
And the luckier lot, betide you." [*The Gypsies Metamorphosed*]

March 7

[March 7] It is the *social* and not the solitary state under which man in fact lives and therefore must be considered by those who write with comprehensive & wholesome views, and not merely to indulge useless speculations & the trick of fantasy. The moralist, who ponders to reform, the statesman, who plots to rule the state, must always adapt

[26] In the left margin, beside the last five lines of verse, are sketched a profiled head and a full view. "(Social Feelings.)" is centered under "unaided developement" at the bottom of the page.

their reasoning to *society*, as such. And may safely abandon every utopian scheme which expects the true perfection from the unaided developement of the human intellect.

[21][27] And it is in itself a most noble and magnificent subject,[n] and one to which all others seem tributary, which is here offered to the discussion of the wise. Not the preference of any one part of education, not the contested merits of any science or art, nor the counsels of an intriguing cabinet, nor a disputed theological point—are opened to our examination; but, how the combined energies of many millions of coexistent agents may be brought to act, with their proper infinite influence, continually in the direction of their sure interests, for time and eternity; and how the improvement which is gained may be kept, and the separate and conflicting energies, ↑may be↓ reconciled, and that ⟨the⟩ Mind shall reap all the fruits of the toil⟨s⟩ing of the body—to see how this may best be done is the design of all speculation upon this head. And every man who gives his unbiassed thought to this view will deem it worthy of sedulous attention and profound pursuit. Indeed it should seem no slight or ephemeral concern if we recollect how many have been occupied in solving these problems and with what poor success. The philosopher immured in his cell, the King on his throne, and the statesman in his senate have for ages professed to concentrate their researches and wisdom on this one study. But despite their deep-laid policy, they may still look out from their windows upon bloodshed and battle, upon fraud and vice, upon the deep and dark depravity of a race, whom their compassionate wisdom pretended to restore. It is possible [22][28] that we may come to the conclusion that it is indeed a subject of such vast compass and reach, as to outrun and baffle the struggling conceptions of man, and leave his sagacity at fault in the device of antidotes to the evil. It is possible that if the filmed eye of human understanding were purged to percieve clearly, it would only discern insurmountable obstacles in the way of perfection. God and man know how hopeless is the inference we derive from the past; but the dura-

[27] "(Social Feelings)" is centered under "wisdom pretended" at the bottom of the page.

[28] "(Social Feelings)" is centered beneath "And thanked" at the bottom of the page.

tion and events of the plan, which may take a novel course from other moral revelations — we do not know.

Note. The proper mode of pursuing this train of thought, would be to state, in a more definite manner, the advantages and condition of that state of society which would result ↑from↓ an entire harmony and cooperation of its parts, and, to shew why this effect has not, & cannot, be brought about; hence to deduce legitimate rules of conduct for the rational philanthropist; — and thus, at least, to clear our own notions upon so broad and intricate topics. I have given 9 or 10 pages now to *social feelings* or subjects connected with them and am inclined to think it were better to complete the remarks at another date. March 7.

[March 8]

1 In the dead of night on Castel-haye
An hundred torches gleamed
And their light sparkled far away
To the cave where Wallace dreamed.

2 From the rock *he* lifted his plumed head
And gazed upon the light; —
He shouted, and grasped his iron blade
And thanked our lady for the sight.

[23][29] 3 "God prosper *us*!" the hero cried
As he belted his sinewy limbs
"God prosper *us*" ⟨the caves⟩ ↑a voice↓ replied
From ⟨its⟩ ↑an↓ hundred caverns dim.

4 O'er rock and hill with rapid stride
The Scottish giant hastes
And now he climbs the mountain side
Wh⟨ere⟩ose ⟨the⟩ beacon lit the wastes

5 What stays his steps on Castel-haye?
What pageant maketh here?
— The English lords, and their array,
Are holding wassail ⟨to⟩ near

[29] "(Ballad)" is centered beneath "over" at the bottom of the page.

6 And that gay company are loud
In merriment and glee;
And dancers light, and barons proud,
Swell the full revelry.

7 In wanton mood the English Earl
Bade the Scotch dogs be brought;—
"Here in our face each rebel churl
"Shall add unto our sport."

8 In chains the rueful captives came,
And ⟨the⟩ laughter shook the hall,
And the dance and the wine and merry game
Went louder over all.

[24][30] 9 But hark! to the warlike peal
Of a Scottish clarion loud;
—And a giant form, with dazzling steel,
Broke in upon the crowd.

10 A cry of fear, a dying yell,
And a clank of broken chains!
—Lo! where the best of Britain fell
The pride of Scotland reigns.

March 8

If it be good to die, it is an ill thing to live; but many, who in the regret of a vexatious disappointment, or in the tedium of indolence, confess the last, will hardly be brought to invite or consent to dissolution. They act unwisely and inconsistent↑l↓y; Yea; but much may be said to sanction the last proposition which does not establish the first. For what is this *life*, which is so lightly esteemed & so jealously guarded? A few dark hours poisoned by evil, and clouded by anxiety whose good consists in this that in prospect they are invariably brilliant with hope, and the light leaves them as we arrive at them only to go on and gild those in advance. Thus the decieved being is led on till his eager pursuit is checked by the infirmities of age, and

[30] Figures of two warriors with shields and swords appear in the right margin beside the last two lines of verse. "(Death)" is centered beneath "the Urn" at the bottom of the page.

he falls down in the path, a dotard,—seeking to warn others who pass on incredulous and mock him. Life;—it is a few hours spanned out from the eternity of years—in which the soul may glean a few truths, comprehend the meaning of joy and of grief, pluck its own lot out of the Urn of fate, and descend to the grave [25][31] to write another Memento Mori on the history of the World. Such is the account of human life which the inquirer borrows from the voluptuary. It must be remembered that it is he who in his light & vapid hours calls the existence of the soul—a painted bubble, a rain bow, to be seen & lost,—that, in his melancholy ones, gives this false view of the same condition. Both are sufficiently distorted images, and the proper fruit of a reason & imagination which have been disordered by the intoxication of pleasure.

Those who have considered the condition of man with other views, and fair attention to the revelations of Divine Providence have another reply—Life is the spark which kindles up a soul and opens its capacities to recieve the great lessons which it is appointed to learn of the Universe—of Good—of Evil—of accountability—of Eternity, of Beauty, of Happiness. The inestimable moment in which ⟨it⟩ the history of past ages is opened, its own relations to the Universe explained, its dependence and independence shewn; the time to teach itself the affections and to gratify them, to ally itself in kindly bonds with other beings ⟨in the world⟩ of like destiny; the time to educate ⟨itself for⟩ ↑a citizen of↓ unknown spheres; the time to serve the Lord.

And is it good to die? to exchange this precious consciousness capable of such sublime purposes for an unknown state—(of which all that is seen is appalling); perhaps for a gloomy sleep? Is it good to be forced away against our will and through extreme suffering, from the vital body, and give up that organ of our enjoyments & sufferings to the worms, while what shall befall the soul we cannot tell? We shudder when the question is made, and terror, terror breaks down the vain refinements of [26][32] philosophy, and the fences of affectation.

Reason bids us ask who is the being that forces away the mind

[31] "(Death)" is centered beneath "terror breaks" at the bottom of the page.
[32] "(Drama)" is centered beneath "nothing" at the bottom of the page.

into this unknown state? Nature & Revelation have taught us something of this being. We are reduced to put our views of death entirely upon ⟨h⟩His character & will, ⟨of this⟩ and Death will become more or less terrible according to our notions of the lord of Death.—

Thus have I fulfilled enough of my design in this book to authorise my dedication on the first page. This shall not prevent me from ⟨pursuing⟩ ↑resuming↓ the topics upon the slightest indications of my Noömeter.

March 9. In connexion with the remarks on the Drama (Wide World, No 3.) it should be further, said, that this art is the most attractive, naturally, of all. The others speak to man from a distance, through cold & remote associations. The literature of a generation generally addresses but a scanty portion of Society; of their cotemporaries, history & poetry are confined to a few readers; philosophy & science to still fewer; but the buskined muse comes out impatient from these abstractions to repeat in a popular and intelligible form the productions of the Closet, to copy the manners of high & low life, to act upon the heart; and ⟨by⟩ succeeds, by thus avoiding the haughty port of the Parnassian queens, to draw the multitude by the cords of love. Folly wins where wisdom fails; and the policy of adding to our attractions even at the cost of some wit, is seldom repented. This is the excellence of the drama which pretends to nothing more than to be a true picture of life.

[27][33] The origin of Fiction is buried in the darkness of the remotest ages. If it were a question of any importance, perhaps its secret springs are not yet beyond the reach of the inquirer. To paint what is not, should ⟨be[?]⟩ naturally seem less agreeable to the mind than to describe what is. "Nothing," (said the author of the Essay on the human Understanding) "is so beautiful to the eye, as truth to the mind." But if we look again, I apprehend we shall find that the source of fable, is *human misery*; that to relieve one hour of life, by exciting the sympathies to a tale even of imaginary joy,

[33] "(Fiction)" is centered beneath "imaginary persons" at the bottom of the page.

was accounted a praiseworthy accomplishment; and honour & gold ⟨rewarded⟩ were due to him, whose rare talent took away, for the moment, the memory of ⟨the⟩ care⟨s⟩ ⟨of life⟩ ↑and grief↓. Fancy, which is ever a kind of contradiction to life & truth, set off in a path remote as possible from all human scenes & circumstances; and hence the first legends dealt altogether in monstrous scenes, and peopled the old mythology and the nursery lore, with magicians, griffins, and metamorphoses which offend the ear of taste, and could only win away the credulity of a savage race, and the simplicity of a child. Reason ⟨however⟩ soon taught the bard ⟨how⟩ that the deception was infinitely improved by being reduced within the compass of probability; and the second fictions introduced imaginary persons into the manners & dwellings of real life.

[28][34] In the northwestern part of the Arkansaw Territory, in the village of Colombo,[35] there has often been remarked a fiery red appearance in the atmosphere, long after the twilight has faded, and sometimes lasting for several hours until midnight. In that mountainous district, many of the phenomena of ⟨n⟩Nature are presented in such striking and unusual forms, that an occurrence of this description excites far less apprehension and alarm than would attend it in other regions. But this appearance had not failed to awaken a degree of Curiosity, somewhat unusual, at the first occupation of the district by the French and American settlers from the banks of the Missisippi. From the Indians, who seemed acquainted with the sight, they gathered some leading hints on which they formed, each for himself, a popular account of the Red-lights. But this industrious people, entirely occupied in clearing the country, and procuring a hard subsistence, were soon familiar with the phenomenon, and ceased to be anxious concerning it. Meantime, there was no man of education or leisure in the neighbourhood, who might investigate the causes of the wonder, and set right the vulgar errors respecting its nature. Continued in

[34] "(Tale)" is centered at the bottom of the page beneath "future termination."

[35] Inside the cover of his College Theme Book Emerson made a sketch of a village with this name. See p. 162, n. 1. If Emerson "continued" this "Tale" as he apparently intended to, the rest of it has not been located.

March 10 No talent is more prized, in society, than that sagacity which, from passing events, draws just & profound conclusions regarding their future termination. The names of Burke, Fox, [29][36] and Pitt deservedly rank high in the world's esteem from the success of their political predictions. For it argues a singular elevation of mind to generalize so calmly in the conflicting interests and partialities of fortune, to see something inevitable in the almost fortuitous concurrence of affairs, to cast a die into the whirl of events, and rest in confidence of its return. This, however, is but a faint approach to the majesty of that remarkable foresight which was exhibited in the early ages of the world, and termed Prophecy. For the one is of inferior origin, and depends altogether upon a shrewd comparison of present with past events, and a critical attention to the bias and results of a form of government, of a national character, of a popular excitement. The other grasps at indications which are invisible to other eyes and possesses a new faculty of communication with the universe. It does not follow the general progress of things to a general result; but singles out, with admirable distinctness, the one man or event, for which its lips were opened; and, entirely destitute of any manifest clue to its knowledge, describes, with a precision not to be mistaken, the character, circumstances, and use of things which are buried in a futurity of many ages. It sensibly elevates our notions of the human mind, to discover in it this latent capacity of reaching through the accidents of time, to ascertain a destiny beyond the possibility of crass accidents [30][37] to change. It is a capacity which every soul looks to enjoy hereafter, and its developement here is a signal distinction from the hand of Providence and an earnest to the soul of an unclouded vision to come. Twenty five hundred years (2534) ago, the prophet Isaiah stood up on the banks of the Dead Sea and looked towards Babylon,[n] and denounced upon the Queen of the Earth his melancholy vengeance—"How hath the golden city ceased! Thy pomp is brought down to the grave, and the noise of thy viols; the worm is spread under thee and the worms cover thee. All the Kings of the nations, even all of them lie in glory, every one in his own

[36] "(Prophecy)" is centered beneath "destiny beyond" at the bottom of the page.

[37] "(Prophecy)" is centered beneath "offers of Rev⟨i⟩elation," at the bottom of the page.

house; but thou art cast out of thy grave like an abominable branch. Howl ye, howl ye, for Babylon!" — Fate is fulfilled; Babylon is as silent as the Jewish seer; the owl, the cormorant, & the bittern usurp the dwellings of her hundred thousand sons; her formidable and overbearing power has become the shadow of a shade; her character, her place and memory have passed away from the earth and her only undying memorial is the song of the awful minstrel which portended her fall, and a proverbial name which has gone out among men as the monument of ruin & wrath. The proper treatment of this fine subject should be to consider its nature in the mind of the *prophet*, to enter somewhat more seriously into an historical view, — of the interval between the Word & the fulfilment, of the opportunities of the prophet and the circumstances of the fulfilment, and from these deduce the high evidence which prophecy offers to Rev⟨i⟩elation, and compare the [31][38] same with the evidence of miracles, &c. &c.

(Perhaps you have never lifted the torch to the nocturnal orgies of Bacchus, of vice, of lust, — but was the inclination & the heart as pure as the hand? has mean and paltry prudence never witholden the gift of charity? Perhaps the important domestic duties have been well & duly discharged but has human pride, (the most absurd & contemptible feeling, in the nature of things, that can be) never tossed the head over the humbler destiny of a fellowman?)

Sabbath Evening, March 10

We complain of change and vicissitude. Say rather, there pursues us always an eternal sameness, an unchanging identity. Did not Caesar and the men of Rome see the same stars, suffer from the same storms, feel the same infirmities? Were they not chilled, wet, and warmed, by the same variations of weather, were they not hungry, athirst, ragged & unfortunate, like the men of this month? Our common conversation but translates theirs, just as we apply to ourselves their addresses to the elements or to the feelings. The world,

[38] Between "the" and "evidence" in the first line, Emerson computes the number of years since the prophecy of Isaiah by adding "712" to "1822" and arriving at "2534" as the sum. "(Conclusions)" is centered under "the Assyrian" at the bottom of the page.

the universe is just the same; only, each man's mind undergoes a perpetual change, and the vainglorious dreamer attributes to Nature and Fortune the alteration which transpires within himself alone. The Ocean heaves up his stormy pride alike against all through each age of empire;—the Assyrian, the Jewish, the Grecian, the [32] Roman, the Vandal, the Turkish, the British, the American;

> "Time writes no wrinkle on thine azure brow;
> Such as Creation's dawn beheld, thou rollest now."
> [Byron, *Childe Harold's Pilgrimage*, IV, 182]

How is it that we preserve so accurately the knowledge of events and minds coeval with the Pyramids? How know we the history of the causes of private ambition or public outrage? It is because every man bears within him a record of other men's motives; inasmuch as there is engraven upon his soul passion & perception of outward things—which tend every where to the same effects, so he can form fair & probable judgements of the manner in which—comfort, plenty, power, all which are comprehended in ↑the possession of↓ a Crown would act upon him. The Egyptian priestess who had washed her sacred robe, the crafty Greek at Delphi who had succeeded indifferently well in his oracular riddle, the Corinthian merchant who added in his books another talent as his future dues from the extravagant proconsul—all felt in their repose the same kind of satisfaction which pleases me in closing another book.

March 10, 1822.

Wide World 6

1822

The missing Wide World 5 would presumably have covered the gap from March 10 to April 14 when Wide World 6 begins. The dated entries here run from April 14 to July 10, 1822.

The manuscript of fifty-six pages is composed of a single gathering of fourteen folded sheets hand-stitched, making up a notebook of twenty-eight leaves. Like that of the other Wide Worlds the paper is foolscap folded folio, but here two sizes of sheets have been used. As a result twelve leaves are approximately 17 x 20.5 cm; the other sixteen leaves are approximately 15 x 19.2 cm. The pagination in the journal runs from 1–52 rather than from 1–56 because of a repeated pagination: after the normal numbered sequence from 1–9, the numbers 6–9 are repeated before the pagination returns to order with the page numbered 10. This irregularity in sequence is indicated in the present text by the subscript numbers 1 and 2, added respectively to the first and second appearance of the repeated page numbers.

[1][1] ["Maximus partus temporis,"[2] quoth giggling Vanity. "Burn the trash," saith Fear.]

Wideworld No. 6

"There the Northern light reposes
With ruddy flames in circles bright
Like a wreath of ruby roses
On the dusky brow of Night" [R. W. E.]

[1] The journal title is enclosed in an elliptical, shaded, fringed figure. In the left margin, from "Wideworld" to "(DEDICATION.)" is a pencilled profile of a man's head. A small, very rough, pencil sketch of a man's head and shoulders follows the date.

[2] "The greatest production of [your] time" (Ed.).

Boston, April 14, 1822.

(DEDICATION.)

In aforetime, while to the inhabitants of Europe, the existence of America was yet a secret in the heart of time, there dwelled a Giant upon the South Mountain Chimborazo, who extended a beneficent dominion over hills and clouds and continents, and sustained a communication with his mother—Nature. He lived two hundred years in that rich land, causing peace and justice, and he battled with the Mammoths, and slew them. Upon the summit of the mountain, amid the snows of all the winters, was the mouth of a cave which was lined with golden ore. This cavity, termed "The Golden Lips" admitted downwards into the centre [n] of the mountain which was a vast and spacious temple, and all its walls and ceilings glowing with pure gold. Man had never polluted it with his tools of art. Nature fashioned the mighty tenement, for the bower of her son. At midday, the vertical sun was perpendicular to the cavity, and poured its full effulgence upon the mirror floor; ⟨and⟩ its reflected beams blazed on all sides from the fretted roof, with a lustre which eclipsed the elder glory of the temple of Solomon. In the centr||e|| of this gorgeous palace, bareheaded and alone, the Giant Califor||n|| [2] performed the incommunicable rite, and studied the lines of destiny. When the sun arrived at the meridian, a line of light traced this inscription upon the wall—"A thousand years, A thousand years, and the Hand shall come, and shall tear the Veil for all." Two thousand years have passed, and the mighty progress of improvement & civilization have been forming the force which shall reveal Nature to Man. To roll about the outskirts of this Mystery and ascertain and describe its pleasing wonders—be this the journey of my Wideworld. The ⟨h⟩*Hand* shall come;—I traced its outline in the mists of the morning.

To Melancholy.[3]

I Sable Goddess, clad in weeds,

[3] Emerson wrote vertically in the left margin upward, from the fifth line of stanza III (below) to the second line of stanza I (above): "'If I did know / A hoop to hold us staunch, from edge to edge / Of the world I'd seek it.' / Ant. & Cleop." "(Melancholy)" is written at the bottom of the page, slightly below and to the right

Nurse of wo, and midnight deeds,
Whose tattered pall the sighing night-wind bears
When thy slow step forsakes the sepulchres
Amid this starless, moonless Night
I call thee now from weary flight
To ⟨|| . . . ||⟩fold thy ponderous wings and soothe
thy savage might.

II I know a brow with furrows deep,
I know an eye whose lightnings sleep,
Far ⟨from the haunts of men, we lonely⟩ ↑in the
lonely woods, that form I↓ met
By starlight, when the summer dews ⟨were⟩fell wet;
But who had knit his lofty brows!
— Thou Goddess, and th⟨y⟩' austerest vows
That ever bowed the frame, in penitential
house.

III And truly this one is my friend,
And we shall love till life doth end,
For both have courted Melancholy long,
Until we learned to love the plaintive song;
We part from men and follies vain,
↑With rose wreaths↓ ⟨And gentle⟩ Friendship
binds the twain
And thou ⟨sad Melancholy!⟩ ↑O dark eyed
Daemon↓ consecrate the chain!

[3][4] Tuesday Evg Apr 16

It is strange that a world should be so dear which speculatively and seriously we acknowledge to be so unsatisfying and so dark. Not all its most glorious array when Nature is apparelled in her best, and when ⟨a⟩Art toils to gratify, — not the bright sun itself, and the blazing firmament wherein he stands as chief — can prevent a man,

---

of the last line of verse. The stanza numbering is Emerson's. The last four lines, originally in pencil, have been written over and revised in ink.

[4] "(VAIN WORLD)" is centered beneath "attracting" at the bottom of the page.

at certain moments, from saying to his soul—"It is vanity." No wild guesses, no elaborate reasoning can surmount this testimony to the familiar truth, that the human spirit hath a higher origin than matter, a higher home than the earth; that it is too capacious to be always cheated with trifles, and too long-lived, to amalgamate with mortality. But this is more strange and unaccountable; that in a bad world at which all are content to rail, the mind should rarely look up, of its own accord to seek the consolation of a better hope; that true and rational pleasure should never dictate an early fondness to anticipate and weigh these expectations; while on the contrary it is *now* left to *pain*, to physical or mental *distress*, to drive us reluctantly upon this *hard formidable* prospect of our happiness & perfection. No honest and noblc aspirations to fulfil the duties of our highest sphere, to meet with the Divinity, find place within us;—but contemptible bodily pain which we have not the courage to encounter, or the force of mind to despise, sets upon idle wishing for a better world, ⟨for⟩from so mean a motive as to escape a transitory pang of this. It plainly shews that though there be a spirit, it is narrowly crowded & mingled with coarse & sordid *clay* which can be tickled with the straws & baubles of a ⟨sh⟩dazzling world and easily moulded to its vain purposes. It was found by philosophy that luminous matter wastes itself ever; it is true without a metaphor of this shining world which goes on decaying and still attracting by its false lustre.

They called the pope's court at Avignon the western Babylon—circum 1310–40.[5]

[4] It is matter of great doubt to me whether or not the *populace* of all ages is essentially the same in character. I am not a competent judge to decide if inconsistent institutions will affect & alter the prominent features of the moral character. There can be no question that from both the poles to the Equator, under every sun, man will be found *selfish* and comparatively indifferent to the general welfare whenever it is put in competition with private interest. But in China

[5] This sentence is crowded to the right of "(VAIN WORLD)" in the bottom margin.

as in Venice, will faction & cabal always watch to check the continuance of every administration, good or bad? Will vulgar blood always rebel and rail and against honourable, virtuous, and opulent members of the same society? Will the good always be in peril from the misdeeds & menaces of the bad? In the answer to these interrogations, truth leans reluctantly towards the affirmative. This is certain that war is waged in the universe, without truce or end, between Virtue & Vice; they are Light & Darkness, they cannot harmonize. Upon Earth they are forcibly consorted, and the perpetual struggle which they make, separates by a distinct line, Man from Man, throughout the world.

The facts relative to the penitent processions in Italy at the commencement of the 15th Century prove a different populace. See Sismondi Vol 7[6] [*Histoire des Républiques Italiennes au Moyen Âge*]

Copy of a letter silly[7]

[Letter omitted]

[6_1][8] Apr. [20] 1822—Scarcely any thing in history creates such a fascination as the narrative of stratagems & political slights with which its pages in some periods abound. The record of the triumphs of eloquence hath a similar charm; but if unsupported, eloquence generally fails of any lasting or prospective effect; and in its best examples as in Rienzi, Cicero, & Demosthenes, the excited hopes which we ⟨for⟩ build upon the enthusiasm attending immediately upon its display, are wofully disappointed by the languid result. —Its misfortune is that it gratifies by its novelty, and therefore wear↑ie↓s ⟨out⟩ by use, so that it can be ⟨only⟩ employed to great ad-

[6] This paragraph is crowded into the space between the close of the previous paragraph and the beginning of the next.

[7] The spacing and size of "silly" suggest that it was added later by Emerson. Following this word, "[to Motte]" is written in pencil, probably by Edward Waldo Emerson. Emerson later drew crisscrossed cancellation lines through the letter, which continued to the center of p. [6_1]. The letter, on pp. [4], [5], [6_1], is printed in full in *L*, I, 108–109. Page numbers [6], [7], [8], [9] are repeated, as indicated by subscript numbers.

[8] "(Letter to Motte / Cunning)" is centered from "which" to "⟨being⟩" at the bottom of the page.

vantage ↑only↓ where any thing is to be decided by a violent & brief effort and must be set aside when the object to be attained, demands a patient exertion or series of persevering exertions.[n] But Cunning is a weapon which does not rust with time, and it is the only quality which of itself without ⟨being⟩ the aid of power [7₁][9] or wealth can attain them both, and maintain a permanent & progressive interest in society. It conveys the most agreeable idea of Power to see a solitary individual, by the ⟨mere⟩ ↑native↓[10] force of intellect, setting at work numerous & mighty engines in the midst of intelligent society; working in various ways upon the passions & interests of many men, and inducing them to do what but yesterday appeared contrary to their views & profit; gradually extending the numbers & purposes of his agents in every direction,[n] and by the energy & uniformity of his individual views concentrating, with exquisite skill, ⟨the⟩ a thousand operations upon one design; — Managing a whole community as the Architect controuls his builders so that each ⟨ignorantly⟩, ↑solely bent on↓ doing his own part, is yet subservient to a harmonious whole. A man of these comprehensive powers is emphatically a host in himself, and commonly proves of better service to a party than an organized army or a full treasury. Why? because without the immense risk & uncertainty attending the use of that dreadful instrument ↑the Army↓ which may be turned against yourself and may be broken; and without the difficulty, odium, or temptation which wait upon the other, the sagacity of a⟨n⟩ rational, consistent, & collected individual can convert to its own advantage these great instruments which are so painfully procured. Innocent VI sent into Italy the Cardinal Albornoz to recover & add to the possessions of the Church, without troops or treasures,[11] and the Cardinal found at his arrival but two castles acknowledging allegiance to the pope.[n] ⟨w⟩When Urban V required of the legate an account of his administration he sent him by way of answer, a Chariot completely filled with the keys of the cities & castles he had reduced to submission. Italian annals are fertile in similar characters, and their longsighted & profound

[9] "(CUNNING.)" is centered beneath "Castracani &c &c" at the bottom of the page.

[10] Inserted in pencil.

[11] "or treasures" is encircled by Emerson.

intrigues, and the perfect success of bold & consummate stratagems; as, for instance the plot which ensnared & ruined the army of Bileggio ⟨at⟩ ↑sent to↓ the siege of Bologna by Bernabos Visconti; the pretended sickness of *Azzo* the Archbishop—(See Wideworld No. 5.); the revolution of Genoa; the exploits of Castruccio Castracani &c &c. In other history take

↑"Jesuits are a people who lengthen the creed and shorten the decalogue." Abbé Boileau↓ [12]

[8₁][13] the achievements of Carthaginian Hannibal; of Belisarius. These present a much more moving picture to the mind when the feats of cunning are exhibited in War,—because in that event the eyes of men are wide open and the ablest & noblest are naturally thrust into the foremost places, so that it argues great powers of dissimulation and artifice to decieve hostile vigilance & break up their coalitions. The ballads of every nation attest the instances of this skill and the popular admiration which pursues them. Fraud circumvents force; the lion was taken in flaxen toils. The activity & skill of an humble individual neutralizes or destroys the efforts of superior might, & superior resources; as the light footed Mercury, in classic lore, ↑when he had↓[14] purloined the thunderbolts↑, ↓⟨and⟩ safely defied the vengeance of Jupiter.
April 20.—

Saturday Evg [April], I rejoice in the full and unquestionable testimony which certifies the sufferings of Martyrs, as the most undeniable merit of the human race; it proves the existence of a consistency & force of character which might else to common minds appear chimerical. Martyrdom is a triumph of virtue which the daily concerns of life ought never to set aside from the Memory. In those moments when a desperate view of the wrong side of society will

[12] Charles Boileau, Abbé de Beaulieu (d. 1704), author of *Homélies et Sermons sur les Évangelist du Carême* (Paris, 1712). The quotation is crowded to the right of "(CUNNING.)" at the bottom of the page.

[13] "MARTYRDOM" is centered beneath "atone for the" at the bottom of the page.

[14] The insertion and following cancellation are in pencil, apparently by Emerson.

sometimes totally unsettle our convictions and reason almost leans to doubt and Atheism,[n] because the world is frail or mad, this saving recollection comes up like an angel of light to assure us that men have suffered the fierceness of the torture, have endured, & died for the faith and that these could therefore abide in the road of virtue unswerving, could disdain and deny the blandishments of vice & the petty considerations of worldly pride. They are happy; for if man can in aught atone for the great transgression, they [9_1][15] have paid a redeeming ransom, and blood for blood they have answered for the sin of their race. To keep inviolate the divine law, they have broken over the law of nature & the native fears of man and have dared to immolate this mysterious existence and to try the gulfs of futurity. This is a sacrifice which must be acceptable in the eye of God; for every mind in the universe strikes in sympathy with the nobleness of the deed, and from the necessity of its nature, applauds.

It is a mournful reverse to turn from this belief, and it is fatally favourable to an opinion of degeneracy to cast an eye upon the surface of society in order to the inquiry whether any traces of this best human spirit can be discerned. Watchman, what of the night? [Isaiah, xxi, 11]. Watchman what of the night? And what are the objects which your scrutiny detects? — The frivolous & flattered heart; the glistening & pampered eye; Pleasure sauntering forth in pursuit of wicked & riotous gratification; Passion & Folly, lust, & pride seeking indulgence in the earth; Fashion sacrificing[n] virtue & principle, body & mind to the fear of man. Mammon abandoning the love of men, the peace of conscience, & the hopes of heaven to an accursed & engrossing pursuit of short-lived wealth; and[n] behind all these a crowd of indolent & passive men who are content to sleep with the dull or mock with the profane wasting the measured hours of life, and losing the season allotted to secure heaven, in a lethargy without excuse or hope. And these are the fellow men and the children of martyrs! — Is there one ↑think you,↓ in all this enormous & lightheaded throng who will give his body to the axe for ⟨the⟩ a testimony ↑t↓o⟨f⟩ the truth. In your parlours, ⟨&⟩in the circles which dance in the saloons of fashion, in all who devote life to the contemptible "solicitudes of

[15] "(Martyrdom)" is centered beneath "philosopher. But" at the bottom of the page.

dress" and to the worse indulgence of appetite, — is it probable, is it possible that I shall find one solitary man ready to renounce these happy vanities and to die for his opinion. It certainly is from this inauspicious glance at society that this doubt is derived which, I make no question, has often damped the sanguine hopes of the enthusiast & sobered the speculations of the moral philosopher. But I shall nevertheless declare in [6_2][16] answer that I think there are hundreds. I hold a higher opinion of this wonderful being whom God hath made in his own image than to believe that if properly excited to his duty when the fires of persecution raged he would basely neglect or surrender his sacred opinion. Such minds are grossly culpable, who, in the possession of such divine energies, forsake and betray them to the seduction of vanity, sloth, & sin. — Have you not one generous sigh, one secret aspiration for the stern glories of Martyrdom? Not one bold sentiment, that, if need were, you would claim with zeal the saint's crown of thorns? Think not that your faith ↑only↓ wants the proof of a religious proscription, of a day of intolerance & massacre. There is a cross erected, a discipline ordained. — Crucify the lusts of the flesh, the desire of the eye, &c &c[.]

Hush, ye vain thoughts that clamour where ye lurk,
Ye silly vanities, & pampered lusts,
⟨Y⟩The little throbs of exstacy, which beat
To Joy's light song — unseasonable now —
Farewell, and carry your harsh music hence
An Abortion this

April 1822

In the eternal & enchanting variety of sky & season, amid the softness of the first vernal airs, there is yet a melancholy voice which makes itself heard, teaching the vanity of joy, the neighbourhood of remorse; saying that Nature acts the part of a deciever, when in this scene of human danger & fate, she wears so gay & gorgeous apparel.

[16] Page number repeated. From this page [6_2] on, Emerson numbers consecutively to the end of the journal, p. [52]. To the left of the verses are two pencil sketches, two men's heads in profile; to the right are two other pencil sketches, a man's face and a profile. "ABORTIONS" is centered beneath "This wide" at the bottom of the page.

Upon a field as beautiful as the plains of Eden, painted & perfumed with flowers, and bright with morning dews, two armed hosts of men array their lines to murder each other. This is a mockery of God's beautiful creation; but this is an emblem of the whole world. In the spicy gardens and beneath the orange groves of the Indies the abused captive sighs & toils. The intoxicating gales which please the sense with odours [n] ↑as you sail upon the waters of↓ Arabia & Africa waft in the same course the chained slave to the land of his captivity. This wide vegetable creation whose bud [72][17] & bloom and fruit delight the heart with beauty, & support the life of man, does also nurse in its expanding leaves the seeds of corruption; and man shall find as he lifteth up his eyes to enjoy his wide dominion that there lurks amidst this abundant Paradise an infant pestilence growing up to be a Minister of Vengeance and the enemy of the nations.

—Now here again is another detached morsel intended to be merely the first lines of a long treatise upon fate & life, &c, but it is cropped in the bud by the fiend Caprice; and I must gallop away to some new topic which my fantastic Genius may suggest[.]

Something Silly.

There died an old man at St. Mary's the Pier
And his body was buried from a beautiful bier
But his wife the next night was assailed by his ghost
Which she saw in the doorway, but did not accost.

That evening the lamps in the street were all lit
And though the rain poured, they did not intermit;
While the wide dusky puddles, by reflection, that shone,
Still blushed to *reflect*—that it was not their own.

That light dimly poured through the glass window-pane
Dust-coated by time, but new-washed by the rain.
And the crooked rays fell on the lady's new cap
And her features portending some dismal mishap

[17] Page number repeated. A very rough sketch of the full-length figure of a woman is pencilled vertically in the margin to the left of the stanzas. "JOKE." is centered beneath "pleasing" at the bottom of the page.

The ghost of her spouse in the corner did stand
Gently holding the ghost of his hat in his hand
He made a low bow; she stared at the ghost
And he suddenly turned himself into a post!

April [28, 1822]

Speculative men are prone to remark that the world presents no variety; that this age beholds the same characters & the same scenes from which the elder moralists deduced ominous or pleasing conclusions; that while [8₂][18] modes & forms change, the principle remains substantially the same. A mingled principle, they call it,—a wayward compound of good & ill, wherein some find more to blame, & others more to praise; but all complain, that it proves itself, at bottom, every where alike, producing, for its results, on the surface of society, a monotonous and unpleasing aspect. There is another view of human affairs which bids them complain if they list, while it fiercely admonishes them that while they murmur at this weary calm they ought to be thankful that the storm is not loosed and this uniform peace broken up by the dreadful activity of the unchained elements.

This ordinary tenor of society, this mixture of the good & bad, may be called the balance & equilibrium of the world, which when restored, gives the common peace to mankind. But there has been a stage in human history, (God in heaven avert its return,) when this balance has been overturned, when in the eternal combat of the Good & Evil Principle, the ⟨e⟩Evil hath prevailed, and; in the strong rebellion of depravity, Virtue went nigh to be extirpated from mortal dwellings. This may be called the unnatural state of society. In the divine appointment, it was by such a storm that the Jewish Commonwealth became a wreck; and the man who at this day looks over that frightful & blotted page of history, is amazed at such a representation of fellow-beings, and is oppressed by the conviction that in that awful departure Εντ↑ε↓υθεν εκβαινωμεν,[19] in parting with their Divinity, they had parted also with the ↑remains of↓ human character, & those

[18] Page number repeated. "VARIETY" is centered beneath "example, &" at the bottom of the page.

[19] "Let us go out from here" (Ed.).

forsaken miscreants acted under diabolic delirium. That war finds no resemblance, no copy in any other period of earthly history; and those who look for repetition & ceaseless analogies from age to age, may sigh, if they will, for such another interruption of the order of events. (Note. In the above may first be named the French "Reign of Terror" as an example, & then the old sentence of "More terrible anecdotes" &c)

[9_2][20] There is another unnatural state of society & the reverse of this ill-starred iniquity; ⟨th⟩I mean *that*, where, for a brief period, too much go⟨d⟩od prevails, to be consistent with the condition of human frailty, & the attraction of worldly temptations. It can only attend the strong & sustained excitement of a new & zealous sect, of a select & enthusiastic society; and though its *permanence* is fabled, it can endure only through one, or perhaps two generations. (Adduce examples.) Sunday Evg Apr 28, 1822

[May 1, 1822] In a former page I said something of the uniform character of the populace, of all ages & nations. It may be well to record every deviation from their distinguishing general features as a remarkable exception which must flow from remarkable varieties in government or information. It has been said that the 14th. Century set in storms. Italy was the most remarkable nation which then figured in the world, and it is a singular fact that there prevailed at that period a deep conviction throughout that & other countries that the end of the world was at hand. It is not precisely known whence this superstition originated, but it was wofully corroborated by the tremendous public calamities which fell, plague on plague & war on war, upon the nations of Christendom. ⟨By⟩In those extended pestilences which diminished the numbers of mankind one third, (?) a singular providence was observed, that almost every personage eminent for virtues & popular esteem to any great degree, was swept [10][21] off by the malady, while all the bad & all feared & detested men were spared. Next to this the exterminating wars which raged between France & England & then between the Italian republics, which had

[20] Page number repeated. "POPULACE" is centered beneath "esteem to" at the bottom of the page.

[21] "POPULACE" is centered beneath "for the" at the bottom of the page.

loosened the bonds of the social state and introduced vice & profligacy public & private beyond all measure & example, had left this mournful impression upon the public mind that the Crimes of Men were thus visited with signal retribution portending the speedy arrival of Eternal Judgement. It may be added that the loss to the Christian cause of Jerusalem which might have been regarded as a Palladium of hopes & redemption, & the already tottering ruin of Constantinople while the borders of Europe ↑from side to side↓ were menaced by the hosts of the Caliphs dispirited every wider prospect of joy & aggrandizement. These melancholy feelings in society broke out in the most uncommon & striking manifestations of a prevalent sense of ↑human↓ desolation which the world ever saw. One Italian city poured out almost its whole population, men, women, & children, clothed in white garments to swell the enormous procession of penitents which thronged all the roads to the churches & shrines & filled the air with wailings for sin & passionate invocations of mercy. This peaceful train went from city to city until they diffused far & wide this religious enthusiasm. In every warlike city those active warriors were seen exchanging helmet & the mail for the Cowl, & the martial word of command for the psalm of penitence.

[11][22] The occupations of ⟨men,⟩ ↑Commerce↓ & the havoc of war ceased for a time, & were absorbed in this tumultuous devotion. All men seem to have buried their distinctions & animosities in an oppressive sense of desperate depravity, and to have gazed in each others faces with the confidence of mutual misery under the cloud of vengeance which blackened overhead. That dismal popular imagination passed away; they returned each man to his several service; one, to his ship & commerce; another to his plough, a third to the sword & massacre; the phantom & the fear were soon forgotten and they began anew the race of depravity. Such is the anecdote of the populace in one age & country and which finds no obvious parallel in other portions of history. I do not know that ↑a↓ modern faction or mob might be wrought up to exhibit such a representation as this; but it is plain that it would require a discipline as extraordinary to reduce them to this; it would require that they should be degraded

[22] "POPULACE" is centered beneath "contention" at the bottom of the page.

to an equal prostration of guilt to that which weig[h]ed down the pride of the Italian cities in order that men with the common virtues of society should confess to such unpardonable load of crime. A consideration of the ecclesiastical & political history of the Middle ages will certainly establish the opinion that modern Europe boasts a state of society beyond comparison more composed, virtuous, & tranquil. The extravagant perpetrations of a church faction upon life & property went beyond all bounds, and often exceeded even savage ferocity. The Greens & Blues of Constantinople, the Blacks & Whites of Florence, distinctions founded on some idle & forgotten freak equalled in their contention the devilish horrors of the [12][23] French Revolution. Now this last is a solitary & awful example, in modern times, of popular fury, & the result, some say, of ages of misrule; whereas the seditions we have named, & a multitude of similar ones, were looked upon in their era as ephemeral & not very uncommon. These views strongly corroborate a remark of the Edinburgh Review, that after the horrors of a revolution have become in a degree familiar, some of that reluctance to their return, which men feel, is worn off, since they partake of the nature of ↑a habit of intoxication↓ or deep play. Moreover, the acuteness & mental activity of the Italians forbids us to draw any rash conclusions touching a better diffusion of knowledge at this day and ↑seems to↓ reduce⟨s⟩ us to the mortifying conclusion that the peace of Europe of right belongs to the perfection of its *police*. There is no such mixture of disagreeable truth, in the quiet of our own nation. The entire internal repose of this country owes nothing to vigorous restriction or armed law. The spirit of the people is peace, & the sword at its side is for ornament rather than use. I will not believe that it is ignorance to esteem my birthright in America as a preferable gift to the honours of any other nation that breathes upon Earth. The Genius of Britain treads with fear upon an unsound & perilous footing[,] burning beneath with flame to an unknown extent. And America has inherited the free step & unconstrained attitude which her parent hath lost by age. May 1 1822

Dum a dum, now, but the book *does* grow better.

[23] "POPULACE" is centered at the bottom of the page beneath the transposed Latin phrase and above this Latin passage is a faint profile sketch.

The Ancients' idea of Fate is thus expressed by Seneca [*Dialogues* I, 5. 8]. "Ille ipse omnium conditor et rector scripsit quidem fata sed sequitur. Semper paret, semel jussit."[24]

[13][25] May 3

Habit is a thing of compound character which forges chains for human nature at the same time that ↑it↓ announces ⟨the⟩ ↑its↓ consistency & independence. It is a thorough & perfect servitude, but man voluntarily imposed it upon himself. It is a noble foresight which at once determines upon actions that will be perpetually proper, and makes one resolution answer for a thousand, and once made, binds with divine force. When we consider it as an *instrument*—put into the hands of Vice & Virtue, which both may wield to certain, to vast[n] advantage, we shall have an adequate idea of its importance in the constitution of human life. In childhood it is given into the power of all to make choice between Virtue & Vice to whom he will commit th⟨is⟩e service of this magic Wand.

Sunday Evg [May 5] In the Morning of life, among the first voluntary ⟨actions⟩ exertions, every action is solitary & independent, the effect of the opening consciousness of free agency; and if the being continued to renew & change its condition, its operations would still be dissimilar & solitary; but *Habit* is the necessary result of the human constitution. Opposite & contrary wants are not felt, but the same set of desires which were felt & gratified return again & demand the same exertion; so that the individual finds himself compelled by the necessity of his nature to repeat certain actions at regular intervals, and thus learns from his bodily wants, the meaning of Habit. Reason directing always the operations of the body, & forming that mysterious connection ↑which exists↓ between matter & spirit, the mind soon learns to apply this new rule to its own faculties. At stated impulses, a train of ideas is regularly excited. &c But this

[24] "Although the great creator and ruler of the universe himself wrote the decrees of Fate, yet he follows them. He obeys forever, he decreed but once." (Emerson first wrote "Semel jussit, semper paret," but then numbered the phrases to indicate their transposition.)

[25] "HABIT" is centered beneath "learn the" at the bottom of the page.

leads us rather too far from the plain considerations of the subject—

Being, as it is, something which grows out of our present human condition, it is difficult to separate habit from Nature & determine upon its abstract character. It appears to be imposed as a part of the human education; Man, who in the Universe of intelligent Souls, is an infant but just admitted to that vast & unknown commonwealth, is placed upon earth to learn the first elements of existence. We do not [14][26] trust a child with the management of himself; and man, in this primal stage, has not acquired the command of his faculties; they[n] are put under the wholesome restraint of Habit. In a higher condition, when the first lesson of existence hath been learned, the force of Habit may be removed, & the Spirit administer absolutely its properties & powers. Each movement of the Archangel is perhaps free & independent of every former one. These speculations are not entirely fruitless, because they ⟨let us into⟩ ↑teach us↓ the nature of Habit, that it does not necessarily form a part of a rational being; that it is actually a protection to human nature from wildness & irregularity of action; that seeing how potent an instrument it is, we do not abuse or tamper with it. (The body is the prison of the mind, because, perhaps in its infancy it could not be safely free; so Habit, I concieve, may be instituted as a requisite restraint—⟨put this above⟩ So armour is necessary to the protection of ⟨ordi⟩ mortal warriors; but to the miraculous might of David ↑in the struggle with Goliath↓ it was despised as an incumbrance.) [For "Habit" see "Hartley on Man," "Butler's Analogy," "Buckminster's Sermons"—and when I have seen these, I will write more.] Spare us!

⟨Amid⟩ May 7, Tuesday Evg. Amid my diseases & aches & qualms I will write to see if my brains are gone. For a day or two past we have had a wind precisely *annual*; which I discover by *this*, that I have a return of the identical thoughts & temperament which I had a year ago. But this Sun shines upon & these ill winds blow over—a changed person in condition, in hope. I was then delighted with my recent honours, traversing my chamber (Hollis 9) flushed & proud of a poet's fancies, & the day when they were to be exhibited; pleased with ambitious prospects & Careless because ignorant of the

[26] "HABIT" is centered beneath "even" at the bottom of the page.

future. But now I'm a hopeless Schoolmaster just entering upon years of trade to which no distinct limit is placed; toiling through this miserable employment even without the poor satisfaction [15][27] of discharging it well, for the good suspect me, & the geese dislike me. Then again look at this: there was pride in being a collegian, & a poet, & somewhat romantic in my queer acquaintance with ⟨Gay;⟩ and poverty presented nothing mortifying in the meeting of two young men whom their common relation & character as scholars equalised.[n] But when one becomes a droning schoolmaster, and the other is advancing his footing in good company & fashionable friends, the cast of countenance ⟨at⟩on meeting is somewhat altered. Hope, it is true, still hangs out, though at further distance, her gay banners; but I have found her a cheat once, twice, many times, and shall I trust the deciever again? And what am I the better for two, four, six years delay? Nine months are gone, and except some rags of Wideworlds, half a dozen general notions &c I am precisely the same World's humble servant that left the University in August. Good people will tell me that it is a Judgement & lesson for my character, to make me fitter for the office whereto I aspire; but if I come out a dispirited, mature, broken hearted miscreant,—how will Man or myself be bettered? Now I have not thought all this time that I was complaining at Fate although I suppose it amounts to the same; these are the suggestions only of a disappointed spirit brooding over the fall of castles in the air. My fate is enviable contrasted with that of others; I have only to blame myself who had no right to build them. Waldo E.

"And there is a great difference whether the tortoise gathers h/im/er/self within⟨to⟩ h/is/er/ shell hurt or unhurt."[28]

I shall bless Cadmus, ⟨of⟩ ↑or↓ Chod, or Hermes, for inventing letters & written language—You, my dear little wideworld, deducing your pedigree from that pretty event.

Mowna Roa, mountain in Sandwich Isles was seen by Mar-

[27] "SELF" is written beneath "which a" at the bottom of the page.

[28] The sentence follows the signature and is crowded into the space between the preceding and following paragraphs.

chand[29] at the distance of 53 leagues ie. 159 miles — Greatest distance at which a terrestrial object hath been seen from the level of the sea.

[16] Trust not the Passions; they are blind guides. They act, by the confessed experience of all the world, by the observation within reach of a child's attention, contrary to Reason. It were madness & manifest perdition for a man who beheld from the shore a stormy & ranging ocean darkened by clouds & broken by rocks — to cast himself into a boat upon it without oar or helm ↑to be tossed to savage shores perhaps, perhaps to famine, perhaps to the wild wilderness of waves, inevitably to death↓ for no other purpose but to gratify a moment's caprice. But this is the strict history of one who trusts himself to the government of passion. He voluntarily puts away from him that godlike prerogative[n] which distinguishes him from the beasts, and which determines & fortifies his actions and throws himself into the wild tempest of temptation & vice, into the direct commission of those crimes which human & divine laws have fenced round & forbidden. He has become another being, and under this strange metamorphosis he dares & delights in enormities at which his calm mind but now shuddered. He has made himself accountable & perchance execrable for high handed wickedness from which a moment's firmness would have extricated him entirely; he had made himself liable to new temptation, and fatally easy to the triumphs of Sin.

We take our impressions of the world from the *average* results of our own limited experiments. These form our general notions from which we reason in cold moments. But we always derive a transient & partial prejudice from the last contact which we had with it. We feel a low & miserable humiliation when we have been in company with beings of that worst sort — like John of Cappadocia in "Decline & Fall," or Glossin in Guy Mannering or Clodius at Rome. This is by far the most tremendous character, (in species), which can be found. Another portrait of it is Richardson's Love-

[29] Étienne Marchand (1775–1793), whose travels were recorded by Charles Pierre Claret, Comte de Fleurieu, *A Voyage Round the World, Performed during the Years 1790, 1791, and 1792, by Étienne Marchand . . .*, transl. from French (London, 1801).

lace. It is a worse being than Byron's personifications; the pirate Cleaveland[30] is of Byron's kind, with the laughing devil in his sneer, but is hardly so dreadful in many respects as these; because[n] the character of which I speak exactly comes up to the best limit of human nature at the same time that it appertains more to the fiend: Byron's have redeeming gentle affections; — these exhibit the gentle affections only to laugh at them, and shock you by butchering [17][31] human beings & divine things in a *genteel* way, — in becoming popular in proportion as they become outrageous. The frequent acquaintance with these pictures hath a dreadfu↑l↓l tendency in roughly wearing off the moral delicacy by such a familiarity with profanity & abomination. To my imagination, the analogy always presents itself between the history of these & that remark of Buchanan at the temple of Juggernaut "that the vultures were shockingly tame."[32] But I am tired of this doleful delineation. I turn gratefully to the opposite circumstances. ⟨The⟩ ↑I saw a↓ toll-taker ⟨after⟩ recieve⟨ng⟩[n] his debt from two men who had walked a mile on purpose to pay the owed fees, has an agreeable impression of the honesty of all passengers which extends itself to trust the next petitioner with ease & confidence.[33] A frank avowal of fault in one who hath injured you, puts you in humour with the world, and a fine moonlight specimen of nature makes you loth to lose her beauty. Hence it follows that our conclusions upon human nature are transitory & prejudiced, and often contradictory and that only we can speak with authority when in philosophical coldness & abstraction, we weigh well the opposing interests & determine upon Man as an universal idea of which few & cautious things must be said to be said safely. — The day labourer is easily seduced by a high reward & liberal treatment, to think well of the rich, by a festive impulse, to imagine himself patriotic.

(All this might be as well continued as not.)

[30] Captain Clement Cleveland, in Scott's *The Pirate*.

[31] "(CHARACTERISTICS)" is centered beneath "age. But mine" at the bottom of the page.

[32] In describing the approach to the temple of Juggernaut in India, the Reverend Claudius Buchanan wrote: "The vultures exhibits [*sic*] a shocking *tameness*." See the review of his *Christian Researches in Asia*, *Quarterly Review*, VI (December 1811), 450.

[33] Emerson evidently did not complete the revision of the sentence.

May 12 ⟨I have a nasty appetite which I will not gratify.⟩[34]

May 13. In twelve days I shall be nineteen years old; which I count a miserable thing. Has any other educated person lived so many years and lost so many days? I do not say acquired so little for by an ease of thought & certain looseness of mind I have perhaps been the subject of as many ideas as many of mine age. But mine approaching maturity [18][35] is attended with a goading sense of emptiness & wasted capacity; with the conviction that vanity has been content to admire the little circle of natural accomplishments, and has travelled again & again the narrow round, instead of adding sedulously the gems of knowledge to their number. Too tired and too indolent to travel up the mountain path which leads to good learning, to wisdom & to fame, I must be satisfied with beholding with an envious eye the labo⟨u⟩rious journey & final success of my fellows, remaining stationary myself, until my inferiors & juniors have reached & outgone me. And how long is this to last? How long shall I hold the little acclivity which four or six years ago I flattered myself was enviable, but which has become contemptible now? It is a child's place & if I hold it longer I may quite as well resume the bauble & rattle, grow old with a baby's red jocky on my grey head & a picturebook in my hand, instead of Plato and Newton. Well, and I am he who nourished brilliant visions of future grandeur which may well appear presumptuous & foolish now. My infant imagination was idolatrous of glory, & thought itself no mean pretender to the honours of those who stood highest in the community, and dared even to contend for fame with those who are hallowed by time & the approbation of ages. — It was a little merit to concieve such animating hopes, and afforded some poor prospect of the possibility of their fulfilment. This hope was fed & fanned by the occasional lofty communications which were vouchsafed to me with the Muses' Heaven and which have ⟨occ⟩ at intervals made me the organ of remarkable sentiments & feelings which were far above my ordinary train. And

[34] The sentence is heavily cancelled. The reading was secured from an enlarged negative which was then studied under magnification of about 19 power. The "y." in "gratify" appears on page [19], since Emerson ran over the edge of the page.

[35] "SELF" is centered beneath "above" at the bottom of the page.

[19][36] with this lingering earnest of better hope (I refer to this fine exhilaration which now & then quickens my clay) shall I resign every aspiration to belong to that family of giant minds which live on earth many ages & rule the world when their bones are slumbering, no matter, whether under a pyramid or a primrose? No I will yet a little while entertain the Angel.

Look next from the history of my intellect to the history of my heart. A blank,[n] my lord. I have not the kind affections of a pigeon. Ungenerous & selfish, cautious & cold, I yet wish to be romantic. Have not sufficient feeling to speak a natural hearty welcome to a friend or stranger and yet send abroad wishes & fancies of an ⟨alliance⟩ ↑friendship↓ with a man I never knew. There is not in the whole wide Universe of God ⟨one being⟩ (my relations to Himself I do not understand) one being to whom I am attached with warm & entire devotion,—not a being to whom I have joined fate for weal or wo, not one whose interests I have nearly & dearly at heart;—and this I say at the most susceptible age of man.

Perhaps at the distance of a score of years, if I then[n] inhabit this world, or still more, if I do not, these will appear frightful confessions; they may or may not; it is a true picture of a barren & desolate soul.

(Be it remembered that it was last evening that I heard that prodigious display of Eloquence in Faneuil Hall, by Mr Otis[37]—which astonished & delighted me above any thing of the kind I ever witnessed.)

I love my Wideworlds.

[20][38] May 14. Two things may be noticed here which are anecdotes of Italian manners at the date 1412. "Squarcia Giramo, ranger to Jean Marie Visconti, (of his father Jean Galeaz Visconti, I intend to speak again,) who had nourished his dogs with human

[36] "SELF" is centered at the bottom of the page beneath "Wideworlds."

[37] Harrison Gray Otis (1765–1848), former Federalist Senator from Massachusetts.

[38] "HISTORY" is centered beneath "whether the pleasure" at the bottom of the page.

flesh was his principal favourite. When victims failed, he declared that he would avenge the death of his mother to which he had contributed more than any one & he gave up to be torn to pieces by his hounds John de Posterla, Antoine Visconti, his brother Francis, & a great number of Gibelin gentlemen. He delivered up to them also the son of John Posterla aged only twelve, but when the boy cast himself on his knees to ask pardon, the dogs stood still & would not touch him. Squarcia, with his knife stabbed the child & the dogs refused still to taste of his blood & his entrails." ——

"The Emperour Sigismond & the Pope John 23d visited Cremona & the emperour pardoned Gabrino Fondolo, tyrant of this city. When they were both ascended to the top of the steeple of Cremona, where almost all Lombardy & the majestic course of the Po ⟨displayed⟩ opened to their view, Gabrino Fondolo, who had already obtained by a black perfidy the sovereignty which he enjoyed, concieved for an instant the thought of precipitating the emperor & the pope from the top of the tower to occasion in Christendom ⟨&⟩an unexpected revolution, from which he might profit. This same tyrant being beheaded at Milan 11 years after by order of Philippe Marie declared dying that his only remorse was for having weakly renounced that thought." (1414) Sismondi⟨s⟩ is very diligent in collecting anecdotes; it is singular that in narrating the death of John Huss, 1415, which he does at some length, he should make no mention of that remarkable prophecy, "Post centum annos" &c. Such an omission leads you to suspect that an author has not read all. (See a better story of this in "Bennett's Memorial.")

My body weighs 144 pounds.——In a fortnight I intend, Deo volente, to make a journey on foot. A month hence I will answer the question whether the pleasure was only in the *hope.*

[21][39] When the angels of Ambition & War have sounded upon the earth, when the famished eagle screams for food and the standards of the nations soiled with blood are lifted from the dust shewing at once the proof & the promise of carnage, new sets of feelings take place in the human breast which amaze & contradict speculation. Then

[39] "WAR" is centered at the bottom of the page beneath "Athens!"

is exhibited the mind's power of accomodation to the tone of things, of becoming all things to all men. It divests itself of its moral tenderness, it becomes hardened to outrage. It dips its finger in blood to paint faces on the wall. There was an ideot who ⟨wept⟩ because ⟨one⟩ ↑when a mower↓ tickled him with a ⟨hair⟩ ↑blade of grass, wept,↓ and straightway mangled himself with a scythe. So the mind in this tempest of affairs passes without an interval from extreme softness to shocking insensibility. There are some vices which, in a peculiar manner, desolate the foundations of virtue & blunt the moral sense; so war, which is a licence of all the passions, bears with it, destruction of body & soul. It is an unnatural & inhuman institution, which was borrowed from the brutes. This is the Calamity of War.

FALL OF THE SENATE. Rome was taken by Narses AD 553 and after a period of 13 centuries the institution of Romulus expired.[40]

I ⟨Oh⟩Go hide the shield of War,
The clarion and the spear,
The plume of pride, & scimetar
Vain trophies of a bier
They have digged a thousand graves
In Marathon today
Their ⟨wail⟩ ↑dirge↓ is sounded by the waves
Which wash the slain away
The hearth is forsaken, the Furies are fed
Make, Maidens of Athens! your wail for the dead.

[22][41] II The Persian's golden car,
And image of the Sun
In flashing light rolled fast & far
O'er echoing Marathon
He mourns his quenched beam

[40] These lines are framed and crowded into the space to the right of the last word in the preceding paragraph and the first line of verse.

[41] Written vertically in the left margin beside stanzas II and III:

"The *dog* of Charles did *madly* comprehend
New. Mil.'s beginning, Galileo's end."

"GOOD BYE" is centered beneath "my late whispered" at the bottom of the page.

His slain & broken host
He curses glory's dream
Which lured him to be lost
His rose-wreath is dyed with a bloody stain
And the Genius of Asia shrieks Shame! to the slain.

III "Io! Minerva"! Hail
What Argive Harp is dumb?
The triumph loads the gale
The laurelled victors come!
There's a light in Victory's eye
Which none but God can give
And a name can never die
Apollo bids it live
The daughters of Music have learned your name
And Athens, and Earth, shall reecho your fame.

May 24th 1822

And now it is Friday at even, and I am come to take leave of my pleasant Wideworld, for a little time, & commence my journey tomorrow. I look to many pleasures in my fortnight's absence, but neither is my temperament so volatile & gay, nor my zeal so strong as to make my expectations set aside the possibility of disappointment. I am so young an adventurer, that I am alive to regret & sentiment upon so little an occasion as this parting; though one would judge from my late whispered execrations of [23] the school that a short suspension of its mortefications would be exceedingly delightful. I may also observe here that I had never suspected myself of so much feeling as rose within me at taking leave of Mrs E. at the water side and seeing so delicate a lady getting into a boat from those steep wharf stairs among sailors & labourers; and leaving her native shore for Louisiana without a single friend or relation attending her to the shore, and seeing her depart.—For myself I was introduced to her upon the wharf. Her husband behaved very well. God speed them! *

* She is dead & her husband also, a thousand miles away from their kindred. 1824.

[May 24, 1822] Mem. certain lines in "Ant. & Cleop." about a "hoop of affection so staunch" &c find it.[42] How noble a masterpiece is the tragedy of Hamlet! It can only be spoken of & described by superlatives. There is a deep & subtle wit, with an infinite variety, and every line is golden. May 24, 182⟨4⟩2

Sunday Evening June 9th. If a man could go into the country but once, as to some raree shew, or if it were indulged by God but to a single individual to behold the majesty of nature, I think the credit & magnificence of Art would fall suddenly to the ground. For take away the cheapness and ease of acquisition which lessen our estimation of its value, and who could suddenly find himself, alone in the green fields where the whole firmament meets the eye at once, and the pomp of woods & clouds and hills is poured upon the mind—without an unearthly animation? Upon a mountain-solitude [24][43] a man instantly feels a sensible exaltation and a better claim to his rights in the universe. He who wanders in the woods percieves how natural it was to pagan imagination to find gods in every deep grove & by each fountain head. Nature seems to him not to be silent but to be eager & striving to break out into music. Each tree, flower, and stone, he invests with life & character; and it is impossible that the wind which breathes so expressive a sound amid the leaves—should mean nothing. But so striking is the ordina⟨ry⟩tion of Providence with regard to the uniformity of human character, that its traits seem to be hardly affected by such wide difference in circumstances as a town & country education. The change from one situation to the other may produce great alterations but the difference of life, little. The embowered cottage & solitary farmhouse display to you the same mingled picture of frankness & meanness, pride & poverty of feeling, fraud & charity, which are encompassed with brick walls in the city. Every pleasant feature is balanced by somewhat painful. To the stranger, the simplicity of manners is delightful and carries the memory back to the Arcadian reign of Saturn; and the primitive custom

[42] See p. 115, note 3.

[43] "COUNTRY" is centered beneath "apt to disgust" at the bottom of the page. Several rough pencil sketches, including a man's head in profile from "character; and" (above) to "as a town" (below), are barely visible on this page.

of saluting every passenger, is an agreeable acknowledgement of common sympathies, & a common nature. But from the want of an upper class in society, from the ↑admirable↓ republican equality which levels one with all, results a rudeness & sometimes a savageness of manners which is apt to disgust a polished & courtly man.

[25][44] Drama.

June 10.

There are two natures in man, — flesh and spirit, — whose tendencies are wide as the universe asunder, and from whose miraculous combination it arises, that he is urged alway by the visible eloquent image of Truth, toward immortal perfection, and allured aside from the painful pursuit, by gross but fascinating pleasure. The worst form under which temptation ⟨att⟩ entices our weakness, is when it plots to make the soul a pander to the sense, by winning the mind to the pleasures of lofty sentiment & sublime fiction, and insinuating amid this parade of moral beauty its pernicious incentives to crime and invitations to folly. It is a fatal twilight, in which darkness is sown with light, until the perverted judgement learns to think that the whole spectacle is more harmonious, & better accommodated to his feeble ↑human↓ sense. But be assured, the light shall grow less and less, and shade shall be added to shade, until the wanderer becomes bewildered and lost. There is no example of this ruinous corruption of the morals by the corruption of the wit so remarkable as the evil influence of dramatic exhibitions. When the feeble defence of this great bad Cause is over ⟨you all well[?] know⟩ ↑every man knows↓ that at the Theatre, the bad passions and corrupt inclinations of the flesh are addressed through the medium of elegant fiction or ingenious allusion; are fomented by the encouragement of company, and the pictures of success; are instructed in their execrable accomplishment, and thereby evil is wrought to the soul of the man in his death, to the world — in his example, to the universe — in adding to the great sum of guilt & misery.

This dreadful result was wisely traced by the early philosopher,

[44] A rough sketch of a woman's head and shoulders is pencilled through five lines of text from "weakness," (above) to "fatal" (below). "DRAMA" is centered beneath "did not" at the bottom of the page.

by the Platonist, by the Gnostic. They did not widely err who proclaimed the [26][45] existence of two warring principles, the incorruptible mind, and the mass of malignant matter. This was a creed which was often damned as heresy by the infallible church; happy if they had never devised a worse. In their attempts to escape from this inherent corruption, and correct the imperfection of nature, they went wrong with delirious zeal; but eternal truth founded the basis of their belief.

And you who consent to be pleased with the falsehearted hilarity of the scenes, and to drink in the poison of depravity from the eloquence of poetry, beware how so transient a charm, hurt your hopes, & set aside your claim to that which is not transient, but enduring. You are pleased for an hour, but will the merry thought or the pleasant imagination arrest the arm which deals judgement to the universe? Will a light fancy of all your gay visions, think you, hang round the throne of the ⟨o⟩Omnipotent to shield your soul from the curse? In the excitement of an earthly crowd and amid the freedom & pageant of a stage, perhaps a bold stroke of profanity or blasphemy was not amiss, and it was not hard to win your approbation.[n] When the Creator of the world shall meet the great assembly of his children and the hosts of heaven & earth look for the testimonies of your gratitude and love — how shall that misspent hour appear! and shall its sweet memory atone for the frown of the Universe, and the anathema of God?

The theory of the drama is, in itself, so beautiful, and so well designed to work good, that we feel forcibly what a pity it is that its concentrating interest, its unequalled power of conveying instruction and the delight inspired by its ordinary decorations should [27][46] be so miserably perverted to the service of sin. It might aid Virtue, and lend its skilful powers to the adornment of truth; its first form was a hymn to the Gods, and a monitory voice to human frailty, & human passion. Now, it seduces to Pleasure and leads on to Death and the shadows of Eternity settle over its termination. —

I think it is pretty well known that more is gained to a man's business by one half hour's conversation with his friend, than by very

[45] "DRAMA" is centered beneath "ordinary" at the bottom of the page.

[46] "DRAMA" is centered beneath "tried" at the bottom of the page.

many letters; for, face to face, each can distinctly state his own views; and each chief objection is started & answered; and, moreover, a more definite notion of one's sentiments & intentions, with regard to the matter, are gathered from his look and tones, than it is possible to gain from paper. It is therefore a hint borrowed from Nature, when a lesson of morals is conveyed to an audience in the engaging form of a dialogue, inste⟨d⟩ad of the silence of a book, or the cold soliloquy of an orator. When this didactic dialogue is improved by the addition of pathetic or romantic circumstances and in the place of indifferent speakers, we are presented with the characters of great & good men, of heroes and demigods, thus adding to the sentiments expressed the vast weight of ⟨their⟩ ↑virtuous↓ life & character—the wit of the invention is doubled. Lastly a general moral is drawn from an event, where all the parts of the piece are made to tend & terminate; this is what is called the distribution of poetical justice, and is nothing but an inevitable inference of some great moral truth, which the mind readily makes, upon the turn of affairs. For greater delight, we add music, painting, & poetry, well aware that the splendour of embellishment will fix the eye, after the mind grows weary. These are the advantages comprehended in the dramatic art. Truths otherwise impertinent, are told with admirable effect in this little epitome of life; and every philosophic Christian must be loth to lose to religion, an instrument of such tried powers.

[28][47] Sunday Evg. June 16

That the declarations of religion cannot claim belief because they are not objects of human sense and may therefore be fabulous is an ancient argument of the Atheist. Its weakness is obvious, and would not seem to require sober refutation if it were not evident that thousands daily build their faith in some sort upon this treacherous ground, and act upon the poor principles to which it leads. The evidence of things not seen, is capable, I presume, of being made out as satisfactorily as any thing subject to the eye of reason; and he that is not persuaded is criminal in wilfully shutting his eyes to the *whole* truth; in not hearing the matter out; and in refusing that effort of

[47] "FAITH" is centered beneath "seen, and" at the bottom of the page.

abstraction which is necessary to learn how to converse upon thoughts without confounding them with things of sense.

In the ordinary concerns of this little world which our senses can perfectly measure and our minds easily comprehend we are continually compelled to act upon faith and having heard from a third, tenth, or twentieth mouth that there is a city called London we send thither our merchandise without ever dreaming how madly we act upon a report which may be a fable. You have never seen the place; you have never seen one of its inhabitants; the bare report came to you, on simple human testimony, which you have often found false, and without any miracle to vouch its truth. And not one of those who ⟨send⟩ ↑act↓ thus boldly on evidence, but would risk his life upon the truth of the assertion that the City of London exists.

You have thus found it possible in one case to believe entirely the existence of something not seen, and to believe it on fallible testimony; [29][48] what now makes the difference between this ⟨subject⟩ ↑truth↓ and those[s] other to which your assent is required. The answer is, that the first are in themselves objects of sense but that the second are only prophecied and promised to be, and are never objects of sense. But the second besides bringing with them the highest internal evidence as that of adaptation, analogy, and naturalness are confirmed by the distinguished & supreme evidence of miracles.

If we take the evidence of testimony upon matters of finite nature and easy apprehension, shall we not rest satisfied with faith in those matters which from their nature transcend the evidence of sense, and which comprehending in their mighty circle the whole moral Universe, the Deity and his attributes, the nature & destinies of the soul and the great revolution of Eternity ⟨?⟩ do surpass the judgement of man and leave it dazzled & blind?

There is an evidence of the things not seen which though it be somewhat subtle does yet bear conviction to my mind of the highest order. It may be stated thus. Every man to whom the Divinity hath imparted this exquisite reasoning faculty, a gift so worthy of a ⟨g⟩God, — is by it compelled to pause often in the crowd of men, amid gaiety sometimes, sometimes amid distress, sometimes in poverty, some-

[48] "FAITH" is centered beneath "events," at the bottom of the page.

times ⟨of⟩ ↑in↓ pride, to find the secret cause of these manifold wonders, and to discover that hidden ⟨o⟩Order which can to his eye harmonize this great confusion of events, principles, actions, characters.

[30][49] In whatever light he attempts to reconcile the apparent inconsistencies which baffle his judgement he must still find himself set at nought in every effort so long as he looks to earth ⟨as⟩only as an interpreter of its affairs,—until he be reduced to sit down desperate & disconcerted, at the doubt of the aenigma. Yes, he will find it necessary to feel after the evidence of *things not seen,* to explain the mazes of mortal things. He sees levity and falsehood weave the fate of beings, for whose habitation the infinite universe was made, and upon whose capricious conduct, by strict laws, eternity is made to depend. He sees the mistakes committed, which last with life, and whose effects *then* begin to be felt—the mistaking of the *means* for the *end* of existence; of the relative estimation of the gift and the ⟨g⟩Giver; of the *prayer*, for the *acceptance*; of life for death. He can behold from what a condition the disorder sprang, and how this moral fabric whose immensity confounds his apprehension, and which was arranged from the divine elements of purity, power, benevolence, justice, & wisdom, came to have its pillars shaken, its design perverted, its almighty perfection undone and lost, in a hideous ruin. Its ruin is tenfold more frightful, from the gigantic proportions which are thus destroyed. Through the cloud of evil which almost hides heaven, he can distinctly discern the Eye of purity that watches the progress, the struggle, and the successive triumphs of vice and virtue; that marks the [31][50] eras of time, and notes the silent approach of the consummation which is to develope the ends of universal & individual conduct; to show why and to what aim nations and ages toiled; to explain the good man's hope, and the sinner's peril and to reduce again to harmony and regular dependence the thousand scenes which vary life & contradict each other.

(It is some months since I read Sherlock's admirable sermon upon Faith which contains the best possible arguments of which the subject is susceptible. q.v.)[51]

[49] "FAITH" is centered beneath "vice" at the bottom of the page.

[50] "GOD" is centered beneath "higher" at the bottom of the page.

[51] The reference appears to be either to Thomas Sherlock (1678–1761), Bishop

↑Up↓⟨O⟩on ⟨the⟩our ideas of God.

Thursday Evg. June 20th 1822

A In the broadest classification we can attempt in our efforts to describe the Universe, there will always be found at the bottom of the system, two varities,—Perfection and Imperfection. Their boundary line is as distinct, as the separation of Vice and Virtue. Earth knows the nature & name of Imperfection; the soul of man converses with it daily; it is the Monster who poisons the cup of human delight; who sees ↑the↓ Paradise of Creation extending far & wide about him; who sits in the midst to shatter the wheels of the mighty structure, & break up the centres of Joy. Corruption is his minister, and Man is his prey. Within the precincts of his dominion, the soul of man inherits its dwelling, but its origin is of higher and divine descent. God [32][52] made man, "and the inspiration of the Almighty hath given him understanding." When the mind extending itself by the impulse of its native energies, laments the weakness which surrounds it here, and cramps its power, when it has learned the loathsomeness of sin and grown at last weary of imperfection, it is its privilege to abandon all low and sordid thoughts, and to ascend to the contemplation and prospect of Perfection.

B A fortunate combination⟨s⟩ of circumstances sometimes gives us the means with our bounded faculties to make an important discovery in the material world, and to reduce to an intelligent scrutiny all the minute organs of an insignificant insect. But the pride which we enjoy in success teaches us that we are unfit for confident progress in higher speculation and the faculties which were adequate to the examination of a worm must sink prostrate in the presence of a God. We dare not seek to estimate the feelings which are in the Mind whose awful energies controul the corners of the Universe, and strike the Imagination dead. Presumption and impiety have not assayed to weigh that wisdom whose decisions cross the infinit⟨y⟩e Creation and comprehend and act upon every part. And it would indeed be a frightful mockery to move the indignation of the most high God for the child of Adam that is a worm to lift himself in this nook of

---

of London, or William Sherlock (1641?–1707), Dean of St. Paul's (see Cameron, *EtE*, II, 153 and 182).

[52] "GOD" is centered beneath "upon" at the bottom of the page.

earth amid the uncounted congregation of God's creatures and attempt to measure that expanse of Omnipotence upon which his bubble is supported, and to [33][53] speak familiarly of those attributes, which do outrun and baffle all comparison and thought.

C Simonides said well, "Give me twice the time, for the more I think, the more it enlarges;"[54] and it is only mathematical truth; for when the subject is infinite, it must be, that, in proportion as discipline enlarges the capacity of the powers to comprehend a portion of the line, so much the more ↑of the line↓ will be continually discerned, extending above and beyond the straining orbs of imagination. It is nevertheless apparent in the munificent endowment of ↑the↓ human intellect, that, provision has been made to enable it to proceed to some distinct knowledge of this Being whom in darkness we adore. Witness some of those admirable demonstrations of *the existence and attributes* which various minds in various ages have fallen upon, and which we record as the best monuments of human wit. And I regard this rather as a glimpse and earnest of the light which shall break upon the soul when its cumbering flesh-bond is broken,—of the glory that shall be revealed—than ↑as↓ any solitary or fortuitous discovery which may stand unconnected with the past or the future. For is it not natural ↑to believe↓, that, *out* of earth, and men of clay,—the Deity is the great engrossing theme which absorbs the wonder as well as the devotion of the disembodied spirits that people his creation? And is it not to be presumed that the soul will be furnished with some understanding of his strength when she enters on the scene where his divinity is displayed? The lisping infant, on earth, stammers the name of God; and shall the Archangel whose gigantic intelligence displays the education of heaven stand silent beneath the very Cloud? Mankind have naturally concieved the joy of that spiritual estate to consist in the satisfaction [34][55] and delight of certain

[53] "GOD" is centered beneath "estate" at the bottom of the page.

[54] This would seem to be an imperfect memory of Emerson's reading in Kennett's *Lives and Characters of the Ancient Grecian Poets.* In the life of Simonides of Ceos, Kennett tells the story of his answer to Hiero, the Tyrant, who asked him "What GOD was." Simonides requested a day to consider the question, then two days, then more. "*Hiero* demanded the Reason of the Delay: *Because* (says *Simonides*) *the more I think on that Subject, the less able I am to explain my Thoughts.*" (part II, p. 47.)

[55] "GOD" is centered beneath "charm" at the bottom of the page.

high intellectual exercises, — of which our best and loftiest contemplations afford some faint symbol. And this notion is natural and consistent with their condition; for they have left the obstruction of a material universe, and dwell now in the majesty of thought, in a grand inconceivable dependence of mind upon the great ⟨s⟩Source of intelligence, and are therefore in a situation to pursue those inquiries which mocked the researches of finite beings, but which invite the study of those to whom the sources of wisdom, and the riches of ⟨things⟩ the unseen state are laid open. In this state, and with these opportunities, a litttle meditation will make it plain, that there can be, in heaven or earth no thought which can so concentrate and absorb the living spirit as the idea of God.

D The subject upon which I have adventured, is apt to lead away and bewilder the imagination, until it mistakes strained metaphors and refined mysticisms for strong conceptions ↑of its object↓.[n] This error, above all, I am anxious to avoid, and shall endeavour to set down as distinctly as I am able arguments grounded directly upon the visible works of the Deity or upon his character as pourtrayed in Scripture.

(Continued on page 36) Boston Babylon

It was to be expected that America should bring to the conflict unwonted national energy from the invigorating solitudes of her clime. We look with confident expectation for something extraordinary by word or deed in the primitive settlers of a large and fruitful territory. For there is a charm in nature that constrains her to [render] [35][56] up a sevenfold blessing of health and life to him who inhales the first breath of her virgin air,[n] and an abundant harvest to him who hath first laid the chain of Cultivation upon the unbroken strength and freedom of the soil. There is certainly something deeply interesting in the history of one who invades the coast of an unknown continent and first breaks the silence which hath reigned there since the creation. As he goes alone to the wilderness and sets his axe to the root of the forest and we reflect th⟨is⟩at this stroke which echoes through the wood begins a dominion which shall never end till this

[56] "AMERICA" is centered beneath "we consider" at the bottom of the page.

green and silent woodland shall groan beneath the feet of a countless ⟨nation⟩ ↑multitudes↓ and ↑shall↓ exchange the ⟨frequent⟩ ↑solitary↓ warble of a bird for the ⟨hum⟩ noise of ⟨men⟩ ↑nations↓, the outcry of human passion, and the groan of human misery. Under these views the settler ceases to be an ordinary adventurer, providing for himself and his son, or his friend,—but becomes the representative of human nature, the father of the Country, and, in a great measure, the Arbiter of its future destinies, ⟨for many generations⟩. We listen to hear the voice of Nature in the sighing of the breeze; we listen for the complaint of Faun, & Dryad,—"Art thou come hither also?" But we moreover look for some signal manifestation of greatness in the subsequent story of the adventurer. His condition is so inspiring to the human faculties, that we anticipate a rapid and perfect developement of them which shall outstrip the ordinary progress of man and send forward ↑over the forest↓ the spirit of civilization and science with ↑unrivalled↓ energy.[n] We can *form* a better estimate of his advantages over his contemporaries if we consider how he is likely to be [36][57] by those ordinary principles which are the inducements to laborious industry among mankind. It was an early lesson of experience that entire change of scene does very sensibly mature and develope the mind. For such an alteration is commonly attended with many circumstances of vivid excitement;—the parting of friends; the breaking up of long domestic habits, which have grown necessary to us as they have grown old; the leaving places, & scenes, with which custom has made us so familiar that we never notice them,—for new regions where the attention is continually commanded by the novelty of the objects.

(Continued)

"Men's failings live in brass; we write their virtues
In water;" Henry VIII [58] [IV, ii, 45–46, misquoted]

Saturday Evg June 29—(Continued from page 34)

E I recur to the consideration of the superiority of this idea,

[57] Is a word omitted before "by"? "GOD" is centered at the bottom of the page beneath "books."

[58] The quotation is crowded after "(Continued)" into the space between the preceding and following paragraphs.

in its influence upon the mind, to all others. Let me ask—with what can it come in competition? What will divert our attention, and attach our affections in the long long Day wherein the faculties shall enjoy an eternal exercise? Perhaps in the communion of departed wisdom and virtue; in the society of Socrates, Plato, and St. Paul. Be it so; it is a rational and authorised hope. We respect and admire the li⟨ves⟩fe & character of these eminent individuals; they appeared to possess an intimate familiarity with the profoundest principles of philosophy, and at the same time a power to express them with the most perfect simplicity in their conversation and in their books. It is natural to look to these [37][59] great masters of mankind as qualified in another state to give us our introduction to its mysteries and joys. But consider a moment, if a celestial spirit could be so besotted, as to prefer the little flights of a spirit which is its peer, to the inconceivable intellect which kindled all and overwhelms all. Let it compare for a moment the history of the two Beings. One lived upon earth its span, and was then swallowed into the multitude of men, leaving no trace of its existence, except, perhaps, a little book, or its name, or its monument. But if your mind be strung to an elevated tone, try to comprehend the history of the Other;—A stream without a source, an age without an infancy,—the mind resorts in vain to its highest antiquity to seek the commencement of the ⟨a⟩Ancient of Days. It can only pursue a few days of his history in the immensity of his works. In a few days he built the world and the firmament, and in the darkness of the Universe he lit the sun; He created man & beast[;] he arranged the seasons and provided for the preservation of the Order established; he arched the rainbow and gathered the clouds[,] the granaries of his hail, of the lightning and thunder. That immeasurable existence upon such an insignificant portion of which the eye of all mankind rests with wonder—we concieve to have been spent in similar employments throughout his infinite [38] kingdom; and that Being is well worthy of prostrate adoration to whom we ⟨|| p . . . ||⟩ ascribe an eternity, every moment of which hath been signalized, by a scheme of preserving providence, by a plan of redemption, by the informing of angelic intellect, or by the creation of a world. One chief reason why the human soul is so prone to

[59] "GOD" is centered beneath "employments" at the bottom of the page.

neglect or avoid this idea, is because it is so unsatisfactory, being almost entirely above the attainment of our weak powers; but, in the upper state, when this weakness is removed, and our faculties are taught to soar up to the very Throne — I need not ask if the mind could be so blind, as to admire the spark, in the presence of that fire whence it came.

Sunday Morn.

F ⟨I⟩On such employments we anticipate the happiness of heaven to depend. ⟨Whether⟩ ↑That↓ any approximation to such spiritual elevation can be made on earth, will be believed by some and denied by others. The reasons why we are no more strongly attracted, are plainly seen, and are lodged within ourselves. The soul is pervaded by a taint of mortality and seduced by the temptations of sense from a devotion to those feelings which disdain to accept a halfway service. Next, we are inadequate to these contemplations, for the reason so often mentioned — our native narrowness and feebleness of ⟨power⟩ mind; because the mind does not yet exist but in an infant state, and waits for a developement [39][60] in another ⟨state⟩ world. But there have been men at various intervals, in the world, who by some remarkable fortune or remarkable effort have rendered themselves less liable to the suggestions of sense, and have, in a manner, departed from the pursuits and habits of men to hold strict conversation with the attributes of Deity, and, in the emphatic language of the Hebrew historian, *to walk with* God. And there are certain facilities for this enlarged communion which sometimes ⟨occor⟩ occur, to give direction & aid to the feebleness of nature. The astronomer who by reason of the littleness of the earth would be able to learn next to nothing of the distances and magnitudes of the heavenly bodies, ⟨is⟩ ↑can↓ yet take advantage of its revolutions a⟨bout⟩ ↑round↓ the Sun, and thus move hi⟨m⟩s instruments about in the universe, across the vast orbit of his planet; so the lapse of ages may sometimes enable the devout philosopher to trace the design of Providence, otherwise above his comprehension, by reducing to a miniature view, a magnificent course of events.

(Continued on page 44)

[60] "GOD" is centered beneath "the existing" at the bottom of the page.

DRAMA We openly confess our design to be ⟨inim⟩ hostile to the stage, and that it is a part of our purpose—not to inquire if the drama be hurtful, but to study whether the existing viciousness of the drama [40][61] be ⟨essential to it⟩ adventitious, and so capable of being eradicated, or whether it be essential to it. It does not become a philanthropist to be concerned lest our inquiries should make out the latter supposition correct but in case of such result it becomes his imperative duty to join heart & hand to attempt its extirpation. Good men have at length learned, that error grown old deserves no respect, and that the moss of age may cover poison and rottenness, as well as the virtues of strength & health. Moreover numberless circumstances remind us how ready Vice has always been to shroud itself under every name of reverence, and how adroit, in adding to the zest of wicked gratification, by perverting to its purpose, the best institutions of mankind. If we succeed in our attempt to prove the active bad influence which the Drama, in its present form, constantly causes, we hope that we shall have done enough in calling the public attention to the magnitude of the disaster. We confide in the virtue of society to remove the evil as soon as it is exposed.

We shall next inquire if a form ⟨of⟩ ↑can be given to↓ the Drama which shall convert its fine powers from the [41][62] servicc of sin to the cause of morals. But if this cannot be done there must be an ultimate re⟨sort⟩↑course↓ to the final cure. Let it not be imagined that this can be any hard or impossible attempt. It may be rapidly brought about by a determined public voice in the higher circles of the community by withdrawing from it that countenance which it has so long borrowed from the indulgence of fashion. True you cannot proscribe it altogether[,] but by outlawing it you may drive it from good company to find its proper association with the brothel and gambling house[,] acknowledged dens of ↑impurity &↓ outrage. ⟨& crime⟩ For I would have it remembered ⟨it is⟩ that the evil complained of is th⟨e⟩at *Sanction* ⟨which⟩ ↑whereby it is↓ enabled ⟨it⟩ to diffuse its sway over good society, and not the badness of the drama itself. For we are not so given to fanaticism as to imagine we can extinguish vice from among mortal abodes.

[61] "DRAMA" is centered beneath "its fine" at the bottom of the page.

[62] "DRAMA" is centered beneath "committed" at the bottom of the page.

Let it not be considered as a fanciful scheme to break down these old forms or that the public voice can be of no effect. That man entertains but pitiful & illiberal views of th⟨e⟩is ⟨race⟩ condition who could distrust the effect of the protest of a community. Events are not committed to foreign and remote agents [42] but God has put ⟨them⟩ into our hands ↑the power↓ to decide our own fate↑s↓. Each generation ⟨recieves⟩ ↑takes in trust↓ from the preceding the care and guidance of the world and each is at free liberty to amend ⟨the⟩ whatever f⟨alsehood⟩↑ault↓ the oversight of other ages may have admitted. And it is a noble spectacle to after generations, and to the distant peoples of this to behold a community rich with the experience of former ages, combining their strength to heave the burden of error, of antiquated immoral custom, at once from their shoulders and distinguish themselves in the history of the world, by those godlike achievements to which nothing but the confederated power of states, is equal. This spirit must produce a great moral bond which overleaps the little local ⟨distinctions⟩ ↑boundaries↓ of mountain or stream, of colour or dress, and compasses with its ample arch a thousand centres of civilization and government. Such an effort was the ⟨energy⟩ ↑Convulsion↓ which broke the slumber of the dark ages and finally established the Reformation. Such an effort commenced and is now perfecting the abolition of the Slave Trade. Such another effort is still demanded to punish with infamy the harlot of literature which is adorned [43][63] with many graces and armed with death.

Nothing is more distinctly seen than the advantage which ⟨follows⟩ ↑accrues↓ to society from these efforts independently of the relief of that evil which caused them, from the spring & energy which it conveys to all the members of the social league. At the same time it must be remembered how rare these earthquakes are, and that it needs some ⟨general⟩ active cause ⟨of an⟩ whose malignity is generally & distinctly felt in order to concentrate an infinity of jarring interests and powers towards a single aim. It must also be remembered that it is necessary individual⟨s⟩ ⟨sho⟩ minds should go before the public to measure & describe the magnitude of the evil and open the eyes of the multitude to their own distress. Luther and Calvin took upon themselves this part in the labour of the ⟨r⟩Reformation and some

[63] "DRAMA" is centered beneath "Conventus" at the bottom of the page.

spirited servant of literature must yet devote his talents to the high purpose of leading the triumph of good principles.

"Give a penny to Belisarius the beggar."

"The Miller of Granchester prayed for peace among the willows; for while the wind blew the wind-mills wrought & the watermill was less customed." Bacon.

"Dordrechti synodus, nodus; chorus integer aeger; Conventus ventus; sessio, stramen, Amen." [64]

[44][65] Saturday Ev.g July 6th 1822.

(Continued from page 39)

The Being which we adore must of necessity be adorable. Where gat we this idea — so different from our other ideas — of somewhat so transcendant & sublime? Did we gather it, as they say, like the fictions of the imagination, by compounding & combining the notions of our memory? No; it differs from them in every respect; in its unlikeness to any of our recollections; in its uniform character in every mind; in the circumstance that it forces itself upon our belief, and never releases the mind from its weight. The only answer which we are compelled to recieve is that the Intelligence who formed our minds adjusted them in such manner as to admit suitable notions of himself from the exhibition of his works, or from the consciousness of our own existence. What must be that Existence to which every star, every leaf, every drop, in the creation, testifies, by their strange & unaccountable formation! Towards that object the eyes of all generations have successively turned, by an universal instinctive impulse; and we are actuated by a portion of the same inspiration when we pronounce the great name of God. And when the mute creation with irresistible force point[s] our inquiries to ⟨h⟩Him, it becomes a truly admirable spectacle to behold this wide sympathy throu[gh]

[64] The three quotations are crowded into the wide bottom margin of the page. The first quotation is from Gibbon, *The Decline and Fall of the Roman Empire* (see *The Works of Edward Gibbon*, ed. J. B. Bury, 15 vols., N. Y., 1907, VII, 287).

Emerson doubtless found the third in J. L. Mosheim, *An Ecclesiastical History, Ancient and Modern . . .*, 6 vols. (Phila., 1797), V, 373, note [h], where it is quoted from Daniel Neal's *History of the Puritans, 1732–1738*, II, 117. Neal gives no author. It may be translated freely: "The Synod of Dort was a knot; the united chorus was sick; the convention was wind; the session was straw. Amen!"

[65] "GOD" is centered beneath "behold" at the bottom of the page.

[⟨46⟩45][66] out nature, of imperfect beings consenting to adore perfection.

In detached unconnected paragraphs I have given form to some of our general & loose notions with regard to Divine worship. Because our minds cannot comprehend him at once, we are obliged to analyse his character, and contemplate it separately under the different aspects in which it appears to us. We first offer our homage to ⟨h⟩Him as children of his Universe[,] as to the Almighty Creator of things; Next we view him in his moral character as having established f⟨or⟩↑rom↓ eternity an immutable rule to guide the actions of all intelligent beings, and as being himself the Eye, which observes, & the tribunal, which judges, of the good or ill observance of that law. ⟨Then⟩ ↑Next↓ we adore him in a peculiar relation which subsists between our race & Himself as the ⟨a⟩Author of a plan of Redemption which makes our erroneous & frail virtue acceptable to Divine purity. Lastly we are accustomed to consider singly those infinite Attributes which compose with their mingled light, ↑the↓ Character of God. I wish to adventure in [46][67] turn, these divine themes. They cannot be treated rapidly, nor should rash hands of levity, of fancy, of weakness, be laid upon the Ark. 9 pages.

(Continued on page 3, ⟨6⟩7 wideworld.)

"Si nulla fuit genitalis origo
Terrarum et coeli, semperque aeterna fuere,
Cur ⟨ante⟩ ↑supra bellum↓ Thebanum, et funera
Trojae,
Non alias alii quoque res cecinere poetae?"[68]
Lucretius [*De Rerum Natura*, V. 324–327].

I know nothing more fit to conclude the remarks which have been made in the last pages than certain fine pagan strains.

[IDEALISM.]

—"Of dew-bespangled leaves and blossoms bright
Hence! vanish from my sight

[66] "GOD" is centered at the bottom of the page beneath "God."

[67] "GOD" is centered beneath "Clarke," at the bottom of the page.

[68] "Besides, if there has been no first birth-time for earth and heaven and they have been always everlasting, why have not other poets also sung other things beyond the Theban War and the ruin of Troy?"

Delusive pictures! unsubstantial shews!
My soul absorbed, one only Being knows,
Of all perceptions, one abundant source.
Hence every object, every moment flows,
Suns hence derive their force,
Hence planets learn their course,
But suns and fading worlds I view no more,
— God only I percieve, God only I adore!" [69]

[Voltaire called Clarke, "un moulin des raisonnements."] [70]

[47] [71] "Venenum in auro bibitur." [72]

July 8th

Before we proceed farther upon this subject let us examine a serious objection which has been gravely advanced in support of the existing establishment[,] to wit[,] that the Theatre is the sewer in which the rebellious vices exhaust themselves, and the preventive of worse outbreakings of licentious passion. This appears to me to proceed on a mistaken principle and if it were true would controvert all which ⟨w⟩I am labouring to prove, that, the theatre is the cause as well as the consequence of public vice. It is supported by an ancient anecdote which carries more weight than if the mistake proceeded from a less responsible source. Cato noticing the shame of a young Roman whom he met coming from a brothel praised him for his wisdom in using such means to refrain from adultery & violation. If we duly consider the inferences from this maxim we must discover that they directly implicate the foundations of our moral relations. They are at war with any tolerable degree of virtue and make the laws of our human condition hard & unjust. Where [48] [73] is the praise and congratulation of youth which all mankind have consented to bestow, if by a necessity of nature it be the season of degraded indul-

[69] "A Hymn to Narayena," lines 8–17, *The Works of Sir William Jones*, 1807, XIII, 308–309. Emerson received the somewhat inaccurate text of this translation of an Indian hymn from his Aunt Mary (*L*, I, 116, n. 22).

[70] Quoted in Stewart's *Dissertation* (*Collected Works*, 1854, I, 296). Stewart has "à raisonnements."

[71] "DRAMA" is centered beneath "condition" at the bottom of the page.

[72] "Poison is drunk from cups of gold" (Seneca, *Thyestes*, 453). The quotation is crowded into the top margin to the left of the date.

[73] "DRAMA" is centered beneath "⟨no weaker⟩" at the bottom of the page.

gence & the appointed hour of crimes which derange the order of society? Rather hide its roses, & song, & pride, and curse it as the miserable celebration of the event whereby man fell, curse it as the orgies which day & wisdom may not behold if its vigour & beauty are to give a sanction to shame. But this was never true. I confide in universal experience that this was never the intent of Providence nor the actual history of life. No; intelligent beings have with cause admired the epoch of unfolding virtues & powers, when Reason shews truth and unperverted con⟨c⟩sience impels to follow it; in general, the only period when good feelings amount to enthusiasm; when devotion & philanthropy spend ⟨themselves⟩their[n] ↑spirit↓ in beneficent plans. And because by our constitution soul & sense are ↑constantly↓ to preserve their equilibrium, producing by their adjustment, the peculiar trial to which our race is submitted, it is the law of our system that the mind & body be developed together & the virtuous confidence & strength of youth be answered by a keener appetite to pleasure. But the proportion is kept; and bad inclinations have no greater power over us than they have in age. In common circumstances then the young man who adheres to duty obeys ⟨no weaker⟩ ↑a↓ command as imperious, as [49][74] he who departs to transgression. But the difference begins here; in old cities of old nations the⟨ir⟩ importunity of temptation becomes tremendous. Virtue grows cold & solitary while vice solicits with the syren voice of taste, & literature, of fashion, & genius. The mighty hand of SHAKSPEAR has consented to add another pulse to the rebellious blood; the sanction of public approbation gives splendour & facility to the poison; and that which is ↑barely↓ countenanced, procures admittance ⟨to⟩ ↑for↓ that which is abominable. Good men are grown so cold as never to interfere a veto which might be decisive. Thus much at a sitting[.][75]

We think it needs ⟨n⟩to say no more upon this idea that youth must be corrupted, but we shall return a moment to the supposition that its public utility is found in being a preventive to worse crimes. It is surprising in an age like this, when the experience of the character of moral turpitude is so /thoroughly/easily/ studied on the dark

[74] "DRAMA" is centered beneath "to a" at the bottom of the page.
[75] Added in pencil.

side of man's history from age to age of ignominy and the features of guilt have been found so uniform and ⟨the⟩ its annals so invariable, that a child can read the lesson, it is surprising to have this benefit ascribed to the Drama. Does not the objector know that in every form vice always subsists by gratification, and that ⟨every several⟩ ↑each↓ gratification adds keenness to its hunger, and makes forbearance less possible? that he who has abstained from scenes & thoughts which foment his lusts is better able to ⟨persevere⟩ ↑resist them,↓ and that self denial requires a less & less effort as it approaches to victory? Is it not plain beyond doubt that the Theatre provokes ↑in↓ him the memory & desire of gratification; and what repenting rake ever dreamed of avoiding his peril by listening to a demoralizing play? Those who [50] advocate it upon this miserable plea, are the votaries which its witchcraft has seduced; and they inwardly know that they acquired within its walls, their early impulses to a pernicious course.

A certain sum of a nation's resources are appropriated to its public institutions and if those establishments be bad so much must be counted as lost to the support of what are useful. The political philosopher makes haste to overthrow such waste establishments & to build up better on their ruins. Perhaps the theatres of the U. States do not cost upwards of 150000 dollars per annum; if so that sum b⟨y⟩uys more mischief than tenfold the sum could repair in the uses of ↑public↓ Charity.

It is difficult to assign the causes of difference in the attainments of two nations. For although the character of the species does obey the grand natural distinctions of the earth, and is found, savage at the poles, & civilized in the temperate zone, yet of nations in the same latitude, one shall be found no whit advanced in knowledge or greatness, & the other shall have arrayed itself with such splendour as to fill an hundred urns with the lustre of its beams. Why is England renowned for arts and arms while an equally high latitude in Russia, and while Norway and the fine climates of North America have languished in barbarism? What imparted that impulse to Greece which may be said to have created literature which has been communicated through Rome to the world? It is a curious spectacle to a contemplative man to observe a little population of twelve or twenty thousand men for a couple of generations setting their minds at work [51] more diligently than men were accustomed and effecting something altogether new & strange; to see them lie quietly down again in darkness, while all the nations of the world rise up to do them a vain reverence; and all the wisest among them exhausting their powers to make a faint imitation of some one excellence of Greece in her age of glory; to see this admiration continued & augmented as the world grows older,[n] and with all the advantages of an experience of 6000 years to find those departed artists never paralleled. It certainly is the most manly literature in the world, being composed of histor⟨y⟩ies, orations, poems, & dramatic pieces, in which no sign of accomodation is discovered to the whims of fashion or patronage. Simplicity is a remarkable characteristic of the productions of all the ancient masters. Upon their most admirable statue they were content to engrave "Apollodorus the Ephesian made it"; and we ⟨ar⟩respect the ⟨simple⟩ republican brevity which, in the place of a studied eulogium upon a drama which had been represented with unbounded applause, simply wrote, "Placuit" (it pleased.)

This last effort of the pen seems to have been tortured out for the mere purpose of ending the book, and I really regret that the sixth wideworld which boasts of several swelling paragraphs, should close its page with so heartless an oration. Giant Californ would contemn the ⟨kernal⟩ gift, whose outside, shews so poor. It should meet an [52][76] honourable fate to consume by the sun-light on his golden altar.

Boston July 10, 1822.

"Let us plait the garland & weave the chi,
While the wild waves dash on our iron strand;
Tomorrow, these waves may wash our graves,
And the moon look down on a ruined land."[77]

The islanders who sung this melancholy song, presaging the evil fates which waited for them — have passed away. No girdled

[76] The quotation from Chaucer is enclosed in an irregular rectangle. Beneath "FINIS" in the bottom margin is a small pen and ink sketch, possibly of tombs.

[77] "Song of the Tonga-Islanders," lines 5–8. See p. 385. Emerson printed the entire poem in his anthology *Parnassus*, 1875, labelling it "Anonymous."

chieftain sits upon their grim rocks to watch the dance of his tribe beneath the yellow lustre of the Moon; the moan of the waves is the only voice in their silent land; the moan of the waves is the only requiem of the brave who are buried on the seashore or in the main. But their memory has not failed from among men; the mournful notes which foreboded their fall have given it immortality. For the⟨ir⟩re is a charm in Poetry, which binds the world, and finds ⟨a⟩its ⟨power⟩ ↑effect↓ in the East and in the West.

"Let me not, like a worm, go by the way." Chaucer.
[*The Clerk's Tale*, line 880]

FINIS.

No 1 1

— The Wide World. —

'Mixing with the thousand pursuits & passions & objects of the world as personified by Imagination is profitable & entertaining These pages are intended at this their commencement to contain a record of new thoughts (when they occur) for a receptacle of all the old ideas that [illegible] partial but peculiar peepings at antiquity can furnish or furbish; for tablet to save the wear & tear of weak Memory & in short for all the various purposes & utility real or imaginary which are usually comprehended under that comprehensive title Common Place book

O ye witches assist me! enliven or horrify some midnight lucubration or dream (whichever may be found most convenient) to supply this reservoir when other resources fail. Pardon me Fairy Land! rich region of fancy & gnomery elvery sylphery & Queen Mab! pardon me for presenting my first petition to your enemies but there is probably one in the chamber who maliciously influenced me to what is irrevocable. pardon & favour me! — & finally Spirits of Earth Air Fire Water wherever ye glow whatsoever you patronize whoever you inspire hallow hallow this devoted paper — Dedicated & signed Jan 25. 1820. Junio. —

Plate I *Wide World 1, page 1* *Text, page 3*

The first page of Emerson's first journal

34

Well, I am sorry to have learned that my friend is dissolute, or rather the anecdote which I accidentally heard
of him shews him more like his neighbours
than I should wish him to be. Perhaps I shall
have to throw him up, after all, as a cheat
of fancy. Before I ever saw him, I wished my
friend to be different from any individual
I had seen. I invested him with a solemn cast
of mind, full of poetic feeling, & an idolater of
friendship, & possessing a vein of rich sober thought;
When I saw [illegible]
[illegible] with the
complete character which fancy had formed and
though entirely unacquainted with him was pleased
to observe the notice which [illegible]
[illegible] for a year I have entertained towards him
the same feelings I should be sorry to lose him
altogether before we have ever exchanged above a
dozen words.

NB By the way this book is of an inferiour character & contains so much doubtful matter
that I believe I shall have to burn the
second number of the Wide World immediately
upon its completion.

Plate II *Wide World 2, page 34* *Text, pages 52–53*
One of the cancelled passages about Martin Gay

38

Books — Inquirenda

Mathers Magnalia.
Dunlop's history of Fiction.
Mattaire.
Swift. Froissart.
Davy's Chemistry
Teignmouth's life of Jones.
Simmons's life of Milton = 3 Vl of Brit. Plutarch
Chaucer
Montaigne's Essays
Germany (Stael)
Drummond's Academical Questions
Price on Morals
Humboldt's work on America
Smith's Virginia
Robertson's S. America
Hist of Philip 2
Life of Shakspeare

Subjects for themes
Destruction of a city. poetry
(Forensic) Whether Civil Government be founded on a compact expressed or implied.
The domestic relations as restraints on an adventurous spirit
Influence of weather on intellectual temperament.
Character of any fancy portrait as for instance

48
44
40
132

Plate III Wide World 2, page 38 Text pages 55–57

An early reading list, a theme list, and a whimsical "portrait"

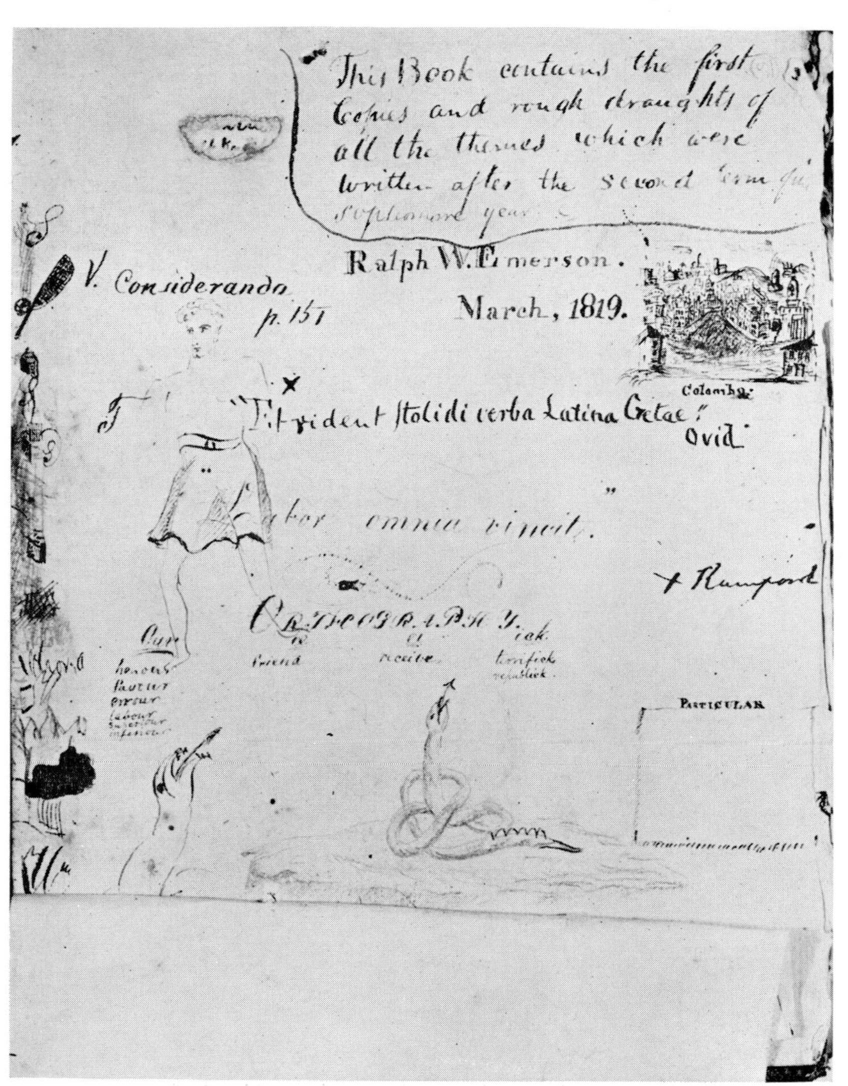

Plate IV *College Theme Book, front cover verso* *Text, page 162*

Perhaps the earliest surviving notebook "page"

3

Regard this character, for a moment, only in
this supposeable way & we shall be inclined
to wonder that men without revelation
merely by the light of reason & nature could
set forth a model of moral perfection
which the wise in any age would do
well to imitate. It might further
form a fine subject for speculation
to point out its faults & wherein would
the difference consist, should modern fancy
endeavour to create a similar paragon
with all the improvements ^with which ^a superior
theology could dignify the mind. But
this is foreign from our purpose.

It will be well at this time ^both ~~at~~
in ~~compliment~~ conformity to custom & propriety of place to
mark the ~~of~~ time of Socrates & observe what immediate influence the ^moral & political state of the age would probably exert upon his opinions & character. The dark
ages of Greece from the first settlement of the Egyptian
& Phoenician colonies to the Trojan War had long closed.
From that ~~[illegible]~~ era the young republics had been growing
in strength population & territory & digesting their

Plate V — No. XVII, page 3 — Text, pages 207–208

A page from Emerson's essay on Socrates

Plate VI *No. XVII, pages 12 and 13* *Text, page 213*

A few of the scores of male heads in left profile which decorate and obscure the early journals

18

In Athens learning was not loved for its own sake but for sinister ends. It was prized as a saleable commodity. The Sophists bargained their literature, such as it was, for a price which ~~was regu~~ always exorbitant was regulated by the ability of the disciple. And this must always happen more or less in the infancy of letters. In a money-making community literature will soon thrive. It will always follow not precede successful trade. The first wants to be supplied are the native ones of animal subsistence & comfort & when these are more than provided for & luxury & ease begin to look about them for new gratification the mind then urges its claims to cultivation

---

From this place to "Detached Sentences" the pages are to be improved by lines, or verses, containing any thing remarkable, either in expression, or sentiment, or remote association, principally quoted, but likewise original ones. The original are distinguished by the letter "O." or Junio or O.

Junio

Plate VII — No. XVII, page 18 — Text, page 215

Emerson's symbols of original authorship

Plate VIII *No. XVII, page 34* *Text, page 229*

Probably the first stage of "King Richard's Death"

Plate IX *No. XVII, page 51* *Text, pages 241–242*

A section of the Pythologian poem, "Improvement"

Plate X — No. XVII, page 58 — Text, page 247

A page of notes and sketches, showing Emerson's different hands

62

King Richard's Death. A Ballad.

1
King ~~Arthur's~~ Richard's days are amaist done
His flitting life that he maun live
The King must bide him to be gone
The Monk must speed the King to shrive

2
King ~~Arthur~~ Richard lies on curtained bed
In ~~[illegible]~~ bluidy Lombard's ~~stately hall~~ stony walls
The setting sun shines dimly red
Oer the proud throng ~~[illegible]~~ who crowd the halls

hurled
curled
furled

3
The bannered pride of Englands host
The dancing plumes of white knighthood's ~~crest~~ bore
Wave wanton oer the parting ghost
To ~~guard~~ fan the dying king ~~no more~~

no more

4
Lo through the crimson curtain's fold
The ghastly frame of the icon king!
Wae wae the day! sair sight behold
Stricken by Sickness weary wing

5
His brow is awful though in death
His throne of death is purple still
But feeble is the struggling breath
His face is wan his heart is chill

~~They gaze upon his burning eye~~
His eye is on another world
Oh why so bright so fixedly
~~[illegible]~~ Doth [illegible]

Continued p. 74

Plate XI — *No. XVIII, page 62* — *Text, pages 294–295*

A later stage of "King Richard's Death"

79

That there is a decline to nations, and a period of semibarbarism ~~Stagnation~~ repose following the decline, is a fact of awful interest whose causes ~~have never been~~ are not fully explained. When E & A. G & I have ~~descended from~~ exchanged that elevation to which they had been raised by wealth literature & the arts for a ~~low level of~~ state of abject ignorance I know that adequate causes have been assigned for their final ruin Perhaps a Conqueror supplanted the pol. inhab. with bar. invad. and actually extir. the ref. of the country. Perhaps the luxury that waits upon wealth corrupted ~~the~~ public virtue ~~while~~ until faction convulsed and ambition ~~enslaved~~ enslaved the people ~~the energies of a free people~~. But I go [illegible] higher and inquire the cause of this submission of a powerful nation to a savage horde, and of mind & virtue to weakness & vice. It does not appear to me that there is any natural necessity that civilization and power should succumb to barbarism. It is on the contrary, a maxim which seems ~~to hold good~~ to be true of the ways of Providence, that to him who has much, much shall be given and It is also true that the arts of a ~~&~~ refined nation do more than supply the deficiency of ~~personal~~ physical courage just as the advantage in a combat with ~~the~~ beasts always rests on the side of man. I should rather regard the downfall of of a mighty empire before the puny force of wild and disunited savages as a special exercise of God's power designed to produce some novel phenomena in human history. Who is he who can assign the precise cause to each great event or who can predict the certain decline of future empires upon the grounds that some empires have declined.

Men are accustomed

Plate XII *No. XVIII, page 79* *Text, page 307*

The revised first paragraph of Emerson's first published work

PART TWO

Miscellaneous Notebooks

College Theme Book

1819–1821, 1822? 1829?

This notebook, untitled by Emerson, contains first drafts of themes that he wrote during his junior and senior years at Harvard, drafts of poems and essays apparently prepared in some instances for college literary clubs, miscellaneous notes, and quotations. It occupies what was originally one half of a hard-covered copybook written in from both ends to make up two sequences, one of which the editors entitle College Theme Book, and the other, occupying the remaining half of the copybook, No. XVIII[A]. Thirty-three leaves have been torn out of the College Theme Book section and penciled numbers have been inserted (probably not by Emerson) in a somewhat careless attempt to include the missing pages in the numbering. An earlier consecutive pagination which ignored the missing leaves has been erased and written over. Front to back writing and penciled pagination for the College Theme Book end with the page numbered 130. In 1823 Emerson reversed the copybook, which was probably already paginated in ink, gave the new front the title "XVIII," and used the space thus obtained for a miscellany until 1829, entering odds and ends of notes and then copies of letters. This section of the copybook is published in its chronological place as No. XVIII[A].

The copybook itself originally consisted of 142 leaves, measuring 17.3 x 21 cm. The section occupied by the College Theme Book comprises 39 leaves, what remains from the original 72 leaves of the first half of the copybook. This section begins with an insert sheet, 17.4 x 15.9 cm, verso blank, pasted to the bottom of the front cover verso. Leaves i–iii are torn out; 3 leaves are torn out between the pages numbered 10 and 15; 16 leaves are torn out between the pages numbered 18 and 51; and 11 leaves are torn out between the pages numbered 54 and 71. In each instance the penciled pagination in the manuscript makes allowance for these missing leaves, inaccurately except between the pages numbered 18 and 51. Writing continues in the volume through the page numbered 114; the pages numbered 115–119 carry the lines for an index, upside down, as though for No. XVIII[A]; the pages numbered 120–125 carry further entries for CTB; pages numbered 126–129 are blank; and the page numbered 130 contains the final entry for this section and the end of the penciled pagination. No. XVIII[A], running from the other end in what appears to be upside down writing, consists of 64 leaves of an original 70 leaves, six of the first eight leaves having been torn away, and completes the total physical volume.

[front cover verso] [1] Ralph W. Emerson.
March, 1819.

This Book contains the first Copies and rough draughts of all the themes which were written after the second term of the sophomore year. [R. W. E.]

V. Consideranda p. 151

"Et rident stolidi verba Latina Getae." [2] Ovid [*Tristia*, V, x, 38]
"Labor omnia vincit." [3] [Virgil, *Georgica*, I, 145]

ORTHOGRAPHY.				Rumford
Our		*ie*	*ei*	*ick*
honour	labour	friend	receive	terrifick
favour	superiour			republick
errour	inferiour			PARTICULAR

[front cover verso—insert] I have thirsted to abuse the poetical character of Mr Wordsworth whose poems have lately been read to me. I fear I shall hardly be able to clothe in language all the droll fancies that this poetry excites in my mind. At once then his poetry is the poetry of pigmies. It belittles the mind that is accustomed to the manly march of other muses. I am pleased with the prettiness, the exquisite prettiness of his verses and with [n] their novelty as long as their novelty lasts but I am soon conscious of a disagreeable sensation which soon becomes intolerable at [the] dwarfish dimensions of all my entertainment and am like a man creeping about in palaces of Lilliput who maugre all the magnificence would fain be on his legs again[.]

He is the poet of pismires. His inspirations are spent light. It is one of the greatest mistakes in the [world] to suppose that that much abused virtue of nature in poetry consists in mere fidelity of representation.

[1] For markings not reproduced, see facsimile, plate IV. The note on Wordsworth is tipped in. The sketches of the snakes and Colombo, in Ceylon, were perhaps inspired by a review of Percival's *Account of . . . Ceylon* (see No. XVIII, p. 349). For Emerson's knowledge of another Colombo, see Wide World 4, p. 110.

[2] "The Getae laugh stupidly at Latin words."

[3] "Work conquers everything."

[1][4] Wo to the youth whom fancy gains,
Winning from Reason's hand the reins.
Rokeby. [I, xxxi, 699–700]

There are two characters in Scott's Rokeby which do honour to his mind & heart & perhaps he has not drawn two better ones in all his ↑poetical↓ works. We have reference to Wilfrid & Edmund. They are both favoured children of Fancy though their situations in life are essentially different; Wilfrid is the peaceful neglected son of a ↑ferocious↓ Border chieftain, a⟨n⟩ ↑rivalled &↓ unsuccessful though pitied lover[.][5]

[June 15, 1819]

2d copy[6] Oh there are times when the celestial muse
Will bless the dull with inspiration's dews,—
Will bid the clowns gross sluggish soul expand
And catch one rapturous glimpse of Fairy Land
'Tis when descending fancy, from the bowers
Of blest Elysium seeks this world of ours
In wayward freak the glittering goddess flies
To make some haunt an earthly paradise
With all her various train in trackless flight
She comes at merry morn or deep midnight
They come at morn & turn their rolling cars
And emulate in speed the flying stars
Then spring to meet the rising God of Day
And ride rejoicing in his golden ray
While in their forms & colours changing shine
All the rich splendours ⟨b⟩Beauty can combine
Then the fantastick train all wide displayed
To earth descending seek some solitary glade.
The airy band in dancing circles go
And round their mistress all their revels show
[2] In their wild pastime wind their feeble horn
Like Zephyr's whispering on a summer morn

[4] Three leaves have been torn out preceding the first numbered page.

[5] The paragraph is crossed out.

[6] The first copy, dated June 10, 1819, is in a manuscript collection of Emerson's Juvenile Verse in Harvard College Library.

Forth to the breeze their golden banners flinging
The silver bells of Fairy Land are ringing
The Dryads listen as they wander by
And Echo faintly answers to their cry
The wandering pilgrim loves the vision well
The hermit views it from his sylvan cell
Th' enthusiast pauses as he ⟨slowly⟩ ↑musing↓ stalks
In the far wild-wood's melancholy walks.
Then will the gazer feel his soul arise
To claim communion with his native skies
Prepares her pinions for ethereal flight
And drinks a wild delirium of delight.
  But ah the dream is fled, the rapture gone,
The awe struck⟨s⟩ wanderer finds himself alone
Where all was Musick all is stillness now
Where all was living glory — the black brow
Of the dark wood-hung mountain. Yes, ev'n there
Where all was graceful motion thro' the air
And thousand hues & forms were streaming fair
Stand the grim rocks immoveable; nor tell
Of ought that happened in that gloomy fell
  Such are the dreams that fancy's children dream
And such their blissful joys & now her child will dream
In heaven's own palaces, then wakes again
To stern reality & mortal pain.
His pleasures are but mocking shades that flee
His pains are bitter even to agony.
[3] For Sensibility rules in *his* heart
And ⟨gives⟩ lends Misfortune a severer smart.
Yet still afflictions love to centre there
And give him up a victim to despair
The world, the sordid world can never know
The racking fierceness of his mental woe
They feel no sharper than corporeal pain
And balms alleviate or give health again
But Disappointment plants in *him* her sting
And rolling years to him no comfort bring.

While tossed unpitied on ⟨lifes⟩↑times↓ stormy wave
He welcomes gloomily his home — the grave.

June 15th 1819.

[June 29, 1819] It is generally the case in all works of literature, ⟨that⟩ and in Poetry in particular that we much oftener meet with works which we can immediately classify as additional productions of a well known school than those which bear the impress of originality. The moment however that a writer of genius has marked out a new path for himself there will be followers enough to enlarge & beautify what his invention has discovered[.]

[4] The pleasure which men manifest & the approbation they bestow upon original merit holds out such an alluring bait to those who have not yet made the experiment that young poets too often find their insignificance established, their time irretrievably wasted, before they discovered their hopes were fallacious. Rather than tread in the good old-fashioned march of Milton or Pope & Dryden, because it is ⟨unfash⟩ old fashioned, they endeavour to acquire popularity in these degenerate times by double-rhymed tender sonneteering; or by ⟨introducing⟩ ↑terminating↓ the common phrases of conversation ⟨into⟩ ↑with↓ rhyme & introducing them into heroick verse, calling it *nature*; or by various other tricks of literary legerdemain equally unworthy of poetry & of patronage. This prevailing mania for originality has ⟨howev⟩ nevertheless accompanied its evils with correspondent⟨s⟩ benefits. Among a large promiscuous assembly ⟨of⟩ there must of necessity be some men of genius — ⟨Man's⟩ The taste of mankind easily distinguishes ↑& rewards↓ their productions ⟨from the rest⟩. Such favour is always followed by the attention of authours to that kind of [5] writing & the fortunate bard soon becomes the head of a numerous school. At ↑the↓ present day Lord Byron, Scott, Moore, & Wordsworth are all founders of distinct schools ↑— as distinct as the *casts* in India.↓ The disciples of the last mentioned poet are generally denominated Lake Poets & have sometimes fallen under the lash of the Edinburgh criticks. Lord Byron's originality is not so much owing to ⟨a⟩ ↑this common↓ desire to please by novelty as to the natural peculiarity of his own character.

The proud feelings of independence which distinguish him seem to have imparted the wish not to be governed by the ⟨caprices⟩ ↑opinions & custom↓ of others but to follow only the dictates of his own caprice. His own wild character as a man stamped the character of his poetry; it is every where saddened by that deep feeling of desolateness & privation which appear to mark his own mind.[n] There is haughty indifference to all that others shall say or think with regard to it as if he wrote only for his own amusement to commit to writing the dark desperate thoughts which were swelling in his bosom. All this intensity of feeling is finely expressed & generally by a perfect simplicity of phrase which is greatly assisted by the frequent use of [6] the inflections of the verb "to be"; add to this that perhaps we cannot find in any poet such a redundancy of monosyllables[.]

A few passages which unassisted memory may furnish will exemplify the remark.

Few years have past since thou & I
Were firmest friends at least in name [7]
["To a Youthful Friend," lines 1–2]

& again in another place ——

Though thou see'st me not pass by
Thou shalt feel me with thine eye
As a thing that though unseen$_5$
Still is near thee & hath been
And when in that secret$_4$ dread
Thou shalt turn about$_3$ thy head
Thou shalt wonder$_2$ I am not
As thy shadow$_1$ on the spot [*Manfred*, I, i, 212–219]

In eight lines here are only five words not monosyllables & even of these not one is three syllables. These marks of simplicity are found throuout his writings & if examined ⟨thei⟩ closely ⟨the are of⟩ extreme fondness for scripture style & phrase is ⟨easily⟩ very perceptible. By many these little characteristicks may be thought to savour of affectation but ⟨candid⟩ ↑a candid↓ read⟨ing⟩er will find nothing which might not be well said by one whose feelings were intense. There

[7] In the left margin, vertical to the quotation, "He that hath bent" is written upward from "Thou" (below) to "Few" (above).

is not that formal manner of saying a trifle which is sometimes though not often found in Scott [7] for instance ⟨where⟩ in Rokeby ⟨where⟩ the simple fact of Edmunds ⟨ap⟩ walking five steps forward to the hearth is thus pompously stated

Due northward from the rugged hearth
With paces five he metes the earth — [VI, vi, 149–150]

But in Byron there is nothing of this; his poetry does not seem laboured but rolls forth the spontaneous effusions of the breast ∧ nor do we often find a line inserted merely ⟨to⟩ for rhyme or euphony [and these natural thoughts are embodied in a nervous style.][8] There is love & a great deal of it, it is true but it is not ↑shown by the sighs & billetsdoux↓ of a simpering miss[,] it is found in the langu[a]ge & ⟨pas⟩ actions of impassioned earnestness[,] it is a guiding principle whose influence counteracts the ↑debasing↓ tendency of vice.

All *his* heroes too are vicious characters but they are so constructed as not to be conducive to immorality; for he places them in situations which few can attain[,] he ascribes to them feelings which none can feel[,] ↑they always have↓ an elevation of sentiment which few minds can long retain & more than that ⟨he makes them⟩ at every turn he displays the bitterness of their misery —

The remark has been sometimes made that sentiments & motives of this exalted kind [8] are evidently forced & unnatural when they fall from the lips of ↑debauchees,↓ bandits, & pirates — perhaps so — but we can concieve of strong minds brought into these situations & it ⟨is⟩ ↑would be↓ cruel to ⟨deprive us of the⟩ ↑sacrifice all the high intellectual↓ pleasures we recieve from the corsair, ↑childe Harold,↓ & the Giaour ⟨by these trivial criticisms⟩ ↑to the↓ gratification of ⟨immaterial⟩ unprofitable cavillings. June 29th 1819

Tune rolls

It is not a peculiarity of our times ⟨to⟩ that ignorant people who↑se↓ ⟨would⟩ ambition it is to be thought wise should continually whine about the degeneracy of the age. However prevalent these complaints of folly & affectation may be now we have reason to believe that analogous personages enlightened ⟨the times⟩ Greece, Rome,

[8] Emerson wrote "above" in the margin beside the bracketed clause, evidently to indicate that it should be inserted after "breast" at the point of the caret.

Italy, & England at former periods when the luminaries of science in each of those nations were at their zenith. Were we not persuaded that these literary demagogues had kindled their flame of superiour information at the tapers of their predecessors we should be inclined to believe ↑Pythagorean doctrine of↓ the transmigration of souls ⟨inculcated by Pythagoras⟩. But we can account for [9] such characters in a simpler manner by substituting the Spleen, Hypochondria⟨ck⟩, & folly for the dogmas of ancient philosophers. — Whatever be the cause & it is immaterial to know we are certain of the effect. These men compass the world representing every where the misery & ignorance & depravity of ⟨modern⟩ the world with aggravating mischief. They studiously seek to exhibit the dark side of humanity as it is at present & then tell you of its faded glory & lost happiness and display every weakness with unmanly & disgusting officiousness which ⟨neither youth admire nor re⟩ ↑honest men would not ⟨repeat⟩↓ magnify. Men of this description are to be found in every department of Society. The temples of Religion, the schools of science, the groves of literature,[n] yes all that men revere are resounding the pharisaical cant of these beings. The great evil is that ⟨men⟩ too many believe them & that they are enlarging their numbers to the detriment of enterprise & progress in literature. The spirit of its patrons & sons is damped by the gloomy representations & prognostications of these Heraclituses ⟨they exaggerate misery & multiply troubles⟩. But liter[10]ature appears to be the great object of their malignity[;] they attack it in every form & in every department. Among other marks their railings are aimed at the comparative pleasures & pains of the modern student. Once when Greece was in * existence the delightful vale of Tempe was the romantick residence of the scholar. The Lyceum & Academy afforded delight as well as instruction to the philosopher; and they will remind you of the Augustan age, when Rome opened her most magnificent villas with eager respect to entertain her orators & poets & historians; when all that was splendid & refined in nature or art was the property of the contemporaries of Pliny & then they display the contrast in the ragged habiliments & universal penury of the modern. If ⟨|| . . . ||⟩once he gains admittance at the luxury of the wealthy it is only the wages of

* 'Tis Greece but *living* Greece no more [Byron, *The Giaour*, line 91].

degraded genius base enough to buy it by servility. But if the sober unprejudiced opinion of truth be given we are persuaded the moderns have lost nothing of the pleasures of literature & have added nothing to the pains of that life—. Honour, wealth, influence are now, always have been, & always will be the reward of distinction in intellectual attainments. ↑For those who think must govern those who toil.↓ Perhaps, nay, positively, the state of society has varied exceedingly since the reign || [11]–[14] ||[9]

[15] [July 26, 1819] ing man's tranquillity by a startling alarm.

If, Sir, this epistle should awaken the generosity & stifle the spirit of inquiry which have occasioned it it will have answered its end & add an additional one to the numberless proofs of the kindness of my countrymen already exerted. Egotism is necessarily its characteristick but I believe ⟨it stands single in my read⟩ the candid will allow that this disgusting peculiarity was never prevalent in my productions.

⟨The⟩Sir, the [n] singularity of ⟨our⟩ the connection that has existed between us render[s] unnecessary the ceremonials of apology for the liberty I have taken in thus abruptly addressing you. But allow me, sir, to add a parting repetition to the sincere professions of esteem & respect which ⟨ever⟩ have always endeared you to

A forgery! [R.W.E.] alias Junius alias R W Emerson

The above was not intended to imitate in the slightest respect the style of Junius which would be presumption but selected only ⟨to⟩ for the subject which it was thought would be *a prolifick one.*

July 26th

[16] [Sept. 1819]

* Ode to Melancholy.

Second Copy

Inexplicable daemon! Melancholy hail!
To these long-hallowed haunts right welcome now

* "Invitation" would be better.

[9] Actually three leaves (6 pages) are torn out here, although the adjusted pagination number accounts for only two missing leaves.

1 Come with thy pensive brow, thy silent wail
To sadden mirth's exuberance none so fit as thou

And Mirth is hateful to the soul's still calm
When she would be herself; the forms of things
2 Wearing Joy's ruddy smile & genial balm
These are not of the song which Melancholy sings.

---

3 Truly she sings of this world's vain renown,
Of glory gone & present bitterness,
The woes encircling mitre, helm, & crown,
Of man's decietful hopes, of man's assured distress.

---

4 Goddess! though hateful to the common eye:
Yet mine has loved to trace thy moody form
Beneath the mustering clouds in the far sky,
And found congenial home amid the raging storm

---

5 And haggard Superstition followed close,
Endeared to thee by a mysterious tye,
For thou wouldst shudder when his phantoms rose
And still wouldst closely cling & follow if he fly.

6 And I will follow thee a li*tt*le t*i*me,
— I deem it madness to be near thee long,
The soul may dote in vigour's earliest prime
And the once wholesome gloom grow deadly & grow strong.

[17] 7 For cloistered Collins was thy favourite child
And captive Tasso & crazed Chatterton
And hapless Petrarch; & in part the wild,
Th⟨e⟩'infuriate Rousseau might claim to be thy son

8 But why invite such gloomy matron here?
— In glad youth's fairy visions, oh tis well
To ponder on vicissitude & fear,
On misery's woeful tale & passion's furious swell.

9 Come then, dread Goddess! from thy caverns foul,
Forsake thy dark retreats, thy cypress bowers,
And all unwelcome company, the owl,
Forsake thy own dark halls, approach & visit ours!

Honorificabilitudinitatibusque

Sept 1819

First Junior Term. ⟨S⟩ Oct 1819[10]

↑"In aforetime I created *Jan* from out of a scorching fire."
Alcoran↓
"Coming events cast their shadows before." [Thomas]
Campbell — ["Lochiel's Warning," line 56]

Our imaginations of all our mental powers are those to whose impulses we are most alive — to whose pleasures we cling most closely. It is with difficulty & reluctance that man brings himself to exercise the reasoning faculties, & the more so when the subject of thought is intricate ⟨&⟩or doubtful. True, by long & frequent habit of disciplining his reasoning powers a man may learn to feel pleasure & satisfaction in these exercises, but [it] is only by long & frequent habits of ratiocination that the pleasure is gained [18] but with regard to imagination it is different. A slight incident will wake its vivacity & when once it is abroad oh how we love to follow its unbidden wanderings. It extends its influence so widely & so variously that it never can weary us with sameness & trifl⟨es⟩ing. — This is sufficiently shown in the universal regard which ↑judicial↓ astrology & the arts, real or pretended, of magick have obtained in every age. Not the illiterate vulgar only have believed but ⟨the⟩ titled power & rational learning have listened with reverent credulity to the responses of the interpreter of the stars.[11] In this enlightened age whose boast it has been that of all others this alone is free from superstition there are but few proofs to warrant the assertion. True it ⟨has⟩ ↑does↓ not as formerly influence the governments of nations. Kings do not

[10] "Digressive Continuity" is inserted at the left margin before this line.
[11] Following "stars" is a tiny sketch of what appears to be a three-legged stool.

tremble now as once in the presence of Magi or Druids [n] but in a humbler sphere it exercises an influence almost as uncontrouled.

For not to rank or sex confined
Is this vain ague of the mind —
[Scott, *Rokeby*, II, xi, 232–233]

In childhood we learn to reverence these tales of wonder & ⟨the thrill↑ing↓ therefore⟩ the thrilling interest which these tales naturally inspire is enhanced by the magnifying medium through which we view them; they have grown with our growth & strengthened with our strength[;] they are ↑inseparably↓ connected with our earliest dreams of happy childhood & come home to the heart bound up in these dear || [19]–[50] || [12]

[51] [June 22, 1820?] have works of taste — we require such works as the Rambler & books of that description, moral & learned & argumentative writers, minds of a firmer make, built up to persuade & convince the stubborn, employing themselves in encountering prejudices & detecting frauds, in checking & chastising profane abuse, & subjecting to controul those ⟨fiery⟩ passions which corrode & fret the soul.

Such works are rare in our american literature & we all feel the deficiency & the want of them is the reproach under which we have long impatiently laboured. Books of an ephemeral nature like the sketch⟨-⟩book will not remedy the evil. Although we feel the beauty of his description, although we love the picturesque glitter of a summer morning's landscape as much as any yet we would willingly exchange the transient pleasure for ⟨one⟩ ↑those↓ of active & salutary effect whose tendency is to instruct & improve rather than to entertain.

June 22d [1820?]

[52] Etsi enim satis in ipsa conscientia pulcherrimi facti fructus erat, tamen mortali immortalitatem non arbitror contemnendam.[13]

Cic[ero]. II Philipp. Sect. XLIV

[12] Sixteen leaves (32 pages) are torn out here with an inaccurate adjustment of the pagination numbers.

[13] "For although in the very consciousness of a splendid deed there was sufficient reward, yet by a mortal immortality should not, I think, be despised."

In all ages self-complacent people prate much about the dignity of human nature. It is a pleasant foible & renders them agreeable declaimers to the little circle about them whose hearts are dilating with satisfaction & even many of those who condemn the boasters after having thus satisfied their consciences sit contentedly down to be pleased & flattered by an enumeration of the graces of their species.

We wish to profess participation in these pleasures, we are glad & proud to see human nature fast advancing in proper paths; but amidst ↑these↓ triumphs of improvement in religion, science, intellect, we cannot look back without mortification and a very superficial knowledge of the history of man will evince the falsehood of their clamouring congratulations.

[53] Look over the whole history & then name the vice, however odious, what degrading enormity, the degenerate perverseness of man has not crouched unto & adored. Remember ⟨the objects of his worship⟩ ↑the direction of his best feelings — religion.↓ He has bowed down to stocks & stones — to things animate & inanimate — to the ghosts of dead men whose lives were bloody & lewd — to beasts & grovelling reptiles, to dogs & crocodiles. But the soul has to revolt at more brutal folly — they have prostituted their obedience & worship, sacrificed their dearest ple⟨asures⟩↑dges↓ of life & fortune, have attempted to abandon their interests & welfare to fiends of hell. Ingenuity has been tortured to drag forth new unimagined objects of horror on whose altars mankind might offer their devotions & repose their confidence.

It is this melancholy & almost unmingled tale of sorrow which makes us glad to meet with occasional causes of joy. We rejoice to see human nature asserting her primitive rights & achieving exploits worthy [54] of her powers. When a brave man is found panting for glory among hosts of unworthy & enslaved country-men & sets up the standard of rightful revolt from usurped or abused power we exult with him to rescue his name from oblivion & surrender it up to the care of posterity a chosen ornament of humanity. Mortali immortalitatem non arbitror contemnendam.[14] Cicero judges well. This high guerdon which is the prize of effort is the strongest of the thousand motives which urge to ⟨duty⟩ action & when ↑its↓ full force

[14] See note 13 above.

is felt it stretches all the faculties to the full & compels the mind to its noblest exertion assimilating it to higher orders of existence. It is the ⟨most⟩ surest preventive to the debasement of which we have spoken & as such should be nourished in the bosom with solicitude[.]

It would indeed be a most humiliating disgrace if after ‖[55]–[70]‖[15]

[71][16] [Feb. 22, 1821] thusiasm. It reminds us of the eternal analogy which subsists between the external changes of nature & the scenes of good & ill which chequer life.[17] Joy comes but is Speedily Supplanted by grief & we tremble at the approach of transient adversities like the mists of the morning fearful indeed & many, but fairies are in them & White Ladies beckoning.

We love

February 22 1821

* We regard these as the miseries of unfortunate climate & where better influences prevail these will be felt ⟨universally⟩ ↑more or less frequently↓ as the inconveniences enumerated in our motto are more or less frequently experienced[18]

[March 1821] On our purposes & motives as scholars.

Although it is common for the Moralist to complain that life is full of purposes whose accomplishment cannot or will not be attained

[15] Eleven leaves (twenty-two pages) are torn out here although the pagination revision accounts for the loss of only eight leaves. Besides prose the lost leaves contained one poem in couplets of at least sixty-five lines, and a shorter one, also in couplets.

[16] In the middle of p. [71] Emerson drew sketches of four men in left profile and a tiny figure of a Roman or Greek soldier.

[17] The middle of this sentence encloses: "1820
1077
743"
Beside "1820" Emerson sketched a *bonnet phrygien*, the cap of Liberty used during the French Revolution. In 1820 there was a popular uprising in Spain, and a revolution began in Portugal. Beside "1077" Emerson drew the head of a crowned king. The date is that of the year when Emperor Henry IV humbled himself before Gregory VII at Canossa.

[18] This passage is evidently a footnote or addition to some part of the lost text between pp. [54] and [71].

& that determinations broken as soon as made are worse than utter disregard to our true interest yet no man will willingly allow that his [72] great plans of life are thoughtlessly formed or may be lightly scattered. Least of all is it to be expected of those who set themselves apart for the culture of the mind & of whom therefore steadiness of purpose is more peculiarly demanded. ⟨It may be well ⟨therefore⟩ ↑then↓ briefly to survey the⟩ ↑There appear to be two↓ chief designs ⟨& intentions⟩ which the scholar proposes to himself as the ends of his pursuits & which it may be well briefly to survey.

There is a goodly picture of splendid emolument and loud approbation held out to induce him to court popularity & present renown — flattering ⟨bribes⟩ prospects ⟨to⟩ ↑from↓ which few can withold their inclination & obedience. It must be recollected however that ↑complete↓ success in these pursuits generally precludes ↑much↓ advancement ⟨to eminence⟩ in severer & solitary studies whose reward⟨s⟩ is reaped later but is more certain, durable & glorious. But as the present pleasure is by far the most satisfactory & the near view of earthly grandeur too dazzling to be coolly sustained by most men this motive is found to outweigh the other & give this direction to our purposes. And it is proper & expedient that it should be so, [73] otherwise must the offices & high places of society be left vacant or badly filled & men derive that improvement from the treasuries of the dead ⟨& not from the⟩ ↑which comes↓ more naturally & usefully [from] oracles of living wisdom.

But there is an ambition which is loftier & purer,[19] which the multitude have not the wisdom to estimate or the genius to attain; the desire to leave something to after-times which the world shall not willingly let die. Th⟨is⟩e ⟨rare &⟩ ↑operation of this↓ sacred feeling hath filled the world with all which graces it; created & perfected the sciences, moulded & polished literature, inspired poetry & invented & decorated the arts. Look at the giant spirits which ↑from time to time↓ have claimed an empire over the mind of man ever since the beginning. ↑Certainly it was a laudable principle which hath animated↓ from Homer & Aristotle, to Bacon & Milton. ⟨We still gaze with added admiration on these luminaries and what were their motives & purposes⟩ They did not write for present fame or for lucre

[19] Emerson sketched three male profiles near the beginning of the paragraph.

or for idle & unworthy purpo[74]ses but accounted it a[n] ⟨honest⟩ desire to look far down into time for the ↑honest recompense[,]↓ possession of a scholar's fame — & posterity has freely given them the undying amaranth. We do not wish to be awed by authority & give up an unmeaning adulation seduced by the name of antiquity but to accord to great names their due honor; & it is safe & wholesome to rest our thoughts on these models lest we ⟨be carried away⟩ [be] ↑won↓ with the less stable beauty of modern letters. It is well to investigate the purposes of these distinguished men that we may copy them or at the least that we may know what is great if we cannot approach it.[20]

March 1821

"Il n'y a que le mechant que soit seul" "Il n'y a que le bon que soit seul." Rousseau

Les plus sublimes vertus sont negatives.

Qui est ce qui ne fait pas du bien? Tout le monde en fait, le mechant comme les autres; — Emile p. 191 [21]

[75] [March 1821] Say not thou, ⟨that⟩ What is the cause that the former days were better than these? for thou dost not enquire wisely concerning this.

Eccles. VII. 10.

The Idol. No. 1

To those who↑se↓ ⟨are eminent in life⟩ ↑prejudices are established↓ my whim⟨s⟩ may be useless to those who are not it may afford instruction; it will be insignificant to none for ⟨the best of reasons⟩ ↑my being is not among them↓. ⟨Disguised as I am in the licensed garb of the anonymous⟩ ↑Concealed & unknown as I am↓, I care not a whortleberry for opinion.

⟨However ignorant the⟩ ↑Perhaps [the]↓ braggart wise of this generation may be ↑ignorant↓ of my history ⟨it is an unquestioned fact

[20] Emerson crossed out all the matter on the page above this point with long crossed lines.

[21] Some of the matter quoted from *Émile* precedes "March 1821" on the page but appears to have been written at another time. The quotations are extracted from Rousseau and do not follow his order. The first sentence is quoted in a footnote by Rousseau from "Diderot, préface du *Fils Naturel*." See J.-J. Rousseau, *Émile ou de l'Education* (Paris, 1876), p. 91.

that I enjoyed⟩ ↑but [n] I recollect passing↓ a pleasant summer in the city of Athens two thousand two hundred & ⟨thirty⟩twenty [n] years ago.[22] The boy-sages of the present day in ⟨beautiful⟩ ↑sweet & becoming↓ imitation of the predecessors for several centuries have ascribed to this period of time & this portion of the world, ⟨during this period⟩ [76] a miraculous excellence. The⟨y⟩ ↑Greeks↓ are supposed to have surpassed ↑all the rest [of]↓ mankind in the invention & perfection of science, in their literature and in the arts. The idolatry which says to them "these be gods" has gone yet further. Their persons must needs be beautiful & their faces divine & perfection seemed to be ⟨lodged⟩ ↑folded↓ in the robes of their dress. I have myself familiarly seen these departed demigods. I have outlived them long & from much experience have a right to decide on a question of fact.

The world is false & the opinions thereof. The present generation are silly beyond all conception; the ancient cumberers of the ground were as sage as they. At that moment however I was not aware of this & assuming the random name of ⟨Pythagoras⟩ ↑Protagoras↓[n] I walked along the noisy streets which have since been honoured with the titles of collonades. I strolled into the market-place & mingled with the noisy crowd of citizens ⟨of⟩ offensive & vulgar in the extreme [77] who were listening to a declaimer on the splendour of the times gone by; furiously summoning up all anecdotes he could imagine, foaming at the mouth with his thefts from Homer, Pisander, & Pindar, to prove the unapproached grandeur of the first ages & the ↑then↓ immaculate purity of Grecian glory, ⟨of⟩ the unstained honour of the rapid Achilles & of Agamemnon King of men. The gaping crowds wretched enough from the disorders of the state separated grumbling at the bad times & fully convinced of the truth of the orator's statements. I passed Socrates & Euripides in the market—the former ↑who↓ was ugly on a broad scale was grinning & moralizing alternately on Euripides who was squabbling angrily with a fish-woman partly to develope her character & partly to procure the breakfast for two oboli. I met Aristophanes on a similar errand with a young Athenian scavenger who was industriously cleaning the im-

[22] Near the top, in the left margin is the addition: " 400
1820
2220" Emerson used these figures to correct his statement.

passable street while the comedian was gathering jests for "The Clouds" from the boy's scurrilous prating.

[78] In a fashionable street the Sophists were parading with trains of fops who were expanding their butterfly apparel to the view or ⟨tucking up⟩ ↑adjusting↓ the ↑folds of the↓ ⟨sena⟩ perfumed senatorial robe in a modish manner. However incompatible with the views of my readers the idea may be of an Athenian Dandy I can assure the public the street was thronged with them talking dialectics & gallantry for punning was not in vogue.[23]

These things could not strike me with overwhelming awe & they are as true as my existence. I have ever since continued to walk the streets of cities great in succession & observe those reputed wise. I cannot forbear to quote the remark of my amusing friend Aristotle *παντων χρηματων μετρον και εμπαιγμα ανθρωπος*.[24]

March 1821

[79] [April 11, 1821] Earl Brodin's Plea.

There is in the centre of Scotland a romantic glen which is called "Brodin's Garden" from a tradition that earl Brodin with a small company ↑of lords, knights, & gentlemen↓[n] held their consultations here during the ↑predatory↓[n] visit of Reginald a Saxon leader who was afterwards repulsed with loss[.]

Fraydon's Essay.

O.[25]

There is a lodge within the embowering glades
Where while these bloody feuds of war did last

[23] Emerson's note at the bottom of the page, in pencil: "Note Dec 1821. Punning was in vogue."

[24] "Man is the measure and the jest of all things" (Ed.). The basic statement, originally made by Protagoras, occurs frequently in *The Metaphysics*, but Emerson appears to have added a twist to it. ἐμπαιγμά (jest) does not occur in classical Greek. It appears in the Septuagint, which Emerson quotes below, p. 187.

[25] One of Emerson's symbols for his own authorship. See p. 215. Several other points indicate Emerson's authorship of the supposed quotation from "Fraydon's Essay." The "O.", like other such symbols, he customarily put after, not before, an original passage; and in the manuscript, "O." stands below and to the right of "Fraydon's Essay." Though a curving line separates the two, the "O." seems designed as a label for the prose passage. Secondly, the interpolations suggest Emersonian composition rather than copying. Finally, there seems to be no writer named Fraydon.

I gathered them who sacrificed repose
To honourable ⟨cares⟩ ↑fears↓ & cankering care.
Their patriot eyes did watch the angry world
From this remote & sylvan solitude
While you slept out the drowsy hours of shame.
O recreant hearts! had not my lion band
Girt the hard iron round puissant limbs
And barred the golden locks of youth in steel
Wasting young years in premature turmoils.
⟨Your laggard feet would⟩
Now would your laggard feet wearily follow
The triumph of the foe on foreign shores;
And dying recollect your land in chains
Then shew your honour is at last awake
In the loud eulogy of those who died
⟨To⟩And consec[r]ate the nook wherein they ⟨dwelled⟩ ↑sat↓,
⟨And⟩To put their noble lives in jeopardy,
Here build a temple of eternal fame.
[80] I was their chief in peril & in peace
For when the ↑grumbling thunder-↓clouds of war
Encircled Albion in ⟨its⟩their horrid folds
And the storm poured its ⟨volleyed⟩ ↑sharp↓ artillery
Yon little host assembled, bid me name
⟨For I was eldest⟩
(Eldest of all) my claims to lead them on;
Proud of the rare distinction I obeyed—
"My refuge hides the banner & the priest
On whom the trust of ⟨Albyo[?]⟩England's host reposes
I vouch the honour of a loyal house
I send four gallant sons to back the claim
I hold the crown to deck my future king.—
These are ↑the↓ sole credentials I ⟨can bring⟩ ↑prefer↓."
They bid me guide their front in arms, & straight
Invested me with badges of command.
For them I sold my seignories & lands.
There are old halls which called me master once

But on my shield are foreign arms escutcheoned
And alien banners hang their Shadows there
The lands which honour forced away from me
Are firmly chartered on another house
By linked rolls of cursed lawyer parchment
And should this honest ruin of their house
[81][26] Call up the souls of my dead ancestors
To tax mine act & ⟨call⟩ ↑brand↓ me profligate
Then would I boldly answer to the charge
Arraying right & Scotland on my side.
Is there not — answer me I charge ye, ⟨men⟩ vipers!
A living principle in glorious lands
Which doth protect adorn improve & /keep/bless/them
And whisper courage in the champion's ear.
If such there be to these high trusts ordained
Th⟨e⟩at spirit will assume a form & speak
In thunder loud on my behalf to ⟨them⟩you.
For I have met ↑⟨met⟩↓ ⟨this Spirit⟩ him in the forest glades,
I've heard his whisper on the secret gale [27]
And felt his awful warnings on my soul
Oh Heaven behold me now a poor old man
Now in the cold complexion of my age
Dragged from the lethargy of closing life
Thus to defend myself & my compeers
From furious envy's merciless assault.
Oh 'twere enough to wake the tiger in me
Were young blood dancing in my veins again
To hear these laggards noted in the war
Grow bold in peace to sting their benefactors
Apr. 11th 1821.

[82_1] [April 17, 1821]
Theme proposed is —

[26] In the right margin, near the top is sketched a profile of a curly-haired man.
[27] The word "too" is written beside "gale" in the right margin.

Why is war so popular a thing, attended as it
is with innumerable miseries?

Idol No. 2

[85_1][28] I understand all languages. I have not disdained to read all the little literatures of mankind and have occasionally conveyed my thoughts to earthly men of every [86_1] mode of speech. It is necessary to say this before I give in the English tongue the tone of a conversation which was held in the French. [82_2] In the long progress of my unrivalled maturity I distinguished particularly the year thirteen hundred & ⟨eighty⟩ ↑1377↓ which was passed partly in England and partly in France. I have thus distinguished it chiefly because I then enjoyed the friendship of Sir John Froissart as true hearted and loyal a gentleman, though he courted kings, as ever existed. Ambitious to know personally him of whom fame said so much I passed myself upon him as a native knight ↑of ↑re↓nown↓ by the name of Simon de Brach. He was free & courteous and (I am glad to acknowledge it) so won my heart that I disguised at once all the mysterious strangeness of my nature and wished myself actually the person whom I pretended to be. When the army was encamped on the plain of Valenciennes I entered Froissart's tent & found him furbishing a sword which was his whole patrimony. "Sir John," said I, "men say that you are skilled in the tongues and have scanned all the chronicles of our monks and all the Greek [83] and latin learning which they tell of. Now tell me frankly, as is your wont, why ⟨it is that⟩ you seek your pleasure in siege and onslaught having all the pleasures of bookmen in your hands?"[29] "Now am I surprised" answered the knight "that you Sir Simon de Brach whom I rede to be not unknowing of church lore should ask this question at my hands but this is my rejoinder. When I was a boy in cap and plume and galloping ↑upon my father's lance↓ right merrily through Voyant's Tower I found upon an abutment of the castle a fair gilt book clasped with golden clasps

[28] The three following sentences Emerson originally wrote at the end of the essay, on pp. [85]–[86]. He preceded them with the direction "To the beginning of the theme prefix the following." He followed them with the date "Apr ⟨2⟩ 17th 1821."

[29] Here is inserted a sketch, presumably of Emerson addressing Froissart, seated and wearing a plumed helmet.

and burnished upon its edges.[30] Without, it was richly ornamented, and gorgeous pictures and illuminations were wrought within. There were portrayed the lineaments of valorous chevaliers and their combats with giants and paynims and with one another. ⟨Over against every picture was a latin page.⟩ Among them I saw the adventures which old Sir Kempis used to recount to me while I sat on his knee and many others which I was curious to understand. Over against every picture was a latin page and I immediately desired to learn to read that I might myself explore the contents. Whereupon I repaired [84] to Father Valtran who was a trusty clerk & had been kind to me and for many years he instructed me so that I learned to read in the latin tongue. All the manuscripts which were in his convent, and there was good store of them, did I study, and I found in them tales of the redoubtable heroes of old; the deeds of Sir Romulus of Rome, ↑Hector,↓ Æneas of Troy, and thereafter came Charlemagne & his peers, & ⟨a⟩Arthur with his Round Table. But when I read these did I desire to be immured in Father Valtran's stone cloister? I trow not. Every line which I read was unto mine ear as the trumpet note which SUMMONED me to battle. I panted to be a man, ⟨to⟩ ↑that I might↓ bestride a good steed, and a chafron of steel. And while I was exercising my youth in martial sports I entertained my time with these tales which I loved to hear, and to tell again. And now Sir Simon think you that it behoves me to love black cowl better than ⟨the⟩ warrior's helmet,—& the cloister than the armed plain?" "Truly Sir John the manner of my amazement is somewhat altered: I now admire ⟨w⟩that the books which holy men busy themselves in writing & reading should be stories of war." "Sir Simon," replied Froissart, "I have journeyed beyond sea to while away tranquil times and to get wisdom. I have seen men in England & in Spain & in Italy ⟨that⟩ and this have I seen [85$_2$] that all men waste their admiration on that which they have not, and God the Creator did make man with the fear of death and with muscles and organs which do avoid pain; so[n] that men do naturally shun war. But[n] they do nevertheless hugely admire those whom circumstances have forced to endure what they shun, insomuch that the⟨y⟩ admiration does in some overcome the fear & they go to war especially in

[30] Emerson sketched this scene further down the page.

youth when the fear is less and the admiration is heightened by the love of painted armour. But hark! Sir Simon, the trumpet!" With that he belted himself and hastily left the tent. You do not find this opinion in his works. He was wiser than his modern fellowmen; he devoted his writings to enlarge their stock of experience and would not tamper with morality though far abler for such an undertaking than they, for how much more than this opinion which I have expressed ⟨do they⟩ have they learned? [31]

Apr⟨2⟩ 17th 1821

[...] [32]

[86$_2$] [33] N.B. I shall only write ⟨two⟩ ↑one↓ more theme [n] while in College[.]

Farewell to Mackenneth high chief of ⟨R⟩Kintail!

[Scott, "Farewell to Mackenzie," line 6]

⟨Mackenneth⟩

⟨The Idol No. 3.⟩

Castles in the air — built, in the near prospect of leaving College —

Idol of many hearts! fair Poesy

shore

[87] [May 8, 1821]

We look for days of joy and groves of peace
Where all the turmoils of ambition cease.
Couched in his cot amid romantic bowers
Domestic visions wing the old man's hours
Then the glad sire shall gather round the door
His ruddy boys to list his fairy lore.
When mellow eve shall paint the saffron sky
And light the Star of Hesperus on high

[31] In the latter part of this paragraph Emerson has sketched a man's bust in profile and labelled it "Sr. J. FROISSART" in block printing. In the right margin is another sketch of a male head.

[32] The passage omitted here has been shifted to its designated place. See note 28 above. The April date actually follows the shifted passage. A pencil sketch of a man's head appears beside the date.

[33] Page [86] actually begins with "mode of speech" in the transferred passage. See note 28 above.

Hush the wild warble of the lonely grove
And charm the hamlet with the tales of love
By every spell to awful ⟨n⟩Nature known
She courts him willing to her sylvan throne;
While o'er his sense the bright enchantment steals
Enamoured ⟨m⟩Memory all her stores reveals.
The star oft seen in youth's rejoicing prime
Rolls back his soul along the tides of time
Recalls the spring time of ↑his↓ health and pride
His ⟨gay⟩*old* companions bounding at his side;
The reckless shout which shook the college hall
The classic lesson potent to appal
The splendid tints which ardent fancy wove
To gild the blushing morning of his love
All these shall rise for memory's brilliant theme
And float in beauty like an angel's dream.
&c &c &c

[88] (This theme is dispensed with . . . I have now closed my college list of themes.—All our old exercises are ceasing in succession, to warn us of the approaching termination of the academic course. For myself I wish it might not move so rapidly; I am in no haste to engage in the difficulties and tasks of the world for whose danger and turmoil, the independance, is a small reward. Thirty or forty years hence if I should live so long, this book will serve as a nucleus for the association of ideas and may recall very vividly all the interest which attached to the projects and fancies of a young writer. It may also recall the characters and intercourse of those who partook of the same studies and fortunes and the larger proportion of whom may at that distant period be buried in the silence of the tomb.

[R. W. E.] May 8th 1821)

Cambridge, Hollis Hall No. 9.

[89][34] The pleasures of Memory. (Written for "The."[35]

---

[34] Few of the remaining entries can be dated exactly, nor can one be sure of their sequence, since Emerson left some pages or parts of pages blank and returned to use them later. A few entries belong to late 1821. Most of them through page [114] belong pretty clearly to 1822. The footnotes supply what evidence exists for dating these entries and those following page [114].

[35] Below "The." is a printed "W" which is repeated in the top margin before

The experience of the world has at length entirely satisfied the moralist that the present is the only unhappy moment and that to the past and the future alone we are to look for enjoyment. The pleasures of memory are not so common nor so exalted as the pleasures of Hope. The latter pervade all the thoughts and designs of a man. They are mingled up in the history of his mind with every plan and every purpose, with judgements on past conduct and inferences drawn from action. Their operation is universal and unvarying. They are alike active at the summit of human power and in the lowest condition of distress. In all circumstances man finds in Hope his chief happiness, and in the extremes of anguish it seldom deserts him. A man without hope is a miserable monument of divine vengeance, an object of horror to his fellowmen & to himself, and a lamentable wreck of human virtues and energies. But deprive a man of the pleasures [of] [90] Memory and you do not ruin his peace or prospects. The memory has been lost under the pressure of a violent disease; the consequences which ensue are mournful but not by any means so terrible as the last. It leaves the mind in the state of infancy, but information may be acquired anew, memory restored to exercise by a new accumulation of knowledge, and the individual pass life with satisfaction. It is not intended to depreciate the pleasures which we derive from memory. We dwell with poetical delight upon the recollections of happy childhood coming to us as they do, softened in the distance. The utility of these pleasures is greater than those of Hope: we build a surer structure upon the judgements we draw from experience, than all the gay castles of hope which are founded in the sand.

We are the instruments in the hands of Deity. Our feet run on

---

the title. There is evidence that Emerson composed this for some meeting of the nameless literary society. The group never found a satisfactory name for itself, and in two instances is simply referred to as "the." The inscription on the flyleaf of the notebook used by the secretaries of the society reads:

"Presented by Br. John G. K. Gourdin
to 'the' ⟨May⟩ April, 1819"

The first page is headed: "Laws and Regulations of the." Emerson read an unspecified essay to the society on February 26, 1821, which may well have been "The pleasures of Memory."

his errands, our tongues speak his Commands. But we are "as petty to his ends [91] ⟨a⟩As is the morn-dew ⟨to⟩ ↑on↓ myrtle leaf, To his grand Sea." Ant & Cleop. Act 3. S. x. [xii, 8–10]

↑Two notions from Hamlet & Lear.↓[n]

It may be you have been sorely tried. The friends whom you trusted have proved false, under the guise of frankness — treacherous. It may be you have "set down in your tablets that a man may smile & smile & smile & may be a villain." [*Hamlet,* I, v, 107–108] Perhaps a more disastrous calamity has befallen you & you have been scared by the dreadful discovery that your judgment was but a parcel of your fortunes & deserted you when they left you naked. ——

— "I am sworn brother, sweet,
To grim necessity, & he & I
Will keep a league till death." Rich. II [V, i, 20–22]

"I hardly yet have learned
To insinuate, flatter, bow, & bend ⟨the⟩ ↑my↓ knee[.]"
[*Richard II,* IV, i, 164–165]

[92] [36] —— "Not all the water in the rough rude sea
Can wash the balm from an anointed King.
The breath of worldly men cannot depose
The deputy elected by the Lord." [*Richard II,* III, ii, 54–57]

Being of God proved from

1) Works of which is else no account
2) Final Causes
   a. in external matter
   b. in mind
3) examination of Atheism

Poets said "Hell was built on spite & Heav'n on pride"
[Alexander Pope, *An Essay on Man,* III, 262]

Pascal [*Pensées*] Part II Art iii. S. V.[37]

[36] The page contains two pencil sketches of male heads, and one of a man walking.

[37] Borrowed by Emerson from the Boston Library Society Sept. 8, 1821. The article argues for the existence of God. Of the list that follows, Emerson read in Bacon's *Essays* as early as Jan. 29, 1820, and he read further in his *Works* throughout the period from December 1820 to July 1821. The next reference is to Thomas

Bacon's essay on Atheism
Brown vol III lect 93
Clarke's demonstr. in Boyle's L.
Hume's Essays
Paley's Nat. Theol.

[93] The Supreme being does not operate always for the immediate short-sighted good of his Creatures[;] the world is full of evil, of passion, which may be perverted[,] of uncontrouled appetites which may be acted upon by innumerable temptations. On these circumstances is built the Science of morality. Shakespeare has admirably described the universal influence of the infinite Spirit by that of the Sun whose light and warmth bring to maturity the healthiest plant and the most poisonous — corrupts the corruptible and nourishes the splendid tribe of Flora with the same beam. It is ours to cooperate, to imbibe, to exert every faculty in opening the soil for the reception of this influence[.][38]

Rabbins said the rock that gave water to the Israelites rolled miraculously along with them thro the desart. Hence in I Cor. [10:4] *ακολουθων*[39] q.v.

Brown (1778–1820), *Lectures on the Philosophy of the Human Mind*, 3 vols. (Andover: M. Newman, 1822). Emerson withdrew volume 1 from the Boston Library Society Sept. 26, 1822, and volume 3 on Dec. 26, 1822. Lecture 93 is entitled, "On the Existence, — the Unity, — the Omniscience, — the Omnipotence, — and the Goodness of the Deity." In Oct. and early Nov., 1821, Emerson read Samuel Clarke (1675–1729), "A Demonstration of the Being and Attributes of GOD: More Particularly in Answer to Mr. HOBBS, SPINOZA, and Their Followers: Wherein the Notion of LIBERTY is Stated, and the Possibility and Certainty of it Proved, in Opposition to Necessity and Fate. Being the Substance of Eight SERMONS Preach'd at the Cathedral Church of St. Paul, in the Year 1704, At the Lecture Founded by the Honourable ROBERT BOYLE Esq." The version Emerson read is unknown, but it may have appeared in volume 2 of Sampson Letsome and John Nicholl, eds., *A Defense of Natural and Revealed Religion* (*Sermons preached at the lecture founded by the Hon. Robert Boyle*), 3 vols. (London, 1739).

Emerson was reading Hume in November 1822. He borrowed Paley's *Natural Theology; or Evidences of the existence and attributes of the Deity. Collected from the appearances of nature* (Philadelphia, 1802), from the Boston Library Society March 2, 1822. (See "Books Borrowed" and "Early Reading List," and *J*, I, 290.)

[38] Between this paragraph and the next is a small sketch of a man's head.

[39] "Following" (Ed.).

A Cardinal said one drop of X's blood atoned for a world's sins. All the rest was superfluous virtue lodged in the Pope's hands to be sold out in Indulgences.

In controversy Luther maintained good works neither end nor means. His disciple Amsdorrf went one step farther & pronounced them impediments to salvation.

[94] Arthur's Dream [40]

Who are they that in blood red robes
Like giants cross the dusky plain?
Their rapid stride by twilight dim,
Tramples the graves of English slain.

Why do they hide their mantled brows,
And shake their lifted hands on high;
What do they do in silence there,
Beneath the dark & clouded sky?

Look, are they men? [n] behold they stoop
And dig a black & ample grave
And build a vaulted tomb below
And ⟨stark⟩ ghosts ↑are↓ gather↑ing↓ round the cave.

See they have done their weary work
I see them round the chasm crowd—
↑God!↓ ⟨Lo! Lo!⟩ their ↑own↓ grave hath ⟨covered⟩ ↑buried↓ them,
—I see the dark and boding cloud. [R. W. E.]

Yon cloud shall be their fringed pall
Yon cloud shall soon be mine
⟨And sow the diamond seed which⟩
For I, in mine ancestral hall
This night my life resign
And

[95] ↑A Treatise on Coaches; in the course, and at the termina-

[40] The poem should be compared with the ballad "King Richard's Death," which originally referred to King Arthur (see p. 294).

tion of which, the careful reader will be treated with some choice words.↓[41]

Nov. 1821

On the advantages ⟨of Study⟩ of knowledge.

Although for the ⟨studious man⟩ ↑scholar↓ to write upon the advantages of study is a thing liable to the complaint which the lion made in the fable, yet as it is the office of the scholar to *write,* & none can be expected to know or appreciate advantages so well as he who hath enjoyed them, it appears proper & reasonable ⟨that we should advo⟩ to discuss this topic.

Could an individual live long enough, other circumstances would suffer that an ingenious mind should discover, alone & unaided, all the truths of science in succession which are now known, and one man should collect for himself all that body of fact & philosophy which the united labours of many men of all ages have at this day accumulated.

The mind always accommodates itself with wonderful ⟨aptness⟩ ↑facility↓ to the discipline whereby it is exercised, and in ordinary cases probably derives its very mould & outline from this action. If then the mind of such an individual as we have supposed be tasked to find out in their proper order the elements & great conclusions of all the sciences by its own sagacious observation, the deductions of reasoning, and the workings of a powerful understanding — to what a state of perfection must the mind needs be carried by the course of this vast employment. Consider what a painful accuracy ⟨must⟩ is demanded in physical researches, how keenly yet comprehensively he must seek and how cautiously combine [96][42] the mass of particu-

[41] Emerson inserted this entry in the top margin apparently as a humorous afterthought in deprecation of the essay which follows.

[42] Some oddities in Emerson's pagination create a problem at this point. Numbers from the back of this double-ender occur on several pages, most of them upside down and in the lower left corner, a few in the normal position. Most of them were quite clearly on the pages before Emerson wrote any entries. This would argue that all entries subsequent to this point were made sometime after January 28, 1823, when Emerson turned this volume upside down and began No. XVIII[A]. But the pages numbered from the other end contain some materials incontrovertibly written early in 1822, and others almost certainly of that year. The only hypothesis that fits the facts is that Emerson numbered the pages of what became No. XVIII[A] some

lars which must determine a general law. He must reduce and simplify continually from species to class and from class to genus with strict precision. When he has amassed ⟨made⟩ a considerable body of material science he must divest himself with rigorous attention of all his habits of feeling and modes of reasoning about matter, in order to come to the study of morals and understanding with correct and unbiassed views. It is indispensabl⟨y⟩e to success in these pursuits that the mind should get rid of all its early & cleaving associations, lest they should embarrass the delicate investigation.

Let this person be esteemed an exemplification of the cultivated powers of the mind. I think no one would question the happiness of such an one. With every thing lofty and noble in the character of his pursuits he enjoys every hour some new discovery which still daily and hourly elevate and expand his ideas filling his comprehension with new relations of objects, new analogies, new tendencies; pouring on him the light of which he had a few glimpses before sufficient to awaken the curiosity which is now satisfied; the laws of one science tending to explain or correct the laws of another and all blending their rays into one beautiful light and that light is happiness. Concieve of his arrival at the state of advancement of the world today[n] and you can hardly imagine aught more grand & celestial than the picture of his intellect. Is ↑pleasant↓ excitement happiness? And will not he be excited who has the secrets of the universe revealed to his admiration and that not to a stupid wonder and ignorant prostration but to powers which have inferred all and can comprehend all[,] which descry the dark links which connect effects with causes and from the study of the workmanship can [97] draw just conceptions of the surpassing intelligence which laid together the lines and atoms of the world. The richly-stored and accomplished mind that has learned to predict the return of the comet, that has found out the principles which bind ⟨together⟩ the universe in their strong bondage, which has detected the subtle economy of light, that has shewed the small passages of the heat and the vast organization which perpetually sends forth the worlds and perpetually returns

time before he actually used it. But since he did not page the "College Theme Book" he used the pagination of No. XVIII[A] to refer to the earlier journal, as on the inside of the front cover and p. [101].

them in their systems; this mind has attuned itself to a sublime harmony, to a familiarity with what is dreadful & grand which fits it for every scene in creation; to look with the friendly eye of acquaintance on the lightning & the thunder; in the once portentous comet to hail a well known visiter from the abyss of space; in earthquake & volcano to trace known effects of known combinations; it fits it for these, for more than these he has reasoned from himself & from the creation & has proved the existence of God; he has learned that an infinite number of intelligent beings exist ⟨with infini⟩ exhibiting infinite variety in their capacities & pursuits; his wisdom has ↑almost↓ rent the veil which covers their destinies; and[n] he hath marshalled their hosts in his mind, only to perform their due function in the /operations/progress/ of ⟨his mental⟩ ↑its↓ powers.

I have said that his tone of mind derived from his knowledge fits him for every scene in creation. By the wisdom which disdains earth & the habits of contemplation which mock at inconvenience or interruption he hath formed a philosophic, a godlike serenity which is not shaken by any occurrence however appalling. He can meet the spirits of heaven or hell unveiled, undaunted. I do not know [98] but that his preparation is sufficiently complete to enable him to meet the Deity. It was the idea of an ancient poet that could we be permitted to behold the machinery of the universe a spectacle so awful would ⟨overwhelm⟩ strike us dead with astonishment and I make no doubt but that if not an equal yet a similar paralyzing thrill would pervade the breast of the ⟨savage⟩ man (if the case could be) who from the ignorance of the savage could at once open his eyes upon all the knowledge which civilized nations have accumulated. Now we ⟨suppose⟩ imagine this effect to be essentially the same ⟨as⟩ ↑with↓ that impotence which shrinks to death in the presence of God; for in both there is a sudden pressure & crowding of a vast idea beyond the strength of the weak vessels until they burst. It is like the musical structure of glass which is broken by too loud a harmony. But when the faculties have been enlarged & strengthened by a constant use they become enured to higher degrees of perfection. Things may be borne however rare & astonishing when custom hath made them familiar. Kings of the East who walked upon floors of gold did not pause at each step to admire the wealth whereon they trod, but moved as upright & majestically as other men. Cherubim fly swiftly through heaven without dropping their wing—though the magnificence of the Universe be centred there, and though the richness of immortal lyres sounded on the air; and though they were enticed to linger by sweet odours that breathe from the gardens of Paradise. Cormorants, plumes, mahogany, & coral; Solomons, seals, flamingoes, and ice!

[99] Harpax dresses his daughters in costly finery. He is fatting cattle to sell.

They choose professors for frivolous merits as if they should 'choose a pilot for rowing in a pond.'

exorbitant usury of memory & mind

Men bring their 'reading raw & undigested.'[43]

And heavenly contemplation is ashamed that aught should distract its bright & burning eye.[44]

[100] *Consideranda.*

1. —"And there is no knowledge which is not valuable." (?) Burke.
2. "A method of discovering truths is more valuable than the truths it has discovered." Playfair.[45]
3. "It is the policy of America to grow and not to acquire." Webster.
4. How can Mr. Hume's Epicurean ⟨ar⟩ reasoning be combated?
5. What effect upon society have the Puritans had?

[43] Beneath this sentence and upside down on the page Emerson drew a rather neat sketch of a chest of drawers with a bowl of fruit, a jar, and an inkpot on top, and a bookshelf with books. Across the page appears a curious group of figures, apparently not related originally, but developed by added lines into a man in left profile tapping with a drumstick upon an object which is both lyre and the elaborate dress of a lady.

[44] Below and to the right of this pencilled sentence Emerson sketched four male heads and the head and shoulders of a man.

[45] John Playfair (1748–1819), British mathematician and geologist. The quotation is probably from his *Dissertation Second, Exhibiting a General View of the Progress of Mathematical and Physical Science since the Revival of Letters in Europe,* which appears in Emerson's "Catalogue of Books Read," dated Sept. 28, 1822. See "Early Reading List."

6. Cannot the Drama be reformed & be made as mighty an Engine of good as it is of evil?
7. The institution of the Sabbath. What made its place good to the ancient pagan world?

[101] 8. Is the modern system of Liberal Christianity a true one? What are its tendencies?

(This & the 5th are related.)

9. Is a man made wise or malignant by a knowledge of the world?
10. Is there an ultimate Standard of Taste?
11. What is the moral & intellectual change that takes place at death?
12. Carnot. Alfred. Roger Bacon. Socrates. Newton. Grotius. Milton. Cicero. Buonaparte. Catiline. Cromwell. Julian. Honorius. Franklin. Playfair. Mackintosh. Watt. Wilberforce. Robespierre. Howard. Canute. Peter.
13. "Give me that man
Who is not passion's slave & I will wear him
In my heart's core, aye in my heart of heart
— a pipe for fortune's finger to play what stop she please."
Shakspear. [*Hamlet*, III, ii, 75–78, misquoted.]

v. p. 137

[102] On the subject of future life, our ideas are very mean & inadequate. Our notions of its happiness are unsatisfying, and take in but moderate portions of greatness & felicity. The best visions of the Christian, ⟨are⟩ ↑correspond↓ cold↑ly↓ & imperfect↑ly↓ to the promises of infinite reward⟨s⟩, which the scripture /contains/reveals/. Many are ashamed or afraid to acknowledge this, fearing lest it be counted a deficiency or blemish in their christian character. Many decieve themselves and mislead others by false raptures, &c. &c. The proper answer to this difficulty lies in the necessity & finite nature of the human constitution, which will not admit of any expansion of ideas proportionate to the truth. ⟨The|| ... ||⟩We think that we have a full idea of what is vast and grand when we task our minds to contemplate the universe; so does the *emmet* count the hillock whereon he has built his mole, vast and high; and our mightiest comprehen-

sion no more reaches the true extent of those joys, than the emmet's notion of *vast*, approaches the greatness of the universe. ↑Political Economy has not contrived means so much as removed obstructions.↓

The Oyster complains that the Universe is a very dark hole. The office which men of science & ⟨let⟩ philosophy do the mind is not to create or sing the beauty of the world but to take down the thick walls of our house & put glass windows instead. The sun and the Universe were shining there before we saw them.

"Victory borne on wings of fire
Waves her red banner in the rattling wind" [James] Beattie
["The Judgment of Paris," lines 187–188]

[103] The piety of ——— is cold & speculative. ⟨He⟩It makes them endure all the changing circumstances of life with silent apathy. The ancient stoics did not hesitate to put an end to their existence whenever they became tired of life. "If the smoke ↑(said they)↓ be troublesome I leave it" and this was a noble and godlike action under their light.[46]

↑If you seek Pisa go to Genoa↓ [n]

Deep in the dungeons of the ⟨Florentine⟩ ↑Genoese↓
Where Mercy cannot hear the captive's cry
Lorn Pisa's thirty thousand warriors lie
And languish; stretched upon stone couches.
At Michaelmas

'Recte sapientis omnia dicuntur quia scit uti solus omnibus.' [47] Cicero.

"Ingentis spiritus res est quum Orientem
Occidentemque lustraveris animo — quum tot
animalia, totam copiam rerum quas natura beatissime fundit, adspexeris, emittere hanc Dei
vocem: Haec omnia mea sunt." [48] Seneca. [De Beneficiis, 7.3.3]

[46] Emerson quotes the same passage from Marcus Antoninus (who is borrowing from Epictetus) in No. XVII, p. [31]. See p. 226.

[47] "All things are rightly said to belong to the wise man because he alone knows how to use them" (Ed.).

[48] ". . . if you survey the East and the West with your thought, . . . if you behold all creatures of earth, all the bounteous store which Nature so richly pours forth, it is the claim of no mean spirit to be able to utter these words of God: 'All these things are mine!'"

'My father made them all.' Cowper. [*The Task*, V, 747]

I shall appeal from the apostle Paul to the Deity. [R. W. E.]

"Not Paul but Jesus" [49] J. Bentham

[104] Tnamurya [50] Oh yes there are on the wing all that ever lived ever suffered ⟨ever died⟩ & waged loved died for that holiest & basest of passions. All are now conscious, what a dread moment of stillness yet we percieve them not. Some one may be watching him, who invoked them so nobly, pointing in their prescience — the prescience of the dead to those *monuments* which may be the landmarks of his future eminence. What is found in the future? Does the kind spirit smile or shed tears? Does he rest with delight which none but spirits know on some goal of glory which his protege is to win in the race of benevolent deeds? Does the guardian see those bright & ever burning thots in the dawning horizon which are as yet concealed from the full sight of mortal friendship? The embryo plans for lessening errors of the obscure — the captive — the ignorant? Hail thee then, oh blessed Incognito, however high thy fate in the records above thy duty here is not degrading. Guard him well. He may, he will repay thee in other worlds Wed[?] morn'g 3 o'clock. You may never choose to exchange the lyre for the *Caduceus*. Before I knew you I did not ask even a dirge. I invoked Nature with rapture to sweep over my grave with her roughest elements; — for there would be the voice of a strange spirit, & there might be a strange light to guide the icy worm to his riot. We then feel as becoming portions of eternity & ask for nothing of time. Yet I do ask the favor of being remembered rather as a dead Cassandra — not prophesying but praying for thy welfare. ⟨were I a seer I wld say, if at any⟩[51] Now that I have made my peace with God for having indulged a sort of doating pride & fondness & come to be able to view you as one among a number who must encounter ills & temptations belonging to a large & incomprehensible plan, I still regret, & know that the coolest observer would do the same that a youth of your easy & poetical habits should be placed in so easy & rhymelike circumstances[.]

Were it optional to get without the precincts of [105] an infinite Being, the design of whose moral creation nature proclaims to be ultimately Virtue, & points to future rewards & punishments with almost universal consent — would it be good taste? Is it good taste to press on our com-

[49] Reference is made to Jeremy Bentham's controversial book, *Not Paul But Jesus*, printed in 1823 with the pseudonym Gamaliel Smith, but circulated earlier in manuscript, and summarized in Bentham's *Summary view of a work, intituled Not Paul, but Jesus: as Exhibited in Introduction, Plan of the Work, and Titles of Chapters and Sections* (London, 1821).

[50] That is, "Aunt Mary" (Mary Moody Emerson). Rusk dates the letter which follows "about Nov., 1821" (*L*, I, 104, n. 12).

[51] The readings of "were," "seer," "wld," and "say" are uncertain.

panions the respect we feel for animal propensities though we mention only those of sleep & eating? Am I misinformed or are not these subjects the most often to say no more tolerated among scholars when they would be joking & merry? A little of this with an occasional boast of *pride* is found among the best probably to accommodate their superiour genius to the multitude of ordinary minds.

That some of the best intellects have been infidels is certain; but ⟨that⟩ does that argue that the natural course of *mind* is to scepticism? Does it not rather go to prove that the legitimate direction is to its Source? But that led astray by passion & superficial science & false philosophy it becomes bewildered? But what else than Spirit emanating from spirit could enable those daring infidels thus to speculate? Are they not a proof of the falsehood of their own theories. Moral & intellectual excellence are not at variance but are necessary to each other. They were embodied in the character & actions of the great model of human nature — and the pursuit of future glory as connected with morals was the object of his mission, not only for a world but himself. Away with your offerings at his shrine if they come not like the emblem of those laid up in the antient ark pure gold & polished without & celestial manna ↑within.↓ His cause is worthy of master spirits & though superior to the decorations of arts & science — yet accepts them & immortalizes their gifts by the sign of the cross. If in heathen ages, *valour* was so often called *virtue,* it is to the credit of Christian times, that every thing grand is allied to morals.

Turn to B[52]

[106] ↑Pomp↓ [n]

Will human nature in its highest refinement ever rise to true dignity? The man who administers justice to his fellow men and is in office like a being of another sphere is himself not a little pleased with the *woolsack* on which he sits. There is nothing which the mind more exults in picturing than scenes of pomp & state magnificance; but separate each of the several circumstances which constitute *pomp* and they are for the most part ridiculous and all of them idle ⟨weal[?]⟩forms. Whence is it that things thus utterly unsubstantial shoud powerfully affect the soul; that [n] the vocabulary which belongs to this class of objects should be in our eyes so beautiful that we are prone to apply it upon slight & inadequate occasions?

We must first observe that th⟨is⟩e passion is universal and that the Negro ↑chief↓ ⟨of the Ivory Coast⟩ is as proud of his painted

[52] The letter continues on p. [107].

canes as the European King of the maces & wands which grace his retinue.

In the next place we should examine its nature & modes of operation, ⟨wh⟩ if it be prejudicial to the welfare or in any manner deeply affecting the history of society. We shall find ⟨that⟩ it to be a harmless & superficial thing, becoming sometimes the ruling passion of individuals and adding ↑the↓ attractions of the crown & the robe to sinful ambition for power & place but not the cause of further evil.

It is that inclination which men have to alter themselves from their true appearance & present a gayer & fantastic aspect. It hides every thing mean & low [107] which necessity forces upon common scenes, & puts out of sight familiar objects or /decks/dignifies/ them with shadowy importance. It is no representation of failings or passions which are in *disrepute* but causes all to breathe the noble, fierce & commanding spirit which naturally strikes the mind ⟨powerfully⟩ forcibly.

(Turn over the page here) A[53]

B Cannot you tell me — have you not looked within the temples of ancient idolatry — I see you at the door & you might turn round & give me (purring about the outer porch) some notices, I say, what is the Cause, that no altar is there to Poets — no incense — no worship; while the inventors of other arts mean & only usefull[,] the warriors & Butchers have their priests & nations of devotees? And yet what everlasting sources of joy does the poetry of the soul supply. It is at the feet of the Muses that the timbrel, the harp, & the sackbut should play. And what notes like these.

"He comes, he comes
The power of philosophic melancholy"

It is for such bards to inspire presentiments ⟨pr⟩described by a Resurrection to a new heaven.[n]

"There is an education of man continually going forward in the whole system of things round him; and what is commonly termed education is nothing more than the art of skilfully guiding this natural progress, so as to form the intellectual & moral combinations in which wisdom & virtue consist." Brown's Phil. Vol II p. 167.[54] Undoubtedly the times colour the common mind, but there

Pass to C

[53] The essay continues at the point marked "A" on p. [108].

[54] Undoubtedly a reference to the same *Philosophy of the Human Mind* by Thomas Brown mentioned on p. 187.

[108] A The principle of this would seem to be that mankind nourish a secret discontent of their own condition and anxious in ⟨their⟩ what they esteem to be their highest occupations to keep out of view the necessary littleness of their nature, they invest the offices of government with fantastic parade. It is curious to see whence they have derived its emblems. They have borrowed the stars from heaven with the crescent & the sun. To gain from nature whatever was terrible or fine they dragged the lion from his lair to signify their power; the eagle from the skies; the dolphin; the crafty serpent; the clouds & the flowers with the angels who were drawn down from the heavens and fairies from the woods to preside over them —[55] all were mixed in splendid profusion for the entertainment of the eye and for the pride of life.

C

were pure & bright spots in those dark nights — (of the Middle Ages) not merely from Comparison, as we find extremely different examples of Virtue under the same Circumstances. There do appear indubitable evidences by the historian of mind making their way without winds & against tides. But what is the cause that after the sleep of ages the human mind should arouse like a giant refreshed by slumber. Here is a succession of events which cannot be connected — surely any more than that night should be the cause of day. This indeed must be among the arbitrary connections of the author of Society. Who cares for poetry?[56]

"Or will the roaring surge when heaved on high
Headlong hang hushed to hear the piping swain" [James] Beattie ["The Judgment of Paris," lines 287–88]

[109] "I beg leave to gratulate my valued Correspondent on finding the secret of attaching so strongly his consciousness to dear mother Earth. The very science you extol is of her mould. True it was very good in Newton to find out so many things about the mechanism of those outposts of Creation. But they are passing — and how few ages & years before Newton's name will be used by the youngsters in some ⟨book⟩ elementary book as Noah's who built the Ark? And tho' his philosophy is connected with a higher, yet the men who travel in his light like motes in the beams

[55] Emerson added the phrase "with the angels . . . over them" from p. [109] and indicated that it was to be inserted at this point.

[56] The question, which is separated from the previous paragraph by double slashes, may, like the lines from Beattie, be an interpolation by Emerson. Both question and verse are in a somewhat different mode of handwriting from that of the paragraph above them.

of the Sun, wander far from that glorious track which will forever mark him in the Church as sitting down to the study of the bible with childlike docility, & applying the same principles of inquiry to those facts as to any physical science. But I meant not to be dull on this occasion. Hasten the banquet & the Viol — let thy heart cheer thee — pursue bravely — it is indeed, it does seem, the very mouldering of talents to hood & cloak up so prudently the love of pleasure & gain. Solomon was great & ventured for the benefit of a world — would they but listen. But avoid weariness of the flesh. Even those arts & studies which are bottomed so broadly on sentiment — these are ugly prototypes which will disturb that cool & calm peace. Give hostages to fortune was the command of a in an age comparatively dark & corrupt to one of his subjects whom fable relates to have stood on the outside of things, in the morning of the day on which he was born, married, & died, when he complained of illusion & disproportion. Hasten to enlarge the territory of the worm. What an aversion to organic, perhaps, if materialism be a fact, percipient happiness & on the vast theatre of lustreless palaces, [110] may be acted the part of Cassock & Crown. Pardon the spleen of a professed .Do you ask if life appear a vapor to those whom old Shakspeare represents in the time of "after dinner dreams"? Let their answer pass who have allied consciousness to another place so strongly as to wish the feeling infinite attached to every moment. Ask the rich imagination of the poet, or of the solidest, if his best visions do not soon become familiar & pall on his better self? Ask the Genius assigned to some incalculable period of time, if he does not foresee the moment when the whole history of this world will pass through the hand of some ancient librarian of Heaven as a scroll! Inquire of the hero who has given glory & freedom to his age, who has been elected to the heights of fame without taking any of its humbler steps[,] whose destiny has mingled the events of the present with the future, that he can make mouths at every thing but the unknown hereafter, & he will own that nothing has filled his lofty vision. "(Answer to *your* 3)" Tnum [57] "So your journal to the country is *jokey*. While the places that Cicero & Virgil trod are met with real or affected enthusiasm the children of God tread on his footsteps with indifference. You should have gone separately; other sprites than Egerian haunt the solitudes of perfect retirement. Or had you feared the "bush," gone among strangers. There is in each individual a stream of thought peculiar & when it habitually mingles with its family it seems

[57] Another anagram for Aunt Mary. The passages which follow are from a letter of hers dated "Friday, [June] 14, 1822," partially printed in Cabot I, 82–83, with additional text which Emerson omitted. Emerson wrote his aunt on June 10 that he and his brother William had made "a pilgrimage on foot" to Northboro, about thirty miles west of Boston, and that he thought his journal of the trip had "too many *jokes* to please" Aunt Mary. The journal appears to be lost. (See *L*, I, 114–115.)

oftener [111] to swell than to wander into new directions. — Can't bear Bracebridge Hall. There seems nothing gained to morals by Caricaturing the eating & drinking of the old General. There must always be those who employ the Butchers & Scavengers. To those who aim high the least habit of dominion over the palate, has certain good effects in this life, not easily calculated, apart from health & intellect & saving the endless mortification of making the mind a labourer (in case of blessed poverty) for anything more than mere comfortable living. Not safe for E to explore the poor old world. The less known of it the better. Even the erudition you tax me with wanting may be beneath attention. Why use a Scaffold if the Executioner be kind enough to free you from the fleshy nook without. The material world is fine as notices of the future imperishable — as instruments of thought."

[112] Upon Egyptian Antiquities

It is pleasant when you hear in autumn the song of the reaper which is a spontaneous expression of joy springing directly from the heart, to revert to former ages and to find in the earliest gathering of the harvest the same pleasant music from those whose bones have slept for ages and whose song hath been echoed back at every ⟨succeeding⟩ annual labour for thousands of years and is echoed back today. The joyous ⟨ploughman⟩ reaper does not know that his coarse melody is but a ↑little↓ verse of the harvest-hymn of centuries, for in each individual it is only the natural result of the moment's cheerfulness.

This is a statement of the principle which should guide our researches into antiquity. We are to trace the affinity of customs in the universal habits of feeling. We are to explain old & foreign peculiarities by the alterations which the mind will experience in different climates & different states of society. We know, for Nature hath told us, that a father rejoices in his children; that a bridal feast is an occasion of joy; that when our friends die, there is grief; that he who kills a tyrant is esteemed brave; and he who is rich in granaries and flocks happier than he who wants them. Joy, sorrow, time, chance, passion, death, pervade all ages and everywhere compose the texture of human life and this knowledge will teach us to understand the complexion and relations of various modes of life. This is the first melancholy lesson of the Scholar.

The utility of these speculations arises from their fine moral tendency. They will come late in the order of pursuit and are not therefore of eminent & indispensable importance ⟨a⟩like [113] other studies. But they come recommended to him who has a ⟨tas⟩ relish for philosophy and moral sentiment for they discover the hidden union of distant periods of time, the influence of one age upon the events of the next, and ascertain "the ⟨cycles⟩ ↑cycle↓ of the moral world." They may not instruct a man how to regulate his business or his life like other sciences but they supply his mind with premises for sublime trains of reasoning.

In going back to the earliest times to the first days of creation we divest ourselves so far as we can of all the new nature which *habit* strong as fate, clinging inseparably to all the old institutions, arts, phenomena, to the very organization of society has woven about us. We must exorcise the demon prejudice. We must quit the city, the house, the ↑cleared↓ road ↑the simplest improvement of civilization↓ and stand up on the banks of the river which no dams have confined amid woods which no axe hath felled in a solitude which none partakes but the invisible Being who has just now made it. I think that person who stands there alone among the trees with his eye on the river & his hand upon his lips is object of interest. He is the venerable head of long & far following generations ↑the germ of↓ whose distant destinies is lodged in him. In him are now kindling the passions which in his sons and his sons' generations shall create more strange & awful scenes than ↑gifted↓ imagination can measure, which shall build up this wilderness into lofty cities in their benign operation & then desolate them in their commotion. He is the only one in the world in whom resides that miraculous combination of corruptible matter contrived ⟨with exquisite⟩ ↑in↓ⁿ omniscient skill ↑with the intricate mysterious mind.↓ⁿ

Have written this over in its proper place—Wide World, No. 4, page 12.[58]

"Men of imagination are dogmatic; Avarice is perhaps the only ruling permanent passion; Patriotism is never"—said Gibbon

[58] Emerson struck through the whole paragraph. The revision appears under date of March 2, 1822.

[114]

14. "Can laughter feed the immortal mind?"

15. Fiat justitia, ruat coelum.[59] (?) e.g. Carnot's defence of the French regicides & Gibbon's account of the policy of Julius. (see p. 26)

16. "There is nothing in the understanding which was not previously in the sense — " was the ancient maxim of philosophy; Leibnitz added a clause which is the great improvement of modern philosophy. — "except the understanding itself." Stewart claims for Locke the same addition.[60]

17. The great warfare in Moral Science is between system (that is deductions from "utility" &c) & sentiment; & in life between calculation & enthusiasm. Upon this & the final theory that shall supersede all others, see — Sir J[ames] Mackintosh on M↑me↓ de Stael's Germany. Ed. Rev. Vol 22 No. 43 [October 1813]

18. Not so much matter *what* as *how* men do & speak. ↑"For forms of govern't, let fools contest," [Pope, *Essay on Man*, III, 303] &c. Style not matter gives immortality[.]↓

19. Monasteries.

20. Fanaticism.

[115]–[119][61]

[120]

21. "*Wise men* are pious & religious, and understand the rites relating to the gods; they sacrifice to the gods, & are acceptable to them; & they alone are the priests." Zeno

22. There is a comparison to be made between the primitive & the subsequent importance of passages (chiefly sacred) of the lives or

[59] "Let justice be done though the heavens fall." Ascribed to Lord Mansfield in the case of "Rex v. Wilkes."

[60] Although Emerson seems to be translating Stewart's quotations from Leibnitz's Latin, his actual source is Madame de Staël's *De l'Allemagne*, as quoted by Stewart in a footnote. See *The Collected Works of Dugald Stewart*, 10 vols. (Edinburgh, 1854), I, 233–234 and 234, n. 1. "Stewart . . . addition" is in pencil.

[61] Pages [115] through [119] contain an index to No. XVIII[A]. See above, p. 161.

language of remarkable persons, ↑at first↓ suggested by accidents, & long afterwards applied by posterity with mighty force, e.g. "He that is not against us is on our part;" [Mark 9:40] & the like; and the predictions concerning St. Peter.

23. Fear nothing; Fear not the gods, man, pain, sickness, death. The Stoic. "Deos nemo sanus timet: furor est enim metuere salutaria." [62] Seneca.

24. "My body, thou art but a little bit of the universe; but my mind ⟨is⟩or reason is neither worse nor less than the gods. Will you not place your good there where you are equal to the gods?" Epictetus
(apud Leland — Vol II p 148) [63]

[121]

25. "Non omnia possumus omnes." [64] [Virgil, *Eclogues*, VIII, 63]

26. The evils of imagination. The detriment brought by it to Xn. cause; in history & at present.

27. I have learned in whatsoever state I am therewith to be content. [Phil. 4:11] [65]

28. Be not deceived, God is not mocked; that which a man soweth that shall he also reap. [Gal. 6:7]

29. Brethren if our gospel be hid it is hid to them which are lost. [II Cor. 4:3]

30. ⟨B⟩Why art thou cast down O my soul & why art thou disquieted within me[?] Hope thou in God for I shall yet praise him ⟨who is⟩ for the help of his Countenance. [Ps. 42:5]

31. Pure religion & undefiled before God the Father is this — to visit the fatherless & widows in their affliction & to keep thy self unspotted from the world. [Jas. 1:27]

32. Moreover it is required of Stewards that ⟨ye⟩they be faithful. [I Cor. 4:2]

[62] "No sane person fears the gods, for it is madness to fear beneficial things" (Ed).

[63] John Leland, *The Advantage and Necessity of the Christian Revelation, shewn from the State of Religion in the Antient Heathen World*, 2 vols. (London, 1764, 1768; Glasgow, 1819). In Emerson's "Catalogue of Books Read," and see "Early Reading List."

[64] "Some limit must there be to all men's faculties."

[65] For this and the other Biblical quotations which follow, the King James version is cited, though Emerson's phrasing is often different and sometimes a mere approximation.

[122]

33. This is a ⟨true⟩ ↑faithful↓ saying & worthy of all acceptation that J. C. came into the world to save sinners. [I Tim. 1:15]

34. For we are workers together with God. [II Cor. 6:1]

35. If ye will do the will of God, ye shall know of the doctrines[.] [John 7:17]

36. He was in the world & the world was made by him but the world perceived him not. [John 1:10]

37. The true intent of asking advice

38. There are no successful hypocrites.

39. Many shall go to & fro & knowledge shall be increased[.] [Dan. 12:4]

40. Stand in awe & sin not. [Ps. 4:4]

41. Our conversation is in heaven. [Phil. 3:20]

[123]

42. Wherewithal shall a young man cleanse his way? by taking heed thereto, according to thy word. Ps 119[:9]

Will a man rob God? Mal. 3. 8.
I have called you *friends*[.] John XV 15
How shall we escape if we neglect so great Salvation[?] Heb II 3
The fruit of the spirit is *gentleness* gentleman, Christian. Gal V. 22
Keep thy tongue from evil[.] [Ps. 34:13]
Phil. I. 18 [66]
Blessed are the pure in heart for they shall see God[.] [Matt. 5:8]
Add to your faith [virtue; and to virtue, knowledge;] II Pet I. [:5]
With the heart man believeth unto righteousness[.] Rom. X. 10.
Arise ye & depart for this is not your rest. Mic. 2. 10
——John XVII 21 [67]
Blessed are the meek for they shall inherit the earth[.] [Matt. 5:5]
And I if I be lifted up will draw all men unto me[.] John XII 32

[124]

—None of these things move me.—

"It is not a vain thing; for it is your life." [Deut. 32:47]

By thy *words* thou shalt be justified & by &c thou shalt be condemned. [Matt. 12:37] *Of the Tongue*

[66] "What then? notwithstanding, every way, whether in pretence, or in truth, Christ is preached; and I therein do rejoice, yea, and will rejoice."

[67] "That they all may be one, as thou, Father, *art* in me, and I in thee, that they also may be one in us; that the world may believe that thou hast sent me."

Lo this is the man that made not God his strength. Ps. 52. 7.

In the multitude of my thots within me thy comforts delight my soul. [Ps.] 94[:19].

And Pharaoh said unto Jacob How old art thou? Gen 47.8

Thou shalt not follow a multitude to do evil. Exod. 23. 2

Evil communications corrupt good manners. I Cor. 15. 33

Surely man walketh in a vain shew surely he is disquieted in vain. [Ps. 39:6]

And let us not be weary in welldoing for in due season we shall reap if we faint not. [Gal. 6:9]

Blessed are the pure in heart for they shall see God.[n] [Matt. 5:8]

[125]

Study to be quiet. I Thess. IV. 11.[68]

He spake as one having authority[.] [Matt. 7:29, Mk. 1:22]

Forgive us our sins. [Luke 11:4]

"It is good to be zealously affected in a good thing." [Gal. 4:18]

They all live unto God. [Luke 20:38?]

[126–129] [blank]

[130]

There be many that say who will show us any good? Ps IV ⟨1⟩6

Because they have no changes therefore they fear not God. Ps. LV. 19

Your father Abraham saw my day. [John 8:56?]

Let no man say when he is tempted I am tempted of God. James I. 13.

What man is he who desireth life & loveth many days? Keep thy tongue from evil & thy lips from speaking guile. Depart from evil & do good. Ps. 34. 12[–14]

— art of prolonging life

The kingdom of God is not in word but in power. I Cor. IV. 20

"Commune with your own heart." Ps IV. 4

Solitude.

O grave where is thy victory. [I Cor. 15:55]

If a man die shall he live again? Job XIV[:14]

Let them first learn to shew piety at home. I Tim. V. 4.

[68] The date "Feb. 1829" appears at the upper right corner of the page and is separated from this quotation by a slash line. The hand differs somewhat, in being finer and more careful. It appears to have been written subsequent to the five quotations on the page, but this is not certain.

No. XVII

1820

Emerson appears to have acquired this notebook in order to collect notes on Socrates and to complete a dissertation on him for the Bowdoin Prize Essay competition of 1820. He soon turned it into a commonplace book and miscellany for "capping" verses, "phrases poetical," occasional verse, and the like, including one poem for the Pythologian Club. The only date in the volume is January 12, 1820, but there are entries as late as October of that year.

The manuscript, of sixty numbered pages, is made up of two gatherings of eight folded sheets each, hand-stitched, with the final leaf of the first gathering and the first leaf of the second gathering cut away, probably before use, since the page sequence is not interrupted. The page numbered 60 is blank except for a sketch and some practice handwriting. The leaves measure approximately 16.6 x 21.7 cm.

[1]No XVII ⟨MAN⟩ Jan. 12th 1820.

⟨Labor⟩On Genius.[1]

The philosophy of the mind has ⟨of late⟩ ↑for↓ years commanded much of the attention ⟨& study⟩ of the /inquisitive/curious/ & the wise. The increasing notice which it obtains is owing much to the ⟨talents⟩ genius of those men who have raised themselves with the science to /general observation/eminence/, but chiefly, as its patrons contend, to the uncontrolled progress of human improvement. However this be[,] the zeal of its advocates, in other respects every way commendable, has sinned in one point; they have laid a little too much self complacent stress on the⟨ir ow[?]⟩ success of their own

[1] Here begins what is apparently the first draft of Emerson's Bowdoin Prize Dissertation of 1820 on "The Character of Socrates." For final text see Edward Everett Hale, *Ralph Waldo Emerson* (Boston, 1904) pp. 57–93.

unassisted exertions & in their just reflections on the ⟨metaphysical quibblings & trifling⟩ ↑ridiculous & trifling speculations↓ of former metaphysicians appear to have confounded sophists & true philosophers & to have been disdainful of some who have enlightened the world & marked out a path for future ⟨progression⟩ ↑advancement↓. [2] ⟨It is probable they are a little⟩ ↑Indeed modern improvement is↓ more indebted to the wisdom of Socrates, Plato, ⟨Xenophon⟩ ↑Aristotle↓ & Epicktetus, Marcus Antoninus,[n] & such ↑of the↓ wonderful men of old than is generally allowed or perhaps than themselves were well aware.

This /remark/idea/ ⟨may not be new but it⟩ was strongly ⟨impressed⟩ ↑confirmed↓ by a consideration of the character of Socrates. In every view ⟨of the subject⟩ that great man's character ⟨will command admiration⟩ ↑is uncommon & admirable↓.[n] To one who ⟨was not familiar with the name of Socrates & who⟩[n] should ⟨take up⟩ ↑meet↓ his faithful biographers Xenophon & Plato without any previous knowledge of the man, the ↑extraordinary delineation↓ & circumstances of ⟨the⟩his biography would appear incredible. It would seem that antiquity had endeavoured to fable forth a being clothed with all the perfections that the purest & brightest imagination could ⟨compose &⟩ ↑conceive or↓ combine ⟨& give it⟩[n] ↑bestowing upon the peice↓ only so much of mortality as to make it tangible & imitable.

[3] [2] Regard this character, for ⟨an⟩a moment, only in this supposeable way & we shall be inclined to wonder that men, without revelation merely by the light of reason & nature could set forth a model of moral perfection which the wise in any age would do well to imitate. It might further form a fine subject for spec⟨ia⟩ulation to point out its faults & where↑in↓ would the difference consist, should modern fancy endeavour to create a similar paragon with all the improvements ↑with↓ which ↑a superi↓our theology could dignify the mind. But this is foreign from our purpose.

It will be well at this time ⟨as⟩ ↑both↓ in /compliment/conformity/ to custom & propriety of place to mark the ⟨age⟩ time of ⟨s⟩Socrates & observe what immediate influence the ↑moral & political↓ state of the age would probably exert upon his opinions & character.

[2] This page is reproduced as plate v.

The dark ages of Greece from the first settlement of the Egy↑p↓tian & Phoenician colonies to the Trojan War had long closed. From that ⟨epoch⟩ era the young republics had been growing in strength, population, & territory & digesting their [4] constitution & building up their name & importance. The Persian invasion had been planned & ⟨begun⟩ commenced by Darius & under Xerxes renewed, rendered formidable, & defeated. The aggrandizement of Greece which followed this memorable war was the zenith of its power & splendour & ushered in the corruption & fall of the political fabrick. The age of Pericles ⟨has⟩ ↑& the times immediately preceding & succeeding have↓ caused Greece to be remembered in history. At no time during the existence of Athens were their arts so flourishing, philosophy so exalted & refined, or their political relations so extensive & respected. The Athenian people were successful & happy at home, reverenced abroad, & ⟨superiour to the Spartans in⟩[n] ↑at the head↓ of the Grecian ⟨Republick⟩ Confederacy. Their commerce was lucrative & their wars few & honourable to themselves. In this mild period it w⟨ere⟩as to be expected that literature & science would grow up vigorously under the fostering patronage of taste & power. The Olympian games awakened the emulation of genius & produced the dramatick efforts of Æschylus, Sophocles, & Euripides, & Aristophanes, & in Philosophy of Socrates & of Plato[.]

[5] Anaxagoras was the philosopher who taught the purity & grandeur of the divinity[,] who wisely discarded the licentious religion of the age & inculcated doctrines of a more exalted nature. But his system was too refined & unconciliating for his age & he dared not divulge in public the elevated sentiments which he entertained respecting heaven & which ⟨the⟩he ⟨pr⟩ instilled into the minds of scholars like Pericles & Socrates[?] Pythagoras the first philosopher had instituted a romantic fraternity[.]

From Diogenes Laertius

Ου μονον ες Περσας ανεβη Ξενοφων δια Κυρον,
Αλλ᾽ ἄνοδον ζητῶν ἐς Διὸς ἥτις ἄγοι.
Παιδείῃ γαρ ἑῇ Ελληνικὰ πράγματα δείξας,
Ως Καλὸν ἡ Σοφίη μνήσατο Σωκράτεος.[3]

---

[3] "Up the steep path to fame toiled Xenophon
In that long march of glorious memories;

Translation

Haud solum ad Persas ascendit Xenophon propter Cyrum
Sed reditum quaesivit in Jovis qui duceret
Doctrina enim sua Graeca gesta ostendens
Ut honestum Sapientia meminit Socratis.

The oracle declared

Σοφος Σοφοκλῆς, σοφότερος Ευριπιδης,
'Ανδρῶν δὲ παντων Σωκράτης σοφώτατος.[4]

The great Origen is of opinion that the devil when he delivered that ⟨opinion⟩ sentence, by giving Socrates those partners purposely obscured his glory while he was in some measure forced to applaud it. (Kennet[t]'s Greek Poets [p. 120]) —

Plato's Distich on Aristophanes
Epitaph

Αἱ | χάριτες | τέμενος | τι | λαβεῖν | οπρ' | ουχι | πεσειται |
Ζητουσαι, | Ψυχην | ευρον | 'Αριστοφανους.[5]

[6] Sophocles (says Kennet[t] [p. 97]) was eight & twenty years younger than Æschylus & twelve older than Eurip.

Sophocle enfin, donnant l'essor a son genie,
Accrut encore la pompe, augmenta l'Harmonie;
Interessa le *Choeur* [chorus] dans toute l'Action;

In deeds of Greece, how bright his lesson shone!
How fair was wisdom seen in Socrates!" Diogenes Laertius,
Lives of Eminent Philosophers, Ch. 6, "Xenophon," II, 58.

In the left margin is a pen-and-ink sketch of the bust of a man in full face. The quatrain is numbered "1" in faint pencil; the other two Greek passages on the page are numbered "2" and "3" respectively, in the same way.

[4] "Wise is Sophocles, wiser Euripides,
But of all men Socrates is the wisest." (Ed.) Emerson is quoting from Basil Kennett, *The Lives and Characters of the Ancient Greek Poets*, 1697, p. 119.

[5] Kennett, Emerson's source, says the distich was composed "as is thought, by Plato," and that it "will make large amends for the loss of his Epitaph." Kennett translates it (p. 132):

"Seeking a Shrine, that ne'er should be Defac't;
The Graces pitch't on *Aristophanes's* Breast!"

De vers trop *rabotteux* [rugged] polit l'expression;
Lui donna chez les Grecs cette hauteur divine,
Ou jamais n'atteignit la faiblesse Latine.[6] Boileau
["L'Art Poetique," Canto III, 75–80]

[7] Like the little waxen /memorial/tablet/ to whose frail keeping Columbus /committed/entrusted/ ⟨the unfolding of⟩ his magnificent ⟨secret⟩ discovery. Of /his/Soc[rates']/ declaration that he knew nothing but his own ignorance an old translator says & in this there seems to me a marvellous fund of knowledge

Archelaus was surnamed Physicus successor to Anaxagoras & Master of Soc[rates] . . .

[7][8] ↑Human Nature wants no such champions↓

The ostentatious rituals of ⟨Egypt &⟩ India which worshipped God by outraging nature though softened as it proceeded west was still too harsh a discipline for Athenian manners to undergo. — Socrates had little to do with these & perhaps his information on the subject was very limited. He was not distinguished for knowledge or general information but for acquaintance with the mind & its false & fond propensities, its springs of action, its assailable parts, in short his art laid open its deepest recesses & he handled it & moulded it at will. Indeed we do not have reason to suppose that he was intimately ⟨acqua⟩ versed in his own national literature, Herodotus, Homer, Thucydides, Pindar, etc. — His profession in early life had perhaps imparted a little of poetic inspiration but his leading feature seems to have been ⟨a⟩ Sagacity — little refinement, little erudition. His genius resembled Aesop[.]

[8] The greatness of the philosopher ⟨was⟩ shines forth in its fullest lustre when we examine the originality, the bold & unequalled

[6] "The *Sophocles*, with happier genius strove,
To raise the Musick, and the Pomp improve;
Gave his just Chorus in the Plot their shares;
And filing rugged Words by nicest Ears,
In *Grecian* Grandeur reach'd that envied height,
Which *Rome* in vain affects, and apes with weaker flight."
(Kennett's transl., p. 102)

[7] After the Boileau quotation Emerson sketched the heads of three men in profile.

[8] Before writing on the page Emerson had drawn rather full sketches of three men, one in an armchair, a second with a heavy beard, and a third with a beard and a turban topped by a crescent.

sublimity of his conceptions. His powerful mind had surmounted the errours of education & had retained useful acquisitions whilst it discarded ⟨the⟩ what was absurd or unprofitable. He studied nature with a chastised enthusiasm & the constant activity of his mind endowed him with an energy of thought little short of inspiration. When he speaks of the immortality of the soul or when he enters on considerations of the attributes or nature of the deity he leaves the little quibblings of the sophists, & his own ↑inferiour↓ strains of irony & his ⟨mind⟩ soul warms & expands with his subject[.] We forget that he is man — he seems seated like Jupiter Creator moulding magnificent forms & clothing them with beauty & grandeur[.]

It seems to have been the aim of his philosophy to have be⟨en⟩come a patriot. He desired to reform his countrymen — he did not wish to flatter them. He saw them sunk deeply almost irrecoverably in moral degradation [n] & still soothed by the ↑miserable↓ voice of flattery & he ventured to address to them the harsh but wholesome precepts of wisdom & virtue[.]

[9] When we reflect how little favourable was the state of Athens to virtue, how much less to extraordinary moral attainments for a frightful voluptuousness had deeply entwined itself in the very vitals of the devoted city we may appreciate the matchless merit of the character of Socrates. To a young man ambitious of distinction the inducements to vice were strong & numberless — to virtue weak & few. ⟨The⟩ Popularity among those unworthy republicans was to be acquired not by self-denying discipline, by hard struggles for preeminent purity & the austere unconciliating virtues of their ancestry, but by bribery, ↑squandered treasury↓, & superiour profligacy & lavish flattery of the corrupt populace.

The progress of debased manners is /well/sufficiently/ marked by the successive character of the comedy from its primal innocence at its institution to the grossness which ⟨disgraces⟩ stains the dramas of Aristophanes[.]

The ⟨religion⟩ ↑infidelity in the popular religion↓ which Anaxagoras entertained but dared not avow & which ↑proved fatal to↓ Socrates was openly proclaimed in the licentious comedy & applauded by the strangely wayward multitude. At the theatre impiety excited strong feeling & bestowed interest on the piece & their gratitude to the poet who could so faithfully amuse them would easily find apologies for ↑even more↓ glaring ⟨faults⟩ ↑impropri↑e↓ties↓. But [10] the philosopher was the teacher of youth ↑who should do away every improper impression↓ & must not be allowed to infringe upon the faith which they had been accustomed to venerate. Besides they came to the lectures of the sage with dispassionate minds & there was no purpose of warm feeling to be answered which /needed the aid/might pardon the introduction/ of profanity. When men came to condemn there were reasons enough to array in argument[.]

The *demon* of Socrates partakes so much of the marvellous that ⟨we⟩ there is no cause for surprise arising from the perverse difference of opinion manifested in its discussion. Those who love to ascribe the most to ⟨the⟩ Inspiration in the prophets of God's revealed religion claim this mysterious being as akin to the ↑ministering↓ spirits of the Hebrew religion. Those who like Xenophon know not of this similarity or those who do not regard it as founded in fact look upon the *Δαιμων*[9] merely as a personification of native ⟨fac⟩ sagacity. Others have Charitably supposed that the philosopher himself was deluded into a belief that he ⟨he⟩ enjoyed a peculiar communication with the Gods by means of this imaginary being; learned their will & ⟨performed⟩ ↑accomplished↓ their ends.

[11] When he entered the world there was a freshness of glory diffused about his country which no after times equalled. The magnificent splendour of their name ⟨do⟩ should seem to astonish the commonwealths. They had atchieved miracles which overshadowed the fame of Hercules & the other heroes of their romance to which they had been taught to look up with admiration. The stupendous success which had now become familiar to them led them to an independence of character the ultimate effect of which was that caprice which we ↑so often find occasion to↓ blame. It was natural that after beholding the full display of their own might which had been so ⟨p⟩effectually exhibited these republicans should acquire a confidence in themselves a fearlessness ⟨at⟩of all contending⟨s⟩ interests about them & which extended from the whole political community to each separate state & from the state to the individual. No wonder that timid prudence should find little room among them ⟨& that⟩ ↑nor↓

[9] "Spirit" (Ed.).

was it extraordinary that an overflowing zeal to approve themselves freemen [12][10] should sometimes make judgements hasty. But we would not apologise for one of the blackest crimes on the page of human history. If any palliation can be offered it is this for a sin ⟨of⟩for which they endeavoured to atone in subsequent sorrow[n] & by the gift of honours to the dead ⟨alas how⟩ ↑splendid if↓ unavailing.

Their Persian war. It was a stern trial of human effort for conquest & for freedom[,] rage & pride conflicting with energetic & disciplined independence.

↑There are↓ Old halls that called me master once
But alien banners hang their shadows there
Upon my shield are foreign arms escutcheoned
The ⟨lands⟩ bartered lands which ruin forced away
Are firmly fastened on another ⟨race⟩ house
By linked rolls of cursed lawyer parchment

[13][11] The ship has been seen off ^ said Crito but the philosopher was unmoved & although h

What is God [?] said the disciples & Plato replied it is hard to learn & impossible to divulge[.]

[14] We come now to his principles of belief as a moral philosopher.[12] — No we don't. — In prison he was directed in vision to seek the favour of the muses. This appears at once utterly incongruous with the views & habits of feeling usual to the philosopher[.] His plain sense, his peculiar mind which would reduce every thing however unpromising to the measurement of square & compass was little conversant with ↑the↓ poet⟨ic⟩'s /visions/golden dreams/ — his airy nothings, his bright personifications of glory & beauty & grandeur — this we know & do not need to be apprised of the philosopher's dismay at this new difficulty but he gave himself little hard labour

[10] In the lower half of the page Emerson sketched the heads of five men and two girls, and a full-length soldier with a plumed helmet. See plate VI.

[11] In the upper left corner Emerson drew a rough sketch of a three-masted ship and an ornate paragraph sign. He filled most of the page with sketches of six male heads, most of them in left profile. In the space to the right of "unmoved" but not as a part of the unfinished sentence, Emerson wrote "Death I. M. pol." See plate VI.

[12] Over "principles" appears a sketch of a building.

by his decision subjecting himself only to the mechanical exercise of ⟨para[?]⟩ versifying Æsop.

Poetry finds its origin in the more delicate features of the soul, in ⟨the⟩ nicer shades of moral distinction [15] a subtle agent which finds its legitimate & blissful circulation in the sympathies of man, in perceptions of beauty ↑& excellence↓ common to only a peculiar order of minds. The mind's eye like that of the body has its various parts differently combined in all. Some reach onward to extreme length, others take in an immense comprehension of objects, & other some are capable neither[n] of long or wide view but are susceptible of exact impressions from the ⟨most⟩ minute & ordinarily invisible.

language of adulation

Archipelago

pro[po]unders of theori[e]s which they could not explain[.]

They were desirous to show themselves freemen amid all their *vices*[.]

"For I have remarked many a towardly word to be wholly neglected or despised in discourse which has passed very smoothly with some consideration & esteem after its preferment & sanction in print." Swift.

[16] One ⟨of the most prominent⟩ leading feature in ⟨the⟩ his history is fortitude; perhaps it was not natural to him but the fruit of that manly philosophy which named fortitude, temperance, & prudence its primal virtues. A mind whose constitution was built up like his, ⟨might⟩ mould↑ing↓ ⟨any virtue⟩ the roughest rudiments into shape & /order/beauty/ might create its virtues & set them in order to compose the aggregate of character. He ⟨did⟩ was not like other men the sport o[f] circumstances but by long habits of forbearance & denial possessed that controul over his ↑whole↓ being which enabled him to hold ⟨that⟩ the same even unchangeable temperament in all the extremes ⟨his fortunes if such a word is practicable such an individual⟩ ↑of life,↓ alike when the young nobility of Greece were proud to follow in his train & when he suffered the death of a criminal. The evidences of this fortitude are familiar. When all the Judges of the Senate betraying an[n] unworthy pusillanimity gave way to the demands of the populace Socrates alone refused [17] to sacrifice justice to the fear of the people & ⟨Al⟩ on

another occasion⟨e⟩ in the forefront of a broken battle Alcibiades owed his life to the firmness of Socrates. It were easy but needless to multiply instances.

Not to forget Mrs Socrates.[13]

"On her white breast a sparkling cross she wore
Which Jews might kiss and infidels adore"
[Pope, *Rape of the Lock*, II, 7–8] [14]

[18] In Athens learning was not loved for its own sake but for sinister ends. It was prized as a saleable commodity. The Sophists bargained their literature, such as it was, for a price which ⟨was regu⟩ always exorbitant was regulated by the ability of the disciple. And this must always happen more or less in the infancy of letters. — In a money-making community literature will soon thrive. It must always follow not precede successful trade. The first wants to be supplied are the native ones of animal subsistence & comfort & when these are ↑more than↓ provided for & luxury & ease begin to look about them for new gratification the mind then urges its claim to cultivation[.]

☞ From this place to "Detached Sentences" the pages are to be improved by lines, or verses, containing any thing remarkable, either in expression, or sentiment, or remote association, principally quoted, but likewise original ones. ¶ The original are distinguished by the letter "O." or Junio or [R.W.E.].[15]

[19] "John! the charges that are objected against the[e] thou oughtest to repel by battel or els by the laws of the land to be drawne hanged & quartered" Apud Godwin's life of Chaucer.[16]

---

[13] There follow a full-length figure, of indeterminate sex but probably male, sketched from the back, and a shrouded figure lying on a crude bench, intended perhaps to represent Socrates.

[14] Quoted in Hugh Blair, *Lectures on Rhetoric and Belles Lettres*, Lecture XXXVIII, "Nature of Poetry. . . ." This was a prescribed text for Emerson in his sophomore year at Harvard.

[15] See plate VII for Emerson's symbol of original authorship.

[16] William Godwin's *Life of Geoffrey Chaucer* (*with Memoirs of John of Gaunt*), (London, 1803), II, 452, listed in "Catalogue of Books Read," and probably read in July 1820.

To an Eagle passing.

Ay, thou winged & cloud cleaving minister
Whose happy flight is highest into heaven
Well may'st thou swoop so near me. I should be
Thy prey & gorge thine eaglets. Now thou art gone
Where the eye cannot follow thee, yet thine
Still pierces downward onward & around
With all pervading Vision. Beautiful!
How beautiful is all this visible world
How glorious in its action & itself &c

[Byron] *Manfred* [I, ii, 291–99]

In the blue depth of the waters
Where the wave hath no strife
Where the wind is a stranger
And the sea-snake hath life
Where the mermaid is decking
Her green hair with shells
And the [Byron, *Manfred*, I, i, 76–81]

[20] Shall we build to ambition? — oh no
x x x x x x x
To Beauty? — ah no; she forgets
The charm which she weilded before
Nor knows the foul worm that he frets
The skin which but yesterday fools could adore
For the smoothness it boasted or tint which it wore.

Herbert Knowles ["The Three Tabernacles," ll. 6, 11–15, misquoted]

You shall be indemnified for the advantage you have abandoned[;] trust it sir they will fall but we shall stand; they are marked out already[;] sons of the morning who exalted themselves above the stars of God shall be brought down to hell. Even now the wheel turneth & the haughty ones with a high look & a proud heart, the fair & the strong, shall be made low. Junio Silly

---

The innocent are gay, the lark is gay
That dries his feathers saturate with dew
Beneath a rosy cloud while yet the beams
Of day spring overshoot his humble nest

Cowper's Task [Book I, 493–96]

"I've aye been vera proud Gentlemen" (he said) "to be a Scots Poet — but never sae proud as just noo."

Peters: letters de Hogg.[17]

[21] He that finds
One drop of Heaven's sweet mercy in his cup
Can dig beg rot & perish well content
So he may wrap himself in honest rags
At his last gasp; but could not for a world
Fish up his dirty & dependent bread
From pools & ditches of the commonwealth
Sordid & sickening at his own success.

Cowper's Task. [Book III, 803–810]

strive
alive
five
hive
shrive

T[18] ‖...‖ done my endeavour my christian Brethren to manifest unto you the unsearchable riches of the Promise; the manifold & marvellous glories of the Ancient of days displayed unto sinful men in the Gospel, all which should encourage & compel us to magnify his name. Lip service is not the homage which he expects. The astonishing benefits of his providence unto you which his preachers vainly seek to enumerate in propounding his religion ⟨un⟩to your credence, the mind he hath bestowed upon you, the crown of daily rejoicing untill your lives' end ↑with↓ which he hath crowned you; all the capacities & joys & opportunities by which you are girded about are clamouring in your ears for a suitable return so far as your little power can reach to be offered unto God. Give to his worship your heart & life. Sacrifice ↑then↓ a goodly oblation on his

[17] Slightly misquoted from John Gibson Lockhart, *Peter's Letters to His Kinsfolk*, 3 vols. (Edinburgh, 1819), I, 135; read by Emerson in Aug. 1820, possibly in the American edition of that year. Letter XII in volume I deals with James Hogg, the Ettrick shepherd, and the quotation is his response to a eulogy.

[18] The "T" is ornately drawn and decorated with human faces. A section cut out of the leaf for pp. [21]–[22] creates the gap in the manuscript.

altar, even ⟨your⟩ the best of your days, the desire of your soul, & the pride of life. Amen Boringtan sermon to ||...|| tievy—Junio—

Whether the objects of his ⟨worship⟩ ↑devotion↓ be the daisy or the polestar. [R. W. E.]

[22] He stood forth like a consul of Rome—as proud as earthly honours could render a man. Junio

Gambol & song & ⟨life's⟩⟨↑youth's↓⟩⟨gay laugh⟩ ↑festival↓
are done
Today the toilsome march must be begun. Junio

Come to my ||...|| here Genii ⟨forlorn⟩ ↑are borne↓
Pavilioned on ||...|| abandoning the morn [19]

Thy hands are reeking with untimely sin
Thy hands are pledged to push a massacre
Thy hands are busy now with parricide
Three things might make a man forswear the world
And waste his manhood in a hermitage [R. W. E.]

Come to my

A fiery soul which working out its way
Fretted the pigmy body to decay
And o'er-informed the tenement of clay
Dryden's Absalom &c [lines 156–58]

And all to leave what with [n] his toil he won
To that unfeathered two-legged thing—a son
Ibid.[20] [lines 169–70]

[23] Come to my mansion [21] house of the forlorn
Well have you known it destitute & torn
Come if you dare come when the winds are high

[19] Some one has cut out what appears to be the figure of a man, leaving only the lower part of his trousers and his feet. The feet are pointed toward Emerson's symbol of authorship [R.W.E.] repeated three times as directive footsteps. In the margin, opposite the mutilation, Emerson wrote "Corrupt" three times in a diagonal column beside an irregular column composed of four instances of his symbol of authorship.

[20] Several sketches follow—of a man with a jar or urn, of a man with a whip, of a man's head and shoulders, and three male faces in left profile.

[21] Two separated words "and abide" are written above "to my mansion" in the top margin.

Go if you will go when Geralde must die
And summon Euphorbus Grave give up thy dead
Think on the thunderbolt think how it sped
When the heaven smitten Titanon bowed his head
If thou art bolder speak thy wishes forth
One witness shall hear from the heights of the north
One pen shall record in the scrolls of the sky
One *arm* shall perform which is powerful on high
Woe to thee! woe! if the daemon fulfil
His oath to Euphorbus of havoc & ill
He stood on a height in ⟨of⟩the fields of the air
Sanctioned by Death; & Destiny was there
In Odin's dread hall in the north of the sky
He doomed thee Euphorbus abandoned to die
He summoned the dead from their coffins to come
And shriek in thy ear their own horrible doom
With the hosts of black hell embattled they came
Blasted & seared with their fiendish flame
Till the hall of the Thunderer rung with the peal
And Nature shrunk back from his chariot wheel
[24] He hung out a comet to point you the way
Which leads to your ruin

"Ex ungue leonem!"[22] said John Bernouilli when he saw Newton's solution of his problem.

Wi coulters & ↑wi↓ forehammers
We garred the bars bang merrily
Until we came to the inner prison
Where Willie of Kinmont he did lie
Apud [Scott] Guy Mannering[23]

[22] "In June, 1696, John Bernoulli [1667–1748] challenged the mathematicians of the world . . . to solve . . . two problems [relating to the theory of gravitation]. . . . On the 29th of January, 1696/7, the challenge was received by Newton from France and, *on the next day,* he sent to Montague, who was then President of the Royal Society, solutions of both problems. . . . It is said that Bernoulli recognised the author from the sheer power and originality of the work; *'tanquam ex ungue leonem'* ['just as (one knows) a lion by its claw']." Louis Trenchard More, *Isaac Newton: A Biography* (New York, 1934), pp. 474–475.

[23] The epigraph to chapter XLVIII. Scott calls it "Old Border Ballad."

Trefoil, vervain, Johns-wort, dill
Hinders witches of their will [24]

— Inscription on Edinburgh Tolbooth. —

A prison is a house of care
A place where none can thrive
A touchstone true to try a friend
A Grave for one alive
Sometimes a place of right
Sometimes a place of wrong
Sometimes a place of rogues & thieves
And honest men among.[25]

Die prophet in thy speech
For this among the rest was I ordained[.] Hen IV
[3 *Henry VI*, V, vi, 57–58] [26]

How like a hateful ape
Detected grinning midst his pilfered hoard
A cunning man appears whose secret frauds
Are opened to the day. — [Joanna Baillie] "Count Basil" [27]

[25] E. for Capping.[28]

(— and Etna flung)
Eternally its pyramid of flame — [Barry] Cornwall's Poems
[Bryan Waller Procter, *A Sicilian Story*, IV] [29]

(— shall ride a feasting long,
In his old velvet jerkin & stain'd scarfs)
Ere we contribute a new cruel garter. Ben Jonson

[24] The couplet is from *Guy Mannering*, ch. III.

[25] Epigraph to *Guy Mannering*, ch. XLIV.

[26] Epigraph to *Guy Mannering*, ch. LIV.

[27] Epigraph to *Guy Mannering*, ch. LVI.

[28] The pastime of capping verses involved replying to a given verse with one rhyming with it or beginning with the same first or last letter. Many of the verses here located come second-hand from Scott's novels; reading the mottoes of the chapters struck Emerson as an antidote to unhappiness (see p. 44). Other verses he doubtless remembered from Byron, whom he read extensively, and Cowper's *The Task*, whose "home-scenes" he liked. But many quotations seem to be taken from other sources than the originals. Where possible, Emerson's presumed source is suggested.

[29] Emerson probably encountered this quotation in a review of *A Sicilian Story* in *The Edinburgh Review*, XXXIII (Jan. 1820), 147.

(And the crackling trunks)
Extinguished with a crash — & all was black. Byron
["Darkness," lines 20–21]

Even dogs assailed their masters — all save one. Idem
[Byron, "Darkness," line 47]

(& beheld)
Each other's aspects saw — & shrieked & died,
Even of their mutual hideousness they died. Byron
["Darkness," lines 65–67]

— (a shallow grave)
Even of the cold earth of our cave. Idem

(Here the self torturing sophist wild Rousseau)
(The apostle of affliction, he who threw)
Enchantment over passion, & from woe. Idem
[*Childe Harold*, III, lxxvii]

— Existent happier in the fly or worm. Id
[*Childe Harold*, III, lxxiv]

Extreme in all things hast thou been betwixt.
[*Childe Harold*, III, xxxvi]

Ere Evening to be trodden ⟨down⟩ ↑like↓ the grass Id
[*Childe Harold*, III, xxvii]

Quath Arthur, "thou heathen cokein
Wende to the devil Apolin!"
The Payen fell dede to grounde
His soul caught Hell-hound —
Morte Arthur [30]

[26] D.

Dark Guido came not all that night while she — Cornwall
[*A Sicilian Story*, VI]

— oer her tearful sight
Drew her white hand to see his raven hair. Idem
[*A Sicilian Story*, VII] [31]

[30] The lines actually occur, with some differences, in "Arthour and Merlin," but Emerson's source may have been responsible for the title he gives.

[31] Emerson probably encountered this quotation and the preceding one in a review of *A Sicilian Story* in *The Edinburgh Review*, XXXIII (Jan. 1820), 148.

Die & endow a college or a cat. — Pope
[*Moral Essays*, "Epistle III," 96] [32]

(I am going to the parliament)
(You understand this bag. — If you have any business)
Depending there — be short & let me hear it
(And pay your fees.) — Little French lawyer apud Guy Mannering [33]

Dark shall be light. — Guy Mannering [Ch. XLI, XLIX]

Delightedly dwells he 'mong fays & talismans.[34]

Doubt & jealousy & fear [35]

Disparked my parks & felled my forest woods
Richard II [III, i, 23] [36]

(Than a successive title long and dark)
Drawn from the mouldy rolls of Noah's ark.
Dryden Absalom & Achit. [lines 301–302]

Daughter of Honour. I have cast mine eye
(Upon thy form; & I will rear this beauty
Above all styles.) (Mammon to Dol. in [Jonson] "the Alchemist") [IV, i, 116–118]

Defy the world's accumulated shock [By Emerson?]

It may be noticed that great men's contemporaries are as great as great men; that Pope's Correspondents write as well as Pope.

[27] A

And Sheriff I will engage my word to you. [1] Hen. IV.
[II, iv, 563] [37]

(Unfit to live or die — oh marbled heart!)
After him fellows drag him to the block. Measure for Measure
[IV, iii, 68–69] [38]

---

[32] Epigraph to *Guy Mannering*, ch. XXXVIII.

[33] Epigraph to ch. XXXIX.

[34] From *Guy Mannering*, ch. III, where it is assigned to "a modern poet."

[35] From *Guy Mannering*, ch. IV.

[36] Epigraph to *Guy Mannering*, ch. V.

[37] Epigraph to *Guy Mannering*, ch. LII.

[38] Epigraph to *Guy Mannering*, ch. LVII.

And to the stir of Commerce driving slow,
And thundering loud with his ten thousand wheels Cowper.
[*Task*, III, 739–740]

An Earthquake reeled unheededly away! Byron
[*Childe Harold*, IV, lxiii]

Aye but to die & go we know not where. Shaks.
[*Measure for Measure*, III, i, 118]

And they drank the red-wine through the helmet barred. Scott
["The Lay of the Last Minstrel," Canto I, iv]

Advance the eagles Caius Placidus. [Henry Hart] Milman
[*The Fall of Jerusalem*]

G

— From his eye
Glares forth the immortality of Hell — Byron
[*Manfred*, III, iv, 77–78]

God & the prophet! Alla Hu! Id.
[*The Siege of Corinth*, XXII, 713]

Good even Sir Priest and so late as you ride
With your [39]

Leap into light [40]

Let us be affectted by what will be true tomorrow a[s] if it were true today

[28] B.

Built the high-pillared walls of Chilminar. Moore
[*Lalla Rookh*, III, 6] [41]

[39] Part of a poem from Scott's *The Monastery*, ch. IX. A pencilled sum, "110 and 75 / 35" two fractions, "25 / 35" and "10 / 35" follow in the manuscript.

[40] This phrase is written diagonally left to right downward and to the right of the pencilled numerals. Presumably this and the following entry were to be read with the capping verses on the next page under the letter "L."

[41] Emerson may have encountered this line in a review of *Lalla Rookh* in *The Edinburgh Review*, XXIX (Nov. 1817), 16 or in the poem itself, which was withdrawn from the Boston Library Society May 10, 1819, and July 1, 1820.

L.

Like the echoes of caves to the voice of a child. [John] Neal
["The Battle of Niagara"] [42]

Lo all my glory smeared in dust & blood. Shakspeare.
[3 *Henry VI*, V, ii, 23]

— Leaped the live thunder; — not from one lone cloud —
Byron [*Childe Harold*, III, xcii]

Lady! A nameless life I lead — Scott
[*Rokeby*, III, xviii, 442]

"No profit goes where is no pleasure ta'en
In brief, sir, study what you most affect" Shakspeare
[*Taming of the Shrew*, I, i, 39–40]

P.

Prowling & gorging o'er carcass & limb. Byron
[*The Siege of Corinth*, XVI, 456, misquoted]

[Q.]

Quavering gaunt hunger's deep carnivorous howl.

[29] Moor Alfaqui, moor Alfaqui,
Though thy beard so hoary be,
The king hath doomed to have thee seized,
For Alhama's loss displeased.
Wo is me Alhama! [Byron, "A Very Mournful Ballad on the Siege and Conquest of Alhama," I, 71–75]

F

Far in the chambers of the west — Scott [*Rokeby*, II, i, 1]

[43] The faery beam upon you
The stars to glister on you
A moon of light
In the noon of night
Till the fire-drake hath o'ergone you
The wheel of fortune guide you
The boy with the bow beside you
Run aye in the way
Till the bird of day

[42] The first word of Neal's line is "As."

[43] The following two stanzas are written in pencil, evidently later than the context. Presumably they were to have been used in the "T" section which follows.

And the luckier lot betide you
[Jonson, song from *The Gypsies Metamorphosed*]

T.

They form — unite — charge — waver — all is lost. Byron
["The Corsair," Canto II, vi, 244]

To Beauty? ah no, she forgets. Herbert Knowles.
[*The Three Tabernacles*, line 11]

To witch the world with noble horsemanship. Shaks.
[1 *Henry IV*, IV, i, 110]

The unblenched bickering of the noontide car. Milman
[*Samor*, Book I, 293–294]

[30] O.

Oh what is intellect? — a strange strange web —
(How bright the embroidery but how dark the woof!
(apud "Peter's letters") [44]

One crowded hour of glorious strife,
(Is worth an age without a name. [Scott] (Old Mortality) [45]

Oh! make her a grave where the sunbeams rest! Moore.
["She Is Far from the Land"]

For a definition & description of poetry which is very good see Ed[inburgh] Rev[iew] LVI No. [XXVIII, (August, 1817)] on "Coleridge's literary life & Opinions."

[46] ⟨The ideas⟩ upon modern poetry in a Review of Campbell's Gertrude of Wyoming are finely written [*Edinburgh Review*] Vol 14 [(April 1809)]

W.

Went clattering down the steeps of night forever. Hogg.

Where the blue wave rolls nightly oer deep Galilee. Byron.
["Destruction of Sennacherib," line 4]

Wae, down, & weary, thy lot shall be

[44] See p. 217, note 17.

[45] Epigraph to ch. XXXIV, labeled "Anonymous," but by Scott.

[46] The following sentence is in pencil and evidently written later than the context.

Epic[47]

Peripatetics	*Stoics*	*Epicureans*	Socrates
		Epicurus	Plato
	Zeno	Lucretius	Aristotle
	Seneca		
	Arrian		
	Apollonius		
	Marcus Antoninus		
	Cato		

[31][48]

Y. You You You

Ye stars! which are the poetry of heaven. Byron
[*Childe Harold*, III, lxxxviii]

You You

"Shew me," says Arrian the Stoic, "a person who is sick & happy, in danger & happy dying & happy, banished & happy disgraced & happy, such a one is a Stoic." "By means of unseasonable divination many duties are neglected." Arrian.[49]

H

He thought as he took it the dead man frowned. Scott.
["Lay of the Last Minstrel," Canto II, xxi]

If you must die, saith Marcus Antoninus, let it be as those who have suffered nothing. If the smoke be troublesome, I leave it. —[50]

"It fanned his cheek it waved his hair
Like a meadow gale in spring
It mingled strongly with his fear
Yet it felt like a welcoming." [Coleridge, "The Rime of the Ancient Mariner," VI, 456–459][51]

[47] Written in a large, ornate hand, and perhaps a false start for the heading "*Epicureans*" below.

[48] Between pp. [30] and [31] two leaves have been cut out.

[49] The first quotation is from Arrian's *Discourses of Epictetus*, Book II, ch. xix; the second from Book II, ch. vii.

[50] A paraphrase of "Marcus Aurelius Antoninus, the Emperor, to Himself," Bk. V, 29. In the last sentence Marcus Aurelius was himself paraphrasing Epictetus as reported in Arrian's *Discourses of Epictetus*, I, xxv, 18, and IV, x, 27.

[51] Quoted verbatim from Scott's *The Monastery*, ch. XII. The errors in this rendition are Scott's.

[32] S.

⟨Of all that now blossom⟩ or gracefully wave
The cypress alone shall b[52]

Alas my friend must leave his pleasant wife

My friend must abandon his ⟨house⟩ ↑wife↓ & his ↑*columned*↓ home
And the groves which encompass his ponderous dome —
Of all which ⟨in beauty luxuriant⟩ ↑now blossom or gracefully↓ wave
The ⟨sad⟩ cypress ↑alone↓ shall weep over thy grave
[R. W. E.][53]

I.

In solitude of unshared energies. C. Lamb

I feel its (i. e. Destiny's) silent billows swell beneath me Milman [*The Fall of Jerusalem*]

I have builded pavilions aloof from the world
Where the houses of heaven their broad portals unfurled
I have summoned strange guests to my palace of wo
The /angels of mischief/swart fiends/ ↑shall rush↓ ⟨from their dread⟩ haunts below
Their hosts in battalions have crowded my hall
The timbrell & trumpet have sounded the call
But the proud hall of Reginald thronged though it be
Hath a space and forever allotted for thee
Come if you will come &c

Though heroes meet no echo answers here
The taunt of vengeance or the scream of fear.

[33] Sic te Diva potens Cypri
Sic fratres Helenae, lucida sidera
Ventorumque regat Pater
Obstrictis aliis praeter Iapyga

[52] These lines were experimental revisions of lines 4 and 5 below.

[53] In the left margin: "President de Thou," presumably Christophe de Thou (1508–1582), first president of the Parliament of Paris.

Navis quae tibi creditum
Debes Virgilium; finibus Atticis
Reddas incolumem precor
Et serves animae dimidium meae.[54] Horat. Od.3 L.I.

Pallida Mors aequo pulsat pede pauperum tabernas
Regumque turres. O beate Sesti
Vitae summa brevis spem nos vetat inchoare [incohare] longam.[55] [Bk. I] Od.IV.
—— nec dulces Camoenas [amores]
Sperne puer neque tu choreas
Donec virenti canities abest
Morosa.[56] Od.viii [Bk. I, Ode IX]

Ausa et jacentem visere regiam
Vultu sereno, fortis et asperas
Tractare serpentes, ut atrum
Corpore combibe⟨tur⟩↑ret↓ venenum,
Deliberata morte ferocior
Saevis Liburnis scilicet invidens
Privata deduci superbo
Non humilis mulier triumpho.[57] Od.xxxi
[Bk. I, Ode XXXVII]
Eheu fugaces, Postume, Postume,
Labuntur anni. x x ⌈Expurgata Horatii⌉
Linquenda tellus et domus et placens
Uxor neque harum, quas colis, arborum

[54] "May the goddess who rules over Cyprus, may Helen's brothers, gleaming fires, and the father of the winds, confining all but Iapyx, guide thee so, O ship, which owest to us Virgil entrusted to thee, — guide thee so that thou shalt bring him safe to Attic shores, I pray thee, and preserve the half of my own soul!"

[55] "Pale Death with foot impartial knocks at the poor man's cottage and at princes' palaces. Despite thy fortune, Sestius, life's brief span forbids thy entering on far-reaching hopes."

[56] "Nor in thy youth neglect sweet love nor dances, while life is still in its bloom and crabbed age is far away!"

[57] ". . . she even dared to gaze with face serene upon her fallen palace; courageous, too, to handle poisonous asps, that she might draw black venom to her heart, waxing bolder as she resolved to die; scorning, in sooth, the thought of being borne, a queen no longer, on hostile galleys to grace a glorious triumph — no craven woman she!"

Emerson wrote "Cleopatra" vertically upward beside these eight lines in the left margin.

Te praeter invisas cupressos
Ulla brevem dominum sequetur.[58]
[Bk. II, Ode XIV]

Huc vina et unguenta et nimium breves
Flores amoenae ferre jube rosae
Dum res, et aetas et sororum
Fila trium patiuntur atra.[59]
Omnes eodem cogimur. Omnium
Versatur urna; serius, ⟨|| . . . ||⟩ ocyus
Sors exitura, et nos in aeternum
Exilium impositura cymbae. Od.iii Lib II.

For all must tread the paths of fate
And ever shakes the mortal urn
Whose lot embarks us, soon or late
On Charon's boat, ah! never to return. — [Philip] Francis' Version. — [*The Odes, Epodes, &c, of Horace*] [60]

[34][61] O ye that live a pleasant life
And ⟨sleep the sleep of joy⟩ pleasant hours employ
Whose merry days are free from strife
And sing the song of joy

King Richard's days are amaist done
His flitting life that he maun live
The King must bide him to be gone
The monk must speed the King to shrive [62]

[58] "Alas, O Postumus, Postumus, the years glide swiftly by. . . . Earth we must leave, and home and darling wife; nor of the trees thou tendest now, will any follow thee, its short-lived master, except the hated cypress." This passage is written vertically upward in the right margin.

[59] "Hither bid slaves bring wines and perfumes and the too brief blossoms of the lovely rose, while Fortune and youth allow, and the dark threads of the Sisters three."

[60] Though Emerson may have taken the translation directly from Francis, it is more likely that he took it from Blair's *Lectures on Rhetoric*, where it appears in a footnote to Lecture XIV, "Origin and Nature of Figurative Language" (see the Philadelphia ed., 1853, p. 154). The translation is written beside and to the right of the Latin original.

[61] Most of the page is filled with pen or pencil sketches, including four male figures in left profile and contemporary dress, two classical heads, and other figures. The full page is reproduced as plate VIII.

[62] These two stanzas seem to be the first stages of "King Richard's Death. A

[35] A magician of might from the Dead-Sea-shore[63] ↑Ho[?]↓ All things are full of labour. Who art thou, O thou Slugard, ⟨Who con coun↑ter↓ ↑acts↓⟩ Who Counteractest the d⟨|| ... ||⟩cres [decrees?] of Nature & Providence.[64]

Phoenix

Gift of the Sun, his golden plumage shone
In Afric's boundless solitudes, alone.[65]

[36][66] We attach in our kindly hours a⟨|| ... ||⟩ life to every thing around us. What man of feeling ever passed from school without personifying his tenses, loving one aorist & hating another? We affix a portion of moral character to all things[.]

Some Spirits who like distant ⟨Saturn⟩ ↑Jupiter↓ delight to encompass themselves with a ring of clouds & mist to swallow up their light

There are more dreadful anecdotes than these. The terrible tradition has come down to us of the divine abandonment of the most holy Temple____when the brazen doors of the sanctuary were burst open without hands & ⟨a sound⟩ the rushing of mighty wings was heard & there came a voice saying *Εξελαυνομεν εντευθεν*![67]

[37] White with unnumbered tents of fair display
The Spartan plain Salutes the rising day[.]

Ballad," which appears in something like final form at pp. 294–295 and 303–304. The first stanza was dropped; the second became the first stanza of the last version. More stanzas appear on p. 235 below.

[63] In pencil. A pencilled sketch of the magician appears below and to the left. On the right and further down is a pencilled sketch of what is apparently a pilgrim.

[64] "↑Ho[?]↓ . . . Providence" is written in a large, loose, boyish hand, which with baffling misplaced quotation marks and parentheses (not reproduced) and other features suggests very early composition. The phrase "Skin for Skin" is omitted from the text. It is written above "(Slugard)" but is in a more mature hand. The initials "J^r I K" are centered on the rule below.

[65] Apparently a later, poetic version of a similar line on p. 231.

[66] About half the page is occupied with four pen sketches of male heads, with the journal entries interspersed.

[67] The conclusion of this solemn jape may be freely translated, "We are leaving here."

—This lowland frame
Stark as the sinews of a mountain man[.] Junio

Does Charles the royal tiara unclasp
Doth Cleopatra lift the slimy asp? [R. W. E.]

⟨writing out[?]⟩ ↑a sublime &c↓ ⟨like ||...|| of old ↑⟨to bless⟩↓, a sublime & striking intellectual personification⟩ without father,[n] ⟨&⟩ without mother, without descent having neither beginning of days nor end of life, king of Salum ↑&↓ priest of the most high God[.][68]

[38][69] It bursts over us like a dreadful dream terrific by the fierce minuteness of circumstance.

Proud is the path, untravelled & unknown,
Which stretches far to Fame's pavilion lone

Crossing the lands & compassing the sea
Pervading nations — what is that to thee?

The gay lark sleeping on a rosy cloud. [R. W. E.]

Fleeter than lions leaping to their prey
Phoenix clad with rich golden plumage the gift of the Sun.
in Solitude, & Grandeur.[70] [R. W. E.]

Calumet
befel
jubilee
jeopardy
behove[71]

IMPORTANT ⟨Freshmen bran⟩dishing their bread[72]
And gravely aiming at a brother's head

[68] The rest of the page contains five sketches of male heads in left profile.

[69] The page has sketches of several male heads, mostly in left profile, and one of a man apparently lying propped up in bed.

[70] "Phoenix . . . Grandeur": evidently another version of the couplet on p. 230.

[71] These words appear in an irregular column in the left margin, running from "IMPORTANT" (above) to "And belted" (below).

[72] The following sets of couplets are evidently an attempt at a comical class poem, like the one on pp. 244–245. Apparently for insertion somewhere, Emerson wrote "challenging scrutiny" upward in the left margin.

2 {And belted Junior⟨s⟩ furbishing ⟨their⟩ ↑this↓ gun⟨s⟩
Mad, squadding, swearing sweating all for fun

Zany

1 {Genius of Sophomores without reproach
Parades the land — a bustling cockeroach!

3 {Whilst Senior Sophisters enjoy the hour
Otium cum dignitate [73] at "the Bower"

interlude

sheltered from reproach & rebuke [74]

Zany

Zany.

[39] Sheltered Shalt

Sheltered

or the wild winds cease their remorseless clamour,

Sheltered

Sheltered

Beginning of Theme on Solitude.

To other worlds by roving fancy led
The minstrel's airy pilgrimage was sp⟨d⟩ed
There musing silent⟨ly⟩ in majestic mood
Abandoned by all things that live he stood
And pondered strange⟨ly⟩ on Nature's low design
Degrading man & all his powers divine [75]

Another.

Mid crowded throngs, by roving fancy led,
The minstrel's thoughtful pilgrimage was sped
Lost to their lowly scenes his soul of pride
Sought its ⟨old⟩ ↑high↓ home to bolder thoughts allied
Now, human virtues proudest ways to scan
Or pondered pensive on the faults of man
But worn & saddened by a load of care

[73] "Leisure with dignity" (Ed.). ("cum dignitate otium," Cicero, *Pro Sestio*, 98.)
[74] Written on an irregular diagonal line, extending into the right margin.
[75] The passage is crossed through.

He sought repose but could not find it there
While the thronged city shook with clamour rude
The angry minstrel sighed for Solitude

Whither do you go? (asked Cyprian timidly as Ippolito rushed by him). "To the theatre, to the gambling-house, to the brothel,"—he roared—"to floods of wine, to songs of madness." [Charles Robert Maturin, *Fatal Revenge; or The Family of*] "Montorio."

[40] poetic

For use — phrases poetical

rescuing & crowning virtue. x "coldest complexion of age." x ill-conditioned. x cameleon x zeal x "booked in alphabet" x cushioned x compunction x beleagured x halidom x galloping x whortleberry x spikenard x staunch x council-chamber x star-crossed x till its dye was doubled on the crimson cross x countless multitudes x abutments x panoply x sycophant smile x kidnapping x beheaded x demigods x signal ↑adj.↓ x Cleopatra x ambidexter x register ↑verb↓ x defalcation x

— The infancy of all nations partakes of the same characteristics. The institutions of advanced civilization diverge widely from each other, & seem to obey no natural & invariable law. One nation does not therefore readily coalesce or even sympathize with the customs & character of another, if these have grown up to a certain maturity. But the first rude efforts of a savage tribe are understood by all, as all men are interested & delighted with the actions & expressions of a child of whatsoever kindred. In this manner the representations of the thoughts [76]

If thou hast a peice of earthen ware, says Epictetus, consider that it is a piece of earthen ware, & by consequence very easy & obnoxious to be broken; be not therefore so void of reason as to be angry or grieved when this comes to pass Quoted by Addison.

habitual to a youthful people must forever attract the interest of Mankind.

1000 years 1000 miles

[76] Emerson stopped to note down the lines from Addison, then completed the sentence.

[41] Detached sentences [77]

"His philosophy was a source of good sense." Indeed the natural effect of his philosophy was to form the accomplished pagan so perfect a man as was compatible with the state of society and a nation of disciples of Socrates would support a state of human advancement which modern ambition & zeal with all its superiority of knowledge & religion may never hope to attain & could Greece have expelled her sophists & corruptors & shewing respect have extended the influence of her ↑most↓ mighty mind till the chastity of her manners restored & the infirmities of her dotage displaced by social virtues[,] the minds of her citizens had been deeply imbued with Socratick sentiment[,] she might have looked on till this day with commendeable unconcern at all the ⟨changes⟩ revolutions that have played around her. A free & a↑d↓mirable commonwealth of philosophers & Philip of Macedon & Mummius of Rome might have slept in obscurity. — We can offer no apology for [42] this idle digression but pleasure of the though[t?] though but in fancy.

of homely virtues — Pandects

Unite & direct to their proper end the wandering energies of the human mind

In the blue depth of the waters
Where the waves have no strife
Where the wind is a stranger
And the sea-snake hath life
Where the mermaid is decking
Her green hair with shells
Oer my calm hall of coral
Came the sound of thy spells [Byron, *Manfred*, I, i, 76–83]

Mont Blanc is the monarch of mountains
They crowned him long ago
With a robe of clouds on a throne of rocks
With a diadem of snow [Byron, *Manfred*, I, i, 60–63]

Mortal to thy bidding bowed
From thy mansion in the cloud [Byron, *Manfred*, I, i, 50–51]

---

[77] See p. 215. Originally Emerson appears to have left the intervening pages blank. Here he inscribes miscellaneous thoughts for the essay on Socrates.

I hear a voice you cannot hear
I see a hand you cannot see[78]
A voice is in my troubled ear
Which thrills with woe & death to me

The voice of autumn calls to me
I hear it in the pines
With solemn cadence mournfully
The swelling strain declines.
The lightning stooped from the cloud
And rent that proud castell
The thunder-clap long & loud
Rung out King Richard's knell.[79]

[43] Improvement

A Poem delivered before the Pythologian Club[80]

Oblivion's veil of weight too long has hung
O'er themes of fancy meet for poets' tongue
Pictures of glory which the bards of yore
Made vocal once vocal alas no more
And why↑?↓ ⟨not vocal⟩ⁿ ask not! the Muses blush to tell
Since gowned monks with ⟨d⟩censer cross & bell
⟨Compressed the free⟩
Clogged the free step & mighty march of Mind
While Rhyme the etherial soul confined
Since then a thousand years have gone their ways

[78] Cf. Scott, *Rob Roy*, epigraph to ch. XVII:
"I hear a voice you cannot hear,
Which says, I must not stay;
I see a hand you cannot see,
Which beckons me away.
Tickell ["Colin and Lucy"]"

[79] Of these eight lines, the first four became stanza 9 and the last four stanza 12 of "King Richard's Death. A Ballad" (pp. 303–304). Emerson may originally have intended the lines "I hear a voice . . . death to me" for the ballad but if so he excluded them from the last version.

[80] A club for "extemporaneous discussion" to which Emerson was elected in June, 1819, composed of "the fifteen smartest fellows" in the sophomore and junior classes (*L*, I, 85). On April 21, 1820, Emerson wrote his brother Edward that he had delivered the poem before the Pythologian Society (*L*, I, 93).

And Time swept off the pride of other days
[↑The gilded palace & imperial tower
In turn have yielded to his palsying power↓]
Rome — child of Jove & mistress of the world —
Her strength is crumbled & her ↑banners↓ furled
Aye the wide world ⟨is⟩was ⟨yielding⟩ ↑hasting↓ to decay
And Grandeur too ha⟨s⟩d flung his wand away.
But thou oh Rome like fabled ⟨p⟩Phoenix fell
And infant nations clamoured out thy knell
Obscured beneath thy mouldering fall awhile
The arts looked forth with new & gladdening smile
But Poesy has lost her early grace
The bloom celestial that adorned her face
Down to this age of proud Advancement vain
The silver fetters of old Rhyme remain —
[44] Shame on the age! Improvements temple high
Towers up from earth ⟨&⟩to comprehend⟨s⟩ the sky
Presumptuous man has stretched his powers so far
He marks the path for every rolling star
Sends Commerce forth to find the polar cave
To unknown climes the colonizing slave
From its wild way the lightning ⟨it⟩He deterrs
And makes the winds his willing messengers
Hurls down ⟨‖ . . . ‖⟩gross Ignorance from his ancient throne
And makes high heaven with pride its fair ↑creation↓ own.
Yet poetry still ⟨rears⟩ ↑hangs↓ her drooping head
By Rhyme's dull powers in hopeless bondage led
Her sons too oft by fair external won
Delight to see the shining shackles on
And while they strive to plant her ancient reig⟨h⟩n
Permit the chafing thraldom to remain.
Oh there were two — their names are writ in heaven
To whom the spirit of the nine was given
Cherish, oh earth, their /names/*dust*/ — above their graves
Triumphal laurel-crowns Urania waves.

For Fairy Land was shook when Shakspeare fell [81]
And Milton's death was jubilee in hell.
[45] But some have ⟨ch⟩ sought them for their guiding star
Dreaming they raise the⟨ir⟩ glory ⟨while⟩ ↑which ⟨th⟩↓ they mar
And Shakspeare's thoughts by servile pilferers drawn
Shine on the pulpit & the stage adorn
Presumptuous ⟨ur[?]⟩ dunce the gem thy folly steals
By singly shining thy vile theft reveals
Borrow not Shakspeare's sentiment of fire
Oh do not tamper with Apollo's lyre!

There is an evil in Improvement's way
Which criticks make in this poetic day
They seek the favour of the uncourtly throng
As men whose independent minds are strong
With judgement weak they find some childish bard
Who rhymes & writes because the times are hard
With blind applause they welcome all his verse
Proclaim the better & defend the worse
No matter when no matter where he strays
'Tis harmless Eccentricity in ways
And fashion's sons [n] will shed their iron te⟨e⟩ars
And weep & wonder when their bard appears
While ⟨|| . . . ||⟩ wisdom weeps & wits may wisely laugh
Like Jews they bow before a homemade calf.

[46] Ages unborn must see the muses rear
The throne of universal empire here
Nor Heaven allows to be developed now
The mighty plans to which the world must bow
The tree of promise blossoms — full & fair —
barb But other plants must claim our present care
garb
astrolabe ⟨How sinks the pride of nations & of kings
And the poor grandeur of exalted things

[81] Between this and the preceding line Emerson wrote a horizontal caret, perhaps indicating an intended insertion.

brutes	What erst provokes Jehovah's bolt of wrath
brutes	Mad Babel's pile — Ambition's earliest path; —
	The boasted splendour of departed Rome
confutes	Or polished Greece, — young Architecture's home —
brutes	Or Egypt's mightier pyramids — even they —
suits	Yield to the slow strong progress of decay,
mutes	Slow sinks their pride ⟨of all⟩ before the ↑giant↓ pile⟩ [82]
pollutes	buried in laurel
fruits	Home of the art & Cradle of mankind
lutes	In solemn grandeur all the soul salutes
salutes	Like thunder swelling o'er the voice of flutes.
computes	

— "As they drifted on their path
There was silence deep as death
And the boldest held his breath
For a time." — [Thomas Campbell] Battle of the Baltic [lines 15–18]

[47] O'er many a land that wails in deep despair
That ⟨over glory⟩ ↑sapphire↓ thrones of empire once were there
O'er gorgeous Glory's unescutcheoned grave
Fate /leads the way/points to ⟨Athens⟩Greece proud/ empress of the wave
Her vig⟨o⟩rous sons[?] dispelled the latent[?] gloom
And welcomed youthful Architecture home
There Sculpture Painting Science loved to dwell
Sculpture &c.
And Musick witched them with volu
Then as he stood celestial & alone
Minerva's aegis turned the god to stone

(Homer's antiquity is proved from Odyss. L.1. ver. 351. & from Iliad L.XX ver 308. [John] Gillie's [*The History of Ancient*] Greece. Item, he flourished before the return of Heraclidae, 80 years after taking of Troy.)

[82] "⟨How sinks the pride . . . pile⟩" is crossed through. The list of words, "barb, garb . . . salutes, computes," was written in the margin to the left of this cancelled passage and the three following lines of poetry.

Lo where Columbus breaks the pitchy cloud
That wraps his time in darkness as a shroud
Come forth young hero at the call of heaven
To thee a task of lofty name is given
Bind wreath of iron round thy youthful brow
Gird up thy loins for Fate's /high message/dread mandate/[83] now
Know ye who ⟨lea⟩ moves the great Columbus on
Who leads the way till the New World be won
⟨It was⟩ ⟨n⟩Not recreant Spain nor favouring human power
For man opposes & the storm-clouds lower
No — it is graven in the book of Fate
Opposing worlds would now oppose too late
[48] Though Earth & sea & Hell itself withstand
Tremendous might would bear him to the land
For those dread arms that built the universe
That sent the planets on their ceaseless course
They are outstretched ⟨to bind the Ocean Storm⟩
⟨And veil dark⟩ ↑gaunt↓ ⟨Danger's terrifying form.⟩ GAUNT[84]
And though in funeral train wave after wave
Unveiled the ↑maddening↓ horrors of the ⟨ocean⟩ ↑⟨threatening⟩↓ grave
Yet their thin bark through heaving mountains strayed
Through unknown wiles of Ocean undismayed
Until the hour in Fate's high ⟨|| . . . ||⟩time was come
The promised land came bursting through the gloom

Rome Muses! if yet ye live & still controul
The mortal melody that wakes[85] the soul
Strike the wild harp till magic numbers swell

[83] Emerson first wrote two dashes, then filled them in with these two variant readings.

[84] In the right margin.

[85] The word "high" appears between "that" and "wakes" in this line, but it is in print writing and seems to have been in its present location before the line was written.

On the glad gale that ⟨knows those numbers⟩ ↑bears them proudly↓ well
Summon the soul of musick from the strings
Which far around the strange enchantment flings
For Rome for Rome the thrilling notes prolong
Unearthly theme demands unearthly song
How did her Genius mount in fearful flight
While blazing splendour mocked the gazer's sight
The startled stars the growing greatness feared
Still favouring Fate the giant structure reared
[Ambition's power each host or hero quelled]
[Till distant lands the towering throne upheld]
[49][86] The hour is come the mandate hath gone forth
And Death & ⟨Pain[?]⟩Havoc hasten from the North
The world's vain homage could not stay thy doom
When kneeling nations hailed "Almighty Rome"
— The thunderbolt is launched Ruin seizes all
And the far islands shook in terror at they fall
O'er climes o'er ages Empire holds ⟨its⟩ ↑this↓ way
⟨Still⟩ westward where Destiny's strange pathway lay
The island Queen recieves the mystic power
And stalls ⟨the⟩his coursers in her Ocean bower
In Albion long the chariot has delayed
⟨While Empire seeks⟩
And fate enlarged the glorious gift she made
She bid her throw the chain of empire round
O'er lands which Roman triumph never found.
And bid Improvement rise on Indian plains
That land of woe & of romantic strains
There in devotion to mysterious powers
The Indian stands in Ganges' holy bowers

[86] Emerson evidently used this page for miscellaneous jottings before writing the verse it bears. The jottings include "ROME" in block letters between "launched" and "Ruin"; and the phrase "In maiden meditation, fancy free." between lines six and seven of the verse. The quotation (*Midsummer Nights Dream*, II, i) appears in ch. XVII in *Kenilworth*. In the left margin near "The island Queen" is a sketch, apparently of Queen Elizabeth, under which the letters "O P T S W" appear.

On the hot sands where human nature fails
&c
Thy name oh Albion shall be honoured long[87]
When thy Improvement has dispelled the wrong
[50][88] The c⟨h⟩ar⟨iot⟩ of Empire rolls ↑for↓ever west.
And lettered Egypt welcomes it to rest
The ⟨Magi⟩ ↑prophets↓ pointed to the starry sky
And bold Improvement reared his fane as high
In that proud land of sages & of Kings
Seek the poor grandeur of exalted things
They reared their piles till mountains sunk in shame
Imperishable monuments of fame
⟨Alighting⟩
High on their tops the sprites of air began
And sung the song of destiny to man
But /hideous/ghastly/ Ruin stooped on dragon wing
On that mausoleum of so proud a King
And Strength & Grandeur strove in vain to save
Their early dwellings from the /inevitable/unyielding/ sullen/hateful/gaping/ grave
⟨But haste & leave the long forsaken climes⟩
Haste leave this hallowed land elder and over time[89]
And westward trace Improvement's march sublime
In polished Greece young Architecture's home
Or the ripe glories of imperial Rome
[51][90] There Sculpture painting ⟨poetry⟩ ↑Science↓ loved to dwell
And heaven-born Musick learned luxurious[n] swell

[87] In the left margin, from "The Indian" (above) to "&c" (below) is a sketch of a man with a bandaged head under which the words "Havoc" and "Hocva" appear.

[88] The page bears sketches of a Pegasus, a flower, various unidentifiable scrawls, and two flying dragons, doubtless suggested by line eleven on the page.

[89] Above "this hallowed" appears "a HAM[?]"; "and over" appears above "land elder"; it is immediately preceded by an "H" which does not appear to belong to the phrase. Emerson's intentions in this substituted and imperfect line are uncertain.

[90] After filling the page with verse and sketches of a female bust and a bird, Emerson pasted in a newspaper clipping of the American eagle emblem, and then attempted a crude pen sketch of it. He also sketched what looks like a blockhouse, which obscures part of his text. The page is reproduced as plate IX.

The holy nine enamoured of the land
On high Parnassus fixed their soft co||m||mand
And pleased Apollo to their Music gave
Divine Castalia's consecrated wave
Land of the Arts thy burning glory fades
⟨Why do Eve[n] ⟨t⟩Thy ↑great↓ Gods forsake their favourite⟩ ↑And Joy abandons thy melodious↓ shades
Thy loud-voiced bards are murmuring tones of woe
Thy heroes quail before a↑n↓ ⟨foreign⟩ ↑infant↓ foe
The /nymphs/Dryads/ leave the haunts they once oft roved
E'en the great Gods forsake the land they loved
Wh⟨at⟩ere[?] fate commands nor men nor Gods gainsay
Nor all the strength of nature interrupt the way
For lo the westering wheels of Destiny
⟨Seek where Italia's fields of glory⟩ ↑Roll on to Rome where fields of glory↓ lie
⟨Rise youthful Rome! the powers of Universe combine⟩
⟨To rear, aggrandise, keep, thy Strength ||div||ine⟩
⟨The world's vain homage could not stay thy doom⟩
⟨When bending nations hailed "almighty" Rome⟩
Though the frail /boast/throne/ of human power decays
The enduring stone transmits thy matchless praise
Shamed Nature shrunk before the sculptured form
Abashed to be surpassed by Man that is a worm
[52][91] Her halls are crowded with a spotless throng
Of living marbles ⟨mid that sto⟩
There stands Apollo

There are fine subjects for poetry which oblivion has too long shrouded — & why? — Poetry ought to be ashamed of the cause[;] it is this. The Monks in their cloisters in the dark ages invented Rhyme by which the[y] endeavoured to shackle poetry or the soarings of the mind. Since that time a long series of years has elapsed & time has swept off in his course all & every thing that was great &

[91] In a space between the poetry and the prose Emerson drew a chariot pulled by a winged horse. The prose passage is in pencil.

splendid in former times: ⟨it⟩he has demolished Rome who was the favourite city of heaven & Mistress of the world & even the world appeared going to destruction & grandeur flung away his wand. From the ruins of Rome many nations rose; & the arts again flourished, but Poetry had lost its charms [53] & even at this ||...|| [92] master *Rhyme* ||...|| of itself since ⟨in⟩ ||...|| ⟨by⟩ under the hand of *Impro* ||...|| influence man has extended & ||...|| astronomy, commerce, politics, has learned to m||ake light||ning rods & ships &c beside overthrowing Ignorance & gratifying heaven. But the reason why these fetter[s] still remain is, first, because they are golden or beautiful second because ⟨truth[?]⟩ some poets have made her beautiful notwithstanding them & therefore others have no conception of her being more beautiful without; again some who have tried to take them off went clumsily to work — Milton & Shakspeare alone suceeded

The unbought admiration of ⟨the world⟩ ↑mankind↓
The grateful joy in human breasts enshrined
The free obedience of the good & brave
The blessing of the emancipated slave
These are the trophies of Brittania's fame
Triumphant Empire destitute of blame
And must they perish in the tide of time
When awful empire leaves her favoured clime
Must mouldering ruin mount her golden throne
Put on her spoils to magnify his own?

[54][93] ||...A||lexander the Great returned ||...|| rad the rajah mounted ||...|| representatives of all the ||...|| ulation & puffed the pride ||...|| arch

Dies Irae dies illa
Solvet saeclum in favilla
Testis Deus et Sibylla [94]

[92] The top right corner of the page is torn off here.

[93] The top left corner of the page is torn off here. Emerson numbered the page "54" to the right of the tear.

[94] "A day of wrath, that day
When world lies waste in fire
As God and Sibyl witness" (Ed.).

You may say what you please of the current rebellion[95]
Tonight the Conventicle drink to a real one
The annals of ages have blazoned its fame
And Paeans are chanted to hallow its name.
Derry Down

Alas for the windows the sophs have demolished,
Alas for the Laws that they are not abolished,
And that *Dawes* could abide the warm battle's brunt
And the Government's[96] ⟨speech⟩ ↑vote↓ it was ⟨all⟩ Gay ↑Lee↓ & Blunt
Derry Down

But this shock of the Universe who could control
Aghast[97] in despair was each Sophomore soul
Save one who alone in his might could stand forth
To grapple with elements — Mr Danforth

Let the Earth & the Nations to havoc go soon
And the World tumble upward to mix with the moon

The third line of the "Dies Irae" (a celebrated medieval hymn attributed to Thomas of Celano) is usually given: "Teste David cum Sibylla."

The lines are scrawled diagonally to the right of a miscellany of words and letters, like "Wm," "E," "Mr," "W" and "Wm Emerson," doubtlessly referring to Emerson's older brother William (1801–1868).

[95] The "current rebellion" appears to have broken out in October, 1820, when "the door between the dining halls of the Sophomore and Freshman Classes was burst open from the Sophomore Hall, . . . articles of furniture from the table were thrown through, and great disorder produced." For their "active part in the disorder," Martin Gay, John C. Lee, and Nathaniel B. Blunt, all sophomores, were suspended and rusticated, and Rufus Dawes, a freshman, was "admonished." In 1823, Samuel Danforth was dismissed with Gay and 34 others for engaging in "a combination to resist the Authority of the College. . . ." ("Records of the Immediate Government of Harvard College," IX, 1814–1822, p. 241, minutes of Oct. 29, 1820, and X, 1822–1829, p. 28, minutes of May 3, 1823.) "The Conventicle," a club established by some members of the class of 1821 after their own rebellion in Nov., 1818, included Emerson, Samuel Alden (the "bishop"), John B. Hill (the "parson"), and Nathaniel Kingsbury (the "archbishop"). The club met irregularly and purely for conviviality, it seems (W. B. Hill, "Emerson's College Days," *The Literary World*, May 22, 1880, reprinted in *EtE*, I, 459–60).

[96] "Government" was the term applied by Harvard men to the college faculty (see Josiah Quincy, *Figures of the Past*, pp. 46, 50, and 52).

[97] "They all ↑were↓" is written beside "Aghast" in the left margin.

Old Harvard shall smile at the rare conflagration
The conventicle standing her pledge of salvation.
Derry Down

[55] The Round Table of Arthur & the iron crown of Charlemagne.

great help
telegraph

Funeral
Real fun

The city was demolished
And the Laws, they were abolished [98]

There
Quid est veritas?
Est vir qui adest

chemistry was developed [99]

Clad in courage he came /on his legs to stand firm/ as an elephant firm/
And a cloak like Apollo's — to keep himself warm

John Grimes was a seller of malt
Which is to say a malt-seller
He was born in a pailful of salt
Or as Shakspeare affirms a salt⟨s⟩cell⟨e⟩ar

But whether he lived in the moon
Or whether he lived in the planets
Alas! it will never be known
Or whether he boarded at Gannett's

My Boots are so tight that I have to get up before light in order to have my feet in readiness to attend the City procession at eleven. [R.W.E.] [100]

[98] Evidently an experimental couplet for the verse on the facing page (p. 244 above).

[99] In left margin.

[100] The "City procession" may refer to a parade by the Harvard Washington

[56] Would'st thou know gentle reader why broad on the wind
Hedge's green summer coat hath its soft skirts resigned
Oh when Time shall have borne us [101]

——To behead a king, to ⟨commit⟩pillage a church, to commit parricide, to eat human flesh, to blaspheme God—are crimes of the first dye and of deep condemnation. The⟨y⟩se are not the practi⟨s⟩ces of every-day transgression; they occur seldom, and are commonly signalized by the swift vengeance of omnipotence. In the last stages of political degeneracy these enormities have become common and uphold a tremendous indication of coming retribution.[102]

[57] Faintly as tolls old Harvard's bell
Our voices keep tune remarkably well
Soon as our eyes grow drunkly dim
We'll cease to repeat this charming hymn [103]
Drink brothers drink the wine flows fast
The tutors are near and the daylight's past

Why should we yet get up to go
There's not ⟨g⟩a glass which is empty now
But when the Wine shall say no more
Oh sweetly we'll rest & snore & snore! [104]
Drink brothers Drink the wine flows fast
The tutors are near & the daylight's past

Oh Sherry wine! this trembling lamp
Shall see us drink up thy surges damp
Tutor of Minerals hear our prayer
And to disturb our fun, forbear

Corps to Boston and back on July 7, 1820. Emerson was not a member of the Corps (see Josiah Quincy, *Figures of the Past*, p. 31).

[101] Possibly Levi Hedge (1766–1844), professor at Harvard, 1810–1832; and author of the textbook on logic which Emerson studied in his sophomore year.

[102] The rest of the page is occupied by sketches of four male heads in left profile.

[103] In the left margin, between this line and the next: "There is not a breath the blue wave to c."

[104] In the left margin, beside the next six lines, are two male heads in profile. "Tho" is written to the left of the upper profile.

Drink brothers drink the wine flows fast
The tutors are near & the daylight's past

Shall see us float ⟨|| . . . ||⟩over th⟨e⟩y⟨re⟩ surges soon
Grant us cool heavens & favouring air [105]

[58][106] Inclement skies that fence Columbia round

Of the Mind Marcus Antoninus propoundeth — "It traverses the whole world & what surrounds it. It contemplates its form & looking forward into eternity, it considers the renovation of the universe at certain intervals." Laid under the table for consideration.

They have dared to commend what ⟨g⟩God hath not commended.
Whether they be as solid as they are sulky [?]

Hark thou mayest hear the dull sound of the industrious worms [n] ⟨a⟩of the sepulchre.

Diomede's head in Heyne's Homer [107]
Whatever
    Whatever
Whatever
Epicurus & his blithe philosophy

Where the decisions of fancy are not traversed by judgement & where the ways of imagination reason doth not contravene

[59][108] There is in the universe of things something which is hard to find, something on which human hands are rarely laid, which is treasured up in profound abysses & which was never intended to be

[105] These two lines, written at the bottom of the page, are evidently proposed substitutes for lines two and four respectively in the last stanza.

[106] The page has sketches of nine male heads in left profile. Some are superimposed upon the notes, or vice versa. Four or five different styles of handwriting appear here, but all of them appear to be Emerson's. The page is reproduced as plate X.

[107] Three etchings of Diomedes, including one of the head and upper torso, constitute the illustration at the beginning of Book IV in C. G. Heyne, *Homeri Carmina* (Lipsiae, Londini, 1802), I (*Homeri Ilias*), 179. None of Emerson's sketches resembles those of Diomedes.

[108] Between the prose and the verse Emerson drew an incomplete sketch of an eagle, like that on p. [51], two male heads in left profile, and a robed figure lying on a rude bench — an improvement on the sketch on p. [17].

freely revealed. Its attributes are stranger than the secrecy of its abode.

Time

Of men by far the most gigantick
Who dwells on this side the ⟨a⟩Atlantic

[60][109]

[109] The page is blank except for a sketch of a male head; "F" written ornately three times; "Friar" written vertically upward twice; and "Mankind" written diagonally downward.

No. XVIII

1820–1822

Emerson used a few early pages of this notebook for notes and quotations about French and Spanish literature, perhaps in connection with a course given by Professor George Ticknor at Harvard. The largest group of entries on a single topic, however, is that concerned with ethical philosophy, from which Emerson derived the final form of his dissertation for the Bowdoin Prize Essay contest of 1821. Other entries include original poems, a draft of Emerson's first published essay, a series of essays on the drama, part of a short story, letters, and quotations. The dated entries run from September 22, 1820 to July, 1822. A notebook kept sporadically between 1823 and 1829 and also numbered XVIII by Emerson is designated by the editors No. XVIII[A] to distinguish it from this one.

No. XVIII, like the College Theme Book, is a bound volume of seventy-five leaves, with a black, hard cover measuring 17.5 x 21.4 cm. The volume has been partially rebound, with a new back cover and fly leaves supplied, but the original front inside cover with its writing exists. Following the new inserted flyleaf, two leaves are cut away. Pagination begins on the recto of the third leaf, though the top half carrying the number is torn away. The Table of Contents on the verso of this leaf lists material for the pages numbered 155 and 156, but this final leaf and the one preceding it are also torn away. The numbering of the existing 150 pages is in sequence through the page numbered 148. The lower half of the leaf for pages 105 and 106 is cut off and the pages numbered 124–126 contain back to front writing, which appears to be upside down in relation to the preceding matter. A second reversed sequence begins with the page numbered 145 and is further complicated by a torn out leaf between pages numbered 148 and 151. Finally, the pages numbered 124, 145, 147, and 151 carry both front to back and back to front writing and therefore are indicated by subscript numbers as repeated pages.

[front cover verso] [1]

mine
wine ⟨Constitut[i]on⟩
divine 33
sign
combine ALFRED SULLY
twine
repine
shrine ⟨Of the United States begun in Bos⟩
sh⟨r⟩ine ⟨ton Jan. 2⟩
hold MILTON
bold
gold
wold
rolled
fold
told slow DEMOSTHENES WASHINGTON
mould bow
behold woe
sold sow
cold low
old grow HENRY IV of France NEWTON
foe
know BUTLER
show
glow
go BURKE
SHAKESPEARE
DRYDEN
BACON
FRANKLIN
JOHNSON MONTAIGNE

[1] Sketches of eight male heads are scattered about on the page, and "SHAKESPEARE" is embellished. Under "⟨Constitution⟩" appears "⟨First Copy⟩"; under "⟨Of . . . Bos⟩" appears "⟨Contemplated and begun⟩"; and under "⟨ton Jan. 2" appears "⟨July 29, 1807⟩"; all the overwritten words are in red ink, and do not appear to be by Emerson.

[1][2] ⟨Motto⟩ No XVIII

Ralph Waldo Emerson.

Boston, Sept. 22d

⟨Motto⟩ *1820*

Where dost thou careless lie,
Buried in ease & sloth?
Knowledge, that sleeps, doth die,
And this security,
It is the common moth
Which eats on wits and arts, and quite destroys them both.

Are all the Aonian springs
Dryed up? [3] Lies Thespia waste?
Does Clarius' harp want strings?
That not a nymph now sings
Or droop they as disgraced
To see their seat & bowers by chattering pies defaced?

BEN JONSON [AN ODE] TO HIMSELF.

1	2	3	4	5	6	7	8	9	0
BC	DF	GH	JKZ	L	MN	PQ	RS	TV	WX

[2] A TABLE OF CONTENTS. PAGE.

Valedictory Poem — scraps —	156
Philosophical Extracts	142
Tnamurya	117
Magician scrap	103
Political condition	134
Dedication	100
Moral Philosophy	7
Grand Motto	6
BIPED	passim
Conversational diffusion &c	130
⟨Moral⟩Ethical Quotations	140
Ethical Extracts	142
Wish	102
Essay on Poetry	39
Drama	51
Arthur	62

[2] Two leaves are cut out before p. [1], and the top of p. [1] is cut off.

[3] At about this point is a deleted sketch of a man's face in left profile.

[3] [R.W.E.] ⟨Spanish Literature⟩French And Spanish 1821
1280
541

"Vasco Lobeira the Author of Amedis de Gaul was a Portuguese born in the second half of the thirteenth century and died in 1325. He wrote in Spanish the four first books of Amadis but by some circumstance — of which no account is given his work was not generally known until the middle of the 14th century." Sismondi's [4]

[R.W.E.] From Sismondi's French translation of Spanish ballad.

Already the armies of Don Rodrigo had lost all courage and fled and already in the eighth assault his enemies were victorious when Rodrigo abandoning his country went out from his royal tent. He went alone unfortunate man — none accompanied him and his extreme weariness did not leave him strength enough to guide his horse. The horse advanced at his own pleasure for Rodrigo did not choose his road. The king being faint ⟨was⟩ ↑is↓ no longer master of himself; he ⟨was⟩ ↑is↓ dying with hunger & thirst and it ⟨was⟩ ↑is↓ pitiful to see him; he ⟨was⟩ ↑is↓ so covered with blood that he ⟨was⟩ ↑is↓ red ⟨as a⟩ like a live coal; his arms ⟨were⟩are spoiled by the stones with which they had been struck & his sword is dented ↑like a saw↓ by all the blows it has given; his helmet all deformed ⟨by[?]⟩ is pushed down over his head; his face is swelled by the toil he has undergone. He ascends to the summit of a hill[,] the highest of those he observes about him[,] & thence he looks down on the defeat of his host; he sees his banners & his standards trodden under foot and covered with dust; h⟨e⟩is ↑eye↓ searches out his captains and he does not see one appear, but the plain is covered with blood which flows

[4] Jean Charles Leonard Simonde de Sismondi (1773–1842), *De la Litterature du Midi de l'Europe*, 4 vols. (Paris, 1829), III, 220–221. Emerson or his mother borrowed vol. III of the 1813 edition from the Boston Library Society on Aug. 25, 1821 and returned it Sept. 8. Vol. I was borrowed on Sept. 15, 1821 and returned Oct. 6. Vols. III and IV were borrowed June 27, 1822, and returned, date unknown. For the translated quotation which follows immediately and continues on p. 254, see the 1829 edition, III, 229–230.

in rivulets. The unfortunate man, beholding this scene, overcome with grief

☞ (Turn to the 6th page)

[4] When collocation is to be corrected, use this zig zag mark[5]

Men at some times are masters of their fates.
The fault dear Brutus is not in our stars
But in ourselves, if we are underlings
[Shakespeare, *Julius Caesar*, I, ii, 139–141]

"The appeals of the early protestant writers to the moral judgement & feelings of the human race from the casuistry & subtleties of schoolmen & monks in middle ages" date the "decline of that worst of all heresies of the Romish church which by opposing Revelation to Reason endeavoured to extinguish the light of both." From Stewart.

For Jesuit Ethics Stewart refers to Mosheim Vol 4 p. 354.
Mosheim Vol 4 p. 18

Hobbes Cudworth, Immutable Morality[6]

Wait occasions, and obey them:
Sail in an egg-shell, make a straw your mast,
A cob-web all your cloth, and pass unseen,
Till you have 'scaped the rocks that are about you.
Motto (Ben Jonson's "Sad Shepherd") [III, v, 9–12 misquoted]

[5] XLIV Chapter of Gibbon's Rome contains an excellent history of Roman institutions[.]

[5] Passages marked with the vertical zig zag which follows are indicated in the notes.

[6] The quotation (inaccurate) and the references to Mosheim, Hobbes, and Cudworth, were all derived from Emerson's reading of Dugald Stewart's *Dissertation: Exhibiting the Progress of Metaphysical, Ethical, and Political Philosophy since the Revival of Letters in Europe*, 1815–1821 (see *Collected Works Of Dugald Stewart*, ed. Sir William Hamilton, 11 vols., London, 1854–1858, I, 40, text, and notes 1 and 2; 38, note 2; and 88). Emerson or his mother borrowed vol. I of the *Dissertation* from the Boston Library Society March 17, 1821, and returned it April 26. Emerson's Bowdoin Prize Essay (see n. 7 below) seems to owe a substantial debt to Stewart's *Dissertation.*

"A General Plan for a Dissertation on the Present State of ethical Philosophy" —[7]
⟨First To for⟩ 1. Introduction — 2. To form an adequate & perfect idea of the present state of the science it is necessary to review its history briefly ⟨3. Present state of it⟩ 4 what has been done for it by the modern philosophers. 5 present state of the controversies which belong to it. 6 State of the general science of Ethics 7. Its tendencies & prospects 8 Conclusion. —

Who invented, who methodized & propagated Ethical philosophy?

What did Socrates, Pythagoras, Cicero, Aristotle,?

What have *the Fathers* done for Ethical philosophy?

What has been done by Des Cartes, Dr [Samuel] Clarke, Dr Reid, Dr Paley, Mr Stewart, Dr Priestl[e]y, Dr Cudworth, Mr Hume Mr

---

Survey the political condition of the world as ethics[;] discover the Lex legum on which legislation is to proceed.

Southern soils lie broad & fair
Beneath the sun, along the deep,
And the spirits of air, with their floating hair
On the glowing clouds of Peru sleep [8]

[6] [Spanish ballad] and shedding torrents of tears speaks thus — 'Yesterday I was king of the Spains (des Espagnes); today I do not own a little farm; Yesterday I had servants and numerous courtiers, today I cannot call a stone of these walls my own. Cursed was the day, cursed was the hour when I was born, when I became heir of so vast a dominion since I must lose the whole in one day. Oh Death

[7] Emerson seems to have started collecting materials for the dissertation early in 1821, since on p. [345] he wrote "Begun Jan 3d 1821" and then jotted down a series of "Detached phrasula" most of which appear in some form in the final essay. It was submitted in July 1821 for the Bowdoin Prize and won one of the two second prizes. It is printed in Edward Everett Hale, *Ralph Waldo Emerson* (Boston, 1904), pp. 97–135.

[8] These lines seem to belong in the poem on Peru on pp. 282–284, at the point indicated by n. 47 on p. 284.

why do you not come, why not remove my soul from this miserable body since now it would be a kindness.

> Ah! if the heart, too confidently raised,
> Perchance too lightly occupied, or lulled
> Too easily, despise or overlook
> The vassalage that binds her to the earth,
> Her sad dependance upon time, and all
> The trepidations of mortality,
> What place so destitute and void — but there
> The little ⟨f⟩Flower her vanity shall check;
> The trailing Worm reprove her thoughtless pride?
> Wordswor[t]h, Excurs. [Bk. IV, 418–26] p. 160

[7][9] When the present system of things began their being & the eternal relations of matter were established the constitution of moral science was yet to be founded. It began with the social ↑human↓ condition; ⟨of man;⟩ with ⟨his⟩ ↑man's↓ first sense of duty to his maker & his fellow man; it has remained a permanent eternal principle whose object is to conduct the human race to their unseen & final destinies. Its developement was later; with rude & unworthy beginnings in which advancement was long scarcely perceptible & always uncertain; & often wandering into hopeless errors↑.↓ ⟨&⟩ ⟨f⟩For a long period of time, it was extricating itself from error, sometimes however making a false step & plunging deeper in gulfs of absurdity & pollution, but it has finally ⟨arrived at a⟩ ↑placed itself on↓ respectable ground in the circle of human knowledge[.]

It were a bold & useless inquiry, & leading back beyond the limits of human information ⟨to ask although⟩ certainly claiming the apology of importance & interest to ask what surpassing mind concieved [8][10] the germ of Moral Science or how it was communicated from heaven to earth. It was a beautiful & ethereal offspring of other worlds & conferred on this by interposition which no discoveries might anticipate.

[9] What follows is the first version of the beginning of the "Dissertation on the Present State of Ethical Philosophy" (see Hale, *Ralph Waldo Emerson*, p. 97). "⟨his⟩ ↑man's↓ . . . destinies" is marked for correction. This and the next six pages have regular pagination but are also numbered 1 through 7 at the bottom of the page.

[10] Sketches of a bust of a Greek or Roman and of a man's face in left profile appear in the middle of the page.

In ↑partially↓ considering the history of moral Science we propose to sketch hastily the achievements of its champions; to stop briefly to indulge our satisfaction at its distinguished triumphs & to notice the memorable questions which ↑have↓ agitated & shaken it; & then proceed to ⟨discuss⟩ ↑consider↓ more at large the Present State of Ethical Philosophy[.]

We find irregular & casual hints of ethical science thrown out by the most ancient Greek poets descending as is supposed remotely from primeval revelation. We know of none however among the first schools of Grecian Philosophy who set himself apart for the sublime purpose of gathering up the relations which bind man to the universe about ↑him↓. Ethics were never separated from the ↑immature &↓ misunderstood sciences [9] of logic & metaphysics. The world was not old enough to have accurately parcelled & distributed [n] her science into professions. The amassed stores of Experience were not then overflowing her granaries, as now, when ages of industry have elapsed & ⟨made⟩ limited & multiplied the offices of her stewards.

Believing as the philosophic ancients appear to have done, that the world as they found it, had forever subsisted & should continue to subsist & that an inscrutable Fate ruled their destinies who might make them at pleasure demi-gods or nonentities after death, they had but scanty encouragement for any grand & holy system which the ardour of virtue might induce them to form. Enthusiasm was chilled by the awful unrevealing silence which prevailed over nature and man and the sanctions which they supplied were ⟨insufficient⟩ inadequate to the support of a great religious faith. Some astonished at the lustre & enchantment with which this visible world was illumined & renewed imagined the possibility of a more intimate connection between man & nature & hence arose [10] the mysteries of Eleusis *[11] & the doctrine of natural magic. ↑Quote from page 120↓ But the high & adventurous ends which these interpreters of nature proposed to themselves were unanswered & afterward perverted in corrupt times. Others were fain to believe the voice of long-descended tradi-

[11] The asterisk is Emerson's sign that the circled matter on p. [120] should be inserted here. See n. 101 on p. 335. The phrase "Quote from page 120" has been added in pencil. In the margin opposite the word "aggrandizement" (below) is a sketch of a man's face in left profile.

tion and awaited the return of the departed Gods with ↑⟨&⟩ the golden age of↓ ample dispensations & ↑piously↓ congratulated themselves on the security of human condition under the protection of Providence. Others threw themselves headlong on the comfortless idea of the administration of Chance & scoffed at the hopes & terrors of all as ⟨visionary & idle.⟩ ↑distempered dreams.↓ To this frail & fleeting order of beings, persecuted by the same natural obstructions to possible aggrandizement, the progress of Ages has unfolded ⟨more fully⟩ & immediate revelation sanctioned a system of morality so complete & divine & its promises attended with presentiments so rich of glory hereafter as to exalt & assimilate the species ⟨above⟩ ↑to↓ the boldest forms of ideal excellence.

---

[11] We must date the reduction of ethics to any thing like a separate system ⟨at⟩ ↑from↓ the time of Socrates. "Socrates videtur, primus ab rebus occultis et a natura ipsa involutis, in quibus omnes ante eum philosophi occupati fuerunt, ⟨deduxisse⟩ philosophiam avocavisse et ad communem vitam adduxisse[.]"[12]

↑This is his peculiar praise.↓ Others before him had been ambitious of dictating laws for the government of Kings & of Empires or had locked up their results & conclusions in costly manuscripts so that their influence ⟨was⟩on the lives of the people was remote & insignificant.

But this patriotic philosopher extended his wisdom to the body of the people in the first city in the world & communicated to his disciples not a mysterious or hierographical scripture ↑to amuse the learned & awe the ignorant↓ but practical rules of life adapted immediately to their condition & little infected with the dogmas of the age. To the inquisitive he unfolded & explained his system and the laws & dependencies of Morals. From him must be derived the modern fashion of ascribing to a single principle the appearance of Virtue. Speaking of things which are just he says "All things are just which

[12] " 'It is [my] view, . . . that Socrates was the first person who summoned philosophy away from mysteries veiled in concealment by nature herself, upon which all philosophers before him had been engaged, and led it to the subject of ordinary life. . . .' " Cicero, *Academica*, I, iv, 15. The following comment "This . . . praise" is added in pencil.

are lawful," a flimsy & fallacious criterion which must of necessity [12] vary under every differ[e]nt government & which sufficiently indicates the ↑then↓ imperfect state of Morals. After the ages of Grecian refinement however when all sciences seem to have burst into premature perfection the Stoics exhibited rational & correct views of ethics. Zeno, ⟨Epictetus maintained &⟩ ↑& long after him↓ his illustrious disciples Epictetus, Arrian, & M Antoninus, maintained the doctrine of a "Supreme intelligence[,] ↑of his universal providence↓ & the obligation we are under to conform to his will & acquiesce in his decisions as necessarily wise & good." * Cicero, though its ornament & herald ↑of philosophy↓ to his age, did little for the advancement of the principles ⟨of philosophy⟩.[n] Cicero loved an elegant philosophy; what was uncouth or profound he polished & simplified; for no man on earth had pictured to himself such high classical & ethereal beauty for the worship of imagination as he. He was an Eclectic philosopher[.]

From these philosophers ethical [13] science was delivered down to the Christian Fathers with all the new motives & sanctions afforded by revelation. With all their schools & disputations the Fathers did little to settle the foundations of morals. They endeavoured to shew a contrariety in the laws of reason & revelation, & to substitute their expositions of the one, for the plain dictates of the other.

They wrote much about them & collected the crude materials for others to analyze.

⟨The Jesuits⟩ The obscurity of the monastic cell & the confined narrow views which were entailed upon each succession of the Roman priesthood were unfavourable to grand apprehensions of moral science & precluded the advancement which might have been expected from their profession and leisure. Some of them were sufficiently familiar with Greek & Roman philosophy to take up the subject on proper grounds but to continue it as it had been begun was beyond the power of minds perverted by bigotry. (Of this hierarchy whatever inspiration [14] some ingenuous disciples might have derived

* Priestley's Heathen Philosophy.[13]

[13] Joseph Priestley (1733–1804), *The Doctrines of Heathen Philosophy Compared with those of Revelation* (Northumberland [U. S.], 1804), from which Emerson quotes in Universe 5, Nov. 20, 1820. See pp. 377–378.

from its imposing Constitution, yet none of its popes was devout or literary enough to write upon these subjects. In the theory of this ecclesiastical government a different & graver character would be expected from the Vicar of Christ.) From the nature of this extraordinary hierarchy great results in intellectual science might be ↑reasonably↓ anticipated from its peaceful & ⟨instructed⟩ ↑educated↓ clergy. No domestic relations interfered nor labours to obtain a livelihood, to deter them[14] from these pursuits; the only ⟨cause⟩ ↑reason to↓ which ↑we↓ can ascribe their failure is—the want of motive. Indeed an enlightened system of morals is so discordant with the popish faith that the *Indian* had gone far beyond them. "If thou beest not at variance" says ↑the lawgiver↓ Menu, "⟨with⟩ ↑by↓ speaking falsely &c." * From the Fathers Moral Science was transmitted to Bacon, to Descartes, and to Hobbes[,] the celebrated author of the Leviathan. The immortal author of the Novum Organum devoted his talents to those departments of Science where commanding intellect was most required ⟨to unravel⟩ [15] to restore ↑the natural↓ integrity and order to the perplexed & misunderstood arts of life and matter. But Lord Bacon's influence has been beneficially felt here as in all other Science. Moral Science will not again be trifled away upon silly and whimsical questions; this man's sound and sagacious philosophy has taught the world lessons of incalculable utility with regard to the method of philosophizing. We hear his praises echoed every day for his services to mankind on this head. Descartes was useful by the spring which he imparted to moral philosophy[.]

Affliction binds men together smoothing away the distinctions of rank and outward circumstances[.]

To Hobbes has been attributed a malevolent Spirit
in his house of cedar and ivory

SORBONNE

The advancement of the collateral ⟨science⟩ philosophy of the mind has matured and improved ethical speculations. It was useless to disclose the defects of education in the culture of the moral powers

* See page 129 for the rest which quotation had better be in a note.

[14] "⟨instructed⟩ . . . deter them" is marked for correction. A sketch of a man's face in left profile appears in the next two lines. The passage "From . . . matter." (below) is added in pencil.

till the knowledge of the mental operations ⟨unfolded⟩ ↑taught↓ ⟨the⟩how they should be /amended/corrected/ & regulated. Unless like the carpenter every man could carry his mathematics in a stick. [R. W. E.]

[16] When the malevolent spirit of Hobbes had given vogue to the selfish philosophy Dr Cudworth and others after him combated him with the establishment of the principles of benevolence. Dr Price wrote to prove that the Understanding judges in questions of moral rectitude and has proved himself one of the ablest champions of truth; he arrives by regular deductions at this most important conclusion, that every wrong action is a step to all that is tremendous in the Universe[.]

The question wherein consists happiness which of all moral questions has most occupied the attention of inquirers is now nearly set at rest by Hume and in a manner very different from that sought by the ancients. ⟨They devoted⟩ They laboured long & uselessly to find felicity in a single quality or circumstance appertaining to human character[.]

[17] Campbell the Poet said to Prof Everett, that it seemed to him that the only chance which America has for a truly national literature is to be found in the *Drama*; that some genius must rise who shall give birth and character to a national theatre. True, the stage must be new modelled and society must undergo some alteration before there can be much hope for such an event.

⟨Vergil hath prophecied the anatomy of his brain — ⟩

Turbidus hic coeno vastaque voragine gurges Estuat.[15]

And if envious critics should describe the anatomy of his brain
for what is self[?] or what is immortality[?]

EBE[16] asks me if I ought to sacrifice my friend to the public good, as Brutus did Caesar. I answer; the duties we owe to one another are nowhere so strict as under the Gospel law. That law is

[15] "Here, thick with mire and of fathomless flood, a whirlpool seethes." *Aeneid*, VI, 296–297.

[16] Edward Bliss Emerson (1805–1834), Emerson's younger brother.

"Love thy neighbour, *as thyself*." Ancient or modern philosophy never prescribed the rule more severely. But no man of great virtuous principle would hesitate a moment to sacrifice *himself* to the good of the community, as did Codrus and Regulus. Therefore virtue demands the sacrifice of his friend.

[18] Modern divines have investigated moral principles where the ancients only speculated upon ethics, have introduced accurate classifications in the place of the imperfect ⟨ones⟩ ↑sketches↓ of antiquity, and have substituted inquiries of immense importance for results comparatively trifling. We would ask, in passing[,] if any ⟨||...||⟩ speculations of Plato or Aristotle[n] can compare with that train of reasoning by which Dr Price arrives at the conclusion that every wrong act is a step to all that is tremendous in the Universe.

A rill which empties bubbling from the heart
In gulfs of evil boundless, bottomless,
And by exhaustion withers life's poor ⟨seat⟩ ↑fount↓
And from its pouring drops reflects a light
⟨Upon⟩Down ↑to↓ the swarthy depths that roar beneath
Therein disclosing to the woeworn heart
What kind of flood its lavish life-blood feeds —
Is this afflicted weeping time of mine. [R.W.E.]

Look at thy tinderbox!

There is no sympathy in the universe, says Bacon, so intimate as that between goodness & truth.

[19][17] In the modern systems of[n] ethical philosophy, the duties whose performance constitutes virtue are ranged under three classes viz. those which we owe to the Deity, those which regard our fellowmen, and those which we owe to ourselves. It founds these duties on the will of the Creator as ⟨gathered from⟩ ↑expressed in↓ the constitution of nature and in revelation. In ascertaining the will of the Deity it does not always proceed on the principle ⟨which shall⟩ that the greatest happiness is intended[,] for ↑that↓ this ↑is fact↓ we cannot

[17] In the lower part of the page is a half-figure of a man in left profile; in the bottom margin are two male heads in left profile.

know, i⟨f⟩t is judged safer therefore to reason from ⟨appearances of⟩ adaptation and analogy.[n] The moral /sense/faculty/? or as others term it the *decision⟨s⟩ of the understanding is recognized as an Original principle of our nature[,] the *intuition*↑?↓ by which we directly determine the merit or demerit of an action. If upon any question which has many relations and dependencies the decision is not prompt or is not given at all it ⟨is⟩ ↑becomes↓ then necessary that the question should be analyzed till this faculty readily decides upon its ultimate principles[.]

[20][18] The Damascus blade.

"Newton saw and unravelled the sevenfold web of light"

There is another distinguishing trait of morals which deserves notice and which has some analogy to the last; that a series of humble efforts is more meritorious than solitary miracles of virtue. The former are unpretending and unnoticed, opposing more obstacles to pursuit with less outside honour to allure imitation; the latter excite applause and as their occasions must occur but seldom, are of less utility to the general welfare[;] for instance the *patience* of an obscure person who endures the peevishness of another ⟨day a⟩for years still preserving ↑his own↓ su[s]ceptibility and at the end feels every emotion of benevolence for the offender is a nobler martyr than Regulus of Rome or Oedipus of Thebes or   for there is that about the constitution of the mind which expands on great occasions of sentiment and strong feeling with adequate power and with such powerful action that on these *emergencies of vir*tue a bad man might do the same. Let any man ask himself in moments of high [21] excitement if himself had been placed in parallel circumstances with   and Rome kneeling at his feet if he could have hesitated a moment in making the proud plunge whose patriotism would be immortal? when Obstruction hath clogged the senses, when the affections are disappointed, when reason itself decays, still

Vide Price on Morals[19]

[18] "⟨Hedges[?]⟩" or "⟨pledged[?]⟩" is written beside "There is another" in the left margin of this page.

[19] Though not keyed to the text, this is pretty clearly a note to "*decision⟨s⟩ of the understanding" in the above text.

Next to these Philosophy explains and defines the rights of man, ⟨self defence⟩ of property, & person, implying the right of self defence, the paternal right. To preserve these to every individual joint consent has created the laws in forming which each member consents to an abridgement of his natural liberty for the purpose of securing the rest. These rights are better understood now than formerly. Before the limits of obligation and right were well known the paternal authority was extended by the laws over the life as well as fortunes of the ⟨offender⟩ son until the father should voluntarily resign it. This dangerous paternal pre⟨g⟩rogative could not be tolerated at this day in civilized nations. The wisdom of experience has determined that such an institution operates to the mischief of both[.]

[22] If in a mountain prospect or a picture, we see a hut distant but a few yards from a superb castle the natural inference of ⟨a⟩the mind is that the inhabitants of the cottage are acquainted with the tenants of the lordlier roof—connected with them by some near ties of service and protection. So in other

We must determine ⟨how perfect is⟩ ↑the perfection of↓ their present state by ⟨for⟩ examining how far they fall short of the condition at which we may reasonably expect human improvement may arrive. After ages of separation from our present being we shall be better fitted to adjust these estimates. ⟨We are⟩ ↑Every man is↓ liable to be misled by our [his] own individual improvement and an individual ↑arrived at the period when every day discern↓ often mistakes the ⟨fast⟩ ↑rapid↓ developement of his powers for ⟨the⟩ an accession of light which has broke upon the age. And in topics of this nature the ⟨facts⟩ minute views which have interested a man are likely to crowd themselves upon his notice so as to occupy a disproportionate part of the picture[.]

There are two Natures[,] moral and material

How does Grandmother Eve

[23]

$$\begin{array}{r} 1821 \\ 1617 \\ \hline 204 \end{array}$$

The impulse to exertion to the enjoyment of our faculties in the greatest possible degree is a very powerful one. It is necessary to the infancy of /knowledge/—science/ and to remove the obstructions of sloth. This principle is manifest in a [.] Very few attempt the experiment of diminishing the strength of a magnet, all prefer to see its power accumulating[.]

Recollect the very simple and summary policy of the reverend Bishop Oradici when Philip II consulted him with regard to the treatment of the Moors[:] "The more you destroy, the less there will remain." Plus on detruit de ses ennemis, et moins il en reste—

Cervantes died only 204 years ago 1821
204
1617

Hannibal gathered 3 bushels of ↑gold↓ rings after the battle of Cannae.

When a Turk's horse started in a bush he would chide him Joinville says with Guides tu qu'y soit le roy Richard? (I) Women kept children quiet with the threat of bringing Richard[.]

(dum Troja fuit,)[20]

And it should be such that it [be] talked of in England for a hundred years to come[.]

[24][21] Boston August 1. 1821
N.B. ⟨||.... Concord ||⟩ Bought a pair of boots

The history of the Minstrels of the middle ages is a singular fact in the ⟨history⟩ ↑annals↓ of human sentiment. It demonstrates the congeniality of poetry to nature and that the ↑rude↓ turbulence of military action does not quench but nourishes the flame of sentiment. Bred in camps or feudal castles under such a wild system of government and wandering from castle to castle to win & exhaust the ostentatious patronage of the barons & the hearty welcome of their serfs, bound by profession to gather up the wildest tales of lawless power, of superstition, of distressed beauty, in an age abounding in these rich legends, his manner of life ⟨was the most⟩ ↑singularly↓ fitted to call up poetical energies[.][22]

[20] "While Troy lived." [Ed.]

[21] In the text in the upper half of the page are sketches of a horse and of the heads and shoulders of two men.

[22] The paragraph may belong with the "Essay on Poetry" beginning on p. 276.

The inhabitants of the burgh San Priamo sent a herald to proclaim in all the streets, that whosoever wished to know the wonders of the other world, should come on the first of May, to the bridge of Carraia or to the quays of the ⟨a⟩Arno. They had prepared upon the Arno boats covered with a scaffolding where they had arranged a representation of the infernal regions with fires, penances, and martyrs. There were men disguised as devils who were horrible to see and others were naked and seemed like souls exposed to divers torments with horrible cries, groans, and storms. The whole combined to form an odious and formidable spectacle. Meantime, from the novelty of the fète, a throng of citizens had assembled, and the bridge which was then of wood, being overloaded with this enormous multitude, fell in, with those upon it. A great number of men were slain by the fall, or drowned in the Arno; many others were wounded, and that which had been said in sport turned to truth "that many went to know the wonders of the other world."[23]

[25] Men

Men have ⟨sought ↑found or↓ motive in c⟩

Richard's Confession. (Continuation of Magician.)[24]

"You were in Palestine[,] Father Gilbert[,] and you often observed the mystery of my conduct. You are a holy man and now listen to what my conscience bids me unfold. I have been visited by an awful guest to remind me of long and dreadful transgression. In Palestine I broke a vow to God and devoted to unholy usage the spoils I had vowed to him; and his avenging Spirit punished the perjured by letting me loose to the dominion of all the cursed vain imaginations and pride of heart which belong to youth. Yes, Father, my youth was ardent that my age might be ripe ↑in↓ agony. ⟨Other men's youth was not like mine;⟩ There was a voice and a language in the sky which spoke to me; the ground I trod, the air I breathed, the waves where I revelled, uttered a sound to mine ear as keenly as if a thousand harps had been struck."

[23] The paragraph sounds like a translation, possibly from Sismondi (see p. 276).

[24] "Richard's Confession" is the title for the following narrative of the King on his deathbed, which parallels at some points the ballad on pp. 294–295 and 303–304. "(Continuation of Magician.)" was evidently intended to refer not to "Richard's Con-

His head was bound round with linen cloth for the penance of the Benedictine scourgeth the head.

The Friar came[;] he was a man well strick[en] in years and his old limbs a little bowed by the weight of seventy Winters. He wore a roquelaire and religiously counted his beads as he approached the bed of death. "My son," said he, "Art thou ready to forsake kingdom and riches, thy household, and all that is thine and resign thy soul to Him that died on the accursed tree?" And he crossed himself as he spake with devotion. Richard the King did not answer a word but he groaned [26] aloud. "Does it repent thee my son," ↑said the abbot,↓ "that thou must leave thy royal estate and diadem of gold and the wicked wishes of sinful ambition and all the outward pomp and seeming of carnal parade? [n] Eschew these vanities, ⟨and⟩ thou shalt exchange ⟨for⟩ them."—"Be still Priest," said the King extending his arm and rising on his couch. "He that is prisoned in marble—will a straw rive his dungeon?" He paused and a sop of honey was offered him, which his parched and discoloured lips seemed to require. But he refused to taste mortal food and turned again to the priest[.]

[Magician][25] Her habits were very singular; she would come to the neighbouring village and while a family were warmly seated about their evening fire they encountered her bright eye and frightful face at the window, where she would remain motionless a moment and suddenly start away and reenter the wood. If pursued she would be found perhaps ⟨stretched⟩ ↑squatted↓ on the heath near her hut twisting a string ↑out↓ of the dead grass and muttering to herself. Once or twice she was found thus, speaking this uncouth rhyme

fession" but to the narrative which follows the "Confession" on p. [26]. For clarity the editors have silently supplied all quotations marks in direct address.

[25] What follows is presumably the continuation of the "Magician" story which Emerson had begun before May 10, 1821 (see p. 55). The first part appears to be lost. The story continues on pp. 284–286 and 302–303. A paragraph on p. 324, referred to as "Magician Scrap" in the Table of Contents, may also belong to the story. The paragraph on pp. 273–274 seems to be a variant of one section. The end of the story is dated Feb. 21, 1822; it appears to have been begun in Aug., 1821. Since there is no discernible point at which Emerson broke off the composition, the pages where it appears are dated 1821, 1822, except for the last two.

Grass, straw, white and grey
Fools may twist ye, El pho rae
Withered flower stems, once on you
Red rosebuds and dais⟨y⟩ies grew
Your leaves are dead ↑and↓ your stalks are dry
Wrinkled hated — so am I

The trees which grew about her dwelling were very lofty and majestic oaks and beeches. In the autumn [27] she would sit beneath the coloured beech until she was covered with the red leaves which the wind ⟨caused to fall in abundant profusion.⟩ scattered from the branches. The peasants sometimes visited her from curiosity and her language was generally severe and abrupt and always mingled with unintelligible terms. At one time her only answer to all who approached her was Avoid, avoid. At another if village tales tell true she darkly hinted the ⟨place⟩ spot where the coming thunder-cloud would strike and designated the victim. After she had occupied the spot about thirty years I came to the town and soon became acquainted with the fame and abode of Uilsa. I watched her often in the town and secretly followed her to her cottage and often hid myself behind the brushwood to observe her motions. At length I went openly to her residence; ⟨she⟩there was no one near and I supposed she had gone to the town or ⟨in⟩to other parts of the wood to pluck berries. But I was pleased with the beauty and magnificent scenery of the place and sat down near a heap of leaves to look about me. Suddenly I was startled by a voice & seeing a motion in the foliage beside me[.]

You may think I was shocked — to see a long bare arm outstretched from the bank and the shrill voice [28] [of] Uilsa not addressed to me as it seemed but screaming to the woods & the sky. "Fall, fall, scarlet leaves! The trees are my servants to cover me with a royal crimson mantle. And am not I a queen of the woods? I scared the wild eagle at the dawn, for the eye of my mother's daughter was fiercer than his. And who is he," she said, turning suddenly upon me, "who comes to the Cave of the Grey Queen? Is the spoon or the doublet or the silver or the gold stolen; have their flocks strayed or sickened or is the magistrate come up that they have hunted out Uilsa again?" I ↑never↓ was so ↑forcibly↓ impressed and awed as with the voice of this ⟨wi⟩woman. ⟨Uil[sa]⟩When she first turned to me her manner was terrifying but my indignation at being confounded with the ignorant staring rustics who now and then sought her out tended to restore my equilibrium. My instant resolution was to ⟨rejoice in⟩ humour her distempered tone of mind and reply to her contemptuous question in similar terms. — "Doth not the Queen of the woods gather the secrets of futurity —— when she reads the ⟨leaves of the⟩ decaying oak-leaves and can she not tell the young man how to guide his steps in life?" "Have ye come to learn fate then? Your habit is goodly, and the lines of your tenement are fair. But why come to the old and withered hag, the decrepit worm which the people of this land fear and contemn? Though I am thus despised and derided, and have lived in a land which is hateful I did not come from the ↑vulgar↓ dust — Uilsa is highly and proudly descended from an hundred weird women[,] fatal and feared daughters of Odin." She stood up and looked to the north as if expecting a sign in the firmament. I expected one myself; I was awed by this strange character and felt a lively conviction of the truth of her claims to supernatural light. As ⟨she⟩ ↑the Sybil↓ stood up between two blasted oaks glaring on me

(Turn to page 48)

[29] Boston Aug 8th 1821

I have been reading Montesquieu's Lettres Persanes.[26] It is a book which answered a very good purpose, if, as I suppose, it was written before modern Essayists (Rambler Spectator &c) were in vogue; for ⟨each⟩ ↑the↓ letter↑s↓ ⟨is a⟩are short unconnected essays on all sort[s] of subjects. One object of the book is to satirize passing events, characters, fashions of Paris. It is no recommendation of the book that he ↑has↓ placed among the first letters in the book, as a lure and attracting point, a sensual one from the seraglio. There is no attempt to preserve any peculiarities of character, though a variety of persons are engaged in the correspondence. Of the *style* I am no judge but the book abounds with brilliant and touching thoughts.[27]

[26] On Aug. 2, Emerson or his mother had borrowed from the Boston Library Society Vol. 5 of *Oeuvres Complettes de Montesquieu*, 6 vols., Paris, 1816.

[27] For the six quotations which follow, see *Lettres Persanes,* ed. Henri Barckhausen, 2 vols. (Paris, 1932): (1) Letter 59, I, 114; (2) Letter 67, I, 127; (3) Letter 141, I, 277–278; (4) Letter 137, I, 267; (5) *ibid.*; (6) Letter 78, I, 155.

"On a dit fort bien que si les triangles faisoient un dieu, ils lui donneroient trois cotes."

"Le coeur est citoyen de tous les 'pays'[.]"

Anaïs, after her introduction to Mahomet's paradise of sensual intoxication, shuts herself up —

"Il y avait plus de huit jours qu'elle etoit dans cette demeure heureuse, que, toujours hors d'elle-meme, elle n'avoit pas fait une seule reflexion: elle avoit joui de son bonheur sans le connaître, et sans avoir ↑eu↓ un seul de ⟨s⟩ces momens tranquilles où l'ame se rend, pour ainsi dire compte a luimême et s'ecoute dans le silence des passions."

[30] As Montesquieu is a quoted oracle in literature and laws it is proper to transcribe these —

"Voici les lyriques que Je méprise autant que J'estime les autres, et qui font de leur art, une harmonieuse extravagance."

Of Epic poems —

"Les connoisseurs disent qu'on n'en a jamais fait que deux et que les autres qu'on donne sous ce nom ne le sont point: c'est aussi ce que je ne sais pas."

Of don Quixote —

Le seul de leurs (Espagnols) livres qui soit bon, est celui qui a fait voir le ridicule de tous les autres.

Many good stories are told pretty well. The satire is conceived ingeniously in the tale of the man who did not sleep for thirty years, and after every other remedy had failed, sent to the bookseller for 6 Volumes of Caussin called "La Cour Sainte." His son, a young scholar, began to read, the company snored at the bottom of the first page and the sick man was sound asleep on the second.[28]

— "et rebus nox abstulit atra colorem." Æn 6.1 271[2] [29]

[31] Those who recommend mathematical studies with the most zeal do not pretend t⟨h⟩o place the objects of the science on higher

[28] Letter 143, I, 291. Most of the rest of the page is taken up with sketches — a man with a club, seven male heads in full face, and two in left profile.

[29] ". . . and black Night has stolen from the world her hues." For what was apparently Emerson's version before he looked it up, see p. 282.

⟨or[?] on[?] equal⟩ ground than morals. ⟨They confess with candour the necessity which directs⟩ ↑When they would direct the pursuits of beings who are ⟨crowded⟩ ↑bound↓ on every side by moral obligations, who⟨se⟩ exist to moral purposes, who can allot but a little time to learn how to spend the rest, they confess all which candour would ask. They admit the necessity which constrains man to accumulate facts which regard the character and condition of his species, the events which have befallen them, and the relations which they have sustained,—and to learn from these the lesson of a perfect life. They allow him to improve those powers and perceptions which are given to soften & adorn life, for the sour misfortunes and accidents of daily occurrence would ↑certainly↓ brutalize, if taste & imagination did not refine it. But when all this knowledge is gained and the region⟨s⟩ of sentiment explored; the objects of mathematical science may surely claim an early attention. [32] We may certainly by this time venture to measure the earth which we tread, to count the number and measure the magnitude of the stars by whose mutual attraction we stand. This is all which the ↑sober↓ Mathematician requires, to give this humble place to his science with regard to its objects—but this is not all the usefulness which is claimed. While they give preference to other learning they require something to prepare the Mind to recieve it; a regulating principle must enter the cloudy & obstructed[30] recesses of the mind to dispel the gloom and clear the chaos and to divide the apartments of the edifice for the proper arrangement of the stores they are to contain. We are told that the road to perfection in moral reasonings which we acknowledge to be the highest intellectual power is best found through that discipline which the mathematics furnish[.][31]

X

An irksome drudgery seems it to plod on,
Through dusty ways, in storm, from door to door.
A vagrant merchant ⟨bare[?]⟩bent beneath his load!

[30] Emerson obscured "cloudy" with a sketched rain-cloud, and filled the middle syllable of "obstructed" with an obstruction.

[31] Following "furnish" is a partially blotted scrawl of what may be "fool"; "John R A?"; and some practice penmanship. Beside the poem is a sketch of a shed, or perhaps a privy.

Yet do such travelers find their own delight;
And their hard service, deemed debasing now,
Gained merited respect in simpler times;
When Squire, & Priest, & they who round them dwelt
In rustic sequestration, all dependant
Upon the *Pedler's* toil, supplied their wants,
Or pleased their fancies, with the wares he brought[.]
[Wordsworth, *The Excursion*, I, 322–331]

[33][32] X Mr Wordsworth's choice of persons lays him open to ridicule, but of this he seems entirely independ⟨a⟩ent. He designed to take man where all mankind meet, above the reach of the arbitrary distinctions of rank or fashion upon the open ground of naked human nature; and it would have been preposterous to have introduced for the purposes of his philosophical dialogue the personages of heraldry. ⟨It is idle to tax a poet with this as a mean fault for no merit attaches to a poet's liberal ⟨catalogue⟩ ↑creation↓ of peers & princes[;] ⟨it is quite as⟩ it requires no more expense of thought to furnish a lord than a peasant.⟩ It were idle to tax a poet with the mean external condition of his characters, whenever it suits his purposes as if nobles & princes, stars & coronets, were not as cheaply obtained in poetical creation as tattered raiment, the cottage, & the poor.

The Excursion is a philosophical poem in nine books connected by a subordinate tale which serves to introduce & change the subject of discussion and forms ⟨a⟩ ↑the 2d↓ part of a larger Poem called the Recluse not yet published ⟨but⟩ which purports to treat of Man, Nature, & Society. The personages of the tale are few and their characters not eventful. We shall give a brief ⟨exp⟩ abstract of this tale. ⟨The author meets⟩ The poem ⟨b⟩opens by a description of ⟨the⟩ ↑a concerted↓ meeting ⟨of⟩ ↑between↓ the Author ↑himself↓ and an old Man called the Wanderer at the ruins of a hut in the woods. The latter relates the story of Margaret the former tenant of the spot whose homely misfortunes form a tale of touching interest. ⟨A wharf⟩ The projected excursion is begun in the second book and the character of the person whom they are about to visit is described. The

[32] About the middle of the page are three sketches of male heads in left profile, one with a turban; "S[r?] John" is written below "philosophical dialogue"; the words "A Madman" run diagonally left to right upward from "Society" (below) to "and forms" (above).

Solitary is a man who has retired from a world which has disgusted him by its untoward events, who loved to madness & has lost the objects of his affections, & who ⟨sought⟩ seeking [33] to substitute new idols for those which are gone [34] is disappointed in all and his distempered mind rejects religion & hope together. When the travellers have reached the romantic Vale they ⟨are cordially⟩ find the Solitary engaged in comforting a child whose parent had just been carried over the hills to his grave and are cordially welcomed. The circumstances give rise to long Conversation in the two following Books "Despondency" & "Despondency corrected" in which the hermit recounts his early history, his love and domestic felicity, the afflictions which blasted it and in which bereavement the meteor light of the French Revolution recalled him to human sympathies from the apathy of despair. Disappointed & mocked there, he carried his fretful visions to America only to return with new disgust. In this secluded dwelling his lacerated affections have settled into a calm depression of mind arising from want of faith in the great truths of religion & want of confidence in the virtue of mankind. This narrative forms the ground of the speculations in Book fourth upon the errors of the Solitary, the miseries of apathy, & the true sources of Consolation & reliance. Book fifth introduces us to "The Pastor" at the Chapel & Graveyard which they have visited. "The ChurchYard among the Mountains" the name of the sixth & seventh Books ⟨is⟩ ↑gives occasion to↓ a series of parish tales after which the clergyman conducts his guests to "the Parsonage" where the conversation is again renewed and turns chiefly upon the character & influence of Manufactures. The ninth book called "The Discourse of the Wanderer" [n] contains an excursion upon the lake and a brilliant sunset[.] The conversation of the party and the parting of the Solitary & his Friends concludes the book.

[35] Ralph W Emerson.

De Anno Sunday Morn Aug 12 1821.

The Reformation proceeded on higher grounds than it would if it should take place ⟨on⟩at the present day. It must be the case in

[33] Underneath "who ⟨sought⟩ seeking" are two words "The [we?]" and "eveter [water?]" in the bottom margin.

general with these events that they come very gradually into notice and respect, & then through the paths of obloquy and ridicule. Most of the sects in the Church however respectable they may now be, have in their origin been examples of this. That religious belief which in any country from its greater prevalence calls itself *the Church* has in long progress of time collected about itself a thousand sons to uphold its banner & ↑who↓ add ⟨all th⟩ beside all their zeal for its support, all their honours & weight as worldly men [n] to give dignity to its creed in the eyes of ordinary inquirers. Owing to the social principles of our condition there is a vast proportion of men, in every country who look to others, & those, the rich and respectable[,] for the direction of their religious opinions. But when a new system of faith is started it is not the opulent or the great who first recieve & /promote/propagate/ it; for these are not generally the most solicitous for truth but are content to be absorbed in the vortex ⟨of⟩ ↑which↓ fashion and eminence have created. But reform and *new light* proceed [36] from intrepid minds of the lower or middle class, and because it originates here, the aspiring and the proud alike disdain it. But the Reformation differed essentially from these in its course and termination[.]

⟨In⟩ Previous ↑to↓ 151⟨5⟩7 when Luther began to declaim against the sale of indulgences, the Roman church possessed a dom⟨ain⟩inion as wide though not as absolute, as at any former period. Europe was subject through all her borders * to spiritual government and brought the homage of all her genius, power, wealth, and splendour to give glory and renown to the hierarchy. Sovereign above all sovereigns Rome derived from the several states the praise of good [n] ⟨government⟩ monarchy, of a well ordered republic, of a powerful senate, or of a mighty and united empire. She was the ⟨one⟩ source of all the talents, honour, and power in the civilized world and sat like Cybele crowned with towers and mother of the gods.

"the earthquake voice of victory"

By the time Wilfred had reached the heath the north wind which had before been resounding faintly in the glens began to blow fiercely and while it rapidly separated the clouds gave indication of a

* Denmark and Sweden

cold night. The sun had set and the stars shone with increased brilliancy through [37] the purified atmosphere. The darkness and the frost hurried our traveller over the barren downs which it will easily be supposed offered few attractions to detain a belated passenger. By reaching to the right he avoided the darker parts of the plain where he supposed the coal pits to lie and which were supposed to make a nocturnal path dangerous. A man of imagination finds a great source of thought in the noise of the wind or the murmur of the stream. Wilfred amused his journey by observing the solemn but varied voices of the breeze as it issued from the hollows of the mountains. Sometimes he compared it to human sounds, sometimes to the shrieks of sea birds till he began actually to believe that the indistinct accents which fell upon his ear were something more than the mountain echoes. At first this was a disagreeable conviction, but though it quickened his ear he found nothing to disprove his first impressions. He ascended a little hillock and stopped to listen, and as the gale died away there was mingled with it an articulate sound which no ear could mistake for the breeze[.][34]

[35] There was a hog ten years ago
A hog a hog a hog
And those who best his story know
Call him the grand son of Magog
However that be, the swine grew up
And roamed about his vaulted sty
Drank swill from Pleasure's brimming cup
And grunted grunts of exstacy.

Ten little pigs, his little sons
Followed their father's daily walk
And much it pleased that good old hog
To teach his smutty sons to talk

An education wise and good
Was his own hobby all his ⟨life⟩ ↑days↓

[34] This paragraph seems to be a variant of part of the "Magician" story, told in the third person rather than the first. See pp. 286 and 302–303.

[35] The poem is written in two columns, the second beginning "But one dark morn . . . ."

To teach them all the joys of mud
And their pork minds with care to raise

But one dark morn of windy March
The cruel hail fell down
Broke thro the sty's protecting arch
And all the boards so brown.

Five little pigs that morning fell
In youth and beauty's pride
And by each other's golden limbs
They laid them down and died

Next day the old hog died of grief
Very insupportable
And one by one the other four

Died uncomfortable.
Oh cruel March that thus didst blow
And cruel clouds to storm
The old hog's ghost & nine little ghosts
Are seen in spectre form.

[38] Few wars are more remarkable than that waged by Florence again[st] Pisa to recover its dominion over that courageous city in the years 1497—1500. In 1500 the French (who were then in Italy, under Louis XII,) undertook to reduce the city to its old obedience; but as their army advanced, the Pisans found means by their affectionate confidence, by their prayers, and by their proofs of indomitable bravery to rekindle in the breasts of their invaders, the kind feelings towards them which had existed in the army of Charles VIII. The French made an assault upon the city and were repulsed. Meanwhile, whatever Frenchmen presented themselves at the gates, were freely admitted, and were even shewn the masked batteries that they might secure themselves and their friends in battle, and were dismissed with presents. The French returned this hospitality by admitting the Pisans to their camp, by refusing to interrupt the convoys from neighbouring cities which entered the gates of the city. Finally, the soldiers refused to fight, and the weapon which Florence

had expected to employ with so much effect, was turned against herself. Florence recieved these tidings with indignation & despair.

(For the whole account, see Sismondi Ital. Repub. Vol 13, p. 100.)[36] [R. W. E.]

A. Its Nativity B. Promise C. Its nature & design D. Rhyme[37]

Men and states change and grow worse after they have reached the perfection of strength, but why they should seems not readily explained. They have added strength to strength until weakness seems excluded from their institutions and when we look to see that great truth exhibited which ⟨is⟩ meets us everywhere in the economy of Providence that to whom ↑there is much,↓ much ⟨is⟩ ↑shall be↓ given[;] a reverse arrests their advancing prosperity and a special decree is issued to contravene the order of nature and to ⟨make⟩ convert vigour into lassitude & to eat ↑into↓ their grandeur with moth & rust[.]

Why said Demosthenes "Action, action, &c"[?] "The reason is plain. There is in human nature generally more of the fool than of the wise; and therefore those faculties by which the foolish part of men's minds is taken are most potent." Bacon. ["Of Boldness"]

[39][38] Essay on Poetry.

A It is the boast of poetry that it has been appreciated in every age of the world. Religion and nature smiled at its nativity, but it has changed its companions a thousand times and taken partners which nature and religion never introduced or commended. ⟨But in⟩ ↑Through↓ all its variety of aspect it has never ↑once↓ slackened its hold on the heart and mind but has preserved its claim entire amid the revolution of moral and political interests and the vicissitudes which have affected government, science, and philosophy. It has been the favourite child—sometimes the spoiled minion of the gentler

[36] Jean Charles Leonard Simonde de Sismondi, *Histoire des Républiques Italiennes au Moyen Âge*, 16 vols. (Paris, 1818). Between Feb. 28 and Aug. 8, 1822, Emerson or his mother borrowed from the Boston Library Society vols. 4–7, and 9–14 of Simonde. Vol. 13 was withdrawn July 20 and returned Aug. 31.

[37] This line, pencilled in above the Sismondi reference, is an outline for the "Essay on Poetry" on the facing page.

[38] In the middle of Emerson's paragraph "A" is a rough pencil sketch of a man's head and upraised arm.

affections but a trifler formidable to its foes ⟨from⟩ by the number of friends which its prattle won.[39] It secured respect by refusing to confine itself to things ⟨as⟩ ↑so↓ humble as fact and science[n] and then ridiculed the lofty pretensions of the professors.

These earthly godfathers of heaven's lights
 That give a name to every ⟨shining⟩ ↑fixed↓ star
Have no more profit of their shining lights
 Than those who walk & wot not what they are"
 [*Love's Labour's Lost*, I, i, 88–91]

B Men engaged in the pursuits of life and the slights, neglect, and cares which vexed them returned them to poetry as the beautiful spirit which should abate or amuse their weariness of life. It was the favourite child of the gentle affections, for it ⟨sprung⟩ adorned the foibles of superstition with romance. The fears of the rustic [40] mistook a ragged bush or a rock for a supernatural being and poetry invested his mistakes with the attributes of truth and gave away virtues, sceptres, and crowns to its own imaginations. ⟨And when⟩ ⟨i⟩In the progress of this airy empire ↑when↓ all the high places, groves, and caverns of the habitable earth had been successively surrendered, the profligacy of poetry /lamented/pined/ that there was no more to squander and with an ingenuity of giving which the material world never rivalled, fairly *imagined* a region for *imagined* beings and triumphed in Fairy Land. This was a policy for statesmen to imitate; and it has accordingly been successfully adopted in bestowing Bounty Lands upon disbanded Armies, and likewise by some individuals endowing colleges with whole estates of this description[.]

C Liberal views of the philosophy of poetry find its adaptation to the faculties of man as the link ↑⟨network⟩↓ between matters of speculation and matters of fact. Poetry is a web ↑of many hues↓ thrown over the dull and tame prospect of life through which ⟨we behold⟩ the same objects ⟨but⟩ ↑are ind⟨i⟩e⟨s⟩finit[e]ly seen &↓ coloured with beauty ⟨and partially withdrawn⟩. ↑We love poetry, as we do the flowers of the field because they supply not the necessaries but the luxuries of life.↓ Its moral design is to relieve the ⟨homely⟩

[39] The sentence is encircled.

↑dreary↓ sadness which gathers so fast over all human pursuits by uniting ⟨their dis⟩ ↑them in their↓[n] distant and shadowy limits ↑where its ends become undefined↓ to ⟨a⟩ brighter scenes. That it ⟨might answer⟩ ↑may fulfill↓ this end it is accessible to all. The truths of philosophy and of science require abstraction and study and what would be to most men a painful effort to comprehend their ⟨|| use ||⟩ ↑nature↓ and learn their use ↑and these do not come to him in an engaging form.↓ But to enjoy poetry a man has but to open his eyes and the whole host of shining images, its frostwork, ⟨array⟩ ↑pageantry↓ of houses, ⟨men and land⟩ ↑castles, mountains, & men↓ [41] will pass before him. It is true that the higher beauties of the art ⟨are⟩ ↑will↓ not be obvious to all and that it may be made a study until the spirit is refined to an exquisite sensibility to the pleasures of sentiment and delicate expression. But the ordinary and common character is open to all and the relish of the ear for melody of rhy↑th↓m⟨e⟩ is a mystery which philosophy resolves into an ultimate principle. And the fine organization by which the soul is fitted to recieve delight from melody and rhythm, is the proper and reasonable indication that it is an art founded on the necessities and ⟨agreeable to the designs⟩ ↑allied to the operations↓ of nature.

D We wrongfully accuse the barbarism of the middle ages for having degraded poetry by ⟨entailing upon future literatures⟩ disusing the lofty cadence of Roman verse and entailing ↑up↓on future literatures the childish invention of rhyme. On the contrary we are inclined to bless the monk and his gentle conception which so fell in with nature and ↑has↓ done such distinguished service to modern literature; which has disclosed a fund of intellectual amusement which the Greek & Roman bard never knew and which perhaps was not adapted to their languages. Has the English language lost anything by it? For those poets whose ⟨subject⟩ ↑genius↓ could not ⟨be⟩ stoop or whose subject could not be confined to rhyme ⟨we possess⟩ and for the drama, we possess a measure which approaches to prose in ⟨the⟩ ease and simplicity while it admits the most beautiful cadences of poetry; a measure which is embalmed and hallowed by the glory of Shakespeare and Milton. The lovers of English poetry will hardly be convinced that the Elegiac Muse of Rome ever uttered a voice so unspeakably tender as some productions of British rhyme or that

Byron has not found a language for deep [42][40] feeling and sublime thought or will ⟨accuse⟩ ↑arraign↓ the ⟨rich⟩ luxurious verses of Moore ↑for↓ ⟨of⟩ frigidness or constraint. Grief and strong passion often play with words and rhyme is not an improper instrument. It is a secondary music and the assistance it affords to ⟨the⟩ memory imprints a thousand beautiful thoughts in the mind which had else been lost. Poetical taste refines and ameliorates the mind and he that has never known the delight of sweet sounds is worse than a brute.

Hanging 4000
900
3100
1821
4921

E We rejoice that there are acquisitions which destroy the praise while they surpass the comprehension of pedantry and that we are suffered to indulge unchecked the course of imagination. In the abundance of thought and the multiplied directions and expressions of human understanding it was consistent with Nature that fancy—the hidden soul of harmony and the most ethereal of all our mental powers should ⟨invent some mode of⟩ ↑seek↓ [to] embody itself in some attractive & appropriate form. For as it is kindled by external objects in combinations which may rarely or never occur again, if you remove its agency all but the remote influence is lost of ↑past↓ events, scenes, and situations which contained picturesque beauty or fine moral character. The leaves fell and the waterfall enlivened the landscape in vain if no voice was taught to repeat the impressions, to renew the brilliant or melancholy sentiments which attached to them ⟨in order⟩ that they might be ⟨perpetuated⟩ ↑remembered↓ through the accidents and smiles of life and rise for a perpetual instance of moral and material analogy. [43][41] When this was effected, Musaeus and Homer ⟨instead⟩ no longer limited ⟨their⟩ to themselves their inspired ideas of nature[,] might inform their countrymen with taste and sublimity, and might transmit through fifty centuries their hymns

[40] In the upper and middle section of the page are a large and a small sketch of a man's head, and one of a man walking.

[41] In the upper section of the page is a pencil sketch of a man's head; in the lower, one of a tholus in ink.

to nature and the tale of Troy to kindle the genius of the distant poet.

F Mankind have always cherished secret or open a grudge against poetry as the spell or disease which palsies activity and enterprise in life. ⟨and unfits the miserable devotee for common duties.⟩ Still ⟨the lovers of poetry⟩ men will abide by it, for in all their professed antipathy or shy affection there is nothing which will stand them in its stead ⟨for it⟩. The love for what is illusory will steal ⟨out⟩ over whatever pains are taken to disguise it. ⟨The fascination of somewhat darker⟩ The belief of things unseen is planted ↑too↓ deep ⟨in the breast⟩ and exerts a fascination too strong to be easily forgone. The belief of things somewhat darker than the storm or somewhat brighter than the day is as old as the mind and will subsist as long; and that which has vital influence sufficient to make the blood creep and the nerves contract and the flesh shiver will surely find itself a↑n adequate↓ language. ⟨We are confident of truth in making the assertion that⟩ ⟨h⟩He who has once enjoyed in any proportionate measure this fine intellectual pastime, if he has ever known fiction warm and elegant enough to decoy admiration and pity from the strict regulation of reason will not be induced to relinquish that gratification by any jeers [44] of ⟨the⟩ frivolous or aphorisms of conceited men. Perhaps it may abate his love of life by quickening his disgust of folly and evil; it may disqualify his mind for ⟨low⟩ ↑coarse↓ and vulgar details of ordinary transactions,[n] but abundant compensation will be provided in the land of the marvelous. It will illuminate the dark road of investigation with indescribable beauty. It will give a tone and sweetness to his feelings which tastes of heaven. It carries him back to enjoy a fellow-feeling with the great of former times[,] with him that left halftold the story of Cambuscan bold. It will multiply his pleasures fast for they depend on slight and common circumstances. So exceedingly delicate is the tenure by which imagination retains its objects that it is not wonderful that those who cannot appreciate them should feel their wonder and ridicule excited at the estimation in which things so frivolous are held. The mind of the poet is enriched with many an old ballad, and disjointed tale, many an idle proverb, and many a quaint obsolete phrase. Trains of pleasing and peculiar thought are excited and embodied by these transient vestiges of former associations and which cost none of that ⟨difficult⟩

sore labour which constructs a mathematical train. The mathematician is satisfied ⟨and well pleased⟩. The poet enjoys more. There is a pleasing momentary delirium which comes over him that surrounds him with paradise and charms him with the idea that he hath created it.

[45] We have stated the views ↑in↓ which poetry ought to be regarded in general but it is not easy in this as in other arts to deduce from general observations upon its nature & character particular rules which ⟨ought⟩ should regulate ↑one of↓ the ⟨composition of a poem⟩ ↑productions of the art.↓ Men have written poems in every manner and in defiance of all rules and succeeded ⟨perfectly⟩ entirely; they have written and conformed perfectly with all the rules and failed.

It adored the Creator with its infant voice and sternly pointed mankind to the workings of Destiny. It commemorated the ⟨dead⟩ men who died at Marathon and Plataea. ⟨It shook the flame of terror and vengeance to alarm the world on the plain of Troy.⟩ On the plain of Troy it took up the torch of national vengeance to alarm the world by its awful splendour. With ominous zeal it resumed the dark fables which pourtrayed a destiny and drew thence its moral of grief and dismay. Impassioned poetry seldom

[46][42] Impassioned poetry affects the mind more forcibly than mere narrative or highly wrought sentiment for all men are alike in common life & must have their passions wrought up before you can trace those interesting distinctions which do prevail. The difficulty which every one percieves ⟨in⟩ when one mind would identify itself with the counterfeit sufferings of another so as to feel & express all which the person described should express, renders this species of poetry rare. The flower of love lies bleeding is one of the few successful attempts of this sort.[43]

Mr Wordsworth is a poet whom we read with caution in whom the eye always is afraid lest it should meet with something offensive at every turn. It subtracts vastly from the pleasure of poetry if you read with this evil timidity. It is like faltering upon a mountain for

[42] In the left center of the page is a large sketch of a crown.

[43] Thomas Campbell, "O'Connor's Child, or, The Flower of Love-Lies-Bleeding" (see *L*, VI, 335). "D D Day" appears in the space between "sort" and the beginning of the new paragraph below.

fear of a precipice. In the midst of an eloquent strain of sentiment or description your admiration is brought up with a noted vulgarism or glaring false taste. To a chastened ear no occasional beauty will make amends for ⟨frequently obtruded⟩ ↑obtrusive↓ deformity; it only serves to aggravate the sin et_1 nox_3 $atra_5$ $rebus_2$ $abstulit_4$ $colorem_6$[44]

Although the theory does not run counter to our own theory of poetry or to any sound views of the art yet experience has not shewn any final decisive success to follow the experiment. On the contrary Mr Southey, Mr Coleridge, & Mr Wordsworth have gained less honour than ridicule by their poetry not because it ⟨did⟩ wanted genius but it wanted nature. The affectation of simplicity was but too apparent; the poetry was too puerile for the taste of their [47] northern countrymen. And the experiment yet remains to be tried[.]

Peru is the land of the diamond stone[45]
Of the silver & of the gold
In the shrine of the Sun, his rites are done,
And the Inca's car is rolled

Day dawned on Para's marble wall
And lit the Inca's jewelled hall
Uprose the offspring of the Sun
And put the anointed garland on
He bade the priests attend his state
And passed beneath the ⟨outer⟩ ↑Eastern↓ gate
Where sacred choirs stood marshalled round
And the palace rung with the lofty sound

Peru is the land of the diamond stone
Of the silver & of the gold
In the shrine of the Sun, his rites are done,
And the Inca's car is rolled.

Nine milkwhite steeds are harnassed on
⟨To the royal car where the beryl shone⟩

[44] See p. 269, n. 29.

[45] The poem is in two columns on the page, the second beginning at "On Peru's fair & ancient shrine . . . ."

To the car, by clasps of the beryl stone
And over his head the menials tie
The crimson knots of his canopy.
Then forth the royal Inca rode
Proudly through the kneeling crowd
Until he reached his shining throne
And left his car, and sat thereon.

Peru is the land &c.

There's a murmur heard from side to side
In that pillared shrine of Peruvian pride
And the crowd divides with haste & fear
As if a foe was approaching here
Ten savage men in iron drest
Straight thro' the shrinking people prest
They strode across the pavement stone
And laid their swords on the very throne.

Peru is the land &c

On Para's fair & ancient shrine
Where 100 lamps of naphtha shine
But the angry burst of the iron chief
Replied to the monarch loud & brief [46]

⟨With fiery rage⟩ ↑Angrily↓ the Monarch rose
And tore the chaplet from his brows
And who ⟨are⟩ ↑be↓ ye that dare intrude
In foreign arms & gesture rude
⟨Upon my presence & profane⟩
↑On Para's old & holy shrine↓
My throne with such defiance vain?
He said; a^{n} chief with hand on high
Was ready with a bold reply

[46] These two couplets are crowded in near the top of the page above the following line. Though they are uncancelled, both their appearance and their incoherence in context argue that they were tentative additions or alternatives, each couplet perhaps designed for insertion at a different place in the poem.

The crowd stood still amazed to view
Such insult fall upon Peru

Southern ⟨Peru is the land⟩ &c[47]

From foreign lands O king I come
In 3-score ships ⟨from⟩thro' Ocean foam
I come to share in Peru's gold
I come to search the gems of old
To pluck the ⟨gold⟩ ↑pearls↓ that deck⟨s⟩ your shrine
And feast my knaves on Western wine
The slave that dares to cross my word
Dies for the deed by a Spaniard's sword.

Peru is the land [&c.]

Fire flashed in the Inca's wrathful eye
He shook his sparkling sceptre high
He smote the Spaniard's plumed head
And felled him to ⟨the earth with speed⟩ ↑his footstool dead↓
The crowd hemmed in the stranger band
And trod them down in the bloody sand
And when the angry deed was done
A shout went up to the glorious Sun

Peru is the land of the diamond stone
Of the beryl and of the gold
In the shrine of the Sun his rites are done
And the inca's car is rolled

FINIS

[48] (continued from page 28.)
with fiery eye and perturbed countenance. I forgot the world I had left and saw nothing but the Spirit of Prophecy and the grove where she ministered. After the pause she resumed "A voice from the sepulchres and caves[,] a voice from the wrinkled rottenness which the earth spurns from her bosom, ⟨to⟩ a voice to the young man from her that has an hundred years and brings judgement from the

[47] See p. 254, n. 8.

palace of souls. Uilsa stood up in her native forest—⟨a panther rushed by fleeing out from the wilderness a thousand wolves ran down by the mountain scared by the hideous lightning and baring the⟩ ↑⟨baring⟩↓ ⟨tooth⟩ ↑⟨to kill⟩↓ ⟨for the panther; the wolves hasted⟩ ↑⟨a strong one of the accursed herd hasted⟩↓ ⟨after the panther, the wild thunder crushed the wolf⟩

A gold caravan travelled down through the wilderness with galloping horses and tasseled elephants from Birmah, they bore away my firstborn to make the son of Uilsa a slave. Did I not wake the mountains with my denouncing scream—calling vengeance from the north? Odin knew me and thundered. A thousand wolves ran down by the mountain scared by the hideous lightning and baring the tooth to kill; they rushed after the cumbrous host. I saw when the pale faces glared back in terror as the black wolf pounced on his victim. I saw them as he dashed his tooth into ⟨his⟩ ↑the Indian's↓ throat and mangled his bones in the sand. They died, and the wild thunder crushed the wolves but one escaped with ⟨the⟩[n] ↑mine↓ infant son ⟨of Uilsa⟩ to the cave of the forest, and nourished him from her dugs. I made my bed in the cavern, my feast with the whelp of a wolf; but there also I mingled in the dance of the [49] Sisters, and heard the voice ↑of↓ a hundred years. Ghosts came to the cave, and my son commanded the snows of the pole. Who is he now but Vahn, the Master of Magicians? But the proud magician forgot the mother that bore him, and the circle of enchantments which he drew was a ring of fiend-dogs to bay at me,—to scare me over the snow-drift in the cold starless night. And when I passed out from the forest there was none who took pity on the old woman of ragged raiment and wild eye. They scoffed & spurned me in the city streets; count and clown turned upon me—Oh Valhalla! The wing of Odin & the wind of the West bore me away to die here. And though I moulder here,—Stranger! there is a spell upon my life which shall make the living & the dead quake, when the thread is snapped, and stir the tempest among the sunny clouds."

⟨S⟩The barbarian paused from the vehemence of her passion and pluck⟨ed⟩ing up some withered weeds ⟨and⟩ threw them into the air as a⟨n⟩ rite to Odin. It was some days afterwards, that I was told that the sympathies of the village had begun to be excited in behalf of this extraordinary vagrant, who had so strongly interested myself, by the desolate and mournful change of aspect which she had lately exhibited. Some of the more respectable inhabitants wished me to seek her out, and tender her a habitation owned within the village. ⟨Some of⟩ ⟨t⟩The peasants were alarmed by the idea that she was about to put an end to her own life, and had intimated such an intention to some people who had carried [50] provisions to her cave. I departed from the town in the direction of the kindlecoal woods, and soon reached those fine shades which never failed to elevate the imagination. Uilsa was not here, nor could my vigilant eye, accustomed to behold her half-concealed somewhere in the neighbourhood of her dwelling, detect any appearance of her. As I left the cavern my attention was suddenly attracted by the loud call of a boy who standing midway up the ascent of the next hill waved his cap to me as he shouted, that Uilsa had gone to the Milboro' pits, and that I must follow her there. This child I had never seen; his dress was somewhat singular for that country, and his message surprised me a little. Still I made no hesitation to set off immediately in the direction he named, for I entertained some apprehensions with regard to the motive which dictated Uilsa's journey to those frightful cliffs. These dangerous places lie in the midst of the coal mines where the mineral soil has been broken asunder to a great depth by an earthquake and often appal the traveller who is gazing at the fine scener⟨e⟩y of that amphitheatre of mountains by the unexpected sight of an abyss yawning open at his feet to a depth which was never fathomed. The peasants who know the passes shun the spot in the dark, and those who are unacquainted with the place generally avoid it even in the day. It was also rendered

Continued on page 72

[51] Drama[48] Oct 21 1821

Mr Editor,

Sir

If it is not trespassing on your liberality to ask admission into your paper for subjects not immediately connected with politics or the news of the day nor interesting ⟨in⟩ ↑with↓ any

[48] The word is in faint orange crayon. By Emerson?

view ⟨of⟩ ↑to↓ trade and yet a subject whose importance is ↑great though↓ not appreciated and is exceedingly misunderstood, — I have before me some papers on the *Drama* which I shall successively send you.[49]

Every scholar who compares the productions of the stage of modern Europe with those of ancient Greece is always disgusted. Every moral man who visits the modern theatre, if he be ignorant or learned is sorely sick at heart. Thousands have mourned over this dark and alarming calamity which is firmly seated in the centre and have deprecated the increasing mischief which threatens society from such high and established grounds. Reason bids us inquire into the nature and causes of the evil and wherein consists the difficulty of removing it and it is dishonourable to the virtue and [52] name of a nation which professes to appreciate the importance of public morals that an enormous pest should be suffered to root itself in the state and no one /zealous/intrepid/ enough to examine the disease and apply the knife. It is the misfortune of America that ⟨with⟩ her sudden maturity of national condition was accompanied with the knowledge of good and *evil* which would better belong to an older country. We have recieved our drama line for line and precept for precept from England and in so doing have inherited a stained and rotten web of corruptions ⟨wh⟩in which a few geniuses have condescended to weave their golden threads but whose ↑whole↓ tissue is consistent in nothing but pollution. But in this country public feeling is much more pure and on this encouragement we build all our hope of reform and improvement. In England they are hardened by long unquestioned custom to survey with indifference this odious spectacle. Indeed I know not what of ⟨flagrant sin⟩ ↑malignant crime↓, of dark enormity, or wide-spread wickedness would startle the public mind there. I am proud and thankful when I contrast this with the ↑uncontaminated↓ innocence of my own country and it ⟨because our prospects are so bright⟩ is this comparative purity joined to the energy of a youthful people [53] still free from the complicated difficulties of

[49] These papers, like the essay on "The Religion of the Middle Ages," beginning on p. 304, were doubtless intended for publication. On Nov. 8, 1821, Emerson wrote to his Aunt Mary, "The *drama* crawls on but clamours for inspiration" (*L*, I, 103). For later thoughts on the drama, see Wide Worlds, 3, 4, 6, and 7, *passim.*

an old government which constitutes the distinction and promise of this nation. We have read in books that the Drama was a beautiful artifice intended to convey Moral lessons in disguise and was thus rendered an useful national institution. But the disguise must be ↑very↓ deep, or else the moral lessons ⟨must⟩ have vanished entirely from the plan as it is exhibited to our generation. It has become scandalous for moral teachers to ⟨attend⟩ ↑visit↓ the Theatre.[50] I am aware that the evil we lament is increased by certain atrocious circumstances which belong to the house rather than the play and are independent of the spirit of the Drama. But if the great Queen of iniquity were cured of her abominations the outcourts of depravity would be cleansed also. ⟨No⟩ Vice never profanes the ⟨house of God⟩ temples of religion with its sensuality; neither would the Theatre be defiled if it were as it ought to be the seat of intellect and the union of sublime genius and morality.

In the ensuing papers I shall recommend the attention of your readers to this subject from ⟨the⟩ considerations drawn from the nature of the drama, slight notices of its history, and chiefly its importance to the American people and ↑hints of the↓ manner of improvement.

[54] Our advantages in pursuing the study of the Drama are great & flattering. The most beautiful relique of ⟨a⟩Antiquity is the productions of the three great masters of ⟨the⟩ Grecian ⟨drama⟩ tragedy. And our knowledge of their stage is made complete by the Comedies of Aristophanes. These last we can well spare from our ⟨study for⟩ ↑inquiry relative to↓ the improvement of our own stage for in this view they only form a picture of the licentiousness of privileged ribaldry. Of the Latin tragedy we ⟨know⟩ ↑have↓ nothing. The French theatre is an imitation of the Greek but without any adaptation to the altered state of modern feeling. Few speculations have so much charm in their nature as these, whose object is how to conduct the dialogue ⟨of⟩ ↑between↓ a man and his fellow just ↑far↓ enough removed from common life to avoid disgust while it must chain the attention and elevate the tone of feeling by its lively delineations and lofty sentiments.

[50] Cf. Emerson to his brother William, April 23, 1819 (*L*, I, 82): "The Government have just made a new law that no student shall go to the Theatre on penalty of 10 Dols. fine at first offence and other punishments afterwards."

Letter 2

An opinion of Mr *Campbell* the celebrated author of Pleasures of Hope has been stated ↑in↓ this ⟨my⟩ country that the only ground ↑on↓ which America can ↑hope to↓ found a truly national literature is the Drama. We are bound to reverence such high authority [55] and at least to examine the ⟨truth⟩ ↑correctness↓ of the position.

Few speculations have such a charm in their nature as this whose object is how to ⟨avoid disgust⟩ conduct the dialogue between a man and his fellow just far enough removed from common life to avoid disgust while it must chain the attention and elevate the tone of feeling.

In the nation which has always been regarded as the model ⟨of⟩in all the arts, the fountain of all polished letters, and the pattern of all time—the Drama was invented and there alone succeeded perfectly. All inquiries therefore upon this subject ⟨tend⟩ begin from Greece. The history & influence ↑of tragedy↓, ⟨the modes⟩ its modes and machines of operation must be explained from these sources[.]

Tragedy by exciting the emotions of fear and of pity tends to correct the same affections in the soul. This has been all along esteemed the philosophy of tragedy with what correctness we shall not pretend to determine, but these ends were answered in Greece and more than this a respect for the Gods was effectually inculcated. The thraldom of superstition was made useful to shackle those whom the light and law of natural religion could not guide and he whom the [56] beauty of moral rectitude could not win, was afraid to face the temple of the Furies and averted his head as he passed by it. But by whom was this powerful influence created over a people whose refined taste kept a watchful eye on the ↑artist↓ ⟨so that it⟩ should not be seduced unawares and never yielded save to the irresistible might of Genius? In what schools did they purchase the subtle art which became in their hands an instrument of such power? This question is the most important which can be asked for it developes the causes of their preeminence. It was not the robed disciple at ease in the Academy who gained the prize of tragedy ⟨a⟩ but ⟨it⟩ ↑Aeschylus↓ was a son of the republic who had fought valiantly at Marathon & Plataea and came bleeding from the battle to assemble in a simple natural plot the personages of old traditions and attribute to them the feelings he had just felt and place them in circumstances in which himself had been placed. Miraculous effects have been recorded of their representation; but by whom and how were they performed[?]

In answer to this we all know how the primitive stage differed from the modern; that all was on a magnificent scale[,] that the actors were transformed to giants and the strength of their voices increased by a metallic mouthpiece. But that which formed their ↑chief↓ distinction were their independent habits of feeling, of sentiment, of invention. This is illustrated by an anecdote of their theatre[:] *Polus* the first actor on the stage was preparing to perform the part of Electra. In this [57] piece Electra embraces the urn ⟨containing the ashes⟩ ↑supposed to hold the remains↓ of ⟨her daughter⟩ Orestes. The Greek actor ordered that the urn containing the ashes of his own son should be brought from the tomb and conveyed ⟨on⟩ to the ⟨stage⟩ ↑theatre↓; and when on the stage this urn was offered to him ↑and the father bent over it↓ he rent the air with no mimic grief or insincere howlings but the whole audience was melted with the moving picture of ↑this↓ grief and lamentation[.]

⟨The heart ↑said Montesquieu↓ is the citizen of every country. Until we have a theatre exclusively our own we can appropriate the tragedies of Greece, we can act over again the dire story of the desolation of Thebes and the misery of her king[.][51]

The language which these facts speak is undeniably this ⟨that the subject of Drama must be such as the audience can enter into warmly and completely[,] that the dramatist must describe not with cold and accurate philosophy but with the strong & rapid pencil of nature[;] that what is wanted in the interest is to be made up in extraordinary beauty and genius of decoration⟩[52]—that a moral influence may be imparted to the drama so that it be connected with a tale into the interest of which the audience enter warmly, it may

[51] Between this and the next paragraph is sketched the head of a man in left profile; to the right appears the name "Robin Adair" with the additional word "yeild" below it.

[52] Besides the horizontal cancellation which begins at "⟨that the subject" the whole passage to this point is struck through; however, "The language . . . this" is necessary to complete the syntax of the uncancelled matter beginning with "— that a moral influence . . . ."

tell of philosophy and sentiment so it [58][53] be sketched with a rapid and glowing pencil[,] and that when the feeble mind grows weary of pure intellect the beauty of scenic decorat↑i↓on must be added. Here no ill-adjusted surfaces of paint and plaster can be vamped up to answer the end but this aid if recieved at all must be administered by the hands of taste and genius.

Letter 3 When the light had failed from the Greek theatre which three /masters/geniuses/ had poured upon it it ⟨was⟩would have ⟨surpassed⟩ ↑violated↓ the common ⟨course⟩ ↑order↓ of events had an equal illumination been rekindled. The frivolous ⟨comedy⟩ ↑Comic Muse hitherto↓ of slight esteem grew into favour and trode fast on the steps of sceptred Tragedy. The witty and offensive Aristophanes parodied the eloquent declamation of Euripides, mimicked the awful port of princes and Gods, and converted the general satire of the old comedians into a vicious personal ribaldry. Finally the civil authority interfered to stop its flagrant abuses.

The tragedy was not inherited by Rome which scrupulously incorporated all the arts of Athens. It was too delicate a treasure to be lightly transmitted by ⟨transaction⟩ instruction or won with

(Turn to page 63)

[59][54] ↑and the moral economy of the universe will abridge such a lavish waste of obligation[?] on a scale↓

Women casualty toward abridge
tow
toward coquetry
brooketh
carnal
abase

[53] Near the end of paragraph one are sketched the head of a boy and the head and shoulders of a man.

[54] The fragmentary sentence was inserted between "From Frodmer's Drama 'The Friends'" and the cancelled verse. For a number of reasons the verse seems to be a disguised address to Martin Gay. There is no dramatist named Frodmer. The title is apparently Emerson's — to describe his own theme. The thoughts parallel others he wrote to or about Gay. "Malcolm" may well be a substitute for "Martin." The words in the left margin, arranged in the pattern of an indented quatrain, are suggestive, though by no means indicative. Line two is heavily cancelled. In the middle

From Frodmer's Drama "The Friends"

⟨Malcolm, I love thee more than women love⟩
Your ⟨And pure and warm and equal is[?] the feeling⟩
Your ⟨Which binds us and our destinies forever⟩
Your ⟨But there are seasons in the change of⟩ times
Yours When strong excitement kindles up the light
Of ancient memories

V. Is.30C Your shops are shut for a few hours

Pour commenter une nouvelle prenez
The moon as seen through the poplars which garnish a town awakens no very —[55]

Such is the fact when sin has entered into a man. And you shall see his conduct; how he ⟨will⟩shall abridge his ascriptions of praise and teach his heart deeper & darker lessons of degeneracy, contract frightfully human feeling & tender mercy, and train up his children in the way they should not go until the long suffering even of the Most Merciful is ⟨closed⟩ /ceased/exhausted/. And his sun hath gone down while it is yet day—hath gone down in sudden & terrible whirlwinds[,] the stormy day of divine displeasure[.] There he lies red with carnage or blasted with lightning. A voice of the mourner, a voice of the orphan and the widow, and a voice of the Archangel[:] woe to the ↑soul of↓ Destroyers[.]

[60] Death If they lie down in sorrow it is a bitter omen that they will rise in wrath

"For it is reasonable to suppose that in proportion to his present indulgence and forbearance and the rectitude of his administration will be his final severity toward the incorrigible & ungrateful abusers of his mercy & compassion" Mellen.[56]—This is in perfect analogy with the Eternal adjustment of things. The more serene is the air, the more perfect & glorious the calm which covers Nature[,] in so

---

of the verse is much practice penmanship, of the sort that sometimes accompanies difficult composition. A sketch of a figure wearing an elaborate headdress appears in the right margin. The words "When" and "When" are written one below the other beneath this sketch.

[55] "Pour commenter . . . no very —" is in pencil.

[56] Probably John Mellen (1722–1807), a minister, and author of *Doctrine of the Cross of Christ* (Plymouth, 1785), and various sermons and discourses.

much the more terrible will be the tem↑p↓est & the cloud. And if God be merciful and the sinner presumptuous; if the light be strong & grace abundant and the transgressor multiply trespasses & crimes and in the face of heaven be brutally lavish of guilt — in such measure shall the vials of indignation be poured out. "Offence's gilded hand may shove by justice." [*Hamlet*, III, iii, 58]

Is it nothing to stand up and say God hath made me — The Creator still sits in the heavens continuing his forming work, fashioning new tenements for immortal souls, and sending them by generations on the Earth until the Great Catalogue of conscious beings shall be filled & he shall say[,] It is enough[.]

"to seal sanctify and invest the Son in office and authority as priest & king of the Ch[urch]. and judge of quick & [dead]." [Mellen?]

Does he deny that a merciful God will punish[?] — let him go back four thousand years and behold a large ship upon a solitary deep. Save in that ship there is no living voice in the world[;] there is no cry of woe, no burst of laughter — there *was* laughter and loud mockery ⟨at⟩ ↑when↓ the prayers of the righteous ⟨which⟩ ↑ascended to↓ implore⟨d⟩ ⟨heaven's⟩ ↑God's pardon↓ ⟨to forgive⟩ ↑ton↓ the⟨ir⟩ blasphem⟨y⟩ers; but the windows of heaven were opened, the fountains of the mighty waters were broken up, and the laugh of the impious and his ⟨bitter⟩ wailings were [61] drowned in the pouring storms. An outcry went up from a million perishing wretches for mercy — but the Ark and eight thankful persons remained alone. [R. W. E.]

(“Moreover it seems morally fit ↑whereby the honourable society called Christian↓ and necessary that the wise and righteous governour of the world should call rational creatures to an account for their actions." Mellen)

The first Covenant with Adam has all gone by, says Mellen, "The primitive fashion of this world is passed away, the traces of the ancient garden of God are obliterated, he has chiefly forsaken the temple of the human heart and man himself the lord of this lower world is changed some how analogous to the fall of this part⟨s⟩ of God's creation."

— Mr S. Reed saith in Oration Aug 1821 — "The people of

the golden age have left us no monuments of genius, no splendid columns, no paintings, no poetry; they possessed nothing which evil passions might not obliterate, and when the heavens were rolled together as a scroll the curtain dropped between the world and their existence."[57]

Men live as if a curtain should be drawn between this scene of things & all after[-]existence. Perhaps they believe they shall live again—but there is no recollection beyond the grave. In vain; there is a recollection—and an account; there are a thousand connecting cords stretching from this world to the next. Every action here of merit & of demerit, reaches out the dark valley to the centre of a mightier system with all its attendance of consequences & conditions infinitely various. Your actions have gone on before you & united themselves with fearful alacrity to their final recompenses [R. W. E.]

The absolution of the priest

[62][58] King Richard's Death. A Ballad.

1 King ⟨Arthur's⟩ ↑Richard's↓ days are amaist done
His flitting life that he maun live
The King must bide him to be gone
The Monk must speed the king to shrive

2 King ⟨Arthur⟩ ↑Richard↓ lies on curtained bed
In ⟨Dighton⟩ bluidy Lombard's ⟨stately hall⟩
stony walls
The setting sun shines dimly red
O'er the proud throng ⟨bewailing all⟩ who crowd
the halls

[57] From the oration by Sampson Reed (1800–1880) presented for the M. A. degree at Harvard, Aug. 29, 1821. Emerson got his brother William, a classmate of Reed's, to borrow and copy the manuscript.

[58] Besides miscellaneous markings, there are in the left margin a sketch of King Richard's death scene, a rhyme list—"⟨merled⟩ hurled curled furled hurled PURLED", "1821
1550
271", a sketch of a man kneeling at an altar, and a sketch of what seems to be the apse of a chapel. The letters "G J S F C A W" appear in the right margin just above line 13. The context suggests that "King Richard's Death" may have been begun in 1821. It was completed in Feb. 1822 (see pp. 303–304). The page is reproduced as plate XI.

3 The bannered pride of England's host
The dancing plumes ⟨of⟩[n] ↑which↓ knighthood⟨s⟩
⟨crest⟩ ↑bore↓
Wave wanton o'er the parting ghost
To ⟨guard⟩ ↑fan↓ the dying ⟨warrior's rest⟩ ↑king
no more↓

4 Lo through the crimson curtain's ⟨|| . . . ||⟩fold
The ghastly frame of Alb⟨y||n||⟩↑ion↓'s ki↑n↓g!
Wae wae the day! sair sight behold
Stricken by Sickness' weary wing

5 His brow is awful though in death
His shroud of death is purple still
But feeble is the struggling breath
His face is wan his heart is chill

6 ⟨They gaze upon his burning eye⟩
⟨His eye is on another world⟩
⟨Oh why so bright so fixedly⟩
⟨⟨Turns⟩ Doth Arthur's eye⟩
Continued p. 74

[63] (Continued from page 58)
the spoils.

⟨When the⟩ In France ⟨in⟩during the dark ages the Castle of feudal chieftains witnessed a second rude drama the name and character of which is all that remains. The *Mysteries* served to shew that it was a natural expression of the human feelings.[59]

In England the progress was somewhat similar but the first productions which were marked ⟨with⟩ for fame are works of prodigious power and ⟨whose⟩ ↑their↓ origin is sudden and unaccountable. From an obscurity which none had illuminated since Chaucer's era there suddenly issued a series of elegant and /powerful/original/ performances equal in power to the masterpieces of Greece and adorned by a strain of such delicate feeling and the wisdom of solid

[59] "F Peck" is pencilled at the right between the paragraphs in a large, ornate hand.

and rare philosophy in verse wherein was breathed ⟨out⟩ the very melody of nature to arrest the soul withal[.]

Over all this fair miracle a hideous corruption was spread which made every page offensive. It is wonderful how intimately health and poison[,] beauty and destruction[,] can combine and no-where shall we find such a fatal illustration. ↑Angel &↓ The inhabitants of England have sat down rejoicing in the light which Shakspear's genius hath shed around them, unconscious or careless of the defilement which attends it until the soul is blunted to the sense of [64] moral turpitude. Shakespeare has had the same pernicious popularity ⟨w⟩as the false prop⟨et⟩het enjoyed who accompan⟨ied⟩ying his indulgences for crime with pretended messages from heaven easily wins the proselyte to those offences to which he is most prone. Shakspear assumed the commanding attitude of bold unrivalled genius; men saw that the inspiration was genuine and few were so scrupulous as to ask if all were pure. From Shakspeare you can cull a volume of poetry nearly approaching to sacred inspiration, and it is for this very reason that the whole mass has wrought incalculable mischief. In a reformed theatre Shakspeare should find no place; Macbeth may be terrible, Othello sublime, and Lear pathetic, but is vicious, Iago is filthy and Edgar disgusting. Those who came after Shakspeare found it eas⟨y⟩ier to copy the deformity of their master ↑than his beauty.↓ ⟨with⟩ They degraded themselves by grossly pampering the filthy appetites of the corrupted and earned their bread by this beastly poetry. This is the character of the dramatists Massinger, Otway, Beaumont, Fletcher. We can only learn from these what to shun.

⟨We turn from this catalogue of proscribed books to seek if there be any which [65] can be admitted to a purified stage.⟩ Shall we be told that Shakspeare painted nature as he found it[,] that we only see here what we see elsewhere in the scenes of life daily[?] No he paints nature not in innocence and its primitive condition but not until it has become depraved itself and its exhibition will deprave others. Nor is the general moral which is to be deduced from the whole pure. Many have thought that in Falstaff the most genius is manifested. But this debauchee is drawn for a favourite and wins approbation for his humourous sensuality. This is deplorably wrong.

↑I own↓ I admire the surpassing genius of Shakspeare but I detest his . The statue is colossal but ⟨the⟩ ↑its↓ diabolical features poison ⟨the⟩ ↑our↓ admiration[n] ⟨we feel⟩ for the ⟨strength⟩ Genius which concieved and the skilful hand which carved it[.]

Letter IV. We come now to the consideration of the subject in new relations, apart from its Greek or English history and shall only presume to ask the question if it can be established in this country on a pure foundation.

America, ⟨is a land of experiments⟩ from the ⟨peculiar⟩ circumstances of its late discovery and natural advantages has been a land of experiments. Here is set forth for the benefit of the world the exhibition of a free republic and the result is to be set down in the books of [66] human experience. In the ⟨Countries⟩ ↑Kingdoms↓ of Europe the arts have crept along with the ↑necessities of the↓ people and unit⟨ing⟩ed with their character in its gradual ⟨progress⟩ formation. The⟨y⟩ ↑nations↓ have occupied their mountains and rivers so long that time and not art has taught them their use and best improvement. But here we have brought the ⟨ac⟩ body of wisdom which these industrious nations have for ages accumulated to apply it with extraordinary advantage in a new and magnificent country. Nor do we find that the moral and intellectual condition ⟨varies essentially⟩ ↑falls behind the↓ natural in its peculiar distinction. The present generation ⟨of men⟩ in this country are ↑for the most part↓ the descendants of a race who were by necessity discreet, diligent, and moral men who fled from poverty or oppression ⟨or to repair shattered fortunes⟩; and I shall not be called to prove so trite an assertion as that an old government involves more misery and vice in its existence[60] than a new one. It were idle then to talk of founding a new and reformed theatre in the unclean regions of England or Holland or Spain while at the same time we ⟨may⟩ shall be suffered to say that the same project Is feasible and rational here[.]

It should not strictly imitate that drama which has elsewhere been successful. France failed in this, she paraphrased the Greek tragedy without [67] an⟨d⟩y alteration to adapt it to the change[,] to the reverse of manners, customs, opinions and feeling with which

[60] The phrase is circled, as though for revision.

it was to coalesce. And hence we have a pure and classical but to English ears a cold and insipid drama. The taste of France has been ruled and dictated by the Academy or the national sentiment would have recoiled from the blind admiration which has been accorded to Corneille and Racine.[n] If the taste of the audience could not ↑be↓ moulded to the love of Euripides there are already in the English language some pieces which would be proper for the purpose. Milton's Masque of Comus contains the finest strains which Milton ever wrote. There are a few /performances/productions/ of modern genius which stand equally high, and first the sublime dramatic poem of Lord Byron — Manfred. Mr. Milman's ⟨Samo[r]⟩ Fall of Jerusalem is full of interest and powerful poetry. But one thing is still more auspicious to our wishes than all these[:] I mean the genius of our countryman the author of Percy's Masque.[61]

⟨Some⟩ It may be said that it is anticipating matters to talk of establishing a new theatre altogether different from the old while as yet we have no drama to produce upon the stage. But public feeling does not follow the direction of ⟨the⟩ authors but the author follows public feeling and catches the tune of the times and relies on this implicit obedience to its will to ingratiate himself in the world.

[68] If once the will of the community be publicly expressed that the Theatre is immoral and patronage inexpedient they will open a field of exertion for American genius which assuredly will not lie barren. Competition will not fail to ensue where success is ↑made↓ valuable. Such a provision will not only substitute purity in the place of vice but will ⟨ensure⟩ supply the imperfections and remove the reproach which have accrued to our American literature. They would wake a note from the wild which would be novel and startling as the savage it celebrates. There are subjects of sufficient interest in American history to dramatize, and in time these would [be] search out. Till then there is an unexhausted treasury accumulated in other ages

[61] By J. A. Hillhouse (London, 1819, New York, 1829). Emerson evidently borrowed his views from the review of *Percy's Masque* in *The North American Review*, XI (Oct. 1820), 384. Compare the language: "This work appears, from the title page, to be printed from a London edition, but we learn that the author is a countryman of our own. We are glad to meet with so respectable a production in this department of literature from the pen of a native writer. . . ." The review did not identify Hillhouse as the author.

and other climes. "The heart," says Montesquieu "is the citizen of every country." We can consent to be awed by the tales of the old time. We can act over again the desolation of Thebes and the misery of her king, nor will the human mind refuse for the first time this three thousand years to be excited by the war of Troy.

"Ask the earth & it shall tell thee, that it giveth much mould whereof earthen vessels are made but little dust, ⟨whereof⟩ ↑that↓ gold cometh of. So is the course of this present world." II Esdras VIII

[69] Of all the Sciences the Science of the Mind is necessarily the most worthy & elevating. But it cannot precede the others. Natural Philosophy & Mathematics must be sought in order to gain first the comforts of civilized life and then the data whence our moral reasonings proceed. It is an old saying that all are a circle and necessarily depend one upon another[n] — that great improvements in astronomy involve a knowledge of Math. & so of the others. We exist to moral purposes and are proud to call ourselves intellectual beings — hence one would say leave matter to the beasts that are only matter and indulge your peculiar & distinguishing faculties. — But then our reason and all our mental powers are called into as active exercise in demonstrating the properties of matter as the properties of mind; and the beasts are alike incapable of both. — So your plea confutes itself. With regard then to the study of Nat. Phil. I do not think any one study so contributes to expand the mind as our first correct notions of this science — when we first know that the sky is not a shell but a vacant space[,] that the world is not still & a plain but a little globe performing as one of a system immense revolutions. And then to our comfort in this life the art of Chemistry has contributed amazingly. Our cloths are bleached[,] our cooking assisted by this ⟨art⟩ ↑science↓ in some of their most essential operations. The Arts and Sciences must be appreciated by their use and judging by this criterion many which have undue attention must be put behind us. ⟨Define⟩ ⟨Define⟩

Define them

Mathematics occupies itself in proving the equality of one quantity to another

Chemistry in discovering the elements which compose bodies & combining them again

Nat. Phil. in discovering the laws which regulate the different properties of matter

Metaphysics in ↑ascertaining &↓ defining the faculties of the Mind

Polit. Economy ascertains the /laws/means/ which form & preserve the Wealth of Nations

Moral Phil.

Medicine in discovering the peculiar structure of the human frame & the means of restoring its order

[70] Tnamurya—

You are right. It was a most uninteresting lecture. It was pointing at the place and times where God first revealed to this dark earth other worlds, and what may be more stale — a moral Government — his own being and attributes — all that could civilise and ornament society. What gives the skies their glory — science ⟨the⟩ its repute — politicks their weight — history its value — and poetry its inexpressible charm. To undermine the miraculous pillars of Judaism, is therefore the favourite object of the deist; — he sees on its deep foundations is raised the structure of Christianity. That the pomp of rites and sacrifices & the glorious oracles of prophecy met in one united blaze of evidence and fulfilment in the rites of Christianity and the catastrophe of Calvary. Or may they not be called evidences a priori contrasted — or in distinction from that invincible host which every succeeding age has marshalled. (It is a perfect peice of irony.)[62]

There is a plausible analogy I know which /describes/makes/ the growth of a nation like the growth of a man ⟨and if which at first⟩[n] whose youth is reared in necessity & labour so that the hands are nerved with strength and the frame established by temperance; successful toil is ⟨accor⟩ attended by wealth; wealth induces luxury, and luxury disease. The analogy is broken by the immortality of the nation which admits ⟨the acquisition of many characters⟩ ↑of many revolutions↓ and may thus boast a variety of ⟨forms⟩ ↑character↓ irreconcileable with the mortality of man. The nation may fluctuate from

[62] The style, the thought, and the lack of real revision in this passage argue that it is copied from one of Aunt Mary's letters. Rusk conjectures that it may be a draft or copy of one of Emerson's letters but omits it because of its "uncertain status" (*L*, I, 105, n. 13).

time to time and ⟨linger in its⟩ ↑one age may hold an↓ opinion, ⟨an age⟩ which the next renounces; during[n] one age the nation may decay and during the next may rise with the ⟨freshness⟩ impulse of a revolution to the vigour of a youthful people.[63]

[71] A puissant nation amid the rage of faction or war, should stand steadfast as a castle founded on a rock against ⟨it⟩which the storm pours & the mighty wind blows in vain and when the fury of the tempest is spent its battlements & banners shall shine out again in the morning /splendour/ray/ immoveable & beautiful as before to gladden the hearts of those who love its prosperity.

Like the sauces of the Epicure, who flavours his viands with nauseous juices, which, unmixed, no appetite could bear, so vice, ⟨compounded⟩ forced into combination with virtue, allures men to embrace it who would abhor it, if [it] were without mixture. "Vice to be hated, needs but to be seen." Venenum bibitur in auro.—[64]

born
forlorn
torn
worn
morn
thorn
scorn
shorn

1 I love thy music, mellow bell,
I love thy iron chime
To life or death to heaven or hell
Which calls the sons of Time

Thy voice its annual welcome /sings/sang/
To Freedom's holiday
And woke old Night with solemn clang
In Peril's hour forlorn

2 Thy voice upon the deep
The homebound ⟨sailor⟩ ↑sea boy↓ /hears/hails/
It charms his cares to sleep
⟨Rejoicing⟩ ↑It cheers him↓ as he sails

⟨It calls men to the house of God⟩
⟨It wails the lowly dead⟩
And mid this mortal Strife
I hear thee call to me

[63] See p. 307, n. 79.
[64] "Poison is drunk from cups of gold." Seneca ,*Thyestes*, 453.

My bark shall come o'er the waves of life
Home to Eternity[65]

[72] (From page 50)

Still more fearful by being connected with some superstitious tales; and it was believed that the soil ↑had↓ first opened to swallow up an Indian enchanter and his abominable accomplices who had treated with the Evil Spirit. In my way thither after a walk of about a mile and before I had reached the open plain I was crossed by a villager who informed me that he was in pursuit of "the witch-woman," ⟨who had gone ahead⟩ for there had been a large *ottar-snake* lying ⟨in⟩ ↑among↓ the rocks ↑several days↓ which had gone towards the Pits, and it was feared that Uilsa's course might lead her to the vicinity of that formidable animal. It may be supposed that this intelligence did not tend to delay my steps or ⟨allay⟩ ↑remove↓ my fears. At length after a rapid walk we escaped from the ⟨darkness and confined prospect⟩ ↑confined prospect and narrow road↓[n] of the woods, by reaching the verge of the forest, and on rising a little from the valley, the first object which struck my eye, at the distance of half a mile across the plain, was a figure which I knew to be Uilsa. She appeared to be advancing rapidly in the same direction which we were pursuing, and which led directly to the precipices. ↑To↓ our[n] instant shout which was echoed back to us from a thousand ⟨quarters⟩ ↑hill tops↓—she paid no attention. Again, we lost her view, in running round a rock with head[73]long haste, & when we had at length passed this last obstacle, we shuddered as we discerned distinctly the enormous serpent, which we had feared, coiled up in immense folds, close to the edge of the chasm towards which the frantic woman was fast approaching. Terror, which took away my voice, did not prevent me from seeing every object with the most minute accuracy. I saw Uilsa, remarkable for her majestic gait advancing on the fatal spot, apparently conscious of her proximity to the monster but with her eye unusually bright fixed upon the dark clouds in the north. She came within a few yards of the snake, and stopp⟨ed⟩↑ing↓ abruptly[,] rais⟨ed⟩↑ing↓ both arms to the sky[,]

[65] A later, revised version of this poem, dated 1823, appears in a manuscript collection of Emerson's Juvenile Verses in Harvard College Library.

stood up like a giantess and cried aloud, "Art thou come, Minister!" The next moment that terrible animal was wound around her, tightening his terrific folds while his victim seemed struggling with superhuman strength and her hand grappled with the head of her destroyer. Suddenly they sunk and I rushed to the mouth of the abyss and ⟨heard⟩ ↑listened, as there murmured up↓ from its depths a loud cry to Odin from the suffocating gripe of the Serpent.

THE END.

Feb 21 1822

[74] From page 62

⟨They gaze upon his burning eye⟩
⟨— His eye is upon another world⟩
⟨A fiend is sweeping through the sky⟩

tread
head
lead
fed
wed
said
dead
bed
thread
bread
spread
shed
sled
stead

6 The dying King hath raised his head
⟨He leans⟩ Upon his hand he rests his brow
And ⟨fiercely⟩ sorrow o'er his aspect shed
A mournful shade of anguish now.[66]

7 King Richard spake to the lordly throng
That watched about his vaulted bed,
— "Bid the bards sing the battle song,
"And chaunt the requiem of the dead.

8 "My fate is written on the cloud
"Which sails upon the murmuring wind,
"Long hoarded vengeance weaves the shroud
"And mercy lingers far behind.

9 "The voice of Autumn calls to me,
"I hear it in the pines;
"In solemn cadence mournfully,
"The swelling strain declines.

10 "It speaks of crime, it speaks of woe,

[66] The stanza and the rhyme list are written vertically in the left margin.

"And ⟨|| . . . || among⟩ ↑⟨mischief⟩ murder done in↓ distant climes
"O God! wipe out the shame I know
"And hide it from the future times."

11 Hark to the thunder's echoing roar
Which shakes that iron pile
⟨They feared as darkness gathered⟩ ↑Wo! for the storm still darkenes↓ more
In stately hall and narrow aisle

12 The lightning stooped from the cloud
And rent that proud castell
The thunderclap long and loud
Feb 1822. Rung out King Richard's knell. The end

[75] Boston, July 22, 1822.[67]

In those periods of the world which have witnessed the decline of nations renowned in arts and arms, there is something remarkable, which philosophy does not perfectly explain. We regard without emotion the gradual rise of a small community which from a little success derives encouragement to enterprise, and repeats and increases its efforts as they seem to be warranted by the inherent strength of the body, until it asserts its claims to national dignity and greatness. But when it has tasted the sweets of literature and splendid Arts, which follow in the train of wealth; when the inventions of luxury have elevated society so far above the savage state—it is

[67] What follows on pp. [75]–[87] is in substance about two thirds of what became the essay "Thoughts on the Religion of the Middle Ages," Emerson's first published work, which appeared over the initials "H. O. N." (the last letters of Emerson's full name) in *The Christian Disciple*, New Series, IV (Nov.–Dec. 1822), 401–408. Emerson must have reorganized it sometime after Sept. 23, 1822, when he wrote: "I desire to make a plan for my View of the Religion of the Middle Ages" and went on to describe the plan. The revision involved shuffling a number of sections and completing others. Presumably Emerson submitted either the plan or the article shortly afterwards, for the magazine noted in the Sept.–Oct. issue (p. 400, n.) that "G. and H. O. N. . . . have been received." Since it also urged readers to send in all articles for the subsequent number by Dec. 10, one may surmise that Emerson presented it by that date.

strange to see him abandon in succession all those privileges and distinctions which ⟨it⟩ ha⟨s⟩ve cost him so much toil to attain, and to lose his estimation of those improvements which had been before so justly appreciated. Egypt and Arabia, Greece and Italy have renounced that superiority which distinguished them from barbarous nations and descended to a humiliating level of ignorance & abjectness. I am aware that adequate causes can be assigned for the final ruin of all these states; that a barbarian conqueror supplanted the polished inhabitants with savage invaders and thus actually [76] exterminated the ⟨taste⟩ refinement of the country. But I go up higher to inquire the cause of this rapid submission of a powerful nation to an unskilful horde. The blow has been death, the fall has been accomplished before; else a nation with the ⟨advan⟩ uncounted advantages of civilization would be thoroughly impregnable to the assaults of such an enemy. In the midst of its power and glory it is in a condition to despise foreign war of any description. It was th⟨at⟩e ↑same↓ generation which gained for Greece all the reputation of its Arts, that repelled with such valour the enormous hosts of Persia. I think it strange that ↑the people which↓ has been so powerful should not ⟨continue⟩ preserve its authority. It is not true that its readiest course is to vice and weakness; for to him that has much, much shall be given and a powerful government ⟨is⟩ always has inclination & ability to grow stronger. There seems to be a direct ordination of Providence that men and states shall grow old & decay; that the purposes of mutability & frailty shall be answered in nations & events as well as individual histories and some imposed necessity of infancy ↑and decay↓ to greatness. ⟨and of⟩

Men are accustomed to reason loosely and to say that the generations of men like the leaves of the forest, follow each other in regular order and uniform character; that great differences in their comparative history [77] do not exist, or are less than they seem, and depend on accidental causes, easily assigned. I confess I see no just reason to hold such views of a race which exist to purposes which they themselves cannot comprehend, and fulfil by their being, designs of which the secret reposes in eternal Benevolence. It seems no wise improper to suppose that God intended to /give/assign/ one order of circumstances as the field of character to one generation and a different order to another. We do not know our relations to the universe, but it seems highly probable that the divine administration and its results on earth are opened to the inspection of ten thousand intelligent beings; and it will consist with these purposes to change the spectacle by causing certain revolutions in the internal affairs of the scene. Not percieving ourselves the connection which binds events, we are unable to discover how far a sublime uniformity may prevail, or whether the seeming disorder may not be like the series of a drama a harmonious succession of events.

a From whatever causes it has happened, we are sufficiently sure of the fact, that for a period ↑of↓ eight or ten centuries the human mind ⟨was⟩ endured a melancholy captivity, and blindly pursued certain miserable ends while society languished under barbarous ignorance & barbarous institutions. In some parts of this ample desert [78] the absurdity seems to grow to an unnatural extent. God drew around them yet darker the veil which concealed the light of truth. In the forms and dogmas of the prevalent religion something more than a common effort of credulity even in a dark age seemed ⟨to be⟩ necessary to digest such barefaced mummery. It may be worth while to devote a few pages to the consideration of the state of religion during the middle ages.

b [68] The sum of political freedom enjoyed in the different portions of Europe was very unequal. In Italy it was very considerable because Commerce had raised a counterpoise to the privileges of the Nobles. In France, Spain, & England it amounted to nothing. Germany seems to have possessed somewhat more than her neighbours by reason of the divisions which gave each individual greater public importance. But over all the countries which in that ⟨dim⟩ ↑disastrous↓ twilight ⟨calle[d]⟩ pretended to civilization, was diffused the levelling principle of a great religious establishment; all were equalised by a common submission of the freedom of opinion to the ordinances of the councils and court of Rome. The task of its discussion is rendered simpler by the necessity which reduces

(Next page but one.) [69]

[68] To the left is a small sketch of a bearded man.

[69] In the printed article Emerson discarded the first version of the beginning of the essay, pp. [75]–[76], and used the one which follows on p. [79]. See plate XII.

[79] That there is a decline to nations, and a period of semi-barbarous ⟨stagnation⟩ ↑repose↓ following the decline, is a fact of awful interest whose causes ⟨have never been⟩ ↑are not fully↓ explained. When E & A G & I have ⟨descended from⟩ ↑exchanged↓ th⟨e⟩at elevation to which they had been raised by wealth, literature & the arts for a ⟨low level of⟩ ↑state of abject↓ ignorance I know that adequate causes have been assigned for their final ruin. Perhaps a conqueror supplanted the pol. inhab. with bar. invad. and actually exter. the ref. of the country. Perhaps the luxury that waits upon wealth corrupted ⟨the⟩ ↑public↓ virtue ⟨while⟩ ↑until↓ faction convulsed and ambition ⟨shackled the energies of a free people⟩ ↑enslaved the people↓. But I go up higher and inquire the cause of this submission of a powerful nation to a savage horde, and of mind & virtue to weakness ⟨of⟩& vice. It does not appear to me that there is any natural necessity that civilization and power should succumb to barbarism. It is, on the contrary, a maxim which seems ⟨to hold good⟩ to be true of the ways of Providence, that to him who has much, much shall be given, and it is also true that the arts of a ⟨ci⟩refined nation do more than supply the deficiency of ⟨personal⟩ ↑physical↓ courage just as the advantage in a combat with ⟨the⟩ beasts always rests on the side of man. I should rather regard the downfall of a mighty empire before the puny force of wild and disunited savages as a special exercise of God's power designed to produce some novel phenomena in human history.[70] Who is he who can assign the precise cause to each great event or who can predict the certain decline of future empires upon the ground⟨s⟩ that some empires have declined. Men are accustomed [80] itself to an examination of the influence of the Roman hierarchy upon private life.

The operation of the institutions of government and religion ⟨is often⟩ upon the life and character of the citizen is often remote and insignificant. The bond hangs so loosely, or is set aside by other near and engrossing interests that it enters very little into the education of the mind and heart. But these systems bear no analogy to the institution of which we speak. The policy of Rome if it approached any thing, would more easily find a parallel in ancient Egypt or

[70] The paragraph on pp. 300–301, "There is . . . youthful people," appeared in the printed version at this point, with some changes.

modern India than elsewhere. Instead of counting the individual, like other governments, as a cipher, as a mere theoretical abstraction, valuable only as he added one to an amount, the ecclesiastical authority entered into a personal and intimate acquaintance with its subject, unclosed the secrets of his heart as none else but his Maker had done, and thus laid upon his actions a command of irresistible force. Wherever the practice corresponded to the theory and each rank of the community was supplied with its appropriate guardian, and none but cultivated minds exercised the functions of the Church, it is manifest that the independence of society was wrested away, & human conduct obeyed by necessity the systems prescribed [81] by fallible men.

A man whose moral sense is delicate can not read the ecclesiastical history of Europe without extreme pain. By its unnatural mixture with the remains of paganism Christianity was first corrupted. The distinctions of office in the church which were necessary to its early wants were next made use of by the artifice of ambitious men to build up their own greatness. Gregory the great * was undoubtedly /deluded by/the victim of/ names, by the title of vicar of Christ, and successor of St Peter, by the keys of heaven &c to add his powerful support to an unprincipled usurpation of the dearest rights of men. But it is not till we have advanced further in the history of Rome that we turn to execrate the steps that led to such flagrant ⟨enormity⟩ ↑abuse of power & the blasphemy of writing the name of God to deeds of the devil↓. The severe Hildebrand, whose epoch marks the consolidation and maturity of the sacred monarchy, was ambitious & tyrannical, but his successors in office were something worse. Christianity was disgraced by the spectacle of its guide↑ance↓ and government being lodged in the hands of weak intellect. The memory of John 22 is particularly distinguished by the circumstances of his election. "Le nouveau pape," says Sismondi, "ne put ↑s'↓empecher de dire à ses confrères, que leur choix fut tombée sur un âne." The schism which the Italians ridicule as the seventy years' Captivity of Babylon was not more remarkable for the bad contentious spirit which it fostered than for the voluptuousness which

* Pontiff from 590 A. D. to 604 AD.

characterised the court of Avignon. (Quote also here 13 Vol Sismondi, 70 p.)[71]

[82] It was the singular fate of Rome ↑twice↓ to become the capital of European civilization and empire and the magnificence of the first hardly surpassed the pontifical glory. It was likewise its singular fortune to see its portentous grandeur balanced by a double desolation. There are two distinct periods recorded in its history, when its miseries proved as unexampled as ever its glory had been. I allude to its disastrous history in the fourth and ⟨in⟩ ↑at↓ the ⟨commencement of the sixteenth⟩ ↑close of [the] 15↓ century.

(These are to be described.) For one see Gibbon, for the other Sismondi[.]

What is the result of this? It is plainly true that [...][n] a law which recognises all the highest principles of human mind higher than any other system had ever pretended to establish and from its theoretic character should produce an Optimism in government—does in fact under this form add infinitely to the sum of human calamity not only by its own mismanagement & tyranny but by letting loose all the worst passions upon society until the very elements of civil order are broken up, and the decency of civilized life outraged. The character & office[n] of the pope was venerable in theory.—A man exalted above his fellows by his learning, piety, and dignity and by his age and habits made superior to their passions and ⟨disputes⟩ able to decide or conciliate their boisterous disputes; to awe by his dignity the factions to peace; rich to administer the charity of the church; sacred to represent its divine majesty—this[n] was the arduous responsibility of the bishop of Rome. If this system of ecclesiastical power had been the result of a regular deliberation and the election of the popes been secured in proper hands, ↑then↓ although the idea of a wise & sincere papist may be somewhat problematical to a protestant, there certainly would have been a powerful check imposed at once upon that unruly licentiousness which ↑has↓ disgraced & ruined that form of religion.

[83] But ⟨this⟩like other systems of government, it grew up gradually, its faults & its virtues gained strength together until it was too late to amend without the risk of overturning it forever. The

[71] See p. 276, n. 36.

election of the pope was finally wrested from the people & lodged in the consistory—the fairest theatre of intrigue & corruption which was ever beheld. So that Christendom recieved its spiritual fathers without a power of assent or dissent from the bribed hands of a band of men who bore holy titles indeed but whose hands were deeper in iniquity than any cabinet which ever deliberated. The popes of the 15 Century were bad men enough but the character & vices of Alexander VI are below the decency of criticism.

The successor of St Peter and the Vicar of Christ was ↑a↓ thousandfold more the servant of the devil than any ↑contemporary↓ man of influence except his own household. With such a prelate for their spiritual head if their belief in this religious system was not warm & sincere ⟨& still worse if it was⟩ is it natural, does it come within the compass of probable events that the heart & the morals should be very pure? Was there no apology for iniquity, no plea of example upon which human frailty, ever ready to lean upon a reed, could lean [?] [n] And if there were sincere believers, as who can doubt, is it not still worse, for how could they act upon perfect principles and with clear notions of moral goodness while they had to reconcile the infallibility of their bishop with his most exceptionable life?

To be soundly explained

[84] But with innumerable faults of doctrine and innumerable consecrated examples of bad living the Roman Church distinguished itself by its strict adherence to sanctimonious forms. ⟨The⟩ There was a saving virtue in the sign of the cross; a thousand romantick & fabulous charms in the string of beads, in the royal golden rose, in the relics of a hundred saints and the Ave Mar⟨y⟩ies, which the worshipper did not understand; a genuflexion was an act of merit [n] and a worthless unction secured the reversion of eternal bliss. ⟨We there⟩ It is not remarkable therefore that we should discover that aspect of religion which in the darkest periods of this history pervades ⟨the⟩ society and marks the habits of bad men no less than the good. We find lawless soldiers and men distinguished for their atrocity prostrated at the altar with peaceful citizens & pious men recieving absolution from a priest & departing to sin again. What was the result of this system? It is manifestly a pleasing apology for a bad heart

and it jumps with the universal tendency of human infirmity, which /seeks/is fain/ to make a compromise with heaven of a few acts or sacrifices of religion instead of the difficult and endless labour of preserving virtuous principles. These are the two characteristics of the religion which caused its pernicious influence and which may be discerned and with precisely the same effects in another religion. I[.] It introduced a low state of morals ⟨in⟩among the teachers of religion & thence directly downwards [85][72] through every class of the laity. Next it commanded a superstitious observance of forms which by transferring ⟨the⟩ religion from the soul to the ceremony satisfied the conscience and relaxed the salutary terrors which reason & revelation address to vice. This is the character also of the Mahometan Religion. Pal⟨y⟩ey has pointed out the policy of that system as a military code, and more recently Mr Hallam has shewn the ↑internal↓ causes of its diffusion. It bears also in ⟨its⟩ the history & present condition of its professors a common character with that degraded form of our better creed of which we speak; its ministers are corrupt, & its forms supersede the necessity of virtue in public opinion; and therefore public disorder & private violence lay waste the fairest regions of the world. Until its power was shattered, and persecution began to wake its fires it seems never to have been strongly influential or sincerely believed. Forms float upon the surface of society, principles act at the core. But of this system the forms were most devotional; and the principles, blind & bad.

The enemies of the Church of Rome seem ever to be most scandalized by ⟨the⟩ its ambitious assumption of temporal power. This was the crying sin which offended the laity, for it came in competition with their interests; and this wrought its downfall. If the church of Rome had never abused the trust committed to them as temporal lords, this accusation might have rested with ↑a↓ ⟨the⟩ barbarous age. To legislate for mankind, & preside in the execution of laws is that office among men which demands the largest [86] share of wisdom & genius. The solemnity & responsibility of an assembly ⟨for⟩ of lawgivers ⟨admits to itself with propriety⟩ ↑favour rather than oppose the admission↓ of the minister of religion. While the statesman stands

[72] The lower middle part of the page has a faint pencil sketch of two struggling male figures. Between "ambitious" and "assump-tion" is sketched a basket.

there as the contriver of means to produce certain ends, & the scholar to ⟨relate⟩ describe the systems which have prevailed, he himself must represent the cause of morals & religion and regulate and correct the schemes of ingenuity or experience. But as soon as he passes the bound of sanctity and profanes his consecrated character with secular ambition he has surrendered that charter of circumstances which delivered him from temptation and has invited the approach of every lawless desire and every extraordinary danger. This did the Roman clergy and their civil character ranks no higher than their moral one and was the concomitant & cause of its degradation. Notwithstanding the current proverb of that age—"It is good to live beneath the crooked staff,"[73] their government was oppressive and seemed only mild in comparison with the iron law of the posterity of the Goths. It was mild only where it was weak⟨;⟩. ⟨f⟩From the nature of its constitution it was precarious, and dependent upon the superstition of the neighbouring potentates; it was exposed to their violence and bought their forbearance by threats, by persuasion, & by art. Its policy therefore could never exercise in such circumstances a fierce tyranny which would arm vassal & lord against it & complete its ruin. But where its power had grown firm & fearless, in the walls of Rome and within the [87] Patrimony of the Holy See, the violent spirit of oppression & civil rapine broke out with unrestrained force.

It should be observed in justice to the Roman Church that its religious system is far better adapted to the purposes of social order than any of the systems we have named. We complain that it keeps down the mind by arbitrary restraints not that

(For the rest of this essay, see the complete
Essay on the Religion of the Middle Ages.)

A great question which is at the bottom of the disputes which shake the Christian World is that of the original condition of man, and whether the fall of Adam affects the moral estate of his children. To place it upon its proper grounds, is a matter exceedingly difficult & elusive, because we must always assume the position that our notions of morals are not perfectly arbitrary but rest upon the eternal foundations of the universe nor could have been other than they are.

[73] See p. 329.

But it appears to my mind, to involve a contradiction of which the orthodox defenders of the faith are not perfectly aware when they state the fundamental articles of their creed. Thus, they object to the bold projection of any theories which may at all militate with the human rules of morals and yet also accuse you if judging by [88] those very rules you arraign God's formation of men with evil dispositions as Calvin has described them to be.

Thoughts upon the Religious tendency
of different states of Society.

It would be difficult to believe that the progress of society from the savage to the civilized state, and the different occupations growing out of their circumstances which distinguish vast portions of the human race—can take place without the care & command of Providence. Men may deem the ⟨little⟩ ↑domestic↓ actions & events of each day too sordid & insignificant to deserve the notice of Infinite Mind. But when they remark four or five great modes of life into one or other of which all individuals necessarily fall & that through all ages these continue the same, they are forced to believe that God is concerned in their perpetuation. Or if it jar with ⟨our⟩ ↑any man's↓ notions of human liberty to suppose a Divine interference with our institutions, he will not think the time ⟨was⟩lost ⟨to⟩in ⟨reviewing⟩ examining the tendency of the habits ↑& opinions↓ formed by these circumstances. The savage & Pastoral, the Agri[89]cultural, the Commercial, & the Military modes of life are so thoroughly unlike each other, that if we attribute any powerful influence to circumstances, we must expect to see the Mind ↑exhibit↓ ⟨under⟩ very different character according to its education in these conditions. And if this be admitted, that, a man's moral character may be affected by these circumstances; by accidents, in fact, over which he has no control—then, human responsibility is lessened and the burden of our sins shifted on to the shoulders of Fate. Anxious to solve these doubts, & to vindicate the ways of God to man, we propose to ⟨consider⟩ ↑examine↓ somewhat in detail, the consequences of ⟨each of these⟩ the several states of Society. I begin with Savage life.

If we consider the readiest means of cultivating proper dispositions towards the Deity, which I take to be the mark & standard of Religion, we shall find that conversation & reading are the two modes that are the most common & efficacious. Both of these are denied to the Savage ↑who is↓ ⟨This class of men are⟩, to a proverb, unsociable. Vexation, hunger, & grief are constitutionally silent, as comfort, festivity, & joy are voluble. Now when it is remembered that all mental education[,] the training of a mind to think for itself[,] [90] depends upon these two means, it will be seen that the cruel sufferings of the barbarian⟨s⟩ which deny him ⟨an⟩ opportunity to inquire after these imposes at the same time a tyrannical ↑hopeless↓ ignorance upon his mind instead of a speculative turn which would supply the want of books. Leisure, which is elsewhere the parent of speculation, in the forest loses its charm; for the ferocity of war & the chase is immediately exchanged for an immoveable languor. Mind is feebly developed while sleep & sense divide the manhood of the barbarian until he grows old & his children slay him. These circumstances are most unfavourable to the mild nurture of religion which though it may favour & reward the vow of poverty yet stands in need of the sympathies & instructions of men. The past which has been forever adding evidences to the truth of our faith and treasures to the sum of our knowledge has subsisted in vain for the savage. No codes hath he against revenge or parricide, no gospel to preach accountability or peace. Civilization, which is founded upon the accumulation & transmission of knowledge, not only leaves him out of her ample limits, but is (he complains,) his invincible foe. ⟨Nevertheless under⟩ ↑Notwithstanding↓ the pressure of all these disadvantages the savage has a system of theology. Indeed so natural is the idea of God or it springs so inevitably from other trains of thought, that no [91] nation is without [it]. But the complexion of this system proves only that men visit heaven with [the] same feelings ⟨with⟩ which they carry about them upon earth. Examine the gods of all barbarous nations, you will find ↑that↓ their characters ⟨to⟩ offend against every article of Moral law; you will find thieves, murderers, adulterers, & liars, enshrined in heaven by the zeal of ignorance; and these ↑motley deities↓ form the best illustration of the religious influence which a savage life promotes. Faithful imitations of the example of such gods occur⟨s⟩ daily among their votaries. And if ↑in defiance of the impediment of fortune↓ even[n] the wretched history of this portion of men ↑exhibits↓ great virtues & noble spirits ⟨have ↑⟨at⟩↓ sometimes adorned the wild⟩ their ↑solitary↓ greatness shines with a miraculous light from its powerful contrast with darkness & crime.

The besetting sins of men vary with the climate wherein they live, and the characters of the pagan heavens vary in like manner. We have spoken above with reference rather to Northern idolaters but ⟨an⟩ analogous errors pervade the religious systems of all the savages on the globe. War and intoxication are familiarly attributed to the northern lust & knavery to the milder character of the southern gods. Ages go by, & generation after generation of uncultivated men implicitly recieve↑s↓ this pitiful substitute for a divine Revelation until our wonder is excited at the purposes of providence. We shall not hazard any remarks upon[74] this topic until we have fulfilled our design ⟨of⟩ by examining the influence of the other states of society[.]

[92] 2. Agriculture is the venerable mother of all the arts and the foundation, among them, of civilized society. For, this first banded men together, to make conventions for the security of property, and this also will last the longest, because when the world is too full for pasture or hunting, men must ⟨still⟩ derive their whole subsistence from the ground. Of course, in the very planting of the human race, ⟨it⟩ a mode of life to which a vast portion of them should always be devoted could not pass without notice. "God Almighty first planted a garden" and appointed this for the residence of the first pair. Thenceforward, the fields have ever been considered as the favourite abode of virtue & the love of the gods. Athens & Rome were filled with an immoral & blasphemous mob, but the philosopher comforted himself with the idea, that Justice on her flight from the city had tarried in the fields. A reputation for solid qualities of mind has been conceded to the husbandman by universal consent. He is deemed trustworthy, reflecting, substantial, & pious; headstrong perchance in his bigotries, but for like reasons /firm/constant/ in his affections & principles. The quietness & regularity of his task or more probably his dependence upon the contingencies of

[74] The phrase "But we leave these unfinished to hurry" is interlineated above "we . . . upon" as an apparently incomplete revision.

sun & rain give rise to his frequent contemplations upon the cause & the manner of his blessings.

[93] "He who hath a wife & children" said Bacon "has given hostages to fortune;"[75] experience declares the same of the tiller of the land. He does not readily abandon his plough & his barns, for untried changes; for, he must stay to sow the furrows which have been opened, or reap the harvest he has sown, or store the harvest he has reaped: — it is a continual pressure of tolerable cares, which do not permit him to sleep or to depart. It is at once a life too laborious to ⟨admit⟩ ↑indulge↓ the ⟨indulgence⟩ ↑license↓ & profligacy of wealth, & too comfortable to harbour the desperate repinings & rebellion of poverty. In a condition therefore which of itself directs the thoughts & hopes to God, ⟨it⟩ ↑the soul↓ is kept aloof from the opposite tendencies of a worldly spirit. ⟨All⟩At the same time the contamination engendered & propagated among a vulgar crowd such as throng the precincts of a city has no field in the thin & scattered population of farms. Experience amply justifies the conclusion that the advantage of moral purity in all ages has decidedly rested in the peasantry. "Virtue is like a rich stone best plain set."[76] The ⟨country⟩ peasant is rude & plain, but he is virtuous. And this is in consonance with the ordinary balance of human affairs, wherein vice is consorted to splendour, & virtue is clothed in weeds. It may be well farther to examine where religious wars & furious sects have sprung and raged[,] whether in the thickly crowded suburbs or in the shelter of groves.*

(It might be remarked that Religious Zeal rather characterizes particular Centuries than Professions.) Age of Italian Republics was a superstitious age. Charles I American Revolution

[94] III. Commercial nations in all ages have borne a like character. Commerce seems to be the parent of civilization, and it is of consequence to understand its effects upon men's minds. ⟨To support the navies of Tarshish & England which cover[n] the ocean⟩ Exactly the opposite principles to those which constitute savage life, prevail here. Savages by reason of the entire listlessness of charac-

* Vide the quotation from Zoroaster's Zendavesta, p. 100 of this book.

[75] "Of Marriage and Single Life."

[76] Bacon, "Of Beauty."

ter bury in oblivion the moral law; the busy throng of seaports are so wholly engrossed in the prosecution of ⟨their⟩ trade that they find no leisure for Religion. Trade involves numberless schemes, incessant attentions to the particular plans of daily business calculations upon future contingencies, watchful notices of the probable ⟨results⟩ effects [n] of passing events. None of the merchant's affairs remind him forcibly of another world, while they involve him in the inextricable labyrinth of this. The hard-run competitions in which he is daily engaged, edged by interest, usurp all his powers in fear lest his rival win the advantage. Obliged to hazard much he is ⟨induced⟩ ↑tempted↓ to hazard all & to force his end in the last resort by the sacrifice of integrity. In this battle of men's interests, ⟨things⟩ actions which, in equity, are absolutely wrong, in law & in practice come to be familiar & respectable. Fair & honourable dealings are found for the most part in the commercial intercourse of nations because, in the main, honesty is the best policy. [95] But the upright merchant is not necessarily a religious man. Overt breaches of human laws are by no means the only transgression for then the mass of society would be ↑no↓ doubt blameless. The most common sins of civilized life are ⟨the forgetfulness of love to our neighbour; & too inordinate sensual indulgence⟩ ↑selfishness & sensuality↓. The first is manifested on innumerable petty occasions by thoughtless or wanton wounds of another's feelings, reputation or interest; & the second by neglecting to impose on ourselves a rigid temperance. Manifestly no law can controul these; and every circumstance of their occupation encourages the growth of them. In the history of religion many periods are found wherein zeal has reached such a pitch that men have exposed their lives to the stake and perhaps the popular ferment has raged to a greater extent in a city in such times than in the country. But this is no contradiction to the general statement that the c⟨u⟩ommercial life is less devout than agricultural⟨,⟩.[n] ⟨It rao⟩ Religious frenzy like every other unruly excitement can only be supported[,] certainly cannot reach its last extravagance ↑except↓ among a mob. And commonly the same deeds are to be expected from an inflamed mob whether the excitement be of a political, personal, or religious, kind. We repeat therefore that popular excitement entrenched under the pretence of religion does not enter into the question.

It may be remarked in general that wherever a man's success appears to depend ↑chiefly or wholly↓ on himself, in that proportion he commonly is negligent of superior beings. Thus a man who drives a profitable trade, and safely reckons upon his assiduity & skill to secure[n] his livelihood, without a momentary qualm springing from the thought of his destiny, loses part of his Unconcern and[77] [97$_1$] timidly acknowledges the omnipresence of deity when he comes to launch his wealth on the seas, & remembers that the profoundest foresight cannot always chain the storm. V. p. 95[.]

[96] Aaron Burr's Defence[78]

I stand up here to answer for my life. I see before me a crowded assemblage of power, wealth, and knowledge, of able, proud, and honourable men, without one friendly eye to take my part by one glance of kindness. The eloquence of the bar, the wisdom of the court, the license of the press, and the prejudices of the people have been levelled with extraordinary activity against a defenceless individual. These evils are dreadful to one who has less at stake than I have, whose house or land is in peril, whose affections or character have been insulted. But when an injured man who has been dragged down from an honourable station and from domestic happiness by wicked men, ⟨and s⟩ ↑has↓ most of these ↑blessings↓[n] taken away and the rest put in jeopardy, and his hold on life loosened; — at that time, to see all that he loves and honours in his country, ⟨anxiously⟩ ↑eagerly↓ waiting to push him off the precipice, — it is ↑a↓ very hard ↑&↓[n] trying situation. A man's fortitude must depend on somewhat more than physical courage, to bear him up; — on something like innocence.

Before I proceed to defend myself by ⟨an⟩ answering ⟨the false charges⟩ ↑calumnies↓ ⟨of⟩ ↑with↓ which I am ⟨arraigned⟩ ↑charged↓ I must give vent to my feelings on the general process. B↑r↓iefly then, my fellow citizens, it is a most atrocious outrage upon my character & my heart. Any other crime, any other suspicion than this, I could boldly have defied. But to be charged with plotting the ruin of my

[77] Emerson wrote the rest of the sentence at the top of p. [97$_1$].

[78] On Nov. 3, 1821, Emerson or his mother withdrew from the Boston Library Society vol. I of *Reports of the Trials of Colonel Aaron Burr . . .*, 2 vols. (Phila., 1808). It was returned Nov. 8.

country, that country which was the idol of my hope & affection, the one sole object, next to God, to which I have devoted the strength & studies of all my life—the malice of this accusation, I confess ⟨overcomes me⟩ ↑I cannot bear↓. That country I was taught to love from my cradle. I saw her Genius though youthful walking [97₂] like a giant among her mountains, nourishing his strength in silence until the hour should come of his going forth, to battle the ⟨old⟩ ↑old & fiery↓ dragon of English tyranny. With his hundred thousand sons, I also, in that day of trial, bade him Godspeed. I saw him when he trampled his enemy under foot, and this land rang through its borders to the shout of triumph. I was prouder, in that moment, of my American lineage, from a rude & republican stock, than ↑was ever↓ the royal descendant of an hundred kings. My resolution was taken to devote all my powers to the service of my country & the honor of my fellow citizens, I have been cruelly disappointed of my honest desires. While I rejoiced in my success in promoting the welfare ↑of the state↓ I have been accused of designing ⟨the⟩ ↑its↓ destruction. Abandoned men have concerted against me so successfully as to bring down the whole weight of ↑the↓ public indignation at my doors. Rebellion, murder, & war have been attached to my name, until the whole people cry out upon me as a monster of crimes. Fellow citizens I demand the rights of Justice. That I had enemies I knew; that I had friends & competitors whom the rage of party feeling or the cross accidents of life had turned into enemies, I have long known. But I did not know that the personal hostility of any man or men in the Union was so fierce against me that nothing could quell it but my blood. That hatred has blighted my fair prospects of honour

Turn to the 108 page

[98] [79] Upon the plain, upon the hill
Troy's painted standards idly blew
Beneath the Mount her host stood still
By Ida's foot in order due

Old Priam's royal car drew nigh

[79] The manuscript suggests that this and the next three poems were written down about the same time as "The Maniac's Verse" which follows them and is dated Nov. 19, 1821.

like gold clouds in a wintry sky
Until amid the armed band
The monarch bade the chariot stand.

I I dreamed the world was young [80]
And life was passing fair
For Hope aye smiled and Sirens sung
And flowers on lurking Care were flung
And Nai⟨d⟩ads warbled to the enchanted air

II A phantom grasped the Urn
Which holds the fate of man
I saw gay Youth approach to learn
And the dark lot indignant spurn
Wherein the lines of fate engraved in fire did burn.

III I plucked from thence my lot
And broke my golden dream
Pleasure and ⟨Hope⟩Love were straight forgot
Low at my feet their garlands rot
While Hope's faint star yet shone with cold & cheerless beam.

When Jove's grey daughter beldame Care
On crimson couches first was laid
Her thousand wrinkled children there
Scowled on poor Man ⟨by [?]⟩to all betrayed.

There was a little Fairy then
Of crooked form whose name was S
Who bade the miscreants join to form
A smiling cherub hight *Caress*

[99] A lady-bird sat in a dainty blue-bell
To hear the wind ring in the flower
"I'll live all my life in this purple shell
My stars! what a beautiful bower!"

[80] Above and to the right is the numeral "15" in an elaborate circle. Written at age 15?

I'll bring my crimson family here
To dine on honey and leaves
And list to the wind as it warbles near
In the edge of the neighbouring sheaves
So spoke red Lady bird on the leaf &c [R. W. E.]

[Nov. 19 1821] THE MANIAC'S VERSE [81]

1 To pluck the rose, to pluck the rose
In dainty meadows wildly growing
To cull ↑the↓ woodbine in its wanton twine
Ere reapers begin their mowing;

2 To climb the rock, to climb the rock
Through the sweeping mist of the rainy morn
And look at the dismal fields below
With pride of station most forlorn

3 To brave the gulf, to brave the gulf
As it madly howls in ⟨the⟩ drear sea caves
Outswim the shark as he dashes dark
In the doleful uproar of the waves

4 For this to live, for this to live
The maniac boy shall seek no more
In ⟨greener fields⟩ ↑wilder scenes,↓ in another world
His ⟨weary⟩ ↑love↓ shall burn, his soul shall soar.

[R. W. E.]
Nov. 19 1821

[100] Dedication.

Quem fugis? Aut quis te nostris complexibus arcet?
Haec memorans, cinerem et sopitos suscitat ignes.[82]
Virgilian lot. [*Aeneid*, V, 742–743]

This song to one whose unimproved talents and unattained friendship have interested the writer in his character & fate.[83]

[81] "MINIST" is written in the right margin beside stanza 2.

[82] " 'Whom fleest thou, or who bars thee from our embraces?' So speaking, he rouses the embers of the slumbering fires. . . ."

[83] The song seems almost certainly addressed to Martin Gay.

By the unacknowledged tie
Which binds us to each other
By the pride of feeling high
Which friendship's name can smother

By the cold encountering eyes
Whose language deeply thrilling
Rebelled against the prompt surmise
⟨Confessed⟩ ↑Which told↓ the heart was willing;

By all which you have felt and feel
My eager gaze returning
I offer to this silent zeal
On youthful altars burning,
All the classic hours which ⟨come⟩fill
This little urn of honour;
Minerva guide & pay the pen
Your hand conferred upon her. [R. W. E.]

"He who sows the ground with care & diligence, acquires a greater stock of religious merit than he could gain by the repetition of ten thousand prayers."

Zendavesta ap. Gibbon [*Decline and Fall of the Roman Empire*]
Vol I p 325 c.8

[101] Life and death of ⟨red⟩ the little red bobbin-maker.

Happy red Robin
Making white bobbin
Whistled the time away
How could Robin rejoice
Amid such a noise?
For he lived on the London quay.

Poor little Robin
Suddenly sobbing
Said that his bobbin was broke
He had twisted it wrong
While singing a song
And the grief did young Robin choke

Robin's dog Daisy
Quickly ran crazy
Primroses being in bloom
So he laid down & died
At red Robin's side
And bobbin grew over their tomb.

[102] Among the rest a small unsightly root
But of divine effect he culled me out
The le⟨f⟩af was darkish, and had prickles on it,
But in another country, as he said,
Bore a bright Golden flower; but not in this soil: —
[Haemony] Comus [ll. 628–632]

Translation of Montaigne to Mons Charron
May fortune bless thee
And friends caress thee
Remote from care but loved by me
The gifts of Pleasure
In boundless treasure
Not witheld but poured on thee
Garlanded with roses
At eve thy friend reposes
Yet looks for joys that boundless be. [R.W.E.] [84]

Yet knowing their advantages too many
Because they shall not trail me through their streets
Like a wild beast, I am content to go.
Samson Agonistes. [ll. 1401–1403]

There I suck the liquid air
All amidst the gardens fair
Of Hesperus and his daughters three
That sing about the golden tree.
Comus. [ll. 979–982]

[84] The poem is, as Emerson makes perfectly clear by his symbol of authorship, original. Charles L. Young asks how Emerson at this point could have even known the name of Charron, Montaigne's editor (*Emerson's Montaigne*, 1941, p. 84). Emerson or his mother had withdrawn Montaigne's *Essais*, vol. I, from the Boston Library Society Sept. 7, 1820. He could have found some discussion of the relations between Montaigne and Monsieur Charron in Stewart's *Dissertation* (*Collected Works*, 1854, I, 105–106).

[103] "There was a laughing devil in his sneer,
That raised emotions both of rage and fear;
And where his frown of hatred darkly fell,
Hope fled the place, & Mercy sighed Farewell."
Byron. ["The Corsair," I, ix, 31–34]

[Magician?] [85] I am alone; the company of man is hideous to me; I have no amusements, the games of the world cannot interest one who is bound ↑by affection↓ to what is ghastly and loathsome to you. You are incredulous,—but there is no gentleness in my breast, for I cannot foster the vipers & tigers which sought to devour me, I love better the ⟨sweet⟩ ↑real↓ asps & crocodiles which issue from the bounteous bosom of nature and come foaming with congenial destruction. The order of life which you enjoy is reversed with me. I ha⟨s⟩ve assembled around me in ⟨disgusting⟩ ↑rich↓ profusion all which you shun, and things which are nameless in the haunts of civilized man, they are found only where damned rites are done in Libya, and beyond the Ganges;—I contemplate what is horrible; I banquet on the nauseous, I sleep in the slimy embraces of adders and reptiles and I shall die by the festering of venomous wounds which the worm sucks daily & the sun mortifies.

[104] [He looked out of the windows of heaven &]

["The late Dr Doddridge whose praise is in the churches for" &c Mellen]

Aedepol & Boruno.

(Ald. Wit is thy merchandise; and thy light wares
Are folly & chicane; and right or wrong
These thou dost barter like all other stuffs
For food & shelter comfort and repose.
The wise are pampered with the choicest viands
Of understanding and thy lettered lore;

For these, their ready gratitude can give
Honour and goodly credit in the world.
The weak & simple are seduced by lies,
By gilded pills of flattery, by shews,

[85] The following paragraph may have been intended for Emerson's "Magician" story. See p. 266, n. 25. It is called "Magician Scrap" in Emerson's Table of Contents.

And gaudy spectacles which Folly prompts;
For these they give the gold their labour earned.

Bor. Why should they not? I look upon the world
As at a stone whereon men whet their wits
And after, live but by their exercise.
For wealth is nought save only in its use
He that hath craft converts it into blessings
But with blank eye wealth will not profit fools

[86] I work no wrong by these conceited drones
If I unlock their swoln bags of gold.
Welcome, I speed their lazy time with glee
Obsequious — win their silly selves from thought
And bless their dulness with my pageantries.
Why should abundance grudge my small return?

Ald.) Opinion is the stronghold of thy fortunes
The weak idolatry of fops and fools
Whose feathery weight the wind shall sweep away
[105] Forms the frail fabric of thy flourishing hopes.
Hail! folly's victim, hail most doughty champion
Abate thy fiery fever of success
For thou must hug the image of despair
And wrap thy cold lust in Death's icy robes
And wail delusion's comfortless event
Nor friend nor son shall waste affection bring
To share thine anguish in sweet sympathy. [R. W. E.]

[to brook	abate	trepan
loll	swoln	psalter
carnal	drenched	Enrich
knives	abortive	Jeer
obsequious	quick ie li⟨f⟩ve	crib
lascivious	balloon	hoodwinked][87]

[86] In the left margin: "Hale" — perhaps a hastily jotted note in reference to the author of the book indirectly quoted on p. 329. The word "fools" of the preceding line is written large in the left and in the right margin.

[87] The list of words is in the left margin, from "Forms the frail fabric" (above) to "and policy" (below).

For a fine Essay upon Balance of Power and policy of Modern Europe V. Edin. Rev. Vol 1, pp 370 &c || . . . . . || [88]

[106] [89] It cannot stand with prelacy &c to keep his horse withal

Oh! what thinks he whose parted soul
From many thousand years looks back on life
Upon the span whose transient dye
Colours the long eternities which roll
Beyond him, now, with being, rife,
And still looks forward through the waste of years
On the far billow of existence borne
Youth is the fault [n] whatever curs pretend
The fault that boys & nations soonest mend.

Elegance
|| . . . . . || [90]

[107] Entombed, Crotona, in thy temple aisles
The dead Bayardo mourned by Florence sleeps.
Enamoured glory o'er the marble smiles
Smiles at the deed his adversary weeps [By Emerson?]

"Life is short and art is long;" some few are wise, many are foolish; some waste their admiration and others husband their wit. These are the truisms which we are prone to use in ⟨our⟩the first sour speculations which dawn upon our minds. Each man thinks he hath broached the doctrines of wisdom when the beam of a star which hath shone on all else at last lights on him, and is pleased with himself until time hath taught him that knowledge is common and ideas are old. The child is proud of his toys till he knows that other children play with ↑the↓ same or better; the [n] man is proud of his honours till some rivals equal and others outgo him and a pri⟨s⟩ze yet brighter is presented to his grasp. This is the life of man — one vain progress from imagined happiness to real disappointment and an endless repetition of the same career.

[88] The rest of the page is torn off.

[89] In the left margin, the word "Elevation" is partially overwritten by "It cannot"; the words "Elis" "Ellis" "Horace" and "Holly" run diagonally left to right upward from "Upon the span" (below) to "Youth is the fault" (above).

[90] The rest of the page is torn off.

The ages that are gone by stand still on their far and solitary grounds and cry down unto man[,] Ye are vanity[.] [108][91] [Burr] and renown; I can never more attempt to acquire that honest esteem in the world, which every highminded spirit pants after; I must renounce forever all things for which I have been proud to live; I must die,—because the merciless voice of faction craves for my blood. But Beware, beware, my countrymen! it will not sink into the earth, but will cry from the ground for Revenge.

Far in the west where the Sun declines
There's a land where youthful glory shines
⟨It⟩ Youthful nation wakes to life
In the iron chain of its mountain land
The axe is laid to the forest tree
The domes of towns are piled to heaven
And far already swells the sound

I saw men gathered in a vaulted hall
And faction's angry ↑whisper↓ murmured ⟨ran⟩ around
And the hoarse cry of thousands

Savages are in general sour & selfish because their hardships & long wanderings in search of food tend to chill & extinguish the gentle affections. But some fortunate youth bounding over the mountains & enlivened by the splendour of a summer morn, may occasionally feel the expansion of social thoughts within him which for want of ⟨a better⟩ other objects will fix upon inanimate objects—upon the mountains or the clouds & endow them with life & thought or on the Sun & call him God of Day. Such is the origin of idolatry & idolatry is the first step to a pure & philosophic religion.

[109][92] Arabia is the country of the horse—fleeter & gentler there than elsewhere; of the camel—happily named the ship of the desert, who will transport a weight of 1000 lb, & whose flesh is fit

[91] In the left margin, mainly beside the verse, are three sketches of a man's head in left profile. In the right margin, after paragraph one, is a man's head, but with a mouth like a dog's, and what appear to be wings. See p. 318 for the first part of Burr's defense.

[92] The separated words "ASIA" and "MAHOMET" appear in the bottom margin.

for food, his hair for weaving, his dung for fuel, & even an extract of his urine is a valuable salt; of the Bedoween, who from the first year of recorded time up to this moment has preserved his savage Ishmaelitish independence, who is lavishly hospitable & a ferocious robber, nominally the subject, yet insults the towns & plunders the caravans of the Turk. The Arab neither laughs nor weeps. Mecca & Medina his holy cities are small poor places of populations about 20,000 apiece. But a law of Mahomet ordained that every Mussulman should visit Mecca once in his life. This wise or fortunate command is the source of all the internal commerce of Asia. Annual fairs are held there to which caravans which grow to armies resort & Mecca contains, so long as the fair lasts, a vast population of [.]

The Geography of Asia is thus generally sketched. The Centre of the Continent is a vast table of elevated land, the greatest continued elevation on the globe. From this descend all the rivers on each side. On the western ⟨side⟩ descent lie all the countries comprehended in anc[ient]. Persia. On the south it descends towards the vast plains of Indostan & the Indian Ocean. This broad territory lies open to the torrid sun whilst every cooling Northern blast is kept off by the ridge behind. The Northern side slopes down into Siberia which is colder than the same latitudes in Europe ⟨by⟩because all gales from the equator are interrupted by the high Mountains to the South. And to the ⟨West⟩ ↑East↓,[n] it comes down with all its streams to China & the Yellow Sea.

[110] 1 I spread my gorgeous sail
Upon a starless sea
And o'er the deep with a chilly gale
My painted bark sailed fast & free

2 Old Ocean shook his waves
Beneath the roaring wind
And the little keel of the mariner braves
The foaming abyss & the midnight blind

3 The firmament darkened overhead
Below the surges swelled
My bark ran low in a watery bed
As the tempest breath its course compelled

4 I took my silver lyre
And waked its voice on high
The wild blasts were hushed to admire
And the stars looked out from the charmed sky

5 Bear me then, ye wild waters!
To ⟨a⟩Apollo's Delphian isle;
My name is Music, in Càstalie known
Where bowers of joy for the Nine do smile.

[111][93] Among the old Saxons of the continent customs & phrases are remarkable. In a part of the Eccles[iastical]. States the⟨y⟩ ↑judge↓ fenced the court with hazel ropes "in the name of God & the Suzerain. Right do I bid ye; Unrighteousness I forbid ye—once—twice—thrice." An Anglo Saxon made a protest against judgement, thus. 'Before Egil quitted the field of violated justice he pronounced aloud the solemn ban—"Bear witness for me thou Arinbiorn, and thou Thorder and all ye men who hear my words liegemen & lawmen and all the commonalty!—I forbid all the lands which Biarn Bryniolfson held.—Let them not be sown or tilled. I forbid thee Bergaunund and all other men, indwellers & outdwellers, thanes & thewes. And he who doth so let it be avenged upon him as one who breaketh the law, who angers the gods, and who disturbs the peace."' Ed. Rev. [XXXVI, Feb. 1822] No 72. p. 304[94]

"they [the land and the lieges] were sworn to be his with weapon touch, according to the old law." [*ibid.*, 298]

[12 men wise & weary] [*ibid.*, 297]

"Churchmen have been wrongfully abused. In the feudal ages they were meeker & milder than the temporal lords. 'It is good to live beneath the crooked staff was the proverbial boast of the subjects of the prelates of the empire, &c'" E. R. 72 p 308.

[93] In the left middle of the page is a small water-color sketch of a man, combining dark shades of red and green with gray and black to make a commendable picture. At the bottom right is a large smudged area, perhaps from black crayon. The quotations following the first paragraph are written around and below the sketch.

[94] Emerson is quoting from a review of Sir Matthew Hale, *The History of the Common Law of England* . . . (London, 1829). The court was not fenced with "hazel ropes," but "by hazel wands connected by ropes" (p. 303). "in the name of God . . . thrice" is quoted from p. 308.

"Men of transcendant talents may force their way through tracks of their own." E. R. [*ibid.*, 340]

⌊"It is a poor merit (said Ed Rev. of Dr Herschell's making new terms of astronomy) to invent words in him who has discovered worlds."[95]⌋

[112][96] On the Affections.

It is well to withdraw the mind from a survey of the convulsions of the political world and trace their sources in the passions of individuals. If it is a refined and ennobling employment to examine the literature of different nations and /enjoy/follow/ the flights of different muses it is more refined to trace out the moral influence which created them and the reciprocal influence which they formed in the age to seek out the reasons why they give pleasure. Ethics has a bearing on legislation. In the history of a country we refer to our knowledge of the Science in judging where good laws were enacted and where it was otherwise[.]

Morality is constituted the rule by which the world must live. It is immensely important that the laws of a nation be conformable to it. Moral corruption struck the blow at Assyrian and /Roman/ Grecian/ magnificence and is sapping the stability of European kingdoms

[113] Utility is the *object*, expediency the law of legislation.
Prof Frisbie

The Magna Charta and the Regulations established in 1686 form the whole of the written constitution of Great Britain so that the Constitution rests rather on the just analogy of administration than on any written code. Hence the eternal disputes in parliament about what is constitutional. Idem.

"Under the rose here"
[Fletcher] Beggars' Bush. [II, iii, 149] iron

[95] I (Jan. 1803), 430, in a review of Herschell's *Observations on the Two Lately Discovered Celestial Bodies*, 1802.

[96] The page has a number of sketches of male heads in left profile and one of a king on horseback, all of which were on the page before the writing. The remaining pages in the journal are largely taken up with sentences, paragraphs, or quotations, most of which turn up in Emerson's "Dissertation upon the Present State of Ethical Philosophy" (see Hale, *Ralph Waldo Emerson*, pp. 97–135).

Is the preservation of the Universe a continual miracle? Is there no fallacy therein?

iron den

Cover Nature with darkness, the world with ruin. Convert the splendour of Genius into idiocy. Make the hoary head of age a mock and substitute for the incomprehensible grandeur of a holy religion, silly whims of superstition. Cease to arrest the progress of decay, and observe, while you may, the tremendous operation. — Then you may safely claim the administration of Chance. DARK DARK DARK DARK.

[114] Influence of Modern Essays as Tatler Spectator &c &c upon Morals.[97] ——

Much has been done in the higher ranks of modern society by the English periodical Essays.

Ranked with the elegant classics of the age they have penetrated into society where treatises professedly moral would never have come. Much has been claimed for the Spectator in rooting out, first the lighter follies of fashion and afterwards striking an effectual blow at vice of graver character as gaming, duelling, and others. This real good, ⟨to⟩done to mankind has not been over-rated and the authors of the Tatler, Spectator, Rambler, & Adventurer deserve ⟨great praise⟩ ↑the praise which Socrates acquired.↓ They have diffused instruction by unfolding, in pleasing forms, the excellence of Virtue; [n] and by taking advantage of that principle in our nature which induces us to enjoy with satisfaction and delight pictures of finished virtue * they [n] have censured vice with wit and recommended virtuous principles in moral strains so artfully that they could not displease. "The good and the evil of eternity are too ponderous for the wings of wit." says Dr Johnson [98] but the unnecessary ⟨obstructing⟩ load ↑and obstructions↓

* We find a great deal of incidental beauty in poetry & prose originating in this principle. Cite B Jonson's fine fiction.[99]

[97] Emerson's idea owes something to the fact that Stewart addresses himself to the influence of Addison and *The Spectator* and *The Tatler* upon morals (Stewart, *Dissertation, Collected Works*, 1854, I, 333–336).

[98] From the *Life of Milton* (see *Lives of the English Poets*, ed. G. B. Hill, 1905, I, 182).

[99] See p. 343.

of [115] depravity may be removed and the way prepared for science to soar[.]

This is combating vice in its high places with its own weapons. The most abominable evil becomes seductive by ⟨its⟩ ↑an unnatural↓ union with elegance and corrupt genius has accomplished immense mischief by insinuating what we abhor with what we admire. It is just that virtue should avail itself of the same advantage and embellish moral beauty with intellectual charms. Here there is no disgusting repulsion or antipathy to be overcome[;] they combine perfectly and in their results we should anticipate from mankind a creation of demigods[.]

The commissioned apostles of peace to the world were seen arming the nations of Europe ⟨in⟩to a more obstinate and pernicious war than perhaps any ever before kindled[,] pursued ↑with fatal hostility↓ through seven successions of bloodshed and horror till ⟨the⟩its dye was doubled on the crimson cross; not contented with this the ambitious popes were embroiled in perpetual disputes or negotiations with the ↑crowned↓ subjects of the church and from every contest reaped some new robbery to enrich

[116] Of Inductive Philosophy

When Bacon's Inductive philosophy ↑had↓ triumphed over Aristotle and ⟨when⟩ ↑the authority of↓ the Gre⟨ek⟩↑cian↓ Sage began to decline multitudes united to accelerate his fall. ⟨In the rage ↑⟨mania⟩↓ ↑⟨zeal⟩↓ which prevailed In⟩ The indignation of the zealots against his errors went beyond bounds and proceeded to abolish his empire in those departments where it deserved to remain entire. Such violent zeal will probably cause a reaction at some future period. The Ethics of Aristotle are little read and serve only to astonish the occasional student with the comprehension of view and the advancement of knowledge which they contain. Aristotle takes different views of morals and pursues different trains of ideas from the moderns; he occupies himself long, in ascertaining definitions and in drawing ↑the boundary↓ lines of moral & mental philosophy and thus manifests the infancy of the science that he is employing himself on [—] something which was new and strange ⟨to mankind⟩ [—] but discovers an intellect which was acute to devise and vast to comprehend[,] an intellect which belonged to that unequalled series commencing with Socrates & Plato alone ↑among the sons of Adam↓ qualified to institute and methodize the SCIENCE of morality.

[117] Tnamurya.

If I were a Poet this night would inspire me. And though I should say nothing new of her lunar majesty — of the dazzling beauty of the world over which she presides, as though her province was peculiarly adapted to her sceptre — yet I should retouch the portraits of others. I would add in no obscure place of the picture, the grave I saw opened to recieve Youth, beauty, sense, and affection. The sun was just gone but its radiance was left — the moon full orbed had ascended over the place of graves. This individual tomb — so obscure — what is it in a busy world like this, you will say — ? What too the sun — the moon in a universe so vast! How sweet is this musick below. —— If you do not think me too ↑fond of↓ sepulchral scenes, I may describe another ↑March 1817.↓ x x x On all sides surrounded with the beauty of Vertumnus what shall I say to one whose taste I have known in his early days somewhat morbid to his decorations. And yet a poet; merely in compliment to the profession I must talk of the posies of nature. If you were as plumigerous as the Muses, you might visit the ⟨v⟩Vale and hear the songs of the grove echoed by the little Tritons of Neptune, who is suspected of holding a small court in the neighbouring lake, — if indeed his sedge-crowned Majesty ever inhabits less than the "vasty deep." If not, you could people a sylvan scene with nymphs or fairies, and Mab might send her followers after moonbeams.

Hitherto you have had no associations with retirement — for you

"The spring may yet
"Distill her dews and from the silken gem
"Its lucid leaves unfold."

[118] I began in jesting with poetry, end with respecting it. Those who paint the primitive state of man's creation are sweet poets; those who represent human nature as sublimed by religion are better adapted to our feelings and situation; but those who point the path to the attainment of moral perfection are the guardian angels. But this is no easy poetic task. The lowly vale of penitence and humility must be passed before the mount of vision, the heights of virtue are gained. Therefore we so often hear the warning voice of high-toned moralists against the seductions of the vagrant flower-clad muse. May yours if she should continue and prune her wings be sanctified by piety, and I shall not blush to decorate my age with a sprig from your garland. But let pass the flowerets of nature and art or deck them with sepulchral dews when we think of departed genius. Alas!

for us who know their worth, for you whom they would have cherished, and for society, their light is departed. Would ⟨we⟩you know the worth of earthly blessings, visit the tomb of genius, learning, and influence. What avails these highest sublunary gifts! ↑May 1818.↓ x x x x I rejoice in Shakespeare's empire as far as it is reckless of that learning which some dotards make a merit of; but as sustained on the sensual, regret and abhor his dominion. It is for a still brighter era to erase his deformities and possibly set a mightier magician over the witcheries of fancy. But to me — to his old admirers nothing could supply his place.[100] x x x x There does appear a soul in Nature; and when we clothe it in a human form, its head is lost amongst clouds — we behold we live only in her ⟨spirits.⟩ ↑skirts.↓ If she raises a nation to her bosom, but a few ages and she covers it beneath the sod of barbarism and forbids a mourner to trace its history.

[119] Again she weeps over its ashes and sends some favourite to remove the pall and bring to light its past glories. In every region she had altars whether ensanguined with blood or decked with flowers. If we were to continue the personification, we might say she acted like a wise parent in mingling the Northern nations with the South that the hardihood of those might be softened ⟨with⟩ by the refinements of these. — Though with some it might be questioned whether the arts were always given by her in love or as toys to children for a temporary diversion and which often prove a bane. x x x You can see Price on Morals and you will find that his theories have no more to do with the history of the science than the nature of a turf has to the different owners from which it has passed. ↑1821↓ x x x x

Here spirits of inspiration are abroad tonight. I have been to behold the wonderous aspect of nature. Do we love poetry as we do the flowers of the field because they supply not the necessaries but the luxuries of life — and give presentiments so rich of an existence where all cares and labours cease. Fancy celestial gift is to the mind what these are to earth. "Imagination penetrates the Sciences — they supply analogies to poetry and history decorates it." "There were of old perhaps more intimate relations between Man & Nature than now exist. The mysteries of Eleusis: the religion [120] of Egypt, the system of emanations of the Hindoo, the Persian adoration of the elements, the harmony of the S. y. ↑Pythagorean↓ⁿ numbers — are vestiges of some curious attraction which united Man to the Universe." Blessed is our condition — we recognize with scientific delight

[100] In *J*, I, 108, this passage on Shakespeare is erroneously attributed to Emerson, rather than to Aunt Mary.

these attractions — but they are material — yet they are the agency of /God/Deity/[n] and we value them not as our relations near and dear but subservient to the ⟨great and grand⟩ ↑vast↓[n] relations we seek and pant after in moral affinities and intellectual attractions from his moral influence.[101] We love nature — to individuate ourselves in her wildest moods, and to partake of her extension, and glow with her colours and fly on her winds; but we better love to cast her off and rely on that alone which is imperishable. Shakspeare has admirably described the universal influence of the infinite spirit by that of the Sun whose light and warmth bring to maturity the healthiest plant and the most poisonous — corrupts the corruptible and nourishes the splendid tribe of Flora with the same beam. What an illustration and of what a truth! It is ours to cooperate — to imbibe — to spread forth every faculty for this influence to open the soil though by the hardest labours[,] by martyrdom if need be — that much may be taken. What an endless approach to the fountain of light have the pious began! After ages of onward and onward ascent then you can better discourse of the history of morals.

[121][102] Morals coeval with existence — where did its records begin? Melchisedec might have been in distant worlds a priest of natural theology. Right and wrong have had claims prior to all rites — immutable and eternal in their nature; what connexion has Christianity with their primitive state involves inquiries endless & perhaps useless. That this scheme seems a provision[,] a medicine for diseased, disturbed beings[,] is clearly discovered in all its parts. That it places before its adherents a higher destiny than what awaits those who expect the awards of justice — that is that the order of beings whom we call angels are on the original plan of fulfilling their obedience and recieving the favour covenanted by the Creator. While to the order so frail so afflicted and so hazardous as man the rewards of grace — a magnificent plan has been laid for him.

The Supreme Being does not operate always for the immediate

[101] "more intimate relations . . . moral influence" appears with few changes and without quotation marks in the printed essay (Hale, *Ralph Waldo Emerson*, p. 100). "the religion of Egypt . . . moral influence" is encircled in pencil, for insertion after "natural magic" on p. [10]. See above, p. 256. According to the printed version, the quotation is from Madame de Staël.

[102] A pencilled sketch of a man in right profile appears in the last paragraph.

↑short-sighted↓ good of the individual; the world is full of evil, of passions which may be perverted, of uncontrouled appetites which are acted upon by innumerable temptations. On these circumstances is built the science of morality.[103] Shakspeare has admirably and so forth

[122][104] Tnamurya 2 Part[105]

Philosophical devotion, like for instance the enthusiasm of the poet, is the transitory effect of high spirits, great leisure, fine genius & a habit of study & contemplation: but notwithstanding all these circumstances, an abstract invisible object like that which *natural* religion alone presents to us, cannot long actuate the mind, or be of any moment in life. To render the "passion of continuance, ↑and endure its supremacy↓ we must have some method of affecting the senses and imagination and must embrace some **historical* as well as *philosophical* account of the divinity. Popular superstitions and observances are found to be of use in this particular." This is the finest thing which Hume himself could say — delightfull testimony to the theist and devotee. x x x x In the little pageantry which will pass before us some ideas may arise from forms of beauty to ⟨tea[ch?]⟩light the combustibles of fancy. And fancy though a trull [123] sometimes may be converted into a ministering spirit.

---

* Historical — the Christian theist glories in the tangible evidences of his religion — but he has still stronger hold on future provisions from the adaptation of his mind to these — and to commune with the author and supporter of his mental and moral powers. And nothing is more true than in every pursuit or object of mind or appetite there is no real satisfaction but in contemplating the Author of nature & revelation and approximating to him. x x x x Imagination is an universal love of conceptions, images, and pictures of all kinds for their own sake, and rejoices in producing them ad infinitum for the sole pleasure of viewing the⟨ir⟩ pageantry. Darwin is an example of vivid imagination existing quite separate from poetical sentiment or moral enthusiasm. For strength of stimulus the poetry of sentiment is certainly preferable to that composed of mere pictures like Darwin's or of observation like Pope's. But, as the understanding of the Reader is passive in perusing poetry of sentiment, the means of excitement are soon expended

[103] The paragraph to this point — and perhaps the preceding paragraph, or a part of it — was evidently intended for insertion on p. 335, after "that alone which is imperishable."

[104] In the top left margin is sketched the head and shoulders of a man; in the top right margin, a man in left profile.

[105] For the first part, see pp. 333–334.

[124_1] [106] Tnamurya (Fancy illumines the dark road of investigation with indescribable beauty. It is immortal — it forsakes not the soul when reason herself decays. — When the senses close, when the affections are disappointed, she remains to aid the eye of faith beyond the grave — to kindle new prospects, — to renew the soul by her magical influence.) [107]

[126] [108] And his teeth were set so prominent that he seemed to talk outside of his face. [R. W. E.]

Anagram ☞ (I AM NO IAME CRAVEN.) [109]

Foxcroft, said the miser!

When I entered the room I found the object of my search stretched at length on his bed and apparently near his end. The ⟨room⟩ ↑chamber↓ was small and furnished with the dismal furniture of sickness and the means and articles which remained to poverty were cramped up with sufficient skill to give comfort to the dying man. But for himself — the first glance shewed him independent of these cares and one whose ↑departure↓ was not likely to be disquieted by the want of them. There was a visible air of satisfied composure written upon his countenance and perhaps somewhat that indicated grandeur of /mind/purpose/ and ⟨evidently one whose thoughts⟩ ↑it plainly appeared his↓ heart & contemplation were removed immensely from the trifles of circumstances about him. He recognized me at once & signed me to a seat by his bedside. When his attendant had retired he immediately addressed me. "I am perfectly aware that I can live but a little longer and I must exert my remaining strength to explain to you what would else appear extravagant in my conduct.

[106] Pages [124], [145], [147], and [151] have back to front as well as front to back writing, here distinguished by subscript numbers.

[107] The entry labeled "Tnamurya" is crowded onto the top of the page, the rest being occupied by the end of the sketch described in n. 108 below, and by miscellaneous notes.

[108] The sketch beginning "When I entered . . ." runs backwards from p. [126] to p. [124_2] and appears upside down in relation to the preceding matter. Other reversed matter appears on pp. [145]–[148] and [151]–[152]. The first sentence on the page may relate to the sketch. The anagram and the next sentence seem to be isolated entries. All three appear to have been written after the sketch was begun. A male head in left profile appears at the top right.

[109] This appears to be an unsuccessful anagram of the letters, written on the facing page, "on a n a m e i r a n" — possibly from ἄμειραν, to rob some one of his share, or portion.

From the time of the first application to the throne for leave of emigration & priveleges I esteemed myself called of God to bring about the establishment of a nation in the unsettled wilderness. I was admonished by visions in [125] the night, by whisperings of the Spirit in the day. I was young & enthusiastic but I could not be mistaken. There were omens speaking an unequivocal language which crossed me in all places. I traced them in the accidents of conversation, in the ground, & in the trees of the forest and read them in the evening cloud. You have heard of the mysterious character of my mother Elspeth for ⟨t⟩she was known and noticed among all the settlers. She instructed me in ⟨the⟩ signs & omens and all which I saw ⟨spoke a single⟩ ↑concurred↓ in one positive interpretation. And had she never taught me, I must have been blind ⟨to⟩indeed to the doings of fate if the frequency of these strange manifestations had not opened my eyes to their import. It would be long to enumerate them as you could not comprehend their principle & useless, for I trow by token God has not revealed himself in these latter days. But I saw my life was devoted by Providence to promote this great design and immediately obeyed my weird. Thrice was its accomplishment threatened with a defeat. The first leader of the expedition died & it was put by & forgotten; then the plan was altered & Holland was thought preferable, again many designing men interfered and impeded it. But I lived only for this & God did by my instrumentality triumph over his enemies. And when finally they reached their ⟨country⟩ ↑destination↓ spread themselves through the country, to earthly eyes it seemed still to stand upon a tottering & perilous bottom. Yesterday the firm foundation of an empire was laid which hath gloriously determined the destinies of the nation. Today its honours are branching to the skies and mixing with the stars in the eyes of the whole world and tonight [124_2] shall bear me to other worlds[,] the humble ambassador of ↑its↓ success⟨ful mission⟩[n] to give up my account of its /condition/progress/. Young Man[,] remember that it was my boast & pride when in the arms of death that the disease which is bearing me away on its irresistible wings was found first in the diligent labour to plant a colony in America." Here he ceased to speak and I offered him immediately a draught which his parched & discoloured lips seemed to demand. He withstood my purpose exclaiming "Mortal food is not for me[,] I must taste the banquets of heaven." His mind appeared to be intoxicated with the destiny which he considered himself appointed to fulfil. What he uttered further were incoherent exclamations of rapture but savouring rather of delirium than reason, and when the clock struck twelve he expired in ↑shrieking↓ an unintelligible word.

His hair stood up negligently, like forks.

"Perhaps I shall want the twine," said the Miser. "Yes, take it" answered Miranda. The careful man gravely undid the knot & pocketed the string.

The roseleaf was not doubled under her

Every nerve which God hath strung in that country is stretched and quick to oppose you.

The moon as seen through the poplars which flourish in a large city awakens no very

Gingerbread the baker was forthwith summoned

AARON BURR!!

[127] We must be the fervent scholars of this Science if we survey with becoming attention its tendencies and objects. It operates directly to obliterate the impure lines which depravity, error, and example have written upon the human mind; and having erased these first impressions, thus abolishing crime which is by them engendered, to substitute the precepts and sentiments which promote the happiness of man, whose exercise generates tranquil and /pure/ unaltered/ enjoyment and which the divine Being will justify and reward. Happiness is incompatible with the consciousness of danger and liability to evil; the sense of insecurity poisons the passing delight with the constant apprehension of its loss. Now nothing can shake the peace of mind which dwells with unblemished virtue; it is perpetually advancing ↑with security and satisfaction to himself↓ to new revelations of intellectual splendour and moral sublimity. It is making of men demigods (at whom the buffoon and the fool may loll their tongues harmlessly.) the peremptory voices of eloquence.

"to imitate the orderly disorder of nature" V.Vol V. B Jonson [110]

[110] The edition is uncertain. Harvard College Library had Peter Whalley's edi-

the first tables of the law which now lie mouldered in shivers on mount Sinai

[128] Assyrian Roman and British Magnificence

↑Sublimity of character must spring from sublimity of motive.↓

The ponderous fashions of former times are passed away. The learned do not separate & seclude themselves from all that is accounted light & trivial to devote their time & talents to a solitary subject gathering up all the lights which have come within their reach on whatever topic to concentrate all, no matter how remote the correspondence, upon the illustration or at all events the discussion of the peculiar theme. Latterly it is not considered a sin for the most frivolous essayist to lay rash hands on Morals & despatch the subject in a chapter & return with equal gravity to the examination of a play or a poem. "The good & the evil of eternity (says Dr Johnson) are too ponderous for the wings of wit." Still we look upon the change of literary opinion which we have mentioned as an unquestionable proof of the universal diffusion of knowledge ⟨connected with⟩ ↑belonging to↓ these pursuits.

In general I believe it will be found that our *admiration* is bestowed on the qualities, among all those that are desirable, which we ourselves least possess. [R. W. E.]

[129] "Admiration is the foundation of all philosophy; Inquisition the progress; and Ignorance the end."[n] [By Emerson?]

It is proper to state the chief conclusions to which experience has led & to name the desiderata yet remaining to the elements of the Science. By so doing we shall most distinctly survey the subject proposed. Mark the great epochs of the fool![111]

Most of the political iniquity which exists is owing to the absurd plan of grounding all government on the "social compact"

As long ago as Menu enlightened morality was taught in India.*

* These Indian doctrines are quoted in Notes to Curse of Kehama.[112]

---

tion in 7 vols., London, 1756, and Emerson would later withdraw this. The next most likely edition is Wm. Gifford's, 9 vols., London, 1816. His own library includes a 6 vol. edition, London, 1716.

[111] Emerson added the sentence later, doubtless as a facetious comment.

[112] *Southey's Poetical Works* (London, 1847), p. 591.

"If thou beest not," says this lawgiver exhorting to truth, "at variance by speaking falsely with Yama the subduer of all[,] with Va⟨vi⟩ivswata the punisher, with that great divinity who dwells in the breast,—go not on a pilgrimage to the river Gangu nor to the plains of Curu for thou hast no need of expiation[.]"

[130] It is only from a⟨n⟩ ↑very↓ extensive Comedy in the departments of literat⟨y⟩ure, that the tone & character of prevalent conversation which belonged to any ⟨country⟩ ↑period↓ can be ↑faithfully↓ transmitted. Hence we are obliged to ⟨draw our comp⟩ derive our ideas of the colloquial intercourse of Rome & Greece, when we institute a comparison between theirs & ours, from[113] the influence which their political condition would be supposed to exert and from the diffusion of knowledge we know them to have enjoyed. Here, modern society will be found to ⟨excel⟩ ↑outstrip↓ the maturest progress of both these Nations. In every family of ordinary advantages in the middle rank of life the great questions of morality are discussed with freedom and intelligence[,] introduced as matters of speculation but as having foundations of certainty like any other science. And in the lowest orders the occurrences and events of the day are debated, the prudence or folly of political and private conduct examined and all with a reference to known principles of ethical science. Anciently, such views were confined to the small circles of philosophers. Out of the schools, they were regard[e]d as things of remote & partial interest[n] much as we regard the useless subtleties of the schoolmen.[114] Now, these questions are connected with the domestic arrangements of every household, and are ⟨mingled⟩ ↑associated↓ with the recollections of his childhood [131] and home which every man ⟨carries about with him⟩ retains and acts upon afterwards. This diffusion of the knowledge accumulated on these topics though it does not add new terms ↑of technical value↓ to the *Science* nor unfold delicate discoveries to the subtle metaphysician is yet the true and best interest of philosophy for it marks the boundary line of truth and speculation; it settles its foundations deep

[113] "Hence . . . ours, from" is marked for correction.

[114] Emerson marked "as things . . . schoolmen" for correction and then made the correction by underscorings and numbers.

in the opinions of men; ^{n} and thus gives the only legitimate immortality to its conclusions and system.

*[115] In the Sciences which ↑display and↓ measure the material world great advancements may hereafter be made and what are now imagined to be profound and ultimate discoveries may at a distant period be regarded as rude and immature speculations ^{n} at the surface[,] ↑and the fabulous tales of alchemy may become true↓; but it is not so with moral Science. What is known now of the good and evil propensities of the heart and of the modes of correcting and regulating them was known two thousand years ago to every sagacious and experienced man. All that has been done is the tracing with precision the lines of the system in order to make them correspond with their known relations.

This fact is abundantly proved by the notorious circumstance which almost always attends the promulgation of a philosophical theory[,] that [132][116] authors start up to prove that it is the same opinion which Pythagoras or Plato or Epicurus propounded before. I mean to say that the ↑primeval↓ Druid * speculated with Druid much as a modern philosopher with all his imagined immensity of improvement converses with his friend upon ordinary topics of moral science —

"I believe however every one will agree with me, that, notwithstanding this resemblance, delicacy of taste is as much to be desired and cultivated as delicacy of passion is to be lamented and to be remedied, if possible. The good or ill accidents of life are very little at our disposal; but we are pretty much masters what books we shall read, what diversions we shall partake of, and what company we shall keep. Philosophers have endeavoured to render happiness entirely independent of every thing external. That degree of perfection is impossible to be attained; But every wise man will endeavour to place his happiness on such objects chiefly as depend upon himself; and that is not to be attained so much by any other means as by this delicacy of sentiment. When a man is possessed of that talent, he is more happy by what pleases his taste, than by what gratifies

* Pythagoras has been supposed to have borrowed his systems indirectly from the Druids.

[115] The asterisk indicates that Emerson intended what follows to be inserted at some other point in the essay.

[116] Before writing the quotation on the page, Emerson had sketched four male figures. One and possibly two of them are soldiers; one is labelled "Druid"; and another, done in full face, wears a Byronic collar.

his appetites, and recieves more enjoyment from a poem or a piece of reasoning, than the most expensive luxury can afford." Hume's Essays Vol I page 3.[117]

[133] It is a fine fiction expressed in these lines from Ben Jonson[118] Quere ? what ground is there for them?

When to the structure went more noble names
Than the Ephesian temple lost in flames
When every stone was laid by virtuous hands;
And standing so (oh that it yet not stands!)
More truth of Architecture there was blazed
Than lived in all the ignorant Goths ⟨are raised⟩ ↑have razed↓.
[*Prince Henry's Barriers*, ll. 49–54]
pro aris et focis.[119] curb. boisterous.

Whenever the Roman church has prevailed, I believe it has been its peculiar operation—to

Whether events change character or merely develope it[120]
develop

"Human Reason never yet from unquestionable principles or clear deductions made out an entire body of the law of nature. If a collection could be made of all the moral precepts of the pagan world many of which may be found in the Christian Religion that would not at all hinder but that the world still stood in ↑as much↓ need of a saviour & his morality."
Locke

The sand of the desert and the weed on the rock contribute ⟨to⟩ the↑ir↓ portion of attraction to the order of the Universe, so, in the moral world every fact and instance whether glory or reproach attaches to it should contribute argument and proof to the truth of Christianity. [R. W. E.]

[134₁][121] The course of our remarks leads us now to take notice of the influence of the present advanced state of Ethics on political Science [135₁] This influence is not subtle or /unsuspected/difficult to

[117] "Of the Delicacy of Taste and Passion," *Essays and Treatises on Several Subjects*, 2 vols., London, 1772, I, 4.

[118] See Emerson's note, p. 331.

[119] "For altars and hearths." [Ed.]

[120] To the left of this penciled entry is a figure of a man seated in a chair.

[121] In the top margin is a male head in left profile. After the first sentence is a

be traced/ but is perfectly plain & obvious. After the decline of the Roman Church the lower orders of Europe had no Indian Bramin to tell them that in the eternal ⟨variety⟩ ↑rounds↓ of transmigration their souls could never rise above the jackal; and the license which the Press immediately brought tended directly to enlighten & emancipate them. Such books as Machiavel's Prince, if designed to favour them or not could not fail to open their eyes to the bondage under which they /lived/groaned/. When at length moral discussions which before were strange & unintelligible ↑to their ears↓ began to be understood & they comprehended the nature of property & government things were in a train for amendment & popular investigation could not be diverted. There could be little hope left to an oppressive despotism after the peasant had learned that the professed object of the robed & reverenced legislator was "to repress all those actions which tend to produce more pain than pleasure & to promote all those which tend to produce more pleasure than pain."[122] [134_2] To the diffusion of this knowledge through the lower orders of Society must be attributed in the first place the rise of the commons in the monarchies of Europe which began the demolition of the feudal system; in the second place the science of representation; & lastly the rebellion of the people against the throne which has everywhere manifested itself either in dangerous symptoms or in actual revolution. To the Statesman this crisis becomes alarming who surveys the national embarrassments with regard to their immediate consequences & the continent is[123] crowded with politicians portending tremendous events about to ensue. But the Moralist regards this commotion as the inevitable effect of the progress of knowledge which might have been fortold almost from the time of the invention of Printing & which must proceed, with whatever disastrous evils the crisis may be attended, to the calm & secure possession [135_2] of equal rights & laws which it was intended to obtain.

---

large caret, referring to a passage on p. [135_1] marked for insertion here. As the subscript numbers indicate, the printed text follows Emerson's instructions: "Insert this after the words 'political Science.' "

[122] From a review of Jeremy Bentham's *Traités sur les Principes de Législation Civile et Pénale* . . . , *Edinburgh Review,* IV (April 1804), 10.

[123] "who surveys . . . continent is" is marked for correction.

[136] Des Cartes' argument for existence of God.

Whilst I direct the attention of my mind, I percieve myself to be an incomplete being & depending on another; & a being aspiring indefinitely to greater & better things; but at the same time I perceive him on whom I depend to hold all those greater things, not only indefinitely & with power but infinitely the things themselves in himself & so to be God: the whole force of this argument consists in this that I know that it is impossible for me to exist as I am, having in me this idea of God unless God actually exists, God, I say the same whose idea is in me, that is possessing all those perfections which I could not comprehend nor in any way reach with my conception & evidently not defaced by imperfections. From this it is plain enough that he cannot be deceitful for it is manifest ↑from nature↓ that all fraud & deception depend on some defect i.e. imperfection[.] [124]

The voice of Summer sounds [125]

[137] [126] the fates of charm-bound heroes of Araby and the Holy-land

Begun Jan 3d 1821
in no wise

Detached phrasula [127]

We admire the noble office of the moral philosopher — abandoning the world & allying himself to higher intellects in gathering up the relations which bind man to the universe. The boundless extravagance of ungoverned passion [128]
And having duly honored the glories & appreciated the dignity of morality we shall be allowed to glance at the blemishes & imperfections which belong to its history.
Cicero loved an elegant philosophy — what was uncouth or profound he polished & simplified for no man on earth had pictured such high & classic & ethereal Beauty for the worship of imagination as he.

[124] *Oeuvres Choisies,* ed. Louis Dimier (Paris, 1930), I, 119–120. The passage is from Meditation III ["Of God; That He Exists"], but it is likely that Emerson found it not in Descartes but in Stewart's *Dissertation,* where it appears in Latin in a footnote (*Collected Works of Dugald Stewart,* 1854, I, 119).

[125] This appears upside down in the manuscript. Being centered at the top of the page (reading from back to front), it may have been the title or caption for a projected paragraph or essay.

[126] The top margin is occupied by the first printed phrase and three small sketches of male heads in left profile, a pointed archway, etc.

[127] See p. 254, n. 7.

[128] The phrase was added later.

Believing as the ancients did that the world as they found it had forever subsisted & should continue to subsist & that an inscrutable Fate ruled them who might make them at pleasure demi gods or nonen⟨te⟩tities after death they had but scanty encouragement for a grand & holy system.

[138] There seems to have been the first approach to the modern fashion of ground all virtue on a single principle in what Socrates says with regard to things which are just (meaning virtuous). All things are just which are lawful. A very flimsy & fallacious criterion which necessarily varies under every different constitution of government.[129]

		Eternal	
	Pythagoras	590	B.C.
	Socrates	400	B.C.
	Epicurus	340	B C
	Zeno	264	B C
	Cicero dies	43	B C
	Seneca	64	AD.
	Epictetus	94	AD
	Arrian	161	AD
[Luther b1483 d.1546	M. Antoninus	180	AD
Machiavelli b.1469.*	Bacon	1626	AD
Hobbes,b.1588 d 1679]	Des Cartes	1650	AD
	Dr Cudworth	1688	
	Locke	1704	
	Malebranche	1715	
To[tal?]s 17	Newton	1727	
	Hutcheson	1748	
	Hume	1776	

* The system of these fanatical demagogues would elevate the ostrich to a higher rank on the scale of merit & wisdom than the man old & honourable whose parental affection dictates actions of wise & profound calculation.[130]

[129] The following list of philosophers is decorated with some thirteen sketches of male heads in left profile, one of them a bust, and all evidently intended as portraits.

[130] This footnote is at the bottom of p. [137]. That it refers to Luther, Machiavelli, and Hobbes is clear from the printed version (Hale, p. 111) although only Hobbes is there mentioned.

[139] JLG MG

Mr Groves paper in the spectator on the illimitable ↑advancement↓ [of] knowledge in the next life [131]

I cannot tell, but it seems to me that the sciences are in our days striking out a new path for their progress towards perfection

It requires a powerful faculty of generalization to cxhibit a system of morals entire in all its parts, accurate discrimination and freedom from bigotry and little prejudices. The Christian Fathers could not do it.

— the wanton smile of frivolity and the ghastliness of horror.

Ermine — the ermine robe of ceremony — [n]

Unassisted Philosophy never rose to such heights as with Plato and Marcus Antoninus. Christianity has supplyed its defects and corrected it and made a grander system but pure philosophy is not so exalted as then.

"And had we a perfect insight into the constitution of nature, the laws that govern it, and the motions, texture, and relations of the several bodies great and small that compose it; the whole chain of future events in it would be laid open to us" Dr Price on Morals [132]

[140] The message was communicated by the Moon to her high Sheriff of Transmission, who pursuant to order passed ⟨it⟩ to the Sheriff of the Atmosphere in the Earth the following —— Five opinions.

In modern times several attempts have been made to fix upon some ↑general↓ principle or rule of conduct. *Dr Clark* for example asserts that the great rule of morality consists in acting according to the relations of things or the fitness of applying certain actions to certain things or relations of things. *Woolaston* alleges that we ought to act according to truth

[131] *The Spectator*, No. 635, Dec. 20, 1714. Grove's ideas about God's omnipotence, the limitations of mortal knowledge of the cosmos and of God, and the gulf between the visible real and the invisible ideal, may well have influenced Emerson's current thought. What appears to be index material in the top margin, "L J K L M N", is omitted.

[132] *A Review of the Principal Questions in Morals* 2d ed. (London, 1769), p. 35.

or the true nature of things considered as they are & not as they are not; i.e. we ought to treat our kindred, not as strangers which they are not but as kindred which they actually are. *Shaftesbury* maintains like the *Platonists* that the great principle of morality consists in preserving a proper balance among ⟨the⟩all our affections; so that none of them may exert a greater influence than of right belongs to ⟨them⟩ ↑it.↓ An ingenious author *William Godwin* has lately attempted to found a system of morality on this ⟨system⟩ principle, that, in our whole conduct we ought to act towards ourselves & others according to strict justice & that we ought to perform towards every man precisely what is due to him. (Forsyth's Principles of Moral Science.) [133]

6—Dr Paley⟨s⟩ arranges all duties under general Expediency
7 Bentham makes a moral arithmetic & grounds all on Utility See Ed Rev Vol 4 [134]
8 Bentham ranges under the name of the principle of *sympathy & antipathy* all systems which place the basis of morality on the indications of a *moral sense* &c.

[141] "It is a noble and just advantage that the things subjected to understanding have of those which are objected to sense; that the one sort are but momentary, and merely taking; the other impressing and lasting else the glory of all these solemni[ti]es had perished like a blaze & gone out in the beholder's eyes. So short lived are the bodies of all things in comparison of their souls. And though bodies oftimes have the ill luck to be sensually preferred, they find afterwards the good fortune (when souls live) to be utterly forgotten." (From one of Jonson's ⟨costly & pedantic amusements of Elizabeth⟩ ↑masques↓[135]) *

"Nature is never more truly herself than in her grandest forms. The Apollo of Belvidere is as much in nature as any figure from the pencil of Rembrandt or any clown in the rustic revels of Teniers." Burke's Regicide Peace.[136]

* Recollect the forgotten amusements of that age the costly and pedantic Masques of Elizabeth's court.

[133] The paragraph from Robert Forsyth (1766–1846) is quoted in a review of vol. I of *The Principles of Moral Science*, *Edinburgh Review*, VII (Jan. 1806), 425.

[134] Emerson's comment is a brief summary of the ideas in the first six pages of a review of Bentham's *Traités sur les Principes de Législation Civile et Pénale*.

[135] Preface to *Hymenaei*, in *Ben Jonson*, ed. C. H. Herford and Evelyn Simpson, VII, 209.

[136] See *Works*, Boston, 1866, V, 407.

"The good & the evil of Eternity are too ponderous for the wings of wit." Dr Johnson's life of Milton [137]

"That passion which is peculiar to rational nature, the anguish arising from the consciousness of transgression & the horrours attending the ↑sense of the↓ divine displeasure is" &c &c. Milton's life by Jonson.[138]

Εχθρος γαρ μοι κεινος εστιν ομως Αιδαω πυλησιν
Ος Χ'ετερον μεν κευθη ενι φρεσιν, αλλο δε ειπη [139]
Ιλ. Β. IX l. 312 [misquoted]

"The list of Ceylonese snakes is hideous; and we become reconciled to the crude and cloudy land, in which we live, from reflecting that the indiscriminate activity of the sun generates what is loathsome, as well as what is lovely; that the Asp reposes under the rose; and the Scorpion crawls [under] the fragrant flower, and the luscious fruit."
(Edin. Rev. of Percival's Account of Ceylon) [140]

A survey of what has amused mankind[,] of what have been the games of the world would be strange and interesting.[141]

[142] Extracts [142]

— on the moral sense — Our feelings are not in their natural state when we can study their aspects ⟨spontaneously⟩ attentively; & their force & direction are better estimated from the traces which they leave in their spontaneous visitations than from any forced revocation of them for the purpose of being measured & compared.x x where the cause cannot be directly examined its qualities are most securely inferred from its effects.
Ed. Rev.

The amount, degree, or intensity of any pleasure or pain is ascertained by feeling & not determined by reason or reflection.

—— The legislator has but one simple maxim to observe — to repress all those actions which tend to produce more pain than pleasure & to promote all those which produce more pleasure than pain.

We are inclined to think in opposition to Mr Bentham that a legislator will proceed more safely by following the indications of those moral distinctions as to which all men are agreed than if he resolves to set them

[137] See p. 331.

[138] *Lives of the English Poets,* ed. G. B. Hill, I, 180.

[139] "For hateful in my eyes, even as the gates of Hades, is that man that hideth one thing in his mind and sayeth another."

[140] II (April 1803), 146. See p. 162, n. 1.

[141] The note may have been prompted by Forsyth's discussion of the amusements of mankind, quoted in *The Edinburgh Review,* VII (Jan. 1806), 427.

[142] The following "Extracts" are from *The Edinburgh Review,* IV (April 1804), 10–15.

at defiance & to be guided by nothing but those perceptions of utility which he must collect from the same general agreement.

— Of general rules of morality. —— It is in aid of this oversight, of this omission, this partiality, that we refer to the general rules of morality, rules which have been suggested by a larger observation & a longer experience than any individual can dream of pretending to, & which [143] have been accom↑m↓odated by the joint action of our sympathies with delinquents & sufferers to the actual condition of human fortitude & infirmity. If they be founded on utility it is on a utility that cannot always be discovered & that can never be correct⟨ed⟩ly estimated in deliberating on a particular measure or with a view to a specific course of conduct; it is on a utility that does not ⟨suffer⟩ ↑discover↓ itself till it is accumulated & only becomes apparent after a large collection of examples have been embodied in proof of it. Such summaries of utility, such records of uniform observation we conceive to be the general rules of morality, by which & by which alone legislators ⟨&⟩or individuals can be safely directed in determining on the propriety of any course of *conduct*. They are observations taken in the calm by which we must be guided in the darkness & terrror of the tempest; they are beacons & strongholds erected in the day of peace, round which we must rally & to which we must betake ourselves in the hour of contest & alarm. Ed. Rev. Vol 4.

Socrates . . . . videtur, primus ab ↑rebus↓ occultis et a natura ipsa involutis, in quibus, omnes ante eum philosophi occupati fuerunt philosophiam avocavisse et ad communem vitam ⟨re⟩adduxisse [143]

Of the Stoics — There is but little to correct in their ideas of the Supreme, Intelligence, of his universal providence, or the obligation they maintain that all men are under to conform to its will & acquiesce in its decisions as necessarily right & good. — But when they come to the *mind* they deviate from common sense. *Dr Priestl*[*e*]*y* [144]

[144]

It is a profitable rod that strikes sparingly, & frights somewhat oftener than it smiteth. Bp Hall

"I do not think that the divines in reasoning on the Adamic covenant and its hold on Adam's posterity place the matter on its

[143] See p. 257.

[144] In Nov. 1820, Emerson had read Priestley's *The Doctrines of Heathen Philosophy* (see p. 13, n. 1); on June 28, 1821, he or his mother withdrew from the Boston Library Society Priestley's *Lectures on History and General Policy*, 2 vols., 1793, returning them July 19. Vol. 2 was borrowed May 23–June 8, June 20–27, and July 6–18, 1822.

proper grounds. Mellen says he will not concern himself with the *righteousness* of the covenant but merely prove the *fact* and quotes Scripture assertions &c to that end. But it appears to me that the Divine Character of perfect justice ⟨is impeached⟩ ↑laesam est↓ by this mode of stating the case and that *Scripture* must be interpreted in consonance with the character of its Author & not his character by a verse of the Bible. My idea is that one covenant was made with Adam & another with his children; that after Adam had fallen, God determined to continue ⟨his⟩the condition of Adam through endless generations of men; but from the constitution of their nature" [R. W. E.] [145]

Behold yon white balloon whose swelling sides
Lift their light burden on the wanton air
'Tis aptest image of this man of starch
This ribbed puffed up utterer of breath
This paper whale this empty Ædepol.

Not all that heralds rake from coffined clay,
Nor storied prose, nor honied lies in rhyme,
Can sanction ↑(?)↓ evil deeds or consecrate a crime.
blazon

[145₁] [June 25, 1821? 1822?] E D's Album
I saw the sail of Youth sweep o'er the tide,
Gilding dark Ocean with its painted pride;
Bright was its path, beneath the noonday sun
God speed the bark! the shoal⟨s⟩ and rock⟨s⟩ to shun.

Fair on the gale its crimson banner⟨s⟩ waved,
Her foaming sides the yawning sea-gulfs braved;
⟨Hope was the⟩⟨The star ↑is set↓ which lured her o'er the deep⟩
⟨At⟩But yon dark cloud, wherein the thunders sleep,
Hides Hope's bright star which lured her o'er the deep!

June 25

[145] Most of the paragraph is struck through, as though for cancellation. Despite the quotation marks, which are repeated at the beginning of each line, Emerson has clearly written the symbol of his own authorship at the end.

Between this paragraph and the poetry quotation are several doodles.

1822 [146]

EAST AND WEST.

1 Far in the East when Time was young
The Spirit of Empire loved to dwell
In Egypt Arts and Learning sprung
And Music woke her choral ⟨b⟩shell.

2 There in the palace of the Sun
The gorgeous Day, to earth, is born
And o'er the world, its chariot rolls
⟨To⟩Towards the rich West in triumph drawn

3 And to the West shall Empire come
Amid our mountains, stall his steeds.
Here Glory find his final home
And Grandeur write immortal deeds.[147]

[147_1] [148] Oh ye Mariners —
Oh thou that art our queen again.
I wish I were where Helen lies
O Brignal banks are fresh & fair
Hail to thy cold & clouded beam
A lightsome eye, a soldier's mien
His mother from the window looked
Away ye gay landscapes
I climbed the dark brow
He took the tables in his hand
Come to Licoo!
Come away, come away, death.
Allan a dale has no faggot
And whither would you lead
The moorish King
The faery beam
Where dost thou careless lie

[146] The date appears in the margin and seems to have been written down some time after the poem.

[147] In the margin, below and to the left: "JEV."

[148] Of the remaining entries, only the ones on p. [147_1] and two brief sentences on p. [151_1] are written in the front to back order, distinguished here by subscript numbers. The others are written from back to front beginning on the last surviving page of the journal [152] and are printed in that order.

Sweet scented flower!
Merry it is in the good
In the blue depth
Beneath yon silver
If thou wilt let us build
I was a wild & wayward
Silent o Moyle
Farewel a long farewel
Whither thro falling dews
Fare thee well & if forever
When Spring to woods & wastes around
Hence all ye vain delights
The Assyrian came down like the wolf
Ah County Guy.
Three voices are there.
The king is kind.[149]

[151_1] Why do you look after me? I cannot help looking out as you pass [150]

[152][151] We look for days of joy & groves of peace

[149] Nearly all the fragments identified are from the first lines of single poems or of poetic units of larger works. The sources are, in order: (1) anon., "The Queen's Marie" (2) Leigh Hunt, *Descent of Liberty*, III, 529 (3) anon., "Fair Helen of Kirconell" (part second) (4) Scott, *Rokeby*, III, xvi, 9 (5) *ibid.*, I, xxxiii, 1 (6) ? (7) John Logan, "The Braes of Yarrow," l. 25 (8) Byron, "Lachin y Gair" (9) Scott, "Hellvellyn" (10) anon., "Kinmont Willie" (11) anon., "Song of the Tonga Islanders" (12) *Twelfth Night*, II, iv, 52 (13) *Rokeby*, III, xxx (14) *ibid.*, V, xxvii (15) Byron, "A Very Mournful Ballad on the Siege and Conquest of Alhama" (16) Jonson, "Gipsy Song" (17) Jonson, "An Ode to Himself" (18) H. Kirke White, "To the Herb Rosemary" (19) Scott, *The Lady of the Lake*, IV, xii (20) Byron, *Manfred*, I, i, 76 (21)? Charles K. Sharpe (1781?–1851), "Lord Herries' Complaint," quoted at p. 383, where the line is "Under yon silver . . ." (22) ? (23) *Rokeby*, V, xviii (24) Moore, "The Song of Fionnuala" (25) *Henry VIII*, III, ii, 356 (26) Bryant, "To a Waterfowl" (27) Byron, "Fare Thee Well" (28) Bryant, "The Murdered Traveller" (29) Fletcher, *The Nice Valour*, III, ii (30) Byron, "The Destruction of Sennacherib" (31) Scott, "County Guy," *Quentin Durward*, ch. IV (32) ? Wordsworth, "Thought of a Briton on the Subjugation of Switzerland" ("Two voices are there . . .") (33) *1 Henry IV*, IV, iii, 52. Emerson doubtless found numbers (1), (3) and (10) in the review of Scott's *Minstrelsy of the Scottish Border* in *The Edinburgh Review*, I (Jan. 1803), 395–406, where they are quoted.

[150] A reference to Martin Gay?

[151] In the left margin are two finished sketches, one of a young man in full face, the other of a man in left profile, plus unfinished sketches and practice penmanship. Except for the dimeters on p. [151_2] the poetry on pp. [152]–[145_2] is part of the

Where all the turmoils of ambition, cease;
Couched in his cot amid romantic bowers
Domestic visions wing the happy hours
When mellow eve shall paint the saffron sky
And light the star of Hesperus on high
⟨And h⟩Hush the ↑wild↓ warble of the lonely groves
And ⟨wake⟩ ↑charm↓ the hamlet with the tales of love
The placid scene /shall shed its soft/still tending to/ control
To win [152] the stubborn passions of the ↑fiery↓ soul
Then the glad sire shall gather round ⟨his⟩ ↑the↓ door
His ruddy boys to list his fairy lore
[By every spell to mystic Nature known]
[She courts him willing to her sylvan throne]
While o'er his sense⟨s⟩ ↑her↓ bright enchantment [n] steals
⟨And faithful Memory⟩ ↑Enamoured↓ all her stores reveals
The star oft seen in Youth's ⟨enamoured⟩ ↑rejoicing↓ prime
Rolls back his soul along the tides of time
Recalls the spring-time of his health & pride
His old companions bounding at his side
The reckless shout which shook the college hall⟨s⟩
The classic lesson potent to appal
The ⟨golden⟩ dreams which ardent fancy wove
To gild the blushing morning of his love
All these ⟨in turn are busy⟩ ↑shall ⟨crowd⟩ rise for↓ memory's ↑brilliant↓ theme
And float in beauty like an angel's dream.
The old man's steadfast gaze beholds the sky
Ere savage Death shall close his glazing eye

[151_2] Let bounding Fancy leave the clods of eart[h]

---

first version of Emerson's "Valedictory Poem," dated July 1821 (ms. in Harvard College Library). Emerson's Table of Contents lists "Valedictory Poem — scraps — page 156"; but this (and hence p. [155]) is missing, as are pp. [153] and [154].

[152] "Shall shed . . . soft" and "To win" are underscored, perhaps to indicate intended revision.

To riot in the regions of her birth
Where robed in light the genii of the stars
Launch⟨ed⟩ in refulgent space their diamond cars
Or in pavilions of celestial pride
Serene above all influence beside
Vent the bold joy which swells the glorious soul
Rich with the rapture of secure control.

Think on Columbus —— chained — Canst *thou* be
crowned with joy

No more shall the grave
Its tenants enslave
But the just shall inherit
The garland of thorns
Which Virtue hath worn
With the glory ⟨which beams⟩ in its fountain shall burn
of heaven ↑shall↓ unchangeably burn

[148] So when of old in universal sway
The arm of Nemesis was shrined in clay
The earthborn host the giant Titans strove
To rend Olympus from the might of Jove
When Terror reddened on the *Almighty*'s cheek
And even Jove's thunders whispered they were weak

Let not presumption blot our opening page.

When the grave closed o'er Athens' laurelled son
The fair haired Muses wept in Helicon
Be ours that dirge sincerely paid to them
That song for aye shall be our requiem

[147_2][153] So the poor ⟨men who sojourn in the *Moon*⟩ ↑Moon-men
looking out on space↓
A pale, dependent, discontented race
Live without breathing without airs or waters
Weak ragged Desolation's sons and daughters

[153] A sketch of the head and shoulders of a man is inserted in the text after "blessing" (below).

Think what a blessing
And when old Jove dispatched a starveling crew
To man the Moon and try what they could do
The ⟨wretched⟩ ↑dismal↓ scoundrels who arrived there first
Agreed t⟨o⟩' adjourn and forthwith died of thirst

To kindle towns no drunkard there retires
No fires can burn no engines put out fires

[146][154] Here in the halls of fate we ⟨free⟩proudly stand
Youth's holy fires by Hopes broad pinion fanned
And while we wait what destiny betides
Gaze on the forms ⟨of⟩ ↑which↓ fairy fancy guides

Bright Apparitions floating on the air
Who soft approaching claim a guardian care
Shall I see FORTUNE wave her silken robe
Or strong AMBITION comprehend the globe
Or warbling MUSES steal the soul away

With the rich ⟨swelling of seraphic⟩ ↑stores of legendary↓ lay
Shall HONOUR trace the heraldry of fame
Or BEAUTY come as Cleopatra came?
Not to dull sense shall forms like these appear
But conscious feeling finds them hovering near

These are the living principles which weave
Life's treacherous /tissue/web/ to flatter and decieve
Through every age they lead the lot of life.
And grasp the Urn with human fortunes rife

The early minstrel when his kindling eye
Marked the bright stars illuminate the sky
Saw these wild phantoms with those planets, roll
The tides of human fortunes to the goal

[154] In the left margin is a sketch of a man in left profile.

[145_2] There robed in light the Genii of the Stars
Launch in refulgent space their diamond cars
Or in pavilions of celestial pride
Serene above, all influence beside
Vent the bold joy which swells the glorious soul
Rich with the rapture of secure controul

The Universe

1820–1822

The Universe is the first of the many quotation books which Emerson kept. It is numbered from one to eight but contains nine items, since number seven appears twice, differentiated by the editors as "Universe 7" and "Universe 7[A]." The dated entries run from April 1820 to February 1821, but some undated entries belong almost certainly (as the record of Emerson's reading demonstrates) to 1822.

The nine "numbers" that compose the Universe are made up of large sheets folded in the middle but carrying the writing from top to bottom across the fold, thus making two pages out of each sheet. The sheets are paginated in pencil at the top and are somewhat irregular in size, measuring from 19.8 x 32 cm to 21 x 34 cm. Seven of the numbers are made up of two sheets each (four pages); Universe 3 and Universe 7 are composed of only one sheet (two pages) each.

[1] The Universe[1] (A quotation-book) No. 1

Apr. 1820—

Spenser speaking of the massacres committed upon the people of Munster ⟨says⟩ in Ireland after the rebellion paints in the strongest colours though in prose. "Out of every corner of the woodes & glennes they came creeping forth upon their handes, for their legges could not ⟨carry⟩ ↑bear↓ them: they looked like anatomies of death; they spake like ghostes crying out of their graves; they eat the dead carrions, happy w[h]ere they could find them, yea & one another soon after; insomuch as the very carcases they spared not to scrape out of their graves. And if they found a plot of water-cresses or shamrockes, there they flocked, as to a feast, for the time; yet not able long to continue there withall," &c. (Spenser's view

[1] The title is framed in an irregular rectangle.

of the state of Ireland p. 154 Vol VI. works 12 mo 1750 as quoted by Warton)[2]

Queen Elizabeth's Maids of Honour (from [William] Harrison[,] a cotempr. writer.

"Besides these things I could in like sort set down the waies & meanes whereby our ancient ladies of the court doo shun & avoid idlenesse; some of them exercising their fingers with the needle, others in caule-work, diverse in spinning of silke, some in continual reading either of the holie scriptures, or histories of our owne and forrein nations about us, and diverse in writing volumes of their owne & translating of other men's into our English & Latin toong; while the youngest sort in the meantime applie their lutes, citharnes, pricksong, & all kinds of musicke which they use only for recreation sake, when they are freed from attendance on the Queen's Majestie. — How manie of the eldest sort also are skilfull in surgerie & distillation of strong waters; besides sundrie artificial practices, pertaining to the ornature & commendation of their bodies! — There is in manner none of them, but, when they be at home can help to supply the ordinary want of the kitchen, with a number of dishes of their own devising, &c." (Description of England prefixed to Hollinshed's Chronicle.)

The ancient device of Musick under the earth.

"—— Which sure had been a noble hearing & the more melodious for the variety thereof, because it should come secretlie & strangelie out of the earth."

(Hollinshed's Chron) — Thus Milton.

And as I wake sweet music breath
Above about or *underneath.* ["Il Penseroso," lines 151–152]

Verses of Homer sung by him and a chorus of boys before the houses of the rich ⟨man⟩ ↑men↓ in Samos —

Δῶμα προςετραπόμεσθ' ἀνδρὸς μὲγα δυναμένοιο
Ος μεγα μεν δυναται, μεγα δε βρεμει, ολβιος αεὶ
Αυταρ ανακλινεσθε θυραι. πλουτος γαρ εσεισ⟨ν⟩ι
Πολλος, συν πλουτω δε και ευφροσυνη τεθαλυια,

[2] The quotation has not been located in either *Observations on the Faerie Queene* or *History of English Poetry.* It appears, without the bibliographical information, in Matthew Carey, *Vindiciae Hibernicae* (Phila., 1819) p. 79, which was withdrawn from the Boston Library Society Dec. 23, 1819.

Ειρηνη τ᾽αγαθη. οσα δ᾽αγγεα, μεγα μεν ειη,
Κυρβαιη δ᾽αιει κατα καρδοπου ερπεο μαζα.
Του παιδος δε γυνη κατα διφραδα βησεται υμμιν.
Ημιονοι δ᾽αξουσι κραταιποδες ες τοδε δωμα
[2] Αυτη δ᾽ιστον υφαινοι επ᾽ ηλεκτρω βεβανια
Νευμαι σοι, νευμαι ενιαυσιος, ωσε χελιδων
Εστηκ᾽ εν προθυροισι᾽ και ειμεντοι δωσεις ει δε μη
Ουχ εστηξομεν. ου γαρ συνοικησοντε ενθαδε ηλθομεν

Basil Kennett's Version of the same — 1697. —

At our Master's great house Merry Tribe here we stand
To praise his just wealth & applaud his command
Let the bars be knocked off & unlock the proud gate
While Plenty & Peace make their entrance in state
May Joys here like Rivals contend which shall reign
And Ceres with Bacchus the combat maintain
May the Nymph whose sweet charms our young patron have won
Drawn by prancing high Mules ride in triumph to Town
And when the gilt Coach its fair load shall resign
Beneath her gay feet may the bright amber shine.
May her wit to her needle fresh labours afford
And o'er the rich Loom spread the fame of her lord
Thus our visits & vows we repeat through the year
And with the new seasons like swallows appear
In th' porch we wait your boon: say quick will't come or no,
We've a long round to make; when our song's done we go

Vide Lives & Characters of Greek Poets (Kennet[t]'s [pp. 12–13])

Theocritus says of himself what few poets can say

Μουσαν δ᾽οθνείην ουποτ᾽ εφελκυσαμην.[3]

Pope Gregory VIIth's Excommunication of Henry IV.
(Emperour of Germany)

Peter, prince of the apostles, listen to thy servant whom thou hast tutored from his youth & whom to the present hour thou hast freed from the bands of the wicked, who hate me because I am faithful to thee. Thou

[3] "And I ne'er wrote a verse but was my own" (Kennett's transl.). The epigram of which this is line 4 is probably not by Theocritus. Emerson found it in Kennett, p. 143.

canst witness, & with thee can witness the holy Mother of Christ, & thy brother Paul, that unwillingly I was compelled to mount this holy throne. Rather would I have worn out my life in exile than have usurped thy ⟨throne⟩ ↑seat↓ to gain glory & the praise of mortals. By thy favour has the care of the christian world been committed to me; from thee I have the power of binding & of loosening. Resting on this assurance, for the honour & support of the church, in the name of God the father almighty, of his Son, & of the Holy Ghost, I depose Henry, who rashly & insolently has raised his arm against thy church, from all imperial & regal power, & his subjects I absolve from all allegiance to him. For it is meet that he, who aims to retrench the majesty of thy church, should be despoiled of his own honours. ([Joseph] Berington's Abelard & Heloisa)

Queen Elizabeth's infatuation for the Earl of Leicester.

Leicestrius, Elizabethae, cui ob animorum conjunctionem, eamque fortasse ex occulta syderum conspiratione (quam Synastriam Astrologi Graeci vocant) longe charissimus. (Camden. Annales Elizabethae p. 537.) [4]

---

[3] Interiour of Manfred's Tower. ——

Abbot. — What dost mean?
Manfred. — Look there
What dost thou see?
Abbot — Nothing.
Manfred. — Look there I say —
And steadfastly; now tell me what thou seest
Abbot. That which should shake me; but I fear it not —
I see a dusk & awful figure rise
Like an infernal god from out the earth;
His face wrapt in a mantle; & his form
Robed as with angry clouds he stands between
Thyself & me — but I do fear him not. —
Manf. Thou hast no cause — he shall not harm thee — but
His sight may shock thine old limbs into palsy.
I say to thee ⟨r⟩Retire!
Abbot. And I reply —
Never — till I have battled with this fiend —
What doth he here?

[4] "Leicester . . . under Queen Elizabeth (to whom by reason of a certain conjunction of their minds, and that haply through a hidden conspiracy of the stars (which the Greek astrologers term Synastria) he was most dear." [Transl. R. Norton.]

Manf. Why ay . . . what doth he here?
I did not send for him . . . he is unbidden.
Abbot. Alas! lost mortal! what with guests like these
Hast thou to do? I tremble for thy sake;
Why doth he gaze on thee & thou on him?
Ah! he unveils his aspect; on his brow
The thunder scars are graven; from his eye
Glares forth the immortality of hell —
Avaunt! [5] —

(Lord Byron's Manfred [III, iv, 57–79].)

Chaucer

— Chaucer's account of his sufferings written while in prison. —

I, that sometime in delicious houres was wont to enjoy blissful stoundes ↑seasons↓, am now dryve by unhappy hevinesse to bewail my sundrie evils in sorrow. — Thus witless, thoughtfull, sightlesse lookinge, I endure my penaunce in this derke prison, caitiffned ↑captived↓ from frendshippe & acquaintance & forsaken of all that any worde dare speake. — Although I had lyttell in respecte among grete & worthy, yet had I a fair parcel as me thought for the tyme in furthering of my sustenaunce. — I had richesse suffisauntly to weive need; I had dignity to be reverenced in worship. Power me thought that I had to keep fro mine enemies; & me seemed to shine in glory of renown. — Every of tho joys is turned into his contrary: for richesse now have I poverty; for dignity, now am I imprisoned; instead of power, wretchednesse I suffer; & for glory of renome, I am now dispised & fouliche hated.

(Chaucer's Works.) [6]

---

[4] Translation of part of a letter from Cicero to Plancus —

— Go on therefore as you have begun & recommend your name to immortality: & for all these things, which, from the vain badges of outward splendour carry a shew of glory, — despise them; look upon them as trifling, transitory, perishing. True honor is placed singly in Virtue; which is illustrated with most advantage by great services to our country. You have the best opportunity for this in the world; which since you have embraced, persevere, & go through with it. (— [Conyers] Middleton's life of Cicero —)

---

[5] To the left of the last six lines is a sketch of a hooded girl.

[6] Emerson copied the passage erratically from William Godwin, *Life of Geoffrey Chaucer* (London, 1803), II, 475, where the lines are glossed and quoted from *The Testament of Love,* formerly attributed to Chaucer.

xxxxxxxxx

I saw a pauper once, when I was young,
Borne to his shallow grave: the bearers trod
Smiling to where the death bell heavily rung,
And soon his bones were laid beneath the sod:
On the rough boards the earth was gaily flung:
Methought the prayer which gave him to his God
Was coldly said: — then all, passing away,
Left the scarce-coffined wretch to quick decay.

2 It was an autumn evening, & the rain
Had ceased awhile, but the loud winds did shriek
And called the deluging tempest back again,
The flag-staff on the church yard tower did creak,
And thro' the black clouds ran a lightning vein,
And then the flapping raven came to seek
Its home: its flight was heavy, & its wing
Seemed weary with a long day's wandering.

(Cornwall's Poems) [7] —

Close of the Conference between the Jewess Rebecca & Brian de Bois Gilbert.

— While Rebecca spoke thus her high & firm resolve which corresponded so well with the expressive beauty of her countenance gave to her looks, air & manner a dignity that seemed more than mortal. Her glance quailed not, her cheek blanched not for the fear of a fate so instant & so horrible; on the contrary, the thought that she had her fate at her command, & could escape at will from infamy to death gave yet a deeper colour of carnation to her complexion, & a yet more brilliant fire to her eye. Bois Guilbert, proud himself & high-spirited, thought he had never beheld beauty so animated & so commanding. — "Let there be peace between us, Rebecca," he said. — "Peace if thou wilt," answered Rebecca — "Peace, — but with this space between." — "Thou need'st no longer fear me," said Bois Guilbert. — "I fear thee not," replied she; "thanks to him who reared this dizzy tower so high, that nought could fall from it & live . . . thanks to him & to the God of Israel! . . . I fear thee not."

(Vol 20 Ivanhoe. [Ch. XXI)] [8]

---

[7] "Gyges," XXXVI–XXXVII. The two stanzas were quoted in *The Edinburgh Review,* XXXIII (Jan. 1820), 151.

[8] The passage was quoted in *The Edinburgh Review,* XXXIII (Jan. 1820), 34.

[1] — The Universe[9] —No. 2. (Apr. 1820)
— Death & funeral of Spenser —

Obit Edmundus Spenserus, patria Londinensis, Cantabrigiensis etiam Academiae alumnus, Musis adeo arridentibus natus, ut omnes Anglicos superioris aevi poetas, ne Chaucero quidem concive excepto, superaret. Sed peculiari poetis fato, semper cum paupertate conflictatus, etsi Greio Hiberniae proregi fuerit ab epistolis. Vix enim ibi secessum et scribendi otium nactus cum a rebellibus e laribus ejectus et bonis spoliatus, in Angliam inops reversus, statim expiravit, Westmonasterii prope Chaucerum impensis Comitis Essexiae inhumatus, *Poetis funus ducentibus*, flebilibusque carminibus et calamis in tumulum conjectis.[10]

(Camden. Page — 730. —)

After a↑n↓ ⟨quarrel⟩ argument concerning transubstantiation between Erasmus & Sir Thos. More the former borrowed a horse of the latter & returned to Holland. Instead of returning the horse as expected he sent the following

Epigram

Quod mihi dixisti
De corpore Christi
Crede quod ⟨habeas⟩ edas & edis
Nunc tibi adscribo
De tuo palfrido
Crede quod habeas et habes.[11]

(Erasmus — Burnet[t]'s Specimens)

---

[9] The title, in block print, is framed by a careful rectangle.

[10] "Edmund Spenser died, a Londoner by birth, and a scholar also of the University of Cambridge, born under so favorable an aspect of the Muses, that he surpassed all the English poets of former times, not excepting even Chaucer himself, his countryman. But by a fate peculiar to poets, he always struggled with poverty, though he were secretary to Lord Grey, Lord Deputy of Ireland. For scarce had he there gotten a solitary place and leisure to write, when he was by the rebels cast out of his dwelling, despoiled of his goods, and returned into England a poor man, where shortly after he died, and was interred at Westminster, near to Chaucer, at the charges of the Earl of Essex, his hearse being carried by poets, and mournfull verses and poems thrown into his tomb." [Transl. R. Norton.]

[11] "What you told me about the body of Christ — believe that you eat, and you do eat — I write you now about your horse — believe that you have him and you do have him." (Ed.) From George Burnett, *Specimens of English Prose Writers*,

Virgil's Epitaph written just previous to his death

Mantua me genuit; Calabri rapuere; tenet nunc Parthenope:
cecini pascua, rura, duces.[12]

Pedantry of Queen Elizabeth's Time.

The books of antiquity being familiar to the great[,] every thing was tinctured with ancient history & mythology. The heathen Gods, although discountenanced by the Calvinists on suspicion of their tending to cherish & revive a spirit of idolatry came into general vogue. When the queen paraded through a country town almost every pageant was a pantheon. When she paid a visit at the house of any of her nobility, at entering the house she was saluted by the Penates, & conducted to her privy chamber by Mercury. Even the pastry-cooks were expert mythologists. At dinner select transformations of Ovid's metamorphoses were exhibited in confectionary; & the splendid icing of an immense historic plumb-cake was embossed with a delicious basso relievo of the destruction of Troy. In the afternoon, when she condescended to walk in the garden, the lake was covered with tritons & nereids; the pages of the family were converted into wood nymphs, who peeped from every bower; & the footmen gamboled over the lawns in ↑the↓ figure of satyrs. — (Warton) [13]

---

[2] In 1553 Richard Wilson published The Art of Rhetorick, the first English work of criticism. — He saith

Some seek so far for outlandish English that they forget altogether their mother's language. And I dare swear this, if some of their mothers were alive, they were not able to tell what they say: & yet these fine English clerks will say they speak in their mother tongue, if a man should charge them with counterf⟨ei⟩ieting the king's English. Some far-journied gentlemen, at their return home, like as they love to go in foreign apparel, so will they ponder their talk with oversea langu⟨g⟩age. He that cometh lately out of France will talk French English & never blush at the matter. Another chops in with English Italianated, & applieth the Italian phrase to our English speaking; the which is as if an oration that professeth to utter his mind in plain Latin, would needs speak poetry & far-fetched colours of strange antiquity. The lawyer &c x x x The courtier will talk

---

3 vols. (London, 1807, 1813, identical editions), I, 392. Line 4 reads: "Sic tibi rescribo."

[12] "Mantua bore me; Calabria carried me away; Parthenope now holds me; I have sung of pastures, of country places, and of chieftains." [Ed.]

[13] The passage, ascribed to Warton, is in Burnett's *Specimens*, II, 81–82.

nothing but Chaucer. The mystical wise men & poetical clerks, will speak nothing but quaint proverbs & blind allegories; delighting much in their own darkness especially when none can tell what they do say. The unlearned or foolish fantastical, that smells but of learning (such fellows as have seen learned men in their days), will so Latin their tongues that the simple cannot but wonder at their talk, & think surely they speak by some revelation. (As quoted by Burnett) [14]

In 1448 Bessarion [15] one of "the learned Greeks" published "Defensio Platonis contra G. Trapezuntium." M. Ficinus wrote of him as follows. — Tantis utique radiis noctuae sive bubones quidam, ut videtur offensi, sacrum illum Platonis nostri thesaurum non solum spernere ut nonnulli quondam, sed, proh nefas! improbare coeperunt. Verum Bessarion, academiae lumen medelam confestim hebetibus et caligatis oculis adhibuit saluberrimam, ut aurum illum non solum mundum sit et splendidum, verum etiam tractabile manibus⟨que⟩ oculisque innoxium. Hoc vaticinatus Plato, fore tempus multa post secula, regi Dionysio inquit, quo theologiae mysteria exactissima discussione, velut igne aurum, purgarentur. Venerunt jam venerunt secula illa, Bessarion, quibus et Platonis, gaudeat numen, et nos omnis ejus familia summopere gratulemur.

([Humphrey] Hody de Graecis illustribus.) [16]

The following extract is the soliloquy of Bertram as written in the original form of the play by Mr Maturin after seeing the knight of the forest. It was retrenched from the play before its publication.[17]

[3] — Was it a man or fiend? — whate'er it was
It hath dealt wonderfully with me.
All is around his dwelling suitable.

[14] *Ibid.*, pp. 55–56.

[15] Directly above is a small sketch of a male head.

[16] "Annoyed as it seems, like so many night owls, by such beams of light, they began not only to disregard the sacred treasure of our Plato, like many before, but, heaven forbid! to condemn it. But Bessarion, the light of the Academy, straightway presented a most healthful medicine to their dull and darkened eyes, so that its gold was not only pure and shining, but even pliant in the hands and harmless to the eyes. Plato prophesied this, that there would be a time after many centuries (he told King Dionysius) when the mysteries of theology would be refined by most precise examination, just as gold is by fire. They have passed now, those centuries, they have passed, Bessarion, in whose passing the divine spirit of Plato may rejoice, and all of us, his family, most fully give thanks." [Ed.]

[17] The "play" is *Bertram, or the Castle of St. Aldobrand*. In the margin below and mostly upside down are several multiplication problems and what appears to be "B G O 5" written across the numbers.

The invisible blast to which the dark pines groan
The unconscious tread to which the dark earth echoes
The hidden waters rushing to their fall
These sounds of which the causes are not seen
I love for they are like my fate mysterious.
How towered his proud form through the shrouding gloom
How spoke the eloquent silence of its motion
How thro' the barred vizor did his accents
Roll their rich thunder on the pausing soul!
And though his mailed hand did shun my grasp
And though his closed morion hid his feature
Yea all resemblance to the face of man
I felt the hollow whisper of his welcome
I felt those unseen eyes were fixed on mine
If eyes indeed were these. ——
Forgotten thoughts of evil; still-born mischiefs,
Foul, fertile seeds of passion & of crime
That withered in my heart's abortive core
Roused their dark battle at his trumpet-peal.
So sweeps the tempest o'er the slumbering desert
Waking its myriad hosts of burning death
So calls the last dread peal the wandering atoms
Of blood & bone & flesh & dust worn fragments
In dire array of ghastly unity
To bide the eternal summons. —
I am not what I was since I beheld him —
I was the slave of passion's ebbing sway —
All is condensed collected callous now
The groan the burst the fiery flash is o'er,
Down pours the dense & darkening lava-tide
Arresting life & stilling all beneath it.
(Edinburgh Review [XXX (June 1818) 255])

---

[4] Then rose from sea to sky the loud farewell
Then shrieked the timid & stood still the brave
And some leaped overboard with dreadful yell
As eager to anticipate their grave
And the sea yawned about her like a hell
And down she sucked with her the whirling wave
Like one that grapples with his enemy
And strives to strangle him before he die

And first one universal shriek there rushed
Louder than the loud ocean, then a crash

Of echoing thunder; & then all was hushed
Save the loud winds & the remorseless dash
Of billows but at intervals there gushed
Accompanied with a convulsive splash
A solitary shriek — the bubbling cry
Of some strong swimmer in his agony
(Byron's Don Juan [II, 52–53, lines 409–424].)

As for humane laws made to encourage & requite vertue or to check & chastise [n] [vice] it is also manifest that they do extend to cases in comparison very few & that even as to particulars which they touch, they are so easily eluded or evaded that without entrenching upon them[,] at least without incurring their edge or coming within the verge of their correction[,] men may be very bad in themselves, extremely injurious to their neighbours, & hugely troublesome to the world so that such laws hardly can make tolerable citizens much less throughly good men even in exteriour de⟨aling⟩↑meanour↓ & dealing. However no laws of men can touch internal acts of vertue or vice; they may sometimes bind our hands or bridle our mouths or shackle our feet; but they cannot stop our thoughts, they cannot still our passions, they cannot bend or break our inclinations; these things are beyond the reach of ⟨our⟩ ↑their↓ cognizance of their command, of their compulsion, or their correction; they cannot therefore render men truly good or hinder them from being ⟨truly⟩ bad.

([Isaac] Barrow's Sermons.)

June 5th 1820

[1][18] The Universe[19] No 3

June 1820

I remember the players have often mentioned it as an honour to Shakspeare that in his writing whatever he penned he never blotted out

[18] Following "(Discoveries. page 100.)" is a small sketch of a man with what seems to be a whip in one hand and a disc in the other. Beside the first verse of Collins' "Ode" is a figure of a man, with a small pack on his back and with a walking stick, climbing a hill. Beside the second verse is a classical bust of a man wearing a fillet of leaves.

[19] The title is framed in a carefully-drawn parallelogram.

a line. My answer hath been [,] Would he had blotted a thousand. Which they thought a malevolent speech. I had not told posterity this but for their ignorance which chose that circumstance to commend their friend wherein he most faulted. And to justify my own candour, (for I loved the man & do honour his memory on this side idolatry, as much as any.) He was indeed honest & of an open & free nature; had an excellent phantasie, brave notions, & gentle expressions. x x x But he redeemed his vices with his virtues. There was ever more in him to be praised than to be pardoned. (Ben. Jonson's Discoveries.)

From the same

But ⟨of⟩ his learned & able though unfortunate success (Lord Bacon) is he who hath filled up all numbers & performed that in our tongue which may be compared or preferred either to insolent Greece or to haughty Rome. In short within his view & about his times were all the wits born that could honour a language or help study. Now things daily fall: wits grow downward & eloquence grows backward.

(Discoveries. page 100.).

Ode

How sleep the brave who sink to rest,
By all their country's wishes blest!
When spring, with dewy fingers cold,
Returns to deck their hallowed mould,
She there shall dress a sweeter sod
Than fancy's feet have ever trod.

By fairy hands their knell is rung;
By forms unseen their dirge is sung;
Their Honour comes, a pilgrim gray,
To bless the turf that wraps their clay;
And Freedom shall a while repair,
To dwell a weeping hermit there!

Collins.

Sun of the sleepless! melancholy star
Whose tearful beam glows tremulously far
* That show'st the darkness thou canst not dispel
How like art thou to joy remembered well
So gleams the past the light of other days
Which shines but warms not with its powerless rays
A night-beam Sorrow watcheth to behold

Distinct, but distant — clear, but oh how cold!
Byron (["Sun of the Sleepless," Hebrew] Melodies)

Meg Merrilies to Ellangowan —

Ride your ways, said the gipsy, ride your ways Laird of Ellangowan — ride your ways Godfrey Bertram! — This day have ye quenched seven smoaking hearths — see if the fire in you ain parlour burn the blither for that — Ye have riven the thack off seven cottar houses — look if your ain roof-tre||e|| [2][20] stand the faster. Ye may stable your stirks in the shealings at Derncleugh — see that the hare does not couch on the hearth-stane at Ellangowan. Ride your ways, Godfrey Bertram — what do ye glowr after our folk for? — There's thirty hearts there that wad hae wanted bread ere ye had wanted sunkets & spent their life-blood ere ye had scratched your finger — yes — there's thirty yonder from the auld wife of an hundred to the babe that was born last week, that ye hae turned out o' their bits of bields to sleep with the tod & the blackcock on the muirs! Ride your ways Ellangowan. Our bairns are hinging at our weary backs — ⟨see⟩ ↑look↓ that your braw cradle at hame be the fairer spread up — not that I am wishing ill to little Harry or to the babe that's yet to be born — God forbid — & make them kind to the poor & better folk than their father. And now ride een your ways, for these are the last words ye'll ever hear Meg Merrilies speak, & this is the last reise I'll ever cut in the bonny wods of Ellangowan." So saying she broke the sapling she held in her hand, & flung it into the road. ——

(Guy Mannering [Ch. VIII].)[21]

(Patroclus to Achilles.)

Sweet rouse yourself & the weak wanton Cupid
Shall from your neck unloose his amorous fold
And like a dew-drop, from the lion's mane
Be shook to air. —

For Emulation hath a thousand Sons,
That one by one pursue. If you give way,
Or hedge aside from the direct forthright,
Like to an entered tide, they all rush by
And leave you hindmost: there you lie,

[20] Just above the poetry is a sketch of a man with left hand upraised; to the right of the poetry is a sketch of a male head in left profile; in the left margin between the poetry and the next quotation is a harp, with a male head appended.

[21] The passage is quoted in *The Quarterly Review,* XII (Jan. 1815), 504–505, but Emerson may have taken it from a copy which he apparently owned (see "Books lent," p. 58).

Like to a gallant horse fallen in first rank,
For pavement to the abject rear, o'er run
And trampled on.

(Shakspeare's Troilus. & Cres↑s↓ida [III, iii, 222–225; 156–163].)

I know a song by which I soften & inchant the arms of my enemies & render their weapens of none effect. I know a song which I need only ↑to↓ sing when men have loaded me with ⟨chains⟩ bonds for the moment I sing it my chains fall in pieces & I walk forth at liberty. I know a song useful to all mankind; for as soon as hatred inflames the sons of men, the moment I sing it they are appeased. I know a song of such virtue, that were I caught in a storm, I can hush the winds, & render the air perfectly calm.

(Song of a ⟨r⟩*Runic bard* apud Godwin [*Life of Geoffrey Chaucer*, I, 179].) [22]

---

[1] September

The Universe.[23] No 4

From Philip Massinger. (born in 1584) Sept. 1820

(Sforza.)

——All that my fears
Could fashion for me or my enemies wish
Is fallen upon me. Silence that harsh music
'Tis now unseasonable — a tolling bell
As a sad harbinger to tell me that
This pampered lump of flesh must feed the worms.
Is fitter for me. — I am sick. —

("Duke of Milan" [I, iii, 140–146])

——When, therefore thy conscience, like a stern serjeant shall catch thee by the throat & arrest thee upon God's debt, let thy only plea be that thou has already paid it. Bring forth that bloody acquittance sealed to thee from heaven upon thy true faith, straitway thou shall see the fierce & terrible look of thy conscience changed into friendly smiles, & that rough & violent hand that was ready to drag thee to prison shall now lovingly

[22] For "Song of a Runic Bard," see Emerson's "Poetry and Imagination," *W*, VIII, 59.

[23] The title, written in script, is framed in a careful rectangle.

embrace thee & fight for thee against all the wrongful attempts of any spiritual adversary. O heavenly peace & more than peace, friendship whereby alone we are leagued with ourselves, & God with us; which whoever wants shall find a sad remembrancer in the midst of his ill-dissembled jollity, & after all vain strifes, shall fall into many secret dumps, from which his guilty heart shall deny to be cheered though all the world were his minstrel! Go then foolish man & when thou feelest any check of sin, seek after thy jocundest companions, deceive the time & thyself with merry purposes, with busy games feast away thy cares, bury them & thyself in wine & sleep. After all these frivolous offerings, it will return upon thee when thou wakest[,] perhaps ere thou wakest, nor will be repelled till it have shewed thee thy hell, nor when it hath shewed thee will it yet be repelled. x x x x I have seen a little stream of no noise, which upon its stoppage hath swelled up & with a loud gushing hath borne over the heap of turves wherewith it was resisted.

(Bishop [Joseph] Hall's Meditations.)

While the enthusiasm of genius is throwing such a bright & overpowering blaze of glory round Europe shall no kindred brilliancy settle upon the name of America? Has that spirit ceased to inspire which turned this wilderness into a garden? which liberated a continent from degrading subjection to foreign despotism & built up in our institutions a temple where [2] Freedom loves to dwell & before whose altar an emancipated nation can offer up its richest tribute — Freemen's Patriotism. — Cannot the grandeur & magnificence of surrounding ⟨scenery⟩ Nature fill the eye with flame, the heart with phrenzy? Cannot inspiration be breathed from our high mountaintops fringed with the glories of sunbeams. Or can floods of native fire be poured only from the forests ↑of Ettrick↓ & the banks of Ayr? — It cannot be — The music of Scotland was never sweeter than when it rose

From Susquehanna's side, fair Wyoming[.]

It must not be — Enthusiasm was breathed over the land when the fountains of our mighty waters were opened; when four Oceans were first dashed from the rocks of Niagara. It shall float round us as long as those waters roll onward in grandeur, or the rainbow bends like the new-born Goddess of beauty over the surge of that Cataract. *Immortality* shall encircle our *name* &

——— "Glory without end
Scatter the clouds away" ———

Such is the voice of Nature. Such is the voice of God.

(Conclusion of C. W. Upham's oration at
Exhibition Aug. 24, 1820.)[24]

---

[24] For Emerson's reactions to such oratory, see pp. 38–39.

"Here," she said, "stand still here. Look how the setting sun breaks through yon cloud which has been darkening the lift all day. See where the first stream of light fa's — it's upon Donagild's round tower — the auldest tower in the castle of Ellangowan — thats no for naething — See as its glooming to seaward abune yon sloop in the bay — that's no for naething neither. Here I stood on this very spot," said she, drawing herself up so as not to lose one hair-breadth of her uncommon height, & stretching out her long sinewy arm, & clenched hand, "Here I stood when I tauld the last laird of Ellangowan what was coming on his house — & did that fa' to the ground? — na — it hit even ower sair! — & here where I brake the wand of peace ower him — here I stand again — to bid God bless & prosper the just heir of Ellangowan, that will sune be brought to his ain; & the best laird he shall be that Ellangowan has seen for three hundred years. I'll no live to see it, maybe; but there will be many a blithe e'e see it though mine be closed. And now Abel Sampson as ever ye lo'ed the house of Ellangowan, away wi' my message to the English Colonel, as if life & death were upon ⟨guy⟩ your haste!"

(Guy Mannering. [Ch. XLVI])

The /*Shadowing*-out/Promise/ of the "Paradise lost"

—— I ⟨should not choose⟩ — And though I shall be foolish in saying more to this purpose, yet since it will be such a folly as wisest men going about to commit have only confest & so committed, I may trust with more reason ⟨& so with⟩ because with more folly, to have courteous pardon. For although a Poet, soaring in the high region of his fancies [3] with his garland & singing robes about him, might without apology speak more of himself than I mean to do; yet for me sitting here below in the cool element of Prose, a mortal thing among many readers of no Empyreal conceit, to venture & divulge unusual things of my self, I shall petition to the gentler sort it may not be envy ⟨of⟩ to me. I must say therefore that after I had from my first years, by the ceaseless diligence & care of my father, whom God recompence, been exercised to the Tongues & some sciences as my age would suffer x x it was found, that whether ought was imposed me by them that had the overlooking or betaken to of mine own choise in English or other tongue, prosing or versing but chiefly this latter — the stile by certain vital signs it had was likely to live. But much latelier in the private Academies of Italy, whither I was favoured to resort, percieving that some trifles which I had in memory composed at under twenty or thereabout (for the manner is that every one must give some proof of his wit & reading there,) met with acceptance above what was looked for; & other things which I had shifted in want of Books & conveniences to patch up amongst them, were recieved with written encomiums, which the Italian is not forward to bestow on men on this side the Alps, I began thus far to assent both to them & divers of my friends at home; & not less to an inward prompting which now grew daily upon me, that by labour & intent study (which I take to be my portion in this life) joyned with the strong propensity of nature, I might perhaps leave something so written to after-times as they should not willingly let it die. . . . Time serves not now & perhaps I might seem too profuse to give any certain account of what the mind at home, in the spacious circuits of her musing, hath liberty to propose to herself, though of highest hope & hardest attempting whether that Epick form whereof the two Poems of Homer & those other two of Virgil & Tasso are models — are to be kept. x x x x And the Apocalyps of Saint John is the majestick image of a high & stately tragedy, shutting up & intermingling her solemn scenes & Acts with a sevenfold chorus of Hallelujas & harping Symphonies. . . . x x x Neither do I think it shame to covenant with any knowing reader, that for some few years yet I may go on trust with him toward the payment of what I am now indebted, as being a Work not to be raised by the heat of youth or the vapours of wine like that which flows at waste from the pen of some vulgar Amorist x x; nor to be obtained by the invocation of Dame Memory & her siren daughters, but by devout prayer to that eternal Spirit, who can enrich with all utterance & knowledge, & sends out his Seraphim, with the hallowed fire of his altar to touch & purify the lips of whom he pleases: to this must be added industrious & select reading, steady observation, insight into all seemly & generous [4] arts & affairs; till which in some measure be compassed at mine own peril & cost, I refuse not to sustain th⟨e⟩is expectation from as many as are not loth to hazard so much credulity upon the best pledges that I can give them.—

(*Milton's* "Reason of Church Government urged against Prelaty.")

Eulogium of a perfect knight

Speech of Sir Bohort over the dead body of Launcelot du Lac.

And now I dare say that Sir Lancelot, there thou liest, thou were never matched of none earthly knight's hands. And thou were the curtiest knight that ever bare shielde. And thou were the truest freende to thy lover that ever bestrode horse; and thou were the truest lover, of a synful man, that ever loved woman. And thou were kindest man that ever stroke with sword. And thou were the goodliest person that ever came among press of knights. And thou were the meekest man & the gentlest that evere eate in hal among ladies. And thou were the sternest knight to thy mortal foe that ever put spere in rest! —

([George] Ellis' Specimens [of Early English Metrical Romances]. Vol I. p. 387)

Now all is hushed & still as death, — tis dreadful!
How reverend is the face of this tall pile,
Whose ancient pillars rear their marble heads
To bear aloft the arched & ponderous roof,
By its own weight made steadfast & immoveable,
Looking tranquillity. It strikes an awe
And terror on my aching sight. The tombs
And monumental caves of death look cold
And shoot a chilness to my trembling heart.
Give me thy hand & let me hear thy voice
Nay quickly, speak to me & let me hear
Thy voice; my own affrights me with its echoes.

Congreve's ⟨m⟩Mourning Bride. [II, i, 48–59])

Nov. 1820

[1] Nov. 20. 1820

The Universe[25] *No.* ⟨||4||⟩ 5

——For there is danger lest in these works of art which appear like so many ultimate perfections and utmost stretches of human industry, the understanding should be captivated, chained down, or as it were enchanted with them: so as not to converse with other things; but imagine that nothing of the same kind can possibly be effected in any other way; & that no farther improvement can be made except by operating in the same way, with greater diligence, exactness, & a better apparatus. x x x x x x And hence all the more noble inventions, will, if duly considered, be found owing not to slender discoveries, applications, & enlargements of arts; but entirely to chance or accident; whose slow & lingering motion, with which it creeps through ages, nothing can anticipate, prevent, or shadow out beforehand but the discovery of forms.

(Novum Organum Part 2d Sect II. — 31)

Southey's Epitaph on Pizzaro

Here lies Pizarro; —
A greater name the list of glory boasts not;
Toil, nor want, nor danger e'er deterred
This gallant hero from his course. Many a fight he won

[25] The title, written in script, is framed in a careful rectangle.

He slaughtered thousands & subdued a large
And ample realm. Such were Pizarro's deeds,
And fame & wealth & power were his rewards
Among mankind. — There is another world; —
Oh Reader! if thou earn'st thy daily bread
By daily labour, if thy lot be low,
Be hard, be wretched, thank the God who made thee,
That thou art not such as he.

Extract from a Idealist.

We are not satisfied with speaking of the objects of our perception — of what we feel & understand. We seek to attach ideas to mere abstractions & to give being to pure denominations. The dreams of our imaginations become the standards of our faiths. Essences which ⟨our⟩ cannot be [2] defined, substances which cannot be conceived; powers which have never been comprehended; & causes, which operate, we know not how; are sounds familiar to the language of error. Accustomed to them from our infancy we seldom enquire into their meaning. Our early associations form the code of our reason. We forget our first impressions; nor recollect how simple are the elements of all our knowledge. Deluded by his own mind man continues to wander in the mazes of the labyrinth which lies before him[,] unsuspicious of his deviations from the truth. Like some Knight of romance in an enchanted palace he mistakes the fictitious for the real & the false for the true. He is dazzled by the effulgence of the meteor & thinks he sees by the light of the sun. The prisoner who dreams in his dungeon imagines himself walking abroad in the fields or in the streets. He enjoys the sweets of fancied liberty. See how gladly he inhales the fresh air of the morning or embraces the friends whom he loves. He suspects not that the world ⟨whom⟩ which he has revisited exists only in himself; & that he must shortly awake to the conviction of his error — to solitude, captivity, & ⟨error⟩ sorrow. Is there no being who resembles this dreamer⟨s⟩? Is there not one who percieves his own ideas, & calls them external objects; who thinks he distinguishes the truth & who ⟨it⟩sees it not; who grasps at shadows & who follows phantoms, who passes from the cradle to the tomb, the dupe & often the victim of the illusions which he himself has created?

([William] Drummond's Academical Questions.) [26]

---

[26] The quotation is almost certainly taken, not directly from Drummond, but from *The Edinburgh Review*, VII (Oct. 1805), 179–180. See p. 47, n. 20.

Reasonings *a priori.*

The argument a priori has been enforced with singular ingenuity by Dr Clarke whose particular manner of stating it is supposed to have been suggested to him by the following passage in Newton's Principia. "Æternus est et infinitus, omnipotens et omnisciens; id est durat ab aeterno in aeternum, et adest ab infinito in infinitum. — Non est aeternitas et infinitas, sed aeternus et infinitus; non est duratio et spatium sed durat et adest. Durat semper et adest ubique et existendo semper et ubique, durationem et spatium constituit." Proceeding on the same principles Dr Clark[e] argues, "that space & time are only [3] abstract conceptions of an immensity & eternity which force themselves on our belief; & as immensity & eternity are not substances, they must be the attributes of a being who is necessarily immense & eternal." — "These, says Dr Reid, are the speculations of men of superiour genius; but whether they ⟨are⟩ ↑be↓ as solid as they are sublime; or whether they be the wanderings of imagination, in a region beyond the limits of human understanding, I am unable to determine."

(Dugald Stewart's Moral Outline.) [27]

But so is it in the region of the stars, where a vast body of fire is so divided by eccentric motions that it looks as if nature had parted them into orbs & round shells of the purest & plain materials. But where the cause is simple & the matter without variety, the motions must be uniform, & in heaven we should espy no motion or no variety. But GOD, who designed the heavens to be the causes of all change & motion here below, hath placed his angels in their houses of light, & given to every one of his appointed officers a portion of the fiery matter to circumagitate & roll; & now the wonder ceases; for if it be inquired why this part of the fire runs eastward & the other to the south they being both indifferent to either, it is because an angel of God sits on the centre & makes the same matter turn not by the bent of its own mobility & inclination but in order to the needs of man & the great purposes of ⟨g⟩God, & so it is in the understandings of men. ⟨when⟩

(Jeremy Taylor's SERMONS)

---

[27] *Outlines of Moral Philosophy* (Edinburgh, 1793), pp. 156–157. The Latin reads in translation, "God is eternal and infinite, omnipotent and omiscient; that is, he endures from everlasting to everlasting, and is present from infinity to infinity. He is not eternity or infinity, but eternal and infinite. He is not duration or space, but he endures and is present. He endures always, and is present everywhere, and by existing, always and everywhere, constitutes duration and space!" (Dr. Samuel Clarke's translation.)

Stoic Philosophy: — Dialogue between a Tyrant & a Stoic.

Tyrant. You shall die. Stoic. But not lamenting. T. You shall be in chains. S. But not whining. T. You shall be banished. S. But what hinders my going laughing. T. Tell me your secrets. S. No that is in my power. T. But I will throw you into chains. S. What say you, man? You may bind my feet, but Jupiter himself cannot change my resolution. T. I will throw you into prison & strike off your head. S. And did I ever say you could not strike it off? T. I will kill you. S. When did I say that I was immortal.

([Joseph] Priestl[e]y's Translation from Arrian.)[28]

[4] The *following is a beautiful measure.*

The unearthly voices ceased
  The heavy sound was still
It died on the river's breast
  It died on the side of the hill
But round Lord David's tower
  The sound still floated near
It rung in the ladye's bower
  And it rung in the ladye's ear
She raised her stately head
  ⟨And her⟩Her heart throbbed high with pride
"Your mountains shall bend
  And your streams shall ascend
Ere Margaret be our foeman's bride."
  Walter Scott (Lay of the Last Minstrel [I, xviii])

Dreams —

And hither Morpheus sent his kindest dreams
Raising a world of gayer tinct & grace
Oer which were shadowy cast Elysian gleams
That played in waving lights from place to place
And shed a roseate smile on Nature's face
Not Titian's pencil e'er could so array
So fleece with clouds the pure etherial space;
Nor could it e'er such melting forms display
As loose on flowery beds all languishingly lay
No, fair illusions! artful phantoms, no!
My muse will not attempt your fairy land
She has no colours that like yours can glow

[28] *The Theological and Miscellaneous Works of Joseph Priestley*, 25 vols. (London, 1817–1832), XVII, 506.

To catch your vivid scenes too gross her hand.
(Thomson's Castle of Indolence. [I, 44–45, lines 388–400])

If Music be the food of love, play on,
Give me excess of it, that surfeiting
The appetite may sicken, & so die.
That strain again; — it had a dying fall:
O, it came oer my ear, like the sweet south
That breathes upon a bank of violets,
Stealing & giving odour.
(Twelfth Night [I, i, 1–7])

[1] The Universe[29] No. 6. Feb. 1821.

Duke and Viola disguised as Duke's Page

Viola. Say that some lady as perhaps there is
Hath for your love as great a pang of heart
As you have for Olivia: you cannot love her;
You tell her so; must she not then be answered?
Duke. — Make no compare
Between that love a woman can bear me
And that I owe Olivia.
Viola. Ay but I know —
Duke. What dost thou know?
Viola. Too well what love women to men may owe;
In faith they are as true of heart as we.
My father had a daughter loved a man
As it might be, perhaps, were I a woman
I should your lordship.
Duke. What's her history?
Viola. A blank, my Lord; she never told her love
But let concealment like a worm i' th' bud
Feed on her damask cheek: she pined in thought
And with a green & yellow melancholy
She sat like Patience on a monument
Smiling at grief. Was not this love indeed?
Duke. But dy'd thy sister of ⟨thy⟩her love my boy?

29 The title is written in heavy black ink but is not framed.

Viola. I'm all the daughters of my father's house.
(Twelfth-Night or What you will [II, iv, 92–95, 104–118, 122–123].)

Spenser's lamentation.

Full little knowest thou who hast not tried
What hell it is in suing long to bide:
To lose good days, that might be better spent,
To waste long nights in pensive discontent,
To speed today, to be put back tomorrow,
To feed on hope, to pine with fear & sorrow,
To have thy prince's grace, yet want her peers',
To have thy asking, yet wait many years,
To fret thy soul with crosses & with cares,
To eat thy heart with comfortless despairs,
To fawn, to crouch, to wait, to ride, to run,
To spend, to give, to want, to be undone.
(Mother Hubbard's Tale [lines 895–906])

[2] The Nightingale.

Oft when, returning with her loaded bill,
The astonished mother finds a vacant nest,
By the hard hand of unrelenting clowns
Robbed; to the ground the vain provision falls;
Her pinions ruffle, and low drooping, scarce
Can bear the mourner to the poplar shade,
Where, all abandoned to despair, she sings
Her sorrows through the night, & on the bough
Sole sitting, still at every dying fall
Takes up again her lamentable strain
Of winding woe, till wide around, the woods
Sigh to her song, & with her wail resound.
(Thomson's Seasons. ["Spring," lines 717–728])

"These lines are now allowed to be the best in "the Seasons." Ed. Rev.[30]

Number of the Settlers in Massachusetts Bay.

However the number of those who did actually arrive at New England before the year 1640 have been computed at Four Thousand since which

[30] This sentence is added in pencil. The passage may have been called to Emerson's attention by *The Edinburgh Review*, VII (Jan. 1806), 333: ". . . the lines on the nightingale ('Oft when returning,' &c. Spring, 715.) are the most perfect in the Seasons. . . ." (from a review of J. Poulin, transl., *Les Saisons de J. Thomson*).

time far more have gone out of the country than have come to it; and yet the God of Heaven so smiled upon ||the|| Plantation while under an easy & equal Gover↑n↓ment the designs of Christianity in well-formed churches have been carried on that no history can parallel it x x x An howling Wilderness in a few years became a pleasant land accommodated with the necessaries yea & the conveniences of human life; the Gospel has carried with it a fulness of all other blessings; and (albeit that mankind generally, as far as we have any means of inquiry have increased in one & the same given proportion, & so no more than *doubled* themselves in about 360 years in all the past ages of the world, since the fixing of the present period of human life) the 4000 first planters in less than Fifty Years notwithstanding all transportations & Mortalities into, they say, more than an Hundred Thousand.

(Cotton Mather's Magnalia [Christi Americana].) [31]

Lord Bacon's expostulation with Queen Elizabeth on being out of favour.

Madam, I see you withdraw your favour from me; & now I have lost many friends for your sake, I shall lose you too; you have put me like one of those the French call Enfans Perdus that serve on foot before the horse; so have you put me in matters of envy without strength, or without place. and I know at chess [3] a pawn before the king is ever much played upon. A great many love me not because they think I have been against my Lord of Essex; & you love me not because ⟨they think⟩ ↑you know↓ I have been for him: yet it will never repent me, that I have dealt in simplicity of heart towards you both, without respect of cautions to myself; & therefore vivus, vidensque pereo. If I do break my neck, I shall do it as Dorrington did, who walked on the battlements of the church many days & took a view & survey where he should fall: and so, Madam, I am not so simple but that I have a prospect of my overthrow; only I thought I would tell you so much, that you may know it was my faith and not folly, that brought me to it; and so I will pray for you.

(Lord Bacon's letter to the Earl of Devonshire)

The faery beam upon you
The stars to glister on you
A moon of light
In the noon of night
Till the firedrake hath o'er gone you.

The wheel of fortune guide you
The boy with the bow beside you

[31] Hartford, 1820, I, 73–74.

Run aye in the way
Till the bird of day
And the luckier lot betide you.
(Ben. Jonson's Gipsies Metamorphosed.)

An Ode to himself.

Where dost thou careless lie
Buried in ease and sloth?
Knowledge, that sleeps, doth die;
And this security,
It is the common moth
That eats on wits and arts and quite destroys them both.

Are all the Aonian springs
Dryed up? lies Thespia waste?
Doth Clarius' harp want strings,
That not a nymph now sings!
Or droop they as disgraced,
To see their seats & bowers by chattering pies defaced?

[Ben Jonson]

[4] An ode to Melancholy.

Hence all ye vain delights,
As short as are the nights
Wherein you spend your folly;
There's nought in life so sweet,
If men were wise to see 't,
But only melancholy,
Oh sweetest melancholy!

Welcome folded arms, & fixed eyes
A sigh, that piercing, mortifies,
A look that's fastened to the ground,
A tongue chain'd up without a sound.

Fountain heads and pathless groves,
Places which pale passion loves;
Moonlight walks, when all the fowls
Are warmly housed, save bats and owls;
A midnight bell, a parting groan
These are the sounds we feed upon;

Then stretch our bones in a still gloomy valley:
Nothing's so dainty sweet as lovely melancholy.
(In BEAUMONT & FLETCHER's "PASSIONATE MADMAN.")

Extract from "Lord Herries' complaint"

Under yon silver skimmering waves
That saftly rise and fa'
Lie mouldering banes in sandy graves,
That fley my peace awa'.

I plunged an auld man in the sea
Whose locks were like the snaw
His hairs sall serve for rapes to me
In hell my saul to draw.

* Repentance! Signal of my bale
Built of the lasting stane
Ye lang sall tell the bluidy tale
When I am dead and gane
How Hoddom's lord, ye lang sall tell
By conscience stricken sair
In life sustained the pains of hell
And perished in despair.

(Written by C K Sharpe — quoted in
"[Nathan?] Drake's Essays."

[1] The Universe [32] No. 7.

——I once in my early days heard (for it was night and I could not see) a traveller drowning; ⟨It⟩ not in the Annan itself, but in the

* The name of a tower.

[32] The title is framed in a decorated rectangle. The manuscript, consisting of one sheet filled on both sides, is in the Pierpont Morgan Library and is reproduced by permission. At the bottom of page [2] is the accession number "MA 1820." John L. Cooley of Pleasantville, N.Y., gave the manuscript to the Library after acquiring it from Goodspeed's Book Shop in Boston about 1939. Here the record of its provenance stops.

"Universe No. 7" must have been the first of the two quotation books so labelled by Emerson. The quotation from Montesquieu was surely written down about Aug. 8, 1821. Emerson borrowed *Lettres Persanes* from the Boston Library Society on Aug. 2 and returned it Aug. 9. On Aug. 8 he wrote that he had been reading the

Frith of Solway close by the mouth of that river. The influx of the tide had unhorsed him in the night as he was passing the sands from Cumberland. The west wi||nd|| blew a tempest and according to the common expression brough||t|| in the water three feet abreast. The traveller got upon a standing net a little way from the shore. There he lashed himself to the post, shouting for half an hour for assistance — till the tide rose over his head! In the darkness of night and amid the pauses of the hurricane, his voice, heard at intervals, was exquisitely mournful. No one could go to his assistance, no one knew where he was —— the sound seemed to proceed from the spirit of the waters. But morning rose, — the tide had ebbed — and the poor traveller was found lashed to the pole of the net, and bleaching in the wind. ——

(Dr. Currie's letter to Walter Scott.)[33]

LAY^{n} D'YSEULT.

Feuillage épais, verts gazons, doux silence,
Bien invitez à prend⟨l⟩re le repos;
Mais tant revient si douce remembrance,
Que de mes cries j'eveille les échos.

Dans ces scepeuils plantes par la nature,
Fontaine sourd et nourrit mille fleurs:
Las mes soupirs augmentent son murmure
Ses petits flots sont grossis par mes pleurs.

"Lettres Persanes" and he copied several extracts, one of which is identical with the last sentence of the quotation in this "Universe" (see No. XVIII, p. [29]). The only other quotation for which any dating evidence is available is the "Lay d'Iseult," which appears to have been copied from Tressan's *Corps d'Extraits de Romans de Chevalrie* in the spring or early summer of 1821. In Emerson's "Catalogue of Books Read," this is entered shortly before McCrie's *Life of John Knox*, which he borrowed from the Boston Library Society July 19, 1821. Thus this "Universe" appears to belong to the spring and summer of 1821. The dateable quotations in the second "Universe No. 7" which we entitle "Universe 7[A]" and in "Universe No. 8," which are continuous, are Oct. 1821, and Jan.–Feb. 1822.

The existence of two volumes of the same number may be conjecturally accounted for. Like the other volumes of the "Universe," this one shows a horizontal fold mark in the middle; unlike the others it shows fold-marks at the quarter and three-quarter lines. It was evidently folded until small enough for mailing or carrying in the pocket, and Emerson doubtless gave or sent it to a friend. When he began another "Universe" in the fall of 1821 he would naturally have numbered it "7," since he no longer had the first one of that number.

[33] Scott quotes this in his headnote to "Annan Water," one of the ballads in *Minstrelsy of the Scottish Border* (see the reprint of the original edition, London, 1868, p. 294).

Que sait Tristan? . . . Ah, plus d'une victoire
Du los d'honneur lui décerne le prix!
La Table Ronde élève aux cieux sa gloire
Chétive, hélas! il n'entend pas me cris.

(Romans du Comte de Tressan. Vol I) [34]

||[2]|| Il me semble, Usbek, qu nous ne jugeon ⟨pre⟩ jamais des choses que par un retour secret que nous faisons sur nous-mêmes. Je ne suis pas surpris que les nègres peignent le diable d'une blancheur eblouissante et leurs dieux noirs comme du charbon; que la Vénus de certains peuples ait des mamelles qui lui pendent jusqu'aux cuisses; et qu'infin tous les idolatres aient représenté leurs dieux avec une figure humaine et leur aient fait part de toutes leurs inclinations. On a dit fort bien qui si les triangles faisoient un dieu, ils lui donneroient trois cotes.

"Les Lettres Persanes de Montesquieu." [35]

The banquet song of the Tonga Islanders.[36]

1 Come to Lacöo [n] the sun is riding
Down hills of gold to his coral bowers
Come when the wood-pigeon's moan is chiding
The song of the wind while we gather flowers.

2 Let us plait the garlands and weave the chi,
While the wild waves dance on our iron strand
Tomorrow these waves may wash our graves
And the moon look down on a ruined land.

3 Let us light the torches and dip our hair
In the fragrant oil of the sandal tree
Strike the bonjoo and the oola share
Ere the death gods hear our jubilee.

4 Who are they that in floating towers
Come with their skins of curdled snow↑s↓;
They shall see our maidens dress our bowers
While the ⟨m⟩hoon↑i↓ shines on their sunny brows.

5 Who shall mourn when red with slaughter

[34] Louis Elisabeth de la Vergne, Comte de Tressan, *Corps d'Extraits de Romans de Chevalerie*, 4 v. (Paris, 1787–89), VII, 131–132.

[35] Letter 59.

[36] 1. A large "B" precedes this title. The verses are anonymous. The version Emerson printed in Parnassus, 1875, p. 380, has four more stanzas. These may have appeared on a lost page of this "Universe."

Finow [n] sits on the funeral stone
Who shall weep for his dying daughter
Who shall answer the red-chief's moan

6 He shall cry unheard by the funeral stone
He shall sink unseen by the split canoe
Though the plantain bird be his alone
And the thundering gods of Fanfaunoo [n]

[1] Universe [37] No 7[A]

Origin of Fable

L'homme a un penchant naturel a entendre raconter. La fable pique sa curiosité et amuse son imagination. Elle est de la plus haute antiquité. On trouve des paraboles dans les plus anciens monumens de tous les peuples. Il semble que de tout temps la verite ait en peur des hommes et que les hommes aient en peur de la vérité. Quel que soit l'inventeur de l'apologue, soit que la raison timide dans la bouche d'un esclave, ait emprunté ce langage détourné pour se faire entendre d'un maitre; soit qu'un sage voulant la reconciler avec l'amour propre, le plus superbe de tous les maitres, ait imaginé de lui prêter cette forme agreable et riante, cette invention est du nombre de celles qui font le plus d'honneur a l'esprit humain. Par cet heureux artifice la verité avant de se presenter aux hommes, compose avec leur orgeuil et s'empare de leur imagination. Elle leur offre le plaisir d'une découverte, leur epargne l'affront d'un reproche, et l'ennui d'une leçon. Occupé a demêler le sens de la fable l'esprit n'a pas le temps de se revolter contre la precepte; et quand la raison se montre a la fin elle nous trouve désarmés. Nous avons deja prononcé contre nous mêmes l'arret que nous ne voudrions pas entendre d'un autre; car nous voulons bien quelquefois nous corriger, mais nous ne voulons jamais qu'on nous condamne.

(Eloge de Fontaine.)

Mariner's dream

In the slumbers of midnight the sailor-boy lay
His hammock swung loose to the sport of the wind
All watch worn and weary his cares flew away
And visions of happiness danced o'er his mind.

He dreamed of his home of his dear native bowers
And pleasures encircling lifes merry morn

[37] The title is written simply without a frame.

While memory stood sideways half covered with flowers
    And restored every rose but secreted its thorn.

Then fancy her magical pinions spread wide
    And bade the young dreamer in extacy rise
Now Far far behind him the green waters glide
    And the cot of his forefathers blesses his eyes.

[2] The jessamine clambers in flower o'er the thatch
    And the ⟨fl⟩swallow sings sweet from her nest in the wall
All trembling with transport he raises the latch
    And the voices of loved ones replied to his call

A father bends o'er him with looks of delight,
    His cheek is bedewed with a mothers warm tear,
And the lips of the boy in a love kiss unite
    With the lips of the maid whom his bosom holds dear.

The heart of the dreamer beats high in his breast,
    Joy quickens his pulse, all hardships seem o'er,
And a murmur of happiness steals oer his rest,
    "Oh God! thou hast blessed me I ask for no more.

Ah whence is that flash which now bursts on his eye!
    Ah whence is that sound which now larums his ear!
Tis the lightning's red glare painting hell on the sky,
    Tis the crash of the thunder, the groan of the sphere.

He springs from his hammock he flies to the deck
    Amazement confronts him with images dire
Wild winds and waves drive the vessel a wreck
    The masts fly in splinters, the shrouds are on fire!

Like mountains the billows tremendously swell,
    — In vain the lost wretch calls on Mary to save,
Unseen hands of spirits are ringing his knell,
    And the ⟨angel of⟩ death-angel flaps his broad wing o'er the wave.

Oh sailor boy! woe to thy dream of delight,
    In darkness dissolves the gay frost work of bliss,
Where now is the picture thy fancy touched bright,
    Thy parents fond pressure, and loves honeyed kiss?

Oh sailor boy, sailor boy! never again
    Shall home, love, or kindred thy wishes repay,
But unblest and unhonoured, down deep in the main,
    Full many a score fathom, thy bones shall decay.

On beds of green sea-flower thy limbs shall be laid,
Around thy white bones the red coral shall grow,
Of thy fair yellow locks threads of amber be made,
And every part suit to its mansion below.

Days, months, years, and ages shall circle away,
And still the vast waters above thee shall roll;
Earth loses thy pattern forever and aye;
— Oh sailor boy, sailor boy, peace to thy soul!

[William Dimond]

---

[3] *Song of the Clown*

Come away, come away, death,
And in sad cypress let me be laid;
Fly away, fly away, breath;
I am slain by a fair cruel maid.
My shroud of white, stuck all with yew,
Oh, prepare it;
My part of death no one so true
Did share it.

Not a flower, not a flower sweet,
On my black coffin let there be strown;
⟨n⟩Not a friend, not a friend greet
My poor corpse, where my bones shall be thrown.
A thousand thousand sighs to save,
Lay me, oh, where
Sad true lover ne'er find my grave,
To weep there.

(Twelfth Night. [II, iv, 52–67])

The peace of Constance presented a noble opportunity to the Lombards of establishing a permanent federal union of small republics; a form of government congenial from the earliest ages to Italy, and that, perhaps, under which she is again destined one day to flourish. They were entitled by the provisions of that treaty to preserve their league the basis of a more perfect confederacy, which the course of events would have emancipated from every kind of subjection to Germany. But dark long cherished hatreds and that ⟨long⟩ implacable vindictiveness, which, at least in former ages distinguished the private manners of Italy, deformed her national character, which can only be the aggregate of individual passions. For revenge, she threw away the pearl of great price and sacrificed even the recollection of that liberty which had stalked like a majestic spirit among the ruins of Milan. It passed away, that high disdain of absolute power that steadiness

& self devotion which raised the half civilized Lombards of the twelfth century to the level of those ancient republics from whose history our first notions of freedom & virtue are derived. The victim by turns of selfish & sanguinary factions, of petty tyrants & of foreign invaders, Italy has fallen like a star from its place in heaven; she has seen her harvests trodden down by the horses of the stranger and the blood of her children wasted in quarrels not her own; *conquering or conquered*, in the indignant language of her poet, *still alike a slave*; a long retribution for the tyranny of Rome.

([Henry] Hallam's Middle Ages.)

[4] It is an advantageous circumstance for the philosophical inquirer into the history of ecclesiastical dominion, that, as it spreads itself over the vast extent of fifteen centuries, the dependence of events upon general causes, rather than on transitory combinations or the character of individuals is made more evident and the future more probably foretold from a consideration of the past than we are apt to find in political history. Five centuries have now elapsed during every one of which the authority of the Roman See has successively declined. Slowly and silently receding from their claims to temporal power, the pontiffs hardly protect their dilapidated citadel from the revolutionary concussions of modern times, the rapacity of governments, and the growing averseness to ecclesiastical influence. But if thus bearded by unmannerly and threatening innovation, they should occasionally forget that cautious policy which necessity has prescribed, if they should attempt, an unavailing expedient! to revive institutions which can be no longer operative, or principles that have died away, their defensive efforts will not be unnatural, nor ought to excite either indignation or alarm. A calm, comprehensive study of ecclesiastical history, not in such scraps and fragments as the ordinary partisans of our ephemeral literature obtrude upon us, is perhaps the best antidote to extravagant apprehensions. Those who know what Rome has once been are best able to appreciate what she is; those who have seen the thunderbolt in the hands of the Gregories and the Innocents, will hardly be intimidated at the sallies of decrepitude, the impotent dart of Priam amidst the crackling ruins of Troy. (Hallam — Ecclesiastical Power during Middle Ages)

C'est une circonstance singulierement favorable pour constituer un gouvernement fédératif, que celle ou une invasion redoutable menace un peuple libre. La ou règne la liberté le grand principe de force, c'est l'amour de la patrie; et jamais cet amour n'est si passioné, jamais il ne rémue l'ame plus profondément, que lorsque la patrie elle-même est renfermée dans d'etroites limites; que lorsque l'enceinte des memes murs vous présente le berceau de votre enfance, les temoins, les compagnons, les rivaux, au milieu desquels vous devez vous élever, la carriére qui seule vous et ouverte, l'état entier enfin, dont vous pouvez partager la souverainté avec vos concitoyens. Dans les petites republiques, chaque homme s'efforce de devenir tout ce que l'homme peut etre; dans la republique fédérée, tant que la liberté est mise en danger par un invasion, chacun des petits états déploie a son tour toute l'énergie dont il est capable. Il n'y a point de lenteur dans les délibérations, point d'hésitation dans les mèsures, parce qu'un grand intérêt, un intérêt supèrieur a tous les autres, reunit tous les esprits. Il faut se défendre, il faut vaincre, il faut repousser l'invasion, il faut briser le joug de despotisme; l'enthousiasme, dont la puissance est bien supèrieure a celle d'un gouvernement, quelque fort qu'il prétende etre, unit les états séparés, et donne un centre d'action

un

[1] The Universe[38] No. 8

un centre de puissance à cet assemblage de républiques, qu'on représente comme se foible. Les factions qui divisent souvent les villes, se calment pour ne point arrêter l'elan national vers l'indépendance; ou, si elles s'agitent encore, leurs mouvemens restent hors de l⟨a⟩'administration générale; peu importe alors le nom de la faction qui pourra triompher, la masse du peuple marchera toujours vers le meme but. S'il s'agissoit de conquérir ou d'asservir au loin des provinces, les fédérations manqueroient d'union et de force; mais, même a leur naissance, elles sont éminemment énergiques pour défendre leur liberté.

Que l'on parcoure l'histoire de toutes les fédérations, on n'en trouve pas une qui ne soit née au moment où ⟨m'en trouve pas une qui ne soit née⟩ il falloit repousser l'attaque d'un oppresseur; pas une qui n'ait triomphé d'adversaires infiniment supérieurs en nombre et en forces. Les rois de Macédoine furent vaincus par les Achéens, le duc d'Autriche par les Suisses, Philippe d'Espagne par les Hollandois, George III par les Américains. L'example des Lombards est plus remarquable encore; ils n'eurent pas besoin d'une fédération, ils ne firent usage que d'une simple ligue, mal organisée, pour secouer le joug du plus vaillant et du plus puissant des empereurs d'Occident. Tant il est vrai que dans les petits états, où le sentiment de la patrie a toute sa force, l'amour de la liberté est une arme puissante contre le despotisme!

[Jean Simonde de] Sismondi. "Histoire des Répub[liques]. Italiennes du Moyen Age." Tome II Chap xi 175p.[39]

---

[38] The title is framed in part in decorative scroll lines.

[39] This entry was doubtless made between Jan. 27 and Feb. 12, 1822, for

Bad omens attending the Commencement of hostilities when Charles I set up his standard at Nottingham Aug 22, 1642.

There appeared no Conflux of men, in obedience to the King's Proclamation, the trained Bands the Sheriff brought, being all the Guard for his Majesty's Person & standard. The Arms and ammunition were not yet come from York, and a general sadness covered the whole town; the Standard was blown down, the same night it was set up by a strong & unruly wind, and could not be fixed in a day or two, till the Tempest was allayed; this was the melancholy state of the king's affairs when his standard was set up. (Lord Clarendon.)[40]

Character of Cromwell.

He was one of those Men, whom his very enemies could not condemn without commending him at the same time; for he could never have done half that Mischief, without great Parts, Courage, Industry & Judgement; that he attempted those things which no good man durst have ventured on, and atchieved those in which none but a valiant & great man could have succeeded. — He had some great qualities, which have [2] caused the Memory of some Men, in all ages to be celebrated, and he will be looked upon by posterity, as a brave wicked man.

(Clarendon.)[41]

To the Herb Rosemary.

I Sweet scented flower! who art wont to bloom
On January's front severe
And on the wintery desert drear
To waft thy waste perfume!
Come, thou shalt form my nosegay now,
And I will bind thee round my brow;
And while I twine the mournful wreath,
I'll weave a melancholy song,
And sweet the strain shall be, & long
The melody of death.

II Come funeral flower! who lovest to dwell
With the pale corse in lonely tomb
And throw across the desert gloom
A sweet decaying smell.

Emerson quotes from the same volume in Wide World 3, pp. [23]–[24] between those dates.

[40] Either Emerson quoted very freely, or his source was defective. Cf. *The History of the Rebellion*, 6 vols., 1888, II, 291.

[41] *Ibid.*, VI, 91, 97.

Come press my lips & lie with me
Beneath the lowly Alder tree,
And we will sleep a pleasant sleep,
And not a care shall dare intrude
To break the marble solitude
So peaceful & so deep.

III And hark! the wind god as he flies
Moans hollow in the forest trees
And sailing on the gusty breeze
Mysterious music dies.
Sweet flower! that requiem wild is mine
It warns me of the lo⟨w⟩↑ne↓ly shrine
The cold turf altar of the dead;
My grave shall be in yon lone spot
Where as I lie by all forgot
A dying fragrance, thou, wilt o'er my ashes shed.
(H. Kirke White)

(Preface to one of Elizabeth's costly MASQES.)

It is a noble and just advantage, that the things subjected to the understanding, have of those which are ⟨su⟩objected to sense; that the one sort are but momentary and merely taking; the other, impressing and lasting; else the story of all these solemnies had perished like a blaze and gone out in the beholder's eyes. So short-lived are the bodies of all things in comparison of their souls. And though bodies, ofttimes, [3] have the ill luck to be sensually preferred, they find afterward the good ⟨luck⟩ fortune (when souls live) to be utterly forgotten.
(BEN JONSON'S [Hymenaei)]

To a Water fowl.

1 Whither mid falling dews,
While glow the heavens with the last steps of day,
Far through their rosy depths, dost thou pursue
Thy solitary way?

2 Vainly the fowler's eye
Might mark thy distant flight, to do thee wrong,
As darkly painted on the crimson sky,
Thy figure floats along.

3 Seekst thou the plashy brink
Of weedy lake, or marge of river wide;

Or where the rocking billows rise and sink
On the vexed ocean side?

4 There is a Power, whose care
Teaches thy way along the pathless coast, —
The desert and illimitable air,
— Lone wandering, but not lost.

5 All day thy wings have fanned
At that far height, the cold thin atmosphere,
Yet stoop not weary to the welcome land,
Though the dark night is near.

6 For soon that toil shall end;
Soon shalt thou find a summer home, and rest
And scream among thy fellows; reeds shall bend
Soon oer thy sheltered nest.

7 Thou art gone; — the abyss of heaven
Hath swallowed up thy form, yet in my heart
Deeply hath sunk the lesson thou hast given,
And shall not soon depart.

8 He that from zone to zone,
Guides through the trackless air thy certain flight,
— In the long way that I must tread alone,
Will guide my steps aright.

(W. C. Bryant's Poems.)

[4] Close of the "Decline & Fall."

I have presumed to mark the moment of conception: I shall now commemorate the hour of my final deliverance. It was on the day, or rather the night, of the 27th of June 1787, between the hours of eleven and twelve that I wrote the last lines of the last page, ⟨of⟩ in a summer house, in my garden. After laying down the pen I took several turns in a berceau or covered walk of acacias, which commands a prospect of the country, the lake, and the mountains. The air was temperate, the sky was serene, the silver orb of the moon was reflected from the waters and all nature was silent. I will not dissemble the first emotions of joy on the recovery of my freedom, and, perhaps the establishment of my fame. But my pride was soon humbled and a sober melancholy was spread over my mind by the idea that I had taken an everlasting leave of an old and agreeable companion, and that whatsoever might be the date of my History, the life of the historian must be short and precarious.

(Gibbon's Memoirs of his own life and Writings.)
"Miscell. Works," Vol I

Therefore we may compare our student to a man who has a river running through his grounds which divides into a multitude of channels: if he dams up all the rest, the stream will flow in the one he leaves open; if he finds it breaking out into sidebranches, he can keep it within bounds by stopping up the outlets; if he percieves the course it takes ineffectual for his purpose, he can throw a mound across and let it overflow at any gap he judges convenient. The water runs by its own strength without any impulse from the man, and whatever he does to it, will find a vent somewhere or other: he may turn, alter or direct its motion, but neither gave, nor can take it away. So it is with our thoughts which are perpetually working as long as we wake, and sometimes longer beyond our power to restrain. We may controul them, divert them into different courses, conduct them this way or that as we deem requisite, but can never totally prevent them from moving.

([Abraham] Tucker's Light of Nature. p. 13 Vol I)

Deliberation and investigation are like the hunting of a hound, he moves and sniffs about by his own activity, but the scent he finds, is not laid, nor the train he follows, drawn by himself. (Ibid p. 11)

Catalogue of Books Read

1819–1824

Emerson began this record of his reading in December of his junior year at Harvard. Only one date, December 1819, appears in the fragment of manuscript, but the record almost certainly covers, though by no means exhaustively, Emerson's reading from 1819 to 1824.

The manuscript, perhaps originally a part of a small notebook, is composed of two sheets, folded folio and tied together by thread that pierces the left margin. The pages are numbered consecutively in ink, beginning with 9 on the recto of the first leaf and ending with 16 on the verso of the final leaf. The leaves are slightly irregular, with crumbling edges, and measure 15.2 x 9.4 cm. The recto of the first leaf (numbered 9) includes the title.

[9] CATALOGUE[1]—

of Books read from the date December 1819—
in order of time.

Don Juan
Alison on Taste
(E. T.)—Channings In↑au↓gural discourse
Ben Jonson's Life & Every Man in his humour
Every man out of his humour
Joanna Baillie's Plays 1. Vol.
Human life a Poem by [Samuel] Rogers
[Thomas] Campbell's Essay on English Poetry
North American Review, E[dward]. Ev[erett]. Ed[itor].

[1] A bibliography and a chronology of the books in the Catalogue appear in "Early Reading List." The dates there supplied for some readings are questionable or erroneous.

Club Room, NO I.
[Thomas] Blackwa[e]ll's Life & Writings of Homer.
[Robert] Lowth's Lectures on Hebrew Poetry
Sketch Book No. 5
Bacon's Essays
Dacier's Plato's Dialogues I. Vol.
[Scott] Bridal of Triermain
Crabbe — I. Vol
Reread one Vol. [Charles] Rollin [Ancient History?]
Burke's Regicide Peace.
Hobhouse's Illustrations of Childe Harold
[10] [Robert] Bissett's Life of Burke
Edinburgh Review [no.] LXIV
Club Room No 2
Sketch Book No 6th
Asiatick Miscellany
[Scott] Ivanhoe
North American (No 2 New Series)
Warton's observations on the Faery Queen
[Basil] Kennet[t]'s lives & charac[ters]. of Greek Poets
[William] Wirt's Life of Patrick Henry
Trial of Michael Powars!!!
[Joseph] Berington's Abelard & Eloisa
[John] Gillies' Greece — Vol. I.
Johnson Vol. 2 — Prefaces. —
[George] Burnett's Specimens of [English] Prose Writers
Club Room No 3
[James] Harris, Three treatises.
Quarterly Review Nos.
Edinburgh Rev. No LXV
[11] [Thomas] Lyttleton's letters
Ben Jonson's Discoveries
North American Review (No 3)
[Smollett] Peregrine Pickle
[Scott] Monastery —
[William] Godwin's life of Chaucer

[Pierre] Brumoy's Greek Theatre 1 Volume—
(Re-read) [Scott] Bride of Lammermoor
Ben Jonson's—Alchemist—Volpone—Silent Woman
[Jeremiah] Joyce's Scientifick Dialogues
Aristophanes' "Clouds" (Latin Translation)
Euripides'—Polynices & Eteocles Ibid—
[Conyers] Middleton's Life of Cicero
Bacon's Novum Organum.
[John G. Lockhart] Peter's letters to his Kinsfolk.
[William Tudor] Letters on the Eastern States.
First Vols. of old novels. [Scott] Antiquary. Rob Roy &
[Charles Maturin] Fatal Revenge
also Reviews—(College library shut up)

Massinger's Plays ⟨4 Vols 8vo⟩
North American Review
Two Volumes of Swift
North american Review
Two Volumes of Swift
[12] [Henry H. Milman] Fall of Jerusalem
[Scott] The abbott
[Joseph] Priestley's Heathen Philosophy
[William] Drummond's ⟨a⟩Academical ⟨q⟩Questions
[Edward] Everett's Dedication Sermon. March 1821
[Cotton] Mather's Magnalia
[Dugald] Stewart's Dissertation I.
Volume of Swift
Do. of Bacon
Bacon's letters.
Three Vols. of Ben Jonson
[Nathan] Drake's Essays on Tatler &c
[Charles] Symmon's life of Milton
[Francis] Wrangham's Brit[ish]. Plut[arch]. Vol 3
Ed. Reviews &c &c
Byron's Marino Faliero
FEDERALIST
Vol. of Bacon

[Fielding] Tom Jones
1 Vol of Beaumont & Fletcher
1 Vol of Comte [Louis] de Tressan [Oeuvres Choisies]
[Joseph] Strutt's Sports
3 vols of Beaumont & Fletcher
[13] 2 Vols of Comte de Tressan
Vol of Burns
[Thomas] McCrie's life of Knox
[Montesquieu] Persanes Lettres
[Montesquieu] Grandeur et Decadence des Romains
The Judgement — [James] Hillhouse
[Jane Marcet] Conversations on Political Economy
[Moliére] Bou↑r↓geois Gentilhomme
1 Vol. of Baron [Friedrich] de Grimm [Correspondence Littéraire]
1 Vol. of [Jean Simonde de] Sismondi's — Spanish Literature
[Joseph Acosta] Burdens of the Nations
North American Review
II & III Vol. of Sismondi's Southern Literature
[Samuel Webber] Logan
1 Vol. of Sam. Clarke [2]
Hallam's Middle Ages
[Scott] Pirate
Byron's tragedies
5 Volumes of Gibbon's Decl. & Fall
[Thomas] Erskine's Revealed Religion
A[lexander] Everett's "*Europe*"
Reviews, &c
More's Utopia
Sismondi
[14] [Maximilien de Bethune, duc de] Sully's Memoirs. 4 Vols
[Henri] Lemair's Fr. Revolution 3 Vols.
Stewart's Dissertation II Part

[2] "A Demonstration of the Being and Attributes of God," in vol. 2 of Sampson Letsome and John Nicholl, eds., *A Defence of Natural and Revealed Religion.*

[John] Playfair's do parts I & II
[William T.] Brande's do. Chemistry
Captain Cook's Voyages
Life of Burns
1 Vol of Milton's Prose Works
[Scott] Fortunes of Nigel
[Scott] Quentin Durward
[Scott] St Ronan's Well
[Scott] Redgauntlet
[Catherine Marie Sedgwick] Redwood
[Jeremy] Taylor's Holy dying
2 Vols [Edward T. W.] Polehampton's Gallery
[John] Leland's Adv[antage]. & Nec[essity]. of Revelation 2 Vols
Edin[burgh]. N[orth]. A[merican]. Reviews — much.
4 Vols of Gibbon
[James] Mackintosh's Introd. Lecture
1 Vol of Burke
[Levi] Frisbie's Writings
2 Vols of Franklin's Works
Hume's Essays 2 Vols
[15] Boileau's poetic works
Voltaire's Charles XII
[Samuel Mather] Life of Saml[Cotton] Mather
Misanthrope of Mol[iére]
[Edward] Everett's Φ B K Oration
[James] Sullivan's Hist of Maine
[Jeremy] Belknap's New Hampshire

Editorial Title List
Alphabetical Title List
Textual Notes
Index

Editorial Title List

This list follows the arrangement and order originally given to the collection by the Houghton Library. Changes or additions in the original list have been made in order to include only Emerson's holograph journals and miscellaneous notebooks. Thus the volumes of personalia of friends and family members that are not in Emerson's hand have been excluded and other items that were not originally in the collection have been added. Houghton numbers 1 through 91, which were the basis of the 1909–1914 edition, contain the majority of the regular journals and some miscellaneous notebooks. Numbers 91a through 121, almost entirely miscellaneous notebooks, are unpublished but dated volumes, from 1824 to 1875, and account books (1828–1882). The remaining items, Houghton 122 through 197, are unpublished miscellaneous notebooks, mostly undated, and pocket diaries. The journals in the first series run in chronological order from 1819 to 1877 and might be grouped, however roughly, as journals of the 1820's (Houghton 1–22, 91), the 1830's (Houghton 23–37), the 1840's (Houghton 38–58), the 1850's (Houghton 59–74), the 1860's (Houghton 75–85), and with less assurance the 1870's (Houghton 86–90). The dating is only approximate, and there is much overlapping, especially in the later years. Chronology, moreover, is as often as not subservient to ideas in these and all the Emerson journals other than account books, pocket diaries, and memoranda of engagements. The dates are therefore elastic and should be extended to include the later periods in which Emerson reviewed, quoted from, or added to the journals.

If all of Emerson's holograph journals and notebooks are counted, excluding the loose pages of journal material scattered about among the collection, there are 234 items, broken down as follows:

171 regular journals or notebooks;

9 additional journals which are double-enders, or volumes kept at different times but within the same covers and written from

back to front as well as from front to back (Houghton 16.1, 23.1, 44.1, 69.1, 80.1, 98.1, 112.1, 140.1, and 143b.1);

9 notebooks that contain Emerson's copies of the letters or personalia of various friends and family members (Houghton 101, 111, 117, 143c, 145, 146–149);

1 notebook that is late and almost completely unused (Houghton 134);

12 account books (Houghton 112–112j, 143b), and the covers of 1 account book (Houghton 194e);

31 pocket diaries (Houghton 163–193).

To this list are added two items, Emerson's "Universe No. 7" in the Pierpont Morgan Library and the transcript of the miscellaneous notebook "WO (Liberty)," the last item on the list.

EDITORIAL TITLE LIST

HOUGHTON NUMBER	DESIGNATION BY EMERSON OR OTHERS	EDITORS' TITLE	ABBREVIATED TITLE
1	No. XVII [Cabot's A] [1]	No. XVII	XVII
2	The Wide World No. 1 [Cabot's D]	Wide World 1	WW 1

[1] Emerson's numbering of his early journals was sometimes systematic, sometimes erratic, but it may be hypothetically reconstructed. The early regular journals he first designated "The Wide World," and gave each an Arabic number from one through twelve. Journals nine through twelve he later designated by the letters I, K, L, M, and still later sewed them together in a single gathering, changing only the letter I to the Roman numeral IX by adding X, and then enclosing the gathering in a folder with the Roman numerals IX, X, XI, and XII on the outside. The following journal he designated "Wide World No. XIII" and began it with the entry "(Continued from W. 13)" — an error for "W. 12." He then dropped "The Wide World" as a title and used the abbreviation "No." with a Roman numeral through "No. XVI." He temporarily dropped titles completely (see Houghton numbers 17 and 18). Then he used a variety of titles, like "Blotting Book," which was also used to designate commonplace books. He entitled travel journals usually by the place visited. In 1833 he began the long series of regular journals with alphabetical titles, though he did not follow the alphabet systematically.

It must have been some time after he had used the Roman numeral "XVI" for a regular journal that he supplied "XVII" and "XVIII" (twice) for three early miscellaneous notebooks. A close study of the Roman numeral titles in the manuscript

HOUGHTON NUMBER	DESIGNATION BY EMERSON OR OTHERS	EDITORS' TITLE	ABBREVIATED TITLE
4 [2]	No. XVIII [Cabot's B]	No. XVIII	XVIII
5	The Wide World No. 2 [Cabot's E]	Wide World 2	WW 2
6	The Universe No. 1 [Cabot's C]	Universe 1	U 1
6a	The Universe No. 2 [Cabot's C]	Universe 2	U 2
6b	The Universe No. 3 [Cabot's C]	Universe 3	U 3
6c	The Universe No. 4 [Cabot's C]	Universe 4	U 4
6d	The Universe No. 5 [Cabot's C]	Universe 5	U 5
6e	The Universe No. 6 [Cabot's C]	Universe 6	U 6
— [3]	The Universe No. 7	Universe 7	U 7
6f	The Universe No. 7 [Cabot's C]	Universe 7[A]	U 7[A]
6g	The Universe No. 8 [Cabot's C]	Universe 8	U 8
7	The Wide World No. 3 [Cabot's F]	Wide World 3	WW 3
8	The Wide World No. 4 [Cabot's G]	Wide World 4	WW 4
9	The Wide World No. 6 [Cabot's I] [4]	Wide World 6	WW 6
10	The Wide World No. 7 [Cabot's J]	Wide World 7	WW 7
11	The Wide World No. 8 [Cabot's K]	Wide World 8	WW 8

reveals that each title was written after other material had been put on the page. In numbering Houghton 16.1 "No. XVIII" Emerson apparently forgot that he had already used that number for Houghton 4. Why he gave the title "No. II" (Houghton 93a) to a miscellaneous notebook given over to a discussion of God is not clear. A "No. I" may be implied; but lacking positive evidence like that for the existence of "Wide World 5" and "No. XIV" (see below, notes 3 and 5), the editors have not included a "No. I" in the list.

Whatever Emerson's system, there is no evidence to support Professor Bliss Perry's speculation that sixteen early journals are missing. He may well have been misled by the fact that according to Cabot the earliest journal was numbered "XVII."

[2] Houghton 3 is omitted because it is not Emerson's holograph manuscript. It is a notebook containing records of the nameless college literary society of which Emerson was for a time secretary.

[3] In The Pierpont Morgan Library.

[4] Besides the gap in Emerson's numbering, two pieces of evidence point to the existence of Wide World 5. First, Cabot arranged the early journals in what seemed to him to be the chronological order, giving a letter to each volume. Volumes lettered A through G, and I through V exist. The missing H would have gone on to the journal following G. Secondly, there is a chronological gap between Cabot's G and I. G (Houghton 8) has dated passages from February 22 to March 10, 1822. I (Houghton 9) has dated passages from April 14 to July 10, 1822. The volumes immediately preceding G and immediately following I show that at the time Emerson was writing quite regularly in his journal — sometimes as much as six days a week. It seems unlikely that he would have given up the practice for five weeks. The

HOUGHTON NUMBER	DESIGNATION BY EMERSON OR OTHERS	EDITORS' TITLE	ABBREVIATED TITLE
12	The Wide World No. 9 [Cabot's L] [5]	Wide World 9	WW 9
12a	The Wide World No. 10 [Cabot's L]	Wide World 10	WW 10
12b	The Wide World No. 11 [Cabot's L]	Wide World 11	WW 11
12c	The Wide World No. 12 [Cabot's L]	Wide World 12	WW 12
13	The Wide World No. XIII [Cabot's N]	Wide World XIII	WW XIII
14	No. XV [Cabot's O] [6]	No. XV	XV
15	No. XVI [Cabot's S]	No. XVI	XVI
16	[Cabot's M]	College Theme Book	CTB
16.1	No. XVIII [Cabot's M]	No. XVIII[A]	XVIII[A]
17	[Cabot's Q]	Journal 1826	J 1826
18	[Cabot's R]	Journal 1826–1828	J 1826–28
19	Charleston South Carolina, St. Augustine, Florida [Cabot's U]	Charleston, St. Augustine	CSA
20	Mem. for Journal St. Augustine	Memo St. Augustine	Memo SA
21	Sermons and Journals	Sermons and Journals	S and J
22	Blotting Book Y	Blotting Book Y	BB Y
23	Blotting Book No. IV	Blotting Book IV	BB IV
23.1	————	Blotting Book IV[A]	BB IV[A]
24	Blotting Book Ψ	Blotting Book Psi	BB Psi
25	Blotting Book No. III Ω	Blotting Book III	BB III
26	Q	Q	Q
27	Sicily [Cabot's 1]	Sicily	Sicily
28	Italy [Cabot's 2]	Italy	Italy
29	[Cabot's 3]	Italy and France	It and Fr
30	[Cabot's 4]	Scotland and England	Scot and Eng
31	[Cabot's 5]	Notebook 1833	N 1833
32	Visits to Maine, France England	France and England	Fr and Eng

combination of evidence from these journals and from the missing letter H indicates that a journal is lost. The editor of the first edition wrote that "Wide World, No. 5, is missing from the Journals" (*J*, I, 131).

[5] Wide World 9, 10, 11, and 12 were subsequently sewn together and enclosed in a folder with the designations, IX, X, XI, XII, but the Arabic numerals Emerson used appear to have been his original designation.

[6] That No. XIV is missing is apparent from the gap in Emerson's numbering and from his note in No. XV, p. 1: "Continued from p. 40, No. XIV."

HOUGHTON NUMBER	DESIGNATION BY EMERSON OR OTHERS	EDITORS' TITLE	ABBREVIATED TITLE
32.1	———	Sea 1833	Sea 1833
32.2	———	Maine	Maine
33	A	A	A
34	B	B	B
35	C	C	C
36	D	D	D
37	E	E	E
38	F No. 2	F No. 2	F^2
39	G	G	G
40	H	H	H
41	J	J	J
42	K	K	K
43	N	N	N
44	Z	Z	Z
44.1	Z[A]	Z[A]	Z[A]
45	R	R	R
46	U	U	U
47	V	V	V
48	W	W	W
49	Y	Y	Y
50	O	O	O
51	AB	AB	AB
52	CD	CD	CD
53	GH	GH	GH
54	LM	LM	LM
55	ED (England)	ED	ED
56	London	London	London
57	RS	RS	RS
58	TU	TU	TU
59	AZ	AZ	AZ
60	BO	BO	BO
61	BO (Conduct of Life)	BO Conduct	BOC
62	CO	CO	CO
63	DO	DO	DO
64	GO	GO	GO
65	VS	VS	VS
66	HO	HO	HO

HOUGHTON NUMBER	DESIGNATION BY EMERSON OR OTHERS	EDITORS' TITLE	ABBREVIATED TITLE
67	IO	IO	IO
68	NO	NO	NO
69	RO	RO	RO
69.1	————	RO Mind	ROM
70	SO	SO	SO
71	ZO	ZO	ZO
72	VO	VO	VO
73	AC	AC	AC
74	CL	CL	CL
75	DL	DL	DL
76	GL	GL	GL
77	WAR (War & Politics & Washington City)	WAR	WAR
78	VA	VA	VA
79	FOR (Forces and Forms)	FOR	FOR
80	KL	KL	KL
80.1	————	KL[A]	KL[A]
81	ML (Moral Law)	ML	ML
81a	LN	LN	LN
82	XO (Inexorable; Reality and Illusion)	XO	XO
83	IT (Natural History of Intellect)	IT	IT
84	NY	NY	NY
85	ST	ST	ST
86	PH (Philosophy)	PH	PH
87	TO (Intellect, the Guardian)	TO	TO
88	IL (Notes on Intellect)	IL	IL
89	EO (Fate	EO	EO
90	PY (Theory of Poetry)	PY	PY
91	Walk to the Connecticut	Walk to the Connecticut	W Conn
91a	Encyclopedia	Encyclopedia	Enc
92	NP (New Poetry)	NP	NP
93	Collectanea	Collectanea	Coll
93a	No. II [Cabot's P]	No. II	II
94	Blotting Book No. I [Cabot's T]	Blotting Book I	BB I
95	Blotting Book No. II [Cabot's V]	Blotting Book II	BB II
96	School Record Preaching Record	School and Preaching	S and P

HOUGHTON NUMBER	DESIGNATION BY EMERSON OR OTHERS	EDITORS' TITLE	ABBREVIATED TITLE
97	T (Transcript)	T	T
98	L (Concord)	L Concord	L Con
98.1	L (Lectures on Literature)	L Literature	L Lit
99	Naturalist	Naturalist	Nat
100	F No 1	F No. 1	F^1
101	C. C. E.	Charles C. Emerson	CCE
102	Φ	Phi	Phi
103	Δ	Delta	Delta
104	Index Minor (1843)	Index Minor 1843	In Mi 1843
104a	————	Index Summary	In Sum
105	JK	JK	JK
106	Index Major (1847)	Index Major 1847	In Ma 1847
107	Index II	Index II	In II
107a	Platoniana	Index Platoniana	In Plato
108	OP Gulistan	OP Gulistan	OP Gul
109	England and Paris 1847–1848	England and Paris	Eng and Par
109a	Journal at the West	Journal at the West	J West
110	Ψ	Index Psi	In Psi
111	Margaret Fuller Ossoli	Margaret Fuller Ossoli	MFO
112	Account Book (1828–1835) [7]	Account Book 1	Acc B 1
112.1	Warren Lot Hedge Fence	Warren Lot	W Lot
112a	Account Book (1836–1840)	Account Book 2	Acc B 2
112b	Account Book (1840–1844)	Account Book 3	Acc B 3
112c	Account Book (1845–1849)	Account Book 4	Acc B 4
112d	Account Book (1849–1853)	Account Book 5	Acc B 5
112e	Account Book (1853–1859)	Account Book 6	Acc B 6
112f	Account Book (1859–1865)	Account Book 7	Acc B 7
112g	Account Book (1865–1872)	Account Book 8	Acc B 8
112h	Account Book (1872–1882)	Account Book 9	Acc B 9
112i	Account Book (1836–1848)	Account Book 10	Acc B 10
112j	Account Book (1848–1872)	Account Book 11	Acc B 11
113	RT (Rhetoric)	RT	RT
114	EA (England and America)	EA	EA

[7] An additional account book of this period has been destroyed, only the two hard covers surviving among the Emerson papers (Houghton 194e). The front cover is entitled "Ledger" and the back cover includes the date "May 30, 1835" along with other notes, sketches, and mathematical figures.

HOUGHTON NUMBER	DESIGNATION BY EMERSON OR OTHERS	EDITORS' TITLE	ABBREVIATED TITLE
115	Orientalist	Orientalist	Orient
116	BL (Book of Lectures)	BL	BL
117	HT (Henry Thoreau)	Henry Thoreau	HT
118	WA (Country Life; Walking)	WA	WA
119	ΦB	Phi Beta	Phi Beta
120	CR (Criticism)	CR	CR
121	QL (Queries on Literature)	QL	QL
122	S (Salvage)	S	S
122a	Blue Book	Blue Book	Blue B
123	NQ (Notes and Queries)	NQ	NQ
124	Parnassus	Parnassus	Parn
125	Trees	Trees	Trees
125a	Trees	Trees[A]	Trees[A]
126	EL	EL	EL
127	EF	EF	EF
128	Dialling	Dialling	Dial
129	Books	Books Large	Books L
130	Books	Books Small	Books S
131	IM (Index Minor)	Index Minor[A]	In Mi[A]
132	X	X	X
133	Rhymer	Rhymer	Rhymer
134	Old Man	Old Man	Old Man
134a	Morals	Morals	Morals
135	LI (Literature)	LI	LI
136	P	P	P
137	OP	OP	OP
138	OS (Odd Sayings)	OS	OS
139	L (Camadeva)	L Camadeva	L Cam
140	ART	ART	ART
140.1	Man	Man	Man
141	LO (Beauty and Art)	LO	LO
142	Σ (Anecdotes)	Sigma	Sigma
142a	Xenien	Xenien	Xenien
143	Catalogue of Books Read	Catalogue of Books Read	CBR
143a	Meredith Village (1829)	Meredith Village	Mer Vil
143b	Account Book (1853–1854)	Account Book 6[A]	Acc B6[A]
143b.1	Notes on Gardening	Gardening	Garden

HOUGHTON NUMBER	DESIGNATION BY EMERSON OR OTHERS	EDITORS' TITLE	ABBREVIATED TITLE
143c	ABA (Alcott)	Amos Bronson Alcott	ABA
144	ETE (Verses)	ETE	ETE
145	CKN (Charles K. Newcomb)	Charles K. Newcomb	CKN
146	MME 1	Mary Moody Emerson 1	MME 1
147	MME 2	Mary Moody Emerson 2	MME 2
148	MME 3	Mary Moody Emerson 3	MME 3
149	MME 4	Mary Moody Emerson 4	MME 4
153 [8]	Collectanea	Collectanea[A]	Coll[A]
163	Pocket Diary (1820–1847)	Pocket Diary 1	PD 1
164	Pocket Diary (1833)	Pocket Diary 2	PD 2
165	Pocket Diary (1868)	Pocket Diary 19	PD 19
166	Pocket Diary (1848)	Pocket Diary 3	PD 3
167	Pocket Diary (1853)	Pocket Diary 4	PD 4
168	Pocket Diary (1854)	Pocket Diary 5	PD 5
169	Pocket Diary (1855)	Pocket Diary 6	PD 6
170	Pocket Diary (1856)	Pocket Diary 7	PD 7
171	Pocket Diary (1857)	Pocket Diary 8	PD 8
172	Pocket Diary (1858)	Pocket Diary 9	PD 9
173	Pocket Diary (1859)	Pocket Diary 10	PD 10
174	Pocket Diary (1859–1860)	Pocket Diary 11	PD 11
175	Pocket Diary (1860)	Pocket Diary 12	PD 12
176	Pocket Diary (1865)	Pocket Diary 16	PD 16
177	Pocket Diary (1861)	Pocket Diary 13	PD 13
178	Pocket Diary (1863)	Pocket Diary 14	PD 14
179	Pocket Diary (1878)	Pocket Diary 29	PD 29
180	Pocket Diary (1864)	Pocket Diary 15	PD 15
181	Pocket Diary (1866)	Pocket Diary 17	PD 17
182	Pocket Diary (1867)	Pocket Diary 18	PD 18

[8] Fourteen numbered items in the Houghton collection are here omitted because they are not Emerson's holograph manuscripts. These include three notebooks of Emerson's father (Houghton 150, 151, 152), one notebook of his brother William Emerson (Houghton 154), three notebooks of his brother Edward B. Emerson (Houghton 155, 156, 156a), a notebook, a journal, and a versebook of Ellen Tucker Emerson (Houghton 157, 158, 158a), a notebook of Benjamin P. Hunt (Houghton 159), a notebook of Mary Moody Emerson (Houghton 160), a notebook of transcriptions made by Margaret Fuller Ossoli (Houghton 161), and Emerson's Atlas (Houghton 162). Some of these volumes contain notes or marginalia by Emerson.

HOUGHTON NUMBER	DESIGNATION BY EMERSON OR OTHERS	EDITORS' TITLE	ABBREVIATED TITLE
183	Pocket Diary (1869)	Pocket Diary 20	PD 20
184	Pocket Diary (1870)	Pocket Diary 21	PD 21
185	Pocket Diary (1871)	Pocket Diary 22	PD 22
186	Pocket Diary (1872)	Pocket Diary 23	PD 23
187	Pocket Diary (1873)	Pocket Diary 24	PD 24
188	Pocket Diary (1874)	Pocket Diary 25	PD 25
189	Pocket Diary (1875)	Pocket Diary 26	PD 26
190	Pocket Diary (1876)	Pocket Diary 27	PD 27
191	Pocket Diary (1877)	Pocket Diary 28	PD 28
192	Pocket Diary (1879)	Pocket Diary 30	PD 30
193	Pocket Diary (1880)	Pocket Diary 31	PD 31
194	Genealogy	Genealogy	Gene
194a	Laws of Composition	Composition	Comp
194b	Sea-Notes 1847	Sea-notes 1847	Sea 1847
194c	Notebook Miscellaneous	Notebook Miscellany	N Misc
194d	Autobiographical Miscellany	Autobiography Miscellany	Auto Misc
194e	Account Book	Account Book covers	Acc B covers
194f	Index Swedenborg	Index Swedenborg	In Swed
195	Autobiography	Autobiography	Auto
196	Parnassus Scraps	Parnassus Scraps	Parn Sc
197 [9]	The Palimpsest	Palimpsest	Pal
———	WO (Liberty) [10]	WO	WO

[9] The last two numbered items in the Houghton collection are also omitted because they are not Emerson's holograph manuscripts: a commonplace book of Ruth Haskins (Houghton 198), and a notebook of Edward Waldo Emerson (Houghton 199).

[10] This notebook apparently exists only in the form of a transcript in Houghton Library, probably prepared for the 1909–1914 edition, but not used. The original existed as late as 1903 or 1904, when Edward W. Emerson wrote that "One of the most interesting of Mr. Emerson's manuscript books is that which is called *Liberty*. . . . ," and went on to describe its contents (*W*, VI, 332). Because the transcript furnishes some kind of text, and because the original may sometime be found, WO (Liberty) is included in the list.

ALPHABETICAL TITLE LIST WITH HOUGHTON NUMBER

EDITORS' TITLE	HOUGHTON NUMBER	EDITORS' TITLE	HOUGHTON NUMBER
A	33	CO	62
AB	51	Collectanea	93
AC	73	Collectanea[A]	153
Account Books (1–11)	112	College Theme Book	16
Account Book 6[A]	143b	Composition	194a
Account Book covers	194e	CR	120
Amos Bronson Alcott	143c	D	36
ART	140	Delta	103
Autobiography	195	Dialling	128
Autobiography Miscellany	194d	DL	75
AZ	59	DO	63
B	34	E	37
BL	116	EA	114
Blotting Book I	94	ED	55
Blotting Book II	95	EF	127
Blotting Book III	25	EL	126
Blotting Book IV	23	Encyclopedia	91a
Blotting Book IV[A]	23.1	England and Paris	109
Blotting Book Psi	24	EO	89
Blotting Book Y	22	ETE	144
Blue Book	122a	F No. 1	100
BO	60	F. No. 2	38
BO Conduct	61	FOR	79
Books Large	129	France and England	32
Books Small	130	G	39
C	35	Gardening	143b.1
Catalogue of Books Read	143	Genealogy	194
CD	52	GH	53
Charles C. Emerson	101	GL	76
Charles K. Newcomb	145	GO	64
Charleston, St. Augustine	19	H	40
CL	74	Henry Thoreau	117

EDITORS' TITLE	HOUGHTON NUMBER	EDITORS' TITLE	HOUGHTON NUMBER
HO	66	Memo St. Augustine	20
IL	88	Meredith Village	143a
Index II	107	ML	81
Index Major 1847	106	Morals	134a
Index Minor 1843	104	N	43
Index Minor[A]	131	Naturalist	99
Index Platoniana	107a	NO	68
Index Psi	110	No. II	93a
Index Summary	104a	No. XV	14
Index Swedenborg	194f	No. XVI	15
IO	67	No. XVII	1
IT	83	No. XVIII	4
Italy	28	No. XVIII[A]	16.1
Italy and France	29	Notebook 1833	31
J	41	Notebook Miscellany	194c
JK	105	Notebook Sc	194d
Journal 1826	17	NP	92
Journal 1826–1828	18	NQ	123
Journal at the West	109a	NY	84
K	42	O	50
KL	80	Old Man	134
KL[A]	80.1	OP	137
L Camadeva	139	OP Gulistan	108
L Concord	98	Orientalist	115
LI	135	OS	138
L Literature	98.1	P	136
LM	54	Palimpsest	197
LN	81a	Parnassus	124
LO	141	Parnassus Scraps	196
London	56	PH	86
Maine	32.2	Phi	102
Man	140.1	Phi Beta	119
Margaret Fuller Ossoli	111	Pocket Diaries (1–31)	163–193
Mary Moody Emerson 1	146	PY	90
Mary Moody Emerson 2	147	Q	26
Mary Moody Emerson 3	148	QL	121
Mary Moody Emerson 4	149	R	45

EDITORS' TITLE	HOUGHTON NUMBER	EDITORS' TITLE	HOUGHTON NUMBER
Rhymer	133	VA	78
RO	69	VO	72
RO Mind	69.1	VS	65
RS	57	W	48
RT	113	WA	118
S	122	Walk to the Connecticut	91
School and Preaching	96	WAR	77
Scotland and England	30	Warren Lot	112.1
Sea 1833	32.1	Wide World 1	2
Sea-notes 1847	194b	Wide World 2	5
Sermons and Journals	21	Wide World 3	7
Sicily	27	Wide World 4	8
Sigma	142	Wide World 6	9
SO	70	Wide World 7	10
ST	85	Wide World 8	11
T	97	Wide World 9–12	12
TO	87	Wide World XIII	13
Trees	125	WO	—
Trees[A]	125a	X	132
TU	58	Xenien	142a
U	46	XO	82
Universe 1–6, 7[A], 8	6	Y	49
Universe 7	[Morgan]	Z	44
		Z[A]	44.1
V	47	ZO	71

Textual Notes

Wide World 1

4 does not$_2$ or cannot$_1$ **5** herefater in th⟨i⟩es↑e↓ page↑s↓ **6** Lest **9** beneathem | conversation. **11** nevertheless; **15** description. **18** bloak⟨t?⟩dt & ⟨&⟩ cruel **19** umprosperous . . . malice; | vapour, **22** ⟨a gr⟩great **23** morals; **24** nature; | Marlbororough **26** ghostly[?]

Wide World 2

34 a ⟨sel[fish?]⟩ conceited **35** celestrial | (*the Wide World*) [parentheses and underscoring dubious] **36** T⟨e⟩ab⟨e⟩ar⟨een⟩in **38** ⟨‖ruined‖⟩[?] **40** a ⟨the⟩ still **41** ⟨glo[ry]⟩visions | h⟨e⟩is ⟨stretched[?]⟩spirit **44** ⟨it as th⟩ ["as th" has been rubbed but not fully cancelled] **45** vain as, fond | crowns. **48** unbelief. | to Pythagoras$_2$ the conceit$_1$ **50** days. . X **52** that they have **53** thought; | Sun;

Wide World 3

60 ⟨su⟩↑ex↓ccess **61** aching brow$_2$ ⟨of⟩ the Statesman↑'s↓$_1$ | Merchant The art | him; He **62** given instances **69** judgement. | we ⟨deplore . . . is⟩ we **70** We presume **75** of an evil world$_2$ it could not reconcile$_1$ **76** Battle of Lignano 1176 [in pencil] **77** Comasques; **78** valley ⟨.⟩ of | Continued on next page [in pencil, by Emerson?] **80** **displayed* **82** God$_2$ gold$_1$ **87** unknown$_2$ and lost$_1$

Wide World 4

94 society. **99** The oaks | The wall-flower **100** The **101** *mind*, **105** magnificent, subject **111** Babylon;

Wide World 6

Irregular pagination in this journal is explained in the Headnote and in footnote 16 on p. 122. **115** the ⟨bo[ttom?]⟩centre **119** persevering exertion$_2$ or series of patient$_1$ | direction. | pope; **121** Atheism$_2$ and doubt$_1$ | sacrificing, | And **123** odours from **128** to vast,$_2$ to certain$_1$ **129** They **130** equalized; **131** preorgative **132** Because | recievi⟨ng⟩ [this cancellation and the preceding cancellation and insertion are in pencil] **134** blank, [the comma is added in pencil] | thin. **140** approbation; **146** for strong conceptions$_2$ ↑of its object↓ strained metaphors and refined mysticisms$_1$ | air. **147** with ↑unrivalled↓ energy$_2$ the spirit of civilization and science.$_1$ **155** the⟨m⟩ir⟨selves⟩ **157** older.

College Theme Book

162 while **166** mind there **168** the groves of literature$_2$ the schools of science$_1$ **169** The ⟨c⟩ **172** Druids$_2$ or Magi$_1$ **176** an **177** ↑b↓⟨i⟩↑u↓t | t⟨hir⟩wenty | P⟨yth⟩↑rot↓agoras **178** ↑of . . . gentlemen↓ [inserted in pencil] | ↑predatory↓ [inserted in pencil] **182** So | but **183** themes **186** Lear$_2$ & Hamlet$_1$ **188** men!

190 today. **191** And **194** ↑If . . . Genoa↓ [This sentence and the following insertion of "Genoese" are in pencil] **196** ↑Pomp↓ [inserted in pencil] | That **197** heavens. **201** ↑in↓ [inserted in pencil] | ↑with . . . mind↓ [inserted in pencil] **205** Blessed . . . God. [added in pencil]

No. XVII

207 ↑Aristotle↓ [inserted in pencil] Marcus Antoninus [cancelled in pencil] | ⟨will⟩ ↑is un-↓comm⟨and⟩on ↑&↓ admira⟨tion⟩able. | & who [uncancelled] | co⟨mpose⟩↑nceive↓ ⟨&⟩or combine ⟨& give[?] it⟩ **208** in [uncancelled] **211** degradation. **213** sorrow. **214** other some neither$_2$ are capable$_1$ | betraying & an **218** whith **231** ⟨father⟩ **235** ⟨not vocal⟩? **237** fashions son's **241** luxureous[?] **247** worm's

No. XVIII

256 distributed$_2$ & parcelled$_1$ **258** did little . . . principles$_2$ ⟨of philosophy⟩ though . . . his age$_1$ **261** Aristolte | systems$_2$ of$_3$ modern$_1$ | ⟨appearances⟩ of analogy$_2$ and adaptation$_1$ **265** parade. **272** The Discourse of the Wanderer"$_2$ ⟨in⟩ ⟨t⟩The ninth book called$_1$ **273** men. | good" **277** science$_2$ and fact$_1$ | the⟨ir⟩m ↑in↓ ⟨dis⟩them **280** transactions. **283** said; A **285** the [uncancelled] **295** of [uncancelled] **297** features$_2$ ⟨are⟩ diabolical$_1$ ⟨and⟩ poison the ↑our↓ admiration **298** Racine$_2$ and Corneille$_1$ **299** another.— **300** man and if ⟨which at first⟩ **301** During **302** ⟨darkness prospect⟩ [cancelled in ink and pencil] | ↑confined prospect and↓ [added in pencil] | ↑narrow road↓ [added in ink] | Our **309** under | The office$_2$ & character$_1$ | This **310** could lean. | merit. **315** even in the **316** England⟩ which ⟨cover | ⟨results⟩effects **317** agricultural⟨,⟩; | skill ↑as↓ to secure | ↑blessings↓ [inserted in pencil] | ↑&↓ [inserted in pencil] **326** fault a | The **328** ↑East↓ [inserted in pencil] **331** the excellence of Virtue,$_2$ in pleasing forms$_1$ | They **334** ↑Pythagorean↓ [inserted in pencil] | Deity [inserted in pencil] | ⟨great and grand⟩↑vast↓ [cancelled and inserted in pencil] **338** of ⟨its⟩ a success⟨ful mission⟩ **340** "Admiration . . . end." [written in pencil] **341** much as we regard the useless subtleties of the schoolmen$_2$ as things of remote & partial interest$_1$ **342** it settles its foundations deep in the opinions of men;$_2$ it marks the boundary line of truth and speculation;$_1$ | speculations↑;↓ **347** — the . . . ceremony — [added in pencil] **354** ↑her↓ bright enchantment$_2$ o'er his sense⟨s⟩$_1$

The Universe

368 chastised **384** LAV **385** Lacoö **386** Y[?]inow | Y[?]anfaunoo.

Index

Abraham, 62, 79, 86, 98
Abrahamic covenant, 89
Achilles, 177
Acosta, Joseph, *Masoth Hagoyim: The Burdens of the Nations*, 398
Archilochus, 31
Acusilaus, 30
Adam, Alexander, *Roman Antiquities*, 55n, 58
Addison, Joseph, 14, 233; *The Spectator*, 268, 331, 347n; *The Tattler*, 331
Adventurer, 331
Aeneas, 182
Aeschines, 32
Aeschylus, 208, 209, 289
Aesop, 210, 214
Agamemnon, 177
Alba, 77
Alba Longa, 103
Albornoz, Cardinal Gil Alvarez Carillo de, 119
Alcaeus, 31
Alcoran, see *Koran*
Alden, Samuel, 244n
Alexander I, of Russia, 16
Alexander VI, Pope, 310
Alexander the Great, 243
Alfred the Great, 193, 250
Alison, Archibald, *Essays on the Nature and Principles of Taste*, 395
Alps, 85
America, 50, 113, 127, 297, 338
American literature, 298
America, North, 156
American Revolution, 316
Amsdorf, Nikolaus von, 188
Anacreon, 31
Anaxagoras, 208, 210
Angier, John, 57
Anglo-Saxon, 329
Antoninus, Marcus Aurelius, 194n, 207, 226, 247, 258, 346, 347
Apian (Peter Bienewitz), 23
Appollonius, 226
Apollodorus the Ephesian, 157
Arab, 60, 328
Arabia, 60, 68, 305, 307, 327, 328, 345
Archelaus Physicus, 210
Aristophanes, 14, 15n, 177, 208, 209, 211, 288, 291; *The Clouds*, 178, 397
Aristotle, 175, 207, 226, 254, 261, 332; *The Metaphysics*, 178
Arno, 265
Arrian, 258, 346, 378; *Discourses of Epictetus*, 226
"Arthour and Merlin," 221n
Arthur, King, 182, 188n, 245, 294; Prince, 15
Asia, 327–328
Asiatick Miscellany, The, 396
Assyria, 62, 96, 113, 330
Athens, 177, 208, 291, 315
Aunt Mary, *see* Emerson, Mary Moody
Avignon, 117, 309
Azzo, *see* Visconti, Giovanni

Babylon, 111, 112, 146
Babylonian captivity, 308
Bacchus, 112
Bacon, Francis, 13, 24, 152, 175, 250, 261, 332, 346, 381; "Atheism," 187; "Of Beauty," 316; "Of Boldness," 276; *Essays*, 186n, 396; "Of Marriage and Single Life," 316; *Novum Organum*, 21, 259, 375, 397; *The Works*, 186n, 397
Bacon, Roger, 193
Baillie, Joanna, *Count Basil*, 220; *Plays*, 395
Barbarossa, Frederick, 78
Barnwell, Robert Woodward, 38
Barrow, Isaac, 17–19; *Sermons Preached upon Several Occasions*, 27n, 28, 368
"Battle of the books, the," 14
Bayle, Pierre, *The Dictionary Historical and Critical*, 27n, 28
Beattie, James, "The Judgment of Paris," 194, 198
Beaumont, Francis, 296
Beaumont, Francis, and John Fletcher, *Passionate Madman*, 382–383; *Works*, 28, 398
Bedouin, 328

Belisarius, 120
Belknap, Jeremy, *The History of New Hampshire*, 399
Bennett's Memorial, 135
Bentham, Jeremy, *Not Paul But Jesus*, 195; *Summary view of a work entituled Not Paul But Jesus*, 195n; *Traités sur les Principes de Législation Civile et Pénale*, review of, 344, 348
Bentley, Richard (1662–1742), 13; *A Dissertation upon the Epistles of Phalaris*, 27n, 28
Berington, Joseph, *The History of the Lives of Abeillard and Heloisa*, 361, 396
Bernoulli, John, 219
Bessarion, Johannes *or* Basilius, 366
Bible, 87, 89, 178n, 351; *Apocrypha*: II Esdras, 299; *OT*: Daniel, 204; Deuteronomy, 204; Ecclesiastes, 176; Exodus, 205; Genesis, 205; Hebrews, 204; Isaiah, 121; Job, 205; Judges (Song of Deborah), 93; Malachi, 204; Micah, 204; Proverbs, 87; Psalms 203, 204, 205; *NT*: 260–261; I Corinthians, 187, 203, 205; II Corinthians, 203, 204; Galatians, 203, 204, 205; James, 203, 205; John, 204, 205; Luke, 205; Mark, 203, 205; Matthew, 44, 204, 205; II Peter, 204; Philippians, 203, 204; Romans, 204; I Thessalonians, 205; I Timothy, 204, 205
Bienewitz, Peter, *see* Apian
Bileggio, 120
Bisset, Robert, *The Life of Edmund Burke*, 10, 396
Blackwell, Thomas, *An Enquiry into the Life and Writings of Homer*, 396
Blair, Hugh, *An Abridgement of Lectures on Rhetoric*, 56n, 58; *Lectures on Rhetoric*, 35, 215n, 229n
Blunt, Nathaniel B., 244
Boccaccio, *The Decameron*, 27, 28n
Boileau, Charles, Abbé de Beaulieu, *Homélies et Sermons sur les Évangiles du Carême*, 120
Boileau-Despréaux, Nicholas, 13; *L'Art Poétique*, 209–210; *Oeuvres*, 399
Bologna, 77, 120
Bonaparte, Napoleon, 193
Bosphorus, 69
Boston, 59, 91, 146, 157, 199n, 251, 264, 268, 304
Bowdoin Prize Dissertation, *see under* Emerson, Ralph Waldo
Boyle, Charles, 13
Boyle, Robert, 187
Braccia, 86
Brahman, 344
Brande, William Thomas, *Dissertation Third, exhibiting a General View of the Progress of Chemical Philosophy*, 399
Broughton, John Cam Hobhouse, *Historical Illustrations of the Fourth Canto of Childe Harold*, 396
Brown, Thomas, *Lectures on the Philosophy of the Human Mind*, 186n–187, 197
Brumoy, Pierre, *Théâtre des Grecs*, 397
Brutus, Marcus Junius, 260
Bryant, William Cullen, "The Murdered Traveller," 353; "To a Waterfowl," 353, 393
Buchanan, Claudius, *Christian Researches in Asia*, 132
Buchanan, George, *The History of Scotland*, 27
Buckminster, Joseph, *Sermons*, 129
Burdino, *see* Gregory VIII
Burke, Edmund, 10, 111, 192, 250; *Letters on a Regicide Peace*, 10, 348, 396; *The Works*, 399
Burnett, George, *Specimens of English Prose Writers*, 364, 365, 366, 396
Burns, Robert, *The Works*, 398, 399; *Life*, 399
Burr, Aaron, 318–319, 327, 339
Burton, Richard, *The Anatomy of Melancholy*, 27n, 28
Butler, Joseph, *The Analogy of Religion*, 129, 250
Byron, George Gordon, Lord, 16, 132, 165–167, 279; *Cain, A Mystery*, 398; *Childe Harold's Pilgrimage*, 16, 58, 113, 167, 221, 223, 224, 226; "The Corsair," 225, 324; "Darkness," 221; "Destruction of Sennarcherib," 225, 353; *Don Juan*, 367–368, 395; "Fare Thee Well," 353; *The Giaour*, 167, 168; "Lachin y Gair," 353; *Manfred*, 34, 166, 216, 223, 234, 298, 353, 361, 362; *Marino Faliero, Doge of Venice*, 397; *Sardanapalus, a Tragedy*, 398; "Siege and Conquest of Alhama," 224, 353; *The Siege of Corinth*, 223, 224; "Stanzas to Augusta," 78; "Sun of the Sleepless," 369–370; *The Two Foscari, a Tragedy*, 398; "To a Youthful Friend," 166

Cadmus, 130
Caduceus, 195
Caesar, Augustus, 70
Caesar, Julius, 20, 65, 70, 75, 112, 260; *De Bello Gallico*, 31
Californ, Giant, 115, 157
Callinus, *Odes*, 31
Calvin, John, 313
Cambridge, 10, 52, 184
Camden, William, *Annales Elizabethae*, 361; *Annales rerum Anglicarum et Hibernicarum*, 27n, 28, 32, 364
Campbell, Thomas, 260; *The Battle of the Baltic*, 238; *An Essay on English Poetry*, 395; "Gertrude of Wyoming," 225; "Lochiel's Warning," 171; "O'Connor's Child," 281; *The Pleasures of Hope*, 289
Cannae, battle of, 264
Canossa, 19, 174n
Canute, King, 193
Capping of verses, 220–227
Carcano, Landolphe de, 77
Carey, Matthew, *Vindiciae Hibernicae*, 359n
Carnot, Joseph François Claude, 193(?)
Carnot, Lazare Nicolas Marguerite, 193(?), 202
Castalia, 11
Castruccio Castracani degli Antelminelli, 120
Cataline, 193
Catholic Church, Roman, 273, 307–308, 310, 311, 312, 344
Cato, 154, 226
Caussin, Nicolaus, *La Cour Sainte*, 269
Cervantes, 264; *Don Quixote*, 269
Chaldeans, 78
Channing, Edward Tyrrell, 50; *Inaugural Discourse*, 395
Charlemagne, 182, 245
Charles I, of England, 316, 391
Charles VIII, of France, 275
Charron, Pierre, 323
Chateaubriand, François René, 6, 46
Chaucer, Geoffrey, 56, 295; *The Clerk's Tale*, 158; *"The Testament of Love,"* 362; *Works*, 27n, 28
Chemistry, 299, 300
China, 83, 117, 328
Chod, 130
Christian Disciple, 304n
Christianity, 193, 203, 308, 343, 347
Church Fathers, 254, 258, 259, 347
Churchill, John, Duke of Marlborough, 24
Cicero, 13, 118, 193, 194, 199, 254, 258, 345, 346, 362; *Academica*, 257; *Philippics*, 172, 173; *Pro Sestio*, 232
Claret, Charles Pierre, *A Voyage Round the World*, 131n
Clarke, Samuel, 154, 254, 377n; "A Demonstration of the Being and Attributes of God," 187, 398
Claudius, 131
Club Room, 396
Codrus, 261
Cogan, Thomas, *A Philosophic Treatise on the Passions*, 28
Coleridge, Samuel Taylor, 282; "The Rime of the Ancient Mariner," 226
Collins, William, "How sleep the brave," 369
Colombo (Arkansaw Territory), 110, 162n
Colombo (Ceylon), 162n
Columbus, Christopher, 210
Comasques, 77
Commerce, 306
Como, War of, 76–78
Concord, 264
Condottieri, 86
Congreve, William, 44; *The Mourning Bride*, 375
Constantine, 69
Constantinople, 126, 127
Contrast, 14, 60, 68
"The Conventicle," 244
Cook, James, "Voyages," 399
Corfu, 71
Corinth, 113
Corneille, Pierre, 298; *Mélite*, 40
Cornwall, Barry, *see* Procter, Bryan Waller
Cowper, William, *The Task*, 44, 195, 216, 217, 220, 223
Coxe, William, *Memoirs of John Duke of Marlborough*, review of, 25
Crabbe, George, 396
Cremona, 77, 135
Crito, 213
Cromwell, Oliver, 193
Cudworth, Ralph, 254, 260, 346; *Treatise concerning Eternal and Immutable Morality*, 253
Currie, James, letter to Sir Walter Scott, 384

D., E., 351
Danforth, Samuel, 244
Darius, 208

Darwin, Erasmus, 336
David, 129
Davy, Sir Humphrey, *Elements of Agricultural Chemistry*, 56n; *Elements of Chemical Philosophy*, 56
Dawes, Rufus, 244
Death, 107–109, 292
Delphi, 113
Demosthenes, 13, 118, 250
Descartes, René, 254, 259, 346; *Oeuvres Choisies*, 345
Diderot, Denis, *Le Fils Naturel*, 176n
Dimond, William, "Mariner's Dream," 386–388
Diogenes Laertius, 208; *Lives of Eminent Philosophers*, 209
Dionysius, 30
Drake, Nathan, *Essays . . . of the Tatler, Spectator and Guardian*, 383(?), 397
Drama, 65, 193, 260
Druid, 172, 342
Drummond, Sir William, *Academical Questions*, 47, 56n, 57, 376, 397
Dryden, John, 165, 250; *Absalom and Achitophel*, 17, 218, 222
Dudley, Robert, Earl of Leicester, 361
Dunlop, John Colin, *The History of Fiction*, 55, 56n

Edinburgh Review, 28n, 29n, 47, 55, 56n, 57n, 127, 202, 220, 221n, 225, 326, 329, 330, 344n, 348, 349, 350, 353, 363, 367, 376, 380, 396, 397, 399
Egypt, 14, 15n, 62, 87, 97, 113, 305, 307, 334
Electra, 65, 290
Eleusis, mysteries of, 256, 334
Elizabeth I, 240n, 348, 359, 361, 365, 381, 392
Ellis, George, *Specimens of Early English Metrical Romances*, 374
Eloquence, 46
Emerson, Edward Bliss (brother), 6n, 260
Emerson, Edward Waldo (son), 22n
Emerson, Mary Moody ("Aunt Mary," "Tnamurya"), 30n, 32, 49, 199, 287n, 334n; letters of, 61, 89, 195–196, 197, 198–200, 300, 333–334, 336, 337
Emerson, Ralph Waldo, Bowdoin Prize Dissertations, 25n, 206n, 253n, 254n; *Parnassus*, 157n; poetical phrases, 233; Pythologian poem, 10, 25, 235–242, 243; "Thoughts on the Religion of the Middle Ages," 287n, 304n. *See also* "Chronology," xlvii–xlix, *and* "self," *under* DISCUSSIONS below

DISCUSSIONS: Aaron Burr's defense, 318–319, 327; advantages of knowledge, 189–192; agricultural life, 315–316; America, 146–147; Anglo-Saxon law, 329; antiquity, 200–201; Asia, 327–328; astronomy, 5–6, 23; changelessness, 112–113; characteristics, 131–132; charity, 44–45; climatic influence, 50, 156; commercial life, 316–318; contemplation, 33–34; contrast, 59–61; cunning, 118–120; death, 107–109; degeneracy, 167–169, 173–174; "Dissertation on the character of Socrates," 206–215, 234; "Dissertation on the Present State of Ethical Philosophy," 254, 255–264, 330–333, 334–336, 339, 341–342, 343–344, 345–351 *passim*; drama, 65–66, 109, 139–141, 150–152, 154–156, 286–291, 295–299; eloquence, 7–9; exilaration, 19; faith, 141–143; the fall of Adam, 312–313, 350–351; fiction, 109–110; future life, 193–194; genius, 206–208; God, 144–146, 147–149, 152–153; greatness, 100–102; growth of a nation, 300–301; habit, 128–129; happiness, 339; history, 134–135; improvement, 115; independence, 6–7; inductive philosophy, 332–333; the infancy of nations, 233; influence of modern essays, 331–332; Italy, 82–86; Judgement Day, 47–48; life, 326–327; literary fashion, 340; martyrdom, 120–122; mathematical studies, 269–270; mental powers, 171–172; Middle Ages, 66–67, 67–71, 73–74; moral character, 117–118; morality, 340–341, 343; moral philosophy, 341–343; morals, 335–336; moral science, 339, 340; nature, 122–123, 138–139, 334–335; passion, 131; pestilence, 15–16; the pleasures of memory, 184–186; poetry, 63–65, 165, 242–243, 264, 276–282; pomp, 196–197, 198; progress, 46; prophecy, 111–112; providence, 92–93, 96–97; the Reformation, 272–273; religion, 49, 61–62, 67, 71–72, 74–76, 78–80, 86–88; religion of the Middle Ages, 304–312; origins of religion, 327; religious tendency of different states of society, 313–318; savage life, 313–315; scholars, 174–176; science, 299–300; self, 10–11, 15, 33, 37–38, 39,

40–41, 46–47, 52–53, 54–55, 94–95, 99, 129–130, 133–134, 137; sin, 292–294; social feelings, 97–99, 102, 104–106; society, 124–127; spirit, 116–117; spring, 11–12; virtue, 23–24; vision, 99–100; war, 135–136; wealth, 80–81; Wordsworth's *The Excursion*, 271–272

DRAMAS: "Aedepol and Boruno," 324–325; "The Friends," 292

INDEX HEADINGS: "Abortions," 122n; "America," 146n; "Asia," 327n; "Astronomical reveries," 5n; "Bacon," 21n, 24n; "Ballad," 103n, 106n; "Barrow," 17n; "Barrowistical," 17n, 18n; "Byron," 16n; "Characteristics," 132n; "Comets," 22n; "Conclusions," 112n; "Country," 138n; "Cunning," 118n, 119n, 120n; "Dark Ages," 66n; "Death," 107n, 108n; "Drama," 108n, 140n, 150n, 151n, 154n, 155n; "Everett," 12n; "Exhilaration," 19n, "Fairy land," 10n; "Faith," 141n, 142n, 143n; "Father Ambrose," 43n; Fiction," 109n; "Futurity," 24n; "Gay," 21n; "God," 143n, 144n, 145n, 147n, 148n, 149n, 152n, 153n; "Good-Bye," 136n; "Greatness," 100n, 101n, 102n; "Greece," 12n; "Habit," 128n, 129n; "Hark rascal," 94n; "Henry IV," 19n; "History," 103n, 134n; "Independence," 6n; "Joke," 123n; "Lapland," 24n; "Letter to Motte," 118n; "Lottery," 17n; "Mahomet," 327n; "Martyrdom," 120n, 121n; "Melancholy," 115n; "Mind," 26n; "Notes to Hudibras," 24n; "Pestilence," 26n; "Picture," 19n, 26n; "Populace," 125n, 126n, 127n; "PQ," 19n; "Pride," 95n; "Prophecy," 111n; "Providence," 92n, 93n; "Pulpit eloquence," 7n, 8n; "rolling Universe," 26n; "Roman," 20n, 26n; "Rome," 26n; "Samor," 7n, 26n; "Self," 130n, 133n, 134n; "Social Feelings," 96n, 97n, 98n, 104n, 105n; "Spring," 11n, 12n, 26n; "Tale," 110n; "Trash," 93n; "Vain World," 116n, 117n; "Variety," 124n; "Virgil," 26n; "Virtue," 23n, 26n; "Vision," 99n, 100n; "War," 135n; "Webster," 9n, 26n; "White Ladies," 26n; "WX," 19n

POEMS: "Arthur's Dream," 188; "Behold yon white balloon," 351; "By the unacknowledged tie," 322; "Come to my mansion," 218–219; "Deep in the dungeons," 194; "Earl Brodin's Plea," 178–180; "East and West," 352; "Entombed Crotona" 326 (?); "Faintly as tolls," 246–247; "Far in the west," 327; "The Genius of the Universe," 66–67; "Go hide the shield of War," 136–137; "The Grave," 72–73, 74; "Grass, straw, white and grey," 267; "Hark rascal," 95; "Hush, ye vain thoughts," 122; "Idealism," 81–82; "I dreamed the world was young," 320–321; "I have builded pavilions," 227; "I love thy music," 301–302; "Important ⟨Freshmen bran⟩dishing," 231–232; "Improvement," 235–242, 243; "Indian Superstitution," 50n; "In the dead of night," 106–107; "I saw the sail of Youth," 351; "I spread my gorgeous sail," 328–329; "John Grimes," 245; "King Richard's Death," 188n, 229, 235, 294–295, 303–304; "The Knight rode up," 103–104; "Life and death of the little red bobbin-maker," 322–323; "The Maniac's Verse," 321; "May fortune bless thee," 323; "My friend must abandon," 227; "Not all that heralds rake," 351; "Ode to Melancholy," 169–171; "Oh there are times," 163–165; "Oh! what thinks he," 326; "Old halls," 213; "Perhaps thy lot," 40; "Peru," 254, 282–284; "Proud of the rich," 88–89; "A rill which empties," 261; "Solitude," 232–233; "There died an old man," 123–124; "There was a hog," 274–275; "There was a little city," 29–30; "Thy hands are reeking," 218; "To Melancholy," 115–116; "Upon the plain," 319–320; "Valedictory Poem," 353–357; "We look for days of joy," 183–184 (*see also* "Valedictory Poem"); "When bounding Fancy," 35, 36–37 (*see also* "Valedictory Poem"); "You may say what you please," 244–245; fragments, 230–231

STORIES AND SKETCHES: "The Idol. No. 1," 176–178; "Idol. No. 2", 181–183; "Journey to Logyle," 19–20; "Magician," 55, 266–268, 273–274, 284–286, 302–303, 324 (?); "Richards's Confession," 265–266; "the village of Colombo," 110; untitled, 337–339

SYMBOLS OF ORIGINAL AUTHORSHIP AND PSEUDONYMS: "H.O.N.," 304n; "Junio," 4, 5, 14, 26, 215, 218, 231; "Junius," 169; "O.," 178, 215; "[R.W.E.]," 63, 71, 114, 162, 169, 184, 188, 195, 215,

218, 227, 231, 245, 252, 260, 261, 276, 293, 294, 321, 322, 323, 325, 327, 340, 343, 351
TRANSLATIONS: 252–253, 254–255, 265
Emerson, William (brother), 199n, 244n, 288n, 294n
Enfield, William, *Institutes Natural Philosophy*, 15, 23
England, 13, 53, 101, 113, 125, 127, 156, 168, 181, 287, 295, 296, 297, 298, 306, 316, 330
English language, 278
English literature, 278, 287
Ennius, Quintus, *Annals*, 31
Epictetus, 194n, 203, 207, 258, 346
Epicoreans, 226
Epicurus, 247, 342, 346
Erasmus, 364
Erskine, Thomas, *Remarks on the Internal Evidence for the Truth of Revealed Religion*, 398
Euphrates, 68
Euripides, 177, 208, 209, 291, 397; *Electra*, 80; Europe, 14, 15n, 50, 68, 83, 126, 127, 273, 287, 297, 306, 307, 308, 309, 328, 330, 332, 344
Everett, Alexander Hill, *Europe*, 398
Everett, Edward, 6, 12, 13, 14, 34, 37, 43, 44, 47, 48, 49, 55, 260, 395; *An Oration pronounced at Cambridge before the Society of Phi Beta Kappa*, 399; *A sermon Preached at the Dedication of the First Congregational Church in New York*, 397; quoted, 15
Evil, 93, 124

"Fair Helen of Kirconell," 353
Fairy-land, 4, 11, 26, 277
Federalist, The, 397
Fénelon, François de Salignac de La Mothe-, *Les Aventures de Télémaque*, 56n, 58
Ferrara, 77
Fiction, 93–94, 109
Fielding, Joseph, *The History of Tom Jones*, 398
Fletcher, John, 296; *Beggar's Bush*, 28n, 330; *The Nice Valour*, 28n, 353. *See also* Beaumont
Florence, 74, 84, 86, 127, 275, 276
Fondulo, Cabrino, 135
Fontaine, Jean de la, *see* La Fontaine, Jean de
Fontenelle, Bernard le Bovier de, 13, 40
Forsyth, Robert, 349n; *The Principles of Moral Science*, review of, 348
Fosbrooke, Thomas D., "British Monachism," 15n
Fox, Charles James, 111
Framingham, 43
France, 13, 14, 125, 181, 275, 295, 297, 298, 306
Francis, Philip, *The Odes, Epodes, &c, of Horace*, 229
Franklin, Benjamin, 193, 250; *Complete Works in Philosophy*, 399
French literature, 40, 54, 252, 288
French Revolution, 127, 174n; Reign of Terror, 125
Frisbie, Levi, 23, 24, 330; *A Collection of the Miscellaneous Writings*, 399
Froissart, Jean, 55, 181, 182, 183n; *Chronicles of England, France, Spain, and the Adjoining Countries*, 28

Gannett's, 245
Gavalesca, Guido Grimaldi de, 77
Gay, Martin, 22, 38, 39, 40, 52–53, 54, 94–95, 130, 244, 291n, 321 , 353
Genoa, 84, 194; revolution of, 120
Germany, 75, 85, 306
Ghibelline, 135
Gibbon, Edward, *The History of the Decline and Fall of the Roman Empire*, 131, 152n, 201, 202, 253, 309, 322, 393, 398, 399 (?); *Miscellaneous Works*, 393
Gillies, John, *The History of Ancient Greece*, 30, 31, 238, 396
Gloriana, 11
God, 9, 60, 61, 62, 63, 66, 76, 79, 86, 88, 117, 122, 124, 140, 142, 151, 185, 186, 187, 191, 195, 201, 217, 247, 261, 281, 293, 305, 306, 313, 314, 315, 318, 327, 329, 335, 338, 345, 351
Godwin, William, *Life of Geoffrey Chaucer*, 215, 362, 371, 396
Goliath, 129
Gorham, John, *Elements of Chemical Science*, 42
Goth, 312
Gourdin, John G. K., 185n
Gray, Mr., 43n
Greatness, 100, 101
Greece, 14, 68, 69, 74, 79, 80, 97, 113, 156, 157, 167, 168, 177, 208, 289, 305, 307, 330, 341
Greek, 181

Greek literature, 11, 12, 13, 181, 287, 288, 290, 291, 295, 297
Greek philosophy, 256, 258
Gregory I, Pope, 308
Gregory VII (Hildebrand), Pope, 19, 24, 174n, 308, 360
Gregory VIII (Maurice Bourdin, *or* Burdino), Anti-Pope, 77
Grimm, Friedrich Melchior von, *Correspondance Littéraire*, 398
Grotius, Hugo, 193
Grove, Henry, 347
Guadalquiver, 68
Gutterson, 58

Hale, Sir Matthew, *The History of the Common Law of England*, review of, 329
Hall, Joseph, quoted, 350; "Meditations," 372; quoted, 350
Hallam, Henry, 311, *The State of Europe during the Middle Ages*, 388–389, 398
Halley, Edmund, 23
Hannibal, 120, 264
Harris, James, *Three Treatises*, 396
Harrison, William, 359
Hartley, David, *Observations of Man*, 129
Harvard College, 3, 94; Athenaeum, 24, 25; Exhibition, 38–39; Hollis Hall, 26n, 129, 184; Rebellion, 244; Stoughton Hall, 54
Hastings, Battle of, 27
Hawkwood, Sir John de, 86
Hecataeus, 30
Hector, 182
Hedge, Levi (?), 246
Hellanicus, 30
Henry IV, of France, 250
Henry IV, of Germany, 19, 174n, 360
Henry V, of Germany, 77
Heraclidae, 238
Heraclitus, 168
Hermes, 130
Herodotus, 14, 15n, 31, 210
Herschell, Sir William, *Observations on the Two Lately Discovered Celestial Bodies*, 330
Heyne, Christian Gottlob, *Homeri Carmina*, 247
Hiero the Tyrant, 145n
Hildebrand, *see* Gregory VII
Hill, John Boynton, 57n, 58, 82n, 244n
Hill, Joseph Bancroft, 57n, 58
Hillhouse, James Abraham, *The Judgement, a Vision*, 398; *Percy's Masque*, 298
Hindu, 334
Hindustan, 14, 15n, 50, 328
Hobbes, Thomas, 253, 260, 346, 347n; *Leviathan*, 28, 259
Hobhouse, *see* Broughton
Hody, Humphrey, *De Graecis Illustribus*, 28, 366
Hogg, James, 217, 225
Holinshed, Raphael, *Chronicles*, 359
Holland, 297
Holy Land, 345
Homer, 175, 177, 210, 279, 359; *Iliad*, 238, 349; *Odyssey*, 31, 238
Honorius, 193
Honorius II, Pope, 77
Hooper, Nathaniel Leech, 58
Horace, 13; *Epistles*, 90; *Odes*, 31, 228, 229
Howard, 193
Howard Benevolent Society, 49
Humboldt, Alexander, *Personal Narrative*, 56n, 57; *Researches concerning . . . America*, 56n, 57
Hume, David, 192, 254, 260, 336, 346; *Essays and Treatises on Several Subjects*, 187, 343, 399 (?)
Hunt, Leigh, *Descent of Liberty*, 90, 353
Huss, John, 55, 135
Hutcheson, Francis, 346
Hyde, Edward, Lord Clarendon, *The History of the Rebellion*, 391

Idealism, 153, 376
India, 165, 210, 259, 308, 340, 344
Indian Ocean, 328
Indians, American, 110
Innocent VI, Pope, 119
Iphigenia, 65
Irving, Washington, *Bracebridge Hall*, 200; *The Sketch Book*, 172, 396
Isaiah the Prophet, 89, 111
Israel, 86
Italy, 73, 83, 85, 86, 88, 103, 118, 119, 125, 127, 168, 275, 305, 306, 316

Jeffrey, Francis, 47n
Jerusalem, 126
Jesuits, 120, 253, 258
Jesus Christ, 61, 89, 188, 259
Jew, 113
Job, 98

John of Cappadocia, 131
John XXII, Pope, 308
John XXIII, Pope, 135
Johnson, Samuel, 250; *Life of Milton*, 331, 349; *The Rambler*, 172, 268, 331; *The Vanity of Human Wishes*, 97; *The Works*, 396; quoted, 340
Joinville, Jean de, 264; *Memoirs of John Lord de Joinville*, 28
Jones, Stephen, *Biographica Dramatica*, review of, 28n
Jones, Sir William, "A Hymn to Narayena," 154n
Jonson, Ben, 17, 44, 220; *The Alchemist*, 222, 397; *Every Man in his Humour*, 395; *Every Man out of his Humour*, 395; "Gipsy Song," 353; *The Gypsies Metamorphosed*, 104, 225, 381–382; *Hymenaei*, 348, 392; *Life*, 395; "An Ode to Himself," 251, 353, 382; *Prince Henry's Barriers*, 343; "Sad Shepherd," 253; *Silent Women*, 397; *Timber, or Discoveries*, 368–369, 396; *Volpone*, 397; *The Works*, 397; quoted, 339
Joyce, Jeremiah, *Scientific Dialogues*, 397
Juggernaut, Temple of, 132
Julian the Apostate (?), 193
Julius, master-general (?), 202
Junius, 169
Juvenal, *Satires*, 18, 31

K., Mr., quoted, 9
Kennett, Basil, *The Lives and Characters of the Ancient Grecian Poets*, 28, 145n, 209, 210n, 360, 396
Kepler, Johannes, 23
Kett, Henry, *Elements of General Knowledge*, 56n, 57
Kingsbury, Nathaniel, 244n
"Kinmont Willie" (anon.), 353
Knowles, Herbert, *The Three Tabernacles*, 216, 225
Koran, 171

Lacroix, Silvestre François, *Elements of Algebra*, 56n, 58
La Fontaine, Jean de, 43; "Eloge," 386
Laguna, 77
Lamb, Charles, 227
Lane, Jonas Henry, 57n, 58
Lapland, 24
"Lay d'Iseult," 384–385
Lee, John C., 244
Legnano, Battle of, 76
Leibnitz, Gottfried Wilhelm von, 202
Leland, John, *The Advantage and Necessity of the Christian Revelation*, 203, 399
Lemaire, Henri, *Histoire de la Révolution Française*, 398
Lignano, *see* Legnano
Linus, 31
Livy, 49, 50n
Locke, John, 13, 193, 202, 343, 343, 346; *A Common Place Book*, 26n; *An Essay Concerning Human Understanding*, 56n, 58, 109; quoted 343
Lockhart, John Gibson, *Peter's Letters to His Kinsfolk*, 28, 29n, 217, 225, 397
Logan, John, "The Braes of Yarrow," 90, 353
Lombardy, 77, 85, 135
London, 142
Lothrop, Samuel Kirkland, 58
Louis XII, of France, 275
Lowth, Report, *Lectures on the Sacred Poetry of the Hebrews*, 396
Lucian, *Works*, 32
Lucretius, 226; *De Rerum Natura*, 153
Luther, Martin, 55, 188, 273, 346, 347n
Lyttelton, Thomas, *Letters of the Late Lord Lyttelton*, 396

McCrie, Thomas, *Life of John Knox*, 384, 398
Machiavelli, Niccolò, 346, 347n; *The Prince*, 344
Mackintosh, Sir James, 193, 202; *A Discourse on the Study of the Law of Nature and Nations*, 399
Magi, 172
Magna Charta, 330
Mahomet, *see* Mohammed
Maittaire, Michael, ed., Homer, *Ilias*, 55, 56n
Malebranche, Nicolas de, 346
Mansfield, William Murray, Lord, 202n
Mantua, 77
Marathon, 32, 281, 289
Marcet, Mrs. Jane (Haldimand), *Conversations on Political Economy*, 398
Marchand, Étienne, 130–131
Marlborough, *see* John Churchill
Martial (Marcus Valerius Martialis), *Epigrams*, 49, 50n
Massinger, Philip, 296; *Duke of Milan*, 371; *Plays*, 28, 29n, 397
Mathematics, 299

Mather, Cotton, *Magnalia Christi Americana,* 55, 56n, 381, 397
Mather, Samuel, *Life of . . . Cotton Mather,* 399
Maturin, Charles Robert, *Bertram, or the Castle of St. Aldobrand,* 366–367; *Fatal Revenge, or the Family of Montorio,* 233, 397
Mecca, 328
Medicine, 300
Medina, 328
Melampus, 31
Mellen, John, 292, 293, 324, 351
Menu, 259, 340
Metaphysics, 300
Middle Ages, 65, 127, 264
Middleton, Conyers, *The Life of Marcus Tullius Cicero,* 28, 29n, 362, 397
Milan, 77, 86
Milman, Henry Hart, *The Fall of Jerusalem,* 223, 227, 298, 397; *Samor, Lord of the Bright City,* 7, 225, 298
Milo, 20
Milton, John, 6, 13, 165, 175, 193, 243, 250, 278, 280; *An Apology Against a Pamphlet Called a Modest Confutation,* 39, 40; *Areopagitica,* 12; *Comus,* 298, 323; *Il Penseroso,* 359; *Paradise Lost,* 40, 99, 373; *The Prose Works,* 397, 399; "Reason of Church Government urged against Prelaty," 41, 374; *Samson Agonistes,* 323
Mississippi River, 110
Mitford, William, *History of Greece,* 87
Modena, 77
Mohammed (Mahomet), 60, 68, 269, 328
Mohammedanism, 311
Molière, Jean Baptiste Poquelin, *Le Bourgeois Gentilhomme,* 398; *Le Misanthrope,* 399
Montaigne, Michel Eyquem de, 250, 323; *Essais,* 56n, 57, 323n
Montesquieu, Charles de Secondat de, 290, 299; *Considérations sur les Causes de la Grandeur des Romains et de leur Décadence,* 70, 398; *Lettres Persanes,* 268–269, 383n, 385, 398; *Oeuvres Complettes,* 268
Monza, 85
Moore, Thomas, 165, 279; *Lalla Rookh,* 223; "She Is Far from the Land," 225; "The Song of Fionnuala," 353
Moors, 264
Moral philosophy, 300, 341–343
Moral science, 187, 202, 255, 259, 330, 333, 339, 340
Moral sense, 60
More, Sir Thomas, *Utopia,* 398
"Morte Arthur," 221
Moses, 62
Mosheim, Johann Lorenz von, *An Ecclesiastical History,* 152n, 253
Motte, Mellish Irving, 25, 118
Mowna Roa, 130
Musaeus, 279
Mussulman, 328

Nameless literary society, 185n. *See also* "The"
Naples, 103
Narses (478?–?573), 136
Natural philosophy, 299, 300
Nature, 230, 279
Neal, Daniel, *History of the Puritans,* 152n
Neal, John, "The Battle of Niagara," 224
Newton, Sir Isaac, 79, 101, 193, 198, 219, 250, 280, 346
Noah, 8, 62, 79, 198
North American Review, 29n, 56n, 298n, 395, 396, 397, 398, 399
Northboro, 199n
Norway, 156
Nottingham, 391
Novare, 77

Oedipus, 262
Old South Church, 44, 49
Olympus, 75
Oracula Sibyllina, 43
Origen Adamantius, 209
Otis, Harrison Gray, 134
Otway, Thomas, 44, 296
Ovid, *Tristia,* 162

Paestum, 27
Paley, William, 254, 311, 348; *Natural Theology,* 187
Palmyra, 65
Papacy, 188, 309, 310, 312, 332
Paris, 268
Parma, 77
Parnassus, 11, 64
Pascal, Blaise, *Pensées,* 186
Paul, Saint, 98, 148
Pavia, 77
Pedagogue's Map of Europe, 16
Pendragon, 11, 15, 27

Percival, Robert, *Account of . . . Ceylon*, review of, 162n, 349
Pericles, 208
Peripatetics, 226
Persepolis, 65
Persia, 62, 75, 97, 305, 328, 334
Pervigilium Veneris, 49
Peter, 193
Peter, Saint, 203, 308, 310
Pherecydes, 30
Phoenicians, 13, 208
Philip II, of France, 264
Pindar, 177, 210
Pisa, 74, 84, 194, 275
Pisander, 177
Pitt, William, 111
Plaisance, 77
Plataea, 281, 289
Plato, 13, 148, 207, 208, 209, 226, 261, 333, 342, 347; "Distich on Aristophanes," 209; *Works*, 396
Playfair, John, *Dissertation Second: General View of the Progress of Mathematical and Physical Science*, 192, 193, 399
Pliny, 168; *Letters*, 32
Plymouth, 55
Poetry, 64, 165, 242, 264, 276
Polehampton, Edward T. W., and John Mason Good, *The Gallery of Nature and Art*, 399
Political economy, 300
Polus, 290
Pompey, 20
Pope, Alexander, 165, 336; *An Essay on Man*, 186, 202; *Moral Essays*, 222; *The Rape of the Lock*, 215
Poulin, J., *Le Saisons de J. Thomson*, review of, 380n
Powers, Michael, *Life of Michael Powers . . .*, 396
Prague, 55
Price, Richard, 260, 261; *A Review of the Principal Questions and Difficulties in Morals*, 51, 56n, 57, 262, 334, 347
Priestley, Joseph, 254; *The Doctrines of Heathen Philosophy*, 258, 350, 397; *Lectures on History and General Policy*, 350; *The Theological and Miscellaneous Works*, 378
Prince Arthur, 15
Procter, Bryan Waller (Barry Cornwall), "Gyges," 363; *A Sicilian Story*, 220, 221
Prometheus, 71
Protagoras, 177, 178n
Providence, 52, 86, 87, 88, 89, 92, 93, 96, 108, 111, 138, 155, 230, 257, 276, 305, 307, 313, 338
Pyramid, 113
Pythagoras, 48, 168, 177, 254, 334, 342, 346
Pythologian Club, 235
Pythologian Poem, 10, 25, 235–242, 243

Quarterly Review, 12, 14, 15n, 25, 27, 28n, 29n, 132, 370n, 396
Queen Mab, 4, 15
"The Queen's Marie," 353
Quintilian, 13

Rabelais, François, 38
Racine, Jean Baptiste, 13, 298
Raleigh, Sir Walter, *The History of the World*, 29n; "Of the Place of Paradise," 28; "A Vision on This Conceipt of the Faery Queene," 27
Rambler, 172, 268, 331
Reed, Sampson, quoted, 293–294
Reformation, 55, 151, 272, 273
Regulus, Marcus Atilius, 98, 261, 262
Reid, Thomas, 254
Religion, 62, 276, 317
Reports of the Trials of Colonel Aaron Burr, 318n
Richard I, of England, 264
Richardson, Samuel, *Clarissa Harlowe*, 131–132; *The History of Sir Charles Grandison*, 28, 29n
Rienzi, Cola di, 118
Robertson, William, *The History of America*, 56n, 57
Robespierre, Maximilien François Marie Isidore de, 193
Rogers, Samuel, *Human Life: A Poem*, 395
Rollin, Charles, *Ancient History* (?), 396
Roman literature, 11, 181, 278, 288
Roman philosophy, 258
Rome, 6, 16, 20–21, 69, 70, 74, 79, 84, 112, 113, 131, 136, 156, 167, 168, 218, 239, 243, 262, 273, 291, 306, 309, 315, 330, 341
Romulus, 136, 182
Rousseau, Jean Jacques, *Émile ou de l'Education*, 176
Rumford, 162
Russia, 69, 156

Saint Martin, valleys of, 78
Saint Peter's, Church of, 16
Samos, 359
Sandwich Isles, 130
San Priamo, 265
Saracens, 68
Scholar, 189, 200
Science, 299–300, 341–342
Scotland, 178
Scott, Sir Walter, 43, 165; *The Abbot*, 42, 397; *The Antiquary*, 397; *The Bridal of Triermain*, 396; *The Bride of Lammermoor*, 44, 397; "County Guy," 353; "Farewell to Mackenzie," 183; *The Fortunes of Nigel*, 89, 399; *Guy Mannering*, 58, 131, 219, 220, 222, 370, 373; "Hellvellyn," 353; *Ivanhoe*, 363, 396; *Kenilworth*, 240n; *The Lady of the Lake*, 58, 353; *The Lay of the Last Minstrel*, 58, 223, 226, 378; *Minstrelsy of the Scottish Border*, 384, review of, 353; *The Monastery*, 223, 226, 396; "Old Border Ballad," 219; *Old Mortality*, 225; *The Pirate*, 132, 398; *Quentin Durward*, 353, 399; *Redgauntlet*, 399; *Rob Roy*, 235, 397; *Rokeby*, 163, 167, 172, 224, 353; *St. Ronan's Well*, 399; *Waverley*, 28, 29n
Search, Edward, *see* Abraham Tucker
Sedgwick, Catherine Maria, *Redwood*, 399
Seneca, 203, 226, 346; *De Beneficiis*, 194; *Dialogues*, 128; *Thyestes*, 154n, 301
Sforza, 86
Shakespeare, William, 13, 57, 101, 155, 187, 199, 243, 250, 278, 297, 334; *Antony and Cleopatra*, 115n, 138, 186; *Hamlet*, 138, 186, 193, 293; *I Henry IV*, 36n, 222, 225, 353; *III Henry VI*, 220, 224; *Henry VIII*, 147, 353; *Julius Caesar*, 253; *King Lear*, 186, 296; *Love's Labour's Lost*, 277; *Macbeth*, 296; *Measure for Measure*, 222, 223; *Midsummer Night's Dream*, 240n; *Othello*, 296; *Richard II*, 186, 222; *Taming of the Shrew*, 224; *Troilus and Cresida*, 371; *Twelfth Night*, 353, 379–380, 388
Sharpe, Charles K. (1781?–1851), "Lord Herries' Complaint," 353, 383
Sherlock, Thomas (?), 143
Sherlock, William (?), 143, 144n
Siberia, 328
Sigismund, of Hungary, 135
Simonides, 145
Sinai, Mt., 86
Sismondi, Jean Charles Léonard Simonde de, 265n; *De la Litterature du Midi de l'Europe*, 252, 398; *L'Histoire des Républiques Italiennes au Moyen Âge*, 78, 118, 134–135, 276, 309, 389–390, 398; quoted, 308
Smith, Gamaliel, *see* Jeremy Bentham
Smith, John, *The Generall Historie of Virginia and the Summer Isles*, 57
Smollett, Tobias George, *The Adventures of Peregrine Pickle*, 396
Social compact, 340
Social feelings, 106
Social race, 102
Society, 98, 104
Socrates, 25, 31, 148, 177, 193, 207–215, 226, 234, 254, 257, 331, 333, 346
Solomon, 199
"Song of the Tonga Islanders," 157n, 353, 385
Sophocles, 80, 208, 209
Sorbonne, 259
Sortes Virgilianae, 17n
Southey, Robert, 282; *The Curse of Kehama*, 340n, 341; "Epitaph on Pizarro," 375; review of Fosbrooke's "British Monachism," 15n
Spain, 297, 306
Spanish literature, 252
Spectator, 268, 331, 347n
Spenser, Edmund, 364, 380; *The Faery Queene*, 29n, 31; "Mother Hubbard's Tale," 380; *View of the State of Ireland*, 27, 358–359
Stackpole, Joseph Lewis, 58
Staël, Madame de (Anne Louise Germaine baronne de Staël-Holstein), 335n; *Corinne, ou L'Italie*, 28; *De l'Allemagne*, 202
Steele, Sir Richard, *Spectator*, 268, 331, 347n; *Tatler*, 331
Sterne, Laurence, *Tristram Shandy*, 22
Stewart, Dugald, 254; *The Collected Works*, 202; *Dissertation: Exhibiting the Progress of Metaphysical, Ethical, and Political Philosophy*, 154n, 253, 323n, 331n, 345n, 397, 398; *Elements of the Philosophy of the Human Mind*, 79n; *Outline of Moral Philosophy*, 377
Stoic, 203, 226, 258, 378
Strutt, Joseph, *Glig-Gamena Angel-Deod, or*

the Sports and Pastimes of the People of England, 398
Sullivan, James, *The History of the District of Maine*, 399
Sully, Maximilien de Béthune duc de, 250; *The Memoirs of the Duke of Sully*, 398
Swift, Jonathan, 14, 55, 214; *The Works*, 57n, 397
Symmons, Charles, *John Milton: The Prose Works, with Life*, 56, 57n, 397, 399(?)

Tabarin, Hugo de, 36
Tacitus, *Histories*, 89
Taillefer, 27
Tarshish, 316
Tatler, 331
Taylor, Jeremy, *The Rule and Excercise of Holy Dying*, 399; "Sermons," 377
Teignmouth, Sir John Shore, Lord, *Life of Sir William Jones*, 56, 57n
Temple, Sir William, 13
"The," 184, 185n.
Theater, 288, 298
Thebes, 262
Theocritus, 13, 360
Thomas of Celano, *Dies Irae*, 243, 244n
Thomson, James, *The Castle of Indolence*, 379; *The Seasons*, 380
Thou, Christophe de, 227n
Thucydides, 210
Ticknor, George, 35, 36, 40, 43, 47, 54
Tnamurya, *see* Mary Moody Emerson
Tressan, Louis Elizabeth de la Vergne, *Corps d'Extraits de Romans de Chevalrie*, 384, 385; *Oeuvres Choisies*, 398
Trojan war, 77, 208
Troy, 182, 238, 280, 281
Tucker, Abraham (Edward Search), 4; *Abridgement of the Light of Nature*, 4n; *The Light of Nature Pursued*, 394
Tudor, William, *Letters on the Eastern States*, 28, 29n, 397
Turkey, 69, 113, 264, 328
Tuscany, 85

Upham, Charles Wentworth, 38; quoted, 372
Urban V, Pope, 119

Vaivswata, 341
Valhalla, 26, 27
Vandal, 113
Venice, 71, 86, 118
Verona, 77
Vicenza, 77
Vico, castle of, 77
Virgil, 199, 365; *Aeneid*, 260, 269, 321; *Eclogues*, 17, 203; *Georgics*, 25, 162
Visconti, Bernabò, 120
Visconti, Giovanni ("Azzo"?), 120
Visconti, Giovanni Galeazzo, 134
Visconti, Giovanni Maria, 134
Vision, 100
Voltaire, 154; *Adelaide de Guesclin*, 47; *History of Charles XII, King of Sweden*, 399

Walker, John, *Rhyming Dictionary*, 57n, 58
Warren, John C., 12
Warton, Thomas, 365; *History of English Poetry*, 359n; *Observations on the Faerie Queene*, 359n, 396
Washington, George, 250
Watson, Robert, *The History of the Reign of Philip II, King of Spain*, 57
Watt, James, 193
Webber, Samuel, *Logan, an Indian Tale*, 398
Webster, Daniel, 9–10, 192
White, Henry Kirke, "To the Herb Rosemary," 353, 391–392
"White Ladies," 19, 174
Wilberforce, William, 193
Wilkes, John, 202
Williams, 58
Wilson, Richard, *The Art of Rhetorick*, 365
Wirt, William, *Sketches of the Life and Character of Patrick Henry*, 396
Wordsworth, William, 162, 165, 281, 282; *The Excursion*, 10n, 27, 29n, 255, 270–271; "Thoughts of a Briton on the Subjugation of Switzerland," 353
Wotton, William, 13, 14n
Wrangham, Francis, *British Plutarch*, 56, 57n, 397

Xenophon, 207, 212
Xerxes, 78, 208

Yama, 341
Yellow Sea, 328

Zendavesta, 316, 322
Zeno, 202, 226, 258, 346
Zoroaster, 316